FROMMER'S
A GUIDE FOR THE
DISABLED TRAVELER

The United States,
Canada,
& Europe

by Frances Barish

S0-ACO-486

Published by Frommer/Pasmantier Publishers
A Division of Simon & Schuster, Inc.
1230 Avenue of the Americas
New York, NY 10020

ISBN 0-671-47359-X

Manufactured in the United States of America

*Although every effort was made to ensure the accuracy
of price information appearing in this book,
it should be kept in mind that prices
can and do fluctuate in the course of time*

CONTENTS

MAPS

INFLATION ALERT: I don't have to tell you that inflation has hit the United States as it has everywhere else. In researching this book I have made every effort to obtain up-to-the-minute prices, and for the most part, I believe I've succeeded in obtaining reliable data. Nevertheless, prices do change in the course of time, and proprietors of establishments sometimes do change price policies. Therefore, it's fairly obvious that I cannot guarantee that each and every price will remain unchanged during the lifetime of this book.

A GUIDE FOR THE DISABLED TRAVELER

The Reason Why

THIS IS A GUIDE for travelers whose baggage includes some special equipment—a wheelchair, crutches, a cane, or maybe a pacemaker. Its basic criteria are set for people who can't walk at all, and so it's also a source to anybody for whom normal mobility presents a problem. And, because the world tends to lump everything under that umbrella phrase "handicapped facilities," my research also turned up information on special arrangements available for travelers with impairments of sight and hearing as well as mobility, and that information has been included here, too.

Having a physical disability need not take you out of the running when it comes to travel. As a paraplegic, I know that the urge to experience the delights of travel didn't disappear just because I became disabled. But we *do* have to do it differently: we can't be that compulsive traveler who decides to go to Europe tomorrow, or wing it to the Coast tonight. The world isn't ready for us to be that spontaneous just yet. So, among the things that make travel possible and pleasurable for someone who is disabled is a careful plan, based on lots of good reliable information. That is what this book is all about.

It should prove more useful than other books on the subject. For one thing, it covers in detail far more places than any other guide for the disabled traveler —15 major cities in the United States, Canada, and Europe, as well as three of the Hawaiian Islands. It cites specifics about entrances, ramps, elevators, and actual door widths to bathrooms and rest rooms in individual hotels, restaurants, theaters, nightspots, museums, tourist sites, airports, and bus and train stations. For the cities themselves, it covers transportation possibilities and the type of terrain, and much other specialized information that you need to know to decide whether that place is for you or not.

Knowing that one person's architectural barrier is another person's challenge, I have made no attempt at too many qualitative judgments. This book has "just the facts" that will help prevent any unpleasant surprises in light of individual needs. Since readers will have their own special criteria for accessibility, the specifics can be used to make a personal assessment of "Can I get there?" and "Can I stay there?" and "Can I get around there?".

One thing I hope this book has done is remove the tedious process of research that planning a trip involves, when you have to start from scratch to find out the things that have been included here. To go that route can turn into enough research, sometimes contradictory and puzzling, for a 12-credit course!

It avoids the litany of lists that often passes as information in other books; the individual access guides to countries, cities, airports, hotel chains, airlines, trains, and buses they refer to—and leave it at that—are often obsolete. Where I have used an access guide already in print, it is only as *one* of the secondary sources, and the data has been culled and double-checked with disabled people on the spot, so that information is up-to-date as we go to press.

ABOUT THIS BOOK: The general chapters deal with the planning and the getting there information that should be especially useful if you are not an experienced traveler. Knowing how to go about booking your transportation; what to expect on planes, trains, or buses; or making sure that the accommodations will be suitable for you are vital to the success of any trip. You can find out here how to get cars with hand controls or vans with wheelchair lifts when you get to your destination, as well as useful telephone numbers for such things as organizations that can give you answers to special questions or help in emergencies.

The places included were chosen for suitability for people who have mobility difficulties or, in a couple of cases, for their irresistible appeal—even when they are not so convenient. Since there is as wide a range of ages, budgets, and interests among disabled people as among any other group of globe-trotters, there is a broad spectrum of activities and price categories of hotels and restaurants included. Each of the "place" chapters is a self-contained guide, covering how to get there, where to stay, how to get around when you are there, where to eat, and what to see and do. All of it, of course, with specific reference to steps, ramps, elevators and rest rooms—the banes and blessings of environment for somebody in a wheelchair—plus all the other information that would be included in a regular guidebook.

Because all you'll need to know about any one place is included within one chapter, you can make it a *traveling* guide that goes along on each excursion. Since you obviously won't need to know about London while you're in Hawaii, for instance, may I suggest a practical way to take along just the section you need? Yes, grit your teeth and actually take a book apart! Unlike other guides, this is not one with a dust cover that looks as if it has to be carefully stored away on the shelf. In this one, it's fairly easy to pull out a complete chapter from the binding in one piece; tuck it in your hand luggage, where it'll be a boon and not a burden.

Because I have never been comfortable using travel guides that give everything a symbol, there are no cryptographic references. You won't have to leaf continuously to a key, printed in some other part of the book, to find out whether a particular hotel, restaurant, museum, or theater is accessible to a wheelchair. It's all spelled out in unabbreviated plain English, right there in the same paragraph, along with all the other things you need to know about the place, such as location, prices, telephone number, hours, and any other pertinent hints or warnings.

This is a book written from the viewpoint of a permanently seated traveler who has moved around a couple of continents on business and pleasure, both accompanied and alone. I know the one thing that really can't be included in plans is flexibility: one hotel is *not* as convenient as another, one guest room is not at all as suitable as the one next door. We cannot jump on a public bus, nor dive down the subway. So it must all be known and arranged in advance, and I hope this guide provides you with a lot of the knowledge you'll need. Not everything has come up roses overnight, but there's literally a world of difference in the world out there from just a few years ago. Go see!

And one last personal word about that much-maligned device, the wheelchair. I believe that there's a lot of the self-fulfilling prophecy about the expression *"confined* to a wheelchair." Let's look at it another way, since it can be a case of whether the cup is half-empty or half-full. The wheelchair is actually an important device for making the world accessible, and for many people the wheelchair offers that freedom of mobility. What you need to know to take advantage of it is what I have tried to provide in this book.

Part I

THE BASICS

Chapter 1

THE VIEW FROM DOWN HERE

1. The Attitude Factor
2. The Accessibility Mystique
3. There Ought to Be a Law . . .

"CAN SHE WALK?" The question was addressed to my husband by a flight attendant on a plane as we headed for the Caribbean.

"No, but I *can* talk," was my rather affronted reply.

That happened less than ten years ago—one of my initial experiences as a disabled traveler—but I doubt if any flight attendant would ask the question that way today.

Those years have brought changes in both legislation and attitudes through the combined efforts of militancy and advocacy by disabled consumer groups and their supporters. The world is opening up for the traveler who has a physical disability: transportation, accommodations, and the attitudes of people in general are helping the integration. And this is just the beginning, really. As the rigidity of the old attitudes is loosened by legislation and fades away with the passage of time, there should eventually be a new generation of people around who'll take the disabled traveler completely for granted.

To modern society, freedom to travel is almost a part of the Bill of Rights. And, just as in education, employment, and housing, it's an area where today's disabled population should be determined not to be left out. Government figures show there are nearly a million Americans of working age alone who use wheelchairs for their mobility. Other aids to mobility are used by many millions more. In the decade of the 1970s, the "new survivors" of disabling trauma, and I count myself among them, have pushed statistics on people with chronic disabling conditions to one in every seven Americans. And we look for freedom to travel alongside those other six, of course.

1. The Attitude Factor

In order to be taken for granted, the disabled traveler has to be visible. If *you* take it for granted that you will be able to travel, that you're going to be just another passenger, guest, visitor, sightseer, along with all the others—except that you get some special attention now and again—you'll be influencing your own attitude as well as the attitude of others.

It's true that there are still some places where ordinary citizens rarely see a person in a wheelchair negotiating the streets and curbs, and they stare. If it's *me* they are looking at, I'm pleased, because the next time they see somebody in a wheelchair on the *street* (there may be a lot of disabled poeple who never leave home), they may be a little less surprised.

In dealing with people you encounter en route, on the transportation networks, in hotels, at theaters, in museums, on the street, or anywhere else, you may need their special attention or assistance, so it helps to have an understanding of any problems *they* may have in dealing with *your* problem. Most of them will be sincerely trying to help, but they are sometimes handicapped themselves by concepts and guidelines about disabled people in general, or by a lack of communication on your part of what your individual needs really require from them.

Keep in mind that your aim is for things to work to *your* advantage: soft words and an upbeat attitude can usually bring out the best in others and get you where you want to go, the way you want to do it.

There are always pioneers and trailblazers, thank goodness. I hear with admiration about paraplegics who parasail, of wheelchair riders who hitchhike, and of amputees who ski and climb mountains. But an attitude of "because it's there" is *not* a necessary qualification for a disabled traveler: planes, trains, buses, boats, ferries, hotels, motels, resorts, restaurants, museums, theaters, movie houses, amusement parks, and National Parks are all readily available. And in researching this guide, I was surprised at how much has been done in efforts to accommodate disabled travelers.

So we can't go everywhere, do everything as if we had no physical limitations, but there's still more than enough out there to fill a lifetime of experiences and pleasures and memories.

2. The Accessibility Mystique

To talk about "disabled" people in general terms, of course, is as dangerous as making generalizations about "men" and "women," but there are a lot of needs that are shared in common.

We do know that what most people with impaired mobility want is a level entrance or a decent ramp, elevators to upper floors or basements, a bathroom door that's wide enough for a wheelchair, and some grab bars in the right places, among other things.

We *do* know that people with impaired vision need braille in the right places and some indication of where obstructions are.

We *do* know that people with hearing impairments need the means to communicate and to understand what is going on around them.

And all of us need other people who are aware of our limitations and differing requirements, and who are willing to change their habits and routines for us.

After that, there are a lot of differences.

Does a short paraplegic in a junior-size wheelchair need the same access features as a six-foot quadriplegic, for instance? How is the "accessibility" of a place assessed for somebody with plenty of upper torso strength and energy, who can get a wheelchair into and up practically anything, versus somebody who weighs 200 lbs. and who doesn't have much muscle? And how about somebody in a wheelchair traveling alone, compared to somebody who is traveling with a companion possessed of a working pair of both legs and arms?

Accessibility is certainly relative

So lists of what's "accessible" beg a lot of questions. For instance, most of us who use wheelchairs need to know that doorways are wide enough, that there aren't flights of steps to get into buildings, that a room has space for a wheelchair to maneuver. Where the word "accessible" is used in this book, it means all those things. But it also includes the details of obstacles as well, since there are those who are not at all discouraged by a few steps if they are traveling with a companion, or even if they are alone.

I have not hesitated to include rear or side or staff entrances where they provide easier access than the main one, nor to include service elevators as a means of access to a restaurant, for instance. A word about that . . . I have known people who use wheelchairs who won't go to public places if it means going through the kitchen in a restaurant, or using the freight elevators, for instance. I don't agree with that, unless the lack of regular access is in violation of the law, as it would be in the case of a federal building or one constructed with federal funds. There are restaurants that I definitely consider worthwhile visiting, even if I know I have to go up or down with the meat and vegetables. I've met some of the nicest people on those routes!

The reason you won't find any reference here to "handicapped facilities," even though it is a commonly used phrase, is because I belong to the school of semantics that understands "handicap" to mean the architectural barrier—*not* the paralysis. I prefer the term "disabled" to distinguish certain people from those who have no physical impairment. But be prepared to talk in those other terms if you have to. And to tell the truth, I'll use "handicapped facilities" any time, if they're there. Or even take a "handicapped room" in a hotel (do they ever stop to think how odd that sounds, I wonder?).

3. There Ought to Be a Law . . .

To people unfamiliar with the details, it may seem they have heard a lot about what's been done in the United States in recent years on behalf of the disabled population. True, there *was* a lot of legislation passed and regulations written in Washington in the 1970s regarding the accessibility rights of disabled people. Milestones that these were, their application was only to areas where federal funds were involved: there was no mandate for the private sector to plan or construct buildings that are accessible to people in wheelchairs. And, of course, it's primarily the private sector we're dealing with when we travel.

We're covered at the airports, since many of them received federal subsidies and are under the jurisdiction of the Department of Transportation. For air travel, the Civil Aeronautics Board requires that no air carrier discriminate in its services against the disabled person (although definitions leave a lot to be desired). And for train travel, Amtrak is also regulated, to a certain extent, as far as its provisions for disabled passengers are concerned, because of its federal support.

But what do we find in those places untouched by federal government regulations? Well, it's not simply a case that all federally related architecture and transportation is open to us—and the rest is not. In at least 33 states, accessibility legislation and standards in varying degrees apply to privately owned buildings that are used by the public. And some municipalities have passed ordinances or amended building codes to require access for physically disabled people to publicly used but privately owned buildings. Curb cuts are often required when new sidewalks are laid down, or old ones reconstructed. There's sometimes a long wait, though, since only the new is affected, and not the old, existing buildings and sidewalks.

When they get around to it, how do architects and builders decide what the "accessibility" features are going to be, and how are they going to be designed? Many conform to specifications approved by the American National Standard Institute (ANSI) for "making buildings and facilities accessible and usable by physically handicapped people."

Then again, some don't. For example, there may indeed be a ramp, but it may be too steep, unless there is help for the person in a wheelchair from one or even two others. Many hotels with level or ramped entrances and elevators between floors call themselves accessible when the bathroom doors are too narrow for a wider wheelchair, and when there are no grab bars. The door to a guest room in a hotel may be wide enough, but the furniture is arranged so that no wheelchair can be moved around inside. I recently encountered a "handicapped" room in a prominent hotel in which I almost had to sleep in the "accessible" bathroom, since the furniture placement made it impossible to get into the bedroom until one of the two beds had been taken out.

However, as is often the case, things *can* be made to suit you with a little friendly persuasion.

Very often, and with all the best will in the world, developers, hoteliers, and corporations put the "experts" to work and forget to consult anybody who is disabled. This results in things like door peepholes and window latches placed too high to be used by people in wheelchairs. Or the guest room door is wide enough, to be sure, but much too heavy for somebody to push or pull open from a sitting position. There are even elaborately adapted rest rooms with every aid imaginable, but the stall door opens *in*ward. Sometimes the grab bars are there, but they are so far away you'd have to be an orangutang to reach them. And what do you do with a toilet that has a spring-loaded seat?

Every disabled traveler has a special "horror" story, but it's usually told for laughs. Or should be. Patience and a sense of humor are absolute essentials to pack along in the baggage. So if you haven't done much traveling yet, these are just warnings and not at all meant to discourage.

Because it's needed in the private sector, where the laws and ordinances don't apply, large national groups like the National Easter Seal Society and the Paralyzed Veterans of America conduct active and effective campaigns in the continuing education—and sometimes battle—for the removal of the architectural and attitudinal barriers faced by the disabled population when they try to enter the mainstream. All of this has certainly begun to make a difference to the environment that the disabled traveler finds.

Legislation is only one of the things that's needed. Attitudes can be barriers that need to be removed as well, and sometimes all it takes is exposure to the notion that people who happen to have a physical disability are looking for similar services and pleasures as everybody else.

Out there in the mainstream, very visible traveler, what are you going to find and how best to plan for it? On your mark . . .

Chapter 2

ON YOUR MARK . . .

The Practicalities of Transportation & Lodging

**1. Traveling by Air
2. Traveling by Train 3. Traveling
by Bus 4. Traveling by Car
5. Cruise Ships 6. Hotels and Motels**

DISABLED TRAVELERS ARE NO DIFFERENT from any others when it comes to the variety of personal choices of how to plan and how to go. This guide has been compiled primarily for the person who wants to travel alone or with a companion. (The possibilities of going with a group of other disabled people are outlined in the last chapter.) Even if you go independently, though, it doesn't mean you have to do *all* the planning alone: a travel agent is a very convenient means of access to the sometimes complex business of making reservations. Agents can save you time and money, too, since they usually know where the bargains are to be found. Their services add no cost to your trip: their commissions are paid by the airlines and hotels.

So why *not* just call a travel agent, and sit back? Well, most travel agents know a lot about travel, but most have little feel for what's needed for a disabled traveler, let alone where to find *your* special requirements. The exception may be the organizers of group tours for disabled travelers, some of whom handle individual trips as well. (See the list in the last chapter.)

It's essential you have some facts at your fingertips before reservations are made by the agent, who has no secret source to find out what would be right for you in particular. Some are more knowledgeable than others. One organization that can guide you to an agent with some experience in handling arrangements for disabled travelers is the **Society for the Advancement of Travel for the Handicapped (SATH)**, 26 Court St., Brooklyn, NY 11242 (tel. 212/858-5483). They may be able to refer you to an agent in your area.

To plan your own trip, or to work with a travel agent to ensure that the best arrangements are made, here's an outline of what to expect in the way of transportation and accommodation.

TRANSPORTATION

1. Traveling by Air

Many readers may have often traveled by air and understand how it's done. What they would probably like to tell the first-time flyers is that it *can* be done, that the airlines *are* geared to handle disabled passengers ... and that no two airlines are likely to do it the same way!

There are basic procedures, even though they may vary from airline to airline, and even within an airline: the system, after all, is made up of individuals who have perhaps understood things a little differently from each other, or prefer to do the required operation in some way that's proved more practical. At any rate, airline personnel now take it for granted that disabled people will be among their passengers, and from airport skycaps to airline captains, you'll find total acceptance.

It is highly unlikely these days that any domestic airline will require you to produce medical certification that you are fit to travel, but there are still differences between airlines in their requirements, so make sure about what those requirements are when you make your reservation. For instance, Pan American Airways has a policy that disabled passengers must be accompanied: I experienced the application of that rule first-hand, when I arrived at the airport for a flight to London, but final decision rests with the flight's captain, and in my case he decided I would be allowed to board on my own, since I probably appeared to be independent and accustomed to traveling alone. The return trip alone on Trans World Airlines presented no such problem.

PLANNING: First, remember that *every* traveler has a hassle every now and again with the airlines, whether it be about reservations, seating, cancellations, weather, overbooking, or lost baggage. Let's hope that your trips are trouble-free, but if there are problems, it need not be because you are a disabled passenger. As a matter of fact, let's make your trip so well-planned that you have fewer problems than anybody else!

The keys to getting off on the right foot (as it were) are in your communicating and confirming. Each airline has its own special services and regulations, so ask a lot of questions, especially if it is a charter flight. Then tell your travel agent or the airline reservations desk what you will need. It's a good idea to travel, if you have a choice, at less busy hours. This gives airline personnel time to give you more attention. And take a direct flight, whenever possible, to avoid multiplying the inconveniences of getting on and off more than one plane per trip.

You cannot tell too much to the person making your reservation: the information needed *should* then get into the computer and down the chain of personnel who will be handling you from check-in to destination, and that includes any connecting airline as well, if you are making a change somewhere along the way. However, it never hurts to check the airline once, or even more, in the days before you leave, on what the reservations system is telling about you. If it's not quite right, you can have it corrected; if it *is* correct, you'll have some peace of mind.

You know what you are capable of—a lot, a little—in the way of mobility, and you should make sure that the airline knows, too. Clarify what "wheelchair" terms you are using: Are you traveling with your own wheelchair? Or do you need an airline's wheelchair? How much assistance will you need? Can you walk at all? Can you stand? Will you need lifting in and out of your seat? Is your wheelchair motorized?

If you use a wheelchair, or don't want to climb steps, check on whether your flight will have jetways for boarding at departure and for deplaning at your destination. (Jetways are those expandable corridors that connect the terminal with the plane door all on one level.) If the reservations agent can't tell you, ask to speak to the supervisor: this information should always be available. Not all airports have jetways, so ask about procedures for getting you on and off the plane. If you can't manage stairs, these will usually involve the use of the narrow boarding chair used by most airlines to carry you up the steps to the plane door and down the plane aisle to your seat. A couple of airlines use lift devices. Whatever the system, airlines usually make sure there is plenty of capable assistance on hand.

Although you will have a choice of seating in smoking or non-smoking sections of the airplane, airlines have their own policies about the seats to be assigned to non-ambulatory passengers, In coach class, it is often the bulkhead seats on the aisle, that is, the first row. If there is more than one coach section, as in the wide-body planes, your seat will usually be close to the plane door. Although, this isn't always the door used at the destination, airline personnel will take care of getting you the extra distance down the aisle. In some aircraft there are now certain aisle seats that have movable armrests, so that transfer is simplified (more details later in this section). If you can walk and will want to use the lavatories, ask for a seat that is conveniently located.

If you are taking a motorized wheelchair, you must make sure your questions to the travel agent or airline agent are answered very clearly, since airline policies can differ on this subject. Gel or dry-cell batteries present no problems for the airlines, but they are more costly and less efficient for you. So if you want to take your wet-cell battery along, make sure about the policy of the airline you plan to fly with. The U.S. government clarified the confusion caused by a lot of airlines that considered wet-cell batteries hazardous. According to federal regulations issued in 1982 by the Department of Transportation's Materials Transportation Bureau, wet-cell batteries can be carried under certain conditions. This has been reinforced by a recent recommendation of the Airline Pilots Association (the pilot generally has the last word on who and what goes on board).

If the battery remains attached to the wheelchair, the battery caps must be tightly secured, the battery terminals and cables must be taped securely, and the battery must be secured to the chair. Some airlines require that the chair be containerized in their own equipment—a very good reason for planning ahead and arriving early at the airport.

Some disabled people who normally use motorized chairs for independent mobility in their jobs or for around their neighborhoods, often opt *not* to travel with this very expensive piece of equipment if they plan to rent one at their destination, or they have a companion on the trip.

Respirators with dry-cell batteries are allowed on aircraft, but there are no outlets for those that depend on electricity. Always mention if you use a respirator when making reservations. It's a good idea to check with your physician before flying if you use a respirator, since the extremely low humidity in the airplane cabin may cause some discomfort.

BOARDING THE PLANE: Plan to arrive in good time at the airport, since you will be boarded ahead of other passengers. When you check in, make sure you have a baggage tag for your wheelchair if it is traveling with you, and reconfirm that a narrow aisle chair will be available at the gate to get you to your seat if you are unable to walk. An airline agent in the check-in area will usually assign somebody to take you to the gate if you need assistance to get there.

Everybody goes through the security check these days before arriving at the departure gate. If you are in a wheelchair, you will be checked over with a hand-held detecting device rather than through the gateway used by ambulatory passengers. Your hand baggage will go through the normal checking equipment.

The one procedure followed by all airlines is pre-boarding of disabled passengers. If there is a jetway to board the plane from the gate, ask to be taken as far as possible in your own wheelchair, since it is so much more comfortable and maneuverable than the airline's narrow boarding chairs: although normal procedure on most airlines is to transfer you from your wheelchair to the aisle chair at the door of the plane, see if you can be taken on board and as close to your seat as possible before transferring, if it is a wide-bodied aircraft. This is not usually possible on narrow-bodied craft.

Your own wheelchair will then be taken down to the baggage hold of the plane. Make sure that it is identified in some way and that all removable parts, such as armrests, are securely fastened. I find it a good idea to take removable footrests into the cabin since they can be damaged in the airplane hold. And, of course, you will take anything not attached to the chair, such as cushions, into the cabin with you, as well. Because you will be so busy attending to the job of transferring and getting to your seat, have someone make sure that the chair has been taken to the hold and *not* back into the terminal (it sometimes happens!), or, if you are traveling alone, get assurance from the flight attendant who will be helping you when you board. Don't hesitate to become a bore on this subject! On some airlines you may be given an escort ticket, which should be given back to the flight attendant, so that it can be handed to the agent who will meet the plane, to indicate that special assistance is needed.

Don't be surprised if the attendant puts a blanket on the seat before you sit on it. This is a procedure that is followed for faster evacuation in emergencies. The attendant may also ask you how you would like to be moved in case of an emergency. Again, this will not happen every time, since the policies are somewhat inconsistent.

At one time, all crutches and canes had to be stored away once the disabled passenger was seated, but new policies, mostly due to advocacy by associations of the blind, now allow those aids to be stored under the passenger's seat, providing that they don't protrude into the aisle or into the emergency exit passage.

Blind travelers are alerted by the public address system to the lighted signals for "fasten seat belts" and "no smoking," and the attendant explains the layout of the aircraft and the location of call buttons, for instance. Frontier Airlines provides flight information in braille. Hearing-impaired passengers can read emergency procedures in instruction sheets available at each seat.

Guide and hearing dogs are allowed to travel on board free of charge with their owners. It is usual for a window seat to be assigned so that the dog is not in the way of the other passengers (This is only applicable to domestic flights—check quarantine regulations if you are going overseas.)

ARRIVING: If you will need assistance when the plane lands, if you want your own wheelchair brought from the hold to the door of the plane (rather than taken to the baggage area), or if you are making a connecting flight, remind the flight attendant in good time before landing. In fact, tell as many on-board personnel as you can to ensure that your special needs will be radioed ahead from the cockpit to the airport. Get a confirmation that this has been done.

Disabled passengers are customarily the last to be deplaned, and you will often have to wait even longer at times while your wheelchair is brought from the hold. Just plan not to be in a hurry. Messages sometimes get mixed up and the wheelchair may be taken to the baggage area instead, so be prepared also to use an airport wheelchair to get from the plane to the terminal if this happens. This is common practice overseas.

There will always be a skycap or airline agent to go with you to the baggage area and then to whatever transportation you are using to leave the airport. If you have made an international trip, the escort will assist you through customs and immigration formalities as well.

AIRPORTS: Air terminals at all major cities in North America are generally well equipped with facilities for disabled passengers. Elevators, and at least one or two adapted rest rooms, accessible to wheelchairs, can usually be taken for granted in the large airports. Lowered and amplified phones are not universal but are found in many terminal buildings. Similarly in the major European cities. Smaller airports haven't quite caught up yet, but assistance is usually provided when the airline has given notice of your arrival.

Again, the best way to get what's best for you is to let everybody know exactly what you need: it's often impossible for them to tell just by looking at you. The desire to help and do the right thing is nearly always there.

Your escort will know the best way to get to the baggage area and out of the terminal, even if it seems rather roundabout at times, so that stairs and escalators can be avoided if you use a wheelchair. If the escort is an airline agent, a tip is not necessary, but if a skycap has provided you with escort assistance, and if he has been particularly helpful, a tip according to his service is called for.

IMPROVEMENTS IN AIRCRAFT: For anybody who is not configured vertically, the environment inside the cabin of any airplane, whether it be wide-body (jumbo) or narrow-body, is not ideal. Space is at a premium; most coach section aisles are only 22 inches wide and knee room between rows is not for the long-legged. Among the most frustrating aspects of any airplane cabin, large or small, have always been both the rigid armrests that are difficult to get around for transfer from a chair, and the impossibility of either reaching or using the toilet if you can't walk.

Something *is* being done about *some* of those things now, mostly due to the efforts of the Access to the Skies program of Rehabilitation International USA (RIUSA) and consumer advocate groups. It was the Access program that also developed prototypes of on-board wheelchairs to be considered for use by airlines. The improvements made so far include equipping new planes and retrofitting existing fleets with two or more movable armrests in each aircraft. A few airlines already have adapted toilets and on-board wheelchairs; others are still considering which chair to buy.

United Airlines was the first carrier to operate planes with all those options for more accessibility in its new fleet of 19 Boeing-767 wide-body planes that are flying, at the time of writing, out of New York (LaGuardia and Newark Airports), Chicago, Boston, Detroit, Los Angeles, Portland, San Francisco, and Washington (Dulles). For the first time, toilets on the new planes have wider doors and more floor space and are equipped with grab bars and faucets that allow for one-hand operation. The area adjacent to the lavatory can also be made into a ten-square-foot privacy area with the use of a curtain. The new Stowaway chair carried on board United's 767 planes allows passengers who can't walk to reach the lavatory. It is also used for getting on and off the plane.

American Airlines and Trans World Airlines also plan on-board wheelchairs and access to the lavatories on their 767s, which already have movable armrests. Both airlines are installing movable armrests in many of their other planes as they are refurbished. TWA plans access features for its DC 9-80s, and Pan American is putting movable armrests in their DC-10s as they are renovated and are evaluating lavatory access and on-board wheelchairs. World Airways has plans to equip its entire fleet eventually with movable armrests, on board wheelchairs, and accessible lavatories, as well as emergency procedure cards in braille and sign-language video screening of orientation and announcements. Air France and Air Canada are among the non-domestic airlines that have already bought on-board wheelchairs.

Other airlines which have plans for installing movable armrests include Eastern, Northwest, USAir and Western, but they have no plans at present for on-board wheelchairs or lavatory access. Although some airlines don't have plans for improving the accessibility of their aircraft, the ones making the adaptations are among the major carriers with fleets that constitute the larger percentage of planes flying.

If you have a choice, go with the airlines that have considered the needs of disabled passengers and let them know why. Writing a letter to the president of the company can be influential in its future plans, especially if you have had a good flight and have received considerate attention from the airline's personnel.

The future of air travel *is* looking brighter. The Boeing Company, the world's largest aircraft manufacturer, has long-range programs for accessibility improvements and has designed options available to airlines that buy Boeing planes, including the existing 747, 727, and 737, as well as the new 767 widebody and 757 standard-body planes. Douglas Aircraft also plans to offer to the airlines options that include movable aisle armrests, which many airlines have already installed on their DC-9s, DC Super-80s, and DC-10s. The next generation aircraft cabin from Douglas will offer improved lavatory access with wider doors, curtained privacy areas, and even a cantilevered toilet for lateral transfer from an on-board wheelchair . . . but that's a few years away, so don't wait for it before you decide to travel.

The Airbus, made in Europe, includes the wide-body A-300, which is designed with one of the largest lavatories aboard any commercial aircraft flying today. It is located at the rear, where privacy can be provided, and it has a sliding door as standard equipment. Airbus is the only aircraft manufacturer that also offers its own design of on-board wheelchair as an option to the airlines. You'll find the Airbus used primarily overseas, but they are flown in the United States by Eastern Airlines, although the domestic carrier does not have on-board wheelchairs for access to the lavatory for non-ambulatory passengers.

INTERNATIONAL AIR TRAVEL: For the last two or three years, fortunately, members of the International Air Transport Association (IATA) have been following fairly standardized procedures in the handling of disabled passengers. There is said to be more emphasis by international carriers on medical clearance, but a new system instituted by IATA could help smooth the way, particularly for the permanently disabled traveler. It is the **Frequent Traveler's Medical Card (FREMEC),** issued by the airlines' medical department, which will give information on the nature of your disability and the kind of assistance generally needed. A physician's statement is *not* required. Once you have the FREMEC card, it is generally accepted as medical clearance by all carriers who belong to IATA.

Policies about seeing and hearing dogs are similar to those on domestic airlines, but, of course, many countries have strict quarantine regulations about the entry of dogs.

The convenience of jetway boarding and deplaning is less frequently found overseas, so be prepared for other means of entry and exit, most of which involve being carried. Some airports use the catering truck, which has a hydraulic lift, rather than the staircase, and though this is considered undignified by some disabled travelers (not by me), it is a safe and convenient way to get on board. SAS and KLM are evaluating a boarding stairway equipped with a movable platform lift. Transportation across airport aprons has to be provided, too, since planes often park a long way from the terminals. This can be by regular mini-buses (again, calling for you to be carried aboard either with or without a chair), or by vehicles with a wheelchair-lift.

All the other procedures and precautions outlined earlier in this section apply to traveling by air overseas. You'll find plenty of assistance provided, as well as escort through airport formalities and to the baggage and exit areas if you are in a wheelchair, or if you make a special request for physical assistance.

IN GENERAL: One of the first things to take into account when traveling by air is that at present most airplane lavatories are going to be out of bounds if you cannot walk, unless you happen to fly one of the new planes that have on-board wheelchairs and larger lavatories. There are no generalizations to be made about how to deal with this inconvenience, since you'll know your own needs best. However, remember there are nearly always accessible rest rooms at most airports, and they may be the last ones you'll get to for a few hours. Depending on the length of your flight, you'll obviously make provision for your own needs in this respect. Some travelers restrict their liquid intake in the hours before flight time. If you want to ensure that this partial dehydration is not detrimental to your health, consult your doctor, who may be able to suggest some other method. Despite the temptation, it is a good idea to delay accepting any of the drinks or beverages offered on board until you are within reasonable distance of airport facilities at your destination and can finally enjoy them!

One thing that often doesn't get enough attention from passengers traveling with such expensive equipment as a wheelchair, especially a motorized one, is the question of lost or damaged baggage. Airlines provide a maximum liability of $750 per passenger, and this would include a wheelchair. Although it is highly unlikely that total replacement would be called for, you may want to consider getting Excess Valuation Insurance that is sold at baggage counters and costs about 50 cents per $100 value. Always inspect your chair as soon as you get it at your destination so that any damage can be reported before you leave the airport.

It probably can't be said too often that it's a good idea to have a carry-on bag with you that contains at least 24 hours' supply of any medication and anything else you may need if your baggage goes astray, for some reason, and doesn't catch up with you until later. (I always travel under the assumption that it *will.*)

For Further Information

Among the booklets with information about air travel for disabled passengers are: "Access Travel: A Guide to Accessibility of Airport Terminals," from Access America, Washington, DC 20202; "Consumer Information about Air Travel for the Handicapped," from TWA, 2 Penn Plaza, New York, NY 10010; "Handicapped," from United Airlines, P.O. Box 66100, Chicago, IL 60666; "Care in the Air," from the Air Transport Users Committee, 129 Kingsway, London WC2B 6NN, England; "Incapacitated Passengers Air Travel Guide," from the Traffic Services Administrator, International Air Transport Association (IATA), 2000 Peel St., Montréal, PQ, Canada H3A 2R4 ($4).

TDD toll-free telephone numbers have been installed to assist hearing-impaired travelers by American Airlines (800/543-1586, in Ohio 800/582-1573), United Airlines (800/323-0170), and Trans World Airlines (800/421-8489, in California 800/252-0622). Pan American's TDD telephone number is 202/659-5454.

2. Traveling by Train

Trains may *not* be the first thing you think of as the means to get from here to there, but there are a number of journeys for which they are eminently convenient and spare you the trouble of traveling to and from airports. Since I am a New Yorker, the obviously convenient ones that come to mind are the runs between New York and Washington, D.C. (with Philadelphia in between), and from New York to Boston, all on Amtrak Metroliners. Or the Amfleet trains that go from Washington and New York north to Montréal and Toronto in Canada. Then there are the long-distance trains with enticing names like the "California Zephyr" (Chicago to San Francisco), and the other Amtrak Superliners that traverse the wide open spaces of the West. You can also take your car to Florida on Amtrak's new auto train service that runs between Lorton, Virginia (near Washington), and Sanford, Florida (near Orlando).

Traveling on all those lines is feasible for passengers in wheelchairs to differing degrees. Federal regulations required Amtrak, the national railroad corporation, to make all trains accessible to disabled passengers by 1984, but gave the system another ten years to convert the stations. However, most major stations have already been adapted or provided with equipment to assist boarding, so a train trip becomes a real possibility.

Amtrak's Turboliners and Amfleet cars that are used on short- to medium-distance routes have features that enable passengers in wheelchairs to travel quite comfortably. The Superliners on the long-distance western routes have specially designed sleepers. Since there is often only one seat, sleeper, or wheelchair space on each train, advance checking is important.

PLANNING: Procedure is to notify or make reservations, in advance, with the local Amtrak office or call toll-free 800/USA-RAIL. For hearing-impaired travelers the toll-free TDD number is 800/523-6590, except in Pennsylvania, where it is 800/562-6950. Let them know what kind of assistance you will need. For instance, if you use a wheelchair or need to be met with a wheelchair, arrangements will be made for a redcap to escort you from the station entrance to the train. Confirm that your departure and arrival stations have adequate provisions if you are in a wheelchair: at some stations there is level boarding access from a high platform to the train; at others, a hydraulic lift will be used to board you. The double-deck Superliners are accessible by ramp from ground level to the lower deck, where the special accommodations are located. Your request for assistance will be handled by a Special Service Desk that will make all the arrangements and then call you to confirm them.

SPECIAL ACCOMMODATIONS: Different passenger cars have different facilities. The Amfleet trains on the short- and medium-distance runs have a snack bar or club car that has one swivel seat with a fold-down armrest for easier transfer. You may remain in your wheelchair, if you prefer. The rest room in the car has a wide entrance and large turn-around space inside and is equipped with grab bars. The car attendant will serve you food and beverages at your seat.

The exception to trains with these features are the high-speed premium fare Metroliners that operate between New York City and Washington, D.C., which are older and do not have special accommodation for wheelchairs, although there is wide aisle space in the club car, where you can transfer to a swivel armchair. Stations served by the Metroliner all have high platforms that allow level entry and exit from the cars. There are no accessible rest rooms in the trains on Metroliner routes.

The Turboliners that operate in New York State and between New York State and Canada have one seat for disabled passengers in the club car, for which you need only pay the regular coach fare if you are disabled. This also applies to any companion attendant. There is enough room in this area of the car so that you can stay in your wheelchair if you prefer. The rest room near the assigned seat or space is accessible.

On the Superliners in service west of Chicago, each sleeper car has one bedroom that is the width of the car and has its own private rest room with plenty of turn-around space. The Superliners also have coach accommodation with a swivel seat that has a movable armrest for easy transfer. This special seat is located near the accessible rest room, and there is also space in the car to remain in the wheelchair if you prefer.

Seeing Eye and Hearing Ear dogs are allowed to travel in Amtrak passenger cars without extra charge, and conductors will make sure that deaf or blind passengers know when they have reached their destination.

DISCOUNT FARES: When the one-way coach fare is at least $40, Amtrak offers a 25% reduction to disabled passengers who have an acceptable ID, which can be as a member of an organization, a physician's letter, or a government agency document.

"Access Amtrak, A Guide to Amtrak Services for Elderly and Handicapped Travelers," is available from the Office of Customer Relations, Amtrak, P.O. Box 2709, Washington, DC 20013.

ACCESSIBLE STATIONS: Stations that Amtrak considers suitable for disabled travelers because they have high platforms or are equipped with lifts, are:

Alabama
 Anniston
 Birmingham
 Tuscaloosa

Arkansas
 Little Rock

 Texarkana

California
 Bakersfield
 Davis
 Fresno
 Fullerton

 Glendale
 Los Angeles
 Martinez
 Oakland
 Ocala
 Pasadena
 Pomona

Redding
Riverbank
Salinas
San Bernardino
San Diego
San Jose
San Luis Obispo
Santa Ana
Santa Barbara
Stockton

Connecticut
Hartford
New Haven
New London

D.C.
Washington

Delaware
Wilmington

Florida
Clearwater
Jacksonville
Miami
Orlando
St. Petersburg
Winter Haven

Georgia
Atlanta
Gainsville
Savannah

Idaho
Boise
Pocatello

Illinois
Bloomington
Champaign-Urbana
Chicago (Union)
Effingham
Kankakee
Kewanee
Springfield

Indiana
Fort Wayne
Indianapolis
South Bend

Kentucky
Tri-State (Catlettsburg)

Louisiana
New Orleans

Maryland
Baltimore
Baltimore/Washington
Airport
Columbia

Massachusetts
Boston (South Street,
Atlantic Avenue,
Sumners Street)
Springfield
Worcester

Michigan
Battle Creek
Dearborn
Detroit
E. Lansing
Flint
Jackson
Kalamazoo
Port Huron

Minnesota
Duluth
St. Paul

Mississippi
Canton
Grenada
Jackson
McComb
Meridian

Missouri
Jefferson City
Kansas City
St. Louis
West Quincy

Nevada
Las Vegas

New Jersey
Newark

New York
Albany

Buffalo (Exchange Sta.
Depew Street)
New York (Pennsylvania
Sta., Grand Central Sta.)
Plattsburgh
Poughkeepsie (Highland)
Rochester
Syracuse
Utica

North Carolina
Charlotte
Fayetteville
Greensboro
Hamlet
Rocky Mount
Raleigh

Ohio
Cincinnati
Cleveland
Lima
Toledo

Oregon
Portland

Pennsylvania
Altoona
Erie
Harrisburg
Johnstown
North Philadelphia
Philadelphia
Pittsburgh

Rhode Island
Providence

South Carolina
Charleston
Columbia
Florence
Greenville

Tennessee
Memphis

Texas
Austin
Dallas
Fort Worth
Houston
Longview
Temple

Vermont	Lynchburg	**West Virginia**
Montpelier Jct.	Newport News	Charleston
St. Alban	Petersburg	Prince
White River Jct.	Richmond	
		Wisconsin
Virginia	**Washington**	La Crosse
Alexandria	Centralia	Milwaukee
Charlottesville	Seattle	Portage

TRAINS OUTSIDE THE UNITED STATES: Train travel in the U.S. *is* feasible. Elsewhere, it still presents all sorts of obstacles.

Canada

For instance, although Canada's VIA RAIL system is in the midst of long-term plans for coast-to-coast accessible train travel, it currently has only one high-level platform (at the Montréal station) and 11 major stations where there is lift equipment for boarding "full service" trains (Calgary, Edmonton, Halifax, London, Montréal, Ottawa, Québec City, Toronto, Vancouver, Windsor, and Winnipeg).

VIA's new main line train, the LRC (Light and Rapid and Comfortable), runs at present only between Montréal and Toronto but is planned for other routes. In these new trains, seats can be removed to allow wheelchair space with tie-downs, and there is an accessible rest room. Food is served to passengers if they wish.

Europe

Although some countries are aware of the problem and are making plans to adapt their trains and stations, it's too early yet to detail much improvement. You will see in the chapter on London that British Railways makes a number of different arrangements to carry disabled passengers. Denmark is working on plans for a boarding lift and compartments with removable seats to make room for wheelchairs. In France, French Railways has policies and facilities for disabled passengers, but there is still no means of level entry to most trains for non-ambulatory passengers (except to TGV trains). Facilities include portable steps that are less steep than the regular entry for passengers who are mobility-impaired, but who are ambulatory. The crack TGV (*Très Grande Vitesse* —Very High Speed) trains have one location in the first-class cars in which it is possible to stay in one's wheelchair for second-class fare. They run between Paris and Nice, Avignon, Belfort, and Grenoble, with stops in between.

Elsewhere it is a matter of being carried aboard if you do not walk. This is usually my mode of using European trains—I am fortunate to have a very fit traveling companion who can carry me up the steep steps into the train—but if you do it that way, too, make sure your wheelchair is in a place recommended by the conductor so that you don't arrive at your destination without it (as happened to me in Venice!).

3. Traveling by Bus

One of my favorite ways to travel around the country before I became disabled was by bus. Nothing comes close to it if you want the actual traveling from one place to another to be part of the experience of seeing different places and meeting different people. It also costs less than other modes of transportation. If you can't walk at all, however, it is not a feasible way to travel alone. You'll need a companion who can carry you on and off the bus, because those steps are steep and the aisles are only 14 inches wide, although some of the newer buses have kneeling mechanisms that lower the steps for easier boarding.

The major bus companies do offer special fare plans to disabled people who bring along a companion to assist them: Greyhound's is called the *Helping Hand Service*, Trailways' is the *Good Samaritan*. Both will transport two passengers—one disabled, one assistant companion—for the price of a single fare. A doctor's certification that you cannot travel alone is required to qualify you for either program.

For disabled people who use a wheelchair, but who can stand and walk a few steps, it becomes possible to travel on the bus alone, and the personnel of both major bus companies are ready to assist with boarding. Folding wheelchairs, or other special equipment such as walkers, are carried free of charge as baggage. Greyhound does not carry motorized chairs, but Trailways has facilities for them on some of their buses, so check.

Rest rooms can cause problems, as always. The on-board rest room at the rear of the bus is probably not feasible for most disabled passengers, but a number of bus stations have been equipped with accessible rest rooms. For the wheelchair passenger who can stand, the lack of accessible rest rooms is less of a problem than for those who need the special facilities of wider doors and other equipment.

When you call the bus company for schedules, alert them that you are disabled and then arrive at least 30 minutes before the scheduled departure time. It goes without saying that traveling at less busy times, like midweek, will be less of a hassle. Whenever you travel, your departing station will alert your destination that you require assistance.

FOR FURTHER INFORMATION: For brochures on the special programs write to **Greyhound Lines**, Section S, Greyhound Tower, Phoenix, AZ 85077, and **Continental Trailways**, 1512 Commerce, Suite 500, Dallas, TX 75201. Greyhound's toll-free telephone number for hearing-impaired travelers is TDD 800/345-3109. Both Greyhound and Trailways allow seeing and hearing dogs to travel with their owners without extra charge.

4. Traveling by Car

Traveling by car is certainly to be recommended as a means of mobility from here to there, and for a way to spend a vacation just touring.

PRIVATE CAR: If you have your own self-operated car, van, or RV, it can be assumed that you don't need much advice on traveling by road: you must know most of the ropes. And it can be assumed that your vehicle has all the adaptations that make it convenient for you. However, if you want to check out a comprehensive booklet that lists factory options, special equipment, driving aids, equipment installation and maintenance, and agencies nationwide with their services, among other things, contact your local AAA Club for "The Handicapped Drivers Mobility Guide," or write to the Traffic Safety Dept., American Automobile Association, 8111 Gatehouse Rd., Falls Church, VA 22407. This booklet also includes the states that have reciprocity on special parking permits, and they are listed as Alabama, Arizona, Colorado, Connecticut, Idaho, Illinois, Indiana, Iowa, Kentucky, Maine, Maryland, Minnesota,

Mississippi, New Hampshire, New York, North Carolina, Oregon, Pennsylvania, Utah, Vermont, Virginia, West Virginia, and Wyoming. You'll know if you drive a lot, however, that state laws do not always apply to local municipalities.

If you plan to travel in your own recreational vehicle, you can get all kinds of information from **AWill/AWay RVers Association,** an organization formed for the specific purpose of providing travel assistance to disabled RV owners. They'll give you a checklist of things related to the vehicle, to medical needs, and access information, if you give them your route and let them know a month before you plan to leave. Send a stamped, self-addressed envelope to AWill/AWay RVers Association, 59 Tahattawan Rd. Littleton, MA 01460.

There's no mode of travel undertaken by anybody with a mobility problem in which the question of rest room accessibility is not a prime concern. The road is no exception. One of the most useful booklets ever published is "Highway Rest Areas for Handicapped Travelers," which lists over 800 rest areas across the country (except Hawaii and Oregon) that are marked with the international symbol of access. It is published by the President's Committee on the Employment of the Handicapped, Washington, DC 20210. The New York State Thruway has its own directory of accessible rest rooms, and it's available from the Chief Engineer, New York State Thruway Authority, 200 Southern Blvd., Albany, NY 12209.

RENTAL CAR: You may consider renting a car, either in advance so that it will be waiting for you at the airport, or when you arrive at your destination, for a day or two of excursions. If you don't need hand controls, you can obviously follow the regular routines of booking and choosing the car you want with the agency of your choice. Always get confirmation in writing.

The companies that can provide hand controls in some major cities in the U.S. at no extra cost are Hertz, Avis, and National. It's harder to find hand controls available in Canada, and they are rare in Europe. Advance notice for a car equipped with hand controls varies with the company and so do the cities where they are available.

Sometimes it is possible to take along your own hand controls to install on a rented car, but you must make absolutely certain that this is permitted by the agency in that particular city and on the kind of car that you have requested. Make sure, of course, that you specify *exactly* what kind of car you'll need, especially if you will be handling your own wheelchair when a two-door car is essential.

Hertz and Avis can provide both left-hand and right-hand controls. National has only left-hand controls available. Information on availability of cars with hand controls is readily available by calling the toll-free telephone numbers. In the U.S. these are: **Avis,** 800/331-1212; **Hertz,** 800/654-3131; **Hertz International,** 800/654-3001; and **National,** 800/328-4567.

Advance notice is always needed of course: Avis requires three weeks; Hertz, 10 days; National, two days. Hertz and National require cars to be returned to the original locations. Avis does not.

All regular requirements apply to disabled drivers—a driver's license specifying that you use hand controls, of course, if that is the case. If you have a disabled driver identification or special parking permit from your local authority, take it along with you, since many places do accept them. It may be just as well to check this out with the local Motor Vehicle Bureau when you arrive.

PLANNING ROUTES: Route plans and maps are provided free to members of the American Automobile Association (AAA) and other automobile clubs. The major oil companies also provide maps and route plans, but not to the extent they once did. However, you can write for free planning to: **Mobil Travel Service,** 106 Hi-lane Rd., Richmond, KY 40475 (allow three weeks for reply to your request), and to **Texaco Touring Service,** P.O. Box 1459, Houston, TX 77001. The **Exxon Travel Club,** P.O. Box 3633, Houston, TX 77001, will provide such information to members (a nominal fee is required), or through their Touring Service Office in New York City at 1251 Avenue of the Americas, (tel. 212/398-3000), if you can go there in person.

5. Cruise Ships

Much more than a mode of getting from here to there, of course, ocean liners these days are cruise ships either part of the time or all the time. The most popular routes are from the East Coast (New York or Florida) to Bermuda, or island-hopping in the Caribbean; or from the West Coast to other exotic places that include Hawaii and Alaska. What's going where and when can be found in travel sections published periodically by most newspapers. Travel agents are usually knowledgeable on the subject of cruises (although they may not know anything at all about how accessible they are to a passenger who is disabled).

There are many disabled people who have their favorite among the cruise ships and consider it a great way to spend a vacation. It does rather depend on the degree of your physical mobility, since most ships are only partially accessible to somebody who is not ambulatory.

One big barrier aboard ships in general are the bulkheads, or risers—the partitions that protrude anywhere from seven to eleven inches from the floor. All ships have them between cabin and bathroom (except for special accommodations on the *Queen Elizabeth II*). Most ships have bulkheads at the entrance to the cabin as well. And, of course, they are always at doors between the interior and the decks. Some ships make provision for this by having portable ramps.

At present, Cunard's *Queen Elizabeth II* is the only ship that has a good degree of accessibility, with some staterooms designed for passengers in wheelchairs, good-sized elevators between decks, and ramps that can be put down to all the public facilities such as dining rooms. In the *QE II's* special cabins, there is no bulkhead at the bathroom door, which opens outward, and there is room to maneuver a wheelchair in the bathroom and grab bars at the toilet and tub.

In all other ships, doorways to bathrooms are only about 20 inches wide and most have bulkheads. The Norwegian Caribbean Line's *Norway* has no bulkheads on cabin doors, and the Norwegian American Line's *Sagafjord* and *Vistafjord,* and the Carnival Cruise Line's *Tropicale* are cruise ships that have degrees of accessibility that have made them popular with disabled travelers. It all depends!

All cruise lines require a physician's letter stating that you are able to travel. Most require at least one companion if you are minimally ambulatory, and sometimes even two companions if you're not. There are also restrictions as to size and type of wheelchair that can be used on board. So, obviously it is important that all these things are checked out and reconfirmed before you make a booking.

Going ashore at ports of call sometimes offers problems if the docks cannot accommodate large ships. (A new dock at St. Thomas in the Virgin Islands was opened at the end of 1983, allowing the largest ships, such as the *Queen Elizabeth II* and the *Norway,* to tie up downtown.) When a tender has to be used in some ports, ships' crews are often accustomed to assisting disabled passengers, even to the extent of carrying wheelchair plus passenger into the tender (but this rather depends on the weight involved!). Find out where this situation is going to be necessary and get confirmation in writing that you will be able to get ashore, if you intend to explore on land.

Most cruises include land sightseeing as part of the package. If you are unable to board a regular tour bus, ask the cruise line what arrangements you can make for private transportation, if you want it. Travel agents who specialize in group tours for disabled travelers (see the last chapter) are often knowledgeable, through direct experience, about which ships offer the most convenient and comfortable cruises. Many of them are also willing to handle individual travel arrangements as well as groups.

For descriptive brochures of the ships and their cruise schedules you can write direct to: **Carnival Cruise Lines,** 3915 Biscayne Blvd., Miami, FL 33137 (tel. 305/576-9220); **Cunard Line,** 555 Fifth Ave., New York, NY 10017 (tel. 212/661-7777); **Norwegian Caribbean,** One Biscayne Tower, Miami, FL 33131 (tel. 305/358-0670), and **Norwegian American Cruises,** 29 Broadway, New York, NY 10006 (tel. 212/422-3900).

6. Hotels and Motels

Lesson number one for the first-time traveler: The international symbol of accessibility does not accessibility make. This is not to discourage but to forewarn.

Many hotel and motel chains request all new or remodeled properties (which are mostly franchises), to have at least one or two "accessible" rooms and to make public rooms barrier-free. However, each chain has its own definition of "accessibility," and you can't take it for granted that just because one establishment in the chain has "accessible" accommodation, all the others in the chain will have the same. For instance, Best Western has a list of eleven standards, five of which will qualify a motel to carry the wheelchair-access symbol in the directory. But among those five standards could be special parking and lower public drinking fountains—and need not mean grab bars in the bathroom. Ramada allows its properties to use the symbol if it meets at least one of three standards. One of them is that public areas have ramps and wide doors, so theoretically that is all you could find there.

Howard Johnson's, however, claims that the access symbol on the motor lodges in their directory means that they have 36-inch doorways into rooms and bathrooms, and grab bars at the toilet and tub, as well as a ramp from parking to sidewalk and building entry.

So, check, check, and check beforehand. Take nothing for granted!

Hotel and motel directories that carry a symbol indicating wheelchair accessibility (*their* criteria) are: Best Western, Holiday Inn, Howard Johnson's, Quality Inn, Ramada Inn, Rodeway, and TraveLodge.

Hilton, Hyatt, and Sheraton do not indicate in their directories which of the properties have wheelchair access, but the policy of these chains is the encouragement of at least one or two rooms that can be used by disabled guests.

Here are the addresses of the major chains that indicate accessibility in their directories and their toll-free reservation numbers, including some for hearing-impaired TDD users:

Best Western International, Travel Guide Dept., P.O. Box 10203, Phoenix, AZ 85064 (tel. 800/528-1234); **Holiday Inn, Inc.,** 3796 Lamar Ave., Memphis, TN 38195 (tel. 800/238-8000 TDD 800/238-5544); **Howard Johnson's,** 222 Forbes Rd., Braintree, MA 02184 (tel. 800/654-2000, TDD 800/654-8442); **Quality Inn,** P.O. Box 767, Dept. TD, Silver Springs, MD 20901 (tel. 800/228-5151); **Rodeway Inns,** 8585 Stemmons Freeway, 400 South, Dallas, TX 75247 (tel. 800/228-2000); **Ramada Inn,** P.O. Box 590, Phoenix, AZ 85001 (tel. 800/228-2828); **TraveLodge International,** Inc., Marketing Dept., 1973 Friendship Drive, El Cajon, CA 92090 (tel. 800/255-3050, in Kansas 800/332-4350, in Alaska and Hawaii 800/255-6411).

Westin Hotels will send a list of their hotels that have "facilities for the handicapped," if you write to 2000 Fifth Ave., Seattle, WA 98121.

The major chains that do not indicate accessibility in their directories, but which do have wheelchair-accessible rooms in most of their hotels, are **Sheraton Corporation,** 60 State St., Boston, MA 02109 (tel. 800/325-3535); **Hyatt Corporation,** 1 Hyatt Center, 9700 West Bryn Mawr Ave., Rosemont, IL 60018 (tel. 800/228-9000); **Hilton Hotels,** 9080 Wilshire Blvd., Los Angeles, CA 90210. Hilton reservations can be made through your local Hilton hotel or by calling 213/278-4321.

If you telephone the central reservations system of a hotel chain via an 800 number, keep in mind that the person who answers the phone has only general computerized information. Be prepared to call the hotel directly for details about accessibility. Remember also that when you inquire about accessibility in a hotel and its guest rooms, it is highly likely that the person who answers the switchboard, and even the staff in the executive offices, will not be able to tell you whether the entrance from the street is flat or if there is one step; or, if there is more than one step, exactly how many there are. If they say, "only about two or three," you'll realize that their concepts are different from yours!

Be persistent but friendly if you are inquiring about a hotel that is not included in this book (which tells you exactly how many steps, if there are any). If you are told "yes, we have handicapped rooms," ask what that means: Is the door to the bathroom wide enough for your wheelchair? Are there assistive devices in the rooms, if you need them? Another good question is, how far is it from the elevator? In large hotels, the journey down the corridors, nearly always heavily carpeted, can be one of the most tiring aspects of your whole trip. It's also better to be on the lower floors of a hotel in case of emergencies, and be sure when you register that your presence and your room number is known to management for the same reason.

If there's a restaurant or coffee shop which you plan to use, ask if there are steps to get there.

One other thing to remember is that there may be only one or two of the "accessible" rooms in each hotel or motel, so there's another reason to plan your travel in advance.

When you arrive, check out the room before you register. This is common practice in Europe, but is not taken so much for granted in the U.S.

Chapter 3

GET READY . . . GO!

Planning Is the Key

**1. Before You Leave Home
2. When You Arrive
3. About this Book
4. The $25-A-Day Travel Club**

YOU'VE DECIDED where you want to go, the transportation is booked, and the hotel is reserved, if you're a planner—and it's highly recommended that planning be done as carefully as can be, even if it's not really your style. Spontaneity and nasty surprises often go together when you're not in a position to "wing" it.

1. Before You Leave Home

But that's not the end, of course. There's planning for packing, for medication, for supplies, for travel-type equipment, for insurance perhaps. And don't forget to check your passport if you're planning to go abroad.

Here are some guidelines, but many more will come out of your own needs and the suggestions of other people who have already done a bit of traveling.

WHAT TO PACK: It would seem unnecessary to point out to a disabled traveler, already handicapped with extra baggage of some sort or another, from cane or even more to wheelchair, let alone with the problem of mobility, that the answer to what to take is "as little as possible."

High on the priority list, of course, is any special equipment that you absolutely must have as your umbilical cord away from home. Work around how much space *that* takes up in the baggage, and you'll know how much room you have left for other things. If I'm traveling in anything but a private car, my baggage criterion is what I can carry on my wheelchair and still be able to wheel myself around. That's usually a suitcase that fits across the armrests (desk arms reversed), sized to be secure and not cumbersome, and lightweight, of course. Others prefer the backpack route, using the handles and back of the chair. Even if there are two of us, one able-bodied, my aim is still just one suitcase so that the wheelchair becomes a cart: everything, including me, gets easily around large airports and railroad stations. Smaller hand luggage can hang on the handles or sit on my lap.

For air travel to Europe, economy flight passengers can check two pieces of luggage (the wheelchair doesn't count) free of charge on a system that now calculates the space they occupy rather than the weight. Length, width, and depth must not exceed 106 inches, and each individual case may not exceed 63 inches in overall dimensions. Besides the main piece of luggage that you won't have access to until you reach your destination, remember, you'll doubtless have a smaller "carry-on" bag. There are many available now that have handy outerzippered compartments and will slip under the airplane seat. Maybe you'll be able to get everything you need in this, and you can have all your possessions within sight all the time!

If I'm traveling by air, I always plan for my carry-on bag to have everything I'll need for 24 hours, including supplies and medication, in the expectation (unfulfilled so far, fortunately) that my baggage is on some other plane or didn't get off when I did. You don't have to be disabled to take this precaution, of course, but it may be more important for *you* to know that you can manage for at least 24 hours while your baggage may be catching up with you.

If you are going to a large city, there probably won't be too much trouble finding regular pharmaceutical or medical supplies when you get there, rather than taking enough with you for the whole trip. You don't need to be reminded to take enough medication plus a little extra, but if you take tranquilizers, narcotics, or sleeping pills with you overseas, make sure you have it properly labeled and carry prescriptions with you or a physician's statement to show to Customs inspectors.

There won't be any advice here on the methods of packing. I have my own ideas, but I know there are lots of others that must suit the people who use them, and the basic premise is always what you will find convenient. The one personal hint I will include, because I find that other people often don't do it, is to take *only* the amount of toiletries or cosmetics, that will be needed on the trip, and transfer that quantity from the original package or bottle into something else. Of course, never take a glass bottle if you can help it; plastic bottles in every size and shape for every function can be easily found and are inexpensive.

HANDY DEVICES: Among the things in my 24-hour emergency carry-on bag is always a narrowing device for my wheelchair, it is eternally useful for public rest rooms that have not been adapted for wheelchair access, or for hotel bathrooms that are not according to expectation, and even for airplane or train aisles, so that I can reach the seat sometimes in my own wheelchair.

If you use a sliding board for transfers, you'll want to keep it available and not packed in your checked luggage, not only for unforeseen situations, but again, just in case that baggage in the hold doesn't arrive when you do.

Most people have their own favorite, indispensable, assistive device, like the wheelchair narrower or the folding "grabber," but if you use a wheelchair, there are also things that you should take in case of emergencies, such as a wrench, a screwdriver, a tire repair kit, even a spare inner tube, and I've seen spare axles also recommended as take-alongs.

An inflatable mattress packs small and may come in handy if you're going to be near the water or a pool. An inflatable cushion can also be useful, if you want to use one of those molded plastic chairs, found in so many hotels, as a tub or shower chair.

A small, lightweight hotplate and pan, if you need to sterilize any equipment, is useful rather than having to make arrangements with the hotel kitchen.

Besides items directly related to your disability, pack a small mirror in case the one in the hotel is too high. A flashlight may be a comfort if you are in unfamiliar surroundings in the dark, and the light switch is not where you would like it to be.

If you are taking small electrical appliances or a respirator to Europe, you'll need a converter for the different electrical current that is used there.

No need, of course, to remind you to check out your wheelchair or other equipment mechanically before leaving home.

EQUIPMENT: There are places where respirators, Hoyer lifts, and other equipment can be rented, but they are not always easy to find. The referral organizations mentioned in each chapter may help you to locate them.

For travelers who need respirators, Lifecare's 18 U.S. offices provide equipment and service, as well as make arrangements with airlines. Regular customers can also get information on where equipment and services can be found overseas. Call or write for the nearest office to **Lifecare,** 55505 Central Ave., Boulder, CO 80301 (tel. 303/443-9234).

INSURANCE: It's a good idea to make sure you are covered by insurance for emergencies—medical, baggage, cancelled charter flights, etc.—when you leave home base, particularly if you are going overseas. Check on whether your present medical insurance coverage, for instance, can be used in other countries.

Among companies with special programs to supplement your regular insurance and help with any emergency costs, either in the U.S. or in Europe, are **Assist-Card International,** 745 Fifth Ave., New York, NY 10022 (tel. 212/752-2788, toll-free outside New York State 800/221-4564); **Carefree Travel Insurance,** 9 E. 37th St., New York, NY 10016 (tel. 212/683-2622); **International SOS Assistance Inc.,** P.O. Box 11568, Philadelphia, PA 19116 (tel. 215/244-1500, toll-free outside Pennsylvania, 800/525-8930); **MedHelp Overseas** and **Health Care Abroad,** 8027 Leesburg Pike, Vienna, VA 22180 (tel. 703/790-5655, toll-free 800/336-3310); and **Near Inc. (Nationwide/ Worldwide Emergency Ambulance Return),** 1900 N. MacArthur Blvd., Suite 210, Oklahoma City, OK 73127 (tel. 405/949-2500, or toll-free outside Oklahoma 800/654-6700).

Insurance policies all vary in conditions, so establish carefully such things as whether you are covered in the United States as well as abroad, whether you are only reimbursed later for expenses you must pay first, whether there is a ceiling on expenses, whether there are any clauses relating to pre-existing conditions, or what kind of medical documentation may be necessary. Some programs also offer 24-hour assistance as well as reimbursement.

The **International Association for Medical Assistance to Travelers (IAMAT),** 736 Center St., Lewiston, NY 14092 (716/754-4883), is a nonprofit organization that can arrange medical care in foreign countries by English-speaking physicians at a prearranged fee.

2. When You Arrive

What most travelers take for granted, or never have to think about much in advance, is how they are going to get around once they get where they are going, how much they can see in the way of tourist attractions, and whether there's anything they won't be able to see even if they want to. It's usually a matter of their own personal choice.

For the disabled traveler those might be very big questions.

TRANSPORTATION: When you arrive at the airport, or even at the bus or train station, there's usually some distance to be covered before you get to your hotel. When you are settled in, there are places you'll want to get to that are beyond "walking" distance. How do you do it?

Among the most common forms of transportation for most people are the airport bus, the sightseeing bus, and the public bus. None of them is for you if you are in a wheelchair. You probably know all about that, though, since it's likely that the situation is the same in your own home town. Even if you have a door-to-door system where you live, instead of public buses with wheelchair lifts, it is rarely available to you in cities where you are not a resident. Some cities do suggest you might register if you are planning a long-term visit, but there are formalities and approvals first, and they take time.

There are exceptions. Of the cities in this guide, New York has wheelchair-lift buses on its main routes, but the system is not perfect. So does Washington, D.C., but they are not to be relied on. Fairly new subway systems in San Francisco and Washington, D.C., can be used by passengers in wheelchairs. In Europe, Vienna and Amsterdam also have subway lines that offer a limited degree of accessibility. But for the most part, the regular public transportation system in *most* cities is not available if you use a wheelchair. And that applies to sightseeing buses as well.

If you normally use special transportation, such as wheelchair-lift vans, there are companies in most large cities that provide them. However, you'll know from your own experience that they are very expensive. Nevertheless, you may want to consider using one to meet you at the airport; you'll find the names of companies listed in this guide for each of the cities covered. So far there seems to be only one city—New York—where you can rent a self-drive van with a wheelchair lift.

Taxis, of course, are the one means of universal transportation found in every city. Rates differ quite considerably, and you will find them noted in most places in this book. They can usually be called by telephone; numbers are noted in each chapter, but you also find them listed in the Yellow Pages of the local telephone directories. Otherwise, in many cities you can pick them up at taxi stands, since there are lots of cities where taxis are not allowed to cruise on the streets. If you can't stand, the transfer from a wheelchair to the back seats of taxis in the United States and Canada is not an easy feat, as you have probably discovered, but you can always request to sit in the front passenger seat (except in London's standard taxicabs, which have no seat next to the driver).

Rental cars are another possibility for getting around in a city where public transportation is not available, but in most places these days parking in city centers and downtown areas is impossible or expensive, or both. However, they are sometimes very useful for short excursions outside the city. If you need hand controls, the cities where they are available are noted.

Boats can be a surprisingly accessible way to see the sights in a city where there is a waterway—river or bay or harbor. Ferries and sightseeing boats are often easily boarded by ramps, and space on the main deck is usually large and obstacle-free so that there is room for wheelchairs to be maneuvered easily.

SIGHTSEEING: There is a growing awareness of the needs of disabled visitors among operators of most of the major tourist attractions of nearly every kind, which translates into ramps and adapted rest rooms when they are being constructed or remodeled. The exceptions are historic buildings that do not lend themselves to the easy removal of architectural barriers, or those that cannot be changed because of landmark status, which means they must be preserved in their original condition. This is the case of historic sites in cities like Boston and Philadelphia, where the National Park Service has done a great deal to make as much as possible available to disabled visitors. This sometimes means a ramp in the rear rather than at the front, or photographic displays of exhibits on upper floors where the only access is by stairway.

The country's major art museums were among the leaders in providing architectural access for disabled visitors. In addition, they usually make special arrangements so that it is easier to get from one gallery to another if the normal route would involve stairs: elevators used to transport exhibits, and not normally used by the public, are often available, and doors normally kept locked can often be opened to give a route without steps to certain parts of the museum. Check these arrangements at the information desk as you go in, and check with guards as you tour, if there seem to be steps or a staircase in your way. Carpeting is the one unwelcome amenity for most people in wheelchairs when they visit museums, since it calls for more strenuous efforts in self-wheeling, but it's rare that more than a few galleries in any museum are carpeted. As far as rest rooms are concerned, most major museums today have at least one facility adapted for use by visitors in wheelchairs.

THEATERS: There is a wide variety of degrees of accessibility in theaters, depending on the age of the building and architectural barriers that can't be changed, as well as fire regulations in the city that may limit wheelchairs in aisles. However, most have tried to provide for disabled patrons as far as they can. In recently constructed buildings, especially performing arts centers such as Lincoln Center in New York and the Kennedy Center in Washington, or the Barbican Center in London, there is good accessibility built into the original architectural plans.

In most theaters, the orchestra section is the only one that can be reached if you use a wheelchair. There is rarely an elevator for access to other parts of the auditorium (except in the newer buildings). In some of the latest theaters, seats can be removed so that a wheelchair can take their place. In the older buildings, it is a matter of either taking "wheelchair locations," which are usually in the rear or on the side aisles, or of transfer to an aisle seat. Some theaters require patrons to transfer and where this is the case, it has been noted in this book.

RESTAURANTS: As for restaurants, there's as much variety in their accessibility as there are restaurants. None has usually made any particular provision for wheelchair patrons, although many have ramped the one or two steps at the front entrance. (One wonders to what extent this is done for the convenience of their deliveries as much as for anything else, but who cares as long as it's there.)

Don't ever plan to use the rest rooms in a restaurant; most are upstairs or downstairs, and the ones that are wheelchair-accessible can be counted on the fingers of one hand, among thousands. If you are "casing the joint" as you pass by, look for a restaurant that has plenty of room between tables, as well as an entrance you can get to and through. Even if the restaurant thinks there's room, there's nothing more annoying than being constantly bumped by the waiters.

There are a great many restaurants included in this guide. The general criteria for selection was ideally either a level entrance or not more than one step. Some with more than one step at the entrance have also been included, if the restaurant seemed to be worth drawing to your attention, and there was an indication that the staff is accustomed to assist. The choice is yours.

3. About this Book

This book covers a lot of places that are great for anybody to visit, but particularly good for a disabled traveler as far as convenience and easy access to places of interest are concerned. Most are where the terrain is reasonably flat. The exception is San Francisco, but it has been included since it provides the visitor with so much that shouldn't be missed, including *some* relatively flat areas and quite a few curb cuts.

Although the places are mostly large cities, three of Hawaii's islands have been included, as well as suggestions for excursions outside some of the cities. They are all on major airline routes, or are easily reached by train, bus, or car (within the United States or Canada).

Details start with "Getting There," from the time you arrive at the transportation terminal, with information about what they are like to get around in, and out of, whether there are accessible restrooms and where they are, and what kind of transportation there is from the terminal to wherever you are eventually heading.

Then there's "Getting Around," which will give you an idea of what the terrain is like, whether there are curb cuts, and details of the transportation facilities.

"Orientation" is planned to give you a quick overview of how the city is laid out, so you can decide about distances and directions, and other general information you may find helpful.

The hotel section of each chapter has tried to give as much information as possible about *all* price categories, but can only provide it where the accessibility is practical—and that means not too many in the budget category, unfortunately. Details about entrances, elevators, and dining rooms are given so that you can decide if a hotel seems accessible for you. Then there are the crucial door sizes, particularly to bathrooms in guest rooms, since hotels sometimes have wide entry doors to guest rooms but much smaller bathroom doors. Also, there is information about location of grab bars, if any, in the bathrooms, as well as other assistive devices provided (in the few instances where they are found).

Some indication of the location and ambience of the hotel is also included, since this is information that I miss in a lot of "accessible hotel" listings elsewhere.

Similarly comprehensive details are given for restaurants and nightspots, along with an indication of their type of cuisine, prices, and hours.

Sightseeing attractions are described so that you can tell not only whether you can get in and around inside, but whether it is a place you want to go to in the first place! Admission prices and hours, as well as the accessibility, will also help you decide and plan where you want to go. Any special arrangements for easier access to entrances, and facilities inside, for people in wheelchairs or for those with visual or hearing impairments, are included.

In chapters on cities with active theater (most in this book), there are full details of how to buy tickets, how to get into the theater, and where you can expect to sit. The special provisions for hearing-impaired patrons is also included, wherever they are available.

And we haven't forgotten the shoppers, either.

All the prices quoted here for hotels and restaurants are, of course, subject to change (and you know in which direction). They will, however, give you an idea of the price level for each establishment. Admission prices to the sightseeing attractions may also have gone up before you get there, but it shouldn't be by very much. Quoting foreign currency conversion is probably taking a chance on accuracy by the time you read it, but the prices will, again, give you an idea of general price categories. You can always check them against the latest conversion rate when you are ready to make plans.

Although this book packs in as much information as you will need to visit these cities, it also refers to access guides and other information specifically compiled for disabled visitors, where they are available. However, be warned that they are often a few years out of date.

Note: Most readers who have hearing impairments will need no explanation of the telephone numbers listed here as **TDD.** For others who don't recognize the reference, they stand for **Telecommunication Devices for the Deaf.**

A FINAL SUGGESTION: Although this book focuses on the availability of access for travelers in wheelchairs (and for others with mobility impairments), I have tried to make it a self-contained travel guide by giving general as well as specialized information about the cities and their sights.

Even so, this information is necessarily condensed because of the number of places covered in the book, so I suggest that you refer to Frommer's regular travel guides for each place for additional general information.

DROP A LINE: In this book, as in all Frommer guides, I invite our readers to participate in future editions. Let me hasten to say that the judgments, opinions, and comments offered here are based on personal inspections and experiences. But change is the very nature of the travel world—accommodations and restaurants appear and disappear, change managements, ownership, and chefs, improve or go to pot. Should you find any of these conditions, please do let me know about it. And don't be shy about sharing with me any especially good discoveries or suggestions of your own. You have my word that each and every letter will be read by me, personally, although I find it well nigh impossible to *answer* each and every one. Be assured, however: I'm listening! Just write: Frances Barish, Frommer/Pasmantier Publishers, 1230 Avenue of the Americas, New York, NY 10020.

4. The $25-a-Day Travel Club

In just a few paragraphs, you'll begin your exploration of the U.S.A., Canada, and Europe. But before you do, you may want to learn how to save money on all your travels—by joining the **$25-a-Day Travel Club,** now in its 21st successful year of operation. It was formed at the urging of readers of Frommer's $-a-Day and Dollarwise travel guides who felt that it would bring together economy-minded travelers all over the world, with benefits to everyone. That's exactly what has happened, and the benefits begin as soon as you join.

Following the budget concept of all our guides, the annual membership fee is low and brings immediate value far beyond the cost. Upon receipt of $14 (for U.S. residents) or $16 (for Canadian, Mexican, and other foreign residents) by check drawn on a U.S. bank or via international postal money order in U.S. funds. to cover one year's membership, we will send all new members by return mail (book rate) the following items:

(1) The latest edition of *any* two of the following books (please designate in your letter which two you wish to receive):

Europe on $25 a Day
Australia on $25 a Day
England and Scotland on $25 a Day
Greece on $25 a Day
Hawaii on $35 a Day
Ireland on $25 a Day
Israel on $30 & $35 a Day
Mexico on $20 a Day
New York on $35 a Day
New Zealand on $20 & $25 a Day
Scandinavia on $25 a Day
South America on $25 a Day
Spain and Morocco (plus the Canary Is.) on $25 a Day
Washington, D.C. on $35 a Day

Dollarwise Guide to Canada
Dollarwise Guide to the Caribbean (including Bermuda and the Bahamas)
Dollarwise Guide to Egypt
Dollarwise Guide to England and Scotland
Dollarwise Guide to France
Dollarwise Guide to Germany
Dollarwise Guide to Italy
Dollarwise Guide to Portugal (plus Madeira and the Azores)
Dollarwise Guide to Switzerland
Dollarwise Guide to California and Las Vegas
Dollarwise Guide to Florida
Dollarwise Guide to New England
Dollarwise Guide to the Southeast and New Orleans

(Dollarwise Guides discuss accommodations and facilities in all price ranges, with emphasis on the medium-priced.)

How to Beat the High Cost of Travel
(This practical guide details how to save money on absolutely all travel items—accommodations, transportation, dining, sightseeing, shopping, taxes, and more. Includes special budget information for seniors, students, singles, and families.)

The New York Urban Athlete
(The ultimate guide to all the sports facilities in New York City for jocks and novices.)

Museums in New York
(A complete guide to all the museums, historic houses, gardens, zoos, and more in the five boroughs. Illustrated with over 200 photographs.)

The Fast 'n' Easy Phrase Book
(The four most useful languages—French, German, Spanish, and Italian —all in one convenient, easy-to-use phrase guide.)

Where to Stay USA
(By the Council on International Educational Exchange, this extraordinary guide is the first to list accommodations in all 50 states that cost anywhere from $3 to $25 per night.)

A Guide for the Disabled Traveler
(A guide to the best destinations for wheelchair travelers and other disabled vacationers in Europe, the United States, and Canada by an experienced wheelchair traveler. Includes detailed information about accommodations, restaurants, sights, transportation, and their accessibility).

Marilyn Wood's Wonderful Weekends
(This very selective guide covers the best mini-vacation destinations within a 175-mile radius of New York City. It describes special country inns and other accommodations, restaurants, picnic spots, sights, and activities—all the information needed for a two- or three-day stay.)

(2) A one-year subscription to the quarterly eight-page tabloid newspaper—**The Wonderful World of Budget Travel**—which keeps you up to date on fast-breaking developments in low-cost travel in all parts of the world bringing you the latest money-saving information—the kind of information you'd have to pay $25 a year to obtain elsewhere. This consumer-conscious publication also provides special services to readers: **The Traveler's Directory** (a list of members all over the world who are willing to provide hospitality to other members as they pass through their home cities); **Share-a-Trip** (offers and requests from members for travel companions who can share costs and help avoid the burdensome single supplement); and **Readers Ask . . . Readers Reply** (travel questions from members to which other members reply with authentic firsthand information).

(3) A copy of **Arthur Frommer's Guide to New York,** a newly revised pocket-size guide to hotels, restaurants, nightspots, and sightseeing attractions in all price ranges throughout the New York area. (4) Your personal membership card, which, once received, entitles you to purchase through the Club all Arthur Frommer publications for a third to a half off their regular retail prices during the term of your membership.

So why not join this hardy band of international budgeteers and participate in its exchange of travel information and hospitality? Simply send your name and address, together with your annual membership fee of $14 (U.S. residents) or $16 (Canadian, Mexican, and other foreign residents), by check drawn on a U.S. bank or via international postal money order in U.S. funds to: $25-A-Day Travel Club, Inc., Frommer/Pasmantier Publishers, 1230 Avenue of the Americas, New York, NY 10020. And please remember to specify which *two* of the books in section (1) above you wish to receive in your initial package of members' benefits. Or, if you prefer, use the last page of this book, simply checking off the two books you select and enclosing $14 or $16 in U.S. currency.

Part II

UNITED STATES OF AMERICA

NEW YORK CITY

The Big Apple

NEW YORK CITY HAS MORE architecturally accessible places and things to see and do than even *exist* anywhere else. So don't bother to count up the things that are not accessible to you. What's available to any traveler with a physical disability is too much—you'll have to make some choice, since it would take many visits to sample even a fraction of what it offers: congested, skyscrapered Midtown, bosky Central Park, old-world Greenwich Village, arty SoHo, Chinatown, and Manhattan Island's encircling waterways are among your options, depending on individual inclinations and abilities. You can get to theaters, the opera, the ballet, concerts, nightspots, and restaurants. You can shop and see the sights. What more could you want in one of the most exciting cities in the world?

It's like no other city, and it's worth a few inconveniences to experience it. So what if there aren't too many curb cuts—the streets are pretty flat, and there aren't many hills to climb. So what if you can't use the subway system—most of the bus routes now have wheelchair-lift buses. So what if there are one or two steps in front of a building—there's usually a lot of willing assistance around. And if you don't feel the energy and the stimulation that comes from its crowds and its density, then you have missed one of the great thrills of a lifetime.

1. Getting There

BY AIR: New York does things in a big way, and so it is serviced by no less than three major airports, two of them international: **John F. Kennedy International** and **LaGuardia airports** are on Long Island, and **Newark International**

is in New Jersey. All three have barrier-free facilities in accordance with the federal standards—level interiors, special parking, elevator access to all levels, accessible rest rooms, accessible telephones, accessible drinking fountains, and accessible dining areas. Jetways provide level, weather-protected exits from the plane door to inside the terminal, and wheelchairs and assistance are available (as outlined in the section on air travel in Chapter 2).

The privately run transportation system of buses between the airports and downtown is not accessible to travelers in wheelchairs, so depending on your disability, you have a choice of private car, limousine service, or rental car ordered in advance, or regular taxicab service. Hand-controlled cars are available at all the airports on advance notice (see the section on car rental in Chapter 2 for details.)

At the time of writing, the cost of a taxi to midtown Manhattan averages $25 from Kennedy and $13 from LaGuardia. From the city to Newark Airport, you'll pay the meter fare and tolls, plus $10; from Newark Airport to New York City (Battery to West 72nd Street), it's $19 to $26.50; East Side, additional $2. From the city to Newark Airport, you'll pay meter fare and tolls plus $10.

Sometimes it is cheaper to take a chauffeured car (ordered in advance). Among the many services available are the Seville Car & Limousine Co., 2109 First Ave., NY 10029 (tel. 212/534-3200) and the Tel-Aviv Private Car and Limousine Service Ltd., 343 E. 21st St., NY 10010 (tel. 212/505-0555). At the time of writing, both average about $20 from Kennedy, $14 from LaGuardia, and $22 from Newark, plus tolls.

At all three airports, disabled parkers can get the lowest available parking rate by presenting any special parking permit from their local authorities to the toll-collector.

Hearing-impaired travelers can get general information on any of New York's airports by calling TDD 800/221-8279 from throughout the continental U.S. From New York State, call TDD 466-7503.

A booklet, "Facilities & Services for the Disabled: Newark International, LaGuardia and Kennedy International Airports," is available at no charge from Aviation Public Services Division, Port Authority of New York and New Jersey, Room 65N, One World Trade Center, New York, NY 10048 (tel. 212/446-7503).

LaGuardia Airport

This is closest to Manhattan and therefore can be the most convenient. Accessible rest rooms are located in the center of the Terminal Building, on both arrival and departure levels. There is a pharmacy in the center of the Main Terminal's departure level that is open from 7:30 a.m. to 10 p.m. daily, except Saturday, until 7 p.m. Telephones are accessible throughout the Central Terminal Building, and volume-controlled telephones are available on both arrival and departure levels. You can reach the Terrace Dining Room by elevator.

Disabled passengers can be picked up at the Arrivals Building on the controlled-access roadway adjacent to the terminal—directions from the garage or metered lot are indicated by the international symbol of access. (This road is normally restricted to buses and taxis, but the driver should tell the police guard that a disabled passenger is awaiting pick-up.) There are special parking spaces on every level of the garage, including the metered sections, with undercover access to the terminal from the fourth level of the garage, reached by elevator from other levels. At LaGuardia, long-term parking charges are much higher than at the other two airports. For exact rates call Meyers Parking

System at 212/429-5380. The TDD number for all information on LaGuarddia is 212/476-0598.

John F. Kennedy International Airport

JFK Airport is the largest, and the farthest from Manhattan. It consists of an International Terminal for departing and arriving flights overseas, and eight other domestic and international terminal buildings under individual airline operation.

Parking in the Central Terminal area: special reserved parking spaces and curb cuts are located in Lots 2, 3, 4, and 6, with access to the terminals. For Northwest, TWA (domestic), Eastern, and British Airways, disabled passengers should be dropped off or picked up at the terminal buildings since there is no direct access from Lots 1, 4, and 5. Call Kinney System for JFK parking information (tel. 212/656-5699).

International Building: You deplane through jetways or via mobile lounges to the second level of the terminal building, then by elevator down to Customs and Immigration. Baggage handlers give special assistance at no charge. Skycaps are available to be employed from the Customs area out to the ground transportation, which is under cover and has ramps and curb cuts. Departure terminals of the various overseas airlines have elevators to the second level where you board the plane—individual airlines make their own arrangements for boarding disabled passengers. There are accessible rest rooms and drinking fountains throughout the International Building. Accessible telephones with volume controls are located in the first floor lobby of the Arrivals Building and on the second floor of the East and West Wing Departures Building.

American Airlines Terminal: The special elevator between levels must be operated by escorting airline personnel. There are accessible rest rooms in the Customs and boarding gate areas.

British Airways Terminal: An elevator in the center of the terminal gives access to both levels. At the time of writing, there are no accessible rest rooms.

Eastern Airlines Terminal: There are ramped curbs at the arrival and departure areas, and an elevator between levels on the north side. Because of steps at some gates, airline personnel are trained to assist disabled travelers. Accessible rest rooms are in the baggage claim area on the arrivals level, and accessible telephones are at each boarding gate area.

Northwest/Delta Terminal: Check-in and plane arrivals and departures are on the second level. Because there is no elevator to the baggage claim area on the lower level, make arrangements with airline personnel to bring your luggage up when you arrive. Accessible telephones with volume control are in front of Departure Gate 8.

Pan American Airlines Terminal: Elevators connect levels. Accessible rest rooms are in the newer portion of both arrival and departure levels, as well as in the Immigration area. In the older section, there is no elevator to the baggage claim area, so you may have to request special assistance. There are specially reserved rooftop parking spaces in Lot 6 linked to the terminal by elevator.

TWA (Trans World Airlines) Terminal (International): Elevators between levels. Accessible telephones are near luggage claim area and Customs Inspection.

TWA (Domestic): Access to planes is via ramp and elevator. Accessible rest rooms are in the baggage claim area and in the center of departure building.

United Airlines Terminal: Easy access to departure level and gates. Baggage claim area is reached by special elevator with an airline personnel escort.

Lower Manhattan

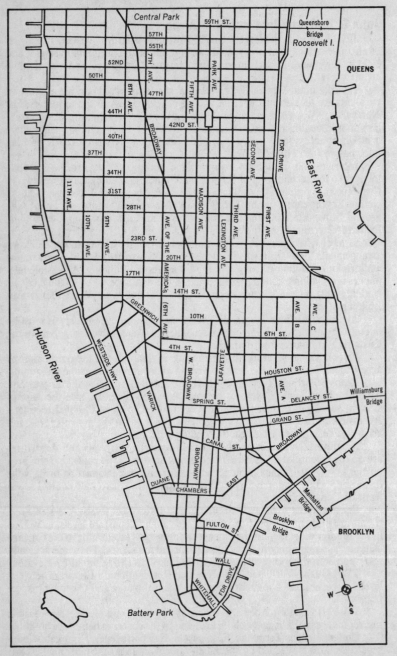

Upper Manhattan

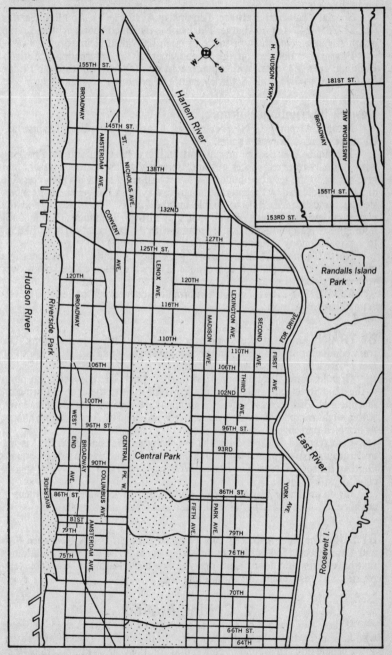

Accessible rest rooms are on the west side of the arrival and departure levels, and in the boarding gate area. Accessible telephones with volume controls are on both levels.

Special Transport Between Terminals: Available by **Autolink Service** (tel. 212/656-2424) at no charge. The van has increased roof height and ramp entry. Arrangements must be made through individual airlines.

Pharmacy: Located on the second floor of the International Arrivals Building; open 7:15 a.m., with a pharmacist on duty Monday through Friday from 1 p.m. to 8:45 p.m., Saturday and Sunday noon to 8 p.m.

Newark International Airport

Newark Airport is in New Jersey, and it has been completely reconstructed and expanded in recent years.

Terminals A & B: The new airport buildings have underground parking with specially reserved spaces at the extreme ends close to the elevators that give access to the terminal buildings. Nearly all the rest rooms are accessible and are so indicated by the international access symbol. Dining and bar concessions are mostly accessible to people in wheelchairs. The pharmacy on the concourse level of Terminal B is open Sunday through Thursday 5:30 a.m. until midnight; Friday and Saturday, 24 hours; with a pharmacist on duty 10 a.m. to 2 p.m., Monday through Friday (tel. 201/961-5797).

North Terminal: This is the original airport building; it has accessible telephones, rest rooms, and concessions. There are reserved parking spaces with curb cuts in Lot 1.

Call 201/961-2154 for detailed information on facilities for disabled travelers at Newark Airport.

BY TRAIN: **Amtrak** trains come into New York City at two stations. The train conductor should have confirmed your arrival in advance for you to be met by Redcap service at either terminal.

Grand Central Terminal on 42nd Street is level. There is a steepish ramp to the 42nd Street exit, and a long level corridor leads to the door at Lexington Avenue and 43rd Street. Tracks and terminal are generally on the same level, with a slight ramp at some. Redcap service is provided by Amtrak at no charge to disabled passengers.

Pennsylvania Station, Seventh Ave. between 31st and 33rd Sts., is the underground part of the new building complex that includes Madison Square Garden, the sports arena. The Redcap will escort you from the track by special elevator to exit level.

If you are leaving by train, call Amtrak at 736-4545 and notify them in advance if you require special escort and assistance at either station.

BY BUS: The **Port Authority Bus Terminal** is on 8th Avenue between 40th and 42nd Streets (564-8484). Long-distance buses arrive at the new buildings that have automatic doors, elevators with low buttons, ramps, accessible telephones, and rest rooms (off the waiting room).

2. Getting Around

If there's one impression of New York City that's always cited by people who have never been there, it is that New York is a city of hustle and bustle. True, people do rush around in New York. But the visitors know better—they leisurely take in the sights and sounds and sensations that are a truly unique experience for anybody from somewhere else.

Mobility impairments aren't much of a handicap, despite the atmosphere of rush: nothing and nobody gets anywhere too fast in New York. The traffic is often slow and bumper-to-bumper, especially at rush hours, and pedestrians can often get where they're going faster on sidewalks, crowded though they are. And "strolling" is one very good way to tour the various districts, since Manhattan Island is only 2½ miles at its widest, and distances are not great within each section.

The topography of Manhattan, generally, is flat, since most of the island's natural hills and dales were leveled as the city spread north from its original site at the southern tip, according to the grid-system street plan that was laid out in 1833. This helps make it easier to get around "on foot."

Curbs do remain a nuisance, except in certain areas where they have been ramped for a variety of reasons. As each new building is constructed, for instance, the new sidewalk must be made with ramped curbs at each corner—and fortunately, there is a lot of building going on. Curbs get ramped, too, when federal funds are used for repaving the streets, so long stretches on First Avenue now have very acceptable curb cuts on all corners. (With bureaucratic perversity, though, the Midtown section of First Avenue north from 51st Street has not been blessed as of this writing.) Because of the number of disabled students who attend New York University, the area around the NYU campus at Washington Square in Greenwich Village has curb cuts. And when the community gets into the act, it sometimes finds funds to make curb cuts, as it did in the busy area on the East Side from 55th to 59th Streets between Lexington and Second Avenues, around Bloomingdale's and Alexander's department stores and a large number of movie houses. There's an odd cut here and there, but in the main, be prepared to negotiate curbs when crossing New York streets.

TRANSPORTATION: When you need to go elsewhere beyond "walking" distance from your hotel, you have a choice of transportation—your own car or van if you've brought it, a hired wheelchair van with a lift, a taxi, or a public bus (on most routes).

Private Cars and Vans

Be warned, cars can be a problem in Manhattan. Rates in parking garages are high, the strictly enforced parking laws in Midtown rarely allow for casual daytime parking, and empty metered parking spots are hard to find. (Disabled New Yorkers usually apply for a special parking permit, but it is a complicated and lengthy process that would probably not be practical for a visitor to pursue.) And unfortunately, the few motels there are in Manhattan do not have facilities for disabled guests. However, don't be discouraged! Some of the hotels have their own garages (not included in hotel rates), and some of the sightseeing destinations have parking facilities (these are noted in the description of the sights).

Taxis

New York City taxis are mostly regular-line sedans; it is as difficult to get in and out of the back seats as in any ordinary car. However, most taxicab drivers are amenable to your sitting in the front passenger seat, where the door is wider and more convenient if you are transferring from a wheelchair. Some Checker cabs are roomier, but may be hard to get into if you are transferring from a sitting position. Taxis cruise the streets, a light on top signalling that they are available. But there also taxi stands outside many hotels, as well as taxis that can be called by telephone. The cruising taxi may present a challenge to flag down if you are in a wheelchair, since a number of drivers don't want to take the extra time and trouble to get out of the cab and put the chair in the trunk (even though it is contrary to city regulations for a cab driver not to stop when hailed). The taxi summoned by a hotel doorman from the taxi stand is a better bet. Calling a taxi by phone is one way to make sure you'll get one, but be patient—it may take a few calls before you are told that there is a cab in your area and is on the way to pick you up. Most of the two-way-radio cab companies accept advance bookings with a fee of $4 over the meter. Radio cabs which can be called on the phone are **Scull's Angels** (tel. IL 7-7777), **Minute Men** (tel. 899-5600), **Ding-a-Ling** (tel. 691-9191), **Skyline Taxis** (tel. 741-1800), and **UTOG Taxi** (tel. 741-2000). The meter on all taxis first drops at $1 and the subsequent charge is by distance (at the time of writing 10¢ for each additional one-ninth of a mile).

Wheelchair Vans

In New York these are run by private companies, and since they are used primarily by people who need transportation to get to work or to medical appointments, or by the social service agencies to transport clients, they are relatively expensive—around $15 for most journeys within Manhattan—and their availability doesn't always coincide with the time you need them. Companies who provide this service include: **American Medical Transportation**, 276 Seventh Ave., New York, NY 10001 (tel. 212/255-3700); **Fred Getz**, 2733 Batchelder St., Brooklyn, NY 11235 (tel. 212/934-0291 or 212/646-1244); **Papi's Transport Inc.**, 2647 Broadway, Suite 45, NY 10025 (tel. 212/662-4094).

This seems to be the only area where you can rent a self-drive wheelchair-lift van with hand controls. For more information write or call **Vanmaster**, 16 Andrews Dr., West Paterson, NJ 07424 (tel. 201/785-2205). Vans must be picked up and returned there. Rates, as we go to press, are $40 per day plus 15¢ per mile, or $250 for one week with a 12¢ mileage charge. The weekend rate (from 4 p.m. Friday to 10 a.m. Monday) is $110, with a 12¢ mileage charge.

Public Transit

Because of parking headaches and the expense of private transportation in Manhattan, the new public buses equipped with wheelchair lifts, which run on most routes, have brought a degree of liberation to mobility-deprived dis-abled New Yorkers. The accessibility of the public bus system is a recent phenomenon, mandated by the use of federal funds, and achieved only after long years of battle by disabled consumer groups in the city.

There are two kinds of new buses, denoted by the wheelchair accessibility symbol on the back door: one made by General Motors, the other by Grum-man. The GM bus has the better lift, so take it in preference to the Grumman, which is identified by its name on the front, and its very dark windows. (Old buses, however, are still in use, so you will have to look for the new ones with the back door symbol if you want to get on with a wheelchair.) A map of the city's bus lines is available from the **New York Visitors Bureau** at 2 Columbus Circle and 59th St. (tel. 397-8222). You can also write for one direct to the **Metropolitan Transit Authority**, 347 Madison Ave., New York, NY 10017. To get information on bus routes, call the MTA at 330-1234.

If you've never used a wheelchair-accessible bus, here are a few guidelines. Flag the bus down as it approaches so that the driver will bring it close to the curb. You enter through the back door, where the steps can flatten out into a wheelchair lift, operated by the bus driver. When you roll on to the lowered lift, lock your brakes. The driver will also raise a safety barrier before raising the lift to bus floor level. Inside the bus, there are special locations where seats can be raised to make room for you, and there are automatic locking devices for the chair on the floor. The driver will give you an envelope in which you are supposed to mail in your fare (at present 90¢), or you can give your fare—in coins—to another passenger to put in the box at the front of the bus (the driver is not allowed to handle money). Tell the driver where you want to get off, and if you recognize the stop as you approach, press the signal at your side to remind him. In getting off, just reverse the boarding procedure. Have patience, though, and don't try to get anywhere in too much of a hurry since you will undoubtedly encounter a bus or two with a lift that is "non-operative."

A free brochure, "The Guide to Riding Wheelchair-Accessible Buses in New York City" is available from the **Eastern Paralyzed Veterans Association,** 432 Park Ave. S., NY 10016 (tel. 212/686-6770).

A word of warning on bus travel at rush hours—don't!

Unfortunately, New York City **subways** cannot be recommended, even for disabled visitors who can negotiate steps and escalators, since stations and trains are rather rundown and congested and not conducive to pleasant traveling. Since access to the subway system is only by stairs or escalators, it is not a possible means of transport for people in wheelchairs.

3. Orientation

LAYOUT: New York City is made up of five boroughs, but the one I'm talking about here is Manhattan, an elongated island, roughly 2 miles wide and 12 miles long. **Midtown** describes a general area (east to west) from the East River to the Hudson River, and (south to north) from 34th Street to 59th Street. Here are the United Nations, the Empire State Building, Rockefeller Center, the Broadway theaters, most of the hotels, many of the restaurants and the major department stores. **Downtown** (south of 23rd Street) are Greenwich Village and the Chelsea districts; farther south is Little Italy, Chinatown, and SoHo. The ultimate in **Downtown,** ending in New York Harbor, is what was once called the financial district, but now is undergoing a lively revival—new office buildings (the World Trade Center among them), reconstructions (South Street Seaport), and a mix of residential and commercial structures going up on landfill, called Battery City.

East and West designations for the numbered streets signify east and west of Fifth Avenue, which ends at Washington Square Park. Below that, it's a bit more complicated, but a good map will help navigation.

Back in Midtown, and heading north, is what gives New York its breathing space—**Central Park** stretching to 110th Street, with acres and acres of playing fields, woods, promenades, and lakes.

AREA CODE: The telephone area prefix for all of New York City is 212.

INFORMATION AND REFERRAL: For regular tourist information about New York City and events, call, write, or visit the **New York City Convention**

& Visitors Bureau, Two Columbus Circle, NY 10019 (tel. 212/397-8222). Hours are 9 a.m. to 6 p.m. on Monday to Friday, 10 a.m. to 6 p.m. on Saturday and Sunday. There is also an Information Center in Times Square.

"Access New York City" is a detailed guide to accessibility of hotels, restaurants, theaters, museums, tourist sites, and special services for disabled people. Copies are available free of charge from the Junior League of the City of New York Inc. 130 E. 80th St. NY 10021 (tel. 212/288-6220).

Organizations concerned with the needs of disabled people and which provide an information and referral service include **The Center for Independence of the Disabled in New York, Inc. (CIDNY),** 853 Broadway, NY 10003 (tel. 212/674-2300, Monday to Friday, 9 a.m. to 5 p.m.); and **The Easter Seal Society,** 2 Park Ave. (Room 1815), NY 10016 (tel. 212/532-8830, Monday to Friday, 9 a.m. to 5 p.m.).

4. Where to Stay

When you read that New York City has the largest number of hotel rooms of any city in the United States—77,000 in Manhattan alone, and new hotels opening in 1983 and 1984 to add another 3500—you might be excused for thinking that it's no problem to find accommodation in the Big Apple. The problem with most of them is that they don't belong in a guide for disabled travelers. Most of the older, smaller hotels were built before "accessibility" was even a word, and the majority of those have *not* been adapted for visitors in wheelchairs or with other disabilities. Hotels built or renovated in the current building boom of the last five years have recognized the need, thank goodness, although of necessity their rates are higher.

In general, hotel prices are higher in New York than in any other city in the country. Budget rooms with special features are hard to find. Look for **weekend package rates,** which include meals, sightseeing, theater tickets, and other extras. These are always changing, so it's best to call the hotel, or write to the New York Convention and Visitors Bureau, 2 Columbus Circle, New York, NY 10019, (tel. 212/397-8222) and ask for the "New York City Packages Directory," which will give you hotels' current offerings.

Needless to say, there must be advance planning, particularly in New York City's "high season," which runs from about April through October. The prices quoted here are subject to change, depending on the season and the demand. All rates are subject to a New York City Room Tax of 8¼%, plus a $2-a-day occupancy tax.

Not surprisingly in a small congested island, there are few motels, as the rest of the country understands them, and none have any special facilities for disabled guests. So if you come by car, you will have to use the hotel garage, which is an added cost, of course.

A general note about New York City hotels as far as amenities for disabled guests are concerned: only a handful have amplified telephones, none have braille information, as far as we have found, and I have discovered only one that had ceiling hooks for lifting devices in guest rooms. Level entrances, ramps, wider bathroom doors, and bathroom grab bars are usually the "facilities" provided.

HOTELS THAT OFFER SPECIAL FACILITIES: These are usually the newest and, as I said, in the higher price category.

In Midtown on the East Side is the **Grand Hyatt,** Park Ave. at Grand Central, NY 10017 (tel. 212/883-1234, toll-free 800/228-9000), with the striking mirrored facade that has given a totally new look to East 42nd Street. Forty-five of its rooms have a 30½-inch bathroom door in the guest rooms and grab bars in the bathrooms. There is a level entrance from 42nd Street through the walkway leading to Grand Central Station, where there is a door marked with the wheelchair-accessibility symbol. A special elevator from here goes to the lobby, and from there the regular elevators go to all floors. There are ramps to two of the lobby restaurants—the Crystal Fountain and Trumpets—but not to the Sun Garden where there are steps. Public rest rooms have 30-inch entry stalls with grab bars. Rooms rent from $110 to $115 single, from $135 to $180 double. Weekend packages are available.

An hotel on the East Side that has been completely renovated, keeping disabled guests in mind, is the **Halloran House**, 525 Lexington Ave. at 49th St., NY 10017 (tel. 212/755-4000, toll-free 800/223/0939). It now has 12 guest rooms with 30-inch bathroom doors and ceiling hooks over the bed, tub, and toilet for removable trapezes, which the management provides (give advance notice). There is a portable ramp for the two steps at the entrance. The restaurant, coffee shop, and bar are all on the same level as the lobby, where the past is recalled with dark wood, marble floors, and chandeliers. There are phone extensions in the bathroom and bedside control for the TV. The services of a concierge are useful and available. Rates are from $93 to $108 single, $108 to $123 double. Children under 18 can stay free in the same room, and weekend packages are offered.

The one hotel with special facilities that has been around a long time—and has the elegance to prove it—is the **Plaza**, overlooking Central Park on Fifth Ave. at 59th St., NY 10019 (tel. 212/750-3000, toll-free 800/228-3000). Designated a city landmark, its French Chateau architecture and much of the interior splendidly demonstrate the ideals of the Edwardian age when it was built. In keeping with the architecture, the striking entrance on Grand Army Plaza has a sweeping flight of steps, but the side entrance on 58th Street is level from the street. The door there is kept locked, so it is necessary to call ahead. There are eight special rooms with 34-inch bathroom doors and grab bars at the toilet and the bath. The telephone can be amplified, if you give the management advance notice. And when you arrive, ask for their special reference handbook for disabled guests, which details the hotel's services and the accessibility of the area surrounding the hotel. The dining rooms—the Palm Court, the Edwardian Room and the Oak Room—are all easily entered from the lobby. Single rooms are $90 to $255, doubles $135 to $275, subject to change. Reduced weekend rates are offered at times, as well as special weekend packages.

The **Drake**, 440 Park Ave., NY 10022 (tel. 212/421-0900), is another landmark hotel that has recently been renovated in comfortable and elegant European style by the Swissotel chain. There are two guest rooms with wide doors and grab bars in the bathroom. Entrance to the hotel is level, and there are two guest rooms with 30-inch doors to both guest room and bathroom, where there are grab bars. (Management recommends Rooms 215 and 604 for guests in wheelchairs). Rates are $110 to $155 single, $125 to $170 double. There are weekend packages that offer good value.

Centrally located on the West Side, on the Avenue of the Americas (Sixth Avenue) between 53rd and 54th Streets, the **New York Hilton**, 1335 Ave. of the Americas, NY 10019 (tel. 212/586-7000), has ten specially designed rooms with 31-inch bathroom doorways and grab bars at the toilet and tub. The restaurants are accessible—elegant Hurlinghams and the Kismet cocktail lounge from the lobby, Sybil's (a club with live entertainment) by elevator at the 53rd Street side, and the Cafe New York, open 24 hours a day, can be reached in the lower concourse by using the service elevator.

There is an International Visitors Desk in the lobby, information, signs, and menus are multilingual, and cashiers can exchange foreign currency. Rates here run from $73 to $113 single, from $95 to $113 double or twin. The Hilton has a **Rainbow Weekend package.** Reservations can be made by calling direct or the Hilton Reservation Service in your area.

One of the largest hotels of its chain is the **Sheraton Center New York,** also on the West Side and centrally located at Seventh Avenue and 52nd Street, (tel. 212/581-1000, toll-free 800/325-3535), and always buzzing with activity. There are steps at Seventh Avenue, the main entrance, but the 53rd Street entrance by the garage is level with the lobby. There are three rooms here with a 30-inch bathroom entry and grab bars. At the lobby level is the Cafe Fontana, a large continental-style cafe with trees and fountains, and the Italian restaurant Ranier is accessible without steps. The public rest room on the third floor has a 30-inch entry door and a 36-inch stall door. Rates here are $72 to $115 for singles, from $72 to $135 for doubles, subject to change. There are many vacation packages available.

At the **New York Sheraton,** Seventh Ave. at 56th St., NY 10019 (tel. 212/247-8000, toll-free 800/325-3535), the entrance is level, and there are two guest rooms with bathroom doors 35 inches wide and grab bars in the bathroom. If you don't need too many assistive devices, it is worth noting that *all* the guest rooms at the New York Sheraton have 34-inch entry doors and 29-inch bathroom doors. Sally's, the disco bar, and the Falstaff Restaurant are accessible without steps; the Pavilion Coffee Shop has a slight ramp. Public rest rooms have 36-inch entry doors and 33-inch stall entry. There are special family weekend packages, and regular prices are $64 to $120 for singles and $75 to $135 for twin-bedded room, subject to change. Desk clerks are multilingual.

In the more moderately priced category, too, is the **New York Statler,** 401 Seventh Ave., NY 10001 (tel. 212/736-5000), farther south on the West Side near Madison Square Garden and Pennsylvania Station, close to Macy's and Gimbels department stores. It is a large hotel, one of New York's oldest, now being extensively renovated by the Dunfey Hotel chain to restore some of its earlier elegance. Current plans call for two rooms on each floor to be available for disabled guests. At present there are six special rooms available with grab bars in the bathroom. However, *all* guest rooms in the hotel have 33-inch entry doors and 29-inch bathroom doors. The entrance on 33rd Street is level and the Seventh Avenue entrance is ramped. All restaurants are accessible through level entrances from the hotel, including the Haymarket Restaurant, the main dining room, the pub-style Penn Bar Restaurant, and the Lobby Bar, a casual restaurant.

With the building of the World Trade Center, the historic tip of lower Manhattan Island has become a focal point of activity after decades of deterioration and will be even more enlivened with the completion of Battery Park City on landfill in the Hudson River. The **Vista International,** 3 World Trade Center, NY 10048 (tel. 212/938-9100), is the first hotel to be built in this part of Manhattan in a century and a half. It is the flagship of the Hilton International chain in the U.S. and is popular with overseas business travelers as well as weekend vacationers.

Its 18 rooms for disabled visitors have doors wide enough for any wheelchair to get to the bathroom, where there are grab bars. Telephones are amplified. The entrance on West Street near Liberty Street has a ramped curb cut, and the entrance to the lobby is level from the street. Restaurants can be reached without steps—the American Harvest Restaurant on the second floor, a series of five intimate rooms serving traditional American dishes; the glass-enclosed and popular-priced Greenhouse Restaurant, also on the second floor; the Vista lobby lounge for light meals and cocktails, with a marvelous view of the sunset across New York Bay; and the Tall Ships Bar off the lobby level.

NO "SPECIAL" ROOMS BUT COULD BE FOR YOU: Back uptown, there are a number of hotels that have reasonable accessibility to guest rooms and restaurants, even though they do not necessarily have special features. You can judge for yourself if the doorways and facilities would suit you.

Among them on the East Side, the most glamorous is the new **Helmsley Palace Hotel,** 455 Madison Ave., NY 10022, between 50th and 51st St. (tel. 212/888-7000, toll free 800/221-4982), which has combined the historic landmark Villard Houses facing Madison Avenue with a high-rise tower behind, a controversial combination architecturally, but a harmonious marriage on the inside. It has some of the finest public rooms in New York City in the restored splendor of the neo-Renaissance Italian palazzo town house that forms the imposing facade around a cobblestone courtyard on Madison Avenue, directly opposite the back of St. Patrick's Cathedral. The entrances from 50th and 51st Streets through the new tower are level with the street, the lobby, and the elevators.

Bathroom entry in all guest rooms is 29 inches wide, and the restaurants—the Trianon, the main dining room on the second floor, and Harry's Bar at the lobby level—are accessible without steps. Although the spectacularly restored Gold Room, Madison Room, and Hunt Bar in the original town houses are not on the same level as the elevator, the hotel staff is very willing to help patrons in wheelchairs down the half dozen steps to reach the landmark part of the hotel. It is very well worth the trip! Breakfast, or especially afternoon tea, taken in the gold-leafed walls of the Gold Room, or among the original La Farge murals of the Madison Room looking out over the couryard, is a unique experience in New York. The dark-paneled Hunt Bar on the same level was once the mansion owner's dining room and evokes a similar sense of the past. Public rest rooms on the elevator level on the second floor both have a special stall with a 30-inch door. The Helmsley Palace has a system to alert its multilingual staff to the location of disabled guests. Other amenities include: a concierge service and a parking garage underneath the building. All rooms have remote-controlled TV; appointments are sumptuous enough to rate single rates from $115 to $195, and $135 to $215 for doubles, subject to change, with weekend packages available here too.

A second Helmsley hotel that has opened in the past few years is the **Harley of New York,** 212 E. 42nd St., NY 10017 (tel. 212/490-8900, toll free 800/221-4982), which has a level entrance from the street to the lobby and elevators. Again, no rooms are specially designed, but bathroom doors in all the guest rooms are 32 inches wide. TV can be remote-controlled from bedside, and there is an extra phone in the bathroom. There are no steps to either Mindy's, the full service restaurant that overlooks an open-air landscaped plaza, or to Harley's New York Bar in the lobby. Rates are $125 to $175 single, $145 to $195 double.

On the same side of town, and across the street from the United Nations on the East River, is the **UN Plaza Hotel,** one of New York's newer hotels, on First Avenue at 44th St., NY 10017 (tel. 212/355-3400, toll free 800/228-9000). It has a level entrance, and all guest rooms have a 28-inch bathroom door. The Ambassador Grill and Lounge, up steps from the lobby, can be reached by the main elevator to the second floor, with a change to the service elevator. Public rest rooms have one stall with 30-inch doors and grab bars. It is a relatively small hotel (290 rooms), and the multilingual staff can often give more personal service than in the larger establishments. Rates are $105 to $140 single, with $20 extra for double occupancy, and there are special rates for weekend packages.

Still on the East Side, and centrally located at Park Avenue and 50th Street, is the venerable **Waldorf-Astoria,** 301 Park Ave., NY 10022 (tel. 212/ 355-3000, or Hilton Reservation Service), with its not-so-venerable grand-entry staircase to the lobby. However, the 49th and 50th Street entrances are at street level through the building-wide driveway in the middle of the block, where cars unload guests and luggage. A ramped entry leads to elevators, which go to the lobby and the hotel floors.

Guest rooms here have the tighter squeeze 26-inch doors, (but not a total barrier for some wheelchairs, especially those that have narrowing devices). The famous Peacock Alley nightspot is level with the lobby; Oscar's Coffee Shop can be entered from the street at Lexington Avenue at 50th Street and is one of New York's most up-scale coffeeshops, decorated as an indoor garden and probably worth a visit even if you don't stay at the hotel. Rates, subject to change, are $75 to $160 single, $110 to $195 double.

At the **Middletowne Harley,** 148 E. 48th St., NY 10017 (tel. 212/755-3000, toll free 800/221-4982), recently converted from an apartment building, there are generously sized rooms with fully equipped kitchens (the hotel has no restaurants). Bathroom doors are 27 inches wide. There is one step to the lobby from the street. Rates, subject to change, are $80 to $90 single, $95 to $105 double or twin. Monthly rates are available, on a two-month minimum.

Among the smaller hotels (and therefore lower rates) that some disabled travelers may be able to use, even though there are no special facilities, is the legendary **Algonquin,** 59 W. 44th St., NY 10036 (tel. 212/840-6800), in the theater district. European in flavor and famed for its literary Round Table memories of Robert Benchley, James Thurber, and Dorothy Parker among others, the Algonquin is still favored by theater and publishing celebrities. Bathroom entrances in guest rooms are 26 inches wide; the entrance to the hotel has one step to the lobby. Restaurants on the lobby floor are level and include the famous Rose Room and Oak Room. Single rates go from $66 to $86, doubles from $75 to $85, and $78 to $94 for a twin-bedded room. There is free parking on weekends if you stay at least two nights.

In Midtown, the **Beverly,** 125 E. 50th St., NY 10022 (tel. 212/753-2700, toll free 800/442-8436; N.Y. State 800/223-0945), has a level entrance and bathroom doors in guest rooms that are 26 inches wide. Rates are $79 to $99 single, and $89 to $109 double. There are good weekend packages and a parking garage across the street.

Still on Lexington Avenue, at 47th Street, there is the **Roger Smith,** 501 Lexington Ave., NY 10017 (tel. 212/775-1400), which has fairly spacious rooms and 27-inch bathroom doors. (Note that the elevator, though, is only 27½ inches.) Single room rates are from $59 to $76, and doubles from $71 to $88, subject to change.

And a good-buy-at-the-price is an older, refurbished hotel in the theater district on the West Side, the **Century-Paramount,** 235 W. 46th St., NY 10036 (tel. 212/246-5500), which has a level entrance, and the bathroom doors in all 700 guest rooms are 34 inches wide! There are no stairs in the public areas, and all doors are very wide. Double- and twin-bedded rooms range from $50 to $60, singles from $40 to $50, subject to change.

5. Restaurants (Mostly Midtown)

When a New Yorker discusses the question of where to eat, it's very often in terms of "Do you want to eat Italian food?" Or Chinese, Greek, Hungarian . . . or any other national cuisine from Afghan to Vietnam. There are literally thousands of restaurants in Manhattan, and you could sample a different region's cooking every night for years.

You'll find out sooner or later, though, that it's not inexpensive to dine out in New York City, so perhaps it's better to be prepared. Most of the best—but also most expensive—places are in Midtown. Restaurants in Greenwich Village, SoHo, Little Italy, and Chinatown—all good dining—are included in their respective sections under "New York's Neighborhoods" in this chapter.

Although location is a consideration for visitors with mobility restrictions, we have listed the Midtown restaurants here by price, since it might be best to pick what fits your budget first, then see what may be in a convenient area. Do remember that even in the most expensive restaurants, you can often enjoy a pre-theater dinner, or lunch of course, for less. A telephone call in advance will ensure that a suitable table will be available when you arrive, even if you're not making reservations. Most of the more expensive restaurants, of course, require reservations. A phone check on Sundays is also a good idea since some places may be closed. All prices quoted here are subject to change (usually upward!). Parking and rest room facilities are mentioned only where they are accessible.

DINNER FOR AROUND $50: Considered by many to be the ultimate in French restaurants in New York City, **Lutece**, 249 E. 50th St. (tel. 752-2225), is in a town house where the ground-floor dining room and garden can be reached from the street level. (There is no elevator to the dining room upstairs.) Lunch is prix fixe at $24, and dinner is in the range of $45 plus wines.

Another kind of New York ambience is at the **Four Seasons**, 99 E. 52nd St. (tel. 754-9494), spacious and elegant in one of the city's more admired modern structures, the Seagram Building. The dining room is on the second floor, and although there is no public elevator, advance notice will arrange for you to reach the restaurant level via the service elevator. The men's rest room on the ground floor has a 31-inch stall door (the women's is only 22 inches). Four Seasons prices match its size and elegance, but the food makes it one of the best restaurants in New York. In the Pool Room, à la carte entrées range from $22.50 to $38, in the Bar Room from $14 to $21. However, prix fixe before- or after-theater dinner, served from 5 to 6:30 p.m. and 10 to 11:30 p.m., Monday through Saturday in the Pool Room, is $26.50. The Four Seasons is closed on Sunday.

Newer on the New York scene, since it is in a new hotel, the Grand Hyatt at 42nd Street and Grand Central, is **Trumpets** (tel. 850-5999), reached by elevator from the hotel lobby. The continental menu has à la carte entrees from $16 to $20. Closed Sunday.

You actually have to leave Manhattan for this one, but it is included here since it has spectacular views of Lower Manhattan and New York Harbor, along with its rather spectacular prices. It's the **River Cafe**, 1 Water St., Brooklyn (tel. 522-5200). On a firmly moored barge, nestled under the Brooklyn Bridge on the Brooklyn side of the East River, it has only one step at the entrance and then is level inside. There is valet parking. Dinner entrées à la carte range from $16.50 to $32, ($6 to $18 at lunch). Sunday brunch is served from 11:30 a.m. to 3 p.m., with entrees from $6.50 to $18.

DINNER AROUND $35: Take a deep breath and enjoy some more of the most notable restaurants in the country. (Quite a few of the "in" places you might have heard of before you arrive in New York are *not* comfortably accessible, and so are not included.) Don't forget, you can have the same surroundings and the same food for less money at lunch.

The **Tavern on the Green,** right in central Park on the West Side at 67th St. (tel. 873-3200), is one of the most glamorous interiors ever seen in the middle of parkland greenery. It is level throughout, and the dining areas add up to a lot of square footage. There is valet parking. Entrees range from about $12 to $20, but you can also get a hamburger or a salad for less. And in the warm weather you can sit outdoors, overlooking the park's meadows.

Another dazzling New York dining experience is 107 floors higher than the meadows in Central Park. It's at the top of the World Trade Center at the southern tip of Manhattan and it's called, aptly enough, **Windows on the World** (tel. 938-1111). In the Restaurant, the main dining room, window tables involve a step or two, but from anywhere in the room, the very tall windows allow an expansive panorama on a clear day. The staff is experienced in serving patrons who have mobility problems, and will tell you the best way to reach the restaurant from the building's concourse when you call for a reservation. If you are in a wheelchair, they will sometimes escort you to the level entrance near the special elevator (though this is not always in operation), or they will get you down the four steps. The restaurant serves dinner from 5 p.m. to 10 p.m., Monday through Saturday, at a prix fixe of $24.95, with an à la carte selection as well. Even though I've included this restaurant in the dinner category, also worth noting is their very popular buffet on Saturday, noon to 3 p.m., and Sunday, noon to 7:30 p.m., served in the same grand dining room, for $17.95, which includes as much as you can eat of the hot and cold buffet dishes, as well as dessert and coffee. Reservations are advised. Unfortunately, the other sections of Windows on the World—the Hors d'Oeuverie and the City Lights Bar—can be reached only by a flight of steps. There is free parking for Windows on the World patrons in the underground garage at the World Trade Center.

Still "on top" of things, you can have a cocktail, or dine and be entertained, 65 floors up at the RCA Building in Rockefeller Center (entered from the Plaza midblock between Fifth Avenue and Avenue of the Americas on 49th or 50th Street). There are great views from the two restaurant/nightspots here, the **Rainbow Room** (tel. 757-9090) and the **Rainbow Grill** (tel. 757-8970). The cocktail lounge of the Rainbow Room is on the same level as the elevator at the 65th floor, and it has great views to the north over Central Park and beyond. If you want to spend the evening dining to music by a dance band, the staff will escort you to the restaurant level through a pantry entrance to avoid steps. Entrees à la carte range from $13 to $18. There is a pre-theater dinner served from 5 p.m. to 6:30 p.m. at a prix fixe of $17.50, and also a $14.95 Sunday brunch served from 11 a.m. to 3 p.m. In the Rainbow Grill, facing south on the same 65th floor, there are some tables on the same level as the entrance, and you'll get a cabaret with your dinner if you are there for the 9:15 p.m. show (cover charge is $8 during the week and $10 on weekends); à la carte entrees are about $14 to $18. For reservations call 755-8970. You can get some spectacular views from the South Lounge cocktail room here that has a level entrance from the elevator. Opens at 5 p.m.

DINNER AROUND $25 (WEST SIDE): Sardi's, 234 West 44th St. (tel. 221-8440), has a level entrance and dining room. It is, perhaps, the best-known theatrical restaurant anywhere, and its dinner entrees range from $8 to $18, with a late-dinner menu (after 9 p.m.) for after-theater dining until 2 a.m., when it can be as busy as any other time!

The **Hotel Algonquin,** 59 W. 44th St. (tel. 840-6800), is in the Broadway theater district, too, and is very popular with theatrical and literary personalities. It has one step at the entrance, and the dining rooms, the **Oak Room** and the **Rose Room,** are level with the lobby. Dinner entrees range from $11 to $17; there is an after-theater supper served after 9:30 p.m. You can enjoy the atmosphere of the Algonquin, too, by having a cocktail or taking tea in the cozy lobby.

In the nine dining rooms at **Mamma Leone's,** in the theater district at 239 W. 48th St. (tel. 596-5151), everybody is treated like a member of a big happy Italian family. Although there are two steps at the front entrance, there is a side door, level with the street, that can be opened for you. Complete dinner, with very generous portions, is $17.95, and there is also a buffet Italiano lunch ($8.95) if you are going to a matinee.

Closer to Fifth Avenue is the unusual dining experience offered by the Japanese restaurant, **Benihana of Tokyo,** 15 W. 44th St. (tel. 683-7120), where everything is cooked at your table in a hibachi. There is a level entrance and interior. Dinner, from $8.25 to $12.25, includes appetizer, soup, entree, salad, rice, and tea; à la carte lunch ranges from $4.25 to $6.25.

If your tastes tend toward Indian dishes, **Raga,** in the Rockefeller Center area at 57 W. 48th St. (tel. 757-3450), is one of the most elegant Indian restaurants in New York. It has a level entrance and interior. Entrees are $8 to $15.

And you don't *have* to have borscht, caviar, or blinis, but you can if you want to, at the **Russian Tea Room,** 150 W. 57th St. (tel. 265-0947), a favorite with musicians, dancers, and performers (it's next door to Carnegie Hall.) It has an atmosphere and food that's worth a little extra trouble. The entrance is level from the street, but the revolving door will be broken down if you are in a wheelchair, and although the tables are snugly placed, it's definitely possible to negotiate the interior. Entrees à la carte range from $13 to $21. After-theater supper is served from 9:30 p.m. to 12:30 a.m. Sunday is dinner only from noon to 1 a.m.

DINNER AROUND $25 (EAST SIDE): La Bibliotèque, 341 E. 43rd St.
(tel. 661-5757), with a view over the United Nations building, must be approached from Second Avenue. It has a level entrance and interior at street level. Dinner entrees from $9 to $19.

La Bonne Bouffe, 127 E. 34th St. (tel. 679-9389), is a typical French bistro in atmosphere, and it has a ramped entrance from the street to a level interior. Dinner entrees range from $11.25 to $14.50.

Bienvenue, at 21 E. 36th St. (tel. 684-0215), is close to Fifth Avenue, near B. Altman and Lord & Taylor department stores. It has a level entrance though the interior is smallish with 28-inch aisles. If you go to lunch, arrive early or late to avoid waiting in line. Complete lunch is $5 to $10, complete dinner $13 to $19.

Hunan, 845 Second Ave. at 46th St. (tel. 687-7471), is noted for introducing the hot and spicy Chinese Szechuan cooking to New York. There is a level entrance, and validated parking is available. Entrees average $8.75.

Chalet Suisse, 6 E. 48th St. (tel. 355-0855), has a level entrance. Its authentic Swiss food includes fondue, $11, or a full prix fixe dinner at $26. Closed on weekends.

DINNER AROUND $15 (WEST SIDE): The West Side is traditionally more casual than the East Side, and there are moderately priced restaurants on every block in Midtown, especially in the theater district. Some with level entrances are:

Cafe Madeleine, 405 W. 43rd St. (tel. 246-2993), located in the new theater neighborhood between Ninth and Tenth Avenues, is a great place for after-theater supper with soups, cheese, pâtés, French breads and desserts, and inexpensive French-style snacks at any time of the day. Open from 8:30 a.m. to midnight on weekdays and from 10:30 a.m. to midnight on Tuesday to Saturday. Sunday hours are 10:30 a.m. to 8 p.m. Closed Monday.

King Crab, 871 Eighth Ave. at 52nd St. (tel. 765-4393), is very popular since it is located near the theater district and is well known for its fresh seafood dishes that range from $6.50 for broiled fish to $12.95 for Alaskan king crab legs. Open from noon to 3:30 p.m. for lunch on weekdays, and for dinner every day from 5 p.m. to midnight.

On a block of many restaurants, **La Fondue,** 43 W. 55th St. (tel. 581-0820), is among the least expensive, specializing in, of course, fondues that range in price from $4.25 to $9.95. There's a five-course dinner, with cheese dishes, for about $11; steaks, chicken, and burgers are also on the menu. Open every day from 11:45 a.m. to 1 a.m.

DINNER AROUND $15 (EAST SIDE): **El Parador,** 325 E. 34 St. (tel. 679-6812), is a popular Mexican restaurant that is always busy for dinner. Reservations are not accepted. Because this restaurant is near the Institute of Rehabilitation Medicine, the staff is familiar with patrons in wheelchairs. There is one step at the entrance and tables in the front part of the restaurant are level with the entrance. À la carte entrees range from $9.50 to $10.50.

Wylie's Ribs & Co., 891 First Ave. at 50th St. (tel. 751-0700), specializes in Texas-style barbecue ribs, with entrees $6.50 to $10.50. Level entrance from street, one step to the dining areas inside.

Xenia, 871 First Ave. at 48 St., (tel. 838-1191), is a Greek restaurant with a level entrance and interior. The garden is also accessible without steps. À la carte entrees range from $7.25 to $12.

The Market at Citicorp Center

The Citicorp Building, a relatively new skyscraper that fills the block between Lexington and Third Avenues at 53rd Street, has an indoor "market" around its skylit atrium where a number of restaurants serve a variety of international menus. Nearly all of them are accessible to people in wheelchairs.

The level entrance to the building is from the Lexington Avenue side, and there are elevators that give access to the lower level where most of the restaurants are located.

Avgerinos (tel. 688-8828) is a Greek restaurant with two tables at the level entrance; the rest are up one step. Dinner entrees range from $8.95 to $10.95.

Les Tournebroches (tel. 935-6029) has a French rotisserie menu, with entrees from $10 to $18. The entrance and interior are all on one level.

Charley O's (tel. 752-2102) is also level, and its traditional American food ranges from brunch on weekends ($6.95) to complete dinners ($9.95 to $13.95).

Alfredo's specializes in Italian food (pasta is $4.95 to $7.95) and complete Sunday brunch is $7.95.

Slotnick Daughters (tel. 935-1744) is a coffee, sandwich, and pastry cafe with a level entrance.

Healthworks (tel. 838-6221) is also level from the lower floor concourse and is a self-service salad restaurant with main dishes from $2.75 to $4.95.

On the street floor level of the Market there is Nyborg Nelson (tel. 223-0700), where the specialty is Scandinavian open-face sandwiches ($2.85 to $4.95) and cold plates ($5.25 to $7.50.)

DELIS: It's difficult to discuss New York restaurants without mentioning its famous Jewish delicatessens, the "delis," where pastrami, corned beef, and chopped liver sandwiches, among dozens of others, can be a complete meal. Although you'll find them scattered all over town, some of the best-known, all with level entrances and cozily placed tables, are: Stage Delicatessen, 834 Seventh Ave. (tel. 245-7850; Carnegie Delicatessen, 854 Seventh Ave at 55th St. (tel. 757-2245); Second Avenue Delicatessen, 156 Second Ave. at 10th St. (tel. 677-0606), which is completely kosher and where braille menus are available; and Kaplan's at the Delmonico, 59 E. 59th St. (tel. 755-5959). Sandwiches generally range from about $4.95 to $7.95, and in most of the delis you can also get hot entrees from about $8 to $12.

6. The Sights

Whether you are going "on foot," by car, by taxi, or by bus—are you ready to see the sights?

There are probably more symbols of New York City whose names are familiar to people who have never seen the originals than of any other city in the world: the Statue of Liberty, the Empire State Building, Radio City Music Hall, the United Nations, and Central Park must all ring bells of recognition. Others of more recent vintage like Lincoln Center (the Metropolitan Opera House is here) and the World Trade Center (for a brief moment the world's tallest buildings) are almost as well known. And the disabled visitor can enjoy nearly all of them—given enough ambition and energy!

ROCKEFELLER CENTER: Right there in the middle of it all is the group of buildings that symbolizes the optimistic hopes of the Great Depression. The construction of Rockefeller Center was completed during the early 1930s and became one of Manhattan's most famous focal points.

The RCA Building, at 30 Rockefeller Plaza, is between Fifth Avenue and Avenue of the Americas, and between 49th and 50th Streets. The Rockefeller Center Garage has entrances on 48th Street (eastbound) and 49th Street (westbound) with elevators to street level. The best view of the RCA Building from street level is from the Fifth Avenue sidewalk (opposite Saks Fifth Avenue), through the Channel Gardens, planted with magnificent displays of seasonal blooms—spectacular particularly at Christmas and Easter, but gorgeous at any time. There's a short level promenade around the gardens, and directly in front of the RCA Building is a sunken plaza which becomes a skating rink in winter and a restaurant in the summer. You'll find steps here up to the street level, but it's only a short back-track to Fifth Avenue, where you can come around to the RCA Building via either 49th or 50th Street. Entrance to the building itself is level, and there is an information desk just inside the door.

This is the home of the National Broadcasting Company, and the NBC network has its East Coast studios here. These days, not too many television shows originate from New York, but the NBC studios are accessible and there are wheelchair locations. Check for anything that may be going on here while you are in New York (tel. 664-3055); sometimes tickets to afternoon shows are distributed on the street at lunchtime. The guided tour of Rockefeller Center includes a number of places that would be difficult for a wheelchair user, but ask at the guided tour office on the ground floor for details of the tour and decide if it is feasible for you. The **Observation Roof** here is accessible, but you will have to be the judge if the surrounding wall (about 40 inches high) will obstruct your view or not. However, there are great views from the 65th floor cocktail lounge and restaurants, the **Rainbow Room** and the **Rainbow Grill**, which are detailed in the restaurant section of this chapter. On the street level, there are many accessible small shops both on the ground floor and in the extensive underground concourse (reached by attended elevator). Remember that most of them will be closed on the weekend.

Radio City Music Hall

Also here in Rockefeller Center is the world's biggest theater (6000 seats), now restored to all its 1930s Art Deco splendor after nearly being torn down a few years ago. Radio City Music Hall has a level entrance on the Avenue of the Americas at 50th Street, and the lobby and orchestra seats in the auditorium are level too. Wheelchair places are available for the performances (now not usually movies)—"spectaculars" such as celebrity concerts of popular music and revues. It is advisable to call the Guest Relations Department (tel. 582-8370) in advance to make sure you can have a wheelchair location if you want one. Rest rooms, reached by accessible elevator, have stall doors that are 25 inches wide.

New York Experience

And still in Rockefeller Center, at the McGraw-Hill Building, 1221 Avenue of the Americas, between 48th and 49th Streets, there's an exhibit called *The New York Experience* that provides a great introduction to New York City. It is a dazzling multi-screen tour of the city, past and present, with spectacular special effects. Enter from the 49th Street entrance (level), and ask the elevator starter to notify the exhibit staff that you need to be escorted to the theater via special elevators. (Arrive about half an hour before show time.) There are wheelchair locations inside the theater. Shows are every hour on the hour from 11 a.m. to 7 p.m. Monday through Friday, 11 a.m. to 8 p.m. on Saturday, and from 12 noon to 8 p.m. on Sunday. Adults $3.90, children under 12 $2 (tel. 869-0345).

UNITED NATIONS: Across town, on the East River between 42nd and 48th Streets, lies the headquarters of the United Nations. The tall, slab-like building is the **Secretariat**, the "office" building, with the low, curved-roof **General Assembly** building alongside. At the visitors' entrance, 45th St. at First Ave., there is a curb cut and a ramp that avoids the ten steps normally used to reach the General Assembly Building, which has a level entrance. Disabled visitors can use elevators during the guided tours that begin every ten minutes, daily from 9 a.m. to 4:45 p.m. Adults $3, students and servicemen $1.75, children $1.25 (under 5 not admitted on tours). You can attend meetings of the General Assembly and councils when they are in session—five wheelchair spaces are available—by applying for tickets in the lobby; they are given out on a first-come first-served basis just before meetings begin. Call 754-7713 between 9:30 a.m. and 5 p.m. to find out about meetings in advance. There is headphone equipment on which you can listen to simultaneous translations of the discussions in different languages.

Handicrafts, ethnic dolls, and gifts of all kinds from most of the member nations are available in fascinating variety in the **Gift Center** on the lower level, reached by accessible elevator from the lobby. Here, too, is the U.N. Postal Service, where you can buy special U.N. stamps for mail posted in the building. You can also use the **Delegates Dining Room,** reached by elevator from the lobby, which is open to the public Monday through Friday 11:30 a.m. to noon and 2 to 2:30 p.m. Rest rooms in the General Assembly Building have been recently redesigned to fulfill American National Standard Institute (ANSI) standards of accessibility. Visitors Service telephone number is 754-1234 if you need further information.

STATUE OF LIBERTY NATIONAL MONUMENT: In preparation for Miss Liberty's 100th anniversary in 1986, the Statue of Liberty is undergoing much needed repairs, but will be kept open while they are done, according to the National Parks Service. There is an elevator to the observation platform (wheelchair-accessible) for a spectacular view from here on Liberty Island in the middle of New York harbor. Call 732-1236 for Statue of Liberty information.

To reach Liberty Island, take the Circle Line Statue of Liberty Ferry (tel. 269-5755) from Battery Park at the southern tip of Manhattan—wheelchairs can get on board.

CIRCLE LINE CRUISE: If you're not visiting the Statue of Liberty, you can get a great view of it during one of the most enjoyable ways to see Manhattan—from its rivers and harbor. You can do this by taking a three-hour cruise on the easily boarded Circle Line boats: it's an impressive reminder that Manhattan is, indeed, an island surrounded by navigable waters. The cruise gives you a perspective on New York that even many natives don't have.

The Circle Line cruise begins at Pier 93 at the foot of West 43rd Street, reached by westbound crosstown bus (wheelchair-accessible) on 42nd Street (M 107), by taxi, or by car (there is a parking lot with reasonable charges). All boats have wide boarding ramps, and crews that are very willing to assist. Certain boats have accessible rest rooms at the main deck level—you can check on the schedule for these by calling 563-3200 (also the number for all enquiries). Circle Line boats operate seven days a week during the season, which runs from the end of March until mid-November; boats leave more frequently from June through Labor Day, when they depart every 45 minutes between 9:45 a.m. and 5 p.m. To take advantage of summer evenings and skyline views by sunset, a shorter two-hour twilight cruise around the tip of Manhattan, with pre-dinner cocktails and music, is being planned at this writing. Once you are on board you'll find that the main deck is level. A recommended spot if you are in a wheelchair is at the stern of the boat (the popular bow deck is up some steps), but the view is just as good and the guided tour commentary just as easily heard. The refreshment stand is in the center of the main deck. Cost is $8.50 for adults, $4 for children under 12 (subject to change).

INTREPID MUSEUM: Close by the Circle Line pier there's a newcomer to the Hudson River waterfront—the famous World War II aircraft carrier *Intrepid,* now permanently berthed at Pier 86 at the foot of 46th Street. The huge ship has been converted to a Sea-Air-Space museum crammed with 20th-century technology in the form of airplanes, rockets, and satellites. And it's completely accessible, including the rest rooms! There are large elevators between decks, and the ramp from the dock is a gentle slope into the lower section. Open 10 a.m. to 6 p.m. Adults $5, senior citizens $4, children under 12, $2.50 (tel. 245-0072).

WORLD TRADE CENTER: After seeing Manhattan from the ground and sea level, you should take a look at it from the roof—on the 107th floor of the World Trade Center. The twin towers, downtown where the Hudson River meets the Harbor, soar over their surroundings, a place where you can often look *down* on a helicopter as it buzzes around below you!

The **Observation Deck,** accessible and glass-enclosed, is on the top of Number Two Tower. Take the express elevator from the lobby direct to the 107th floor. (An open roof deck, on the 110th floor, is reached by a 23-inch-wide escalator.) Rest rooms here have 30-inch stall doors and grab bars. The observation levels are open from 9:30 a.m. to 9:30 p.m. daily, with an admission fee of $2.50 for adults, $1.25 for children (tel. 466-7377). There are breathtaking views to be had, too, from the restaurant complex at **Windows on the World,** which is on the 107th floor of the other, Number One, Tower of World Trade Center. (See the restaurant section of this chapter for details.)

The **World Trade Center Concourse,** at street level, is a spacious mall on one level that offers a variety of restaurants and shops. Most appealing are the Market Dining Room and the Big Kitchen, where there's a seemingly endless offering at the Delicatessen, the Bakery, the Oyster Bar, and the Grill. There are no steps at either restaurant. Accessible shops on the concourse include branches of uptown's F.A.O. Schwarz, the famous toy store, and Alexander's department store.

If you go by car, there's an underground garage entered from West Street, with elevators to the concourse level and the lobbies of either building (Red garage to 1 World Trade Center and Yellow garage for 2 World Trade Center; there are two "handicapped" spaces in each). Street parking at the Liberty Street entrance to 2 World Trade Center has 12 spaces for cars with special vehicle identification. Curbs are ramped around the buildings.

MORE DOWNTOWN SIGHTS: While you are at the World Trade Center you should take in some of the other Lower Manhattan sights. This is the historic section of the city, the site of the original Dutch settlement of Nieuw Amsterdam, the heart of colonial New York, and today the financial center of the world (Wall Street, the New York Stock Exchange). It's undergoing quite a rebirth, with old streets being swept away and replaced by shiny high-rise office buildings.

But the history is still there. It was in this area that General George Washington was inaugurated as the new nation's first president. Head toward Broadway if you are leaving from the World Trade Center and go south to Bowling Green (really used for bowling by the Dutch), now restored to the way it looked in the 19th century. Then go over to Broad Street, where it meets Pearl Street, and at 54 Pearl you'll see **Fraunces Tavern,** one of New York's rare remaining colonial houses, built in 1719 and a tavern since 1763. George Washington was an habitué and here in the Long Room in 1783 he bade farewell to his officers at the end of the Revolutionary War. It is now a restaurant on the ground floor and a museum upstairs (but no elevator). There are four steps at the entrance, but you can get assistance from the doorman for these and for another two steps to the dining level, if you want to eat in the restaurant (tel. 428-1776). Rest rooms on the main floor each have stalls with 30-inch doors that open out. Parking is one block from the entrance.

If you go north on Broad Street, you'll come to legendary Wall Street, where the Dutch built a wooden palisade to protect the colony from Indian attack. Now, Wall Street is synonymous with the nation's finances. Looking west, you'll see the spires of **Trinity Church,** which dominated the skyline when the church was completed in 1846, but now completely overshadowed in the narrow streets by neighboring buildings. The church itself has four steps at the entrance, but assistance is available. The interior is accessible, and an Acoustiguide tour will fill you in on its history. (The churchyard is where Alexander Hamilton and Robert Fulton are buried.) Open from 7 a.m. to 6 p.m. Monday through Friday, and from 7 a.m. to 4 p.m. on Saturday, Sunday, and holidays.

At the corner of Wall and Nassau Streets (the extension of Broad Street), is the **Federal Hall National Memorial,** fronted by a statue of George Washington to mark the site where he took the oath of office as the nation's first president in 1789. It was also the site of the first U.S. capital, where the first American Congress adopted the Bill of Rights. The present building dates from 1842 and houses a very fine museum of the Colonial and Early Federal periods. There is a ramp at the Pine Street entrance and the interior is accessible. Wheelchair locations are available in the auditorium, where one regular feature is a film on Washington's Inauguration. Open from 9 a.m. to 5 p.m. Monday through Friday. Admission is free. Call 264-8711 for information.

Diagonally across the street (at the corner of Broad and Wall Streets) is the **New York Stock Exchange,** which has a ramped entrance. There is a level entrance to the lower level of the Visitors Gallery where you can watch activities on the trading floor. A multilingual guided tour (every half hour Monday through Friday, 10 a.m. to 4 p.m.) will give you some idea of the inner workings of this scene of seeming chaos. (Call 623-5168 for information.)

Still in the money, go two blocks north to 33 Liberty Street, where the **Federal Reserve Bank of New York** has the country's largest stock of gold in its vaults. The interior is accessible and has elevators between floors. Take the free guided tour, on banking days at 10 a.m., 11 a.m., 1 p.m., and 3 p.m., to see the gold vault and the currency operations; you must reserve at least one week in advance. Write to the Public Information Department, Federal Reserve Bank of New York, 33 Liberty St., New York, NY 10045, or call 212/791-6130.

Turn on Liberty or Maiden Lane toward the East River until you come to South Street, at New York's historic waterfront of clippers and sailing ship days. The **South Street Seaport,** the heart of New York's maritime commerce in the 19th century, underwent an ambitious restoration and is now a lively complex of restaurants, cafes, specialty stores, and pedestrian malls. At the Visitors Center, 12 Fulton St., (tel. 669-9426), there is one small step at the entrance.

Some of the pedestrian-only areas have been newly cobblestoned, but there are smooth sidewalks for easier wheeling. At the **Fulton Market** building, which houses restaurants, cafes, and gourmet shops, there is a level entrance and elevator access to the upper floors. **Schermerhorn Row** and the **Museum Block** buildings have low steps at the entrance, but levels inside are sometimes separated by one or more steps. Sidewalk cafes and food stalls outdoors are easily accessible. The TransLux Seaport Theater at 210 Front St. (tel. 608-7882) has a wheelchair-accessible entrance on Water Street, which has an elevator to the auditorium, where there are two wheelchair locations. There is a wheelchair-accessible rest room near the Water Street entrance. The theater shows a multiscreen presentation called **"South Street Venture"** every hour on the hour from 10 a.m. Admission is $4 for adults and $2.50 for children under 12.

The old ships that are berthed at Piers 15 and 16 between Maiden Lane and Fulton Street are not easily boarded, but the open piers are easily accessible; they are level and the wide planks have smooth pathways made of plywood. There are outdoor jazz and folk music concerts here during the summer, and free tickets are available on a first-come first-served basis. Scheduled to open some time in 1984 on Piers 17 and 18 is a Victorian-style pavilion with a grand arcade and 120 restaurants, cafes, and retail stores that should have level access and elevators between floors.

If you drive to South Street Seaport from Midtown, take the East River Drive (also called FDR Drive) to the South Street exit. There are commercial parking areas along South Street and elsewhere in the area.

CENTRAL PARK: All great cities have their famous parks, but it is almost a surprise to find one as large as Central Park right in the middle of this crowded island. You certainly will be able to see only a fringe of it "on foot," but it will be enough to get the flavor. Most of the pathways are paved, and you can keep your route fairly level by looking for alternatives when the one ahead seems hilly—paths go off in all directions. There are entrances all round its perimeter, of course, but if you are coming from its southeast corner, at Fifth Avenue and 59th Street, the entrance here will take you through the Zoo (the current refurbishing is scheduled to be completed in 1985), the Children's Zoo (there is a ramped entrance), and onward in any direction, through meadows and wooded areas where New Yorkers will be picnicking, sunbathing, bird-watching, roller-skating, kite-flying, playing instruments (solo or combo), bicycling, jogging, performing mime, dancing on stilts, or absolutely anything that might take their fancy in the particular season you are there. On summer evenings there are free open-air concerts by the New York Philharmonic and the Metropolitan Opera; you can take up a place anywhere on the large meadow where the performances are given. And lots, lots more. Daily reports of what's going on in the park can be had by calling the recorded message on 755-4100.

You'll find details of how to get tickets for the free New York Shakespeare Festival in July and August at the Delacorte Theater in the Park in the Off-Broadway Theater section of this chapter.

NOTE: If you wonder what happened to the famous **Empire State Building** in our sightseeing suggestions, just consider it as a skyline silhouette only! Though a mecca for thousands of tourists every year, the Observation Roof here is not an ideal place for a visitor in a wheelchair—the wall around the open platform is quite high, and the glass-enclosed level is five steps up with a narrow gangway.

7. Museums and Art Galleries

New York City's position as the capital of the art world is even stronger today than when it took over from Paris in the late 1950s, and its lively art galleries and museums in uptown, midtown, and downtown in SoHo attest to its preeminence. It's a pleasure to note that enough of them are accessible to satisfy the most ardent art lover. Fortunately, too, most have the good sense not to carpet their floors entirely, a boon to wheelchair users.

METROPOLITAN MUSEUM OF ART: One of the world's great museums, this long-established, venerable institution has been "jumping" in recent years. It is located on Fifth Avenue, between East 80th and 84th Streets (actually, it's *in* Central Park). Although it has a most awesome flight of steps at the main entrance, the museum is easily entered either from street level through a door just south of the steps, behind the fountain pool, or from the underground garage. From the garage, where there are reserved spaces for disabled visitors, there is a curb-cut access to the elevator that takes you to the level of the museum's main elevator.

The Information Desk, in the center of the Great Hall by the main entrance, can provide a brochure on the museum's facilities for disabled visitors, including the location of the accessible rest rooms. There are braille and enlarged print materials as well as programs available for visually impaired visitors (call 879-5500, ext. 3561, for a recorded message listing programs). Nearly all the major exhibits can be reached by elevator, though a few of the smaller galleries are accessible only by stairs. (But since it would take you days to see the whole museum, you'll probably have to miss some of the galleries anyway!) Guards are helpful and can direct you via the enormous elevators used primarily to transport the artworks. Elevator attendants can give you further directions. The restaurant on the main level, near the elevator in which you arrive from the street level, has been recently refurbished and is open from 11:30 a.m. to 4 p.m. In the Cafeteria, help with trays is available. Where the Reflecting Pool used to be, there is now a full-service restaurant with a few steps down.

Museum hours are Tuesday 10 a.m. to 9 p.m., Wednesday through Saturday 10 a.m. to 4:45 p.m., and Sunday 11 a.m. to 4:45 p.m. The museum is closed on Monday. There is a suggested admission of $4 for adults and $2 for students and senior citizens. Call 535-7710 for recorded information, and 878-5512 for details of concerts and lectures. The TDD number is 879-0421.

MUSEUM OF MODERN ART: In Midtown at 11 West 53rd St. (just off Fifth Avenue), the Museum of Modern Art is just that—modern paintings, sculpture, drawings, prints, architecture, photography, and industrial design from the 1880s to the present—plus a cinema that shows classic movies and a Garden Terrace restaurant. Its exhibit space has recently been more than doubled. The entrance is level with the street and all exhibits are accessible by ramp or elevator. For the hearing-impaired visitor, there is a TDD telephone available at the lobby information desk, and some of the gallery lectures have sign-language interpreters. (Call TDD 247-1230 for all museum information.) For the visually impaired visitor, touch is permitted for a selection of sculptures —details from the information desk. MOMA, as it is known to itself and New Yorkers, is open Monday, Tuesday, Friday, Saturday, and Sunday from 11 a.m. to 6 p.m., Thursday till 9 p.m., and closed Wednesday. Admission is $3 for adults, $2 for students with valid ID, and 75¢ for children and senior citizens. Tuesday is "pay as you wish" day. Admission includes entrance to the movie.

SOLOMON R. GUGGENHEIM MUSEUM: On Fifth Avenue between 88th and 89th Streets (tel. 860-1313), the Guggenheim specializes in modern paintings, sculpture, and graphic arts that are housed in a very unusual, once-controversial building designed by Frank Lloyd Wright. The interior is a spiraling ramp, six floors high! It's best, of course, to begin at the top of the ramp (reached by elevator) and then you can slowly descend the gently sloping ramp as you view the continuous exhibits on the walls. The Museum Cafe, for lunch and snacks, is on the ground floor and is accessible. A public garage on 89th Street gives a 15% discount with a validated museum ticket. The Guggenheim is open daily, except Monday, from 11 a.m. to 5 p.m., Tuesday until 8 p.m. Admission is $2, students with ID and visitors over 62, $1.25, children under 7 are free. Admission is free on Tuesday evenings from 5 to 8 p.m.

MUSEUM OF THE CITY OF NEW YORK: Further north, on Fifth Avenue at 104th Street, is the fascinating Museum of the City of New York (tel. 534-1672), which tells the story of New York's development from a Dutch trading post to America's great metropolis. The exhibits here include period costumes, prints and photographs, as well as theatrical memorabilia. There's a ramp at the 104th Street entrance, and the interior is accessible on all levels by elevator; it is open Tuesday to Sunday, 10 a.m. to 5 p.m. Adults $1, students 50¢.

COOPER-HEWITT MUSEUM: If you want to imagine what it was like to be a 19th-century industrial tycoon, steel magnate Andrew Carnegie's mansion still stands at the corner of Fifth Avenue and 91st Street and now houses the Cooper-Hewitt Museum, the Smithsonian Institution's National Museum of Design, with the most important collection of decorative arts in the U.S. It is accessible, even though the 64-room mansion was built in 1901: the few steps at the front entrance have been ramped, and assistance is available. Interiors are accessible and there is an elevator between floors. Even rest rooms, for a change, are accessible, with 30-inch stall door and grab bars. If you call in advance (tel. 860-6868), it is possible to use the staff parking lot on the property.

FRICK COLLECTION: A gem of an art museum, also housed in a 19th-century mansion, is the world-renowned Frick at Fifth Avenue and 71st Street. There are six steps at the entrance, but the risers are shallow and the treads between them are wide enough for a wheelchair base. The staff is willing to assist, particularly if you call in advance (tel. 288-0700) and go when they are not too busy. Also, request prior permission for use of the staff elevator. This beautiful mansion, with its greenery and fountains, is not too much altered from its days as a residence: the exquisite medieval collection and other priceless paintings of European masters, from the 14th to 19th centuries, make it an absolute must for any art lover. For details of concerts and lectures (held October through May) call 288-0700. Open Tuesday to Saturday 10 a.m. to 6 p.m., Sunday 1 to 6 p.m., closed Monday and major holidays. From June to August, closed Tuesday. No children under 10 admitted, and those under 16 must be accompanied by an adult. Admission $1, Sunday $2.

WHITNEY MUSEUM OF AMERICAN ART: In contrast, and close by, is a famous museum of modern artworks, the Whitney Museum of American Art, 945 Madison Ave at 75th St. (tel. 570-3600), which houses the largest collection of 20th-century American art at any public institution in the country. It is accessible, except for rest rooms, by level entrance and elevators between floors. There is a restaurant for light refreshments in the sunken sculpture court, reached by elevator. Open Tuesday 11 a.m. to 8 p.m., Wednesday to Saturday 11 a.m. to 6 p.m., Sunday noon to 6 p.m. Adults $2; children under 12, senior citizens, and college students, free. Admission on Tuesday evening 5 to 8 p.m. is free.

AMERICAN MUSEUM OF NATURAL HISTORY: One of the world's great scientific institutions and, perhaps, one of New York's most popular is the American Museum of Natural History, Central Park West between 77th and 81st Streets. There are endless exhibits, movies, and activities here about Man and Nature, and all are accessible to the mobility-impaired visitor. As usual with such venerable edifices, there is a sweeping flight of steps at the main entrance, but from 77th Street, or from the parking lot at 81st Street (with reserved "handicapped" spaces), entrances are ramped and accessible to elevators to all floors. There is a cafeteria in the basement. Rest rooms on the second floor have 30-inch stall doors and grab bars. Open Monday to Thursday and Sunday, 10 a.m. to 5:45 p.m.; Wednesday, Friday, and Saturday, 10 a.m. to 9 p.m. Admission is on a pay-as-you-wish basis with suggested rates for adults $3, children $1.50. Free on Friday and Saturday between 5 and 9 p.m.

The **Naturemax Theater,** with its four-story screen, shows special movies such as *To Fly, The Living Planet,* and *Man Belongs to the Earth* daily from 10:30 a.m. (Call 496-0900 for the schedule for these or for other scientific and natural history movies.) The theater has space in the rear for people in wheelchairs. Ticket prices, which are additional to museum admission, are adults $3, children $1.50.

Alongside the museum is the **Hayden Planetarium,** reached from the same ramped entrance on 81st Street, or from the interior of the museum. The dome of the accessible auditorium serves as the screen for the Zeiss VI projector, which reproduces the intricate movements of the stars and planets with breathtaking realism. The frequently changed shows are narrated by planetarium astronomers. There are wheelchair locations in the auditorium. Since the planetarium is adjacent to the museum, it is possible to use the museum's accessible restrooms (second floor). Shows on weekdays are at 1:30 p.m. and 3:30 p.m.; Saturday at 11 a.m., 1,2,3,4, and 5 p.m.; Sunday at 1, 2, 3, 4, and 5 p.m. Adults $3.25, students with ID and senior citizens $2.25, children up to 12 $1.50. For information, call 873-1300.

MORE MUSEUMS: New York City's treasure chest of museums of all sorts is a large one. Among the many others that have reasonable accessibility are:

The **American Craft Museum,** 55 W. 53rd St. (tel. 397-0630). There is a level entrance from the street, but two steps between the two levels on the first floor. An elevator gives access to the upper floor. Open Tuesday to Saturday 10 a.m. to 5 p.m., Sunday 11 a.m. to 5 p.m. Adults $1.50, children 75¢.

The **Asia Society,** 725 Park Ave. at 70th St. (tel. 288-6400), has a level entrance and an accessible interior. There is a lift available to avoid the six steps to the Starr Gallery. The auditorium has wheelchair locations, and rest rooms have 30-inch-wide stall doors and grab bars. Open Tuesday to Saturday 10 a.m. to 5 p.m., Thursday to 8:30 p.m., Sunday noon to 5 p.m. Closed Mondays. Admission $2.

International Center of Photography, 1130 Fifth Ave. at 94th St. (tel. 860-1777), has six 6-inch steps at the entrance. The interior is accessible. Open Tuesday to Friday noon to 8 p.m., Saturday and Sunday noon to 6 p.m.

Jewish Museum, 1109 Fifth Ave. at 92nd St. (tel. 860-1888). There is a portable ramp available on advance request over two 6-inch steps. The interior is accessible, and the rest room stall door is 29 inches wide. Open Monday to

Thursday noon to 5 p.m., Sunday 11 a.m. to 6 p.m. Closed Friday and Saturday. Adults $2; students with ID and children under 16, $1; seniors "pay-as-you-wish."

Museum of Broadcasting, 1 E. 53rd St. (tel. 752-7684), has a level entrance from the street and an elevator to the museum. Open Tuesday to Saturday noon to 5 p.m., Thursday noon to 7:30 p.m. Adults $2, seniors and children $1.

ART GALLERIES: Besides the museums, New York is replete with art galleries. The most recent center of the avant garde is the SoHo area, and I've noted the galleries there in this chapter's SoHo section. In Midtown, and somewhat more formal in style, though not necessarily in art, is the area along East and West 57th Street, which the *New York Times* called "the city's main drag for art." From the Avenue of the Americas to Park Avenue, more galleries line 57th Street and its bordering streets than can be found in the rest of the U.S., and the art shown here is some of the world's best. Many of these galleries are located in large elevator buildings that provide easy access from the street.

Among the 57th Street galleries that show contemporary artists are (working eastward from the Avenue of the Americas): **Terry Dintenfass,** 50 W. 57th St., 10th floor, (tel. 581-2268); **Marlborough,** 40 W. 57th St., 2nd floor, (tel. 541-4900); **Betty Parsons,** 24 W. 57th St., 3rd floor (tel. 247-7480); **Pace,** 32 E. 57th St., 2nd and 3rd floors, (tel. 421-3292); and **André Emmerich,** 41 E. 57th St., 5th and 9th floors (tel. 752-0124).

More traditional art is to be seen at the **Hammer Galleries,** 33 W. 57th St., 1st and 2nd floors (tel. 644-4400). Both traditional and contemporary artists are shown at **Wally Findlay Galleries,** 17 E. 57th St., 1st and 2nd floors (tel. 421-5390).

Specifically what is on, and where, can be found in the Sunday edition of the *New York Times.*

8. It's Entertainment Time

New York City is one place where they never roll up the sidewalks: there is too much going on for it to shut down even for a minute. There are plays, movies, concerts, the opera, the ballet, nightspots, theater workshops—everything that makes it the entertainment capital. And, best of all, it shouldn't be too much of a problem for you to enjoy it all.

GETTING TICKETS: If you want to see a play or a musical on "Broadway" (the term is loosely applied to all the major theaters located on or near Broadway in the Times Square area), a concert at Carnegie Hall, or an opera or ballet at Lincoln Center, some advance planning is essential. You can find out what's on from the **Quarterly Calendar of Events,** published by the New York Convention and Visitors Bureau, 2 Columbus Circle, New York, NY 10019. Or, if you can't get the *New York Times* in your area, the Sunday "Arts and Leisure" or "Guide" section contains all details.

Write for tickets as far in advance as you can: nearly all theaters accept credit card reservations. If you wait until you get to New York, you will probably have to use a ticket broker. (You'll pay more for your tickets and won't always have the guarantee that you can get aisle seats, for instance, if you need them, or any ticket at all for what you want to see.) You should make a note of the 16 theaters run by the Shubert Organization, since they offer a substantially discounted ticket price ($7.50 at the time of this writing, but subject to change) both to patrons in wheelchairs who will use the wheelchair location in the aisle, and to their companions (who must sit in the adjoining aisle seat). You can order tickets for any Shubert theater (noted in the following list) by calling Telecharge at 212/239-6200 (additional $2 per ticket for charging). Theaters charge full orchestra ticket price for wheelchair locations.

Most theaters have good accessibility to the orchestra level. When you are getting tickets at any theater, specify "wheelchair location" or "aisle seat" if you can transfer from a wheelchair. (Word of warning on transferring: there's usually not much room between the rows.) The New York City fire laws rule that any person in a wheelchair not able to transfer to an aisle seat must be accompanied by an able-bodied person.

It is possible to ask—and sometimes get—aisle seats (if you need them) at the half-price **TKTS Booth (Times Square Theater Center),** Broadway and 47th St., but be warned that this usually involves waiting on line. Half-price theater tickets are sold here for the day of the performance only, beginning at 3 p.m. for evening shows, at noon for matinees, for shows that are not sold out.

Don't forget that tickets on weekdays and Wednesday matinees are cheaper than on weekends. (Orchestra seats for a Broadway musical currently are $40 week nights and $45 on weekends; for a play, $30 to $32.50.)

Some long-running shows are put on "twofers," which entitle you to buy tickets at discount prices. You'll find "twofer" slips at some hotel desks, restaurant cashier booths, some shops, and for certain at the Visitors Bureau at Columbus Circle (tel. 397-8222). You'll then go the theater box office and buy admission tickets at discount prices by presenting the "twofer" slip.

For theatergoers with hearing impairments, there are now infrared sound enhancement systems installed in many theaters. They have been noted where they are available in the following list, along with the other special facilities.

"BROADWAY": In the following list of theaters, it is assumed that, unless otherwise noted (1) the entrance is level, (2) the orchestra level is accessible without steps, and (3) the rest rooms are *not* accessible.

Ambassador Theater (Shubert), 215 W. 49th St., NY 10019 (tel. 239-6200). The main entrance has two steps, but the side entrance is level; there are eight wheelchair locations in the orchestra. Assistance is available.

Belasco Theater (Shubert), 111 W. 44th St., NY 10036 (tel. 239-6200). The entrance has one 4-inch step and one 8-inch step (assistance available), and there are four wheelchair locations in the orchestra.

Bijou Theater, 209 W. 45th St., NY 10036 (tel. 221-8500). There is a level entrance and six wheelchair locations.

Biltmore Theater, 261 W. 47th St., NY 10036 (tel. 582-5340). The main entrance has three steps and there are four wheelchair locations.

Booth Theater (Shubert), 222 W. 45th St. NY 10036 (tel. 239-6200). There is a level entrance and two wheelchair locations in the orchestra. Infrared system available.

Broadhurst Theater (Shubert), 261 W. 47th St., NY 10036 (tel. 239-6200). The entrance is level, and there are two wheelchair locations in the orchestra.

Broadway Theater (Shubert), 1681 Broadway (near 53rd St.), NY 10019 (tel. 239-6200). The entrance is level, and there are four wheelchair locations in the orchestra.

Brooks Atkinson Theater, 256 W. 47th St., NY 10036 (tel. 245-3430). There is a level entrance and two wheelchair locations in the orchestra. Infrared system available.

Century Theater, 235 W. 46th St., NY 10036 (tel. 354-6644). Patrons in wheelchairs enter by an escorted route through the Century Paramount Hotel, which has a level entrance and accessible elevators. Call in advance for escort, and arrive 15 minutes before curtain time. There are 20 wheelchair locations.

Circle in the Square, 1633 Broadway, NY 10019 (tel. 581-0720). At the level entrance, on 50th Street between Broadway and Eighth Avenue, there is an escorted elevator to the seating area. There are two wheelchair locations in the orchestra.

City Center Theater, 131 W. 55th St., NY 10019 (tel. 246-8989). The main entrance near Seventh Avenue has one step, and there are five wheelchair locations in the orchestra. Porters are available to assist patrons into standard aisle seats if you call in advance.

Cort Theater (Shubert), 138 W. 48th St., NY 10036 (tel. 239-6200). There is a level entrance and two wheelchair locations in the orchestra.

Edison Theater, 240 W. 47th St., NY 10036 (tel. 757-7164). The entrance is level, and there are five wheelchair locations. However, transfer to aisle seat, if possible, is requested by management.

Ethel Barrymore Theater (Shubert), 243 W. 47th St., NY 10036 (tel. 239-6200). There is a level entrance and two wheelchair locations in the orchestra.

Eugene O'Neill Theater, 230 W. 49th St. NY 10019 (tel. 246-0220). There is a level entrance, and two wheelchair locations in the orchestra.

46th Street Theater, 226 W. 46th St., NY 10036 (tel. 246-0246). The entrance is level. There are four wheelchair locations in the orchestra, but management encourages transfer to aisle seats.

Gershwin Theater, 1633 Broadway (at 50th St.), NY 10019 (tel. 586-6510). Although the entrance is level and there is an elevator to the seating area, there are steps to all seating, including the four wheelchair locations. Special assistance is available.

Golden Theater (Shubert), 252 W. 45th St., NY 10036 (tel. 239-6200). There is a level entrance and one wheelchair location in the orchestra. Infrared system available.

Helen Hayes Theater, 240 W. 44th St., NY 10036 (tel. 944-9450). The entrance has one 4-inch step and three 8-inch steps, but assistance is available. There are two wheelchair locations in the orchestra, but the management encourages transfer to the aisle seats, if possible.

Imperial Theater (Shubert), 249 W. 45th St., NY 10036 (tel. 239-6200). The entrance is level, and there are four wheelchair locations in the orchestra.

Longacre Theater (Shubert), 220 W. 48 St., NY 10036 (tel. 239-6200). There is one 4-inch step at the entrance, and two wheelchair locations in the orchestra. Infrared system available.

Lunt-Fontanne Theater, 205 W. 46th St., NY 10036 (tel. 586-5555). The entrance is level, and there is one wheelchair location in the orchestra. Infrared system available.

Lyceum Theater (Shubert), 149 W. 45th St., NY 10036 (tel. 239-6200). There is one 4-inch step at the entrance and two wheelchair locations in the orchestra.

Majestic Theater (Shubert), 247 W. 44th St., NY 10036 (tel. 239-6200). The entrance is level, and there are four wheelchair locations in the orchestra.

Mark Hellinger Theater, 237 W. 51st St., NY 10019 (tel. 757-7064). The entrance has one 2-inch step, and there are two wheelchair locations in the orchestra.

Martin Beck Theater, 302 W. 45th St., NY 10036 (tel. 246-6363). The entrance is level, and there are four wheelchair locations in the orchestra.

Minskoff Theater, 200 W. 45th St., NY 10036 (tel. 869-0550). There is a level entrance to the lobby; the elevator to the seating level requires staff escort. There is also access by elevator from the underground garage. The orchestra has six wheelchair locations.

Music Box Theater, 239 W. 45th St., NY 10036 (tel. 246-4636). The entrance is level, and there is one wheelchair location.

Nederlander Theater, 209 W. 41st St., NY 10036 (tel. 921-8000). The entrance has one step, and there are 12 wheelchair locations in the orchestra.

Neil Simon Theater, 250 W. 52nd St., NY 10019 (tel. 757-8646). There is one step at the entrance, and two wheelchair locations in the orchestra.

The New Apollo Theater, 234 W. 43rd St., NY 10036 (tel. 921-8558). The entrance is level, and there are four wheelchair locations in the orchestra.

The Palace Theater, Broadway at 47th St., NY 10036 (tel. 757-2626). The entrance is level. Management policy is that patrons in wheelchairs who cannot transfer to aisle seats will be seated in the side aisles.

Plymouth Theater (Shubert), 236 W. 45th St., NY 10036 (tel. 239-6200). There is a level entrance, and two wheelchair locations in the orchestra. Infrared system available.

Princess Theater, 200 W. 48th St., NY 10036 (tel. 586-3905). There are steps involved in going to this theater, but assistance can be arranged by calling in advance. The recommended entrance is at 1576 Broadway (at 48th Street), where you can take the elevator to the back entrance of the theater on the second floor. (At the main theater entrance there is one 8-inch step and a 28-inch wide corridor, followed by the need to go up and down three 8-inch steps. Call 586-3903 in advance to arrange for assistance at the back entrance. There are four wheelchair locations in the orchestra.

Royale Theater (Shubert), 242 W. 45th St., NY 10036 (tel. 245-5760). The entrance is level, and there are three wheelchair locations in the orchestra.

St. James Theater, 246 W. 44th St., NY 10036 (tel. 398-0280). The entrance is level. There are six wheelchair locations in the orchestra, but management encourages transfer to aisle seats, if possible.

Shubert Theater, 225 W. 44th St., NY 10036 (tel. 239-6200). There is a curb cut on the street and a level entrance to the theater, which has eight wheelchair locations in the orchestra.

Virginia Theater, 245 W. 52nd St., NY 10019 (tel. 977-9370). There is a level entrance to the lobby and eight steps to the orchestra (assistance available). There are no wheelchair locations, and transfer to aisle seat required.

Winter Garden Theater (Shubert), 1634 Broadway (near 51st St.), NY 10019 (tel. 239-6200). There is a level entrance and four wheelchair locations in the orchestra.

LINCOLN CENTER FOR THE PERFORMING ARTS: This impressive group of theaters, concert halls, and other buildings related to the performing arts, was built on the West Side, in the vicinity of Broadway and 65th Street, when its location was considered off the beaten track. Now, 20 years later, it is the hub and a magnet because of its treasure of cultural activity—opera, ballet, concerts, and drama. Here is the world-renowned Metropolitan Opera House, the New York State Theater (home of the New York City Ballet and the New York City Opera), Avery Fisher Hall (home of the New York Philharmonic), the Juilliard School of Music and Drama, and the Vivian Beaumont and Newhouse Theaters. The Library of the Performing Arts here has also become a lively spot to spend some time browsing or listening.

Because the complex is of relatively recent date, Lincoln Center's buildings provide good facilities for disabled patrons with mobility, hearing, and visual impairments. A detailed brochure (also available in braille) "Tips for the Physically Handicapped: Accessibility Guide" is available free from the Lincoln Center Public Information Department, 140 W. 65th St., NY 10023 (tel. 877-1800). For patrons with hearing or speech difficulties, general information is available by calling TDD 877-1805, serviced from 10 a.m. to 5 p.m. on weekdays.

In **ordering tickets** for any of the performances at Lincoln Center, you should specify "wheelchair location" if you wish to stay in your chair, and confirm before the performance that you will be arriving. Details follow for each building. If you come by car or taxi, use the lower level concourse, which has access by elevator to all theaters.

The **Metropolitan Opera House** (box office, tel. 362-6000; administration, tel. 799-3100, ext. 2207) has 16 seat locations available for patrons in wheelchairs in the orchestra and dress circle—regular seats are removed so that you can wheel into place. You should call the administration office the day before the performance to confirm removal of the seat. Accessible rest rooms are on the dress circle level. All levels can be reached by large elevator. For the visually impaired, program notes are provided on cassettes or in braille for many performances, and braille libretti are available on loan in the Belmont Room before performances. Score Desks in the family circle (no view of the stage) are available for $2 (call 582-7500).

The **New York State Theater** (box office, tel. 870-5570) is the home of the New York City Ballet and the New York City Opera. There are eight wheelchair locations in the orchestra. Rest rooms are accessible. Notify the manager's office (tel. 877-4700) so that the special wheelchair-accessible door in the concourse (where you will ring the bell) can be opened for you. There is an elevator from here to the auditorium.

The **Vivian Beaumont Theatre** (box office, tel. 787-6868; credit card reservations, tel. 874-6770) has two wheelchair locations in the orchestra. The best way to reach the auditorium (because there are steps at the main plaza entrance), is to use the taxi ramp from West 65th Street where there is an elevator from the entrance door to the theater on the underground concourse. Call ahead (tel. 787-6868) to have an attendant meet you there one-half hour before the performance. The rest rooms on the orchestra level are wheelchair-accessible.

At the smaller **Newhouse Theatre** in the same building as the Vivian Beaumont (box office, tel. 362-7600) there are no wheelchair locations, but the entrance to the auditorium is via the same route as the one to the Vivian Beaumont (see above). Call ahead to the box office to request assistance at the locked door on the concourse. Rest rooms are accessible.

For hearing-impaired patrons, the New York State Theater has installed infrared listening devices which may be rented for $2. Detailed synopses of the operas are available by calling the **Theater Script Center for Hearing Impaired** (TDD 763-6154, regular number 241-8166), or by writing to Dept. H., New York City Opera, New York State Theater, Lincoln Center, NY 10023.

Home of the New York Philharmonic, **Avery Fisher Hall** (box office, tel. 872-2424) has six seats that are removable for use as wheelchair locations on the first, second, and third tiers (call the day of the performance to have the seat removed; tel. 580-8700). Rest rooms are accessible on all levels. The infrared listening system for hearing-impaired concertgoers is also available here at a rental fee of $2. There are impaired-hearing headsets to telephones in the rest room vestibules at the Plaza and Orchestra levels. You can reach the lobby of Avery Fisher Hall (box office and a restaurant) from the street-level plaza driveway. If you arrive through the lower concourse by car or taxi, the door to the elevator there is opened 30 minutes before performance. You can arrange earlier entry to the restaurant by calling 580-8700.

Alice Tully Hall (box office, tel. 362-1911; administration, tel. 362-1900) is the home of the Chamber Music Society of Lincoln Center. There are 12 seats in Box C, at the street level, that can be removed to accommodate wheelchairs. You should call the manager's office for advice on arrival and assistance before attending the performance. The infrared listening system headsets are also available here at a $2 fee.

Even if you are not planning to attend any performances at Lincoln Center, it's a place to go just to look around. (Best to avoid curtain times.) The central focus of the center is the large open fountain plaza, and you can get there by car or taxi on the access road from 65th Street at Broadway or Columbus Avenue. From the plaza there is level and ramp access to the box offices of the Metropolitan Opera House, Avery Fisher Hall, and the State Theater (there are steps to the auditorium at the Met and State Theater from this level). Avery Fisher Hall also has restaurants, a gift and book shop, and rest rooms at the plaza level, and the Met has a gift shop near the box office (all accessible to non-patrons).

Another Lincoln Center building accessible from the plaza is the **Lincoln Center Library**, a branch of the New York Public Library, a vast storehouse of performing arts resources. It is located on the North Plaza between the Met and the Vivian Beaumont Theater. Here's the reflecting pool with Henry Moore's monumental bronze sculpture *Reclining Figure,* as well as Calder's large steel stabile *Le Guichet.* Looking up at the opera house as you pass in front of it, you see the large and impressive paintings by Marc Chagall that fill the tall windows fronting the plaza. "Strolling" around the plaza level (there are a few gentle ramps), you'll come to the **Guggenheim Bandshell** in Damrosch Park, south of the Opera House, where free concerts are presented during the summer, weather permitting. Call 755-4100 for information. Also in the Lincoln Center Plaza from mid-August through Labor Day, there's a three-week open air festival of performances of all kinds; call 877-1800 to hear what's happening.

ALSO FOR MUSIC LOVERS: Once threatened by the bulldozer, **Carnegie Hall,** 154 W. 57th St., NY 10019 (tel. 247-7459), is now a landmark building. Surrounded by the steps synonymous with its era, it now has a wheelchair lift (hydraulic) at the Seventh Avenue entrance. Arrangements must be made in advance with the manager's office (on weekdays, the same day as the performance; on Friday, for weekend performances). The orchestra level is the only one accessible; there are no elevators to other levels. Three wheelchair locations are provided at the back of the auditorium.

And if you like your opera light, in the style of Gilbert & Sullivan and Sigmund Romberg, the **Eastside Playhouse,** 334 E. 74th St., NY 10021 (tel. 861-2288), home of the Light Opera of Manhattan, has one step at the entrance and two wheelchair locations. Call in advance for assistance.

OFF-BROADWAY THEATERS: Though not as inexpensive as they once were (but still under $20 top ticket, and often much less), these smaller theaters scattered throughout Manhattan, are still where experimental, not-so-commercial theater with undiscovered, exciting talent can be seen. Because they are small and usually in buildings converted from other uses, the Off-Broadway and Off-Off-Broadway theaters are not the most accessible places, but there are some that you might find you are able to attend. You'll find listings in the newspapers, and a phone call can determine if it will be accessible for you:

Circle Repertory Theater, 99 Seventh Ave. S., near Sheridan Square in Greenwich Village (tel. 924-7100), has one step at the entrance and ten wheelchair locations in the front row of the orchestra where regular seats can be removed on advance notice.

Circle in the Square Downtown, 159 Bleecker St., in Greenwich Village (tel. 254-6330), has a level entrance and one wheelchair location. Other seating is up one to nine steps (this is a theater-in-the-round auditorium).

Cherry Lane Theater, 38 Commerce St., in Greenwich Village (tel. 989-2020), has a level entrance and an accessible auditorium, but no specific wheelchair locations.

Lucille Lortel Theater, 121 Christopher St., in Greenwich Village (tel. 944-9300), has a level entrance from the street, one step up to the seating area (assistance available), but no wheelchair locations.

Harold Clurman Theater, 412 W. 42nd St. (tel. 695-5429), is one of the many theaters on the recently created 42nd Street Theater Row. The entrance is level, and there are five wheelchair locations in the orchestra.

Manhattan Theater Club, 321 E. 73rd St. (tel. 472-0600), has two steps at the entrance (assistance available with advance notice). Wheelchair locations are in the last row of the main theater and in the front row of the Cabaret.

The **Public Theater,** 425 Lafayette St. on the eastern edge of Greenwich Village near Astor Place (tel. 598-7150), is included here because there are seven—count them, seven—theaters in this landmark building, and although the entrance has seven steps, the staff is young and strong and eager to assist. Some of the seven theaters are more accessible than others, but there is usually a good choice of performances, and you should check which theaters are available for you, depending on your needs. There are elevators between floors.

New York Shakespeare Festival

If you are in New York in the summer, don't miss the *free* performances of the New York Shakespeare Festival, held outdoors in the Delacorte Theater in Central Park under the aegis of the Public Theater. In recent years, the festival has presented two different productions, one in July and one in August, and they can be among the best you'll see anywhere. Special consideration for the disabled patron and a companion include availability of tickets without waiting in a long, long line: go straight to the box office of the Delacorte Theater in the park on the day of the performance and ask for front row seats or for a wheelchair location. Performances are usually at 8 p.m., but you must be in place by 7:45 p.m. Go around 6 p.m. or earlier to get your tickets and take a picnic supper to eat al fresco. You can reach the Delacorte Theater by car (there's a public parking lot nearby, off the main park drive northbound, near the Belvedere Castle), or "walk" in from the East Side entrance to the park on Fifth Avenue at 79th Street, or from the West Side at Central Park West at 81st Street. The theater is about in the middle of the park, equidistant from either direction.

MADISON SQUARE GARDEN: The latest version of New York City's "Garden" arena for all kinds of sports and spectaculars (Ice Capades, Westminster Dog Show, basketball—New York Knicks, Harlem Globetrotters—and lots more) is at 33rd St. between Seventh and Eighth Avenues (tel. 564-4400), above the Pennsylvania Railroad Terminal, which is below street level.

You'll find the schedule of events in any entertainment directory, or in the Quarterly Events Calendar published by the New York Visitors Bureau. The garage entrance is on 33rd Street. The level entrance is at Eighth Avenue and 33rd Street (officially called 8 Pennsylvania Plaza), and you can get directions from the staff here for the best route to other areas of the garden. There are wheelchair locations at all seating levels (must be reserved in advance), and the Garden personnel are familiar with the seating locations and other facilities for disabled visitors. On all levels, the men's rest rooms have a 28-inch stall entry; the women's rest rooms have a 30-inch stall entry and grab bars.

9. New York's Neighborhoods

There are many sections of New York City that are worth exploring, and *can* be explored, for their unique atmosphere, different from each other and different from the rest of the city.

SOHO: This area gets its name from "So" (south of) "Ho" (Houston Street—in New York pronounced House-ton). In recent years it has become the lively center of the avant garde, especially in the art world. It happened because artists and writers and others in the creative arts, moved into what were then low-rent lofts in the area's old cast-iron commercial buildings. SoHo stretches from Canal Street to Houston Street, west from Lafayette to West Broadway; it's just north of Chinatown and just south of Greenwich Village. It's a true—and "in"—New York experience to stroll on Saturday or Sunday among the art galleries, trendy boutiques, and small restaurants, many of them reasonably accessible if you want to go in. West Broadway is one of the main "drags." If you are coming from uptown you can get to SoHo on the number 5 bus on Fifth Avenue marked West Houston, and take it to its last stop.

Vigorous and anti-establishment paintings and sculptures are to be seen in galleries, and here's just a selected few of many: **Leo Castelli, John Weber, Mary Boone, Sonnabend Gallery,** are all at 420 West Broadway (near Spring Street), in an elevator building with two steps at the entrance. **O.K. Harris,** 383 West Broadway (tel. 431-3600), has one step, then three, at the entrance. The interior is accessible. **Paula Cooper,** 155 Wooster St., near Houston St. (tel. 677-4390), has a ramped entrance and an accessible interior.

Among the restaurants in SoHo that you'll find reasonably accessible are: **Central Falls,** 478 West Broadway (tel. 533-9481), which has a ramped entrance and an accessible interior. This combination art gallery, restaurant, and bar has live classical music at Saturday and Sunday brunch from 1 to 4:30 p.m. (reservation necessary). Brunch entrees are $6 to $10, regular dinner entrees $9 to $13.50. Open seven days from noon to midnight. **Berry's,** 180 Spring St., (tel. 226-4394). Two steps at the entrance; this is a lively European-style restaurant and bar, with dinner entrees $10 to $15. Brunch on Saturday is noon to 3 p.m., Sunday 1 to 4 p.m. **Spring Street Natural Restaurant,** 149 Spring St., (tel. 966-0290). Everything on the menu here is homemade from natural ingredients. There are two steps at the entrance. Brunch entrees are $4 to $9. Open daily 11:30 a.m. to 2 a.m. **Raoul's,** 180 Prince St., (966-3518). One step at the entrance. This was once a neighborhood bar and is now a popular restaurant serving French dishes, entrees $11 to $21 à la carte. Open daily for dinner.

GREENWICH VILLAGE: "The Village," as it's known to most New Yorkers, retains its Bohemian atmosphere even though struggling artists and writers have bypassed it for some years because of the soaring rents. But its elegant town houses, twisting back streets, ethnic restaurants, and Italian coffeehouses provide a fascinating setting for "strolling" and watching the passing show, sipping espresso or capuccino in the coffeehouses, or seeing an off-Broadway play. Its boundaries are roughly from 14th Street south as far as Houston Street, and east to west from West Broadway to West Street at the Hudson River.

The area around **Washington Square Park** (at the southern end of Fifth Avenue) has its curbs well-ramped, since this is also the campus of New York University where there is a large number of disabled students. The park itself has the same level throughout, so you can wander around—there's always a lot going on in the way of chess games, music-making, young people seeking the "action," and local residents taking the sun with their children. Take a map and set your own itinerary—a fixed "route" around the Village is a contradiction in terms, especially west of the Avenue of the Americas.

From Washington Square Park you can take MacDougal Street on the south side, the center of the Bohemian groups in their heyday 50 or 60 years ago. (The Provincetown Playhouse is here, noted for its presentation of Eugene O'Neill's early plays.) The coffeehouses in this area still have the flavor of those days, all with level entrances but "cozy" interiors: on MacDougal Street, the **Cafe Dante** is at No. 81, and the **Cafe Reggio** at No. 119; level and roomier is **Cafe Lucca**, 228 Bleecker St., where it crosses the Avenue of the Americas.

A traditional-style Italian restaurant on the same street is **Villa Mosconi,** 69 MacDougal St. (tel. 609-0390), which has a level entrance. Dinner entrees here are from $6 to $11. Departing from the Italian flavor of much of the Village for a more American tradition is the **Derby Steakhouse** at 109 MacDougal St. (tel. 475-0529), well-known by Villagers for its steaks, with prices ranging from $9 to $15. It is open daily for dinner.

Bleecker Street is one of Greenwich Village's main streets, full of small cafes, restaurants, Italian groceries, small theaters, and nightspots. At no. 285 is the **Tavola Calda da Alfredo** (tel. 924-4789), which has two small steps at the entrance and a reasonably spacious interior. There is a $12 minimum per person here, and it is open for lunch and dinner except Tuesday. Alfredo's original Village restaurant, **Trattoria da Alfredo,** is farther west at 90 Bank St. (tel. 291-2930). This one has a level entrance and a roomy interior. (Because of its popularity you should make sure you have a reservation here.)

Two blocks east of MacDougal, still south of Washington Square, is Thompson Street where you'll find a number of restaurants that are reasonably accessible: **Rocco's,** 181 Thompson St. (tel. 677-0590), has one step at the entrance. It's a smallish restaurant in the old Italian style, with entrees from $6 to $9, and is open daily for lunch and dinner; **Un Rincon de España,** 226 Thompson St. (tel. 260-4950), has one step at the entrance and a spacious interior. Its dishes are, of course, Spanish, served in a Spanish ambiance complete with flamenco guitar music. Entree prices range from $10 to $17.50, and it is open daily for dinner; next door is **Mexican Village,** 224 Thompson St. (tel. 475-9805)—it has one step at the entrance and is "intimate" inside. Long popular with Villagers, it serves traditional Mexican food, with combination plates from $6 to $8.50, and is open daily for lunch and dinner.

The Village is noted for the number of its fine Italian restaurants, and yet another, which is accessible, is **Ennio & Michael Ristorante,** 504 LaGuardia Place (tel. 677-8577), one block west of Thompson around the corner from Bleecker. It has a ramped entrance. Entrees are priced from $9 to $18. Closed Monday.

If you head west out of Washington Square along Waverly Place, you'll come to one of the Village's grander restaurants, the **Coach House** at no. 110. It has been here a long time and has the very cozy atmosphere of a private home. Reservations are essential. Complete dinners are from $26.50 to $32, and there is à la carte choice as well. The entrance has one small step.

LITTLE ITALY: One area of New York City that nurtures its links to the old country with a special devotion is just south of SoHo and has Grand Street at its center. Its narrow streets are lined with small groceries, pastry shops, and restaurants with an emphasis on Neapolitan and Sicilian specialties. Not many curb cuts here for wheelchairs, but Little Italy should be experienced, even if you do it from the roadway, where the traffic moves reasonably slowly through the narrow, one-way streets. (Attempting to park in these streets is not to be recommended!)

Have an espresso coffee and a delicious pastry at **Ferrara's,** 195 Grand St., on the sidewalk or inside (over a ramped entrance); or at **Cafe Roma,** 385 Broome St. (one step at the entrance). You can have a full lunch or dinner at one of the many restaurants that have reasonable accessibility and roomy interiors, such as **Angelo's,** 146 Mulberry St. (one small step at the entrance); at **Luna's,** 112 Mulberry St. (one of its two entrances is level); **Puglia,** 189 Hester St. (one step at the entrance); or **Vincent's Clam Bar,** 119 Mott St. (level entrance). Most of the Little Italy restaurants do not accept reservations.

CHINATOWN: Edging into Little Italy these days is an expanding Chinatown, but its original neighborhood south of Canal Street densely packed with thousands of Chinese-Americans, is still the most popular tourist spot and for good reason. There is no way anyone can park in its maze of winding streets, some of them no more than wide alleyways, but a driving tour will give you the flavor if you just want to have a look around from the car.

If you do go to eat, getting there by taxi or by parking your own car in a garage, you'll find a few restaurants that are accessible (always a surprise, since most of them are downstairs or upstairs in the old non-elevator buildings of this area). On your way to the restaurant, window-shop to see the exotic vegetables, herbs, and other foods.

Foo Joy, 13 Division St. (tel. 431-4931), has one step at the entrance and is roomy inside. Unpretentious decor, but unusual Fukienese dishes, ranging from $5 to $8. **Hong Fat,** 63 Mott St. (tel. 962-9588), has one small step at the entrance to a crowded, inexpensive restaurant specializing in Cantonese noodle dishes. **Hee Seung Fung,** or **H.S.F.,** 46 Bowery (tel. 964-1204), has a level entrance and is noted for its dim sum, the collective name for a variety of filled dumplings and other bite-size delicacies, served until 4 p.m.

10. Shopping

For lots of visitors, shopping is among the "musts" of a vacation in New York. It would be impossible to list the multitude of smaller shops that can be visited, but it will be obvious to you as you pass by whether it's a place you can, or want, to get into. Here we'll concentrate on the larger stores, since their entrances and interiors are not quite so obvious from the street.

Near Central Park, at the corner of 58th Street and Fifth Avenue, there is the famous fashion store, **Bergdorf Goodman** (tel. 753-7300), where you should use the employee entrance on 57th Street and will be able to get assistance from the security guard or customer service. Inside there are two steps to some departments on the street floor, but all other floors can be reached by elevator. Across the street at 10 W. 57th St. is **Henry Bendel** (tel. 247-1100), equally well known for its fashion style. It has a level entrance and an elevator to all floors.

On the east side of Fifth Avenue at 57th Street is the legendary **Tiffany's** (tel. 755-8000) for jewelry and gifts. It has a level entrance and elevators to all floors. Next door to Tiffany's 57th Street entrance is **Bonwit Teller** (tel. 593-3333), reopened on a small scale a couple of years ago but still just as famous as ever for high-style fashion and a large cosmetics department. There is a level entrance from the street to the main floor and to all elevators. Rest rooms on the lower level and the fifth floor are accessible for wheelchairs.

Legendary as a trend-setter, **Bloomingdale's** is at 59th Street and Lexington Avenue (tel. 705-2073). Go to the level entrance on Third Avenue if you want to get to most of the floors via the elevators. (At Lexington Avenue there is a flight of steps between the street-level departments and the rest of the store.) Accessible rest rooms with 30-inch stalls are located on both the seventh floor and in the women's rest room on the fourth floor.

Back on Fifth Avenue, near Rockefeller Center, **Saks Fifth Avenue** (tel. 753-4000) has level entrances both on the avenue and on 50th Street, and elevators to all floors. The separate Saks Gifts and China Shop on 50th Street has steps; the Luggage and Linen Shops on 49th Street are level from the street.

Lord & Taylor, on Fifth Avenue at 39th Street (tel. 391-3344), has a level entrance, elevators, and lots of fashion and furnishings. A few blocks south, at 34th Street, is the venerable **B. Altman** (tel. 689-7000), one of New York's oldest (but up-to-date) stores. If you want to avoid the step at the Fifth Avenue entrance, you'll find it level at the Madison Avenue entrance. There are elevators to all floors.

The world's largest department store is **Macy's**, at 34th Street and Broadway (tel. 971-6000). It stretches for one huge block over to Seventh Avenue, and you can get in from either end at level entrances. The street floor has steps between the two ends of the store, but all other floors in the Broadway and Seventh Avenue Buildings are joined by gentle ramps that you probably won't even notice. Elevators go to all floors from either end of the store. The restaurants—and you might need refreshment if you try to "do" the whole store—are the Fountain on the fifth floor of the Broadway Building, and P.J. Clarke's, which is in The Cellar on the lower level (reached by elevator). For reference, the women's rest room, on the sixth floor in the Seventh Avenue building, has a 28-inch stall, with grab bars; the men's rest room, on the seventh floor of the Seventh Avenue building, has a 26-inch stall, with grab bars.

A block away at 33rd Street and the Avenue of the Americas is the entrance (level) to **Gimbels** (tel. 564-3300), Macy's traditional rival and almost as large. There are elevators to all floors.

On the block between the two department stores, tentatively planned for late 1984, will be the city's first multi-level mall—**Herald Center**—where the stores and restaurants on eleven floors will feature a different theme, each reflecting the special atmosphere of an area of New York City.

ANTIQUES: The auction house of **Christie's**, 502 Park Ave. at 61st St. (tel. 826-2888), is accessible, with elevators between floors. The **Manhattan Arts & Antique Center**, 1050 Second Ave. (tel. 355-4400), is an enclosed mall with over 60 dealers. The entrance at the 56th Street end of the building is level from the street, and the interior is level. **Sotheby Parke Bernet**, 1334 York Ave. at

72nd St. (tel. 472-3400), has a level entrance from the street, and large elevators give access to different floors.

WASHINGTON, D.C.

America's Home Town

ONE OF THE GREAT things about Washington, apart from its sightseeing attractions, comes from its prominence as the seat of our federal government: the city became a role model for all the architectural accessibility legislation enacted there in the 1970s. It isn't by any means a model city in that regard, but many of its sights, monuments, and museums are run by branches of the federal government, and were among the first public institutions in the country to be adapted for people with disabilities.

Government mandates did not apply to private enterprise, of course, but general awareness has provided enough hotels and restaurants to make a vacation here convenient and enjoyable. The flat terrain makes it easy to get around if you're wheeling or walking: curbs are well ramped along the Mall, where there are many of the buildings you will want to visit, and around the Capitol Building, seat of Congress and the Senate. The newest subway system in the country is a model of public transport available to disabled passengers (thanks in part to persistent local consumer groups).

As a place (it doesn't really have city status but is a separate entity known as the District of Columbia) that was designed and built from scratch for a specific purpose, Washington offers the greater part of its treasures within a compact area so sightseeing does not involve great distances. No claustrophobia either, since skyscrapers are forbidden in the central district to keep the Capitol dome visible from anywhere. And while you're visiting the grand buildings and monuments along the wide boulevards and grassy malls, you can enjoy the splashing fountains of the plazas and the millions of flowers that always seem to be in bloom.

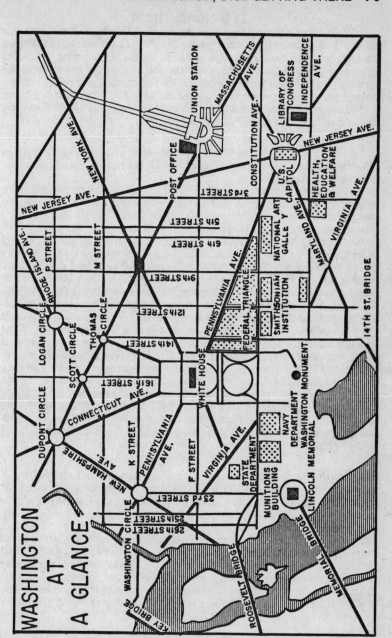

WASHINGTON AT A GLANCE

1. Getting There

Washington is the southern tip of the so-called Northeast Corridor created by the I-95 highway that stretches on the East Coast south from Boston through New York and Philadelphia. As the capital of the nation, it has also become the hub of transportation services and roads from anywhere in the country. It's 240 miles from New York City, for instance, and can be reached from there by car on major turnpikes all the way; by fastest train in 2 hours and 49 minutes, and in one hour's flying time. Interstate routes are well marked and connect easily from any direction.

BY AIR: You can arrive in Washington by air at either of three airports—Washington National (domestic flights) and Dulles or Baltimore-Washington International Airports.

Washington National Airport (tel. 202/783-5488) is by far the most convenient to the center of town, just across the Potomac River in Virginia, and you can take the accessible Metro rail Blue Line from there into the "District." The station is opposite the North Terminal (see details of the Metro that follow in the "Getting Around" section of this chapter). National Airport has a level entrance with wide automatic doors, and the interior is level with access by ramps and elevators. Rest rooms with 36-inch stall entry and grab bars are available. Other facilities include lowered and amplified telephones, and low water fountains. **Baltimore-Washington International Airport** (tel. 301/859-7100) is in Maryland. The entry is level through wide automatic doors. Specially equipped rest rooms are located in the Medical Service Section; they have 32-inch entrance and grab bars. Sky Cap escort is available for use of the elevator between levels and through the security areas. A lowered telephone is across from the Delta Airlines desk at Pier C. **Dulles International Airport** (tel. 703/471-7838) has a level entrance through wide automatic doors. There are elevators between levels, and the rest rooms on the street level have 32-inch-wide stall doors and grab bars. Lowered phones are available.

Regular bus transfer service to downtown is not accessible to wheelchairs at any of the airports. Taxi fares, either metered or by prior arrangement with the driver, will be about $10 from National, $30 to $35 from Dulles, and $35 to $40 from Baltimore-Washington International.

BY TRAIN: Amtrak service from all points brings you into **Union Station** at Massachusetts Avenue and North Capitol Street near the Capitol Building. At present, the main building is closed to the public until the historic structure is checked out for potential hazards. Until it is reopened, the entrance and exit to the tracks underneath the building is directly from the street. All Amtrak procedures outlined in the chapter on train travel apply, and arrangements will be made for you to be escorted to and from the tracks once you have notified Amtrak in advance of your departure plans. On arrival, the conductor of your train is responsible for making arrangements for you to be met at Union Station. The **Amtrak Information and Reservation** telephone number is 484-7540, toll-free 800/523-5700. There is a Metrorail stop at Union Station.

BY BUS: If you are able to use the major services (see the section on travel by bus in Chapter 2), getting to Washington by bus is very convenient, since you'll arrive right in downtown. The **Trailways Terminal** at 12th Street and New York Avenue (tel. 202/737-5800) has an interior accessed by ramp and elevator. To use the specially equipped rest room in the ticket plaza area, you must obtain the key from the Customer Service Office. Redcaps are available 24 hours a day. The curb at 12th Street and New York Avenue is ramped. The **Greyhound Terminal**, 1110 New York Ave. between 11th and 12th Streets (tel. 202/289-5100), has a level entrance. Ask ticket agent for the key to the special rest room on the main floor.

BY RENTAL CAR: Hand-controlled rental cars are available at the airports from **Hertz** (toll free tel. 800/654-3131) with five days notice; from **Avis** (toll free tel. 800/331-1212) with two weeks notice, and from **National** (toll free tel. 800/328-4567), which requests "as much advance notice as possible."

2. Getting Around

You'll definitely need a street map, as well as one of the accessible Metro rail system if you are making a first visit to Washington. These maps, and a lot of other very useful information on all aspects of visiting Washington, can be had by writing in advance to the **Washington Convention and Visitors Association**, 1595 "I" St. NW (also often written as "Eye" St.), Washington, DC 20005, or by calling 202/789-7000.

BY CAR: Within the city, be prepared for traffic congestion during business hours and remember that parking lots get full quite early in the day. Street parking is difficult, and regulations are strictly enforced. In addition to traffic tickets, beware the "boots" (metal blocks attached to your front wheels for parking violations) or towing to a city lot, where it will cost a lot to retrieve the car.

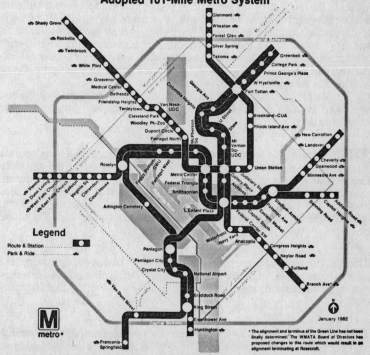

Adopted 101-Mile Metro System

Map Courtesy of Washington Metropolitan Area Transit Authority

BY SUBWAY: Should you decide against driving, there is a relatively convenient and inexpensive way to get around that can take you to most places you want to go. You'll find the nearest Metro station to most of the sightseeing spots listed in the official System Map.

Washington's subway system, known as Metro rail, with its modern, air-conditioned trains and stations, is totally accessible to people with impairments of mobility, sight, and hearing. All stations have elevator access from the street and between levels, and there is level entrance to the trains from the platforms. For the *sight-impaired passenger,* there are bronze hand rails between entrance escalators and mezzanine levels, and the granite edge of the platform provides a distinguishable texture from the tile floor used throughout the rest of the station. Clear voice announcements on station platforms and on board the trains give destination and stop information. For the *hearing-impaired passenger,* pulsating lights along the platform edge warn of the train's approach. Attendants and maps are available at each station to help you find your way. The material you get from the Visitors Bureau will include a Metro map so you can make best use of the system and plan your trip by locating your destination and seeing if you will have to transfer.

At street level you can identify stations by the tall, brown-colored column topped by a large "M," identified with colored stripes indicating the lines—Red, Orange, Blue, or Yellow—that serve that particular station. All lines serve downtown Washington's many points of interest.

Fares on Metro are collected by a computerized farecard, which you buy from vending machines at the stations and which must be inserted in the fare gate to enter the platform. You retain your card, and at your destination insert it again in the fare gate when you exit. If you purchase a $5 farecard but only do $3 worth of riding, your farecard will be returned to you with $2 left on it for more rides. On the other hand, if you owe the system money, you go to an "add-fare" machine at your destination for a supplementary card. All non-rush hour fares are 65¢ regardless of distance traveled, but during rush hours (6 to 9:30 a.m. and 3 to 6:30 p.m. on weekdays) fares depend on time and distance traveled. The farecard will work it out for you!

The Metro system runs from 6 a.m. to midnight Monday through Friday, from 8 a.m. to midnight on Saturday, and from 10 a.m. to 6 p.m. on Sunday. For information, call 637-2437.

TAXIS: One thing to learn early on, if you take taxis, is that they operate without meters on a zone basis. Within one zone charges are $1.70 (subject to change); from one zone to another, fare is $2.45. There's a 65¢ surcharge during the rush hour Monday to Friday from 4 to 6:30 p.m. It is always a good idea to ask the driver in advance what the fare will be to avoid surprises later on, especially when going to the airports. Each extra person also adds 75¢ to the fare.

BUSES: Although there are buses with wheelchair lifts on regular routes, the system cannot be said to be too reliable, and service for disabled residents may be changed, as we go to press, to a paratransit system of door-to-door transportation.

TOURMOBILE: There is a very convenient way to see the sights in Washington, called the Tourmobile (tel. 202/554-7950), but there are four steps to board. If this is possible for you, you can board the Tourmobile at 14 different locations and may get off at any stop to visit monuments or buildings, then get back on the next Tourmobile that comes along to continue the tour. One fare allows you to use the buses for a full day.

SPECIAL TRANSPORTATION: Although the Metro is the cheapest way available to people in wheelchairs for getting around the city, there may be an occasion when a wheelchair-lift van is needed, such as the trip from the airport. Among companies who provide this service are the **Van Go Corporation,** 817 Timber Branch Pkwy., Alexandria, VA 22302 (tel. 703/836-5617); the **Mobile Care Inc.,** 20 Plattsburg Court NW, Washington, DC 20016 (tel. 202/363-6300); and **Murray's Non-Emergency Transportation Service,** 2329 Skyland Pl. SE, Washington, DC 20020 (tel. 202/889-6912).

3. Orientation

There is very much of a small-town atmosphere in Washington, despite some of the broadest boulevards in America, grand art galleries, national monuments, fine restaurants, and all the trappings of a seat of government of one of the world's great powers. Compared to New York, say, it is a relatively quiet place, and easy to get around.

Washington owes its beautiful symmetry to Charles L'Enfant, the Frenchman hired by President Washington to create the nation's capital. His plan envisioned great sweeping avenues crossed by numbered and lettered streets, with spacious circles placed at key intersections (a way also to provide strategic command posts to defend the capital, if necessary). L'Enfant's plan gathered dust until the 1870s when a great part of it finally got built.

The first thing to learn about its layout is that the city is divided into quadrants, with the Capitol at the center of everything. The dome of the Capitol Building is the focal point of most vistas in the District, and provides a good way to orient yourself: it is exactly in the center of the District and can easily be seen from anywhere in the city. The White House, most government buildings, and important monuments lie west of the Capitol Building, as do the major hotels.

Addresses in Washington come with two letters appended: NW, SW, NE, or SE, designating one of the quadrants. As a visitor, here to see the important sights, you will be primarily in the northwest and southwest sections. You must remember that each of them will have a 6th Street and a G Street, for instance, so it's important to know the section letters of each address.

Lettered streets run east-west, numbered streets run north-south. The grid pattern is broken up, though, by avenues named for states that run diagonally across the city, with the primary artery, Pennsylvania Avenue, running on a direct line between the Capitol and the White House (and then continuing on at an angle to Georgetown). Massachusetts Avenue runs parallel to Pennsylvania Avenue and keeps going all the way to Maryland. Constitution Avenue and Independence Avenue are wide, east-west thoroughfares lined with government buildings that run on either side of the Capitol. Between them is the Mall, developed as a focal point of Washington's layout in the early part of this century, that runs as a green swath from the Capitol through the Washington Monument to the Lincoln Memorial, and which is lined by the National Gallery, the Smithsonian Institution, the National Museum, and the Supreme Court building, among many others.

You can locate addresses on the avenues through the lettered or numbered streets. For instance, 1100 to 1200 Massachusetts Avenue will be in the K to

L block (the 11th and 12th letters in the alphabet). On Connecticut Avenue, crossed by numbered streets, a 2100 number would be between 21st and 22nd Streets. In the NW district, the higher the letter, the farther north it is; the higher the number, the farther west. In the SW district, the higher the letter, the farther south the street is; the higher the number, the farther west it is.

Remember, it all ends at the Potomac River: on the other side is Virginia. Don't forget to take a map: nobody promised you it would be easy!

CLIMATE: Washington can be very cold in winter, and heat and humidity are high in summer. Most buildings are *very* air-conditioned in the hot weather, so be sure to take a jacket or sweater to wear indoors. Springtime, especially in April, when the cherry trees are in full bloom, is the most popular season for visitors, but expect some rain. In autumn, the weather is comfortable and generally clear, a good time to visit.

AREA CODE: All telephones within the District of Columbia carry a 202 area code. In nearby locations in Virginia it is 702, and in nearby Maryland, 301.

USEFUL PHONE NUMBERS: Washington, D.C., Convention and Visitors Association, 202/347-0101; Information Center for Handicapped Individuals, Inc., 202/347-4986; Paralyzed Veterans of America Association, 202/872-1300; Easter Seal Society for Disabled Children and Adults, 202/232-2342; Travelers Aid Society, 202/844-2525; American Automobile Association, 202/222-5000; Medical Referral Service (24 hours), 202/223-2200; and Dental Referral Service, 202/686-0803.

4. Where to Stay

Plenty of places to stay, and good accessibility, can be found in Washington's upper-bracket hotels but, as usual, there are fewer selections in the medium-price range, and none to be found in the budget category. Just across the Potomac in Arlington, Virginia, there are motels not too far from the wheelchair-accessible Metro that can take you downtown fast and comfortably, and while prices there are not much lower, parking is free. In addition to the Arlington motels, most of the hotels listed here are in the northwest section of the city, which is where most of the attractions and good restaurants are located. Many of the District's hotels cater to the business traveler who goes home on the weekend, so weekend packages are usually very attractive.

DELUXE (Around $100 and up, double): This price category is where there are the most hotels that have special rooms and good accessibility, but don't forget that special packages can bring the price down considerably.

Relatively new on the Washington scene, on Capitol Hill, the **Hyatt Regency Washington,** 400 New Jersey Ave. NW, DC 20001 (tel. 202/727-1234, toll free 800/228-9000), has a number of rooms with 36-inch bathroom doors, grab bars at the toilet and showers (no bath). The entrance to the hotel is level, and there is an elevator to the reception desk floor. The design of the hotel is the familiar Hyatt atrium style, with outside glass-enclosed elevators. All the restaurants have level access including Hugo's, a rather expensive restaurant on the top floor with a stunning view over the city. Rates are $92 to $116 single, $112 to $136 double.

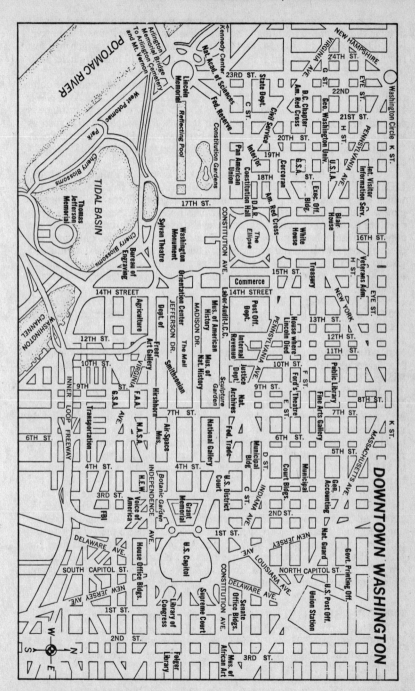

Toward Georgetown and close to Kennedy Center is a new and elegant hotel in the European tradition, **The Four Seasons,** at 2800 Pennsylvania Ave. NW, DC 20007 (tel. 202/342-0444, toll free 800/828-1188), which has five rooms with wider doors and grab bars. Rates go from $110 to $140 single, $130 to $160 double.

A short subway ride from the center of town is what was once the quite rural **Sheraton Washington,** 2660 Woodley Rd. (at Connecticut Ave. NW), DC 20008 (tel. 202/328-2000, toll free 800/325-3535), where the entrance is ramped, and there are many rooms with features for disabled guests such as wide doors, grab bars, a telephone in the bathroom, and lowered peepholes in the entry doors. Rates range from $95 to $105 single, and from $115 to $125 double.

In a great location close to the Mall is **Loew's L'Enfant Plaza,** 480 L'Enfant Plaza SW, DC 20024 (tel. 202/484-1000, toll free 800/223-0888), where every room has a good view in some direction. There is a commercial garage underground that has access to the hotel, and there is also a level entrance to the hotel from the ground level driveway. All the rooms here are considered suitable for guests in wheelchairs as far as size is concerned, but there are none with special adaptations. There is access to the restaurants and also to the extensive shopping complex beneath the hotel. Rates go from $90 to $130 single, $110 to $150 double, but weekend packages here offer rates considerably lower.

The **Mayflower,** 1127 Connecticut Ave. NW., DC 20036 (tel. 202/347-3000), is a Washington institution, and its age and graciousness mean spaciousness. Its location between L and M Streets, with the Farragut North Metro station next door, makes it very convenient. There is a paid parking lot adjacent, with ramped curbs leading to the level entrance of the hotel. Some of the Mayflower's rooms have 32-inch doors to both entry and bathroom. Rates are $65 to $128 single, $110 to $150 double.

Just across the river, the **Key Bridge Marriott,** 1401 Lee Hwy., Arlington, VA 22209 (tel. 703/524-6400, toll free 800/228-9290), is close to the Rosslyn Metro stop, where you can get very quickly to Capitol Hill (though it's slightly uphill, so you may need help if you use a wheelchair). There are great views of the city across the Potomac from all rooms, including two specially designed rooms with 36-inch doors. If you are using a car, parking is free. Rates are $85 to $110 single, $105 to $130 double, but there is a variety of packages that can reduce those rates.

Also in Arlington is **Stouffer's National Center,** 2399 Jefferson Davis Hwy. (Rte. 1), Arlington, VA 22202 (tel. 703/979-6800, toll free 800/325-5000), which is a modern, family-oriented hotel. The entrance is ramped over one step, and there are two special rooms here with 36-inch doors to the bathroom, which is equipped with grab bars. The hotel is two blocks from the Metro. If you have a car, there is free parking. Both single and double rooms range from $95 to $115, with $15 for each additional person in the same room. There are special family plans and weekend packages.

FIRST-CLASS HOTELS (Doubles $80 and up): Two blocks from the White House, the **Capitol Hilton** has a good location at 16th and K Sts. NW, DC 20036 (tel. 202/393-1000), and 12 rooms for disabled guests. Rates are $65 to $110 single, and $85 to $130 double. There are Metro stations on two different lines, both three blocks away.

The Rosslyn Metro stop is right across the street from the **Hyatt Arlington,** 1325 Wilson Blvd., Arlington, VA 22209 (tel. 703/841-9595, toll free

800/228-9000). The entrance is level and access inside is ramped or by elevator. Ten special rooms have 33-inch entry doors and 31-inch doors to the bathroom, which has grab bars. The bedroom is equipped with ceiling hooks for hoisting devices. Four of its five restaurants have level access. Rates go from $77 to $97 single, from $92 to $112 double, with special weekend rates.

Because there are not too many hotels in this category, I'll mention a centrally located hotel, even though it does not have any special features, but *is* spacious. It is the **Hotel Washington,** 15th St. at F St. NW, DC 20004 (tel. 202/638-5900, toll free 800/424-9540). The main entrance has steps, but the others do not. This is a vintage hotel with a lobby that has been given landmark status, and its rooms are comfortably large, with 33-inch doors and 27-inch bathroom entry (door can be removed to allow another inch or two). Rates are $68 to $78 single, $80 to $90 double.

In the West End, four blocks from Georgetown and one block from the Foggy Bottom Metro stop that provides a way to get quickly to the Smithsonian and the Capitol, is the **Ramada Renaissance,** 1143 New Hampshire Ave. NW at M St., DC 20037 (tel. 202/775-0800, toll free 800/228-2828). It is fully accessible with a number of special rooms. Rates are $85 single, $95 double.

MEDIUM-PRICE HOTELS (Doubles under $80): Not too many hotels
in this category with special facilities, but here are some possibilities: The **International Hotel,** 10 Thomas Circle NW, DC 20005 (tel. 202/842-1300, toll free 800/424-1140), is at the junction of M Street and Vermont Avenue, a few blocks north of the White House. It has a level entrance, and there are some rooms with 31-inch doors to the bathroom. Underground parking is available. Rates are $52 to $68 single, $62 to $78 double.

In the same area is a **Holiday Inn,** Massachusetts Ave. at Thomas Circle NW, DC 20005 (tel. 202/737-1200, toll free 800/238-8000, or for the hearing-impaired TDD 800/238-5544), which has special wheelchair-accessible guest rooms. Rates are $56 single, $64 double.

5. Washington Restaurants

Eating places in Washington range all the way from the cafeterias in the historic sights and museums to the "power" houses where national policy is discussed over lunch, and the choice is spread all over town.

Many residents and visitors alike gravitate to Georgetown restaurants in the evening, and you'll find a number of them included here. The cuisine offered in Washington has taken a definite turn for the better in recent years, both in quality and variety, and it's not an easy task to select just a few from the many that are available, even from an accessibility point of view. But here are some, listed by price category.

EXPENSIVE: Among Washington's leading French restaurants is **Le Lion d'Or,** 1150 Connecticut Ave. NW (tel. 296-7972), considered by many to be among the best. It's difficult to get a luncheon reservation here since it is one of the "in" places for the Washington decision-makers, but it is quieter on a weekday evening. You're here for the food, though, not the atmosphere, since the decor is strictly office-building style, and although it is in the basement, there is an elevator available to get there. Since you will be calling in advance for a reservation, make sure they know what your access needs will be. Entrees range from $12.50 to $24 à la carte. Lunch is served Monday through Friday from noon to 2 p.m. and dinner from 6 to 10 p.m. Dinner only on Saturday; closed on Sunday.

The **Americus** at the Sheraton Washington Hotel, 2660 Woodley Rd. NW (tel. 328-2000), has been setting trends for its emphasis on regional dishes from around the country, gourmet style. Dishes change with the seasons. Although this is an expensive restaurant for lunch or dinner, which may cost around $50, there is a Sunday champagne brunch, served from 11:30 a.m. to 3 p.m., that has a fixed price of $16.50. The entrances to both the hotel and the restaurant are level. Although this is "uptown," it is close to the Woodley/Zoo Metro station on the Red Line.

UPPER BRACKET: One institution in Washington eating that has been around for a long time is **Blackie's House of Beef,** 1217 22nd St. NW (tel. 333-1100), which is large, with a number of different dining rooms, some with level entrance, some up one step. There is just one step at the entrance to the restaurant. Most dinner entrees are in the $6.50 to $16.95 range, and the house specialty of prime rib is in the medium range of these prices. Lunch costs less and can include a sandwich menu as well. This is one of a number of Blackie restaurants around town that are open from 11 a.m. to 10:30 p.m. Monday through Saturday, on Sunday from 4 to 10:30 p.m.

You don't have to guess what the specialty is at the **Prime Rib,** 2020 K St. NW (tel. 466-8811), which is two blocks west of the Farragut North Metro stop. This restaurant is popular for business lunches and may be less busy at dinner. Entrees average $15 at dinner, $9 at lunch. The entrance is level. Open for lunch Monday through Friday from 11:30 a.m. until 3 p.m., and for dinner Monday through Saturday from 5:30 p.m. to midnight.

The ambience is glamorous at the **Roof Terrace at the John F. Kennedy Center for the Performing Arts** (tel. 833-8870), which would be worth a sightseeing trip anyway, even if you were not going to a performance. The building is accessible, and elevators service all floors, including the top-floor restaurants, where there are some good views over the Lincoln Memorial. In the main dining room, dinner entrees range from $9.50 to $14.95 à la carte. Lunch is served from 11:30 a.m. to 3 p.m. and dinner from 5 to 9:30 p.m. Late supper is served after 9:30 p.m. The Roof Terrace is open every day.

La Bagatelle, 2000 K St. NW at 20th St. (tel. 872-8677), is a French restaurant with a high reputation for its cuisine served in an intimate atmosphere in a building with a level entrance. Dinner entrees range from $11.50 to $16.50; less at lunch. Lunch is served on weekdays only from 11:30 a.m. to 3 p.m. and dinner from Monday through Saturday from 6 to 11 p.m. Closed on Sunday.

Another French restaurant that has attracted Washington diners for a long while is **Le Provençal,** 1234 20th St. NW, between M and N Sts. (tel. 223-2420). It has a level entrance, and although the four rooms are on different levels, there is seating available without steps. Entrees à la carte at dinner range from about $14.75 to $17.50, and at lunch from $7.50 to $9.50. It is open from noon to 3 p.m. for lunch, from 6 to 10 p.m. for dinner, Monday through Saturday.

More French flair is evident at **La Niçoise,** 1721 Wisconsin Ave. NW, between R and S Sts. (tel. 965-9300), where service is speeded up by the roller skates that all the waiters wear. There is a level entrance. Dinner entrees range from $10 to $18. Dinner only is served, Monday through Saturday, from 5:30 to 10:30 p.m.

Closer to Capitol Hill is a Swiss restaurant, **The Broker,** at 713 Pennsylvania Ave. NW at 8th St. (tel. 546-8300), where the entrance is level and where you can savor the specialties of several regions of Switzerland, including a raclette Valasienne at $11 per person. Other daily specials are priced from $13 to $17.50. The Broker is open daily for lunch from 11:30 a.m. to 2:30 p.m. Monday to Friday, and for dinner from 5:30 to 11 p.m. Monday to Saturday. Brunch is served on Sunday from 11 a.m. to 3 p.m.

MODERATE: There are some hotel eateries worth mentioning in this category, as well as a number of restaurants located in Georgetown.

The **Park Promenade** at the Hyatt Regency, 400 New Jersey Ave. NW on Capitol Hill (tel. 727-1234), is bright and cheerful in its gardenlike atrium setting, which has level access from the street and to the restaurant. You can eat here any time from 7 a.m. to midnight for a variety of meals including breakfast, sandwiches, a light lunch, or a full dinner. There's also a lavish Sunday champagne buffet brunch priced at $16.75 that is served from 11 a.m. to 3 p.m.

In the vicinity of the White House at the Washington Hotel, **The Two Continents,** 15th and F Sts. NW (tel. 638-5900), offers a choice of lobby level or rooftop dining. The restaurant derives its name from the variety of its cuisine, which is a mixture of French and American, with entrees in the $8 to $16 range. Open for lunch Monday to Friday from 11:45 a.m. to 3 p.m., and for dinner daily from 5:30 to 10:30 p.m.

One of the most unusual eating spots in Washington is the **Bread Oven,** 1220 19th St. NW (tel. 466-4264). There's a full menu here, though (and not only what comes out of the ovens), with entrees priced at $6.45 at lunch and $7.45 at dinner. You have a choice of two entrances here, one with one step, the other is level. The Bread Oven is open Monday through Saturday from 8 to 11 a.m. for breakfast, from 11:45 a.m. to 3 p.m. for lunch, tea (yes!) from 3:30 to 5:30 p.m., and for dinner from 5:30 to 10 p.m. Closed on Sunday.

Another unusual setting for eating is **Kramerbooks & Afterwords Cafe,** at 1517 Connecticut Ave. NW (tel. 387-1462), which is both a bookstore and a cafe, located near the Dupont Circle Metro stop. It has a level entrance if you want to go inside, but it is also a sidewalk cafe from mid-March to mid-December. Dishes are the light kind, and entrees range from about $3.95 to $6.95, with a prix fixe dinner for $10. It opens at 8 a.m. and serves food and drink all day long until 1 a.m. Sunday through Thursday, and until 3 a.m. on Friday and Saturday.

GEORGETOWN: There's a wide variety of choices in Georgetown, both in type of food and in price; in checking them out for accessibility, it turned out that quite a few of the best ones were French and most happily were in the medium-price category.

Chez Odette, 3063 M St. NW (tel. 333-9490), is in the center of Georgetown between 30th and 31st Streets, and is Parisian bistro-style, with one step at the entrance. Dinner entrees range from $3.95 to $9.95, and the restaurant is open for lunch from 11:30 a.m. to 5 p.m. (not on Sunday), and for dinner from 5 to 10:30 p.m.

In the Georgetown shopping area there is authentic French cuisine at **Au Pied de Cochon,** 1335 Wisconsin Ave. NW (tel. 333-5444), where there is a level entrance to the main restaurant and a step to the enclosed sidewalk patio. Lunch might average $6; dinner around $8. Open every day for 24 hours.

Not far away and a sister restaurant, the **Aux Fruits de Mer,** 1329 Wisconsin Ave. NW (tel. 965-2377), concentrates on seafood specialties costing $7 to $10. There is one step at the entrance. Lunch is served from 11 a.m. to 4 p.m., and dinner from 4 p.m. to 2 a.m. on weekdays, until 3 a.m. on weekends.

At the eastern end of Georgetown, **La Chaumière,** 2813 M St. NW (tel. 338-1784), has a rustic atmosphere and a level entrance. Lunch entrees are around $4 to $8, and at dinner from $7 to $13. Lunch is served Monday through Friday, and the restaurant is open for dinner until 11 p.m. on Monday through Thursday, and until midnight on Friday and Saturday.

Bistro Français, 3124 M St. NW (tel. 338-3830), is another popular Georgetown restaurant that has a level entrance. There are two rooms, the Cafe Bam Bam and the main dining area, where entrees average $7 to $10. The champagne brunch on Saturday and Sunday is $8.50. It opens at 11 a.m. Monday through Friday, at 10 a.m. Saturday and Sunday, and stays open until 3 a.m. Sunday through Thursday, until 4 a.m. Friday and Saturday.

One exception to the French list is an old Georgetown Tavern, **Martin's,** at 1264 Wisconsin Ave. NW (tel. 333-7370), which serves hearty food at lunch and dinner in a suitably tavernlike and unpretentious atmosphere. The entrance is level. Lunch may cost between $4.95 and $6.95, and dinner up to $10.95.

A northern Italian restaurant in Georgetown, **Candelas,** 3280 M St. NW (tel. 338-0900), has a level entrance and a romantic candlelight setting. The menu is a long one, including pasta of course, and prices range from $6.95 to $10.95. (There is free parking here.) Open Monday through Thursday from 11:30 a.m. until 11:30 p.m., and until midnight on weekends. Sunday, 1 to 10:30 p.m.

If you are in Georgetown and would like an inexpensive snack or light meal in relaxing surroundings, try the **Piece of Cake,** 3116 M St. NW (tel. 341-1854). There is one step at the entrance. It is open from 11:30 a.m. to 2 a.m. every day.

6. Sightseeing

The decision to locate the new nation's capital on swampy land along the Potomac River, ceded by Virginia and Maryland, meant at least one good thing for the disabled visitor nearly 200 years later: the land on which all our national monuments, treasures, and legislature would be built would, at any rate, be flat! A good start, despite the imposing stepped entrances and grand staircases that were the symbol of significant edifices built mostly 100 years ago. But today, with awareness of such things as architectural barriers, the federal government has done its best to get around them, as far as it could, with ramps and elevators. The newest buildings, and especially the new subway system, fortunately kept us in mind when plans were made.

It all goes to make Washington, D.C., a good place for most disabled visitors. What a mobility-impaired visitor can experience in Washington today, compared with ten years ago, is—almost everything. Ramps, elevators, and accessible rest rooms have been installed wherever that was feasible, making the symbols of America's heritage that are so familiar to everyone—the White House, Lincoln Memorial, Washington Monument, the Capitol—places that don't have to be looked at from the sidewalks any more. Ramped curbs are more evident than in many cities, and are to be found particularly around the Capitol Building and along the Mall.

There's such a lot to see that nobody should try to do it all in a few days. Spend a longer time, or be discriminating in what you choose to do, since it could turn into a test of stamina rather than a vacation.

The monuments, museums, art galleries, and public buildings included here do not follow any particular itinerary, since routes will depend on whether you are using a car, taxi, or the Metro. All of them will be easily located on the map since they are in a relatively small area west of the Capitol Building. Which is as good a place to start as any.

From **Capitol Hill** you will be looking west down the Mall, all the way to the Lincoln Memorial on the banks of the Potomac River. On your left, between the Capitol and the Washington Monument, are the National Air and Space Museum, the Hirshhorn Gallery, the Smithsonian Institution, and the Freer Art Gallery. To your right is the National Gallery of Art, the National Museum of Natural History, and the National Museum of American History. If you look down Pennsylvania Avenue as it goes off diagonally to the right of the Mall, you are looking toward the National Archives, the Federal Bureau of Investigation (FBI) among many other government buildings, and eventually to the White House.

The distance from the Capitol to the Lincoln Memorial is a little over two miles, but if you visit everything that is crammed into this relatively short distance, it will turn into quite a marathon!

THE WHITE HOUSE: That famous address at 1600 Pennsylvania Avenue has, of course, been home to every President of the United States except George Washington, and is the oldest public building in Washington.

The Visitors Office of the White House emphasizes that all the rooms toured by the general public are available to disabled visitors, via ramps and elevators where necessary, when the office has been alerted in advance. They recommend that disabled visitors use the Northeast Gate of the White House between 10 a.m. and 12 noon on Tuesday through Saturday. Another way to arrange a White House tour is through the office of your Member of Congress, which should then advise the White House of your special needs when the tour is set up for you. For general information on tours, call 202/456-7140.

The nearest parking lots are on Pennsylvania Avenue at 17th Street, on New York Avenue near 16th Street, and on F Street near 15th Street. Nearest Metro stations are McPherson Square (Blue and Orange Lines) on I and 15th Streets, or Metro Center (all lines) at G and 12th Streets.

THE CAPITOL: Just as it is a focal point for the nation's laws, the Capitol Building, with its domed silhouette so familiar to anybody who ever watches television newscasts, is also the focal point for any visit to Washington. Don't forget, though, that newsmen always refer to events on Capitol *Hill,* and since it does sit on one of the few bumps on the Washington landscape, be prepared for an incline on the sidewalks to the entrance if you are not driving there. This also applies if you come on the Metro, either to the Capitol South (Blue Line) or to Union Station (Red Line) stations, about equidistant on either side. All curbs are ramped! If you need to park your car, request special arrangements from the guard on duty.

The building and grounds of the U.S. Capitol have been under remodeling procedures for some time, although no final definition of their accessibility features has yet been issued by the Capitol Architect's office. At present, you'll find there are entrance ramps at the North, South, and East fronts; under the portico, the entrance is level. Inside there is access to different levels via attended elevator, and in the visitors' gallery for both the Senate and the House there are special wheelchair locations, as well as an audio loop system for hearing-impaired visitors.

One set of wheelchair-accessible rest rooms is located at the Capitol end of the Senate Subway, and there is a lowered phone near the Refectory on the first floor.

Tours are offered every morning except Sunday and Monday. There is a new Special Services Office under the jurisdiction of the Senate Sergeant at Arms through which you can make tour arrangements if you use a wheelchair, are hearing-impaired, or are visually-impaired. Individuals as well as groups can call 202/224-4048 (voice) or 202/224-4049 (TDD) or write to Special Service, Office of the Sergeant at Arms, United States Senate, Room S-321, The Capitol Building, Washington, DC 20510. Arrangements to request the special services can also be made through your Senator's office. This should be done in advance of your visit.

There are accessible restaurants in the Capitol, the Dirksen Senate Office Building, and the Rayburn and Longworth House office buildings, that are open to the public from 8 to 11:15 a.m. and from 1:15 to 2:30 p.m.

The U.S. Capitol is open in the summer from 9 a.m. to 10 p.m. daily, and in winter from 9 a.m. to 4:30 p.m. daily. It is closed on Thanksgiving, Christmas, and New Year's Days.

THE LIBRARY OF CONGRESS: Reached by going under the arch across the street from the Capitol Building, the Library of Congress, at First St. and Independence Ave. on Capitol Hill (tel. 287-5458), is the nation's library, open to anyone over high school age, and containing over 75 million items, including a treasury of absorbing historical documents, a rare Gutenberg Bible, as well as constantly changing exhibits of manuscripts, maps, prints, photographs, and rare books. It has a fairly steep ramp over the three steps at the entrance, but the interior can be toured on all floors with access by elevator. Rest-room stall doors are 28 inches wide. There are guided tours on weekdays between 9 a.m. and 4 p.m. The nearest Metro station is Capitol South.

THE FOLGER SHAKESPEARE LIBRARY: The Folger Shakespeare Library has one of the world's finest collections of Renaissance books and magazines and is, of course, devoted also to the great Bard and his times. Regular seasons of Shakespeare plays are given in the theater, where there are wheelchair locations and one signed performance per run is given. Call 547-3230 for information. The Folger is located behind the Library of Congress at 201 East Capitol St. SW at 3rd St. (tel. 544-4600). The wheelchair-accessible entrance is at the rear of the building (there are 17 steps in front), and a staff member will escort you via elevator to the main floor. It is open from 10 a.m. to 4 p.m. daily (closed Sundays from Labor Day to April 15). There is no admission charge.

THE SUPREME COURT: If you are in Washington any time between the first Monday in October and May or early June, you can see the Supreme Court of the United States in session. It's one of the most impressive shows in town. The building at 1st St. NE, at the corner of East Capitol Street, has a formidable number of steps at the main entrance, but there is a ramp on the Maryland Avenue side of the building. Elevators inside the building give easy access to the Visitors Gallery, to the basement where there are exhibits and a film explaining the workings of the Supreme Court, and to the cafeteria.

Arrive as soon as you can after 9 a.m. when the building opens, if you want to get a place in the Visitors Gallery, which is always crowded, especially on Monday when decisions are often handed down. Court sessions are held weekdays from 10 a.m. to 3 p.m., and you can check the schedule in the local newspaper. For other information, call 252-3000.

When the court is not sitting in the summer, there are lectures about the history of the Court given hourly on the half-hour.

Nearest Metro is about three blocks away at either Capitol South (Blue and Orange lines) or Union Station (Red line.)

THE MALL: Rows of stately elms mark the sweep of the green mall that runs from the Capitol to the Washington Monument and was a key feature of L'Enfant's plan drawn up in 1790. Today it is lined with the many buildings of the Smithsonian Institution complex. Over one hundred curb cuts have been made in the Mall area, which also includes the major memorials (Washington, Jefferson, and Lincoln), Constitution Gardens, the Sylvan Theater, the President's Parks (the Ellipse, the White House and Lafayette Park), West Potomac Park (including the Reflecting Pool), and the Tidal Basin. In addition to the accessible rest rooms and drinking fountains inside the buildings themselves, you will find these facilities also, accessible from street level, near the Sylvan Theater off Independence Avenue near 15th St. SW; in West Potomac Park near the polo field; on the south side of the Reflecting Pool at the Folklife Festival site; and in Constitution Gardens near the lake.

The relatively new Constitution Gardens, constructed for the Bicentennial, is a 42-acre park on the Constitution Avenue side of the Mall that was planned to conform to the prevailing requirements for accessibility set out by the American National Standard Institute (ANSI), and includes accessible rest rooms, curb cuts from Constitution Avenue, and gentle incline grades.

Unless you can get into one of the designated spaces for disabled drivers (where out-of-town special parking permits are allowed,) it is *not* a good idea to park on the Mall itself, where it is illegal before 10 a.m. and a "jungle" after that. Those special parking spaces are at the Washington Monument, in the parking lot off Constitution Avenue, and near the entrances to the Smithsonian Institution (see below). There is also a commercial garage at L'Enfant Plaza, within reasonable distance at 10th Street and Independence Avenue. If you arrive early, you may be able to get one of the wheelchair-designated spaces in the garage under the Air and Space Museum, where rates are reasonable.

On the Mall, you'll find accessible cafeterias in the National Museum of American History, the National Air and Space Museum, and at the National Gallery of Art.

SMITHSONIAN INSTITUTION: We'll talk about the Smithsonian Institution first, since *all* the museums of any significance along the Mall come under its jurisdiction (including the National Zoo, not on the Mall). You can write in advance for an excellent free booklet, "Guide for Disabled Visitors," to the Office of Public Affairs, Smithsonian Institution, Washington, DC 20560. In addition to the Smithsonian Institution itself, this booklet includes accessibility details for the Freer Gallery, the National Museum of American History, the National Museum of Art, the National Portrait Gallery, the National Museum of Natural History, the National Air and Space Museum, the Hirshhorn Museum, the Arts and Industries Building, and the Renwick Gallery. Single copies on cassette can be requested at no cost. Braille and recorded editions of the

Official Guide to all parts of the Smithsonian may be purchased from the Mail Order Division, Smithsonian Institution, Box 2456, Washington, DC 20013, at $2 for the braille edition, $5.25 for a cassette tape.

There are Information Desks in most of the Smithsonian museums and you can also call for information, 202/357-2700, or TDD 202/357-1729, between 9 a.m. and 5 p.m. daily, except Christmas Day. For recorded information on hours and exhibits, call 202/357-1300. Most of the museums are served by the Metro subway system. There are parking spaces on the Mall for disabled visitors with cars displaying identification issued by their home city or state, in each of the following locations: on Jefferson Drive, east of the Arts and Industries Building and in front of the Air and Space Museum; on Madison Drive in front of the Museum of Natural History and Museum of American History; and on Jefferson Drive in front of the Freer Gallery of Art. Every museum has wheelchairs available for use within each museum, and at least one telephone equipped with sound amplification.

For hearing-impaired visitors, a portable loop amplification system is available for use at Smithsonian events from the Office of Elementary and Secondary Education at least 48 hours before the program (tel. 202/357-1697 or TDD 202/357-1696). The Baird Auditorium in the Museum of Natural History is equipped with a permanent loop amplification system for the many concerts and lectures given there. Hearing-impaired visitors may request sign language and oral interpreters for any Smithsonian program or special event. The numbers to call are listed under the individual museum, for requests at least 48 hours in advance of the program. Any other questions regarding the accessibility of Smithsonian programs and facilities should go to the Accessibility Program Manager, Room 3161, Arts and Industries Building, Smithsonian Institution, Washington, DC 20560.

National Gallery of Art

Bearing right as you leave the Capitol, you'll come to the National Gallery that occupies four blocks of Constitution Avenue NW between 3rd and 7th Streets (tel. 737-4215). All of it, the older neoclassic structure of rose-white marble opened in 1941, and the stunning new East Wing opened in 1978 (which you'll come to first at 3rd Street if you're coming from the Capitol) are all accessible to the disabled visitor.

The National Gallery ranks with the Louvre in Paris and with the Hermitage in Leningrad, to offer a whole day's viewing, at least, to the art lover, with a treasurehouse of old masters in the older building and a superb collection of more modern works in the new East Wing. There is a level entrance to the East Wing and an underground concourse, reached by elevator, that connects the two buildings, which have accessible cafeterias for both cafe and buffet service, offering pleasant and inexpensive meals.

If you go directly to the older National Gallery building on Constitution Avenue, there is a ramped entrance on the street level and access to all floors is by elevator. Rest rooms in the original building have 35-inch entrances and 34-inch curtained stalls with grab bars. From April through Labor Day, the gallery is open Monday through Saturday from 10 a.m. to 9 p.m. Other times of the year it is open Monday through Saturday, 10 a.m. to 5 p.m., Sunday 12 noon to 9 p.m. Admission is free. The nearest Metro stop is Archives (Green Line), which is on 7th Street near Pennsylvania Avenue.

National Archives

Located between Pennsylvania Avenue and Constitution Avenue at 8th St. NW (tel. 523-3099), the National Archives building can be reached via the Archives stop on the Metro (Green Line) or, if you're coming from the National Gallery, it is on the other side of Constitution Avenue. Here you can see the nation's most cherished documents—the Declaration of Independence, the Constitution of the United States, and the Bill of Rights. The originals! The Declaration is displayed vertically so it is easy to see from a wheelchair; the other documents are in a case that's four feet high.

If you're looking for roots, this might be the place. On file here are census records from 1790; records of army, navy, and marine services; ships' passenger files with lists of immigrant passengers as far back as 1820; naturalization records; and any other records you care to name. Research hours are 8 a.m. to 10 p.m. on Monday through Friday, 9 a.m. to 5 p.m. on Saturday, closed Sunday and government holidays.

There's a ramp at the Pennsylvania Avenue entrance that has a 37-inch automatic door. Inside, there is elevator access to different levels. Most rest rooms, however, only have 25-inch entry stalls, but there is a wheelchair-accessible stall in the ladies room on the ground floor. Open daily, free of charge, April through August from 10 a.m. to 9 p.m., September through March from 10 a.m. to 5:30 p.m. Closed on most holidays. For information on daily exhibits, call 523-3000.

National Museum of Natural History

The world's peoples and their natural surroundings are the focus of the National Museum of Natural History, at 10th St. and Constitution Ave. NW (tel. 357-2747, TDD 202/357-1696). And it has just about everything, from the largest African elephant to the legendary Hope Diamond—including accessibility. There are actually 60 million objects in the museum's three floors!

The Constitution Avenue entrance is ramped, has automatic doors, and all exhibit areas are reached by elevator. The rest rooms off the Constitution Avenue lobby are equipped with larger stall and grab bars, and there are lowered water fountains in each rest room; lowered telephones are in the Constitution Avenue lobby. At the snack bar, people in wheelchairs may need help to reach items in the center of the self-service carousel. For signed tours for hearing-impaired visitors, the museum requests two weeks advance notice.

A detailed guide to the museum for visually impaired visitors, called, "Touch and Hear," is available free of charge from the information desk or from the Office of Education, Museum of Natural History, Washington, DC 20560, or by telephone 202/357-2747, TDD 202/357-1696.

The nearest Metro station is Federal Triangle (on Blue and Orange Lines), which has an elevator exit at 12th Street, one block north of Constitution Ave. NW. The National Museum of Natural History is open from 10 a.m. to 5:30 p.m. every day, except Christmas Day.

National Museum of American History

Fascinating exhibits of everyday life in the American past, as well as the nation's major scientific, cultural, and technological achievements can be seen at the National Museum of American History, located at 14th St. and Constitution Ave. NW (tel. 357-1481, TDD 202/357-1563). There are level entrances on the Constitution Avenue and the Madison Drive sides of the building, both with automatic doors. All public areas inside, except some part of the bookstore on the first floor, are accessible to visitors in wheelchairs (staff members are willing to provide help in the bookstore). There is a lift to the Railroad Hall for people in wheelchairs, to be operated by a guard. The second floor rest rooms have enlarged stalls. Lowered telephones and water fountains are on the first floor in the Constitution Avenue lobby, and on the second floor in the Madison Drive lobby.

For sight-impaired visitors, elevator control panels are marked with braille symbols and raised numbers, and floor numbers are also indicated in braille and raised numbers on the elevator door jambs. There are free tours in which time for handling artifacts and reproductions is provided. If you have a hearing impairment, sign-language tours are usually scheduled once a week (call for information).

A full-service cafeteria and a fast-food carousel are located in the lower level, reached by elevator, at the western end of the building, and there is an accessible ice cream parlor on the first floor. The museum is open daily from 10 a.m. to 5:30 p.m. Closed Christmas Day.

The nearest Metro station is the Federal Triangle (on Blue and Orange Lines) with the elevator at 12th Street one block north of Constitution Avenue.

National Air and Space Museum

If you turn left down the Mall from the Capitol, you'll come to the National Air and Space Museum on the Mall at 7th St. and Independence Ave. SW (tel. 357-2700). A magnet for most visitors to Washington, it is the newest of the Smithsonian buildings, and is a showcase for the evolution of aviation and space technology—and it is very accessible indeed. The chronicle of man's mastery of flight from Kitty Hawk to outer space fills 23 galleries of spectacular exhibits that include the 1903 Wright Flyer, Charles Lindbergh's *Spirit of St. Louis,* John Glenn's *Friendship 7,* and the *Apollo 11* command module.

Both entrances to the building, from Independence Avenue and from Jefferson Drive, are ramped. Three parking spaces are reserved for disabled visitors in the commercial garage beneath the museum, with regular parking rates. Every level of the building, including the garage, can be reached by elevator, and there are accessible rest rooms and telephones. Wheelchairs can be borrowed for use in touring the museum; and to help people with limited head mobility, there are also clamp-on mirrors available in the cloakroom off the Milestones of Flight gallery on the first floor.

Not to be missed are the museum's movies, especially *To Fly,* a bird's-eye view of America, and *Living Planet,* an aerial tour projected on a five-story-high screen. The films are shown every 40 minutes starting at 10:15 a.m., and admission is $1 (50¢ for students and senior citizens). It is a good idea to get your tickets for the movies as soon as you enter the museum (or even the day before), since this is a very popular attraction. There are three wheelchair locations in the theater, and the theater aide or cashier will admit wheelchair visitors to the auditorium through the east door on the second floor.

A self-service cafeteria is located on the third floor (reached by elevator from the first floor), but people in wheelchairs may need help reaching items in the center of the food carousel.

For visitors with hearing impairments, the Briefing Room where lectures and programs are held is equipped with a loop amplification system; scripts of most films and audio programs given at the museum may be borrowed from the information desk. You can arrange for sign or oral interpreters, giving two weeks' notice, by calling 202/357-1400 or TDD 202/357-2853.

For visually impaired visitors, tours can be arranged so that models or artifacts can be examined by touch. The information desk has a building model with braille labels and also booklets with raised line drawings of aircraft and spacecraft. Braille, large-print, and tape-recorded editions of the museum's brochures can also be requested at the information desk. Tours of some galleries have been recorded on cassettes, and portable tape recorders are available.

The nearest Metro station to the Air and Space Museum is L'Enfant Plaza, with elevator exit at Maryland Avenue and 7th Street SW.

Hirshhorn Museum

Another Smithsonian museum on the Independence Avenue side of the Mall is the Hirshhorn Museum, on Independence Ave. between 7th and 8th Sts. SW (tel. 357-1300). It was the first major museum of contemporary art in Washington, with a magnificent collection of over 6000 paintings and sculptures, in a showcase building for viewing art—including the wheelchair view. The outer galleries of the circle are carpeted in places, but in a solid, flat pile; the sculpture galleries on the inner part of the circular floors are uncarpeted. The entrance for wheelchair visitors is through level swinging doors on the plaza (main door is revolving), and all the galleries are accessible by elevators. Accessible rest rooms and lowered drinking fountains are located on the ground floor. Accessible entrance to the Sculpture Garden is from the Mall (there is a flight of steps from the museum plaza). In the summer, an accessible cafe on the outdoor plaza level serves box lunches.

For the visually impaired visitor, about 30 of the museum's sculptures can be examined by touch. These are marked with a "T" emblem in a circle. A staff member will accompany visually impaired visitors on the sculpture tour on weekdays between 10 a.m. and 5 p.m., but requests for this should be made at least two weeks in advance by calling 202/357-3235 or TDD 202/357-1696.

The nearest Metro station is L'Enfant Plaza, with elevator location at Maryland Avenue and 7th Street SW.

Arts and Industries Building

Continuing down the Independence Avenue side of the Mall, you'll come to the Arts and Industries Building, at 8th St. and Jefferson Drive SW (357-2700), which is devoted to "1876: A Centennial Exhibition," a barrier-free exhibit with one of the country's most extensive collections of working steam engines and locomotives as well as other historic machinery. Visitors in wheelchairs should enter the building through the Victorian Garden entrance on the west side of the building. Rest rooms are equipped with enlarged stalls and grab bars. There is space for wheelchairs in the Discovery Theater that features puppet shows and other programs for children. The nearest Metro station is Smithsonian (Mall exit), with elevator at 12th St. and Independence Ave. SW. Open 10 a.m. to 5:30 p.m. daily.

Smithsonian Institution Building

The castlelike Victorian building that symbolizes the Smithsonian Institution, at 1000 Jefferson Dr. SW on the Mall, is primarily the central information office for the rest of the museums and galleries, but is not to be recommended for visitors in wheelchairs, since entrance to this very old building is a problem. There are no accessible rest rooms. You can get information on the phone, 202/357-2700 or TDD 202/357-1729 between 9 a.m. and 5 p.m. daily. The nearest Metro station is Smithsonian (Mall exit), the elevator is at 12th St. and Independence Ave. SW.

Freer Gallery of Art

On the other side of the "castle" is yet another of the Smithsonian's museums, the Freer Gallery of Art, at 12th St. and Jefferson Dr. SW (tel. 357-2104), devoted to Oriental art, with a brilliant collection of Far and Near Eastern art, including Japanese paintings, Persian miniatures, Korean pottery, Chinese jades, and more. There is also a representative collection of American art, with the largest group in the world of works by Whistler. Visitors who cannot use steps can enter on the Independence Avenue side of the building through the receiving room, which is at sidewalk level. Advance arrangements must be made for this door to be opened on weekends and holidays by calling 357-2101, TDD 202/357-1729.

Exhibition galleries on the second floor can be reached by special elevator with staff escort, and staff help may also be needed for the sales desk, check room, and auditorium, which are reached only by the use of steps.

Nearest Metro station is Smithsonian (Mall exit on the Blue and Orange Lines), where the elevator is at 12th St. and Independence Ave. SW.

There's still more . . .

National Museum of American Art

Art lovers of the American masters have a treat in store at the National Museum of American Art, another part of the Smithsonian complex at 8th and G Sts. NW (tel. 357-3176). The National Portrait Gallery is also here and both are housed in the Old Patent Office Building, completed in 1837, a neoclassic building with long flights of steps on both sides.

However, visitors with limited mobility can enter either side of the building through the garage (but no special parking facilities here), or by ramp from the sidewalk at 9th and G Sts. From the garage level, there is an elevator to the first floor where you'll turn right for the American Art, and turn left for the Portrait Gallery. All interior access is by elevator. Lowered water fountains and an accessible rest room are located on the Portrait Gallery side. The Patent Pending Cafeteria is accessible; during the summer it is located in the outdoor courtyard, reached by ramp from the Portrait Gallery side. Nearest Metro station is Gallery Place (Red Line), with elevator at 7th and G Sts. NW. The National Museum of American Art is open from 10 a.m. to 5:30 p.m. daily.

The Renwick Gallery

Another Smithsonian museum is the Renwick Gallery at 17th St. and Pennsylvania Ave. NW (tel. 357-2531). It is part of the National Museum of American Art, and a showcase for American creativity in design, crafts, decorative arts, as well as exhibits from other countries.

There is a ramp from the corner of Pennsylvania Avenue and 17th St. which leads to the basement where an elevator provides access to all the public galleries. There are no other accessible facilities here. Nearest station is Farragut West on the Blue and Orange Lines of the Metro, with the elevator at 18th and Eye Sts. NW. The Renwick is open from 10 a.m. to 5:30 p.m. daily. Closed on Christmas Day.

The National Zoo

Because this is reckoned to be one of the world's finest and most enjoyable zoos, it deserves mention although its physical location will present difficulties for some mobility-impaired visitors and those in wheelchairs. The Zoo is on the 3000 block of Connecticut Ave. NW, on a hill sloping down to Rock Creek Park, and some of the several miles of walkway are quite steep. It is particularly popular because it houses the two Giant Pandas given to the people of the United States by the People's Republic of China. The best time to catch the pandas is at feeding times at 11 a.m. and 3 p.m. There is a parking lot about 75 yards from the Panda House where spaces are reserved free of charge for visitors whose cars display some official identification of disability issued by their local city or state. This parking lot is at the upper end of the Zoo, near the Connecticut Avenue gate. There is a cafe nearby.

The Cleveland Park Station (east side exit) elevator will bring you to Connecticut Ave. and Ordway St., just under half a mile from the Zoo along ramped level sidewalks. (The other Metro stop, Woodley Park Zoo, is located *downhill* from the Zoo.)

All rest rooms, water fountains and telephones can be used by people in wheelchairs. Group tours for visitors with various disabilities can be arranged in advance by calling 202/673-4955 or TDD 202/357-1696. The Zoo map and supplemental information for disabled visitors are available at the information desk in the Education Building, or by writing to the Office of Public Affairs, National Zoological Park, Washington, DC 20008.

WASHINGTON MONUMENT: It's hard to miss—the tallest edifice in Washington and the world's tallest masonry structure at 555 feet high, on the Mall at 15th St. NW (tel. 426-6839). It was finished 100 years ago, but now you can ride to the top by elevator for what will be one of the finest views of Washington for anybody who is ambulatory. (Window locations are not ideal for viewing from a wheelchair.) There is a public parking lot about 180 yards from the entrance, which is about the same distance as the passenger loading zone. There are 32-inch-wide stalls in the rest rooms on the southeast side of the monument. From the first Sunday in April to the day after Labor Day, it is open from 8 a.m. to 12 midnight; the rest of the year from 9 a.m. to 5 p.m.; closed Christmas Day. The nearest, but not very near, Metro station is Smithsonian (on the Blue and Orange Lines).

LINCOLN MEMORIAL: In perfect alignment with the Capitol, and across the Reflecting Pool from the Washington Monument, is the Lincoln Memorial, in which the 19-foot-square statue of Abraham Lincoln dominates the rectangular Doric temple with its 36 marble columns that represent the states that belonged to the Union when Lincoln died.

In height it is the equivalent of a nine-story structure, with steps all around to match, but in the late 1970s the Parks Department installed an elevator and an access ramp as an alternate access to the 58 steps that run from the sidewalk to the statue chamber. Rest room facilities, telephones, and drinking fountains are fully accessible and can be reached by a gradually sloping walkway with curb cuts at the street. There is parking for visitors in wheelchairs, marked on the east side of the circle roadway. Call 202/426-6895 for information on tours, including sign language tours, which should be arranged in advance by calling or by writing to Lincoln Memorial, c/o National Capital Region, 1100 Ohio Dr. SW, Washington, DC 20242. Tours are conducted at random daily by

National Park Service guides. The Lincoln Memorial is open daily until midnight. Closed on Christmas Day.

JEFFERSON MEMORIAL: The third great presidential monument to be erected in Washington was dedicated only 40 years ago, but now it seems an inseparable part of the Washington landscape, situated as it is in East Potomac Park near the south side of the Tidal Basin, and surrounded in April by cherry blossoms—the eternal picture postcard. The columned rotunda contains the 19-foot bronze statue of Jefferson, standing on a 6-foot pedestal with inscriptions from the great man's writings engraved on the interior walls.

An elevator and ramps to the rotunda have recently been installed from the street level on the west side to make the memorial fully accessible, complete with rest rooms, lowered drinking fountains, and telephones on the lower level. There are designated places in the parking lot and curb cut access to the building.

VIETNAM MEMORIAL: The approach is from the Henry Bacon Drive near the Lincoln Memorial. Plans are in work for granite pathways to be laid down over the grass leading to and in front of the Vietnam Memorial in 1984.

MORE SIGHTS: The **Bureau of Engraving and Printing,** 14th and C Sts. SW (tel. 447-9709), is the place to see where they print dollar bills. Since the tours are extremely popular, especially in the summer, free admission tickets are issued on a first-come, first-served basis, beginning at 8 a.m. There is on-street parking on C Street between 12th and 14th Streets, and a commercial lot at D Street and 14th Street. The entrance at C and 14th Streets is level, and the interior is accessible by elevator and ramp. No accessible rest rooms. Open Monday through Friday, except legal holidays, from 8 a.m. to 2 p.m. Nearest Metro station is Smithsonian.

The **FBI headquarters** is at 935 Pennsylvania Ave. NW (9th St.), tel. 324-3447, and if the "most wanted" are among your interests, this is the place to see exhibits depicting famous gangsters of the 1930s, famous kidnapping and ransom notes, notorious bank robberies, and other displays of the FBI's efforts in fighting organized crime and espionage. In the laboratory there are demonstrations of the latest scientific techniques used in investigations.

There is a ramped entrance on E Street, near 9th Street, and a 32-inch automatic door. Tours start every 15 minutes Monday through Friday from 9 a.m. to 4 p.m., except holidays. There are no steps involved in the tours.

The **National Aquarium** is located in the Department of Commerce Building, Constitution Ave. and 14th St. NW (tel. 377-2825), where it shares the basement with a cafeteria. For the fish fan this is a great collection of familiar and very unusual specimens including moray eels and sharks. There are three steps, which are ramped, at the 14th Street entrance. Rest rooms have 32-inch-wide stalls. Open daily from 9 a.m. to 5 p.m., except Christmas Day. Admission is $1 for adults, 50¢ for children.

The **U.S. Navy Memorial Museum** depicts the history of the U.S. Navy from 1775 to the space age. This wheelchair-accessible museum, all on one floor (and with adapted rest rooms), is located in Building 76, Washington Navy Yard, 9th and M Sts. SE (tel. 433-2651). It is open Monday to Friday from 9 a.m. to 4 p.m.; on Saturday, Sunday, and holidays from 10 a.m. to 6 p.m. Free admission.

Arlington National Cemetery, located on rising ground that was once the estate of Robert E. Lee, is not easily accessible for visitors with mobility impairments. Cars are not allowed in the cemetery, but special permission to drive through the grounds can be obtained at the Park Information Desk (tel. 703/692-0931). The cemetery is directly across Memorial Bridge from the District; it is also a stop on the Metro Blue Line, and on the Tourmobile.

ROCK CREEK PARK: One of the largest urban parks in the world, Rock Creek Park, run by the National Park Service, has 1754 acres of natural, historic, cultural, and recreational facilities in the midst of metropolitan Washington. It extends from the northern boundary of the District at Western Avenue to West Potomac Park, and some of it is accessible to the disabled visitor. The Rock Creek Nature Center, at Military and Glover Rds. NW (tel. 426-6828), has exhibits designed to provide an understanding and appreciation of the natural world. The center and the planetarium are fully accessible, as are the rest rooms. Ramps lead to the auditorium. Open Tuesday through Saturday, 9:30 a.m. to 5 p.m.

POTOMAC CRUISES: If you want to see Washington from a different perspective, you can cruise the Potomac River by boat. Call Washington Boat Lines ahead (202/554-8000) to get information on the time schedules of the accessible boats, which are hydrojets.

7. Out-of-Town Excursions

GEORGETOWN: Although strictly speaking Georgetown is within the District, it is some distance from downtown Washington. Georgetown begins at the western end of Pennsylvania Avenue and lies west of Rock Creek Park and north of K Street. In colonial days, this was a commercial center and slave quarters; now it is a showplace of restored residences, boutiques, restaurants, cafes, antique stores, art galleries, and nightclubs, as well as the location of Georgetown University. It is one of the liveliest "in" areas of Washington.

Georgetown streets and sidewalks are quite narrow, and many are surfaced in brick, so you'll have to decide if you'll be comfortable touring here. If you can, it's a must when you visit Washington.

Among the notable houses in Georgetown is the **Old Stone House** at 3051 M St. NW (tel. 426-6851), one of the few structures that still exist from pre-Revolutionary times and now administered by the National Park Service, which advises that the ground floor and gardens are wheelchair-accessible (one small sill at the entrance to the house). The second floor is reached only by a narrow winding stairway. Staff members in period dress give demonstrations of 18th-century cooking, candlemaking, and other domestic crafts. If you have a hearing impairment, you can make arrangements for a guided tour by calling in advance. There are reproductions of historic items available for touching by visitors with visual impairments.

ALEXANDRIA: Driving from Washington and heading south via the 14th Street Bridge and the George Washington Memorial Parkway, you'll come to Alexandria, a colonial port town where hundreds of lovely old buildings have been restored in its Old Town, centered on King Street (Ramsay House is the Tourist Information Center.) There are antique shops, galleries, boutiques, restaurants in abundance, but be forewarned that there are some cobblestone streets.

MOUNT VERNON: If you continue from Alexandria along Washington Street, it becomes the George Washington Parkway, and from here you can follow the signs to the ancestral estate of George Washington. As with most historic sites, it is not easily accessible for visitors with mobility impairment, but you might just want to drive by this historic spot. There are long gravel paths around the grounds and four steps into the main house, with only a staircase access to the upper floors.

However, the **Mount Vernon Inn,** next to the Main Gate, *is* accessible (including the rest rooms), and has re-created the colonial period in its six dining rooms. Lunch is served from 11:30 a.m. There is also a snack bar, which is open from 9:30 a.m. daily. Mount Vernon (tel. 703/780-2000) is open every day of the year. Admission is $3 for adults, $2.50 for senior citizens, $1.50 for children.

8. Entertainment

Washington was, at one time, as dull a place in the evening as any small town that rolled up the sidewalks after dark. In the last 20 years or so, almost dating, it seems, from the very social- and culture-conscious Kennedys, the lights stay on, and there's theater of all kinds, concerts, and ballet, with active seasons in fall, winter, and spring. In the summer there are outdoor concerts in the parks.

TICKETPLACE: The place to get tickets for many of Washington's top entertainment events at regular prices in advance, or for half price on the day of the performance, is at TICKETplace. The computerized box office is on the F Street Plaza between 12th and 13th Streets NW, across from the 12th Street entrance to the Metro Center subway station. There is a service charge of 50¢ for each $10 of the half-price ticket's face value, and a $1 service fee on full-price tickets regardless of price, cash only. During the summer it is open from Monday through Saturday from 11 a.m. to 7 p.m.; during the winter, hours are 11 a.m. to 5:30 p.m. Tuesday through Saturday, and noon to 2 p.m. on Monday. Phone 842-5387 (TIC-KETS) for a recorded announcement of performances.

THE KENNEDY CENTER: The most active location for music, theater, dance, and film in Washington is the John F. Kennedy Center for the Performing Arts on Rock Creek Parkway and New Hampshire Avenue NW (tel. 254-3600). This huge temple to culture—the Concert Hall (tel. 254-3776), the Opera House (tel. 254-3770), the Eisenhower Theater (tel. 254-3670), and the new Terrace Theater (tel. 254-9895)—was built recently enough to be relatively accessible.

Garage parking arrangements can be made ahead of time by calling 659-9620, and elevators connect the underground garage to all levels of the center. Specially equipped rest rooms are on parking level B. Cars that have official disability identification from any local authority are allowed to park on the east side of the entrance plaza across from the front entrance.

In each of the theaters, a box is reserved for patrons in wheelchairs, and aisle seats are accessible if you wish to transfer. Elevators within each theater service the orchestra, box, and balcony levels. Lowered telephones and rest rooms, with 31-inch stall doors and grab bars, are located on the orchestra levels of all theaters, as well as at the Roof Terrace level. There are lowered telephones in the Concert Hall lobby (first and second floors); in the Opera House lobby (second floor); the Eisenhower Theater corridor; and in the Theater Lounge, the Hall of States, and the Hall of Nations. The restaurants at rooftop level are wheelchair-accessible.

The Kennedy Center gives major cultural events an advance showcase before moving to New York, as well as unique performances of its own since the Concert Hall, for instance, is the home of the National Symphony Orchestra. Prices generally range from $3 to about $25 (for a Broadway musical either on its way into or out of New York). Disabled patrons are offered half-price tickets for many of the events here at any time in advance of the performance, and to find out what will be playing when you are in Washington, write for information to "Two on the Aisle," Kennedy Center, Washington, DC 20566. Enclose 40¢ for postage and specify which month you are planning to visit. You can buy tickets, too, in advance with major credit cards. For current information, call (toll free) 800/424-8504. If you are not attending any performances, there are guided tours daily from 10 a.m. to 1:15 p.m.

ARENA STAGE: At 6th St. and Maine Ave. SW (tel. 202/488-3300), on Washington's beautiful renovated waterfront is the Arena Stage, the home of many "firsts" and noted for its theatrical offerings; it was the first theater outside New York to receive the Tony Award for theatrical excellence. Although it does not have level access (there are two short flights of steps), there is assistance available, and there are wheelchair locations in this triplex of intimate playhouses—the Arena, the Kreeger Theater, and the Old Vat Room. Ticket prices range from $7 to $15 and can be charged to MasterCard or VISA. Rest rooms are not recommended as accessible to wheelchairs.

NATIONAL THEATER: Washington's most prestigious theater, the National Theater, presents dramas and musicals year-round. It is located at 1321 E St. NW, (tel. 628-3393). There is a commercial parking lot nearby. The entrance to the theater is level, and there are six wheelchair locations. Rest rooms are up a flight of steps.

FORD'S THEATER: Ford's Theater, where President Lincoln was assassinated in 1865, is at 511 10th St., between E and F Sts. NW (tel. 426-6924). For performances, the orchestra level is accessible (one small step at the entrance) and there are wheelchair locations, but the Lincoln Museum in the basement can be reached only by a flight of stairs.

Visitors with visual impairments can arrange for a special tour that includes the President's Box, where all the furniture and appointments can be handled. There is also a sign language tour. Arrangements for both should be made by calling in advance. For ticket and performance information, call 202/347-6260. There is a parking lot adjacent to the theater, with a ramped curb.

OUTDOOR EVENTS: Military bands offer outdoor concerts several nights a week in front of the Capitol Building at 8 p.m. during the spring and summer. You'll find listings of the events in the local newspapers.

The Jefferson Memorial and the Tidal Basin in West Potomac Park are the scene for **a Torchlight Tattoo** every night except Monday and Saturday, weather permitting, June through August. It is free and is one of Washington's most impressive pageants, featuring the U.S. Army Fife and Drum Corps and the U.S. Army Precision Drill Team. There is a parking lot near the memorial, but you'd better get there early!

WOLF TRAP: It takes about half an hour by car to get to Wolf Trap Farm Park for the Performing Arts, 1624 Trap Road, Vienna, VA 22180 (tel. 703/938-3800). It is the first and only National Park devoted exclusively to the performing arts, where an indoor-outdoor amphitheater, the Filene Center, is the setting for top performances in opera, dance, symphony, musical theater, country music, and jazz. It was extensively damaged by fire but is in the process of being rebuilt and is scheduled to be reopened in the summer of 1984.

Tickets for Wolf Trap performances range from $6 for places on the lawn on up to about $25 for seats inside. In addition, there are free previews and discussions of the evening's performances at the Tent in the Meadow before the show; free opera and ballet productions on Saturday mornings—box picnic suppers available on the grounds, or an elegant buffet in a dinner tent for about $12. A portable ramp is available for access to the tent platform, which is raised a few inches above the grass. Arrive any time after 6 p.m.

The parking area has designated spaces for visitors in wheelchairs and curb cuts and an access ramp at the unloading zone. Call in advance to arrange for parking passes and for assistance from park personnel to reach the seating areas. Wheelchairs are available on loan, as well as electric vehicles for special assistance from the parking lot to the seating area. Rest rooms are accessible.

Chapter 6

BOSTON

The Hub

**1. Getting There
2. Getting Around
3. Orientation 4. Where
to Stay 5. Boston Dining
6. Sightseeing 7. Entertainment**

"BOSTON IS a walking city" says the city's official guide, but *don't* be turned off! It's only a way of saying that most Boston sights are within a short distance of each other, and that's convenient.

What most people visit Boston to see and experience is the very tangible connection to the nation's beginnings (and it is rivaled only by Philadelphia in the treasures it offers), from the Freedom Trail sites to the gaslit streets of Beacon Hill. But its history is not covered in dust. There's always Harvard, very much history and very much alive. And one of Boston's freshest and newest attractions, Faneuil Hall Marketplace, is a rebirth of a historic site in an exciting modern concept of shopping malls, outdoor cafes, and all kinds of street activity. And when you're finished with the history, there's always the seafood!

For all its historic significance, Boston also has big-city sophistication, with strong cultural credentials in such institutions as the Boston Symphony Orchestra, Boston Pops, and the Boston Museum of Fine Arts. Schools, colleges, medical centers, and research institutions abound, attracting bright young people from all over the country.

If you are not walking, is it a "wheeling" city? Well, there *are* areas that are hilly, like Beacon Hill, but even those can be "done" with a motorized wheelchair, by car, or with a companion with lots of stamina! Even if you are ambulatory but have mobility impairment, consider renting a wheelchair, since many of the older districts have brick sidewalks. And, as anywhere else, historic sites often cannot be made totally accessible to wheelchair users, but most of them can be seen to some degree, and there's much to look at without the need of access to the interiors of buildings.

Boston's own attitude to the needs of disabled visitors is signaled in the city's official Guide Book, which indicates whether hotels and restaurants consider themselves accessible to wheelchairs. The criteria are not spelled out, but it's a useful start. This 112-page guide is published by the **Boston Convention and Visitors Bureau,** Prudential Plaza, Boston MA 02199 (tel. 617/536-4100), and it is part of the Visitor Information Kit (available for $3 by mail, and for $2 at the Boston Visitors Information Booth) that also includes a city map, a Freedom Trail Guide, and a monthly Calendar of Events.

One of the most comprehensive city access guides in the country is the 200-page book, "Access to Boston: A Guide for Disabled Persons," published in 1981 and available at no charge from the Mayor's Commission of the Handicapped, Boston City Hall, City Hall Plaza, Boston, MA 02201. It rates parking, entrance, interiors, elevators, rest rooms, and telephones, and also includes listings of amplified telephones, TDD numbers, restaurants with braille menus, and detailed neighborhood maps designed to show curb cuts, parking facilities, and the location of all sites whose access features are described in that section, as well as important landmarks and public buildings.

1. Getting There

From the days of the Pilgrims in the 1600s when Boston was first settled, the city has been a hub for New England and the East Coast, and later for highways all over the country and airways all over the world. You'll find it easy to get there from practically anywhere by road, bus, train, or plane.

BY AIR: Boston is served by many domestic lines—Air New England, American, Continental, Delta, Eastern, New York Air, Northwest Orient, People Express, Piedmont, Republic, TWA, United, USAir, and World Airways, as well as the international lines Aer Lingus, Air Canada, Alitalia, British Airways, Lufthansa, Northwest Orient, Swissair, and TWA. Overseas charter lines also come into Boston's Logan Airport.

There are few airports that are as convenient as Boston's **Logan International Airport,** which is only three miles from downtown, just across the bay.

Rest rooms have 35-inch stall doors and grab bars at all terminal buildings, located on the second floor of the South East Terminal, on the first floors of the South, North, and International Terminals. There are lowered telephones with volume control devices on the first floor of each terminal. For general information, call 617/482-2930; for parking information, 617/567-5400.

Transportation leaving the airport for downtown can be by private car, rental car, or taxi. The airport limousine service does not have wheelchair-accessible vehicles, and although a few of the MBTA (Massachussetts Bay Transportation Authority) rapid-transit train stations are wheelchair accessible, the airport station is not one of them.

Taxi fare (subject to alteration) for the trip downtown is about $5 to $6.

One private transportation company that services the airport and whose vans are equipped with wheelchair lifts is **THEM Inc. (Transportation for the Handicapped and Elderly in Massachussetts),** 21 Water St., Cambridge, MA 02141 (tel. 617/666-8820).

Hand-control rental cars are available at the airport from **Hertz** (tel. toll free 800/654-3131) on three days' notice, and from **National** (tel. toll free 800/569-6700) on one day's notice.

BY TRAIN: Amtrak trains on the Washington-New York-Boston run arrive at the **South Station,** Atlantic Avenue and Summer Street (tel. 617/482-3660, toll free 800/523-5720). The entrance to the station is barrier-free, and rest rooms at the entry level have 28-inch stall doors (women), and 35-inch stall doors (men). There are grab bars in the men's room (but not in the women's).

BY BUS: The **Greyhound Terminal,** 10 St. James St. (tel. 617/423-5810), has a barrier-free interior. (Rest rooms are down a flight of stairs.)

The **Trailways Terminal** is at 55 Atlantic Avenue (tel. 617/482-6620), in the South Station (also used by Amtrak). There are two parking spaces reserved for the disabled in the lot to the right of the building, and the entrance is barrier-free. Rest rooms with wide doors and grab bars are located near the waiting areas. Accessible telephones with volume control devices are near the rest rooms.

BY ROAD: Even Boston's official guide says that "our network of highways is confusing," but they assure the natives are friendly and urge you to stop and ask the way!

From the west, Rte. 90 (Massachusetts Turnpike) is the clearest route inbound, with exits 18 to 20 for Cambridge and Charles River locations; exit 22 for Prudential Center, Back Bay, and Fenway areas; and exit 24 best for downtown.

From the south, Rtes. 95, 24, and 3 feed in to Rte. 28 East, and to Rte. 93, with the Kneeland Street exit for Back Bay, Theater District; and the Dock Square exit for the airport, waterfront, and Faneuil Hall Marketplace.

From the north, Rtes. 95, 1, and 93 enter Boston, with the Storrow Drive exit for Back Bay, Beacon Hill, and Cambridge; the Dock Square exit for the airport, waterfront, and Faneuil Hall Marketplace; the High Street exit for downtown; the Kneeland Street exit for Chinatown and the theater district. (There are even more detailed directions for getting in and out of Boston in the official guide book.)

When you leave Boston, go north via the Tobin Bridge over the Mystic River to connect with I-93 and I-95. To go south, take the Southeast Expressway (Rte. 3). There are two routes to the west—the Massachusetts Turnpike Extension with entrances at Copley Square, Massachusetts Avenue at Newbury Street, and downtown near South Station; and Rte. 2, picked up from Storrow Drive, that runs on the route through Cambridge to Lexington, Concord, and western Massachusetts.

2. Getting Around

Most guides recommend the subways and your feet as the most practical means of transportation around Boston. Since only very few of the subway stations are wheelchair-accessible, and your feet may not be *your* means of locomotion, let's look at the other possibilities.

TAXIS: Taxis can be found either cruising or waiting at stands. Rates are on a metered basis, with (at time of writing) 90¢ for the first 1/6 of a mile and 20¢ for each additional 1/6 mile. Among the companies that can be called are **Boston Cab Co.** (tel. 617/536-5010); **Boston Independent Taxi** (tel. 617/426-8700); **Cambridge Taxi** (tel. 617/876-5000); **Checker Taxi** (tel. 617/536-5000), and **Yellow Cab** (tel. 617/739-9020). For other taxi information, call the Cab Association of Boston, 617/462-8316.

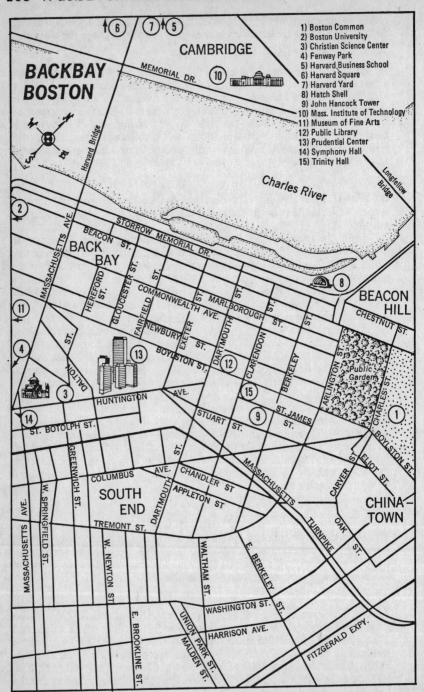

BACKBAY BOSTON

CAMBRIDGE

MEMORIAL DR.

Harvard Bridge

Charles River

Longfellow Bridge

1) Boston Common
2) Boston University
3) Christian Science Center
4) Fenway Park
5) Harvard Business School
6) Harvard Square
7) Harvard Yard
8) Hatch Shell
9) John Hancock Tower
10) Mass. Institute of Technology
11) Museum of Fine Arts
12) Public Library
13) Prudential Center
14) Symphony Hall
15) Trinity Hall

BACK BAY

BEACON HILL

STORROW MEMORIAL DR.

BEACON ST.

COMMONWEALTH AVE.

MARLBOROUGH ST.

NEWBURY ST.

BOYLSTON ST.

HUNTINGTON AVE.

STUART ST.

ST. JAMES ST.

CHESTNUT ST.

Public Garden

MASSACHUSETTS AVE.

HEREFORD ST.

GLOUCESTER ST.

FAIRFIELD ST.

EXETER ST.

DARTMOUTH ST.

CLARENDON ST.

BERKELEY ST.

ARLINGTON ST.

CHARLES ST.

BOYLSTON ST.

ELIOT ST.

DALTON ST.

ST. BOTOLPH ST.

SOUTH END

COLUMBUS AVE.

CHANDLER ST.

APPLETON ST.

TREMONT ST.

GREENWICH ST.

W. SPRINGFIELD ST.

MASSACHUSETTS AVE.

W. NEWTON ST.

E. BROOKLINE ST.

WALTHAM ST.

UNION PARK ST.

MALDEN ST.

WASHINGTON ST.

HARRISON AVE.

E. BERKELEY ST.

MASSACHUSETTS TURNPIKE

CARVER ST.

OAK ST.

CHINA-TOWN

FITZGERALD EXPY.

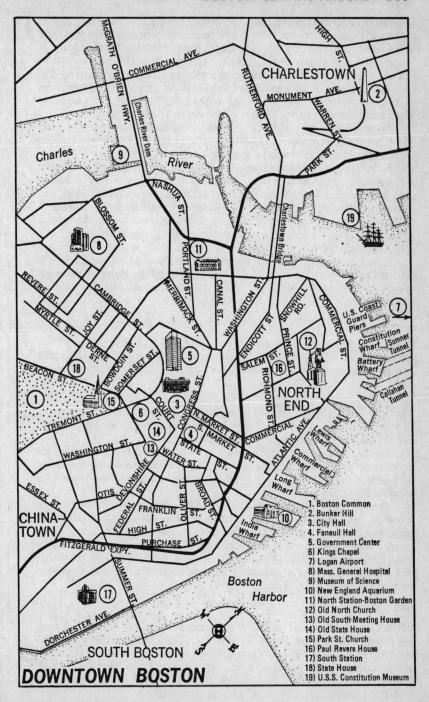

1. Boston Common
2. Bunker Hill
3. City Hall
4. Faneuil Hall
5. Government Center
6) Kings Chapel
7) Logan Airport
8) Mass. General Hospital
9) Museum of Science
10) New England Aquarium
11) North Station-Boston Garden
12) Old North Church
13) Old South Meeting House
14) Old State House
15) Park St. Church
16) Paul Revere House
17) South Station
18) State House
19) U.S.S. Constitution Museum

DOWNTOWN BOSTON

DRIVING AND PARKING: For the visitor, driving around Boston can be confusing; there is a lot of one-way traffic on the older narrower streets, which, to confuse you further, do not have any numerical or alphabetical order.

Parking in Boston is challenging and expensive: in downtown, every curbside space sprouts a pole that bears either a parking meter or a sign saying "No Parking." As new office towers have been built, the number of commercial parking spaces has remained the same as ten years ago. Metered spaces cost $1 an hour, and downtown garages often charge $10 or more a day.

There are a number of public garages in central districts where you can leave the car while you see the sights in the area, and the two largest garages are underground at **Prudential Center** and **Boston Common.**

The **city-owned parking garages** have rates set according to traffic volume and are at St. James Avenue in the Back Bay area, and in Winthrop Square near Summer and Franklin Streets (best for Filene's department store and Downtown Crossing shopping). The Government Center Garage is convenient to the waterfront as well as to North End and the Haymarket. At the time of writing, however, the city is negotiating to sell its garages, which are to be eventually replaced by commercial developments.

Privately owned parking garages and lots can start as high as $2 for the first half hour. There are multilevel garages near the John Hancock Building, Symphony Hall, and the Aquarium. Dock Square Garage is in the Faneuil Hall Marketplace.

RENTAL CAR: Hand-controlled cars are available on three days' notice from Hertz (tel. toll free 800/654-3131), and on one day's notice from **National's** downtown office (tel. 617/426-6830).

PUBLIC TRANSPORTATION: Massachusetts Bay Transportation Authority (MBTA) runs the rapid-transit rail system (some stations accessible), and the buses (inaccessible for wheelchairs).

It also administers a program known as **"The Ride"** that provides door-to-door transportation for disabled residents and long-term visitors, but check with them on availability (617/722-5123), since they are flexible if there is an opportunity to help.

There are accessible stations on three of the city's four rapid transit lines (none on the Green Line). All lines radiate from the center of Boston as subways and then go above ground on trolley lines or elevated railways. However, all stations have vertical or horizontal gaps (or both) of three to six inches between the platform and the cars. Gateways to the platform are 38 inches wide. To get information on routes that are accessible, call the **Customer Service Center** at 617/722-3200.

PRIVATE TRANSPORTATION: Companies that run wheelchair-lift vans are listed in the Yellow Pages. THEM Inc. (Transportation for the Handicapped and Elderly in Massachusetts), which operates "The Ride," also operates privately at a rate of $15 an hour from 8 a.m. to 5 p.m. Monday through Friday, with a supplement for evenings and weekends. THEM Inc. is at 21 Water St., Cambridge, MA 02141 (tel. 617/666-8820).

3. Orientation

For Old World settlement on the East Coast, you can't go much further back than Boston, which was founded in 1630, only ten years after the Pilgrim Fathers landed on Plymouth Rock. You can see the reasons still very much in evidence in its impressive waterfront, which became an important shipbuilding center and a fishing port early in Boston's history. In the center of things, the green oasis of Boston Common dates from the days when it was common grazing ground for colonial sheep.

Around the common are three of the important areas to see in Boston. The area known as **Downtown Crossing** is where most of the Freedom Trail sites are located. Close by, still near the common, is the **theater district** and **China-town.** On the other side of the common is **Beacon Hill,** and to the west of that, also spreading out from yet another side of the common, is **Back Bay,** the only area of Boston that has a grid street system, because it was created about 120 years ago from marsh and tidal flats. Back Bay is a mix of residential, cultural, and commercial activities, including many of Boston's leading shops, as well as an esplanade along the Charles River. Between the common and the water-front is the very active restored area of **Faneuil Hall Marketplace,** and at the waterfront itself, restoration of the whole area is under way with hotels, con-dominiums, and a new Harbor Walk. The **Charles River** separates Boston from **Cambridge.**

Boston's streets just happened, and so you'll find no real pattern: a map to follow as you go is essential. You can get one from the **Visitor Information Bureau,** located at the Tremont Street side of Boston Common (closest parking is the Boston Common Underground Parking Garage), or by writing in ad-vance to the **Boston Convention and Visitors Bureau,** Prudential Plaza, Bos-ton, MA 02199 (tel. 617/267-6446).

There is also a **Tourist Bureau** (tel. 617/367-9275) and a **National Park Service Visitor Center** at 15 State St., (tel. 617/242-5642) opposite the Old State House (nearest parking is at the Government Center Garage or on the Devonshire Street side of the Visitors Center, where there is one parking space reserved for disabled visitors). The Devonshire Street entrance is accessible by ramp, and there are elevators to all floors, with an accessible rest room on the first floor. This is the place to find out about the Freedom Trail and other sites in nearby towns like Lexington and Concord.

An audio-visual show, *Where's Boston?*, gives an insight into the city, with scenes and sounds of the different neighborhoods, museums, sports, and nightlife. It's shown at 60 State St., near Faneuil Hall (tel. 661-2425), daily on the hour from 10 a.m. to 5 p.m., with multi-image screens and quadrophonic sound. Admission is $3 for adults, $1.50 for children under 13, $1.25 for senior citizens. There is curb parking reserved for disabled visitors on Congress Street, near City Hall, with additional parking available in the lot on the corner of Kilby and State Streets, where there are curb cuts. There are no steps at the front entrance, 60 State St. (the door here is 29 inches wide).

You can get a bird's-eye orientation of Boston from the top of two of its tallest buildings. The latest is the **John Hancock Observatory,** in the Back Bay section, 200 Clarendon St. at Copley Sq. (tel. 247-1976), where you see a great panorama from 60 floors up. Parking is available in the John Hancock garage on Clarendon Street and there are curb cuts for the approach to the Hancock Building's barrier-free entrance. An elevator goes directly to the sixtieth floor from street level. The observatory's main entrance is 30 inches wide, but there is another that is 40 inches wide that can be opened on request. Coin-operated telescopes are height-adjustable, and various audio-visual exhibits provide additional information about the city. Rest rooms on the fifteenth floor of the building have stall doors from 28 inches to 33 inches wide. There are accessible telephones on the sixtieth floor. Admission is $2.25 for adults, $1.75 for children from 5 to 15, and $1.50 for senior citizens and students. Hours are 9 a.m. to 11 p.m. on Monday through Saturday, from 10 a.m. to 11 p.m. on Sunday from May to October, and from noon to 11 p.m. November through April. Open daily except for Thanksgiving and Christmas Days.

There's a similarly spectacular view from the top of the **Prudential Tower** just a few blocks away at 800 Boylston St. (tel. 236-3318), although the Skywalk there may not be as convenient for wheelchair users since the coin-operated telescopes are 60 inches high and not adjustable. The Observation Deck here is enclosed, and the sills of the windows are 34 inches from the floor. There are reserved parking spaces on Level Two of the South Parking Garage beneath the Prudential Center. The elevator goes to the fiftieth floor, where there is a level entrance to the observatory. Admission is $2 for adults, $1 for children 5 to 15, and for senior citizens. Open Monday through Thursday from 9 a.m. to 11 p.m., Friday and Saturday from 9 a.m. to midnight, and Sunday from 10 a.m. to 11 p.m.

From either tower you'll see the general layout of Boston, which lies on a peninsula connected by bridges and tunnels to the surrounding area. Looking toward the ocean, you'll see the old wharves (where there are now also apartments, hotels, and marinas), the Mystic River bridge leading north, and to the left of the bridge the Bunker Hill Monument, the beautiful new Waterfront Park, and Faneuil Hall Marketplace. In the center of the peninsula, the large stretch of green is Boston Common and the tree-lined boulevard of Commonwealth Avenue. To the right of Commonwealth Avenue is the Charles River, which separates Boston from Cambridge.

CLIMATE: When you pack for Boston, be prepared for anything: cold winters and hot, sticky summers, but mild and beautiful springs and crisp, clear falls. Don't forget, though, that in the summer, locals will be "down the Cape," and the city will be less crowded. For weather information, dial 936-1234.

AREA CODE: The telephone area code for the Greater Boston area is 617.

INFORMATION AND REFERRAL: Information Center for Individuals with Disabilities: 617/727-5540. Emergency Physician's Service: 617/482-5252.

4. Where to Stay

Boston is no exception to the general rule that the newer (and therefore usually higher priced) hotels are the ones most convenient for people with disabilities. Accommodations with special facilities are listed here, but there are many hotels in all price categories that you'll find listed in the official guide book, especially if you usually find that certain chains are amenable to your particular needs. More than most cities, there is contrast between the gracious style of Old Boston and the sleeker New Boston, with many hotels presently under construction in all areas of the city.

Of course, it's always advisable to book ahead, especially in the vacation months of July and August (many hotels have a toll-free 800 telephone number). In the spring and fall, the popular time for conventions (and Boston is a favorite venue), it is essential to make advance reservations. Parking is available at most hotels and motels, or there are arrangements with nearby garages. Be prepared for the tax of 5.7% on all hotel bills.

Many of Boston's hotels offer dining on gourmet cuisines, as well as lounges and cafes and evening entertainment (see the restaurant and nightlife section of this chapter).

The hotels and motels listed here include the ones in downtown Boston and in Cambridge, convenient to historic areas, that also offer special facilities for disabled guests. There are others included that do not offer special facilities but which have access and wider doors that make them worth considering. In addition, you'll find listed here some that lie farther out, such as at the airport (but still close to downtown), and some "resort" hotels about half-an-hour's drive out of Boston that have special facilities for disabled guests.

Don't forget that all of these establishments offer special packages, primarily on weekends, which you should ask about when you call or write—there may be a free meal or two included or even an extra night's stay. And, as always, be prepared for an increase in the rates quoted here, which are in effect at the time of writing.

DOWNTOWN HOTELS THAT OFFER SPECIAL FACILITIES: Starting with one of Boston's newest hotels (comfortably deluxe and priced accordingly) the **Boston Marriott Hotel/Long Wharf,** 296 State St., MA 02116 (tel. 617/227-0800; toll free for reservations, 800/228-9290), is located on the waterfront and tries to look like an ocean liner heading out to sea. It is near Faneuil Hall Marketplace and Waterfront Park and just across the harbor from Logan International Airport.

The entrance is barrier-free and so is the interior, with elevators to all levels of this multitiered 400-room hotel. Fifty-four rooms have special features for disabled guests, and these include bathroom entry doors 36 inches wide and grab bars at the toilet and bath. Public rest rooms have 34-inch stall doors. The restaurants are all accessible.

Most rooms have views of the waterfront, and rates (subject to change) are $90 to $115 single, $105 to $130 double, with special rates for weekend packages, such as the "Boston Escape," which offers two nights, Saturday breakfast for two, and a Sunday champagne brunch for two for $89.50 per person double occupancy, among other packages. Valet parking is available for an extra charge of $10 a day.

In the brand-new Copley Place complex of hotels, restaurants, and office buildings constructed in 1983 near Copley Square in the Back Bay section, is the **Westin Copley Hotel,** 10 Huntington Ave., MA 02116 (tel. 617/262-9600, toll free 800/228-3000). There is a barrier-free entrance, and in the 40 rooms for disabled guests the entry door is 40 inches wide and the bathroom has a 36-inch entry door that opens outward, with grab bars at the toilet and bath. (*Note:* the regular guest rooms also have 36-inch bathroom doors.) The TV set can be controlled from bedside. Braille is available for hotel information and for telephone use. The public rest rooms have 42-inch entry to cubicles. Restaurants are accessible. Rates (subject to change) are $110 to $140 single, $130 to $160 double.

Rates are slightly lower, but still in the deluxe category, at the **Sheraton Boston,** 39 Dalton St., MA 02199 (tel. 617/236-2000, or toll free 800/325-3535), which is at the Prudential Center in the Back Bay section of the city and adjacent to the Massachusetts Turnpike Extension. There are a barrier-free entrance and elevators to all floors. Some of the 1400 guest rooms have 38-inch bathroom doors opening outward, and bathrooms are equipped with grab bars. All the hotel's restaurants have menus available in braille. The underground parking garage has reserved spaces.

The Sheraton Boston is a large, busy place with four restaurants and a covered passageway to the Prudential Center's shops and boutiques. Each of the rooms provides a spectacular view over Boston. Single rooms range from $86 to $100 and doubles from $99 to $113. Again, there are special packages here, and one, listed at the time of writing, is the "Weekend Splash," which offers two nights in a deluxe room (up to four persons) for $59.90 per night, per room. Some of the restaurants have two or three steps at the entrance, but portable ramps are available.

It's a Howard Johnson's, but the **57 Park Plaza Hotel**, 200 Stuart St., MA 02116 (tel. 617/482-1800, toll free 800/654-2000), is one of Boston's newest hotels and is centrally located downtown near shopping and the theater district, and close to the Public Gardens and Boston Common. Parking in the hotel's garage is free, but mobility-impaired guests should be dropped off in the passenger loading zone, since the ramps leading from the parking garage are quite steep.

There are six steps at the main entrance to the hotel, but there is another entrance on Stuart Street that has a gently sloping ramp. Although the registration desk is in a sunken lobby area, arrangements can be made for you to register elsewhere than at the main desk. The 57 Restaurant, unfortunately, has a lot of steps at the entrance. A number of guest rooms have 31-inch entry to the bathroom, which is equipped with grab bars. Rates are $70 to $80 single, and $80 to $90 double. Don't forget the weekend package, which gives you two nights, dinner and breakfast for two, and other extras, for $74.92 per person, double occupancy (at time of writing).

Although the **Logan Airport Hilton**, MA 02128 (tel. 617/569-9300), is obviously at the airport, remember that Logan is very close to downtown and may be convenient headquarters for a visit to Boston. There is free parking, and the approach and entrance to the hotel is barrier-free. There are guest rooms with bathrooms that have 35-inch entry doors and grab bars. The Appleton's restaurant entry is level and there is a 1:12 ramp leading to the Glass Garden Cafe. Singles here are $60 to $80, doubles $75 to $95.

CAMBRIDGE HOTELS WITH SPECIAL FACILITIES: That architectural pyramid on the banks of the Charles River in Cambridge is the **Hyatt Regency**, 575 Memorial Dr., Cambridge, MA 02139 (tel. 617/492-1234, toll free 800/228-9000). There are 15 rooms on the third floor designed with wide doors; bathrooms have 34-inch doors and are equipped with grab bars. Parking is available for guests at $4 a day, with no in-and-out charges, in a garage adjacent to the hotel. The approach and entrance to the hotel are barrier-free, and all floors are served by elevators. Single rates are $82 to $112, and doubles from $102 to $132, with all kinds of special one-night and two-night packages available. Restaurants are accessible, and the menus are available in braille in Jonah's on the Terrace, open from 7 a.m. to 11:30 p.m.

HOTELS THAT MAY SUIT YOU: Although the hotels that follow here are not deliberately equipped with special facilities, access is relatively easy and bathroom doors are wide.

Beginning in the deluxe category, there is one of the country's most elegant hotels in the grand tradition, the **Copley Plaza**, 138 St. James Ave., MA 02116 (tel. 617/267-5300). It has a barrier-free entrance; guest-room entry is 33 inches wide, and bathroom doors are 29 inches wide. Parking is available at the John Hancock Garage on Clarendon Street for $4 a day. There is gracious ambience everywhere, including the dining facilities, which range from the Palm Court Cafe in the lobby to the gourmet Cafe Plaza, all of which are reasonably accessible. Rates here are $95 to $115 single, $110 to $130 double.

Can you manage with a 27-inch bathroom door? Then there's stylish elegance at the **Colonnade,** 120 Huntington Ave., MA 02116 (tel. 617/424-7000, toll free 800/223-6800). It's deluxe and contemporary, with a European style, located in Boston's Back Bay area across from the Prudential complex and adjacent to the Massachusetts Turnpike Extension. There is parking at the hotel garage, and valet parking is available. The entrance is barrier-free, and all public areas are served by elevators. Rates are $82 to $115 single, $93 to $125 double. Lots of weekend packages.

In a less expensive category, you'll find 31-inch bathroom doors at the **Midtown Hotel,** 220 Huntington Ave., MA 02115 (tel. 617/262-1000), across from the Prudential Center in the Back Bay section. It's also within easy distance of Symphony Hall and the Museum of Fine Arts. There are steps to the restaurant, but otherwise there is level access from the underground garage (free parking) to the hotel. Rates are $48 to $69 single, $58 to $74 double, with good weekend packages that include breakfast and theater tickets.

At the base of Beacon Hill near the Charles River is the **Holiday Inn/ Government Center,** 5 Blossom St., MA 02114 (tel. 617/742-7630, toll free 800/238-8000), which is part of a complex that includes a movie theater and a garage with free parking for guests. There are barrier-free entrances in front and at the side, and all floors, including the garage, are accessible by elevator. Entrances to the guest rooms are 32 inches wide, and bathroom doors are 30 inches wide. Single rates range from $74 and up, and doubles $84 and up, depending on the floor.

Because moderately priced hotels with accessibility are not easy to find, consider whether the three steps at the entrance and a 24-inch elevator door would be a problem for you. The bathrooms in the guest rooms do have 29-inch doors. This is at the **Copley Square Hotel,** 47 Huntington Ave., MA 02116 (tel. 617/536-9000, toll free 800/225-7062), an older but friendly and informal hotel close to many points of interest, and near the entrance to the Massachusetts Turnpike. Parking is available in the adjoining Prudential Center Garage. Singles are $48 to $52, and doubles $60 to $70.

Another moderately priced motel, especially if you're a baseball fan, is **Howard Johnson's Motor Lodge Fenway** at 1271 Boylston St., MA 02215 (tel. 617/267-8300, toll free 800/654-2000). It is adjacent to Fenway Park, home of the Red Sox, and is also convenient to the Back Bay colleges and to the Museum of Fine arts and the Gardner Museum. Parking is available in a lot in front of the motel. There is one step at the entrance and to rooms on the ground floor, with bathroom doors 28 inches wide. Rates are $45 to $57 single, $54 to $67 double.

There is a **Ramada Inn-Boston Airport,** 228 McClellan Hwy., East Boston, MA 02128 (tel. 617/569-5250, toll free 800/228-2828), listed in the Ramada Directory as having "facilities for handicapped travelers." The toll-free reservation number for the hearing-impaired is 800/228-3232. The rates here are $61 single and $71 double.

In Cambridge, in one of its most historic districts, the **Sheraton-Commander,** 16 Garden St., Cambridge, MA 02238 (tel. 617/547-4800, toll free 800/325-3535), is just across the common from Harvard University and is furnished in appropriately neo-Colonial decor. There is a 1:12 ramp that avoids the regular six steps at the entrance. Passenger elevator doors are 27 inches wide, but if that is too narrow for you, the service elevator with a 36-inch door is available for use by guests in wheelchairs. Guest rooms have 33-inch-wide entry doors and 30-inch bathroom doors. Off the lobby is Dertad's, a restaurant noted for its gourmet cuisine, and the Colonial Restaurant, open for breakfast and lunch. Rates at the Sheraton-Commander are $60 to $86 single and $74 to $100 double.

In the moderately priced category, on the Harvard side of the river, is the **Holiday Inn-Cambridge,** 1651 Massachusetts Ave., Cambridge, MA 02138 (tel. 617/491-1000, toll free 800/238-8000), but bathroom doors are only 25 inches wide here. There are two reserved spaces in the motel's free parking lot, and the entrance to the motel is barrier-free. Rates are $52 single, $62 double.

There are wider bathroom doors at the **Holiday Inn,** 30 Washington St., Somerville, MA 02143 (tel. 617/628-1000, toll free 800/238-8000), which is on the Cambridge/Charleston line, near Harvard, Tufts, and MIT, as well as Bunker Hill and the U.S.S. *Constitution.* It is four miles from Logan Airport and about 2½ miles from central Boston. There is a barrier-free entrance, free parking in the motel's lot, and guest rooms with 34-inch-wide bathroom entry. Rates here start at $60 single, $65 double.

The **Harvard Motor House,** 110 Mt. Auburn St., Cambridge, MA 02138 (tel. 617/864-5200) is practically in Harvard Square. It has one step at the entrance and guest rooms with 27-inch bathroom doors. Continental breakfast is included in the price of the room, which is $58 to $60 single, $65 to $67 double, and there is free parking.

RESORTS NEAR BOSTON WITH SPECIAL FACILITIES: Within a half-hour drive of the city, there are resort hotels that offer complete vacation packages as well as special facilities for disabled guests.

About 15 miles from Boston, north on Rte. 128, just off I-95, is the **Hilton at Colonial,** Audubon Rd., Wakefield, MA 01880 (tel. 617/245-9300, toll free 800/882-1653). This is a 200-acre luxury resort, and, for a non-disabled companion, there are things like golf, tennis, and a glass-domed tropical pool (for you too!). The entrance is ramped, and there are a number of guest rooms with special facilities such as 33½-inch bathroom entry and grab bars at toilet and bath. Rates are $47 to $73 single, and $67 to $93 double, with special vacation packages available.

Another country resort about 20 miles from downtown Boston and three miles north of I-95 on the Middlesex Turnpike, is **Stouffer's Bedford Glen Hotel,** 44 Middlesex Turnpike, Bedford, MA 07130 (tel. 617/275-5500). It has 14 rooms with special facilities such as 34¼-inch bathroom doors and grab bars at the toilet and bath. The entrance is barrier-free. Room rates are the same for single and double and range from $86 to $97, with weekend packages ranging from $60 for one night to $125 for two nights per room.

5. Boston Dining

There's more to Boston dining these days than "the bean and the cod." You can eat everything from regional New England fare to American to European and Oriental cuisines.

Yet Boston is still unrivalled for its seafood. Fresh fish and shellfish are landed every day from the fishing boats, and local chefs excel in preparing the fresh lobsters, oysters, clams, mussels, haddock, and flounder, along with a wide variety of chowders and many other seafood delicacies. (The Visitors

Bureau Guide devotes two pages to explaining in detail the seafood to be found on Boston menus.)

Talking of the official guide, you'll find that it includes a *W* in its codes alongside the restaurant listings, which means, in the view of the restaurant, that it has access for wheelchairs, although no criteria are given for the coding. *Boston Magazine,* the monthly that you can pick up at Boston newsstands, also includes the *W* for wheelchair accessibility (again, in the opinion of the restaurant) as well as indications of the price category of the restaurants listed, a useful addition.

I've listed the restaurants according to their price range and the type of cuisine served. As usual, budget eating is not easily found. However, there are innumerable fast food restaurants that you will see on your sightseeing outings that you can easily check out yourself, as well as all the sidewalk cafes in Faneuil Hall Marketplace and elsewhere that are among the delights of warmer weather visits to Boston, and which usually provide easy access. The large population of students in Cambridge also encourages the existence of value-conscious eating places.

It's always a good idea to phone ahead and make reservations, particularly for dinner in the better restaurants. Find out, too, what their parking arrangements are and doublecheck on the particular facilities you need to have a pleasant evening. In Boston, there is a 5% meal tax added to all bills. And, as usual, don't forget that even in the most expensive restaurants you can often eat the same menu for lunch at much lower prices than at dinnertime. Rest room status is *not* included unless it provides facilities for patrons who are in wheelchairs.

CONSIDERED THE BEST ($30 AND UP): The Sheraton Corporation headquarters in Boston has made a showcase out of the new and elegant **Apley's** restaurant in the Sheraton Boston Hotel, 39 Dalton St. (tel. 236-2600) at the Prudential Center. Specializing in "contemporary American" cuisine, it features a variation of the French *nouvelle cuisine* with light sauces and special presentations of the dishes. Delicacies are flown in from all over the world, although New England seafood is also strong on the menu. There is an underground garage and a barrier-free entrance to the hotel. Braille menus are available. Apley's is open for dinner daily from 6 to 10 p.m.

Another stylish hotel restaurant is the **Cafe Plaza** in the Copley Plaza, 138 St. James St. (tel. 267-5300). Amid crystal chandeliers, fresh flowers, and elegant continental menus to match, the Cafe Plaza serves dinner Monday through Saturday from 5:30 to 10:30 p.m., lunch from noon to 2 p.m. Monday through Friday (at lunch, cost will range from $10 to $15). There is parking nearby in the John Hancock garage on Clarendon St., and the hotel and restaurant entrances are barrier-free.

One of the finest French restaurants anywhere is **Maison Robert,** 45 School St. (tel. 227-3370), where there are two restaurants—the formal **Bonhomme Richard** restaurant on the main floor, reached by elevator, and the less formal **Ben's Cafe** on the ground floor. At Bonhomme Richard, lunch is served from noon to 2:30 p.m., and dinner from 6 to 10 p.m. Ben's hours are 11:30 a.m. to 2:30 p.m. for lunch and 5:30 to 9:30 p.m. for dinner. Closed Sunday. In the summer, there is outdoor terrace dining next to the statue of Benjamin Franklin (the Ben of the cafe title) that marks the site of his boyhood home.

Many of Boston's hotel dining rooms get top rating, and another one is **Zachary's** in the Colonnade Hotel in the Back Bay area, at 120 Huntington Ave. (tel. 424-7000). Open for dinner Monday through Friday from 5:30 to 11 p.m., and Saturday until midnight. Closed on Sunday. There is parking available in the hotel garage, and the entrances to the hotel and the restaurant are barrier-free.

UPPER BRACKET (DINNER AROUND $20): Among Boston's many seafood restaurants, there are two which are reasonably accessible to wheelchair patrons. One is **Jimmy's Harbor Side Restaurant,** 242 Northern Ave. (tel. 423-1000), which has a fine view of the harbor. Special children's dinners are available here, too. Lunch is served from 11:30 a.m. to 3 p.m. and dinner from 3 p.m. to 9:30 p.m., Monday to Saturday. Closed on Sunday. Valet parking is available. There is one 7-inch step at the entrance directly into the central dining room; a second dining room facing the ocean is reached by two steps.

Another of the famous seafood restaurants is Boston's oldest (since 1826). It is the **Union Oyster House,** 41 Union St. (tel. 227-2750), between Faneuil Hall and City Hall. There is only a staircase to the main dining room on the second floor, but you can have lunch in the Oyster Bar on the first floor. There is one 2-inch step at the entrance to the building. Lunch is served every day until 5 p.m. Sunday through Friday, and until 6 p.m. on Saturday.

In the North End, on the eighth floor of a converted trade building and with a great view of Boston from high windows, is the **Scotch 'n Sirloin,** 77 N. Washington St. (tel. 723-3677), which features seafood as well as steak. Valet parking is available, and there is one step at the entrance. An attended elevator goes to the eighth floor, where there are two steps into the restaurant lounge and also into one of the four dining areas. Dinner is served from 5:30 to 10:30 p.m. Sunday through Thursday, and until 11:30 p.m. on Friday and Saturday.

Another view of Boston from on high, this time from the thirty-third floor, is from the **Bay Tower Room** of the building at 60 State St. (tel. 723-1666), which is a private executive dining club during the day but is opened to the public 5 p.m. to 10 p.m. daily. Reservations are necessary. There is discounted parking in the 60 State Street garage under the building, with curb-cut access to the building and no steps at the State Street entrance (door here is 29 inches wide). The elevator to the restaurant has 40-inch doors. The restaurant's main entrance is on the thirty-third floor, and a ramp with a slope of 1:7 leads up to the middle-level dining area, and a similar ramp also leads down to the lower-level window seating. Upper-level seating is accessible from the thirty-fourth floor. The cuisine is international with touches of New England.

Still higher, the **Top of the Hub** at the Prudential Tower, 800 Boylston St. (tel. 536-1775), is glass-walled and is a great place to watch the sun set. The emphasis is on seafood, but there are steak and roast beef, too. The lunch menu includes sandwiches and omelets, as well as seafood, with entrees ranging from $4 to $8. Sunday brunch is from 10:30 a.m. to 2 p.m. Hours are 11:30 a.m. to 2:30 p.m. for lunch, 5:30 to 10 p.m. for dinner Sunday through Thursday, and until 11 p.m. on Friday and Saturday. There are reduced parking rates available in the Prudential garage, a barrier-free entrance to the building, and elevators to the top, where there is level entry to the restaurant.

The **Last Hurrah** is in the Parker House, 60 School St., in the Downtown Crossing section (tel. 227-8600). The hotel has a level entrance on Tremont Street, and although there is a flight of steps to the restaurant, a service elevator is available to patrons in wheelchairs, on request. The decor is turn-of-the-century style, and prices for such entrees as Boston scrod or roast beef range from $7 to $10. There is a different chowder on the menu for each day of the week. A "Swing" brunch, with live music on Sunday from 11:30 a.m. to 3:30 p.m., is $13.50. The Last Hurrah is open from 11:30 a.m. to 1 a.m. Monday through Thursday and until 2 a.m. Friday and Saturday.

Copley's, another of the restaurants in the Copley Plaza Hotel, Copley Sq., in the Back Bay section (tel. 267-5300), has Edwardian decor and an international menu in the three intimate dining rooms. There is also a lounge where cocktails and light sandwiches are served. The hotel has a barrier-free entrance, and the restaurant is on the ground floor. Copley's is open for dinner from 6 p.m. to midnight daily, and from 11:30 a.m. to 3 p.m. for lunch. Parking is available at the John Hancock Garage on Clarendon St.

MODERATE (ABOUT $12): Nostalgic decor is popular in Boston, and at **Charley's Eating & Drinking Saloon,** 344 Newbury St., in the Back Bay section (tel. 266-3000), it is Victorian, emphasized by waiters in period costume. The menu here includes steak and fish (entrees from $7 to $10), with very large sandwiches as well (priced from $3.25 to $4). It's just around the corner from the Prudential Center, and there is free valet parking. The entrance has one 2-inch step. Braille menus are available. It is open from 11:30 a.m. to 3:30 p.m. for lunch Monday to Saturday, and from 3:30 p.m. to 1 a.m. for dinner (there are late-night specials if you go after the theater or a concert), and from noon to 1 a.m. on Sunday.

Also near the Prudential Center is **J.C. Hillary's,** 793 Boylston St. (tel. 536-6300), again with turn-of-the-century decor. It is noted for its beef stew, but there are also fish and sandwiches on the menu. Valet parking is available from 6 p.m. to midnight, or there are special parking spaces in the Prudential Center's underground garage. The entrance has two steps and a 28-inch wide door. Rest rooms, up one step, have 36-inch-wide entry and 27-inch-wide stall doors. Braille menus are available. Hillary's is open Monday to Thursday from 11:30 a.m. to midnight, on Friday and Saturday until 12:30 a.m., and on Sunday from noon to 11 p.m.

Near Faneuil Hall Marketplace, there's more turn-of-the-century at **Houlihan's Old Place,** 60 State St. (tel. 367-6377), where the atmosphere is busy and noisy, but fun. Special parking is available nearby on Congress Street and in the Clinton Street garage near the Quincy Market building. The approach to the building has curb cuts, and although you'll see five steps at the main entrance, there is another entrance close by which has a hydraulic lift and a 42-inch door (a buzzer will get staff attention to operate the lift and open the door). There are tables on the main level of the restaurant, but three or four steps to the other dining room and the bar. Rest rooms on the main level have 35-inch stall doors and grab bars. Houlihan's serves light meals during the day and the evening but adds dinners after 5 p.m. Open Monday through Thursday and on Sunday from 11 a.m. to midnight, and on Friday and Saturday until 1 a.m. Sunday brunch is served from 11 a.m. until 4 p.m.

A Boston fixture for a long time, **Dini's Sea Grill,** 94 Tremont St. (tel. 227-0380), serves an extensive menu of seafood, chowders, steaks, and lobster. It's just a few blocks from the Faneuil Hall Marketplace. There are parking garages at 275 Washington Street and 153 Tremont Street, with curb cuts on Tremont Street. The entrance to the dining room is level. Entree prices range from $7 to $12. Braille menus are available here. Dini's is open weekdays for lunch and dinner from 10 a.m. to 9 p.m., and on Sunday from 11 a.m. to 3 p.m. for brunch and from 4 to 9 p.m. for dinner.

In the same Sheraton-Boston Hotel as the elegant Apley's, the moderately priced **Massachusetts Bay Company,** 39 Dalton St. (tel. 236-2600), has a mostly seafood menu. There are special parking spaces in the hotel's underground garage and also on Level 2 of the South Garage under the Prudential Center. The hotel and the restaurant entrance are barrier-free. Lunch is served Monday through Friday from 11:30 a.m. to 2:30 p.m., with a price range of $6.50 to $14. Dinner hours are from 5:30 to 10:30 p.m. daily, with prices from $8.50 to $17.

BUDGET (AROUND $6): There are plenty of hamburger places and delicatessens around that you will come upon as you tour, but among the more notable ones is **Ken's,** 549 Boylston St., at Copley Square in the Back Bay section (tel. 266-6106), which puts emphasis on sandwiches, salads, omelets, steaks, chicken, and fish in a wide range of prices. Open daily from 7 a.m. to 3 a.m., Ken's has a barrier-free entrance and a dining room at street level.

There's Irish fare at the **Black Rose,** 160 State St., near Faneuil Hall Marketplace (tel. 523-8486), with a luncheon buffet for $3.50 Tuesday through Friday from 11:30 a.m. to 3 p.m.

There are a number of **Legal Sea Food** restaurants around Boston; the one in the Statler Office Building, in small cafe style, adjoins one in the Park Plaza Hotel at 64 Arlington St. (tel. 426-5566), but is more casual than the main room there, with lower prices also. There is a ramped entrance from the office building.

Another moderately priced restaurant at Faneuil Hall Marketplace that is accessible is **The Magic Pan,** in the Quincy Market (tel. 523-6105), which specializes in stuffed crepes of all kinds. A 1:12 ramp leads from street level to the first floor of Faneuil Hall, and an elevator with a 35-inch door serves the second-floor location of the restaurant, which has a barrier-free entrance. Rest rooms have 34-inch stall doors and are equipped with grab bars. Menus are available in braille.

INTERNATIONAL: There's a variety of ethnic restaurants in Boston, with emphasis on Italian cooking, especially in the North End. The ones listed here have reasonable accessibility and are in order of price, starting with the more expensive.

Overlooking Boston Common in the theater district is the **Houndstooth Restaurant,** 150 Boylston St. (tel. 482-0722), which features a continental menu with entrees from $8.50 to $15. Open for lunch Monday through Friday from 11:30 a.m. to 2:30 p.m. and for dinner from 5:30 to 11 p.m., with special seating arranged before and after curtain time during the theater season.

An elegant Italian restaurant on the waterfront near the North End is **Stella,** 74 East India Row (tel. 224-3559), with entrees priced from $5.50 to $17.50 at dinner and from $4 to $10 at lunch. Open from 11:30 a.m. to 11:30 p.m. There is validated parking available at the Harbor Tower Garage at 65 East India Row, and barrier-free access to Stella's is by a brick ramp near the Aquarium. Rest rooms have 31-inch stall doors.

There's home-style southern Italian cooking in the North End at **The Pushcart,** 61 Endicott St. (tel. 523-9616), with a price range from $3.25 to $9. Open from 11 a.m. to 3 p.m. for lunch, and from 5 to 10:30 p.m. for dinner Tuesday through Saturday. Parking is available both at the curb and in a lot across the street from the restaurant. There are curb cuts in this area.

Claiming to be Boston's oldest Italian restaurant, also in the North End, **The European,** 218 Hanover St. (tel. 523-5694), has pizzas and complete dinners as well. The entrance has one step.

Crave a Polynesian luau brunch? You'll find it in another of the Sheraton Boston Hotel's restaurants, the **Kon Tiki,** 39 Dalton St., at the Prudential Center (tel. 262-3063), for about $10, served from 11 a.m. to 3 p.m. There's a daily luncheon buffet Monday to Saturday from 11:30 a.m. to 3 p.m. for about $6. Kon Tiki is open every day for dinner from 5 to 11:30 p.m., with meals priced from $10 to $15.

If you're in the mood for Japanese food, there's **Taisei of Japan,** 138 Lewis Wharf (tel. 723-9235), on the waterfront. Although some of the seating is Oriental style on the floor, there is also regular seating. Validated parking is available in a lot on Lewis Wharf. There are curb cuts in the area, and a barrier-free entrance to the restaurant. À la carte entrees range from $5 to $15, and complete dinners are also available. Open for lunch and dinner daily from 11:30 a.m. to 2:30 p.m. and from 5 to 10:30 p.m.

In the theater district there's a German menu with budget prices for lunch and dinner at **Jacob Wirth's,** 31 Stuart St. (tel. 338-8586), with parking in an outdoor lot behind the restaurant. There are two low steps at the front entrance, but the rear entrance from the parking lot has only a low threshold. The main dining room is up a 6-inch step, but there are also tables in the bar area, which is level with the entrance. Open Monday through Thursday from 11 a.m. to 8 p.m., on Friday and Saturday until 9 p.m.

CAFES: Sidewalk cafes often offer easy accessibility, even if there are steps into the indoor restaurant to which they are attached, and they can be one of the most pleasant ways to have a meal. Among them are **Ben's Cafe** at Maison Robert, 45 School St., with a French menu. There are three cafes on Newbury Street in the Back Bay section. The **Cafe Florian,** at no. 85, serves drinks, light meals, or full-course continental dinners. The **Travis Restaurant,** at no. 135, is informal and inexpensive—you can get your sandwiches or hamburgers and take them to the tables out front. More expensive than the foregoing is **Cafe l'Ananas** at no. 279.

Faneuil Hall Marketplace almost looks like one big outdoor cafe in the summer, and one of the most popular places is the **Cafe at Lily's,** overlooking the busy plaza's flower market, which serves light meals from early morning until late at night. You'll find others here, too.

If you prefer your cafes *indoors,* there's always the quiet elegance of the **Promenade Cafe** in the Colonnade Hotel, 120 Huntington Ave. (tel. 261-2800), open for all meals from 7 a.m. to 11:30 p.m.; and you can even have a full English tea among the palms in **Copley's Court** in the Copley Plaza Hotel (tel. 267-5300), complete with watercress and chicken sandwiches, scones and strawberry preserves with cream, hot buttered crumpets, and an English trifle. Both Back Bay hotels have barrier-free entrances, and their cafes are level with the entrance.

EATING IN CAMBRIDGE: Cambridge is so close to Boston that it's easy to reach even if you only go for the dining. You'll rub elbows with students and faculty from Harvard, Radcliffe, and MIT, and there's a wide variety of price categories to choose from.

In the higher-price bracket are the restaurants in the hotels there, but the prices are justified by the cuisine. At **Dertad's** in the Sheraton-Commander Hotel, 16 Garden St., near Harvard Square (tel. 354-1234), there is a continental-French menu with à la carte entrees starting at $12.50. Parking is available in the Sheraton lot or at metered curb spots on Garden Street. The entrance to the hotel has a 1:12 ramp, and restaurant rest rooms have 31-inch stall doors. Open nightly from 6 to 11 p.m., and reservations are necessary.

Two restaurants in the Hyatt Regency Cambridge, 575 Memorial Dr. (tel. 492-1234), are noted for their Sunday brunch. At the **Empress** at the top of the hotel, the menu is Szechuan, Mandarin, and Cantonese, served with a view of the Charles River from 11:30 a.m. to 3 p.m. at $13.75 per person. Also in the Hyatt Regency in Cambridge is **Jonah's on the Terrace** with its Sunday brunch, overlooking either the river or the terrace, from 10 a.m. to 3 p.m., and priced at $14.50 for adults, $10.50 for children under 12. Jonah's also has a Wednesday night seafood buffet for about $12.

Trees and plants bloom under the skylight at the **Atrium Cafe** in Harvard Square, at 50 Church St. (tel. 491-3745), where you can sit by the waterfall amid this garden setting for lunch or dinner, and where the menu features sandwiches, salads, and continental specialties at moderate prices. There is parking in a lot on Church Street or metered at the curb. Rest rooms have 33-inch stall doors. The Atrium is open on weekdays from 11 a.m. to midnight, on Friday to 1 a.m., and on Saturday and Sunday from 9:30 a.m. to 1 a.m.

There's a very Italian atmosphere at **La Groceria**, 853 Main St. (tel. 547-9258) off Central Square. Daytime specials range from $2.95 to $5.95 and dinner entrees from $6.50 to $10.50. Open for lunch from 11:30 a.m. to 3 p.m., and for dinner from 5:30 to 10 p.m., to 11 p.m. on weekends.

AT FANEUIL HALL MARKETPLACE: There's a cross-section of prices in the group of restaurants that make up the **Landmark Inn**, 300 N. Market St. (tel. 227-9660), in the Faneuil Hall Marketplace, on different levels in the building and reached by an elevator with a 36-inch door.

Upstairs is the **Wild Goose,** an elegant room specializing in goose, venison, duckling, and other game, as well as steak and fish. Entrees range from $9 to $15, and dinner is served here from 6 to 10 p.m. Monday through Thursday, until 11 p.m. on Friday and Saturday. Lunch is from noon to 2 p.m. on Monday through Saturday.

The **Landmark Cafe** is an indoor-outdoor sidewalk cafe serving hamburgers, steaks, and ribs, with live music nightly after 7 p.m. Dinner entrees range from $5 to $7, and lunch is $3.50 to $4.50. Open from 11:30 a.m. to 11:30 p.m. In the restored cellar (reached by elevator) is **Thompson's Chowder House** and its seafood specialties. Entree prices start at $7. It is open for lunch Monday through Saturday from 11:30 a.m. to 4 p.m., for dinner Monday through Thursday from 5:30 to 10:30 p.m., and until 11 p.m. on Friday and Saturday. Sunday hours are 4 to 10:30 p.m., with brunch served from 11 a.m. to 3 p.m.

Special parking is available on Congress Street near City Hall, and there is also a parking garage on Clinton Street. There are curb cuts in the approach to the entrance, which has a 34-inch door and no steps. Rest rooms have 33-inch stall doors and grab bars.

6. Sightseeing

For starters, Boston is the city of Paul Revere, the Boston Tea Party, the Battle of Bunker Hill, and all the other historic shrines that signify this is the place where the United States of America began. With the coming of independence, it was the Adams family of Boston that gave the nation two of its early presidents, and with the city's growing prosperity came some of the finest buildings in the country at the time. Recently, 350 years from the beginning, the "New Boston" has emerged, with vast projects transforming downtown and

Back Bay. All these periods of Boston's momentous history make the city a great place to visit, and one that offers a great deal for the disabled visitor to enjoy.

Boston is a leisurely place to see the sights, and most of the major ones can be seen within a period of two or three days. The places included here are only those considered reasonably accessible to people in wheelchairs, or which provide information and special facilities specifically for visitors with hearing or visual impairments. Where there are parking spaces reserved for people with disabilities, these are indicated by the phrase "reserved parking" or "special parking."

Note: There are many sightseeing tours, but none of their vehicles have facilities for passengers in wheelchairs.

KEY TO THE NUMBERED REFERENCES ON OUR MAP OF THE FREEDOM TRAIL:
1.—Faneuil Hall; 2—Faneuil Hall Market; 3—Boston Massacre Site; 4—Old State House; 5—Site of Benjamin Franklin Birthplace; 6—Old South Meetinghouse; 7—Old Corner Bookstore; 8—Statue of Benjamin Franklin erected 1856; 9—Site of the First Public School, 1635; 10—Granary Burying Ground; 11—Park Street Church; 12—Boston Common; 13—State House and Archives Museum; 14—King's Chapel; 15—King's Chapel Burying Ground; 16—Paul Revere House; 17—Paul Revere Mall; 18—Old North Church; 19—Copp's Hill Burying Ground; 20—Boston Tea Party Ship and Museum; 21—Bunker Hill Monument; 22—U.S.S. *Constitution* *("Old Ironsides").*

THE FREEDOM TRAIL:
This is a pre-planned, self-guided tour that takes you past 16 of Boston's significant historic sites; a red line on the streets and sidewalks will tell you that you are still on the trail. It is spread out over an area of three or four square miles in the downtown section and in Charlestown, so how much you cover at one time will depend on your stamina and your own limitations. There are two loops to the Freedom Trail—one through downtown Boston, and the other through the North End.

Boston Common is as good a place to start as any, especially if you go first to the Visitors Information Center on the Tremont side of the Common (there is parking in the Boston Common underground parking garage). The common, incidentally, is as old as Boston since it dates back to the 1630s and is the oldest public area in the United States. In colonial times it was common pastureland and also a militia training ground. The east side of it is a little hilly, but at the west side, facing the formal Public Gardens, you'll find major outdoor events taking place (in the area where British troops were mustered before heading for Lexington and Concord).

The common is bordered by Beacon, Tremont, Boylston, and Charles Streets, and is open from 7 a.m. to midnight. There are six parking spaces reserved for disabled visitors in the underground parking garage beneath the common, with the entrance off Charles Street. There are elevators to ground level. The common is accessible by curb cuts on Tremont, Boylston, and Charles Streets, but avoid the Beacon Street entrance where there are several flights of steps. Most of the pathways throughout the common are paved.

Across the common, Beacon Street leads to Beacon Hill, and although some of the terrain here could present hill-type problems for anybody with mobility impairments, a car or a motorized wheelchair could be the answer.

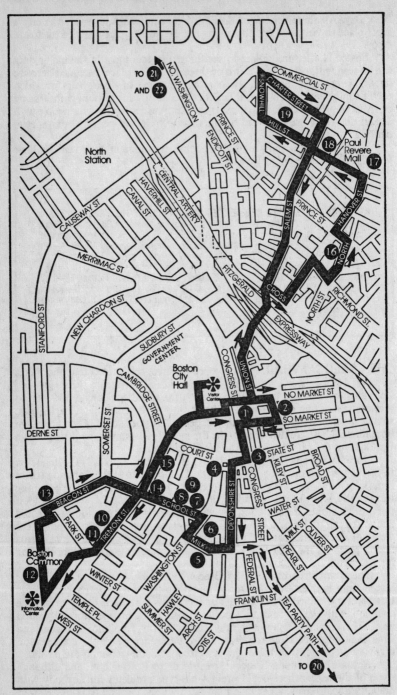

Atop Beacon Hill is one of the first stops on the Freedom Trail: the "new" **State House,** with its impressive gold dome, was actually built in 1795 to replace the smaller "old" State House (also on the Freedom Trail). It is located on Beacon Street at Park and Bowdoin Streets (tel. 727-3676), and is the meeting place of the Massachusetts State Legislature. Its historic credentials are impressive: Samuel Adams laid the cornerstone, and the original dome was once done in copper purchased from Paul Revere. There are five parking spaces reserved for disabled visitors in the rear of the legislators' parking lot, on Mt. Vernon Street, and the barrier-free entrance is directly opposite. Inside, everything is accessible by ramp or elevator, and rest rooms on the second floor have 33-inch-wide stall doors. There's a pamphlet called "Wheeling Through the State House" available at the tour guide station, and there are free guided tours every weekday on the hour from 10 a.m. to 4 p.m.

One of the things to enjoy here is the Archives Museum, replete with old documents, maps, guns, and even copies of the acts against witchcraft. During the winter, the Archives Museum provides signed tours for deaf visitors, and visitors with visual impairments are encouraged to touch some of the exhibits here. The State House and the Archives are open Monday through Friday from 9 a.m. to 5 p.m.

The **Park Street Church,** at the corner of Park and Tremont Streets, is one of Boston's most historic churches, dating from 1809, with its white steeple and original interior. It is open Tuesday through Saturday from 9:30 a.m. to 4 p.m., with Sunday services held at 10:30 a.m. and 7:30 p.m. Curb parking is reserved for disabled visitors on Beach Street between Park and Bowdoin Streets, and there are curb cuts in the approach to the main entrance, which has one step. A level entrance to the right on Tremont Street is usually kept locked but will be opened if you notify church personnel around the corner at 1 Park Street. Services are held on the second floor, but an elevator is available on request.

Just to the left of the Park Street Church on Tremont Street is the **Granary Burying Ground** (it was once the site of a public granary). Some of America's luminaries are buried here, including John Hancock, Samuel Adams, Paul Revere, and Benjamin Franklin's parents (he was born in Boston). It is open daily from 8 a.m. to 4 p.m. but may present some problems, since there are four 8-inch steps at the entrance and rather uneven stone paths inside. However, pause here and consider the significance to American history of those who rest here; it is part of the Boston experience.

Nearby is the **King's Chapel,** 58 Tremont St. (tel. 523-1749), the first Episcopal church in Boston, built in 1754. Now Unitarian-Universalist services are conducted here, and it is open Tuesday through Saturday from 10 a.m. to 4 p.m. The chapel entrance is barrier-free. The historic burial ground adjacent has one 7-inch step at the entrance and stone-surfaced pathways.

Following the red Freedom Trail line you'll eventually come to the corner of Washington and Milk Streets where you see the **Old South Meetinghouse** at 300 Washington St. (tel. 482-6439), used by the early colonists for both religious and political meetings, including those turbulent ones that led to the Boston Tea Party. It has an 8-inch step at the entrance. Today it's a fascinating museum of revolutionary history, even displaying a vial of tea washed up after the Tea Party to emphasize the Meetinghouse's claim that "the Boston Tea Party started here December 16, 1773." Open daily from 10 a.m. to 4 p.m. in the winter, and from 10 a.m. to 6 p.m. in the summer. Admission is 50¢ for adults, 25¢ for children 6 to 16, under 6, free. There is parking available at 367 Washington St.

Next on the official Freedom Trail itinerary is the **Old State House** at 206 Washington St. (tel. 523-7033), a historic gem but an accessibility problem, with nine 7-inch steps at the entrance and a spiral staircase inside. Sorry, wheelchair visitors! But if you *are* able to go inside, you'll find a priceless collection of colonial and revolutionary memorabilia at this original seat of colonial government built in 1712. It is open daily from 9:30 a.m. to 5 p.m. Admission is 75¢ for adults, 50¢ for students, and 25¢ for children.

Even if you don't go inside the Old State House, you can see the ring of cobblestones outside that marks the scene of the Boston Massacre that took place on March 5, 1770, when British soldiers clashed with some protesting Bostonians and five colonists died, an event that signalled the mood for revolution.

One of the most active centers of unrest before the revolution—it was known as the "Cradle of Liberty"—was **Faneuil Hall**, built in 1742 on Merchants Row in Quincy Market (tel. 223-6098) as a market place and meeting hall. It was also built to be impressive, which means atop a flight of steps. Actually, you won't miss much if you don't go inside; the ground floor is a produce market, and the upstairs is used as a meeting hall for state and local civic and political groups. The top floor houses a collection of weapons of the Ancient and Honorable Artillery Company of Massachusetts, but there are no elevators. National Park personnel are available for aid and information. (Now you're next to the Faneuil Hall Marketplace, which is a must for cafes and shopping; details are covered later in this section.)

Faneuil Hall is the end of the southern loop of the Freedom Trail; the northern loop begins at the North End (where most curbs are ramped) on the other side of the Fitzgerald Expressway, at the **Paul Revere House,** 19 North Square (tel. 227-0972). This two-story wooden house is the oldest structure in Boston; it was already some 90 years old when Revere bought it in 1770. You probably don't need to be told about the historic ride of Paul Revere, the silversmith, from Boston to Lexington and Concord to warn the patriots of the advance of the British, but this is where it all started. (You'll see his saddle-bags.) There is curb parking reserved for disabled visitors one block away at 185 Fulton St. and 190 Commercial St. The streets and sidewalks around the house are brick and cobblestone but not *too* bumpy a ride, and there is one step at the entrance, which has a 32-inch-wide door. Inside, the doors vary in width, the narrowest being the kitchen entrance, 29 inches wide, but all the passages inside are at least 36 inches wide. The upper floor is decorated in 18th-century style but is only accessible by a flight of stairs. However, you can see photos of this floor if you can't get there, and will be charged only half the full admission price, which is $1 for adults and 25¢ for children. Visitors with visual impairments are allowed to touch the objects kept behind railings. The Paul Revere House is open daily from 9:30 a.m. to 5:30 p.m. in the summer and from 10 a.m. to 4 p.m. in the winter.

A few blocks away is **St. Stephen's Church** at 24 Clark St. (tel. 523-1230), an historic Catholic church built in 1802. There is reserved curb parking about three blocks away on Commercial Street, and there are curb cuts at the approach to the church. The main entrance has three 6-inch steps, and wheelchair seating is available in the rear of the church and along the main aisle.

If you go through the little park at James Rego Square (which has a statue of Paul Revere on horseback), you'll emerge at the **Old North Church,** 193 Salem St. (tel. 523-6676), perhaps Boston's most famous landmark, since it was from here that the lanterns were hung on the eve of the Revolution to signal that the British were approaching Boston by sea. Built in 1723, it is also Boston's oldest existing church still in use, and was modeled in the style of Sir

Christopher Wren's buildings, with a red brick façade and a tall steeple. There is curb parking available on Hanover Street, although be warned that the streets around this area are very narrow. There is one low step into the church and wide aisles inside, with wheelchair seating in the center aisle. Old North Church is considered "about a five-minute walk" from the Paul Revere House, and fortunately there are quite a few curb cuts in this area, which is known as the North End. Old North Church is open daily from 9 a.m. to 5 p.m.; Sunday services are held at 9:30 a.m. and 11 a.m.

From here the Freedom Trail is all uphill, and at the top is **Copp's Hill Burial Ground,** used as early as 1660, where Cotton Mather is buried along with other early Bostonians, but unfortunately there are six steps at the entrance and brick paths inside that are sometimes quite steep as well as irregularly surfaced. However, if you have made it to the top in a car or by some other means of locomotion, you'll be able to see across the river to Charlestown to the Bunker Hill Monument and the masts of the U.S.S. *Constitution* (*"Old Ironsides"* of the War of 1812)—the next stops on the Freedom Trail.

To reach this part of the Freedom Trail across the river, a suggested route by car from Copps Hill is along Commercial Street, over the Charlestown Bridge, and take a right turn on Constitution Road toward the Boston Navy Yard. You can request to discharge disabled passengers close to the *Constitution,* and there are two special parking spaces in the free parking lot. The U.S.S. *Constitution,* built in 1797, is the oldest commissioned warship afloat. Access to the main deck involves one step followed by a wooden ramp with 1-inch treads every so often, and by another ramp with a 1:4 slope. Although the Spar Deck is the only one accessible to visitors in wheelchairs, there are some interesting things to see here, and admission is free. Objects such as guns and ropes are touchable by visitors with visual impairments. The ship is open daily from 9:30 a.m. to 3:50 p.m. The **Constitution Museum** (tel. 242-0543), is located 200 yards from the ship and an admission fee is charged here of $1.75 for adults and 50¢ for children from 6 to 16. The front entrance has steps but there is a barrier-free entrance at the rear where you can have the door opened by pressing the buzzer. Rest rooms and some of the displays are located on the second floor, reached by elevator. Rest rooms have 34-inch-wide stall doors and are equipped with grab bars.

Refreshment Note: Near the *Constitution* is the **Front Page Restaurant,** 29 Austin St. (tel. 242-5010), with reserved parking spaces opposite the restaurant entrance, which is barrier-free. Rest rooms have 35-inch stall doors and grab bars. The menu features steaks, seafood, and sandwiches at moderate prices. The Front Page is open Monday through Saturday from 11:30 a.m. to 1 a.m., and on Sunday from 11 a.m. to 3 p.m.

It's uphill from here to the **Bunker Hill Monument** (tel. 242-9562), and it probably makes sense to drive there. If you do, ask the guides at the Navy Yard for instructions, since there are narrow one-way streets en route. The 220-foot monument commemorates the Battle of Bunker Hill on June 17, 1775, and since the only way to the top is by climbing 284 steps, you'll probably decide just to drive by or to go and see the exhibits at the National Park Service Lodge at the base of the monument (reached by a ramped approach). There is one step into the building, which has exhibits related to the battle. The women's rest room here has a 30-inch stall door and grab bars. The men's rest room has an outdoor entrance 30 inches wide, also with grab bars.

BEACON HILL: Although it is one of the highlights of most guide books for the Boston visitor, they usually warn that Beacon Hill involves a great deal of walking and climbing. Reluctantly it must be said that details of the elegance and charm of the 19th-century architectural gems of this area on the northern side of Boston Common may not be a feasible part of a guide book for disabled visitors, depending on factors such as the stamina of your motorized chair or of any companion who is pushing your wheelchair, or of your ability to negotiate the red-brick sidewalks. You may want to take a quick pass-through in a car to get its flavor, but be ready for very narrow streets and impossible parking. (The tourist buses don't get there.)

FANEUIL HALL MARKETPLACE: The historic Faneuil Hall Marketplace has been recently renovated to create a miniature city in itself with stores, restaurants, food markets, entertainment, and a lively nightlife. The three 500-foot-long buildings were first opened in 1826 directly behind historic Faneuil Hall, and were the most impressive urban developments of 19th-century America. Now, 150 years after Mayor Josiah Quincy opened the original, it is once more alive with shoppers, eaters, and just people-watchers. The copper-domed center building is named after Mayor Quincy and has restaurants, delicatessens, and sidewalk cafes, as well as food stands of every kind. Under glass canopies on either side is the Bull Market where artisans sell wares of all kinds from pushcarts.

There is reserved parking on Congress Street near City Hall, and parking is also available in the Government Center parking garage on Congress and Sudbury Streets, as well as in an outdoor lot on Commercial Street. There are curb cuts here, but the original cobblestones remain in many parts of the marketplace. In the **Quincy Market Building** are barrier-free entrances at the ends and sides of the canopied areas. Most of the food carts, bars, and small shops under the glass canopy are at street level, although stores and restaurants in the basement down five steps may have to do without your patronage. There are steps, but also 1:10 ramps, into the hall proper, where there are a variety of fast-food counters and a central lobby with tables for eating. You can reach restaurants and exhibits on the third level via an elevator. Rest rooms are downstairs, with narrow stalls.

The **South Market** and the **North Market,** on either side of Quincy Market, house fine restaurants and some rather elegant shops. Both buildings have elevators that give access to the shops on the second floors. The South Market Arcade has rest rooms (located to the left of the entrance) that have 34-inch stall doors and grab bars. There are accessible telephones near the rest rooms.

Hours at the Marketplace are 10 a.m. to 8 p.m. Monday through Saturday, and 1 to 6 p.m. on Sunday, but some restaurants open early for Sunday brunch and remain open until 2 a.m. daily.

WATERFRONT: Although water at one time lapped at the doors of what is Faneuil Hall Marketplace, and clipper ships and fishing boats were once tied to the docks there, the waterfront is now a bit farther away, but it is very much a part of Boston's revival of its historic past. Ramshackle warehouses are being rebuilt as restaurants, apartments, and offices (Marriott's Long Wharf Hotel is here), and there is a new two-mile Harborwalk under construction, which is a trail linking the historic area to the ocean.

Waterfront Park between Long Wharf and Commercial Wharf is a grassy public park directly on the harbor. Parking is available in the Harbor Tower parking garage, or in a lot nearby on Lewis Wharf. There are curb cuts that provide access to the park, but look out for some of the cobblestone crosswalks if you find them difficult to negotiate. Most of the park is on one level although there is a rather steep ramp to the raised fountain area.

On the Harborwalk at Fort Point Channel on Congress Street you'll find the **Boston Tea Party Shop and Museum** (difficult access here) and the much more easily accessible **Children's Museum**, 300 Congress St. (tel. 338-1773, TDD 426-6500), which has lots of touchable interactive exhibits for children of all ages. Reserved parking spaces are in front of the building (behind an orange gate, which is not locked). A ramped entrance and elevator at the rear of the building services all the public areas but must be operated by a special card obtained at the front desk. The height of the exhibits ranges from floor level to 45 inches. The Information Desk has material on the best routes through the museum for visitors in wheelchairs, as well as museum information in braille. Rest rooms have 34-inch stall door and grab bars.

SIGHTSEEING CRUISES: While you're on the waterfront, consider taking
one of the many cruises available around the harbor, or a little farther afield. Most of the boats are accessible for wheelchairs.

Harbor cruises leave from Long Wharf near the Marriott Hotel. For more information call **Boston Harbor Cruises** (tel. 227-4321) or **Bay State Cruise Line** (tel. 723-7800). Costs are around $3 or $4, and sailing times are usually between 10 a.m. and 5 p.m.

The **Massachusetts Bay Line** (tel. 542-8000) sails from Rowes Wharf (farther along Atlantic Avenue) to George's Island daily.

MUSEUMS: Boston museums are among the finest in the country and they
cover a lot of subjects—art, science, transportation, and plant, sea, and animal life.

The **Museum of Fine Arts** in the Fenway district at 465 Huntington Ave. (tel. 267-9300) is one of Boston's popular institutions, noted for an international collection ranging from ancient Egyptian sculpture to contemporary paintings in 200 galleries that can keep you busy for days. Special parking is on Huntington Avenue in front of the museum, and there is a barrier-free entrance at the new West Wing, now the main entrance. All floors can be reached by elevator (but there are four steps to the gift shop). Accessible rest rooms are on the second floor. Details of sign-language tours are available at the information desk, and a tactile tour with portable tape-recorded information is also available. The new West Wing has a tree-lined sidewalk cafe in the atrium, and there is gourmet cuisine in the glass-walled Fine Arts Restaurant on the second floor of the Galleria. Museum hours are 10 a.m. to 5 p.m. Tuesday to Sunday until 10 p.m. on Wednesday; the West Wing is also open until 10 p.m. on Thursday and Friday. Both are closed Monday and some holidays. Admission is $3 for adults during regular hours, $2 for senior citizens, free for children 16 and under. Admission to the West Wing only during the additional hours on Thursday and Friday is $2. There is free admission on Saturday from 10 a.m. to noon. Call 267-9377 for recorded listings of events.

World-renowned for its collection of Italian masters, French Impressionists, American painters, and Eastern art, the **Isabella Stewart Gardner Museum** is in the same district, at 280 Fenway (tel. 566-1401). It is housed in what was Mrs. Gardner's private house (more like a Venetian palazzo), with a breathtaking skylighted courtyard filled with fresh flowers appropriate to the season. There is curb parking and a barrier-free entrance. Access to upper floors, normally reached by staircase, can be arranged by escorted elevator in the rear of the building. Concerts are given in the Tapestry Room on Sunday at 3 p.m., at 12:15 p.m. on Thursday, and at 6 p.m. on Tuesday (except in July and August). The Tuesday and Thursday concerts are free. Hours are noon to 9 p.m. on Tuesday (except July and August), and noon to 5 p.m. Wednesday through Sunday (closed on Monday and national holidays). There is a voluntary admission fee of $1. Lunch and desserts are served in a small cafe. Call 734-1369 for information on exhibits and programs.

One of Boston's most popular sights is the **New England Aquarium** at Central Wharf (tel. 742-8830), which features dolphins, sea lions, giant turtles, sharks, and many other fish in natural environments. If you are driving, take the Dock Square-Callahan Tunnel or Atlantic Avenue exits from the expressway. Parking is available in the Harbor Towers parking garage at 65 East India Row, but there is a rather steep exit ramp from here to the main entrance, which is barrier-free. Because the normal way to view the central tank is from a long and rather steep spiral ramp, make sure before you go in that the freight elevator is available if you need it. An attendant-operated elevator serves the adjacent Discovery Boat, which houses the aquarium's floating auditorium, where there is a sea lion and dolphin show that has level wheelchair locations at the rear. Hours are 9 a.m. to 5 p.m. Monday through Thursday; 9 a.m. to 9 p.m. on Friday, Saturday, and Sunday; 9 a.m. to 6 p.m. on holidays. Admission is $5 for adults, $2 for children; $4 on Friday from 4:30 p.m. to 9 p.m.

Look-and-touch involvement and something for everyone in more than 400 participatory displays ranging from astronomy to zoology are available at the **Museum of Science and Hayden Planetarium** at Science Park (tel. 742-6088), which is on the Charles River between Boston and Cambridge. There are four reserved parking spaces to the left of the main entrance near the planetarium, and curb cuts give access to the main entrance at ground level. Attended elevators serve all the public areas. Rest rooms at the entrance level have 31-inch stall doors. Low drinking fountains and telephones with volume control are on the first floor of the east wing. Braille directories can be borrowed from the ticket counter, where you can also get a guide to the layout of the museum if you are using a wheelchair. With advance notice, arrangements can be made for a tour with a guide who is familiar with the needs of patrons with either sight or hearing impairments. Hours are 9 a.m. to 4 p.m. on Tuesday through Thursday, until 10 p.m. on Friday, and from 10 a.m. to 5 p.m. on Sunday. Closed on Monday from September through May. Admission is $4.50 for adults, $2.75 for children 5 to 16, for senior citizens, and students; on Friday evening $2 for adults and $1 for all others. There are two shows daily in the planetarium, and admission is 50¢ above museum admission.

A short drive of about 8 miles to Columbia Point on Dorchester Bay will bring you to the **John Fitzgerald Kennedy Library** (for information, call 617/929-4523), perched on a hill at the edge of the sea, with a striking view overlooking Boston Harbor and designed by famous architect I. M. Pei. It houses the documents, photographs, recordings, and film clips that commemorate the life and times of the 35th President of the United States. To get there from downtown Boston, drive south on the Southeast Expressway (Rte. 3) to exit 17 (marked Kennedy Library), and follow the signs. There are reserved parking spaces in the free parking lot and a barrier-free entrance with an elevator between floors. Rest rooms on the first floor have 34-inch stall doors and grab bars. The movie theater on the first floor has wheelchair locations. Average height of the exhibits on the lower level is 25 inches. The last showing of the film begins at 3:50 p.m. Open daily from 9 a.m. to 5 p.m. Admission is $1.50 for adults, free for children under 16.

CAMBRIDGE: Across the Charles River is America's most famous college town, Cambridge, where the country's oldest college, Harvard University, and the Massachussetts Institute of Technology (MIT) are located. Harvard Square can be the most lively and stimulating spot you might visit during your trip to Boston. You can drive there from Boston by taking Storrow Drive, Memorial Drive, or Massachusetts Avenue north; or by crossing the Longfellow Bridge and following Broadway north.

Your first stop should be at the Harvard Information Center at Holyoke Center (tel. 495-1573), at the corner of Dunster Street and Massachussetts Avenue, where you can get a detailed map of the university and the surrounding area. Student volunteers conduct guided tours of Harvard Yard from June to Labor Day, but during term time, tours leave from Byerly Hall Admissions Office (off Appian Way). These tours do not go into the buildings.

Stroll down Brattle Street with its great little bookstores and boutiques and see the pre-Revolutionary British neighborhood of Tory Row. At no. 105 you can see Longfellow House (tel. 876-4491), where the books and furniture have stayed unchanged since the poet died there in 1882. The mansion was also used by George Washington as headquarters during the Revolutionary War. Disabled visitors may park in the driveway. The side door has no steps, and major displays are on the ground floor. Open daily from 10 a.m. to 4:30 p.m. Admission is 50¢ for adults, free for children.

There are several important museums at Harvard. One of them, the **Fogg Art Museum** near Harvard Yard at 32 Quincy St. (tel. 495-2387), is known for its collections of Oriental art, late medieval Italian paintings, and French paintings and drawings from the 18th century through the Impressionists. There is metered curb parking on Quincy Street and also in a lot off Prescott Street near the museum's rear service entrance, which has a small ramp (the main entrance has 14 steps). You can also arrange to use the service elevator to reach the upper floor by calling in advance. Open Monday through Friday from 9 a.m. to 5 p.m.; on Saturday from 10 a.m. to 5 p.m., and on Sunday from 2 to 5 p.m. The Fogg Museum is closed on weekends from July 1 to Labor Day.

There are four museums in one at the **Harvard University Museum,** 24 Oxford St. (tel. 495-1910): the Peabody Museum of Anthropology and Ethnology, the Museum of Comparative Zoology, the Botanical Museum, and the Mineralogical and Geological Museum. There is curb parking on Oxford and Kirkland Streets, but disabled visitors can obtain permission to use the university's staff parking lot by calling in advance. Since most of the main entrances have long flights of steps, the best way to enter is through the service door of the Museum of Comparative Zoology on Agassiz Street, which has a ramp with a slope of 1:12. Long flights of stairs also connect the floors of the museum, but advance arrangements can be made to use the service elevator.

Before you leave Harvard Square, take a look at one of its more commercial sights, the **Harvard Cooperative Society (The Coop),** 1400 Massachusetts Ave. (tel. 492-1000), a very large department store with practically everything, and an annex that emphasizes books, records, posters, and original prints. There is metered curb parking and an outdoor lot on Church Street. Entrances on Massachusetts Avenue are barrier-free, and you can reach the Annex on Palmer Street by a connecting enclosed overpass on the third and fourth floors. All floors are served by a public elevator. Rest rooms have 27-inch stall doors. Open Monday and Wednesday through Saturday from 9:20 a.m. to 5:45 p.m.; Tuesday, 9 a.m. to 8 p.m.

BOSTON'S GARDENS: If you need time just to relax, don't forget that Boston is noted for its gardens, particularly **Boston Public Garden** adjoining Boston Common. There are reserved parking spaces in the underground parking garage beneath the common, with a garage entrance off Charles Street. Access to ground level is by elevator. Entrances to the common on Tremont Street, on Boylston Street, and Charles Street have curb cuts, but there are several flights of steps at the Beacon Street entrance. Paved pathways lead throughout the common. The Boston Public Garden is a flower garden that blooms with thousands of flowers in appropriate seasons.

THE PAUL REVERE TRAIL: If you go westward from Boston to Lexington and Concord, you'll be following the journey of Paul Revere on the night of April 18, 1775, to warn the colonists that the British were coming. Today he'd be held up in traffic, so avoid the rush hours when you drive through Cambridge out to Lexington. Take Storrow Drive or Memorial Drive to Rte. 2W, and follow signs to Lexington and Concord. Although it is almost a suburb of Boston now, there's still a small-country-town air about Lexington, whose open common is the spot where the British and colonists first came to blows, and where stands the country's oldest Revolutionary War monument. At the accessible **Visitors Center** on the Village Green at 1875 Massachusetts Ave. (tel. 617/862-1450), open from mid-April to November 1, you can see a diorama outlining and explaining the Battle of Lexington.

The **Minute Man National Historical Park,** Box 160, Concord, MA 01742 (tel. 617/369-2101) takes in both the Lexington and Concord areas and covers the scene of the fighting on opening day of the Revolutionary War in 1775. It includes the Old North Bridge in Concord, the Minute Man Statue, and four miles of Battle Road between Lexington and Concord, which the National Parks Department calls a "Living History" area. There are two visitors centers with exhibits and films that retell the story of the Minutemen and the Battle of Concord Bridge. The **Battle Road Visitor Center** in Lexington is on Rt. 2A in a landscaped park that has a barrier-free entrance, and rest rooms designed to accommodate wheelchairs. Information is printed in extra-large type. The **Fiske Hill Information Station** on Rtes. 2A and 128 in Lexington is barrier-free and offers information about the surrounding area.

The Old North Bridge and the Minute Man Statue are readily accessible, and there are no steps in this area. The path is not paved but is made of hard-packed earth. Interpretive talks are given at the Old North Bridge, and a schedule of the talks is available at the Buttrick Mansion, on the hill overlooking the bridge, which can be entered by a portable ramp over the entrance steps. The park and the visitors centers are open from April through October every day from 9 a.m. to 5:30 p.m., and in November through March on Wednesday through Sunday from 8:30 a.m. to 5 p.m.

BLUE HILLS TRAILSIDE MUSEUM: Located in the 5700-acre Blue Hills Reservation, and operated by the Massachusetts Audubon Society, the Blue Hills Trailside Museum, 1904 Canton Ave., Milton, MA 02186 (tel. 617/333-0690), is a farm/museum that houses live animals and plants with other exhibits on geology, archeology, energy, and natural history. It is open year-round from 10 a.m. to 5 p.m. on Tuesday through Sunday and on all Monday state holidays. There is a $1 admission for adults and 50¢ for children. To get there, take the Massachusetts Turnpike to Rte. 128 South and exit at Canton Avenue, then turn north to the museum. Parking is available in two lots on either side of the museum, and a 1:12 ramp leads to the museum's barrier-free entrance. Rest rooms have 35-inch stall doors. Animals are touchable by visually impaired visitors.

PLIMOUTH PLANTATION: The restoration of the Pilgrim Village of 1627, Plimouth Plantation on Warren Avenue in Plymouth (tel. 617/746-1622), is complete with a modern visitors center and a full-size replica of the sailing ship *Mayflower.* Maintaining authenticity has meant that visitors with mobility problems may find some difficulty, since the pathways are not paved, but they can be negotiable for wheelchairs, with assistance.

The Reception Center is barrier-free—there is an exhibit here—and so is the orientation area, where there is an exhibition and a slide show. Staff members here can direct you to the easier way to reach the houses in the center of the area (bearing to the left of the fort), where some of them have 32-inch entrance doors and either one step, or no steps.

Cafeteria, gift shop, and rest rooms are at the Reception Center and are all accessible.

The replica of the original *Mayflower,* at anchor in Plymouth harbor about a mile from the plantation, re-creates the Pilgrims' voyage. There are dockside exibits here, but boarding the ship is difficult for visitors in wheelchairs.

To get to the Plimouth Plantation from Rte. 3, take the exit marked Plimouth Plantation Highway. It is open daily from April 1 through November 30 from 9 a.m. to 5 p.m. Admission to both the plantation and *Mayflower* is $6.50 for adults, $3.75 for children 5 to 13; to the plantation alone, admission is $5.25 for adults and $2.75 for children.

7. Entertainment

The Shubert Theatre, the Boston Pops, and the Boston Symphony are all well-known segments of the Boston entertainment scene. Even though Boston does not stay up too late, there's other music and theater as well, and there's entertainment in the hotel lounges and many of the restaurants. You can find listings of events in *Boston by Week,* the Tourist Bureau's free calendar of events and, of course, in the local newspapers.

You can get half-price, day-of-performance tickets, as well as regular price advance tickets at the **Bostix Ticket Booth** in the Faneuil Hall Marketplace (tel. 723-5181) for the theater, all music and dance events (as well as museums, historical sites, and tourist attractions around Boston). No credit cards. Bostix is open Monday through Saturday from 11 a.m. to 6 p.m., on Sunday from noon to 6 p.m. You can hear recorded information on the day's offerings by calling 723-5181. There's a cobblestone mall around the ticket booth, so if that is difficult for you to negotiate, it may be better to go there with a companion.

MUSIC: "Going to Symphony" in Boston means **Symphony Hall,** 301 Massachusetts Ave. at Huntington Ave., MA 02115 (tel. 266-1492), where both the Boston Symphony Orchestra and the Boston Pops Orchestra have their concert seasons. Parking is available in a garage around the corner from Symphony Hall on Westland Avenue. Although there are steps (a portable ramp is available) at the main entrance, there is a barrier-free entrance on the Huntington Avenue side. Most of the seating is in the ramped orchestra section, but there is also an elevator to the balcony. (Make sure you make your needs known when you call for reservations.) Rest rooms have 33-inch stall doors.

Seats for the Boston Symphony's winter season from September to April are heavily subscribed, but there are usually some available for most concerts. On eight Wednesday evenings there are open rehearsals at 7:30 p.m., with all seats unreserved at $5. Both orchestras go outdoors for the summer, with the Symphony Orchestra at Tanglewood in the Berkshires, and the Pops to the Hatch Shell on the Charles River Esplanade. To find out who's performing where and when, call **Concert Line,** 353-3810, or **Jazzline,** 262-1300.

A wide variety of concerts are given by major performers in the **Berklee Performance Center,** 136 Massachusetts Ave. (tel. 266-7455). There are two steps at the entrance, and most seating is at the entry level in the orchestra with a ramped floor. Rest rooms, off the lobby, have 29-inch stall doors and grab bars. Again, be sure to mention your seating requirements when calling or writing for tickets.

If you plan to go to performances of the Boston Ballet Company at the **Metropolitan Center,** 268 Tremont St. in the theater district (tel. 542-3600), you'll find a barrier-free entrance and wheelchair seating arranged in the aisles.

The **Hatch Shell** along the Charles River Esplanade, reached by an overpass at Arlington Street, is the location of many free programs during the summer, including the Boston Pops, the Boston Ballet, chamber music, rock groups, and other bands. You'll find the listings in the newspapers.

THEATER: You'll often find Broadway tryouts as well as other performances at the Shubert and Wilbur Theaters in the theater district on Tremont and Boylston Streets. The **Shubert Theater,** 265 Tremont St. (tel. 426-4520), has a barrier-free approach and entrance. Most of the seating is in the sloping orchestra section (the balcony is up a flight of stairs), and wheelchairs can be accommodated in box seats and at the ends of aisles. There is parking available in an outdoor lot, next door to the theater, or in a garage across from the Shubert on Tremont Street.

The **Wilbur Theater,** 252 Tremont St. (tel. 423-4008), is barrier-free at the right-hand entrance of the three front doors. Wheelchair seating is available on the orchestra level in the side alcoves.

HOTEL AND RESTAURANT LOUNGES: A good many of the hotels and restaurants included in this chapter under those headings have live music along with the drinks and hors d'oeuvres. These include the **Plaza Bar** in the Copley Plaza Hotel (piano); the **Scotch 'n Sirloin** (music of all kinds Wednesday through Sunday 9 p.m. to 1:30 a.m.); **Rachel's** in the Boston Marriott Long Wharf, open until 1:30 a.m.; and the **Black Rose** with its Irish ballads. In Cambridge, the **Spinnaker** is the revolving rooftop lounge at the Hyatt Regency Hotel, open until 1 a.m. daily and until 2 a.m. on Friday and Saturday, and at the **Atrium Cafe** there's a harpist adding to the relaxed ambience of the skylit indoor garden.

SPORTS: If you are a baseball fan you'll want to include a visit to **Fenway Park,** home of the Red Sox, at 24 Yawkey Way (tel. 267-8661). Parking for disabled visitors is available in the Red Sox parking lot, across from the ticket office, on the corner of Yawkey Way and Brookline Avenue. Discharging and loading of passengers is permitted on Van Ness Street, and entrances designated for spectators with disabilities are on Lansdowne Street and on Yawkey Way. Seating reserved for patrons in wheelchairs is located behind home plate, and sections 14 and 15 are also used. The stadium has wide aisles, and ramps between seating levels have a slope of 1:7. There are rest rooms with varying degrees of accessibility at street level, with stall doors 29 to 31 inches wide. Some are equipped with grab bars. It is always best, of course, to call in advance to arrange assistance for special needs.

PHILADELPHIA

City of Brotherly Love

FORGET ALL those corny jokes about Philadelphia as a dull backwater of America: in recent years it has become a lively and picturesque city that has kept its long historical heritage in good shape and has developed modern cultural amenities that all go to make it one of the most popular cities for tourists—the disabled tourist included.

The activity that has created this renaissance in Philadelphia has been spurred on by two historic anniversaries—the nation's 200th (in 1976) and the city's own 300th (in 1982)—and the results of that alone are worth a visit. For starters, there's Independence National Historical Park created in the center of Philadelphia (with good curb cuts and enough accessible buildings to keep you well occupied). Then there are other historic centers like Society Hill and Penn's Landing that have been reborn to provide current delights.

Philadelphia has worked hard at eliminating architectural barriers wherever possible—all new public buildings must be barrier-free, and awareness of the needs of disabled visitors has led to efforts to do the best job possible to make the historic sections of the city available (although 17th and 18th century architecture is not easy to convert for ramps and elevators). There's a good cross-section of hotels with ease-of-access features, and enough accessible restaurants in all price categories to provide pleasant dining.

Philadelphia has other things going for it too. It is a natural stopping place between New York (100 miles) and Washington (133 miles), and Atlantic City's casinos and beaches are nearby.

There's a *Guide to Philadelphia for the Handicapped* available free of charge from the Mayor's Office for the Handicapped, Room 143, City Hall, Philadelphia, PA 19102 (tel. 215/686-2798, TDD 564-1782), which includes accessibility information on some of the hotels, restaurants, historic sights, and museums, as well as telephone numbers of special services for disabled people.

For general information and guides to Philadelphia, call or write to the **Convention and Visitors Bureau**, 1525 JFK Blvd., Philadelphia, PA 19102 (tel. 215/864-1976).

1. Getting There

BY CAR: From points in roughly north or south directions, Interstate 95 runs along the Delaware River, and a new section now parallels Front Street in Center City (which is probably where you will be heading). From the west, Rte. 76 brings you downtown via the Vine Street exit. From New Jersey, the Benjamin Franklin Bridge (75¢) joins Camden and Center City via 6th Street.

BY AIR: **Philadelphia International Airport** (tel. 215/492-3333), eight miles from Center City, is served by all major domestic carriers from more than a hundred cities in the country, and by Mexicana Airlines, Pan Am, and TWA for overseas flights. The terminal has been modernized recently and now incorporates special features for disabled travelers: the new garage has designated parking spaces, and there is level access into the terminal building. There are specially equipped rest rooms at several locations. Most individual airline gates are equipped with jetways for level entry and exit to and from planes. You will find taxis at Terminal B.

BY TRAIN: All **Amtrak** trains stop at the **30th Street Station** (tel. 215/824-1600). The conductor on your train should notify the station in advance that you will need assistance on arrival, and you will be met by a porter who will escort you from the platform (level with the train exit) via elevator to the main floor. The station interior is level with the sidewalks. Follow the reverse procedure if you are leaving from here. (See the section on train travel in Chapter 2.)

BY BUS: **Continental Trailways** (tel. 215/972-3333) has a depot at 13th and Arch Sts., which is level throughout. There is one adapted stall large enough for wheelchairs in each of the rest rooms.

The **Greyhound Terminal** (tel. 215/568-4800) is at 17th and Market Sts. There are only escalators from the bus arrival area up to the terminal building, and no accessible rest rooms. If you cannot use the escalators you should be met by car or taxi at the bus arrival area.

Both bus terminals are close to City Hall in the center of town.

2. Getting Around

As a tourist city Philadelphia is quite compact; sightseeing can be done without relying on transportation too much, but to get from one area to another, here is a summary of the methods available to you. If you're going on your own wheels, you'll find that most of the Center City business and shopping area has its curbs ramped, and so has the Independence Historical Park.

DRIVING AND PARKING: Although there is a lot of modern city here and Philadelphia is not *all* 300 years old, many of the streets are still very narrow and leave very little room for parking. All the Center City streets are one-way (except for lower Market Street, the Parkway, Vine Street, and Broad Street).

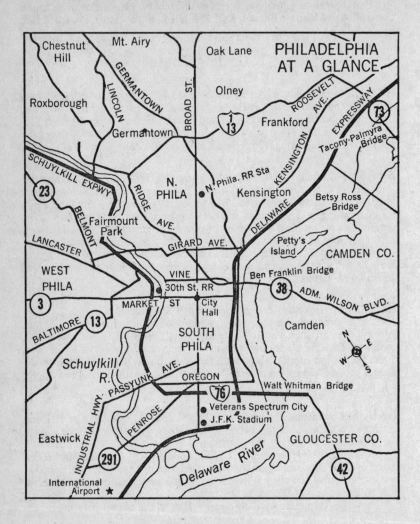

Pennsylvania permits motorists to make a right turn (or a left turn from and to a one-way street) on a red light at most intersections, providing they yield to pedestrians and to vehicles that have the green light.

If you have written in advance to the Convention and Visitors Bureau, the package they send you should include a Center City traffic map. This will also indicate the parking garages and lots.

Many hotels provide free or reduced-rate parking to registered guests, and there are also large public garages where you can leave your car while you tour the area: Independence Park has a 600-car garage at 2nd and Sansom Streets, and there's another large one between 5th and 6th Streets just above Spruce Street. If you are in Society Hill, there is a parking lot, convenient for Head House Square and NewMarket, at 2nd and Lombard. In the middle of town there is an underground garage at Kennedy Plaza below the Visitors Bureau; and near the Academy of Music there are two lots on South Broad Street at Locust. Rates are similar at most garages, with day rates around $6 and an hourly rate of about $1 (subject to change).

RENTAL CARS: Avis (tel. 215/492-3350) is the only rental company with hand-controlled cars available at the airport, or in Center City at 1909 Market St. (tel. 215/563-8980). One week's notice is necessary for booking.

TAXIS: Philadelphia doesn't seem to have as many taxis as other cities, but you will find taxi stands at the airport and at most of the large hotels. Cabs can be called from many companies including **United Cab** (tel. 864-0750), **Yellow Cab Co.** (tel. 922-7180), or **Quaker Cab Assoc.** (tel. 728-8000).

SPECIAL TRANSPORTATION: Services that offer vans with wheelchair lifts include **Accessible Transportation for the Disabled** (tel. 215/352-7785), and **Wheels Medical and Specialized Transportation Service** (tel. 215/627-7065).

PUBLIC TRANSPORTATION: Although the bus system does run vehicles equipped with wheelchair lifts, they do not operate on all routes, and the lifts malfunction quite frequently. Drivers will not pick up wheelchair passengers during rush hours. Subways and the elevated trains are not accessible. The para-transit system of door-to-door transportation for disabled residents is not available for visitors.

3. Orientation

It is just over 300 years since William Penn stepped ashore on a peninsula between the Delaware and Schuylkill Rivers to claim his grant of land from King Charles II of England to set up a colony where his own Quakers and other religious minorities could settle and worship in peace. It became the site for the city he named Phila (love)-delphia (brotherly).

Penn's city is still Philadelphia's Center City today. He laid out the grid street pattern that is still there (it was an unusual arrangement at that time), with five public squares, also still there, now called Penn Center, Washington Square, Franklin Square, Logan Circle, and Rittenhouse Square. At the center of Center City is City Hall, at the intersection of Market and Broad Streets. As it did in Penn's day too, Front Street fronts the Delaware River, and it is from here that the major north-south thoroughfares of the grid are numbered, starting with 2nd Street and going as far as the Schuylkill River at the other side of the peninsula. Today the streets continue across the river to West Philadelphia, and some streets between 24th and 30th appear on both sides. The main intersecting streets that run east to west were named by Penn's architects for trees and plants—Cherry, Filbert, Chestnut, Walnut, Locust, Spruce, Pine.

In Center City a tourist will find most of Philadelphia's attractions, particularly between Arch and Pine Streets. Here are Independence National Historical Park, Society Hill, Penn Center, the area around Rittenhouse Square, and the museums bordering Logan Circle and Benjamin Franklin Parkway. Find your way easily by remembering that addresses on Center City streets add 100 for every block and that Market Street is the start for those streets named South. This means that, for instance, 1534 Chestnut is between

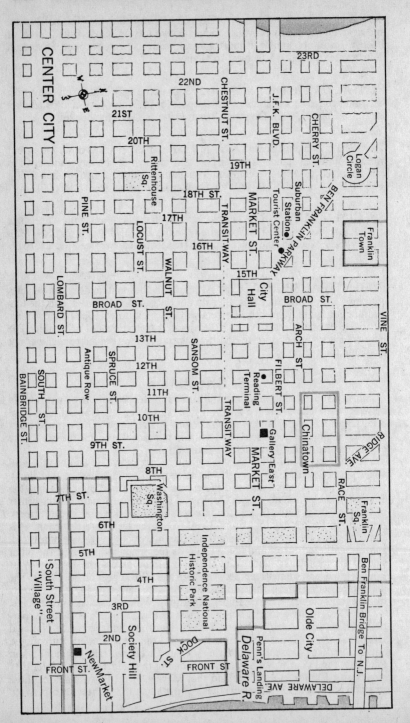

15th and 16th Streets, and 610 South 5th Street is between six and seven blocks south of Market Street.

The colonial city—the city of Benjamin Franklin, Thomas Jefferson, and the Liberty Bell—originally centered along the Delaware River north and south of Market Street, and is now focused on Independence National Historical Park and its immediate surroundings. The area north of Market Street is now known as Olde City. The original city had got only as far as 6th Street by 1776: its early expansion was along the river, which became a center of commerce on its busy docks.

In the 19th century, when many of the museums and other cultural centers were established, the city moved westward to the Schuylkill River and beyond. This was when fashionable society took up residence around Rittenhouse Square in the southwest part of Center City. Many of their Victorian-style homes are still there.

The grand boulevard, Benjamin Franklin Parkway, that runs diagonally, linking City Hall and the 4000 acres of Fairmount Park, was constructed in 1926 to mark the nation's 150th birthday. The settlement of West Philadelphia began when the first bridge was built across the Schuylkill River in the early 1800s, but not until the University of Pennsylvania moved there in 1872 did it become an important part of the city. The 20th century has added skyscrapers to Penn Center in midtown, an impressive shopping and restaurant area.

Philadelphia has combined its most recent urban renewal projects with an awareness of its attractions for the tourist as well: the establishment of Independence National Historical Park and Society Hill are already complete, and the Penn's Landing development on the Delaware River waterfront, as well as the Gallery II complex of shops and restaurants are still underway, all again in Center City, the old stamping ground of William Penn. Which seems to be where we came in. . . .

CLIMATE: Philadelphia has four distinct seasons. Summer tends to be humid, with July and August temperatures ranging between 66° and 85°, calling for light, comfortable clothes. Fall is usually drier—light knits and wools are the best bet, with a sweater or jacket for the evening.

TELEPHONE AREA CODE: Most of the Philadelphia area is 215.

LIQUOR: Liquor can be bought only in state stores, usually open from 9 a.m. to 5 p.m. Monday to Wednesday; until 9 p.m. on Thursday to Saturday. State stores are located at 9th and Chestnut, 21st and Chestnut, and on 5th near Walnut Streets. Delicatessens and licensed supermarkets carry beer and champagne.

INFORMATION AND REFERRAL: Among the organizations that can provide the special information needed by disabled visitors are **The Mayor's Office for the Handicapped,** Rm. 143, City Hall, Philadelphia, PA 19102 (tel. 215/686-2798, TDD 564-1782), and the **Easter Seal Society,** 3975 Conshohocken Ave., Philadelphia, PA 19131 (tel. 215/879-1000).

4. Where to Stay

It is general opinion that there need to be more hotel rooms in Philadelphia —and they are now being provided, though usually the new hotels are in the high-price range. However, advance reservations should ensure no shocks on arrival. You'll find rates, in general, lower than the East Coast average, and the choice is yours whether to stay in Center City or on the outskirts, where there are more moderately priced hotels, and use a car to come downtown and see the sights. There are good, accessible possibilities in both areas. Hotels are listed here by price categories. All the ease-of-access features are noted, and you can assume that special facilities do not exist if they are not included here.

DELUXE: The grande dame of Philadelphia hotels, and indeed one of the most notable in the country, is the **Bellevue-Stratford** on Broad St. at Walnut, PA 19102 (tel. 215/893-1776), a palatial building of grand staircases and high-ceilinged rooms from past eras—but it does have good wheelchair access to all parts of the hotel and in the guest rooms, following recent renovation by Westin International. A ramped entrance, as well as a new garage are being installed even as we write! There are 13 guest rooms with special features that include lower door handles, light switches, medicine cabinets, and closet shelves; 35-inch bathroom doors; and grab bars in the bathrooms. Even the regular guest rooms have 33-inch entry doors and 30-inch bathroom doors. In the public areas, elevator buttons have been lowered, and there are wheelchair-height public telephones, as well as 35-inch stall doors in each public rest room. There is level access to the elevators and to the lobby, which is a hive of activity and is grand enough to have guided tours of its own. They serve high tea here to piano accompaniment, and there are specialty shops, the Versailles Restaurant and Lounge, and the Burgundy Room. Also available and reached by elevator is moderately priced O'Brien's Restaurant on the lower level, open 24 hours a day.

Rates vary, since each guest room differs (though all have deluxe touches, such as eiderdown pillows and extra-fine percale sheets). Singles start at $89 and doubles at $100. However, there are packages that cost less, and you can find out about them by calling Westin toll-free at 800/228-3000.

FIRST CLASS: Opened more recently (for the 1976 Bicentennial), the **Franklin Plaza**, 2 Franklin Plaza, PA 19103 (tel. 215/448-2000, toll free 800/828-7447), is as much a resort as a hotel, and also a popular site for conventions. Its accessibility credentials are good: the entrance is ramped and the interior is level. Elevators have floor indicators in braille. All the guest rooms have 36-inch entry and bathroom doors, and there are 16 guest rooms that have grab bars in the bathrooms. Many have wheel-in showers. Public rest rooms also have this 36/36 measurement. The five restaurants have level entrances. Rates begin at $68 single and $80 double, with weekend packages that include one night and parking for $59 double. The in-house garage costs $6 a day. There is no additional charge for children 14 and under, if staying in the same room.

Even newer, opened in 1983, the **Hershey Philadelphia Hotel,** Broad St. at Locust, PA 19107 (tel. 215/893-1600, toll free 800/523-7800) is centrally located near the Shubert Theater and the Academy of Music. It has a level entrance and interior and elevator access to all floors and public areas. There are 11 guest rooms that have special features such as 33-inch bathroom doors and grab bars. Public rest rooms have the same dimensions. TV can be controlled from the bed in the special guest rooms, which also have a lower door peephole convenient for guests in wheelchairs. There are braille floor indicators in the elevators, and braille menus are available in the restaurants. Indoor parking is available in the hotel garage. Rates at the Hershey are $75 to $95 single, $90 to $110 double.

MODERATE: The **Holiday Inn-Center City,** 1800 Market St., PA 19103 (tel. 215/561-7500), centrally located at Market and 18th Sts., has recently been refurbished, and there are now ten rooms with special features for disabled guests. To allow more floor space in these rooms, one of the two double beds has been removed. Entry and bathroom doors are both 33 inches wide, and there are grab bars at the toilet and bath. Ceiling hooks have been installed to accommodate lifting devices both in the bedroom and in the bathroom. The TV set can be switched on and off from the bed. The entrance and the interior of the hotel are barrier-free, and so are the three restaurants. Double rates are about $71.

An accessible motel on the outskirts of Philadelphia, but not too far away from Center City, is the **Marriott,** City Line Ave. at Monument Rd., PA 19131 (tel. 215/667-0200). This is a resort-type hostelry, spread out over 22 acres. The 20 guest rooms, with wide bathroom doors (31 inches) and bathroom grab bars, open directly onto the parking area for convenience. The main entrance is ramped, the eight restaurants are accessible, and there are public rest rooms with 32-inch stall entry. Elevators are marked with braille floor indicators. Room rates start at $77 single and $87 double.

On the other side of the Schuylkill River, but also not too far away from Center City, is the **University City Holiday Inn,** 36th and Chestnut Sts., PA 19104 (tel. 215/387-8000). There is free parking in the garage, which is on the first five floors of this relatively new motel, and there is access to the lobby by elevator from the garage. There is also a level entrance to the lobby at 36th Street. Six guest rooms have wide bathroom doors and grab bars, and the restaurants and public rest rooms are also accessible. Rates are $61 single, $67 double, children under 12 free in the same room.

One of the more pleasant airport hotels is the **Marriott at Philadelphia International Airport,** PA 19153 (tel. 215/365-4150, toll free 800/228-9290), which has two rooms equipped with wider bathroom doors and grab bars. All the guest rooms have television controls at bedside. There is a ramp from the parking lot to the main lobby, and restaurants can be reached without steps. There is an accessible public rest room near the gift shop. Rates are $75 single, $90 double, but with special weekend packages at lower rates.

On the outskirts northwest of the city, on Rte. 1, is the **Sheraton Inn,** 9461 Roosevelt Blvd., PA 19114 (tel. 215/671-9600). It has a ramped entrance and a level interior, with one guest room equipped with bathroom grab bars and a 33-inch entry. The TV set can be controlled from the bed in all guest rooms. Elevator floor indicators are in braille. There are no dining facilities. Weekday prices vary between $50 and $90 per room, but weekend packages can be had from $43.95 a night, double occupancy.

You can't come much closer to staying near the Liberty Bell than at the **Holiday Inn Independence Mall,** 400 Arch St., PA 19106, (tel. 215/923-8660). The entrance is ramped, and the interior is level. *Every* guest room has a 38-inch entry door as well as a 38-inch bathroom door. The two rooms equipped with bathroom grab bars have 40-inch doors for both entry and bathroom, as well as ceiling hooks for lifting devices in the bedroom. The Packet Restaurant, which serves a buffet lunch for $5.50, is accessible. Room rates start at $62 single and $68 double, with no extra charge for children under 18.

5. Philadelphia's Restaurants

There was a burgeoning of restaurants in Philadelphia to go along with the city's renaissance during the 1970s, and although some establishments came and went with some regularity, things seemed to have settled down somewhat. I've listed those that are likely still to be around by the time you use this book, and, of course, they are also those that have a degree of accessibility. Philadelphia has a 5% tax on all meals.

The price categories mean that full meals run approximately $25 and up for the Haute Cuisine, between $10 and $25 for Upper Bracket, and $8 to $15 for Moderate. Remember that if you want to eat the finest food at less than budget-breaking prices, go to top-bracket restaurants at lunchtime. For meals at so-called budget prices, there are plenty of fast-food outlets and other more casual eateries that you'll come across in your sightseeing. You can check them out as you go by. Rest rooms are not wheelchair-accessible unless noted.

HAUTE CUISINE: Considered by many to be the best in Philadelphia and among the finest restaurants in the country, is **Le Bec-Fin**, recently moved to 1523 Walnut St. (tel. 732-3000), where there is a level entrance. This is a *very* special place. Prix fixe is $55 per person (no credit cards), and reservations should be made at least one week ahead for weeknights, longer for weekends. There are two sittings, at 6 and 9 p.m., Monday through Saturday.

Fine food at less awesome prices can be had at the **20th Street Cafe**, 261 S. 20th St. (tel. 546-6867), which has one small step at the entrance. Just south of Rittenhouse Square in a sophisticated neighborhood, it is very popular, so you should make reservations ahead of time, especially at weekends. Without wine, a full meal at dinnertime may cost about $25 per person. The 20th Street Cafe is open from 11:30 a.m. to 2:30 p.m. and 6 to 11 p.m. Monday through Saturday. On Sunday, it's noon to 3 p.m. and 5 to 9 p.m.

Hotel Dining

Among the more deluxe dining establishments in the leading hotels to be recommended for their cuisine are: The **Versailles** at the Bellevue-Stratford, Broad and Walnut Sts. (tel. 893-1880), which is level from the lobby (the Bellevue-Stratford has installed a hydraulic lift for wheelchairs at the street entrance); the **élan** at the Warwick Hotel, 17th and Locust (tel. 546-8800), where there is a ramped entrance on Locust Street to the hotel and two steps to the restaurant (assistance available); **Le Beau Lieu** at the Barclay Hotel, Rittenhouse Square East (tel. 545-0300), with a level entrance to both the hotel and the restaurant; and **Between Friends** at the Franklin Plaza, 17th and Race Sts. (tel. 448-2000).

UPPER BRACKET: **Morgan's** at 24th and Sansom Sts. (tel. 567-6066) is in a less-traveled area between Rittenhouse Square and the Schuylkill River (which means easier parking) and has just one step at the entrance. The menu is inventive and changes with the seasons, and is served in an elegant but unstuffy setting. A full dinner will cost about $25 to $30; lunch much less. Morgan's is open for lunch from 11:45 a.m. to 2 p.m. on weekdays and for dinner from 5:30 to 11 p.m. Monday through Saturday. Reservations suggested.

Nearer the waterfront is a North Indian restaurant called **Siva's**, 34 S. Front St. (tel. 925-2700), with emphasis on tandoori cooking in a comfortable setting that blends East and West. There is one step at the entrance. A complete meal here will be about $15, but you can eat for less. Siva's is open Tuesday to Friday from noon to 2 p.m. and 5:30 to 10:30 p.m. (Saturday until 11:30 p.m.). Sunday hours are 5 to 10 p.m. It is closed on Monday and for lunch on weekends.

La Truffe, 10 Front St. (tel. 627-8632), is between Penn's Landing and Independence Park, and has just one step at the entrance. Inside the ambience has French provincial charm and a French menu that has won a reputation for the restaurant. Entrees start at $15. It is open Tuesday to Friday from noon to 2 p.m. (except July and August), and for dinner from 6 to 11 p.m. Monday to Saturday.

In NewMarket, the **Dickens Inn** has a Head House Square entrance at 421 S. 2nd St. (tel. 928-9307). It's a relative of the one in London, and there's a spacious dining room with Dickensian overtones and unusual dishes, including many baked on the premises. Wheelchair patrons will not be able to use the general entrance but can get in by going to the bakery attached to the inn and asking them to alert security for special access to the restaurant. Open for lunch from 11:30 a.m. to 2:30 p.m. and for dinner from 6 to 11 p.m. Monday through Saturday. Sunday brunch is served from 11:30 a.m. to 3 p.m., and the pub is open daily until 2 a.m.

There was a time when nobody visited Philadelphia without having dinner at the **Old Original Bookbinder's,** 125 Walnut St. (tel. 925-7027), and it's probably a good tradition to keep alive. Lobster and seafood in large portions are the specialty of this Philadelphia institution. There is a level entrance from the street through the door normally used for exit. It is open for lunch from 11:45 a.m. to 3 p.m. Monday to Friday, and for dinner from 3 p.m. to 10 p.m. Sunday to Saturday.

MODERATE: There are a lot of seafood choices in Philadelphia, and among the more moderately priced is the **Dockside Fish Company** on the Piers at 815 Locust St. (tel. 925-6175). There is a level entrance. The specialty here is seafood grilled in a charcoal oven and entrees are under $12.50, many under $10. Open for lunch from 11 a.m. to 3 p.m. Monday through Saturday, and goes on for dinner until 11 p.m.

The **Sansom Street Oyster House,** 1516 Sansom St. (tel. 567-7683), is in the middle of a shopping area. In addition to the oysters and clams, there's a regular seafood menu as well, and you might be able to have lunch for about $5 and dinner for about $9. Lunch is served from 11 a.m. to 3 p.m. every day except Sunday, and dinner from 3 to 8 p.m. Monday to Thursday and to 9 p.m. on Friday and Saturday. No credit cards.

In Olde City, **Dinardo's Famous Crabs,** 312 Race St. (tel. 925-5115), has its obvious specialty, but also all kinds of seafood as well. It has one step at the entrance. Open from 11 a.m. to midnight Tuesday to Saturday, 4 to 10 p.m. on Sunday.

In a modest storefront further south on 2nd Street (with one step at the entrance) is **Walt's King of the Crabs,** 804 S. 2nd St. (tel. 339-9124), with the obvious house specialty and a faithful following because of its good value for the price. Platters are mostly under $5 and shrimp stuffed with crabmeat around $6. Call ahead. Open from 11 a.m. to 12:30 a.m. Monday to Saturday, 2:30 to 10:30 p.m. on Sunday. No credit cards.

Although there is only staircase access to the upper floor, where there is formal table service, you should try the ground floor gourmet cafeteria at **The Commissary,** 1710 Sansom St. (tel. 569-2240). It's about three blocks from City Hall and open all day long. Since it is a cafeteria, you may need assistance from a companion if you are in a wheelchair, but you'll find it's worth it for any meal of the day. There's also a wine bar on the ground floor with nightly piano entertainment.

If you don't go to **Rick's Cabaret** at **Le Bistro** for the jazz at night, try it for dinner, which leans to Mediterranean dishes (pasta or seafood for around $9). It's in a historic Federal building at 757 S. Front St. (tel. 389-3855), with a clear view of the Delaware River and the Benjamin Franklin Bridge. Entrance is one step up and one step down. There's a metered parking area available.

6. Sightseeing

It's "the most historic mile in America" that most visitors come to Philadelphia to see. That area's connection to the beginnings of the United States as an independent nation holds a fascination for Americans and foreigners alike. The innumerable colonial houses and other buildings of historic significance cannot be made completely accessible to disabled visitors, but it's a special thrill just to see them—still standing as they did when Franklin, Washington, and Jefferson walked the streets of Philadelphia—as well as the Liberty Bell, Independence Hall (where it all started), and the house where Thomas Jefferson drafted the Declaration of Independence.

Philadelphia has some of the country's finest art collections in the Philadelphia Museum of Art, easily accessible to people in wheelchairs, as is the Pennsylvania Academy of Fine Arts, the Franklin Institute Science Museum, and many other sights and attractions that a disabled visitor can enjoy.

Sightseeing areas are compact, and distances are not great. Even a "stroll" from City Hall to the Museum of Art down Benjamin Franklin Parkway is a pleasant 30 minutes—unless you take in all the other sights on the way. Independence National Historical Park can be easily negotiated in the course of a day, and then there's Society Hill, not too far away, for another glimpse of the colonial city. Most of the Center City is fairly flat, and the business and shopping district has ramped curbs. There are also many curb cuts in the Independence National Historical Park. You'll have to climb a little to Society Hill, but nothing is very steep.

Maps and sightseeing information are available from the Visitors Bureau, but it is a good idea to write for any information in advance of a trip since the bureau's building has ten steps at the entrance. The address is **Convention and Tourist Bureau,** 1525 John F. Kennedy Blvd., Philadelphia, PA 19102 (tel. 215/568-1976).

INDEPENDENCE NATIONAL HISTORICAL PARK: This area has a history that goes back to the first settlement, but it assured itself of a place in history by becoming the birthplace of the United States in 1776 with the signing of the Declaration of Independence. The place swarmed with delegates to the Constitutional Convention in 1787, and then became the capital of the country with Congress and the Supreme Court sitting here for ten years until the Capitol in Washington, D.C., was finished. Yet until the preparations for the Bicentennial in 1976, it was a rundown area, with Independence Square isolated in a morass of warehouses and office buildings and the colonial relics looked upon as almost a real estate nuisance. Now, under the care of the National Park Service, Independence Hall is graced with a view from a mall of greenery, gardens replace office buildings, and colonial structures have been lovingly restored. The Liberty Bell has a glass pavillion all to itself (it used to be in Independence Hall) that is totally accessible!

You should go to the **Visitor Center** before you start your tour—it is at 3rd and Chestnut Sts. (tel. 215/597-8974/5, TDD 215/597-8974) and all its facilities, including rest rooms, are available to the visitor in a wheelchair. If you arrive by car, there's a city parking garage on 2nd Street between Walnut and Chestnut Streets, one block from the Visitor Center, with parking space reserved for visitors with mobility impairments. There are curb cuts from the parking garage to the Visitor Center.

Here you can get a map of the area (and information in one of 15 languages if you need it). Displays give an idea of what life was like in 1776 Philadelphia, and the John Huston film, *Independence,* is shown every 30 minutes without charge. It is captioned for hearing-impaired viewers. The National Park Service explains that it is responsible for maintaining the buildings in their *original* condition and, in some cases, creating physical accessibility could destroy the historic character of the buildings. However, the service does stress that interpretive programs, such as the photo album of the second floor of Independence Hall, are being planned as an alternative to actual access. Rangers and volunteers at the Visitor Center have all the latest accessibility information. Wheelchairs are available on loan at the center.

There are curb ramps at most intersections in the park area and the center can provide you with maps showing where they are located. (Care should be taken on the 18th-century brick sidewalks, which are sometimes uneven.)

Although the Liberty Bell Pavilion is the only place, apart from the Visitor Center, that is totally accessible for people with mobility impairments, there are others that are partially accessible, or accessible with staff assistance. These include Independence Hall, Congress Hall, Old City Hall, Franklin Court, Graff House, and Christ Church.

Hearing-impaired visitors can obtain printed scripts for the audio-visual and audio programs at most locations where they are presented.

For people with sight-impairments, park brochures in both braille and large print are available on loan at the Visitor Center. Cassette tape of the park brochure and a player may also be borrowed here. In most buildings Park Rangers can provide detailed descriptions of the buildings and their historical significance.

All facilities in Independence National Historical Park are open from 9 a.m. to 5 p.m. daily (often longer in the summer). There is no charge anywhere.

The Visitor Center is as good a location as any to set off on a tour of Independence Park, especially as you will have acquired the very latest information about what is available for your special needs.

You'll pass some of the park's prime properties in the block of 4th Street between Chestnut and Walnut. Most of these will have to be noted and admired from the outside—but just *think* that it was in **Carpenter's Hall** (the one with the cupola that looks like a salt shaker and has eight steps at the front!) that the First Continental Congress met in 1774 and began the progress to independence. **Pemberton House** is a 100-year-old reconstruction that will show you the kind of home a prosperous merchant had in those days. It now houses dioramas of the military history of the Revolutionary War, but has several steps. **New Hall** is now the Marine Corps Museum, and although there is a portable ramp that can be placed over the steps at the front entrance, there is not much room inside to maneuver a wheelchair.

However, wheelchair-users, take heart! You'll be able to go into **Franklin Court,** underground between 3rd and 4th Streets, with entrances on Chestnut and Market. It's ramped at the entrance, and there is an elevator available for return to the ground floor. This is where Benjamin Franklin's home once stood; since 1976 it has been an imaginative and informative (and fun) museum about the great man who once lived on this very site. Only remnants of the foundations still remain, but there are touch-it, dial-it, and see-it exhibits of his life, his inventions, his philosophies, and his limitless interests.

If you start your tour from the Visitor Center in the other direction, toward Walnut Street, you'll see the 1832 **Philadelphia Exchange** on one corner of 3rd and Walnut (not open to the public), and on the other corner, at 309 Walnut, is the **Bishop White House** from the Federal period, one of the loveliest row houses in the city. It *can* be enjoyed from the outside, but if your disability allows you to negotiate the two steps at the entrance and a staircase inside, there are tours for ten people at a time (make arrangements at the Visitor Center). As you go down this block of Walnut between 3rd and 4th Streets, you'll see a number of other restored row houses adorned with paneled doors and shuttered windows, and carrying the historical insurance markers (small metal plaques) which once helped firemen employed by the insurance companies to identify the houses for which they were responsible. The last one, the **Todd House,** is open to the public but not easily accessible.

The focal point of **Independence Square** (which you'll come to at 5th Street from either Chestnut or Walnut), are three buildings that stand exactly as they did those 200-plus years ago when history was made there—Independence Hall in the center, flanked by Old City Hall and Congress Hall. There are portable ramps available on request (at the East Wing of Independence Hall) for all three buildings, which have two steps at the entrances. You can visit the ground floors, at least, where there is a lot to see; the second floors are reached by staircases.

Independence Hall is open from 9 a.m. to 8 p.m. in the summer and from 9 a.m. to 5 p.m. in the winter, with admittance by guided tours (waiting lines can be lengthy). On the ground floor you can see the most significant room in America's history, where the Declaration of Independence was signed and where the American Constitution was created.

Congress Hall, next door, is where George Washington and John Adams were inaugurated (on the ground floor); and on the other side of Independence Hall is Old City Hall (at 5th and Chestnut), seat of Chief Justice John Jay's first Supreme Court and now used for exhibits describing the judiciary's early years.

It was outside, in what is now Independence Square, that the Declaration of Independence was read publicly for the first time. You can see a free sound-and-light show here in the summer every evening at 9 p.m. that tells the story of Independence Hall.

Now you're close to the only building in the Park that is really fully accessible—the **Liberty Bell Pavilion,** located in the area that was cleared to create Independence Mall behind Independence Square. In the first minute of 1976, the Liberty Bell was moved here from Independence Hall, where it had pealed as independence was originally declared 200 years earlier. The Liberty Bell Pavilion is open from 9 a.m. to 8 p.m. every day in the summer. At night you can see it through glass walls from the outside and hear its history.

While you are in this area, you may want to have a snack and listen to music (if it's lunchtime) at **The Bourse,** an old Victorian building just renovated as a mall around a skylit atrium. There is elevator access to the upper floors, although some of the stores and restaurants are quite small and may present difficulties for wheelchair visitors. The Bourse is open from 10 a.m. to 6 p.m. on Monday, Tuesday, and Thursday, and until 9 p.m. on Wednesday, Friday, and Saturday; from noon to 6 p.m. on Sunday.

If you head down Market Street from Independence Mall, you'll come to the **Graff House,** at 7th Street, where Thomas Jefferson drafted the Declara-

tion of Independence. There is an accessible entrance at the rear. From here
a ramp also leads to the basement, where a short film about Jefferson is shown.
A staircase leads to the upstairs rooms.

PENN'S LANDING: In the other direction, on the Delaware River, is the
very recent development called **Penn's Landing,** a waterfront park on Delaware Avenue between Market and Lombard Streets. It's a reminder that Philadelphia has always been a freshwater port. You can drive into the parking lot
at Penn's Landing from either Chestnut or Lombard, or go across the covered
portion of the I-95 highway between Locust and Spruce. There are several
historic ships berthed here—even one, the *Mosholu,* that you can board and
have dinner on! It has an easy ramp and plenty of room inside for comfortable
dining.

At Penn's Landing, too, is the new **Port of History Museum** with exhibitions on the sea and the city. The entrance is level, and there is an elevator to
the upper floors, as well as wheelchair-accessible rest rooms. It is open from
Wednesday to Sunday from 10 a.m. to 4:40 p.m., with $1 admission.

SOCIETY HILL: This historic area, east of Washington Square between Walnut and Lombard Streets and just south of Independence National Historical
Park, was named for the Free Society of Traders and does *not* designate social
status! As its name indicates, there is a rise to Society Hill from Center City,
so you may want to go there by car or taxi. There is a parking lot convenient
to Head House Square and NewMarket at 2nd and Lombard.

Like much of historic Philadelphia, the Society Hill area had become
decrepit and rundown until a massive urban renewal project turned the hundreds of colonial facades into charming town houses, and even housing developments blend with all the other exteriors. This is the place to see more
Colonial and Federal architecture in a small area than anywhere else in the
country, constructed mostly in the brick that was made from mud easily found
along the Delaware River. There are also Georgian and Federal public buildings and churches as well as homes, and all these historic structures are in good
working order and in daily use. You can learn all about Society Hill on an
evening tour every Wednesday, Friday, and Saturday, leaving from the City
Tavern at 6:30 p.m. It ends at NewMarket after about 90 minutes and costs
$4 for adults, $2.50 for children. For information and reservations, call 564-
2246, and it is advisable to check if the tour is possible for your particular
requirements.

You'll find restaurants and shops around **Head House Square,** a recent
restoration project which dates as a marketplace from 1803 and lies between
Front and 2nd Streets, Pine and Lombard. Streets are not too smooth here, be
warned; there is a curb up to the central area where you'll see Head House
itself, a small brick building with a cupola that once held a fire bell, and where
in summer there are many crafts offered for sale in the open square. Shops and
restaurants around Head House Square have varying degrees of accessibility,
but this is eaily noted as you pass.

A brand-new shopping mall nearby, **NewMarket,** now enlivens the block
between Front and 2nd Streets. The Georgian facades on 2nd Street have been
preserved. It's a multilevel complex of stores and restaurants around two
courtyards complete with waterfall. There are some steep ramps here—and
some steps—and although the entire mall is not accessible for wheelchairs, have
a look at NewMarket while you are in Society Hill.

Also while there, you may want to drop in at the **Perelman Antique Toy Museum**, 270 S. 2nd St. (tel. 922-1070), two blocks from Head House Square. The house actually dates from 1758 but is reasonably accessible. It has one step at the entrance and an elevator inside. It is open daily from 9:30 a.m. to 5 p.m. except on Sunday, when it closes at 4 p.m. Admission is $1 for adults, 55¢ for children.

A block away from Head House Square, on 3rd St. and Pine, is **St. Peter's Episcopal Church**, built in 1761 to serve the residents of Society Hill, and where George Washington sometimes sat in pew 41. There is one step at the entrance, and it is open to visitors from 9 a.m. to 5 p.m. daily. The churchyard contains the remains of many notables including the painter C.W. Peale, Stephen Decatur of naval fame, and Nicholas Biddle of the Second Bank, as well as Indian chiefs who fell victim to the 1793 smallpox epidemic.

OLDE CITY: The area north of Market Street, now known as Olde City, is outside the Independence National Historical Park, but since it is close by you may want to look at a couple of historic gems in this area.

From a distance in any direction, you can see the white spire of **Christ Church** on 2nd Street, half a block above Market. There is a level entrance on 2nd Street and the interior is substantially accessible. This Anglican, then Episcopal, church was built between 1727 and 1754. Here you'll see the font sent over from the Anglican church in London at which William Penn (later the nonconformist Quaker) was baptized, as well as pews used by George Washington and Betsy Ross when they worshipped here.

And another block north, between 2nd and 3rd Streets, is the **Betsy Ross House**, 239 Arch St. (tel. 627-5343). It doesn't have watertight authenticity as the home of the seamstress who sewed the first American flag, but as a small 1750 home that has remarkably survived, it is certainly worth more than a passing glance. It has one step at the entrance and, of course, only a staircase to the second floor and basement kitchen. There is a gift shop on the ground floor. No entrance fee.

If you continue along Arch Street for another block you'll pass **Loxley Court**, homes dating from 1770 to 1800, and still private homes. Across the street is the **Friends Meeting House**, the simple Quaker gathering place, built in 1804 and now showing a series of dioramas of William Penn's life. It has four steps at the entrance, but is all on one level floor inside.

And if you want to see money being made, literally, the **U.S. Mint** is near here, on 5th St. at Arch St. (tel. 597-7350). The entrance is level, and there are elevators between floors. You can take a self-guided tour on weekdays between 8:30 a.m. and 3:30 p.m.

The totally accessible building that houses the **Afro-American Historical and Cultural Museum** is two blocks away, at 7th and Arch Sts. (tel. 574-0380). There is a level entrance and the different levels of the interior can be reached by ramps. There is also an elevator. Rest rooms on the first floor have accessible facilities. This was the first building in the country to have been specifically constructed to display the history of black Americans. It is open Tuesday to Saturday from 10 a.m. to 5 p.m., on Sunday from noon to 6 p.m. Admission is $1.50, half price for seniors and children.

As you wander around Olde City, look in at the **Painted Bride Art Center**, 146 N. Bread St., just off Race St. (tel. 925-9914), which is an accessible art gallery that offers folk or chamber music (at different times!) as well as jazz and poetry.

MIDTOWN: The central area of Center City is the location of many of the large hotels, of City Hall, the Pennsylvania Academy of Fine Arts, the Academy of Music, the Schubert Theater, the skyscrapers of Penn Center, and the fashionable row houses of Rittenhouse Square.

In the center of it all is **City Hall**, at the junction of Broad and Market Streets, with a cupola topped by a statue of Benjamin Franklin, the visual symbol of the city of Philadelphia. Generally, visitors can get a great view from the top, but it is reached only by escalators and a very small elevator. City Hall is being noted here primarily for its accessible rest rooms! These are on the street floor and the fourth floor; access to the building is level at the archway entrances.

If you would like to see some fine exhibits of American painting and sculpture, including Gilbert Stuart and three generations of Peales as well as the later works of Thomas Eakins, Winslow Homer, and Childe Hassam, the **Pennsylvania Academy of Fine Arts (PAFA)** is three blocks north of City Hall at Broad and Cherry Streets (tel. 972-7600).

It is the oldest museum in the country, and the building itself, now a National Landmark, was recently refurbished to accommodate disabled visitors. The level entrance is on Burns Street, where the elevator gives access to the rest of the building. You should call in advance to arrange to come into the PAFA on Burns Street. Other special installations inside include accessible rest rooms and lower drinking fountains. It is open Tuesday to Saturday from 10 a.m. to 5 p.m., on Sunday from 1 to 5 p.m. Admission is $1.50 for adults, $1 for students and seniors. The museum tours, which start at 11 a.m. and 2 p.m. on weekdays (at 2 p.m. on summer weekends), can include a signing interpreter if arrangements are made in advance.

There's a great collection of colonial furniture as well as art at the **Historical Society of Pennsylvania** in Center City, this time south of City Hall, at 1300 Locust St. (tel. 732-6200). It is accessible at the entrance on 13th Street, south of Locust—ring the bell here for the door to be opened. Inside, there is a ramp to the first level and then an elevator to all floors. Open Monday from 1 p.m. to 9 p.m., and Tuesday and Friday from 9 a.m. to 5 p.m. However, it is closed for the month of August. Admission is free.

THE BENJAMIN FRANKLIN PARKWAY: It's along this departure from

the original grid street plan that you'll find a number of top art and science museums, many of which have taken accessibility into account in recent renovations. The parkway was constructed to commemorate the 150th anniversary of independence in 1926, and it goes from Penn Center Station northwest to Fairmount Park in a fairly level stretch of pleasantly floral and leafy surroundings. If you want to leave your car at the Center City end of the parkway, there are parking facilities at the Penn Center Station on 16th Street at Arch. Or, if you want to drive to the neighborhood of Logan Circle, which is the location of the Academy of Natural Sciences, the Free Library, and the Franklin Institute, there are garages at each of these buildings.

The **Academy of Natural Sciences**, on the parkway at 19th St. (tel. 299-1000), has been recently refurbished with major changes in the interior and in the fascinating dioramas and other natural history exhibits. The barrier-free entrance is on 19th Street and there are accessible rest rooms on every floor. It is open from 10 a.m. to 4 p.m. daily. Admission is $2.50 for adults, $2.25 for ages 12 to 18, and $2 for children under 12.

Logan Circle, one of William Penn's original squares, now serves as a traffic circulator around the central fountain. Science is fun-time at the **Frank-**

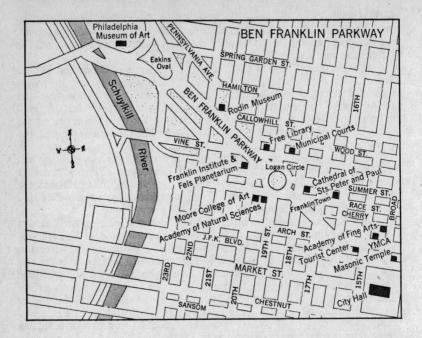

lin Institute here at Logan Circle on the parkway at 20th St. (tel. 448-1000). The building is accessible with a level entrance from the parking lot (the entrance at Winter Street has three steps). Because all the exhibits on the four floors can be reached by several different elevators, it is best to ask the guards for information on getting around. There is at least one accessible rest room on each floor. The Franklin Institute is open from 10 a.m. to 5 p.m. Monday to Saturday, noon to 5 p.m. on Sunday. Admission is $3.50 for adults, $2.50 for students, and $2 for children over 5. The Fels Planetarium (tel. 564-3375) is on the ground floor of the Franklin Institute and is completely wheelchair-accessible. It has shows at noon on weekdays and hourly on Saturday and Sunday, starting at noon. Admission is $1. There is a McDonald's on the first floor.

On the other side of the circle from the Academy of Natural Sciences is the **Free Library of Philadelphia**, at 19th and Vine (tel. 686-5322), where there are always lobby displays, such as medieval manuscripts or other fascinating exhibits connected with the library's rich store. The rooftop cafeteria is one of the parkway's rare eating places. There is parking behind the building, and the library is accessible by ramp at the Wood Street entrance. Inside there are elevators to all floors, as well as to the auditorium. The rest room is accessible. The library is open from 9 a.m. to 9 p.m. Monday to Wednesday, to 6 p.m. Thursday and Friday, to 5 p.m. on Saturday, and from 2 to 6 p.m. on Sunday. Admission is free.

The largest collection of the sculptor Rodin's work outside Paris is in the **Rodin Museum** on the Benjamin Franklin Parkway between 21st and 22nd Sts. (tel. 763-8100). The wheelchair-accessible entrance is well marked, and there are elevators to all floors. Rest rooms are not accessible. The Rodin Museum is open from 10 a.m. to 5 p.m. Tuesday to Sunday; admission is 50¢ for adults and 25¢ for children.

It sits on a hill, so you may want to take your car, or go by taxi, to the **Philadelphia Museum of Art** on the parkway at 26th St. (tel. 763-8100), which has the reputation for having the finest groupings of art objects in America. There are reserved spaces in the free parking lot.

It is accessible by a ramp at the south entrance (Division of Education door), with an education/freight elevator here that takes you to all floors. The public elevator is up a rather steep ramp. The new Stieglitz photography gallery is, unfortunately, not accessible. There *are* accessible rest rooms, and a very good cafeteria with entrees around $2.50. The museum is open from 9 a.m. to 5 p.m. Tuesday through Sunday, and admission is $2 for adults and $1 for students; children under 5, free. Sunday admission is free from 9 a.m. to 1 p.m.

FAIRMOUNT PARK: There is never enough time for a visitor to fully explore Fairmount Park's more than six square miles, the largest of any city park in the country. The best way to sample it is in your own car with the help of a map available from the Convention and Visitors Bureau (1525 John F. Kennedy Blvd.), and it might be a good idea to take your own food along on the trip if you think you'll get hungry. The park covers 400 acres on both sides of the Schuylkill River; there are mansions of old country estates that used to be here, summer playhouses, concert halls, a zoo, Japanese teahouses, and flowers galore.

While you're touring, you may want to stop at some of the places that are reasonably accessible. These include **Memorial Hall** on the North Concourse Drive of the park (tel. 686-1776), one of the original buildings from the centennial, which now houses a huge scale model of life in 1876. It has recently been made totally accessible.

If you follow the Visitors Bureau's suggested tour, the last stop will be the **Zoological Gardens** at 34th and Girard Ave. (tel. 222-5300), which has free parking. It covers 42 acres and is generally well ramped, with level entrances to nearly all of the ten buildings. Wheelchairs can be rented for a nominal fee at the entrance. There are accessible rest rooms. The zoo is open daily from 9:30 a.m. to 5 p.m. in winter, to 6 p.m. in summer, though it is closed on some holidays. Admission is $2.50 for adults, $2 for older students, and $1.50 for children 2 to 11. There's a family admission for $3.50.

UNIVERSITY CITY: If you want to stroll through an Ivy League campus, cross the Schuylkill River and take a look at the University of Pennsylvania in the area of 34th St. at Walnut and Locust Sts. There is parking here at a commercial lot across the street from the University Museum and from the Annenberg Center. Locust Street has been converted to a mall where you'll find refreshment vendors, if you're there about lunchtime.

You can go into the college quadrangles which were built in 1895 in the style of England's Oxford and Cambridge. South, on Spruce Street, you'll find one of the finest archeological collections in the United States at the **University Museum,** 33rd and Spruce Sts. (tel. 898-4000). There is easy entry on South Street through the Kress Wing, and elevators go to all floors. Accessible rest rooms are on the first floor of the Kress Wing. A special feature of the museum is the Nevil Gallery, funded by the Nevil Foundation for the Blind and designed with braille and large print for the visually impaired visitor. Thirty-five objects are mounted on rotating pedestals for touching.

7. Entertainment

Lively entertainment and nightlife were not characteristics associated with Philadelphia in the past, but there's a new vitality, inspired by the national and city birthday celebrations, that provides plenty of activity at night, culturally and otherwise. The best sources for finding out what is on are the "Weekend" supplement of the *Philadelphia Inquirer* on Friday, or the publications you'll find at most hotels and at the Visitors Bureau, or the listings in *Philadelphia Magazine*. This chapter discusses some of the places that seem reasonably accessible for the disabled visitor, and some where you will have to decide for yourself.

MUSIC: The regular season of the world-famous Philadelphia Orchestra is happily supplemented by many other musical events, not the least of which are the pleasant outdoor concerts in Fairmount Park and around Center City.

The **Academy of Music,** Broad and Locust Sts., Philadelphia, PA 19102 (tel. 215/893-1935), is the home of the Philadelphia Orchestra and the Opera Company of Philadelphia, and the auditorium for other concerts and for ballet performances. This is a venerable building, modeled on La Scala in Milan, and accessibility is therefore not ideal, but perhaps possible for you. You can arrange to drive into the South Alley off Broad Street (by calling the manager's office in advance), where there is a ramped entrance on the side of the building. There are a few steps to the proscenium boxes and steepish ramps to the parquet and parquet circle levels. A small elevator to the balcony levels could be used by people with ambulatory difficulties, but is not meant for people in wheelchairs. Rest rooms on the first floor are accessible. The box office is open Monday to Saturday from 10 a.m. to 6 p.m., but tickets to some events are sold out early, so some advance booking might be the best idea. You can also charge tickets by phone with major credit cards (tel. 800/223-0120).

The Philadelphia Orchestra gives free outdoor concerts in the summer at the new **Fredric R. Mann Center** in Fairmount Park on Monday, Tuesday, and Thursday evenings at 8 p.m. from mid-June to late July. The center seats 5000 under cover and 10,000 on the lawn. The building is ramped and has wheelchair-accessible rest rooms. If you come by car, come early to insure convenient parking. During June and August, there is opera and ballet, and at other times in the summer there are free performances of all kinds. For the season's brochure and for ticket information, write to Robin Hood Dell Concerts, 1617 John F. Kennedy Blvd., Philadelphia, PA 19103, or call 567-0707.

At **Robin Hood Dell East,** also in Fairmount Park near 33rd and Ridge Ave. (tel. 215/686-3612), there is a full summer schedule of outdoor performances of all kinds (not all music) on Monday, Wednesday, and Friday evenings at 8 p.m. for a minimal charge. The concert area is accessible, and you can get help with parking if you call in advance. Access to specially equipped rest rooms is ramped. For information, tickets, and prices during the summer, contact the Philadelphia Department of Recreation, Golden Age Building, Belmont and Parkside Aves., Philadelphia, PA 19131 (tel. 477-8810).

There's a lot of other outdoor music in the summer—on Monday evening on Rittenhouse Square and on the steps of the Philadelphia Museum of Art on Thursday, Friday, and Saturday at 8 p.m. Lunchtime entertainment takes place in Kennedy Plaza next to the Visitors Bureau at 1525 John F. Kennedy Blvd., and on Wednesday the Olde Citie Fife and Drum Corps marches throughout the Independence National Historical Park.

There are wheelchair locations for the mostly rock concerts at the **Spectrum** at Broad St. and Pattison Ave. (tel. 389-5000). Special parking is available near the ramped entrances to the main level, where the special seating is located at the rear. There is a fully equipped rest room for disabled patrons and the key should be requested from the usher.

THEATER: Philadelphia often has a Broadway show, on its way to or from New York, as well as other drama and ballet performances.

The **Shubert Theater** at 250 S. Broad St. at Locust St. (tel. 735-4768), has a level entrance but requires transfer from wheelchairs to aisle seats. Besides Broadway shows, the Shubert is the home of the Pennsylvania Ballet Company.

The **Walnut Street Theater,** 825 Walnut St. (tel. 574-3550), has a level entrance. You can arrange to stay in a wheelchair if the theater has advance notice. Audio loops for amplification are available for hard-of-hearing patrons. Performances here include Broadway shows, the Pilobolus Dance Theater, chamber groups, films, and the Philadelphia Composer's Forum series.

The bigger musicals as well as plays and concerts are often at the **Forrest Theater,** 1114 Walnut St. at 11th St. (tel. 923-1515). It has a level entrance, but management requires transfer from wheelchairs to aisle seats in the orchestra.

The **Annenberg Center,** 3680 Walnut St. (tel. 243-6791), on the campus of the University of Pennsylvania, is a complex of four theaters—the Zellerbach, Studio Theater, Hal Prince, and the Annenberg Auditorium Theater. Wheelchair locations are available, and the box office can indicate suitability of seating depending on your requirements. There are accessible rest rooms, but escort is necessary via a staff elevator to the main floor. There is drama, film, dance, and other performing arts at some or all of the Annenberg Theaters year-round.

There's dinner theater at the **Riverfront Dinner Theater** on the Delaware River at Poplar St. (tel. 925-7000), which often presents full Broadway shows on a small stage. The dinner and show tariff ranges from $15.95 to $19.95 depending on the day. The **City Line Dinner Theater,** run by the same management, is at 4200 City Line Ave. at Monument Rd. (tel. 879-4000), and has much the same fare. There is wheelchair access at both, but call in advance so that a table can be rearranged as necessary.

The **Burgundy Theater** in the Bellevue-Stratford Hotel, Broad and Walnut Sts. presents a number of small productions throughout the year in an attractive period-room setting. The hotel is in the process of building a ramp at the entrance, which should be complete by the time you visit. Call the theater at 735-8905 and request "floor section" for easiest access.

You may not be visiting Philadelphia to go to the movies, but if you see something playing that you really don't want to miss, you may like to know that most movie houses are on street level, and many of them allow patrons who wish to do so, to remain in their wheelchairs. A phone call to the particular movie house will give you the information you need. But, as usual, don't expect accessible rest rooms.

SPECTATOR SPORTS: Philadelphia is represented in every major sport, most of which are played at the stadium complex at the end of South Broad Street. The **J.F. Kennedy Stadium** does not have good accessibility but not much goes on there these days. However, the Spectrum at Broad St. and Pattison Ave. (tel. 389-5000), which houses the hockey and basketball teams as well as being the site for the U.S. Pro Indoor Tennis Championships, offers facilities for disabled patrons. There is special parking near ramped entrances to the main level, and special seating on the main level for people in wheelchairs. There is an elevator at this level, and the specially equipped rest room can be used by asking the usher for the key. For information on the '76er basketball games (October to April), call 339-7676; for the Flyers ice hockey games (October to April), call 755-9700.

The Phillies play baseball (April to October), and the Philadelphia Eagles play football (August to December) at **Veterans Stadium,** Broad St. and Pattison Ave. (tel. 463-6000), which is accessible by ramps or elevators. You should call ahead to make special arrangements for seating. For ticket information on Eagles games, call 463-5000, and for Phillies games, 463-1000.

Intercollegiate and amateur events take place at **Franklin Field** in West Philadelphia on 33rd St. below Walnut St. (tel. 396-0961), which has entrances at ground level at the East End Gate. There is also ramped access to wheelchair locations elsewhere in the stadium. Call ahead and make specific arrangements.

Both horse-racing tracks are quite accessible. **Liberty Bell Park,** at Knights Rd. and Woodhaven Rd. (tel. 637-7100), runs harness races in spring and fall. To go by car, take I-95 north and follow the signs. Entrances are level and there are ramps or elevators to all floors. (Don't count on the rest rooms.) Thoroughbred horse racing takes place every day except Monday and Thursday at **Keystone Park** in Cornwell Heights (tel. 632-5770), which has level entrances or ramps and elevators to all floors. The rest rooms here are accessible. To reach Keystone Track, take the Pennsylvania Turnpike to exit 28.

BARS AND BISTROS: There's a lot of lively nightlife in Philadelphia, contrary to rumor, but a lot of it is subterranean or very, very crowded as most nightspots are by definition. However, here are a few places that offer evening entertainment that might have a degree of accessibility for you.

Rick's Cabaret is part of Le Bistro restaurant (see restaurant section of this chapter) 757 S. Front St. (tel. 389-3855), and offers what some consider to be the best jazz in the city. It is open from 5 p.m. to midnight Monday through Thursday; to 1 a.m. on Friday and Saturday. Drinks start at $2 and there is no cover charge.

A bit closer to the center of things at Head House Square, the **East Philly Cafe,** 200 South St. (tel. 922-1813), has one step at the entrance and jazz until 1 a.m. every evening.

Even if you are not staying at that particular hotel, there are many that have recommendable places to relax in the evening. The **Society Hill Hotel** has a bar on the corner of 3rd and Chestnut (tel. 925-1919), with an outdoor section that is a pleasant place to spend some time on a warm evening. In the Warwick Hotel, 17th and Locust Sts. (tel. 545-4655), the **Brasserie Cafe and Bar** is accessible and open all day, and there is live music, mostly jazz, from 9 p.m. to 1 a.m. Wednesday through Saturday, and 8 p.m. to midnight on Sunday. And at the **Bar at the Barclay Hotel,** 18th and Rittenhouse Sq. (tel. 545-0300), you'll find light meals and piano music.

8. Shopping

If shopping is an indispensable part of your vacation, you'll probably find more than enough in Philadelphia that's accessible to you to satisfy the urge. There are some very fashionable boutiques around Rittenhouse Square, as well as shopping malls and department stores that are relatively easy to get around. For crafts, you'll find the **Artisans Cooperative** at NewMarket at 2nd and Pine Streets, open on Sunday, and craftsmen offer their wares outdoors in **Indepen-**

dence Mall on warmer weekends, and at **Head House Square** all day Saturday and on Sunday afternoons April through September.

There are some attractive small specialty shops on the **Chestnut Street Walkway** that goes from Independence Hall to 19th Street, where most cross streets have curb cuts. The mid-block crossings on Chestnut Street here are also level.

The **Market Street East Complex,** on Market St. between 8th and 9th Sts., is made up of the new indoor shopping mall, with 100 stores built on four levels, around a sunken arcade and a glassy atrium, and encompasses a new Gimbels and that Philadelphia institution, Strawbridge & Clothier's. Parking is available in indoor lots that have special parking spaces for disabled people at either end of the Gallery. From the lot at 8th and Market Streets, there are level entries through Strawbridge & Clothier's. The Gallery can be reached from the second and third floors at Strawbridge's. From the parking lot at 10th and Market Streets, take the elevator to the top level of the Gallery where you can then take the glass elevator to all levels. The lowest level of the Gallery has many fast-food restaurants that are accessible, and there are also accessible rest rooms on this level.

Strawbridge & Clothier's, 8th and Market Sts. (tel. 629-6000), has all its entrances level with either the street or the adjoining parking lot. Wheelchair-accessible rest rooms are on the second and fifth floors for women, and on the sixth and Budget floors for men.

Wanamaker's, the store that fills the block between Market and Chestnut, and 13th and Juniper Sts. (tel. 422-2000), was one of the first great department stores in the country and still maintains its preeminent status. It has everything in the most elegant surroundings, as well as level entrances all around the store. There is a doorman at Juniper Street. Elevators give access to all 12 floors. There are accessible rest rooms on the ninth and Budget floors.

Chapter 8

ATLANTIC CITY

Bets and Boardwalk

1. Getting There & Getting Around 2. Orientation 3. The Casino/Hotels 4. Dining in Atlantic City

AT ONE TIME, Atlantic City was just a P.S. to Philadelphia in most travel guides, but now it's much more than that. Transformed since 1977 from a rundown seaside resort, the new gambling mecca has become, it claims, the biggest tourist destination in America, with 23 million visitors a year. If you want to flutter a few quarters—or more, if you want to see some of the most pretentious construction outside ancient Rome at its peak, if you would enjoy top entertainment every night, all combined with a fine oceanfront and a wide boardwalk overlooking some of the cleanest beaches anywhere, Atlantic City's new casino hotels have made sure that you, as a disabled visitor, can be included in everything that's going on here (even though their motives aren't exactly philanthropic).

Everything in the new hotels has been made accessible, by level entrances, ramps to the casino floors, elevators to all facilities, easy access to most of the restaurants, and lots of special rooms.

You will certainly be able to get into the casinos, but, depending on your disability, may need assistance at the slot machines (they don't have any made for wheelchair height!), and blackjack tables are made to accommodate the dealer who is standing up or on a high stool. Baccarat tables are usually lower, as are the roulette tables.

The boardwalk is well maintained and close boarded and is accessible directly from casino entrances or by ramps from the street level. The piers that still remain are level with the boardwalk, and you *can* get to the beach by using the ramps constructed for the garbage trucks—there are quite a number of them.

Accommodations, prices, parking, and other practical arrangements are not always as routine as elsewhere, since things are still a-building and developing, so you should check for the latest information with the **Atlantic City Convention Bureau**, 16 Central Pier, Atlantic City, NJ 08401 (tel. 609/345-7538). You'll also be able to find out what's going on through the monthly *Atlantic City Magazine,* 1637 Atlantic Ave., Atlantic City, NJ 08401 (copies

$1.95 each), which includes wheelchair-accessible symbols in the restaurant listings.

1. Getting There & Getting Around

BY AIR: Atlantic City's two airports are both accessible: Bader Field, one mile from downtown, is the smaller general-aviation airport; the International Airport in Pomona (20 minutes by car or taxi to downtown) serves charter flights flown in by hotel casinos and regular flights of American International Airways and People Express. It is all on one level and there are wheelchair-accessible rest rooms and ramped curbs. A multi-million dollar expansion planned for 1984 will add a transportation center and customs facilities.

BY CAR/VAN: You can reach Atlantic City by car in about 80 minutes from Philadelphia on the Atlantic City Expressway (from the Benjamin Franklin Bridge), and in about 2½ hours from New York via the Garden State Parkway to the Atlantic City Expressway. Private automobile may be the only way for a visitor with mobility impairments to travel to Atlantic City, since none of the public or charter buses that take so many of those millions of visitors are equipped with wheelchair lifts. However, the **Handi-Wheels Transportation Service** (tel. 215/757-3316) runs day trips from Philadelphia and points in Bucks County for groups of 20 people minimum (if you are not part of a group, you may be able to join one; call and ask). Fare is $15 (or $20 if they pick you up), but you get $10 worth of chips from the casino when you arrive.

Once in town, parking can be expensive. If you stay at a casino you will pay for the valet parking, and since there are just too many cars on the streets, the traffic situation is not the best. There are many independent parking lots, but price correlates to demand.

To get around once you have arrived, and if you are ambulatory, you may be able to use the 13-seat jitneys that provide fast and frequent transport the length of Atlantic City for 75¢. They have one step at the entrance and two more steps inside.

You can usually find a taxicab in front of the hotels, or you can call in advance for one to pick you up (find telephone numbers in the Yellow Pages). Local rate is $1.35 for the first one-fifth of a mile, 20¢ each additional one-fifth mile. Each additional passenger is 20¢.

2. Orientation

Atlantic City is on Absecon Island, part of the string of barrier islands along the South Jersey Shore.

A Monopoly board may be the most useful tool in acquainting yourself with the town, and many of the street names will have a familiar ring. Starting at the inlet end of the island, the cross streets are named after American states, beginning with the northern states (Maine, New Hampshire, Vermont) and make their way down the Atlantic coast, into the midwest and south (with a few geographical exceptions). In the "Downbeach" section of town (which is the way natives refer to "south"), most of the streets are named after state capitals. Streets that run lengthwise through the city are named mainly after the seas of the world: Pacific, Atlantic, Arctic, Baltic, Mediterranean, and Adriatic.

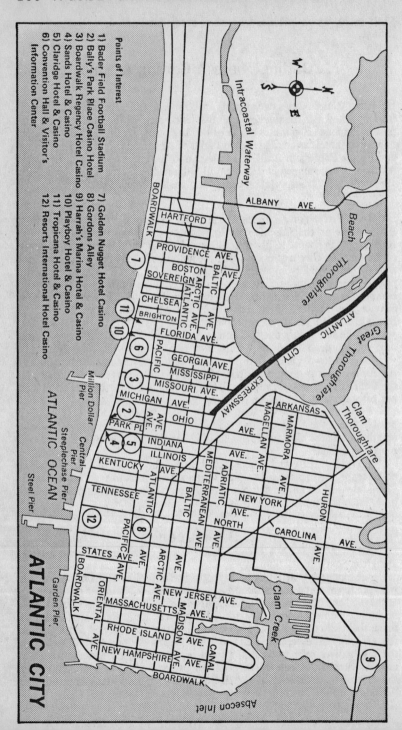

Points of Interest

1) Bader Field Football Stadium
2) Bally's Park Place Casino Hotel
3) Boardwalk Regency Hotel Casino
4) Sands Hotel & Casino
5) Claridge Hotel & Casino
6) Convention Hall & Visitor's Information Center
7) Golden Nugget Hotel Casino
8) Gordons Alley
9) Harrah's Marina Hotel & Casino
10) Playboy Hotel & Casino
11) Tropicana Hotel & Casino
12) Resorts International Hotel Casino

ATLANTIC CITY

Addresses on the lengthwise streets are numbered in blocks of 100 starting at Maine Avenue. The cross streets are designated North and South, divided by Atlantic Avenue, so that 100 South Illinois Ave. is near the ocean, while 100 North Illinois is closer to the bay.

There is no Marvin Gardens.

3. The Casino/Hotels

As grand new buildings, designed to attract *everybody,* the casino hotels incorporated total accessibility in their plans. Not cheap, but that's not a new story. All lined up with frontage on the boardwalk, they have been likened to a line of costumed showgirls, and all of them have at least the 500 hotel rooms required for a casino license.

Certain rules-of-thumb apply to all of them: rates shown for rooms and parking are current at the time of writing and will give an idea of the range to expect. Keep in mind that rates are usually lowest in winter, get a little higher in spring, top out in summer, and drop a bit in the fall. Rates will also vary depending on whether you stay on a weekday or a weekend. All the casino/hotels offer special packages that include accommodation plus various combinations of meals and shows, and they are worth looking into since they can be bargains. Check with individual hotels, or your travel agent, to find out what is available at the time you want to visit.

Casinos are open from 10 a.m. to 4 a.m. on weekdays, to 6 a.m. on Saturday, Sunday, and holidays. Expect to find drink minimums in lounges and theaters with at least $2.75 a drink. The legal gambling age is 21 and casinos are careful to check.

There are no strict dress codes, except for "no bathing suits allowed" in the public areas of the casinos or restaurants. Casual-but-covered is usually good enough. In the better restaurants, jackets are often required, so call first if you want to know.

Your visit to Atlantic City could be for the day, for the weekend (taking advantage of the special packages), or for longer, and there's no doubt you'll find it relatively easy to get around in the new hotels. However, the hotels *are* enormous, so distances between different areas can be lengthy. The list that follows indicates the vital statistics of some of them and includes details of their multiple restaurants as well. Of course, they all have pools in areas accessible from level entrances, but there is no special equipment for wheelchair access *into* the pools.

Each casino has a top-of-the-line restaurant featuring gourmet dining, as well as steakhouses, New York style delis, buffets, and a 24-hour coffee shop. If the restaurants are described as upper-price bracket, it indicates entrees over $16; medium indicates $12; and moderate, between $8 and $12.

RESORTS INTERNATIONAL: Resorts International on the boardwalk at North Carolina Ave., NJ 08404 (tel. 609/344-6000), has level or ramped approaches at all entrances, and 29 guest rooms are equipped with grab bars in the bathroom. All guest rooms have 33-inch entry doors and 27½-inch bathroom doors. Bed units include AM/FM radio and remote control of the color TV. Resorts International got a head start as the first operating casino and works hard to maintain its service and slickness, with five restaurants, 14 shops, the largest casino in town, and a parking capacity of 4000 cars ($8 a day for valet parking, $4 if you park yourself, free self-parking with validation from the casino, restaurant, or theater). Rates at the time of writing for double rooms range from $85 to $120 in season.

The **Superstar Theatre** holds 400 for dinner but many, many more when headliners perform, and when tickets, which range from $15 to $35, should be reserved well in advance (call 609/340-6434 for information and schedules). It is accessible via a wheelchair lift, and the interior is level. There's a revue here during afternoon matinees, and early and late evening shows, as well.

The restaurants are all considered accessible, except perhaps the Oyster Bar (no low tables). **Capriccio, Le Palais,** and the **House of Kyoto** are in the upper price brackets. Average entrée is under $8 in the **Celebrity Deli,** the **Cafe Casino,** and in the **Wedgwood Pavilion,** which also has an all-you-can-eat buffet for $7. There are rest rooms (on the same level as the restaurants) that have 36-inch stall doors.

BALLY'S PARK PLACE: Don't be too disheartened when you hear that the centerpiece here is a continuous grand escalator from the casino level to the restaurants on the sixth floor! There *are* elevators. Bally's Park Place, Park Place at the Boardwalk, NJ 08401 (tel. 609/340-2000, toll free 800/257-8546), has level entrances and 22 rooms with 33-inch bathroom doors and grab bars in the bathrooms. Regular guest rooms have 33-inch entry and 29-inch bathroom doors. The TV can be controlled from the bed, and the telephones can be amplified. There are public rest rooms that are designed for accessibility. At the time of writing, rates for single or double rooms range from $105 to $135 in the summer season. There are packages, though, that are worth looking into.

Parking charges, as with everything else, are subject to change, but in the multilevel indoor garage it is currently $4 a day, free for four hours with validation from the casino. Most of the eight restaurants are considered accessible (with wide price ranges). The **Oyster Bar** and **Ice Cream Parlor** have only counter service. In the upper bracket are **By the Sea** (a prix fixe dinner is $25) and **Prime Place Steak House.** In the medium range are **The Greenery** coffee shop; the **Sidewalk Cafe,** which has a dinner buffet for $9.95; and **Park Place Deli,** which features a $7.95 supper, but also serves sandwiches and hamburgers that average $4.95.

THE CLARIDGE: This is a conversion of one of Atlantic City's landmark hotels that has even built a new wing to match the brick of the old one, and everything has a strong British theme. The Claridge is on the Boardwalk at S. Indiana Ave., P.O. Box 448, NJ 08401 (tel. 609/340-3400, toll free 800/257-8585), and has a ramped entrance and 24 rooms with 32½-inch bathroom entry and grab bars (the regular guest room bathroom is only 24½ inches). Public rest rooms have 33¾-inch stall entry doors. There are braille floor indicators in the elevators, and braille menus are available in the restaurants. Valet parking is free for registered guests, otherwise the charge is $8 for 24 hours. The room rates at the time of writing are around $85 double and vary with the seasons and the time of the week. Again, look into special packages.

Claridge restaurants considered wheelchair-accessible are the upper-bracket **London Pavilion,** which also has a buffet lunch and Sunday brunch for $14.95, and the **Hyde Park,** open 24 hours, in the moderate price range.

The pool in the health club on the eighth floor is smaller than in most of the other casinos, and health club activities cost $5 extra.

THE SANDS: The Sands Hotel and Casino at Indiana Ave. and Brighton Park, NJ 08401 (tel. 609/441-4444, toll free 800/257-8580), has entrances that are level or ramped and 24 guest rooms with 32½-inch bathroom entry and grab bars. Regular guest rooms have 33-inch entry doors and 29½-inch bathroom doors. There are public rest rooms that have 36-inch entry and stall doors. The elevators have braille numbers for floors, as well as a tone signal to indicate floor arrival. Room rates vary with the season, of course, whether you stay during the week or on weekends, and by as much as $30 depending on whether you have an ocean or a city view. Subject to change, midweek rates range from $69 to $99 double; $79 to $109 on Friday, Saturday, and holidays. Packages, however, can start at around $45 per person for room, dinner, and the show. There is valet parking, but the hotel won't commit itself to a printed rate. Restaurants considered wheelchair-accessible are the higher-priced **Mes Amis,** the **Brighton Steak House** (which has a country brunch for $11.95), and the more moderately priced 24-hour **Park Garden Cafe.**

Best entrance for the theater is at the side, and there are wheelchair locations inside for good sightlines of the shows.

PLAYBOY: Giant rabbit ears atop the 22-story tower easily identify this hotel from a great distance. It is at the Boardwalk and Florida Ave., P.O. Box 1558, NJ 08404 (tel. 609/344-4000, toll free 800/621-1116), has a level entrance and 25 special rooms with bathroom grab bars and 35¾-inch bathroom entry doors. All regular guest rooms have 34-inch bathroom doors. Public rest room dimensions are a 32-inch entry and a 33½-inch stall. If you need telephones that are amplified, request rooms 716 or 816. The casino here is on three levels, with a wall of windows facing the ocean.

Room rates vary with the season, the day of the week, and the view, but doubles range from $90 midweek to $105 at weekends, and up. Parking is in the garage under Convention Hall (next door, with access directly to the hotel) and hotel policy is to say that "rates vary."

At the restaurants considered wheelchair-accessible, gourmet cuisine puts the **Chat Noir** in the upper price bracket, while the **Golden Steer** and the **Tahitian Room** could be considered in the medium price bracket (there is a $9.25 buffet lunch in the Tahitian Room). The 24-hour **Garden State Cafe** is more moderately priced.

The **Cabaret Theatre** at the Playboy seems to be the one exception to the overall accessibility of Atlantic City hotel/casinos since it has steps inside.

TROPICANA: More low-key than the other hotel/casinos but still opulently luxurious, Ramada's Tropicana is on the Boardwalk at Iowa Ave., NJ 08404 (tel. 609/340-4000, toll-free 800/228-2828). There are two rooms on each of eleven floors that have wide doors and bathrooms equipped with grab bars. All guest rooms have views on three sides. The rest of the hotel is fully accessible to wheelchair guests, including the pool area and the 1600-seat **Tiffany Showroom** dinner theater. The accessible restaurants include the top-price **Les Paris, Il Verdi,** and **Regent Court;** the fast-food buffet at **Summerfield's** where lunch is $7.95 and dinner $8.95, and the **Backstage Deli.** Rates range from $90 to $120.

4. Dining in Atlantic City

Although convenience is built into casino dining, there is a great variety of other restaurants all over town, particularly Italian and seafood restaurants in all price ranges. The ones listed here consider themselves to be accessible for patrons in wheelchairs.

Knife and Fork, Albany and Pacific Aves. (tel. 344-1133), has a reputation as one of the finest seafood restaurants anywhere, although the atmosphere is unpretentious. Expect to pay about $23 per person. Open 5:30 to 11 p.m. every day. Free parking.

Pal's Other Room, 3810 Ventnor Ave. (tel. 344-0366), is an Italian restaurant with a chalkboard menu and entree prices ranging between $8 and $12. Open all year from 4:30 p.m. to midnight.

Dock's Oyster House, 2405 Atlantic Ave. (tel 345-0092), specializes in seafood, of course, with average entree prices between $12 and $16 (lobsters a bit higher). Open for dinner from 5 p.m. until the wee hours, Tuesday through Saturday.

A. C. Charles, 1006 Atlantic Ave. (tel. 348-8227), is an Italian restaurant with reasonable prices, with dinner and luncheon specials every day for under $4. Open from 7 a.m. to midnight every day.

Rib-It, 3700 Atlantic Ave. (tel. 347-0505), specializes in guess-what, as well as steak and chicken, with the average entree under $8. Open from 4 p.m. to 11 p.m. Sunday through Thursday, until midnight on Friday and Saturday.

Chapter 9

NEW ORLEANS

The Crescent City

**1. Getting There
2. Getting Around
3. Orientation 4. Where to
Stay 5. New Orleans Dining
6. The Sights 7. A Festival
City 8. Nightlife & Entertainment**

NEW ORLEANS IS a city to visit for its food, its jazz, its French Quarter, its Garden District, and (if you're brave) its Mardi Gras. *And* it's a city to visit because a disabled traveler can enjoy it to the fullest.

This is something of a paradox: there aren't many cities in America as old as New Orleans, where 150-year-old buildings that are still used as residences and restaurants also have reasonable architectural access. In a way, that's even due to the passage of time: many buildings that originally had entrance steps are now level with the sidewalk, because a century-and-a-half of street repaving has layered the original roadway and sidewalks until they are level with the building entrance! These old buildings, of course, are in the French Quarter, which is probably where most visitors spend most of their time. There are certainly enough hotels here where disabled guests will find good accommodations, and the food, the jazz, the history, and the Mississippi River are right at the doorstep, all readily available to a disabled visitor. Sidewalks leave something to be desired—they are uneven in many places—but there are times during the evenings and in the daytime as well as on the weekends, when you can take advantage of Bourbon Street and Royal Street as pedestrian malls and "stroll" the smoother roadway in comfort, joining the parade of natives and tourists listening to the lively jazz that fills the air through the open windows of the restaurants, stopping off for half-a-dozen raw oysters, a bowl of gumbo or jambalaya, or a French pastry as your fancy takes you at any hour of the day.

And a city that has a public rest room marked with the international symbol of access in mosaic tile *has* to be a good place to go to!

1. Getting There

As a tourist attraction that is a mecca for Americans and foreign visitors alike, and as a historic port that is now the second busiest in the country, New Orleans is a traffic hub that is easy to get to.

BY AIR: The International Airport is served by ten airlines—American, Continental, Delta, Eastern, Lacsa, Northwest Orient, Ozark, Pan American, Republic, and USAir. You arrive at the upper level, as at most airports, and there is an elevator to the baggage claim area on the lower level. Rest rooms in the airport have 30-inch entry doors and 28-inch stall doors.

Taxis will be found at the lower level, and at the time of writing, taxi fare from the airport to the leading hotels in the Central District or the French Quarter is set by the Aviation Board at $18 per person. Rates on buses (limousines) that leave from the upper level is $6 per person, but they are not wheelchair-accessible.

A transportation company that offers vans equipped with wheelchair lifts, and which serves the airport, is **Medicab**, 53 Smithway, Gretna, LA 70053 (tel. 504/367-7720).

Rental cars with hand controls are available at the airport from **Hertz** (tel. toll free 800/654-3131) on five days notice; and from **Avis** (tel. toll free 800/331-1212) on two weeks notice.

BY TRAIN: Amtrak trains from all major cities arrive at **Union Passenger Terminal,** at 1001 Loyola Avenue in the central business district, and not far from the French Quarter. The interior does not have steps, and there is elevator access to all levels. There is one step at the exit to the street. Accessible rest rooms are located near the Loyola Street entrance; tokens for rest rooms may be purchased at the ticket office.

BY BUS: Greyhound and Trailways buses also come into the **Union Passenger Terminal** from all over the country.

BY CAR: The road approach to New Orleans is across the Lake Pontchartrain Causeway on Rte. LA 25. Most hotels provide parking facilities, even in the French Quarter, where there are a number of motels. The AAA's Central Gulf Division is at 3445 N. Causeway, Metairie, LA 70002 (tel. 504/837-1080).

2. Getting Around

BY CAR: The French Quarter is *not* a place to tour by car—the streets are narrow, and there's nowhere to park. A number of the Quarter's hotels are actually motels that offer free parking if you stay there.

BY MINIBUS: You can take a tour of the French Quarter on the small bus that has one fairly low step at the entrance and another one inside—a possibility if you can negotiate those steps, or can be carried on (folding wheelchairs can be left at the entrance of the bus). They also run between the French Quarter and the Garden District. They leave Canal and Bourbon Streets from 6 to 9:30 a.m. and 4 to 6 p.m. on weekdays, or you can board at Bourbon and Iberville

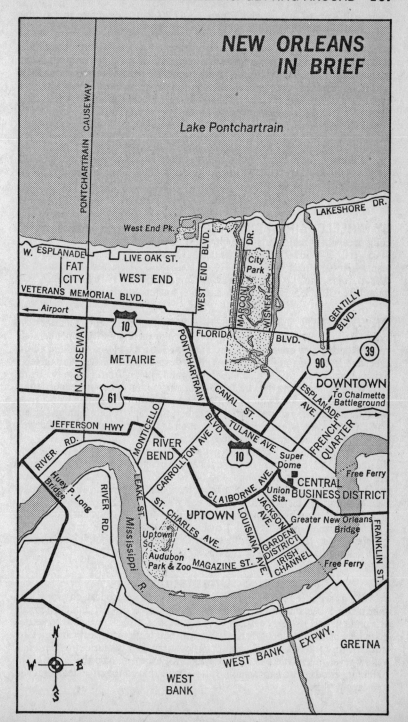

NEW ORLEANS IN BRIEF

Lake Pontchartrain

PONTCHARTRAIN CAUSEWAY

LAKESHORE DR.

West End Pk.

W. ESPLANADE

FAT CITY

LIVE OAK ST.

WEST END

WEST END BLVD.

MARCONI DR.

WISNER

City Park

GENTILLY BLVD.

VETERANS MEMORIAL BLVD.

← Airport

10

N. CAUSEWAY

METAIRIE

FLORIDA   BLVD.

90

39

61

JEFFERSON HWY

PONTCHARTRAIN

CANAL ST.

DOWNTOWN
To Chalmette Battleground

ESPLANADE AVE.

FRENCH QUARTER

RIVER RD.

MONTICELLO

RIVER BEND

CARROLLTON AVE.

BLVD.

TULANE AVE.

10

Super Dome

Huey P. Long Bridge

LEAKE ST.

RIVER RD.

ST. CHARLES AVE.

Mississippi R.

CLAIBORNE AVE.

UPTOWN

LOUISIANA AVE.

Union Sta.

CENTRAL BUSINESS DISTRICT

Free Ferry

Uptown Sq.

Audubon Park & Zoo

MAGAZINE ST.

JACKSON AVE.

GARDEN DISTRICT

IRISH CHANNEL

Greater New Orleans Bridge

FRANKLIN ST.

Free Ferry

N
W ⊕ E
S

WEST BANK

WEST BANK EXPWY.

GRETNA

from 9:30 a.m. to 4 p.m. and 6 p.m. to 12:30 a.m. weekdays, and all day Saturday, Sunday and holidays. Cost at time of writing is 40¢.

BY TAXI: Taxis are plentiful (except at Mardi Gras) and can be summoned, for instance, to go to the Garden District from the French Quarter (about $3.50 on the meter). Cabs that can be called on the phone include **Yellow Cab** (tel. 504/943-2411); **Checker Cab** (tel. 504/525-3311), and **United Cabs** (tel. 504/522-9771).

BY RIVER: River transport is good for sightseeing. There is a free ferry across the Mississippi that has a well-ramped entry. Paddlewheel steamboats are accessible to their lower decks for tours of the harbor and of the bayous. At the moment, they do not have accessible rest rooms, but modifications are being considered. Call **Natchez Steamboat** for information 504/586-8777.

BY WHEELCHAIR-LIFT VAN: Transportation services that offer vans equipped with wheelchair lifts include **Medicab**, 53 Smithway, Gretna, LA 70053 (tel. 504/367-7720), and **Transfer Parking**, 501 N. Cortez, New Orleans, LA 70119 (tel. 504/569-2614 or 504/569-2611). Tours are offered by **Abbott Tours, Inc.**, 2609 Canal St., New Orleans, LA 70119 (tel. 504/827-5920 or toll free 800/535-8550), which has vans for four to six people.

ON YOUR OWN: This is often the best way to tour the French Quarter. The sidewalks are uneven in places, but even though there aren't any deliberately ramped curbs, they are all fairly low. Jackson Square is closed to traffic all the time, and Bourbon and Royal Streets are pedestrian malls on Monday through Friday from 7 p.m. to 3 a.m., and Saturday and Sunday from 10 a.m. to 3 a.m.

Wandering around the Garden District on your own (having reached there by car or taxi from somewhere else), is a pleasant way to spend half a day. Even though there are no ramped curbs here either, the traffic is light enough (except on St. Charles Avenue and Jackson Street on the edge of the District) that you could use the roadway with relative safety.

Note: There are other ways to get around, but none is readily available to disabled visitors. Streetcars or trolleys have two high steps at the entrance and are certainly not for wheelchairs, and the entrance to the famous horse-drawn carriages that are such a colorful part of the French Quarter, calls for nimbleness even in the able-bodied as far as entry is concerned.

The city has a para-transit system of door-to-door transportation for its disabled citizens, but this is not available to visitors since one must be a registered user. (So, if you see the van with the access symbol, it won't be any good hailing it or looking for the bus stop!)

3. Orientation

It's no wonder New Orleans is different. It was a European city for a long time before it became part of the United States; it took no part in the American Revolution; and its early settlers were by no means the Puritans who settled elsewhere on the continent. It has had a constant battle with death and disaster in the form of floods, hurricanes, countless fires, and plagues of cholera and yellow fever (all in the past, thank goodness, except maybe the floods). The different periods of its tempestuous history have shaped the city's temperament and layout alike.

You can get a lot of general information from the **Visitors Information Center,** 334 Royal St., New Orleans, LA 70130 (tel. 504/556-5011). You should probably do this in advance of arrival, since the Visitors Center has three large steps in front (it is one of the very few in the French Quarter that does not have level access). Maps of walking and driving tours are especially useful.

Looking at a map of New Orleans, you'll see that the city nestles in a loop of the Mississippi River, a location that gave it its Crescent City designation. The French Quarter, or Vieux Carré (Old Square), is the original 18th-century settlement and runs between Canal Street and Esplanade Avenue, the river and North Rampart Street—a negotiable distance for exploring on foot, or your own wheels. The central business district, the most modern part of the city by the river, is situated next to the French Quarter on the other side of Canal Street, and the Garden District lies beyond, between St. Charles Avenue and Magazine Street toward the river, and Jackson and Louisiana Avenues. The Garden District is the section that was settled by Americans after the Louisiana Purchase of 1803, when Creole society rejected the newcomers. A completely separate town was the result, with homes built in a lavish style designed to surpass the old city in its grandeur. Loyola and Tulane Universities are further out on St. Charles Avenue. The "Irish Channel," nearer the river beyond Magazine Street, is yet another reflection of the city's past, when it became home to Irish immigrants a hundred-and-more years ago.

As the outlet port for the entire Mississippi Basin, New Orleans prospered and flourished, along with the unique and colorful steamboat life, and the outlying cotton and sugar plantations that lined the Mississippi upriver from New Orleans. The plantation economy, built on slavery, declined after the Civil War, but some of the great houses remain along River Road above New Orleans. For the disabled visitor, however, visits to the plantations are probably not to be recommended, since access to the houses is minimal if not impossible.

TELEPHONE AREA CODE: The area code for all sections of the city is 504.

MEDICAL ASSISTANCE: Most major hotels have doctors on call 24 hours a day. Useful emergency numbers are **Charity Hospital,** 1532 Tulane Ave. (tel. 504/568-3291) for downtown (the French Quarter side of Canal Street), or the **Touro Infirmary,** 1401 Foucher St. (tel. 504/897-7011) on the Garden District side of Canal Street. Call the **New Orleans Dental Association** for dental emergencies (tel. 504/834-6449).

INFORMATION AND REFERRAL: The **Easter Seal Society of Louisiana, Inc.** is at 4631 W. Napoleon Ave., P.O. Box 8425, Metairie, LA 70011 (tel. 504/885-9960).

TRAVEL AGENTS: A newly formed association of travel agents in the New Orleans area, called **TAGNO,** specializes in providing services to disabled travelers. Write for information to John Hunlee, Holmes Travel Agency, P.O. Box 56908, New Orleans, LA 70156, or call him at 504/561-6314.

CLIMATE: New Orleans has a balmy, subtropical climate with an average mean temperature of 70°.

Lightweight clothing is suitable for spring, summer, and fall, with extra sweaters for the winter. The summer can be humid, and rainfall averages 63 inches annually—so be prepared for sudden showers.

4. Where to Stay

THE FRENCH QUARTER: There is a very real sense of the past in New Orleans's French Quarter—not the sanitized, stagelike past of a restoration in a museum, but a "lived-in" feeling that gives it a vivacity and a continuity. Ornamental iron balconies are its architectural "signature," and it is ironic that the entire city, now called the French Quarter, was entirely rebuilt under Spanish rule after a disastrous fire in 1788. The result is a unique district with elements of both cultures, influenced by native materials and the subtropical climate.

The one thing, perhaps, of even more interest to visitors with a mobility problem is that this historic architecture is often more amenable to their needs than many a modern building. As mentioned earlier, the roadway has gradually been layered over the years so that it is level, in most places, with the ground floor of these buildings that have been there for 150 years. The other big plus of this architecture is that it was designed for a lot of pleasant living on the ground floor, though I doubt whether physically disabled people were in mind at the time. The original reason for the serene oases of the concealed courtyards, blooming with greenery and blossoms, was the alternating dust and mud of the poorly drained world outside. Today there are barrier-free entrances from the streets into most of these inner havens where restaurants, art galleries, and merchants serve the city's countless visitors in one of the most pleasant settings in any city.

It isn't easy to convert a building that's one hundred years old, at least, into one that's easy for a guest in a wheelchair. And that's the problem in the French Quarter of course. However, there are some charming hotels and motels that have wider bathroom doors and also level access (but seem to be a bit short on other facilities, such as grab bars). Since the French Quarter *is* really the heart of tourist New Orleans, it's certainly worth a try to stay there if you can.

Perhaps a surprise in today's world of look-alike hostelries are the hotels and motels in the French Quarter that belong to some of the large chains. Every hotel here is in keeping with the Quarter's atmosphere and architecture; where additions have been made to the old buildings, sometimes the old slave quarters as well, it has been done in the spirit and style of the past. Many are built around the old inner courtyards that often serve today for patio dining or for the swimming pool.

Advance reservations are absolutely essential during the fall and winter, and if you're thinking of being there for Mardi Gras, that can be as much as a year ahead. Prices quoted here are in effect at the time of writing; expect them to be higher for Sugar Bowl week, Mardi Gras, and other festival times. Always ask about vacation packages rates, or special weekend rates, since they can save you money. If you are arriving by car, remember that parking is free at the motels (and there are some, even in the French Quarter).

Upper Bracket

You'll get all those lacy New Orleans balconies at the **Royal Sonesta**, 300 Bourbon St., LA 70140 (tel. 504/586-0300, toll free 800/343-7170), a location in the middle of everything. It has a level entrance and some rooms with

28-inch bathroom doors in the guest rooms. TV can be controlled from the bed. Restaurants in the Royal Sonesta are accessible. Rates for double rooms range from $95 to $140 on a regular basis (look into vacation packages).

A very sophisticated French elegance is available—complete with grab bars—at the **St. Louis**, 730 Rue Bienville, LA 70130 (tel. 504/581-7300, toll free 800/535-8741), where there are rooms with 30-inch bathroom doors. Entrance is ramped and restaurants are accessible. Doubles run from $110 to $140.

Moderate

It *is* owned by Holiday Inn, but the **Chateau Le Moyne Hotel** is a charming old building, built around a courtyard as are many of the French Quarter hotels. It is at 301 Dauphine St., LA 70112 (tel. 504/581-1303, toll free 800/238-8000), and because it is a motel, there is free parking available. (Although this is not listed in the Holiday Inn directory as having wheelchair accommodations, I certainly stayed there in a room that has a bathroom equipped with a wide door and grab bars!) Entrance is level with the sidewalk, and access to upper floors is by elevator from the level lobby. Rates for double rooms range from $70 to $88.

The **Holiday Inn,** 124 Royal St., LA 70130 (tel. 504/529-7211, toll free 800/238-8000), has rooms with 28-inch bathroom doors and a level interior. There is one step at the entrance. Free self-parking. Rates are $57 to $75 single, $67 to $85 double.

There's level access to all parts of the **Prince Conti Motor Hotel**, 830 Rue Conti, LA 70112 (tel. 504/529-4172, toll free 800/535-7908), *if* you can use a bathroom with a 24-inch door (entry doors to guest rooms are 32 inches.) There's free valet parking, and the atmosphere here is comfortable and friendly. Doubles cost $60 to $100.

One of the largest hotels in the French Quarter is the long-established **Monteleone Hotel,** 214 Royal St., LA 70140 (tel. 504/523-3341, toll free 800/535-9595), which has a level entrance and interior, and guest rooms with 32-inch entry doors and 27-inch bathroom doors. Rates for a double room range from $80 to $120, but there are packages offered here at considerable savings.

You can't get much more central in the French Quarter than at the **De La Poste Motor Hotel,** 316 Chartres St., New Orleans, LA 70130 (tel. 504/581-1200), where all the rooms have 30-inch bathroom doors. The entrance is ramped and the restaurants are accessible. Rooms are spacious and overlook either the courtyard or some of the other fascinating scenery of the French Quarter streets. Parking is free. Double occupancy rooms begin at $55.

HOTELS OUTSIDE THE FRENCH QUARTER: Although the French Quarter is the usual magnet for tourists, there is also a wide range of hotels near the universities or in the central business district, many new ones built to accommodate visitors to the 1984 Louisiana World Exposition. The reasonably accessible ones are listed here, as well as restaurants you may want to visit. And, of course, there's the Garden District that should be seen if you are to experience a part of New Orleans very different from the French Quarter but with an appealing character all its own.

Many of the large chains already had hotels in New Orleans, and others were built to accommodate visitors to the 1984 World's Fair. They are mostly in the upper bracket, but they do provide many accessible features.

Close to the Mississippi River, the **New Orleans Hilton, 2** Poydras St., LA 70140 (tel. 504/561-0500, or through the Hilton Reservation service in your area), has 15 rooms with 32-inch-wide bathroom doors and grab bars. Entrance from the street is level, and there are level entrances to the restaurants. Access to the elevators from the first floor is ramped. Public rest rooms have 31-inch stall doors, grab bars, and lowered sinks. Guest rooms are spacious, and most of them have fabulous views of the river or the city, and are furnished in a French country style appropriate to the city's origins. There's a lot going on here in the restaurants and nightspots (see the appropriate section of this chapter). Rates for double rooms range from $104 to $132.

Near the Superdome and the central business district is the spectacular **Hyatt Regency New Orleans,** 500 Poydras Plaza, LA 70140 (tel. 504/561-1234, toll free 800/228-9000), with 12 guest rooms that have bathrooms with 33-inch doors and grab bars. The main entrance is ramped and the restaurants have level access. Public rest rooms have 30-inch stall doors and grab bars. One elevator has brailled floor indicators, and there are five pay phones amplified for hearing-impaired users. Rates for both single and double rooms start at $79.

New hotels opened for the Fair include the **Sheraton New Orleans,** 500 Canal St., LA 70130 (tel. 504/525-2500), which has been built with two special rooms per floor designed for disabled guests (56 rooms in all), that are near the elevators. Elevators have both braille and sound-signal floor-indicators. Rates are $98 to $136, double occupancy.

Rooms designed with special features will also be at the **Hotel Interconti-nental,** still under construction at the time of writing. It is at 1001 Howard Ave., LA 70113 (tel. 504/525-5514).

New Orleans hotels cannot be mentioned without referring to the revered **Pontchartrain Hotel,** 2031 St. Charles Ave., LA 70140 (tel. 504/525-0581, toll free 800/323-7500), an institution in the Garden District since 1927. Although "accessible" features were not built in at that time, the rooms are very spacious and beautifully furnished, so that doorways are wide and bathrooms large. The hotel boasts more than two staff members to every room who will provide accustomed and willing assistance at all times, including on the two steps into the dining room. Double rooms are in the $85 to $125 range.

In the moderate-price category, the **Downtown Howard Johnson's,** 330 Loyola Ave., LA 70112 (tel. 504/581-1600, toll free 800/535-7830), is centrally located between the French Quarter (four blocks) and the Superdome (two blocks). There is free parking and a ramped entrance, with six rooms designed with 30-inch-wide bathroom doors and equipped with grab bars. Double rates are $61 to $71.

Also between the French Quarter and the Superdome, the **Ramada Down-town,** 1732 Canal St., LA 70112 (tel. 504/525-5525, toll free 800/228-2828), has eight rooms on the third floor that have wide doors and grab bars in the bathrooms. The two restaurants on the main floor are accessible. Rates here range, according to the season, from $63 to $83 for a double room.

If you have your own car and would prefer to stay on the outskirts of the city where rates are less expensive, consider two Holiday Inns that have wheel-chair-access accommodations. There is one to the east (five miles to the French Quarter), the **Holiday Inn-East Highrise,** 6324 Chef Menteur Hwy., New Orleans, LA 70112 (tel. 504/241-2900, toll free 800/238-5400), and another to the west (four miles to the French Quarter), the **Holiday Inn-Gretna,** 100 West Bank Expressway, Gretna, LA 70053 (tel. 504/366-2361, toll free 800/238-5400). Rates at both are in the $40 to $50 range, with children under 18 free in the same room.

5. New Orleans Dining

RESTAURANTS IN THE FRENCH QUARTER: There are plenty of restaurants in all price categories that are easily accessible. So what to eat?

It's hard to describe the unique dishes of New Orleans since they are like no other, and are rarely tasted in their full glory outside the region. The mix of French, Spanish, and African recipes, with Indian and West Indian vegetables and spices, produces the Creole and Cajun specialties. Seafood is plentiful, and oysters are presented in every conceivable way, as are shrimps, crabs, and crayfish. Gumbo and jambalaya are soups that are meals in themselves. Po-boy sandwiches are another New Orleans specialty, containing practically anything between two halves of a long individual loaf of bread. Menus, of course, include a great many more items than these regional specialties, and you should find dishes and prices to suit you since the choice is so large.

Don't forget that if you are watching the budget, you'll generally find the same menu at the upper-price-bracket restaurants with lower prices at lunchtime than at dinner. You can also have a fine time eating here and there all day long without having a full meal anywhere! It's easy to do, since many restaurants and cafes will entice you as you pass by, and most have easy entry with room enough inside for comfort. Sunday brunch with live jazz is one of the most enjoyable features of some of New Orleans's top restaurants.

In the following listings, rest rooms are mentioned only where they provide facilities for wheelchair-users.

The Top Restaurants

Two or three of these are famous not only throughout the United States, but are also familiar to gourmets in many parts of the world, with justification. Also to be recommended is the fact that they are also among the most accessible of the country's famous restaurants. Prices, of course, are commensurate with their reputations.

There can't be too many people who haven't heard of **Antoine's,** 713 St. Louis St. (tel. 581-4422), even if they haven't read Frances Parkinson Keyes's famous novel *Dinner at Antoine's,* written when she lived in the French Quarter. It wasn't the novel that made Antoine's famous though, since it has been around for more than 130 years and has been run by the same family all that time. It has a level entrance and its interior is a rambling landmark building that goes on for room after room, all in a different decor. Entrees à la carte range from $10 to $18 at lunch and $15 to $35 at dinner. Reservations are essential.

Housed in another historic building, and also noted for its fine food, is **Arnaud's,** 813 Bienville St. (tel. 523-5433). There is one step at the entrance, and a large dining room. Prices for entrees à la carte range from $8.95 to $19. At the Sunday Jazz Brunch, entree prices are around $15. Again, reservations are very necessary.

They don't take reservations at all at another of New Orleans's top restaurants, **Galatoire's,** 209 Bourbon St. (tel. 525-2021), where you can see elegant gourmets lined up in the street at weekends, waiting for a table. (There *are* less busy times, though.) It has a level entrance. Entree prices à la carte range from $10 to $20.

Brennan's is in a building that has been restored to its 1801 elegance, at 417 Royal St. (tel. 525-9711). It has one step at the entrance to the dining room, which surrounds one of those beautiful patios. This is a spot favored for its famous breakfasts—which often turn out to be the only meal you'll want that day. Breakfast and lunch entree prices are in the $12 to $22 range, and dinner, à la carte and table d'hote items, from $17 to $32. Make reservations if you want to go.

Noted for its French-Creole food and its elegant interior is **Broussard's**, 819 Conti St. (tel. 581-3866). It has a level entrance and a level interior. The price range of à la carte or table d'hote items is $15 to $35.

The rare, fine restaurant *without* a French name is the **Rib Room** in the Royal Orleans Hotel, 300 Bourbon St. (tel. 529-7045). The level entrance is on the Royal Street side of the building. Its specialty is obvious, but it does have a wider menu whose à la carte prices are from $17.75 to $22.50 at dinner, and $7.50 to $15.50 at lunch.

Good, Less Expensive Restaurants

The elegance of the **Andrew Jackson**, 221 Royal St. (tel. 529-2603), which specializes in French and Creole cooking, reflects society in the time of its namesake. There is a level entrance, and the folding leaf on most tables is useful for dining from a wheelchair. A complete meal here will cost about $15 to $25 at dinner, and $8 to $15 at lunch. It's popular, so make reservations.

The ambience is as romantic as its name implies at the **Court of Two Sisters**, 613 Royal St. (tel. 522-7261). It has level entrances from both Royal and Bourbon Streets into the beautiful courtyard complete with a wishing well, flowers, trees, and fountains. Depending on the weather and your inclination, you can dine in the courtyard or savor it from indoors. There's a daily Jazz Brunch Buffet here for $15, from 9 a.m. to 3 p.m. Complete dinner prices start at $9.50.

On the edge of the French Quarter across from Armstrong Park (on North Rampart Street), **Marti's**, 1041 Dumaine St. (tel. 524-6060/6216), specializes in Creole cooking, though not exclusively. There is one step at the entrance and a roomy interior. Price range for dinner is from $13 to $21, lunch from $5 to $8.

There's a large menu of Louisiana seafood at **Ralph & Kacoo's**, 215 Bourbon St. (tel. 523-0449), which has a ramped entrance and a large interior. A meal here will cost somewhere between $7 and $15.

Moderate Prices

There are a great many inexpensive places to eat in the French Quarter, and you'll probably come across some that are not on this list as you wander around. Here are some of the best known that have reasonable accessibility.

Attractive and informal for casual eating at any time of the day, **Mr. B's Bistro and Bar**, 201 Royal St. (tel. 523-2078), has one step at the main entrance, but has level access both from the side door or from the public garage around the corner on Iberville Street. There's plenty of room between tables in the spacious interior. There is a large bar section, with tables, for drinks or coffee. Complete dinners range in price from $13 to $18, lower for lunch. It is open from 11 a.m. to 11 p.m., seven days a week.

Casual dining at any time of the day in historic surroundings is a pleasant pastime at the **Gumbo Shop**, 630 St. Peter St. (tel. 525-1486), where the entrance through the courtyard has one low step into the dining room. This is one of the only five buildings in the French Quarter to survive the 1788 fire. Gumbo isn't the only thing on the menu—there's a wide variety of specialties served from 11 a.m. to 10 p.m.—but if you plan to sample gumbo at all, this is where to do it. It costs under $5 and is a meal in itself. Other dishes range à la carte from $7 to $17.

The **Four Seasons,** 505 Royal St. (tel. 525-9751) has two very appealing identities. By day it is a cafe serving coffee and pastry (croissants, too), but in the evening it serves a full four-course dinner, prix fixe at $10.25. The entrance is level, and there is negotiable space between the few tables inside, or on the patio. It's a good "anytime" place, since it's open from 7:30 a.m. to 11 p.m. every day.

Tujague's, 823 Decatur St. (tel. 523-9462), has no printed menu, but its regional specialties are well known and much appreciated by habitués who sometimes ask for the daily menu before they decide if they will stay. Dinner will cost about $8.50, lunch about $6.50. (Rest rooms here have 28-inch doors.)

You can have patio dining at any time of the year (there is an effective heating system when it's needed) in the lovely courtyard of **Zachary Taylor Seafood,** 621 Royal St. (tel. 566-7289). The entrance is level from the street to the patio and the inside dining room. Prices are in the $7 to $15 range.

For an interlude of American-style dishes there's the **Original Melius Bar,** 622 Conti St. (tel. 523-9292), which has one step at the entrance. Lunch is in the $4 to $7 range.

And in the event you have a hankering for some Japanese-style dishes, there's a level entrance to **Benihana of Tokyo,** 720 St. Louis St. (tel. 522-0425), where prices range from $9 to $18.

I've heard that you can't visit New Orleans without eating at **K-Paul's Louisiana Kitchen,** 416 Chartres St. (tel. 524-7394), and to prove it, there always seems to be a line in the street waiting to get in. One of the reasons for this—apart from the marvelous food—is that there are not many tables. This might be a hassle, but you decide. The entrance is level. Prices range from $6 to $12.

There's an haute-cuisine French menu at the **Louis XVI** restaurant in the Marie Antoinette Hotel, 829 Toulouse St. (tel. 581-7000), which looks onto an elegant courtyard. There is one small step at the entrance; the interior is level. Prices à la carte for lunch range from $8 to $17, and for dinner from $20 to $35.

Cajun and Creole dishes are specialties at **Le Bon Creole,** 1001 Toulouse St. (tel. 586-8008), in the Maison Dupuy Hotel. There is a ramped entrance. Good weather dining is also available in the beautiful courtyard. Table d'hote prices are $12 to $25 for dinner, lower for lunch. Breakfast is served, and there is a brunch on Saturday and Sunday.

Eating on a Budget

No "greasy-spoon" diners here, but there are inexpensive restaurants with great food in the New Orleans style.

Oyster-lovers will have a hard time staying away from two restaurants on the same block, **Acme Oyster House** at 724 Iberville St. (tel. 523-8928), which has one step at the entrance, and the level-entrance **Felix** at 739 Iberville St. (tel. 522-4440), across the street. Half-a-dozen raw oysters on the half shell are about $2.25 at both. Acme closes at 9 p.m.; Felix stays open until 2 a.m. Besides the oysters, there's a sandwich menu at Acme, and a selection of Creole and other dishes on the menu at Felix.

At the **Coffee Pot,** 714 St. Peter St. (tel. 523-8215), the level entrance to the patio is through the carriage gate during the day. In the evenings, the big gates are sometimes closed and there is a "step-over" small door that makes it less accessible. There are two steps to the inside dining room. Breakfast is very special here, but lunch and dinner are served as well, when prices range from $3.50 to $8.50, besides multiple varieties of coffee.

Tucked away in the courtyard of the Provincial Motor Hotel is the **Honfleur Restaurant,** 1024 Chartres St. (tel. 581-4995), which has a level entrance at the side of the building that houses the restaurant. The short entryway from the street is cobblestone, but not totally impassable. Lunch prices run from $3 to $6, dinner from $4.50 to $8.

Large portions of hamburgers and steaks are characteristic of the **Cafe Maspero,** 601 Decatur St. (tel. 523-6250), which has a ramped entrance. Prices are in the $3 to $5 range, and it is open until midnight.

A bar with a sandwich menu is housed in historic **Napoleon House,** at the corner of Chartres and St. Louis Sts., with a level entrance. The 1797 house is the one where Napoleon's rescue from exile was plotted and where he was scheduled to live, but never did. It is open until 2 a.m.

Luncheonette-style dining, but good food at reasonable prices, is to be found at **Tally-Ho,** 400 Chartres St. (tel. 566-7071). There is one step at the entrance. Breakfasts around $2 and lunches for $5 are typical. Open midnight to 3:30 p.m. except Monday.

Across from the French Market is **Cafe S'bisa,** 1011 Decatur St. (tel. 561-8354), in an old building with an attractive interior. The entrance is ramped. Prices run from about $8 to $18. Closed Monday.

There are a number of bars-with-short-menus, also located across from the French Market on Decatur Street, an area in the process of revival. They all have level entrances.

Bonaparte's Retreat, at 1007 Decatur, and **Molly's at the Market,** 1107 Decatur, serve breakfast, lunch, and dinner until 9 p.m. Both are open until 1:30 a.m.

And Then There Are Those Cafes . . .

One of the most popular spots in New Orleans at any time of the day—or night—is the **Cafe du Monde** in the French Market (between Jackson Square and the river), 800 Decatur St. (tel. 561-9235), with plenty of tables both indoors and outside on the open patio, all of which is level with the street. The only items served here are coffee, milk, hot chocolate, and beignets (an irresistible cross between doughnuts and fritters covered in confectioner's sugar). A serving of three beignets costs 60¢, which is also the price for everything else. Open 24 hours a day.

La Marquise, 625 Chartres St., is tiny inside, but there's a patio in back as well. Although the front entrance has a very large step and narrow door, both the patio and the inside cafe can be reached without steps from the side entrance. French pastries are the specialty here, as well as croissants and Danish pastries. Coffee is served as well. Everything is available for take-out (for enjoying in nearby Jackson Square). Open every day from 8 a.m. until 5:30 p.m. on weekdays, and 8:30 p.m. on Saturday and Sunday.

The level-entrance **Four Seasons,** 505 Royal St. (see the Moderate Category of restaurants in this chapter), is also a pastry shop during the day where you can have coffee and croissants or pastries until dinnertime.

RESTAURANTS OUTSIDE THE FRENCH QUARTER: There's good
eating all over New Orleans, and you'll find many good restaurants outside the French Quarter in all price categories. Some of the more accessible ones are

listed here by area, in descending price brackets within that regional listing. No accessible rest rooms available unless mentioned.

Downtown

There are a couple of moderately priced restaurants in the downtown area, outside the French Quarter but on the same side of Canal Street.

The **Old Spaghetti Factory,** 330 St. Charles at Poydras Sts. (tel. 561-1068), has just one step at the entrance and lots of space and Tiffany lamps inside. Lunch prices go from $2.50 to $4.50 and dinner from $4 to $6.50. Open from 11:15 a.m. to 10 p.m. Sunday through Thursday, and until 11 p.m. on Friday and Saturday.

At **Chez Hélène,** 1530 W. Robertson St. (tel. 947-9155), you'll find the cuisine described as "Creole with Soul," and prices ranging from $4.50 to $13. There's one step at the entrance. It's a very popular restaurant, so make reservations. Open from 11 a.m. to midnight Tuesday to Thursday, and to 1:30 a.m. on Friday and Saturday; to 10:30 p.m. on Sunday, and to 6 p.m. on Monday.

Central Business District

Two of the restaurants at the New Orleans Hilton, 2 Poydras St. at the river (tel. 561-0500), are accessible from the lobby and one is at the top (the hotel has a level entrance).

Winston's looks like an English country house and accoutrements are stylishly elegant. As you might expect, it is not inexpensive, with a $29 prix fixe dinner served nightly from 6 to 11 p.m.

The more informal **Cafe Bromeliad** in the Hilton has a level entrance through the coffee shop and serves breakfast, lunch, and dinner, which is buffet style on Friday and Saturday, at reasonable prices.

The **Rainforest Lounge** on the 29th floor of the Hilton is well known as an evening spot, but it also serves a $5 buffet lunch from 11:30 a.m. to 2:30 p.m.

Uptown and the Garden District

This area is upriver from Canal and over toward the lake.

Some of the finest New Orleans cuisine is reputed to be found at the **Caribbean Room** of the elegant Pontchartrain Hotel, 2031 St. Charles Ave. (tel. 524-0581), where the staff is very willing to help you negotiate the two steps into the dining room. Lunch entrees are from $8 to $12, dinner entrees are in the $18 to $25 range, and a Sunday buffet is priced at $22. There are reasonably accessible rest rooms here.

On the far side of the Garden District at the corner of Washington Ave. and Coliseum St. is a 100-year-old restaurant, the **Commander's Palace** (tel. 899-8221), which specializes in Creole dishes. It has one step at the entrance and a pleasant patio, level from the street, between two dining rooms. A popular event here is the Jazz Brunch on Saturday and Sunday from 11 a.m. to 2 p.m., where you'll often catch some Dixieland greats. Brunch starts at $10, lunch goes from $7 to $12, and dinner from $20 to $25.

At the **Versailles,** 2100 St. Charles Ave. (tel. 524-2535), the St. Charles Room looks out *on to* the tree-lined avenue that runs through the Garden District. There is one step at the entrance. The menu here is continental, and prices of the à la carte entrees are in the $12 to $20 range for dinner. Closed on Sunday.

Very popular with the locals who often go just for the barbecued shrimp, **Pascal Manale's,** 1838 Napoleon Ave. (tel. 895-4877), has one step at the entrance. The restaurant calls itself an Italian-New Orleans steakhouse, and there are a lot of things on the menu besides the shrimp. Prices for entrées at lunch are $7 to $12, and $10 to $18 at dinner. Open from 11:45 a.m. to 10 p.m. Monday through Friday, and from 4 p.m. on Saturday. Closed on Sunday. (Rest room stall doors are 28 inches wide.)

More Creole dishes and great seafood are on the menu at **T. Pittari's,** 4200 S. Claiborne Ave. (tel. 891-2801), which has one step at the entrance. Dinners are in the $12 to $16 range. Open from 11:45 a.m. to 10 p.m., and until 11 p.m. on Friday and Saturday. (Note that the stall doors on the rest rooms here are 28 inches wide.)

Casual dining and inexpensive prices are to be found at **Petrossi's,** 901 Louisiana Ave. (tel. 895-3404), where there is one step at the entrance. Seafood platters range in price from $3 to $10. Hours are 11 a.m. to 10 p.m. every day except Monday and Tuesday, when it is closed.

KEY TO THE NUMBERED REFERENCES ON THE FRENCH QUARTER MAP: 1. Old Bank of Louisiana; 2. Old Bank of the U.S.; 3. Old La. State Bank; 4. N.O. Court Building; 5. Casa Faurie; 6. The Hermann House; 7. Maison Seignouret; 8. Merieult House; 9. Casa de Comercio; 10. Court of Two Lions; 11. LeMonnier House; 12. Maison de Flechier; 13. Maison LeMonnier; 14. Spanish Arsenal; 15. Pirates Alley; 16. Cathedral Garden; 17. Salle d'Orleans (Orleans Ballroom); 18. Pere Antoine's Alley; 19. The Presbytere; 20. St. Louis Cathedral; 21. The Cabildo; 22. Jackson Square; 23. Pontalba Buildings; 24. 1850 House; 25. The French Market; 26. Old Ursulines Convent; 27. Beauregard House; 28. Soniat House; 29. Clay House; 30. LaLaurie House ("The Haunted House"); 31. Thierry House; 32. The Gallier House; 33. Lafitte's Blacksmith Shop; 34. The Cornstalk Fence; 35. Miltenberger Houses; 36. "Madame John's Legacy."

---

6. The Sights

SIGHTSEEING IN THE FRENCH QUARTER: If you did nothing but wander around the 90-or-so blocks that make up the French Quarter of New Orleans, noting the visual delights of lacy ironwork, secluded courtyards, and a fresh architectural silhouette on every other building, you'd get your money's worth. You'll soon become familiar with its special character—Bourbon Street is rowdy (cheerfully so), Royal Street is classier (with its antique shops)—and the layout is quickly assimilated. There are also quiet residential streets that can resemble a small village in the Old World, sometimes just around the corner from Bourbon Street.

Because it is nearly three centuries since the Quarter was laid out in its grid pattern, the streets are narrow compared to modern cities. Don't look for rehabilitated sidewalks and curb cuts. Even so, there always seems to be a way to get where you want to go. Motorized traffic definitely does *not* have priority here—there are no traffic lights—and many of the streets are closed to traffic for large parts of the day and night. Royal Street and Bourbon Street become pedestrian malls on weekday evenings, and all day after 10 a.m. on weekends. Jackson Square is permanently closed to traffic.

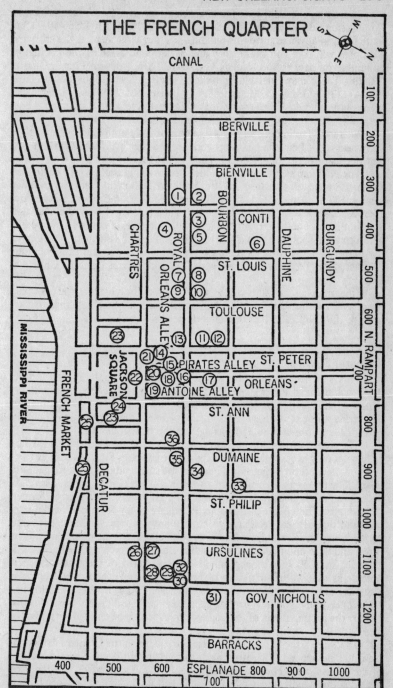

THE FRENCH QUARTER

MISSISSIPPI RIVER

FRENCH MARKET

JACKSON SQUARE

DECATUR

CHARTRES

ROYAL

ORLEANS ALLEY

BOURBON

DAUPHINE

BURGUNDY

N. RAMPART

CANAL

IBERVILLE

BIENVILLE

CONTI

ST. LOUIS

TOULOUSE

PIRATES ALLEY ST. PETER

ORLEANS

ANTOINE ALLEY

ST. ANN

DUMAINE

ST. PHILIP

URSULINES

GOV. NICHOLLS

BARRACKS

ESPLANADE 800

100
200
300
400
500
600
700
800
900
1000
1100
1200

400 500 600 700 900 1000

Map Courtesy of the New Orleans Tourist & Convention Commission

There's an excellent plan for a **walking tour** available from the Tourist Commission, 334 Royal St., New Orleans, LA 70130, (tel. 504/566-5011), but write for it in advance since this building has four large steps at the entrance. This plan will give you the history and background of 36 of the fascinating buildings you pass as you tour on your own. There is also a French Quarter **"Rolling Tour"** map available from the Easter Seal Society, 4631 West Napoleon Ave., P.O. Box 8425, Metairie, LA 70011 (tel. 504/885-9960). It indicates, among other things, which courtyards are open to the public, although it does not indicate accessibility of the buildings themselves.

There are fascinating stories—some historically authentic, some intriguingly hearsay—about the buildings you see, and their past inhabitants. You'll find details in these tour pamphlets and in the regular guide.

The National Park Service conducts free walking tours which begin near Jackson Square at the **Jean Lafitte National Historical Park Information Center,** 527 St. Ann St. (tel. 504/589-2636). They last 1½ hours and leave at 10:30 a.m., 11:30 a.m., 2 p.m., and 3 p.m. The "History of New Orleans" tour does not involve going into any buildings. Guides are, of course, a storehouse of information about the things you see (and you'll hear a bit about Jean Lafitte, the notorious but heroic pirate after whom the center is named). Tours are conducted every day except New Year's Day, Mardi Gras Day, and Christmas Day.

Since many of the sights will be seen only from the outside and accessibility is not a factor, this section of the chapter will deal only with buildings that are open to the public and have a degree of accessibility.

Jackson Square

This is the focal point of the old city and is what gives the French Quarter its French name of *Vieux Carré* (Old Square). The square began as a military parade ground with a gallows in the center where there is now the familiar equestrian statue of Andrew Jackson, after whom it was renamed to honor the hero of the Battle of New Orleans against the British in 1815.

The central, landscaped part of the square itself, enclosed within the iron railings, is only accessible by four steps on the Chartres Street side and by two steps on the Decatur Street side. However, the surrounding street is a pedestrian mall with ramped corners up to sidewalk level, and this is where the action—an all-day bustle of sidewalk artists, musicians, and other performers of all kinds. The buildings that line the square today form one of the most beautiful symmetrical groupings to be seen anywhere in America. The large, handsome red brick buildings flanking two sides of Jackson Square on St. Peter Street and St. Ann Street are the **Pontalba Buildings,** built by the Baroness de Pontalba in 1850 (her monogram, A-P, is entwined in the ironwork), and notable as one of the first rows of English-style town houses to appear in America, designed for elegant living. Study them from the outside—although one is open to the public, it cannot be called accessible. Some of the shops that occupy the ground floors of the houses, however, can be entered with just one step.

The three large buildings that face the square on the Chartres Street side were all built around 1795, after the disastrous fire of 1788 that destroyed most of the original city. They are the Cabildo, St. Louis Cathedral, and the Presbytère, all of which are readily accessible and fascinating for history buffs.

The Cabildo

This easily accessible building at 701 Chartres St. was once the seat of the Spanish governing body after which it is named; it was the setting for the signing of the Louisiana Purchase and has been the city hall and a state supreme court. Today it is a part of the Louisiana State Museum, full of intriguing exhibits that give a marvelous insight into the history and culture of the region. The entry is level with the sidewalk through wide doors. All levels of the interior are spacious and uncarpeted. A large elevator gives access to all floors, and there is assistance available. Open every day except Monday, from 9 a.m. to 5 p.m. Admission is $1.25 for adults and 50¢ for children (under 12, free).

St. Louis Cathedral

Next door to the Cabildo, at 721 Chartres Street, the St. Louis Cathedral once had an architectural unity with the buildings on either side but spires were added later to the cathedral. There is one step at the entrance, and the interior is accessible. It is open from 9 a.m. to 5 p.m. every day.

The Presbytère

Intended to be a residence for the priests from the cathedral next door, the **Presbytère**, 713 Chartres St. is now a part of the Louisiana State Museum. It has a small step at the entrance, wide doors and elevator access to all levels. In the spacious, uncarpeted interiors are permanent exhibits of antique toys, pottery, portraits, and Audubon prints. Outside the Presbytère, you'll see the first-ever iron submarine, launched in 1861 by the Confederate Navy at the start of the Civil War but only used for one trial run. Open 9 a.m. to 5 p.m. Tuesday through Sunday. Adults $1.25, children 50¢ (under 12 free).

Old French Market

On the river side of Jackson Square is the old French Market that runs for about six blocks along the Mississippi. Some of the buildings are very old, some built in 1912. Now, the pleasant, colonnaded buildings you see are the result of the most recent (1975) restoration, which converted interiors into easily accessible restaurants, ice cream parlors, and shops selling candy and pralines, as well as many other gifts and souvenirs. (*Note:* it's in this part of the French Market that you'll find the accessible public rest room.) Some of the French Market is still used as a fruit and vegetable market, and there's an open-air flea market every Saturday and Sunday at the end near Barrack Street. Across from the French Market along Decatur Street, other buildings have been rehabilitated, and there are many street-level cafes and gift shops in this area as well.

Museums and Historic Sites

The Cabildo and the Presbytère are, of course, the major museums, but a few of the other New Orleans museums can be put on the accessible list as well.

The **Historic New Orleans Collection**, 533 Royal St. (tel. 523-4662), is housed in the historic Merieult House, accessible from street level to the ground floor where there are exhibits covering 150 years of the economic, historic, and cultural development of Louisiana. There are other exhibits on the upper floor, and a small elevator is in the planning stages, but it might still be difficult for physically impaired visitors to see the private quarters of the house, which also form part of the collection. Guided tours for visually impaired visitors can be arranged.

The **Musée Conti Wax Museum**, 917 Conti St. (tel. 525-2605), has a barrier-free approach and a wide door. The interior is on one level and exhibits life-size wax figures in authentic costumes and settings depicting New Orleans legends and history. Open 10 a.m. to 5:30 p.m. daily. Admission, adults $3, children (13 to 17) $2, (6 to 12) $1. The rest rooms are approached by a ramp and have 32-inch-wide doors.

The **Gallier House**, at 1132 Royal St. (tel. 525-6722), is an elegant town house that is open to the public and has a small elevator to the upper floors. There is one step at the entrance. It was built in 1860 by James Gallier, Jr., architect of many other famous buildings in the Quarter. Call in advance to ask if your particular requirements for touring the house can be accommodated. Admission is $2.50 for adults, $2 for senior citizens and students, $1 for children 5 to 11, under 5 free.

Exhibits of early medicines and other drugstore memorabilia are on display at the **Pharmaceutical Museum**, 514 Chartres St., which has one step at the entrance and reasonable wheelchair turn-around inside. It is housed in a building that actually was a pharmacy for about 40 years after it was built in the 1820s. Open Tuesday through Saturday, 10 a.m. to 5 p.m. Admission 50¢.

They have recently given new life to the old U.S. Mint Building that runs the length of the 400 block of Esplanade Ave. (tel. 568-6968), and it's all accessible, including the rest rooms. This is the new home of the **Jazz Museum** and the **Mardi Gras Museum**, as well as a multimedia show on Louisiana in the auditorium. Open 10 a.m. to 6 p.m. daily. Admission is $2 for adults, $1 for students, free for children under 12.

Curious about black magic? There's a **Voodoo Museum** at 636 St. Ann St. (tel. 523-2906). Visitors in wheelchairs may need assistance on the single steps between the front room, the courtyard, and back up to the room on the other side of the courtyard. Open 10 a.m. to midnight daily except holidays. Admission is $2 for adults, $1.50 for students, and 75¢ for children.

Riverboat Cruises

You can take a very pleasant two-hour cruise of the harbor aboard the *Natchez*, a sternwheeler that can be boarded by an easily negotiated ramp to its main deck. (There are two other decks but reached only by stairs.) The fare is $8.50 for adults, $4.25 for children ages 6 to 12, children under 6 can go free. It leaves from the Toulouse Street wharf across from Jackson Square. Call 586-8777 for sailing times and other information. At time of writing, there are no accessible rest rooms, but modifications are being considered.

SOME SIGHTS OUTSIDE THE FRENCH QUARTER: There's a lot of New Orleans outside the French Quarter, and lots to see—Basin Street, Canal Street, the Irish Channel, the Garden District, Loyola and Tulane Universities, Bayou St. John, and Lake Pontchartrain—but most of them don't involve a need for accessibility information; you can read about them in the regular guide books and in the tourist office brochures, if you decide to tour by car to have a look at them.

However, there are a couple of places you may want to go by car and then spend some time "on foot," and so I am including them here, along with their accessibility features.

The Garden District

This unique area is the original American section of New Orleans. It was here that American settlers, who arrived following the Louisiana Purchase in 1803 by President Jefferson, began to build elaborately landscaped mansions that were intended to outshine in grandeur the French Quarter houses of the Spanish-French Creole society that had refused to accept the newcomers. Most of the Garden District houses built throughout the rest of the 19th century have the then popular Greek Revival façades, ornamented with local cast-iron work and are set back from the streets on large pieces of land. The very fertile soil produced trees, shrubs, and flowers in profusion—oaks, magnolias, oleander, camellias, bougainvillea, azaleas, wisteria, and roses. Today, the result is a district you can wander through, savoring the beautiful gardens and the variety of architecture of what are still mostly private homes. There are stories attached to many of them, and the regular guide will give you details.

Most nondisabled tourists probably take the trolley ride along St. Charles Avenue to the Garden District from the French Quarter, but unfortunately the trolleys have one high step from the street and another high step inside. The minibus that runs from the French Quarter and tours the Garden District has a wide door and one step from the street. It isn't too far, though, to go by taxi and will probably cost about $3.50 on the meter from the French District to Jackson Street on the edge of the Garden District.

Away from St. Charles Avenue, the streets are fairly quiet, so it's easy to tour slowly. There are no ramped curbs here, but the roadway is feasible for a wheelchair, if you prefer to avoid the curbs. Take a tourist map with you so that you don't venture further than you will find comfortable for the return to the main arteries, where you can find a taxi if you need one.

Longue Vue House and Gardens

Not too far from the center of town, just off the Metairie Road at Bamboo Rd. (tel. 488-5488), you'll find one of the most beautiful garden settings in the area, on the Longue Vue estate. The house, built in the style of the great English country houses, is accessible with a ramp at the entrance and an elevator to the upper floors.

The grounds and gardens are reasonably accessible for wheelchairs, perhaps with a little assistance; the wide, smooth paths are asphalted or bricked. Management is considering making the rest rooms accessible, but they are not so at the time of writing.

You can visit Longue Vue on Tuesday through Friday from 10 a.m. to 4:30 p.m., and from 1 p.m. to 5 p.m. on Saturday and Sunday (closed holidays). Admission to both house and garden is $5 for adults and $3 for students and children; to the garden only, admission is $2 and $1 respectively.

7. A Festival City

There can't be too many people who don't know about Mardi Gras time in New Orleans. However, it is only one of twenty-six festivals throughout the year which include the Sugar Bowl, a Festival of Jazz, a Celebration of Spring, an oyster festival, a catfish festival, and a two-week Bastille Day celebration. You can get a Calendar of Events from the Greater New Orleans Tourist Commission, listed at the end of this chapter. It's difficult to know whether to recommend these festivals as a reason to visit New Orleans, or a reason for a disabled visitor to avoid these particular dates. You'll have to be the judge. If you decide to visit during a festival, make hotel reservations well in advance.

Mardi Gras is the extravagant festival that begins on Twelfth Night (the 6th of January) and continues in growing intensity until the Tuesday before Lent, 45 days before Easter. It culminates on that day, called Mardi Gras (Fat Tuesday) in private masked balls and parties, with elaborate parades through the streets of the French Quarter, crowded to capacity with partying natives and visitors.

Some of the other festivals might be more negotiable for the disabled visitor.

During the **Jazz and Heritage Festival,** which usually takes place at the end of April or the beginning of May, there'll be more than you can imagine of what New Orleans is all about. Famous-name jazz players are among the thousands of entertainers who arrive to perform on the streets, in the hotels, on the steamboats, and at the Fairgrounds Racetrack, 1761 Gentilly Blvd., where there are ten stages offering music of all kinds at weekends. The Heritage part of the festival, also held at the Fairgrounds, includes food and crafts in abundance. At the Fairgrounds, sales booths and performances are located off an asphalt track (but the rest of the Fairgrounds can be quite boggy if it rains). There are no permanent rest room facilities during the festival. Dates and details from the Jazz and Heritage Festival, P.O. Box 2530, New Orleans, LA 70176 (tel. 504/522-4786).

Spring Fiesta, which starts on the first Friday after Easter and lasts for 19 days, is a celebration of the season in the French Quarter, with balcony concerts, an outdoor art show in Pirates Alley (next to the Cabildo), and the "Night in New Orleans" parade of carriages filled with costumed personalities associated with New Orleans history, as well as marching bands—of course! The Spring Fiesta also includes tours of some of the private homes, but most will be out of bounds if you have mobility difficulties, except for the candlelight tours of the patios, which are nearly always on a level with the street. Write for details to the Spring Fiesta Association, 529 St. Ann St., New Orleans, LA 70116 (tel. 504/581-1367).

Yet another **Food Festival** is held in late June or early July, this time in the accessible Rivergate Convention Center, 4 Canal St. (tel. 504/529-2861). There are food-tasting booths for everything that New Orleans food is famous for, and many other creative culinary treats besides, and the finale is a grand gourmet dinner. For details write to the New Orleans Food Festival, P.O. Box 2410, New Orleans, LA 70116. The Rivergate Center has a level entrance and there are elevators to all floors.

8. Nightlife & Entertainment

IN THE FRENCH QUARTER: There *are* things to do at night in the French Quarter that are not related to jazz, but New Orleans's special brand of Dixieland music permeates the night even more than it does the day. Even if you are going to the theater, or just out to dine, you will be surrounded by its contagious, exciting beat coming from every open window on the way. All you really need to become a guest at the nightly party is to wander the streets, especially Bourbon Street's central blocks lined with bars, jazz clubs, strip joints, and restaurants of all kinds. As you stroll the roadway (always a pedestrian mall in the evening) it will be easy to see what is being offered and how accessible it will be for you. There are so many places for all tastes and inclinations.

Jazz, etc.

Of the famous nightspots whose access or otherwise may not be obvious, **Preservation Hall,** 726 St. Peter St. (tel. 523-8939), is perhaps the best-known temple of jazz. Not that it's a temple to look at: it is housed in an old building that nobody has tried to spruce up lately. Access might present a problem, depending on your stamina and your disability, since there is usually a line outside long in advance of the 8 p.m. opening, as well as a 10-inch step inside, and an open room where there are only a few chairs in front and where everybody has to fend for themselves. Admission is $2. If you can't get in, or prefer not to try, there's always the open window.

One enormous courtyard plus two bars, one with nonstop piano and singalong music, makes **Pat O'Brian's,** 718 St. Peter St. (tel. 525-4823), one of the liveliest places in town until 4 a.m. Sunday through Thursday, until 5 a.m. Friday and Saturday. There are some tables level with the entrance to the beautiful patio, the others are up three steps. There is one step to each of the bars on either side of the level courtyard entrance.

And then there's **Bourbon Street,** and more Bourbon Street. You can easily see as you promenade, as already noted, what you'll want to investigate both from an entertainment and an accessibility point of view. The choice is wide and varied.

If you prefer the wide open spaces of the Mississippi for your evening entertainment, there's a **Dinner/Jazz Cruise** on the steamboat *Natchez,* which leaves the Toulouse Street wharf opposite Jackson Square at 6:30 p.m. There is a boarding ramp to the main deck where the entertainment and buffet take place, and both outside deck and enclosed areas are suitable for wheelchairs. Cost of the cruise only is $8.50, children half-price, free under 6 years of age. The cash bar and buffet are optional (entrees at the buffet range from $7 to $12). For sailing times and further information, call 586-8777.

Theater, Opera, Concerts, etc.

There's local theater here, and there are companies who come through New Orleans on national tours. You can find out what's on by calling the **Greater New Orleans Arts Council** (tel. 522-2787). Many of the theaters are reasonably accessible from an architectural point of view, although not always presenting performances.

At the **Toulouse Street Theatre,** 615 Toulouse St. (tel. 522-7852), there is level entry to the auditorium alongside the box office, through a passage normally used by the staff. The small area immediately in front of the stage with tables and chairs, where wine is served, is rather confined, but there is good space in front of the first row of regular seats, and also in the aisle for access to aisle seats. The theater is used for stage shows, concerts, and occasionally films.

OUTSIDE THE FRENCH QUARTER: A bird's-eye view of New Orleans can be had along with entertainment from the tops of a couple of the taller buildings in the central business district. At **Top of the Mart,** you can get live jazz and a 360-degree panorama on the slowly revolving 33rd floor of the International Trade Mart Building, 2 Canal St. at the river (tel. 522-9795). The building has one step at street entrance, and there are elevators to the Top, which has a level entrance. Only drinks are served; there is no admission charge and no cover.

There's a room with a view, too, at the top of the New Orleans Hilton, called the **Rainforest** (tel. 561-0500). From 5 to 7 p.m., the "Supper at Sunset" time allows you all you can drink for $5 on weekdays. After 9 p.m. there's dance music and a spectacular light-and-sound show. No cover or minimum charges.

Pete Fountain, a renowned native son and jazz musician, has moved from the French Quarter into **Pete Fountain's** (tel. 523-4374 or 523-3105), at the accessible New Orleans Hilton at Poydras and the Mississippi River. There is an $18 cover charge at the nightly show (10 p.m.), which includes one drink. Reservations are necessary here. Closed Sunday and Monday.

More jazz at **Le Club** on the third floor of the Hyatt Regency Hotel, 500 Poydras Plaza (tel. 561-1234). Open for cocktails from 6 p.m. to 2 a.m., with three shows each night after 8 p.m. No cover or minimum.

There's entertainment, too, at the **Louisiana Superdome** (tel. 587-3768 for tickets, or 587-3645 for tourist service), the noted sports center that has entertainment spectaculars as well as home games for the New Orleans Saints football team, the University of New Orleans basketball, the Tulane University football, and the Sugar Bowl, always held on New Year's Day. The Superdome has reserved parking for handicapped patrons, and there is a ramped entrance at Gate A on Poydras Street, as well as elevators inside Gate A to the seating. There are specified wheelchair locations, so indicate your special needs when buying tickets. Rest rooms on the third floor have 30-inch stall doors and phones are 45 inches high.

SAN FRANCISCO

The Bay City

IF YOU'RE PLANNING to go to San Francisco, it's probably because you are among the millions who have an image of the city that makes nearly everybody want to go there at least once. Its breathtaking views, charm, quaintness, and cosmopolitan sophistication, all at the same time, make it one of the world's unique cities.

Another thing San Francisco is famous for is its hills (we've all seen those TV shows and movies set in San Francisco, in which cars are parked with their front wheels at right angles to the curbs), so you might wonder if it's a place for wheeling around. It is true that all of San Francisco is not the most convenient city for a person with a mobility problem, but many of the tourist attractions and points of interest *are* available. They are located in relatively flat areas between hills—Fisherman's Wharf, Chinatown, Union Street, Jackson Square, Golden Gate Park, Pier 39, Embarcadero Center, Japan Center, Market Street, and the financial/business areas among them.

San Francisco and its organizations of disabled residents continue to work hard to remove as many of the architectural barriers as possible, and eventually hope to ramp all curbs in the city's commercial and tourist areas; there are already ramped crosswalks along Market Street, in Fisherman's Wharf, the Civic Center, Chinatown, and Embarcadero Center. These are comfortable areas for wheelchair visitors.

The famous cable cars? Well, even when they are put back in operation some time in 1984 after lengthy overhaul, they are still going to be just one of the sights (if you have a mobility impairment) rather than a way to get around.

Write for regular guides and maps (including the BART system) to the **San Francisco Convention and Visitors Bureau**, 1390 Market St., CA 94102 (tel. 415/974-6900), and also request their special guide for disabled visitors as well, published at the end of 1983. For the "Guide to San Francisco for the

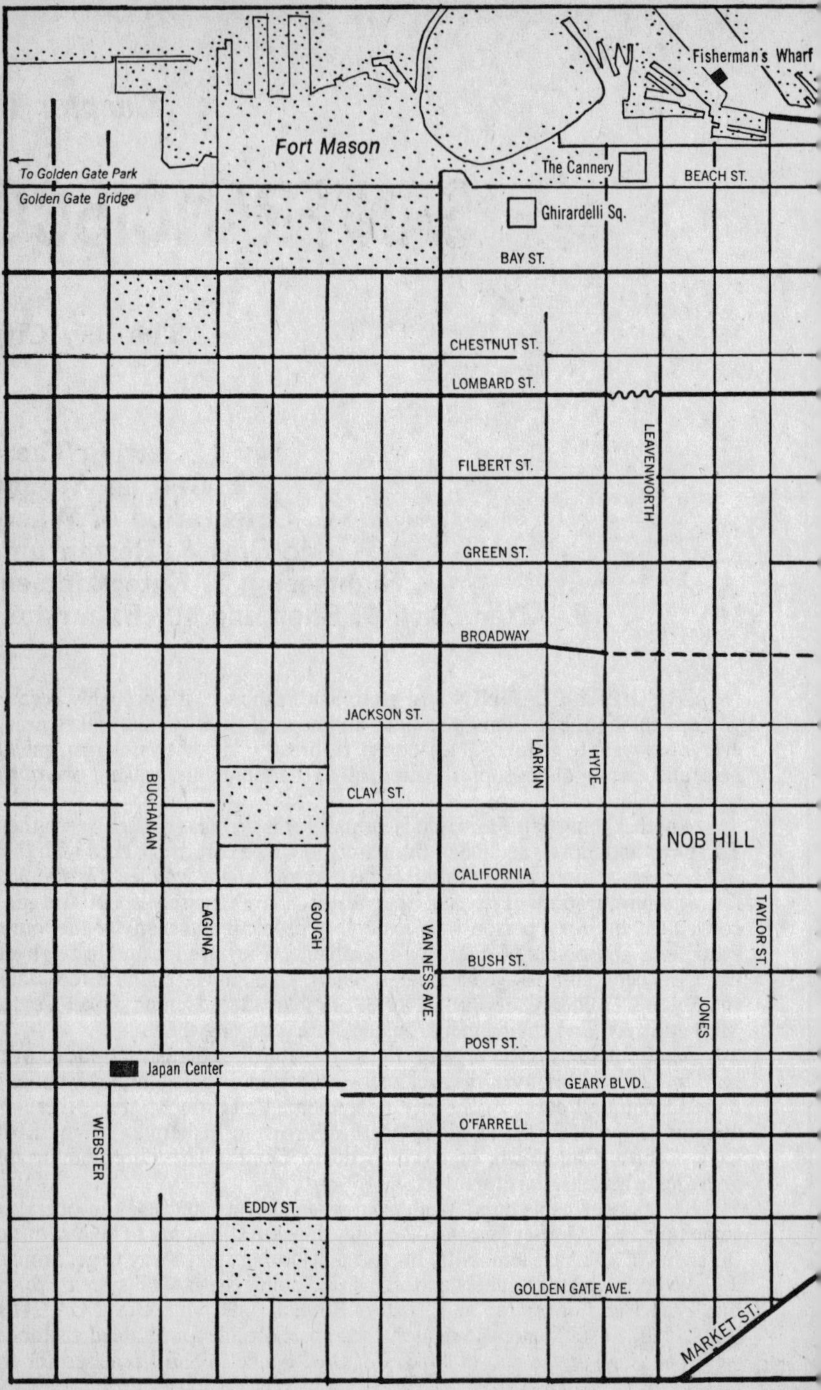

Fisherman's Wharf

Fort Mason

To Golden Gate Park
Golden Gate Bridge

The Cannery

BEACH ST.

Ghirardelli Sq.

BAY ST.

CHESTNUT ST.

LOMBARD ST.

LEAVENWORTH

FILBERT ST.

GREEN ST.

BROADWAY

JACKSON ST.

LARKIN

HYDE

BUCHANAN

CLAY ST.

NOB HILL

CALIFORNIA

LAGUNA

GOUGH

VAN NESS AVE.

BUSH ST.

TAYLOR ST.

JONES

POST ST.

Japan Center

GEARY BLVD.

WEBSTER

O'FARRELL

EDDY ST.

GOLDEN GATE AVE.

MARKET ST.

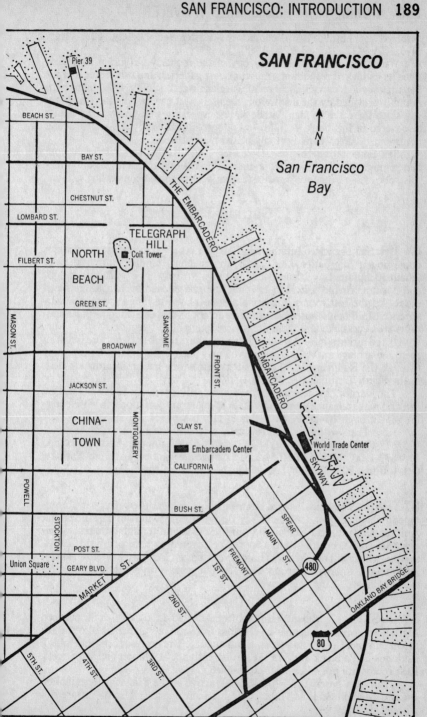

Disabled" (published 1976), contact the **Easter Seal Society,** 6221 Geary Blvd., CA 94121 (tel. 415/752-4888).

When you arrive, pick up a copy of the monthly *California Magazine,* since its listings of restaurants, museums, art galleries, and other events in the Bay area section, carry indication of wheelchair-accessibility. Even though the rating is provided by the institutions themselves, it can be a kick-off guide for you since there are so many other places, especially restaurants, that cannot be covered in this book. A follow-up phone call can verify if your particular needs can be taken care of at any of the places listed.

San Francisco *can* be the city you left your heart in, too—as well as your diet resolutions, since the food is high on its list of attractions. Last, but not least, one of San Francisco's greatest assets is the friendly people who live there.

1. Getting There

BY AIR: San Francisco International Airport is served by almost every major domestic and international air carrier, and is about 16 miles south of the city (about 30 minutes travel time from downtown). A network of curb cuts, ramps, and elevators enable visitors to go easily from the gates to the baggage retrieval areas. All the rest rooms in the main areas of the terminal are wheelchair-accessible (although those near the gates do not have special facilities). Restaurants are accessible, and there are lowered, amplified telephones.

If the airlines have advance notice of your arrival or departure, most of them can arrange any special service you may need while you are at the airport through the Handicapped Travelers Services, which has an information desk in the South Terminal (tel. 415/861-6689).

The journey downtown from the airport will cost about $20 in a taxi. You can also make advance arrangements for special transportation in a wheelchair-lift van through **Medivan,** P.O. Box 34116, CA 94134 (tel. 415/822-2212).

Rental cars with hand controls are available at the airport from **Avis** (tel. 415/877-6725, toll free 800/331-1212), on two weeks notice; from **Hertz** (tel. 415/877-1600, toll free 800/654-3131), on five days notice; and from **National** (tel. toll free 800/328-4567), with advance notice of three days.

BY TRAIN: The long-distance **Amtrak** trains, such as the superliners, terminate in Oakland, just across the Bay Bridge from downtown. The buses that Amtrak runs into San Francisco from their Oakland terminal are not wheelchair-accessible, but the short trip can be covered by taxi, or by the BART system, which will take you to a number of stops on Market Street. For general information, and departure and arrival arrangements on Amtrak, see the section in Chapter 2 on train travel.

BY BUS: The **Greyhound** terminal (tel. 415/433-1500), on 7th St. between Market and Mission Sts., has level access from the bus arrival area to the 7th Street entrance. You'll find a taxi stand outside. The nearest accessible BART station is half a block north of the station entrance at Market and 7th Streets. Rest rooms are not wheelchair-accessible.

Trailways buses (tel. 415/982-6400) arrive at the Transbay Terminal on 1st and Mission Streets. There is a taxi stand outside. Rest rooms are not wheelchair-accessible.

2. Getting Around

Hills or no, there are plenty of San Francisco sights on fairly flat terrain, and whole areas have ramped curbs. This is thanks to the groups of disabled people and organizations that formed the Coalition for the Removal of Architectural Barriers (CRAB) about 10 years ago, and to the financing provided by the city. When you want to venture farther afield, you can take a ride on San Francisco's BART system, which is accessible to passengers in wheelchairs.

PUBLIC TRANSPORTATION: The **Bay Area Rapid Transit (BART)** (tel. 788-BART, TDD 839-2200), has accessible stations and trains in a high-speed network between San Francisco, the East Bay communities, and northern San Mateo County. In San Francisco itself, it has stops along Market Street at convenient locations such as Civic Center, Montgomery Street, Powell Street, and the Embarcadero Center.

BART stations have special elevators to boarding levels, with lowered controls and telephones. The carpeted and air-conditioned trains have level entry, with wide doors and wide aisles. Each station has a rest room equipped for passengers in wheelchairs.

TAXIS: Although San Francisco has plenty of cabs, they are not inexpensive. Fortunately, distances are comparatively short. The meter starts at $2.50 and goes up $1.20 for each mile. Taxi stands can be found at hotels—the St. Francis, Sheraton Palace, Hyatt Union Square, Hyatt Regency, Fairmont, and San Francisco Hilton—and at transportation terminals. They can also be summoned by telephone; among the cab companies are the **Veteran's Cab** (tel. 552-1300), **DeSoto Cab** (tel. 673-1414), **Luxor Cabs** (tel. 552-4040), and **Yellow Cabs** (tel. 626-2345).

SPECIAL TRANSPORTATION: Medivan, P.O.Box 34116, CA 94134 (tel. 415/822-2212), can provide transportation in vehicles equipped with wheelchair lifts.

FERRY: You'll be able to travel to Sausalito, Tiburon, and Larkspur by ferry boats that are accessible via ramps (see Sightseeing section of this chapter).

BY CAR: You don't really need a car to explore San Francisco, but if you want to tour the bay area or take the 49-mile Scenic Drive, you may prefer to rent one for the day if you do not arrive in your own. Three major rental companies have cars with hand controls: **Avis** (tel. toll free 800/331-1212), **Hertz** (tel. toll free 800/654-3131), and **National** (tel. toll free 800/328-4567). (For advance notice to obtain hand controls, see the Getting There section in this chapter.)

When you are driving, remember that pedestrians really do expect to have the right of way—and it really works in San Francisco—and that cable cars, when they resume running, are in the same category. If you go while cable car reconstruction is still going on, try to avoid those streets (the tourist map from the Visitors Bureau indicates the cable car routes). And remember that a car parked on a hill must have its brakes set and its wheels turned to the curb to prevent rolling. Use low gear when driving downhill. Be warned that cars are towed away on certain streets during morning and evening commuting hours.

Most color-coded curb markings restrict passenger cars, but ten-minute parking is allowed in green zones, and after 6 p.m. parking is allowed in yellow zones. You'll find some curbs that designate parking for disabled drivers identified by California license plates. Identifications from states other than California are honored in special parking spaces, but they must be displayed on the dashboard.

3. Orientation

The 49 square miles that it occupies on the tip of the long peninsula between San Francisco Bay and the Pacific Ocean means that San Francisco is one of the smallest of America's "Big Cities." There is nothing left of its Spanish origins, nor of the Gold Rush days of the mid-1800s. Its murky past as the Barbary Coast, when it equalled Shanghai and Marseilles as one of the world's most wicked ports, was vitually wiped off the face of the earth by the earthquake and fire of 1906.

Within the triangle formed by Market Street, Van Ness Avenue, and the waterfront lies nearly everything in the tourist's San Francisco, other than Golden Gate Park.

At the heart of the city is Union Square, the hub of the shopping and hotel district, with a restful and beautiful plaza and park that create an oasis in the traffic jams of surrounding streets. It also has an underground garage for over 1000 cars ($1.50 an hour), but it's difficult to get into on a weekday.

Facing north from here you are looking toward, first of all, Chinatown, the largest Chinese community anywhere outside the Orient; next to it is North Beach, the nightlife area noted for originating topless dancers; between there and the waterfront is Telegraph Hill topped by the Coit Tower, once bohemian, now a respectable high-rent area; and on into the port area of San Francisco, one of the world's largest and busiest; Fisherman's Wharf, replete with seafood restaurants, cruise boats, and the restaurant and shopping center of Ghirardelli Square are toward the Golden Gate Bridge end. At the waterfront end of Market Street, San Francisco's wide main artery, is the Ferry Building at the Oakland Bay Bridge end (where you can get ferries to Sausalito and Larkspur). In the opposite direction down Market Street, toward Van Ness Avenue, is San Francisco's Civic Center, a handsome group of buildings including City Hall, the Opera House and the Louise M.Davies Symphony Hall, around a landscaped plaza.

The mile-wide opening to the bay from the Pacific Ocean has been spanned since 1937 by the Golden Gate Bridge, probably the most-photographed bridge in the world for its graceful single span and spidery cables amid its spectacular setting. It links the city to Marin County to the north. The peninsula's link to the "interior" in the other direction is the San Francisco-Oakland Bay Bridge, its 8½-mile length making it the longest steel bridge in the world.

CLIMATE: Indescribable, they say, of San Francisco's climate, because it is like no other place. Average monthly temperatures range only from 50.7 degrees in January to 62 degrees in September, and San Franciscans usually consider 70 degrees a heat wave. It isn't a perpetual anything, though, since there are very cold days in the summer (rarely below 40 degrees F.) and quite warm ones in the winter. And it can be both on any given day at any time of the year. Foghorns are part of the background music in San Francisco, and it is the fog that provides the city with its natural air conditioner, created by a rare combination of water, wind, and topography. But it is a special kind of

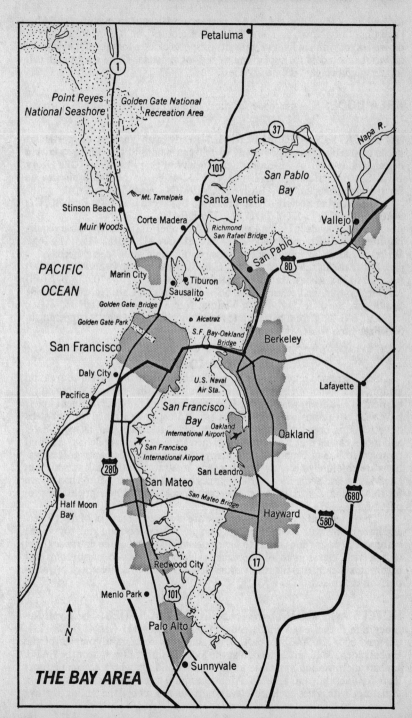

THE BAY AREA

fog and gives the city a stage-set appearance, with mist in one area and blue sky in another. Now you know the kind of clothes you'll want to take: suits or dresses for women, lightweight suits or sports clothes for men; for everyone, all-weather top coat for cool evenings and for showers. There's not much call for very lightweight summer clothes.

AREA CODE: The area code for most of San Francisco is 415.

INFORMATION AND REFERRAL: Ready with answers on particular needs of disabled people, or ready to tell you where to find the answer, are organizations such as the **Easter Seal Society of San Francisco**, 6221 Geary Blvd., San Francisco, CA 94121 (tel. 415/752-4888), or the **California League for the Handicapped**, 1299 Bush St., CA 94109 (tel. 415/441-1980).

The **Hearing Society of San Francisco Bay Area** is at 1428 Bush St., CA 94109 (tel. 415/775-5700, TDD 415/776-DEAF).

The **Independent Living Project** is a free referral service for those requiring attendant assistance, at 4429 California St., CA 94121, (tel. 415/751-8765). Write or call as far in advance as possible outlining your special needs.

Other useful references include: **S.F. Medical Supply** (wheelchair rental) (tel. 922-6123), **Abbey Medical Wheelchair Repair** (tel. 771-3700), **S.F. Medical Society** (physical referral) (tel. 567-6234), **Health Care Network** (mobile health care unit) (tel. 441-4494), **Visiting Nurse Association** (tel. 861-8705).

Call 391-2000 for a two-minute recording telling you what's happening in San Francisco while you're there.

4. Where to Stay

San Francisco hotels are well-geared to catering to tourist and convention visitors, but some of them are in older buildings that present architectural barriers to visitors in wheelchairs. However, many of the older, eminent hotels have spacious rooms with wide doors and at least one entrance without steps or with ramps, even if they don't have built-in "special facilities" as such. Hotel and motel chains that have rooms designed for guests in wheelchairs are well represented in San Francisco, and many of them offer free parking. Reservations are absolutely necessary at any of the hotels during the peak season from late May to late September, and the prices quoted here (subject to change) are for that period. Check for special weekend packages at lower prices. Be prepared for a 9¾% tax on hotel bills.

The hotels and motels included here are in the area north of Market Street and have rooms with special facilities (ramps, wider doors, and grab bars in the bathrooms), or are considered to have reasonable access at the entrance (level or one step), elevators to all floors, and wide entry doors to guest rooms and bathrooms. Before making reservations, it is advisable to doublecheck on facilities you may need.

HOTELS AND MOTELS WITH SPECIAL FACILITIES: The **Hyatt Regency San Francisco**, 5 Embarcadero Center, CA 94111 (tel. 415/788-1234, toll free 800/228-9000), is part of the shopping-restaurant complex of the Embarcadero Mall on flat terrain at the foot of Market Street, near the BART Embarcadero station and close to the Ferry Building, where accessible boats leave for Sausalito and Tiburon. Architecturally, it has Hyatt's soaring atrium signature, with glass-enclosed elevators from the lobby, the setting for live music every evening. There are 11 guest rooms here with wider doors and grab bars in the bathroom. Public rest rooms are wheelchair-accessible, including those at Hugo's, the continental restaurant that has a level entry at the side door. There are other level-entrance restaurants, including Mrs. Candy's in the lobby, and the revolving rooftop Equinox that serves lunch and cocktails. Parking is free on weekends. Rates range from $103 to $153 single, $128 to $180 double.

Part of the Japanese Center and on fairly flat terrain, the **Westin Miyako,** 1625 Post St., CA 94115 (tel. 415/922-3200, toll free 800/228-3000), has ten rooms designed for guests in wheelchairs (30-inch-wide doors and grab bars in the bathrooms). There is a strong Japanese ambience here, naturally; waitresses dressed in kimonos serve Japanese-American dishes in the accessible Bamboo Grove dining room. There are wheelchair-accessible public rest rooms, and public telephones are lowered. Elevators have floor indicators in braille. Rates range from $75 to $95 single, $95 to $115 double.

Facing Union Square is the elegant grande dame of San Francisco hotels and one with good wheelchair-access credentials, the **Westin St. Francis,** Powell & Geary Sts., CA 94119 (tel. 415/397-7000, toll free 800/228-3000). The main building predates the earthquake, and it has preserved the rosewood paneling and crystal chandeliers that belonged to that era. The entrance is level at Geary Street where there is also a drive-in approach. The hotel has three rooms designed for guests in wheelchairs, and the hotel's facilities are accessible by ramps or elevators. The restaurants are barrier-free. Rates here range from $80 to $160 single, $105 to $185 double.

In the area of Fisherman's Wharf is a good choice of hotels and motels belonging to national chains, with accommodations for guests in wheelchairs:

Holiday Inn, 1300 Columbus Ave., CA 94133 (tel. 415/771-9000, toll free 800/238-8000), has special rooms in the new wing with extra large bathroom doors, grab bars, and lowered fixtures. There is a pool here, and parking is free. Rates are $80 to $100 single, $94 to $113 double.

Howard Johnson's Motor Lodge is at 580 Beach St., CA 94113 (tel. 415/775-3800; toll free 800/854-2000, from California 800/652-1527). It has some guest rooms with entry doors to both room and bathroom, which are 36 inches wide, and grab bars. There is a ramped front entrance. Rates are $76 single, $84 double.

There's also a **Ramada Inn on Fisherman's Wharf** at 590 Bay St., CA 94133 (tel. 415/885-4700, toll free 800/228-2828), with three special rooms equipped with extra-wide doors and grab bars in the bathrooms. Parking is free, with elevator access to the lobby from the underground garage. Rates are $82 to $90 single, $97 to $105 double.

The **Sheraton at Fisherman's Wharf,** 2500 Mason St., CA 94133 (tel. 415/362-5500, toll free 800/325-3535), has level access and five rooms designed for guests in wheelchairs. The garage is underground with elevators to the lobby, and there is a pool. Rates are $92 to $111 single, $92 to $126 double.

The **TraveLodge at the Wharf,** 250 Beach St., CA 94113 (tel. 415/392-6700, toll free 800/255-3050), has accommodation for guests in wheelchairs. There's a pool, free parking, and good views of the bay. Rates are $86 to $92 single, $96 to $102 double.

In the neighborhood of Chinatown and the financial district, the **Holiday Inn** at 750 Kearny St., CA 94108 (tel. 415/433-6600, toll free 800/238-8000), is another motel where the rooms have wider doors and grab bars. Parking is free and there's a rooftop pool. Rates are $84 single, $97 double.

On the level stretch of Market Street between 8th and 9th Streets, close to the Civic Center with its museum, theater, and the opera house, is a charming older hotel, recently renovated, which has reasonable rates as well as the convenience of the original spacious rooms and wide doors. It is the **San Franciscan,** 1231 Market St., CA 94103 (tel. 415/626-8000, toll free 800/227-4747), and the entrance is level. Some of the large, airy rooms have the convenience of sinks in the bedroom, as well as grab bars in the bathrooms. It is also conveniently close to BART's Civic Center station. Beppino's Italian Restaurant is accessible off the impressive 1911 lobby of the hotel. Rates are $60 to $85 single, $70 to $95 double.

The **Holiday Inn Golden Gateway,** 1500 Van Ness Ave., CA 94109 (tel. 415/441-4000, toll free 800/238-8000), has a number of rooms with larger bathrooms (equipped with grab bars) and features such as lowered counters, electrical outlets, fixtures, and peepholes. You'll probably need a car if you stay here. Rates are $56 single, $64 double.

NO SPECIAL FACILITIES, BUT SPACIOUS: Preeminent among San Francisco hotels is the venerable **Mark Hopkins,** Number One Nob Hill, CA 94106 (tel. 415/392-3434, toll free 800/327-0200), with a magnificent view from every room. But that's because it is at the top of one of San Francisco's hills; decide if you will be taking a taxi or using your car for this one. Bathroom doors in guest rooms are more than 25 inches wide. There is valet parking and an adjacent garage (entry on California Street) which has level access to the hotel via elevator. The Top of the Mark cocktail lounge is a legendary rendezvous place and is accessible to wheelchair patrons, who can also reach tables next to the windows. Rates here start at $100 single and $120 double.

Also on Nob Hill and obviously in a hilly area at the junction of California and Mason Streets, is the equally renowned **Fairmont Hotel,** 950 Mason St., CA 94106 (tel. 415/772-5000, toll free 800/527-4727). The block-square marble palace has six restaurants, eight cocktail lounges, the city's leading nightclub, and many shops. The garage is adjacent on Powell Street, and the Mason Street entrance has valet parking. The entrance is level via the approach from the Mason-California corner. Doors to guest rooms are at least 29 inches wide. The tower is topped by the accessible Crown Room, reached by an outside elevator known as the Skylift (there is a buffet served here as well as cocktails). Other restaurants in all price categories include the Venetian Room (a lush supper club) and the Tonga (a Polynesian restaurant). Rates at the Fairmont range from $90 to $125 single, and $115 to $150 double (higher in the tower).

On Union Square between Post and Sutter Streets is the **Hyatt on Union Square,** 345 Stockton St., CA 94108 (tel. 415/398-1234, toll free 800/228-9000). Although not in the current Hyatt architectural mode, it is handsome and modern and has recently been renovated. There is level entrance, and guest-room and bathroom doors are at least 25 inches wide. Rates range from $95 to $165 single, $120 to $190 double.

San Francisco likes to preserve its older buildings rather than tear them down, and one of these is the tastefully elegant **Four Seasons Clift,** 495 Geary St. (at Taylor), CA 94102 (tel. 415/775-4700, toll free 800/828-1188), in the downtown Union Square area. It has recently been refurbished and all its rooms have 30-inch bathroom doors (grab bars at the bath only). The entrance to the hotel is level and the restaurant entries are also barrier-free. The Redwood Room and the French Room are open for breakfast and lunch, and the French Room is open nightly for dinner. The Lobby Lounge offers a light lunch and English tea Monday through Saturday. Rates range from $110 to $150 single and $130 to $170 double.

Brand new in 1983, and also near Union Square, is the **Campton Place Hotel,** 340 Stockton St. (between Post and Sutter Sts.), CA 94108 (tel. 415/781-5555, toll free 800/647-4007). It has a level entrance and elevators to all floors. The restaurant has a few steps down at the main entrance, but there is a ramp at another entrance. There are five guest rooms where bathrooms have 36-inch doors and grab bars. Rates are $110 to $179 single, $130 to $190 double.

The city's largest hotel is the **San Francisco Hilton,** 333 O'Farrell St. at Mason, CA 94102 (tel. 415/771-1400; check toll-free number available from your state through 800 information, 800/555-1212, or you can make reservations through the Hilton reservation office in any of the major cities). It is in the Union Square area, two blocks from the Union Square BART station and in the center of the shopping and theater districts. The Hilton has level access, and the bathroom doors in guest rooms are at least 25 inches wide. The garage, entered from Ellis Street, has an internal ramp for cars to floors 5 through 11, where you can park beside your room. There is a heated swimming pool and a sundeck on the 16th floor. Rates at the Hilton range from $69 to $130 single, $89 to $150 double.

5. Restaurants

San Francisco takes its eating very seriously. The standards of cuisine are exceptionally high, and the variety of international offerings is wide because of the city's history as host to many cultures.

You'll be able to enjoy fish and shellfish fresh off the boats at Fisherman's Wharf and at the great seafood restaurants in town. Then there is North Beach and its Italian specialties, and any kind of Chinese cooking you like in Chinatown, of course. San Francisco boasts some of the finest French restaurants in the country, and American-style fare is there too, with its new emphasis on the natural ingredients. No need to go hungry as you shop and browse, either, at complexes like Ghirardelli Square, the Cannery, and Pier 39. You'll find some of their accessible restaurants listed in the Sightseeing section of this chapter.

With more than 2500 restaurants to choose from, selection is not an easy job, but the ones included here are within the triangle of Market, Van Ness, and the bay, which is where you'll probably be most of the time if you are sightseeing or staying in a downtown hotel. They are, of course, establishments that offer reasonable access to people with mobility impairments. All San Francisco restaurants are required to have at least 75% of their tables accessible to people in wheelchairs. It's the rare restaurant, however, that has wheelchair-accessible rest rooms, so you can assume that they are not available unless indicated. Don't forget that lunch can bring an expensive restaurant into the moderate category.

Restaurants are grouped together here by price, but the area they are in is also indicated.

DINNER $25 AND UP: In the neighborhood of Nob Hill in the Stanford Court Hotel is **Fournou's Ovens,** 905 California St. (tel. 989-1910), with a California-oriented menu served in a dining room dominated by enormous tiled ovens used for roasted meats and fowl of all kinds. There is a glass-enclosed conservatory as well. Dinner is served every day, lunch Monday through Friday. The entrance to the hotel has one step.

Also in the Nob Hill area in the Huntington Hotel is the romantic setting of **L'Etoile**, 1075 California St. at Mason St. (tel. 771-1529). Reservations necessary. Closed Sunday.

Near Union Square in the new Pacific Plaza Hotel, you can have fine northern Italian dishes in luxurious surroundings at **Donatello**, Post and Mason Sts. (tel. 441-7182), which serves lunch and dinner daily.

In the Jackson Square area, two blocks from Broadway, is one of San Francisco's most ambitious and innovative French restaurants, **Ernie's**, 847 Montgomery St. at Pacific Ave. (tel. 397-5969), in bonanza era decor with many furnishings salvaged from San Francisco's old mansions. It is one of the few places in the city that requires coats and ties. Reservations are necessary.

Le Trianon, 242 O'Farrell St. near Mason St. (tel. 982-9353), is three blocks north of Market Street and two from Union Square. Owned by Rene Verdon, who was chef at the White House under President Kennedy, it serves classic French dishes in classic French surroundings, and is open daily for dinner only. Reservations are essential.

DINNER $15 TO $25: Peking-style Chinese food in an elegant setting is offered at the **Mandarin**, in Ghirardelli Square on the third floor of the Woolen Mill (tel. 673-8812). Lunch and dinner served daily, and reservations are recommended.

Le Central, 453 Bush St. between Kearny St. and Grand Ave. (tel. 391-2233), is a classic French bistro. They do not accept reservations.

DINNER $7 TO $15: In an old warehouse overlooking the marina and the bay is **Greens**, Building A, Fort Mason Center at Buchanan and Marina. (tel. 771-6222). The fare is vegetarian and extraordinary. You can have a very good lunch here, Tuesday through Saturday, for $3 to $7. Dinner is served on Friday and Saturday only, by reservation. Call ahead.

The place to go for elegant pizza is **Prego**, 2000 Union St. at Buchanan (tel. 563-3305), in the Cow Hollow section of Union Street, a light and airy trattoria that is very popular, so you may have to wait for a table. Pastas here are $6 to $10.

A couple of blocks away is **Mai's Restaurant**, 1838 Union St. (tel. 921-2861), with a Vietnamese menu in an elegant setting. Open for dinner daily, and lunch (except Sunday).

In the financial district, there's a San Francisco institution called the **Tadich Grill**, 240 California St. between Battery and Front (tel. 391-2373). It has an extensive menu of simple but great food, specializing in fish. Closed Sunday.

In the vicinity of Jackson Square, **McArthur Park**, 607 Front St. at Jackson (tel. 398-5700), is a good spot for dinner after the theater, or for lunch after exploring Jackson Square. The gardenlike setting in an old brick building is open for dinner every day, for lunch Monday through Friday. Reservations are recommended.

The **North Beach Restaurant**, 1512 Stockton St. between Union and Green (tel. 392-1587), serves its fine Italian food in an unpretentious setting. Open daily for lunch and dinner.

No New Yorker need go without the typical Jewish deli if they go to **David's**, 474 Geary St. at Taylor (tel. 771-1600), which is open daily from 8 a.m. to 1 a.m., and is especially lively after the theater. It is two blocks west of Union Square. In addition to full meals, delicatessen sandwiches are available for $3.95 to $5.95.

In the Ghirardelli Square neighborhood, **Camargue,** 2316 Polk St. (tel. 776-5577), looks like a Parisian bistro and has a very original menu. House special is a three-course dinner for $12. Open daily for lunch and dinner.

For Northern Indian food in an elegant setting, try the **Peacock,** 2800 Van Ness Ave. (tel. 928-7000). There is a buffet here for $9.50. Dinner served every day, lunch on Sunday to Friday. Call ahead if you use a wheelchair.

One of San Francisco's newest Indian restaurants is **North India,** 3131A Webster St. (tel. 931-1556), located at the bay end of Webster near the Moscone Center. There's room for a wheelchair in the rest room.

Vanessi's, 498 Broadway (tel. 421-0890), is another busy San Francisco institution, lying just north of Chinatown and Jackson Square. It specializes in broiled meat and fish at dinnertime, but has a wide menu all day long, every day (no lunch on Sunday).

BUDGET: For refreshment as you see the sights, there are many places that offer accessibility along with the food, and you can check these out as you go by. You'll find plenty to choose from, especially in the large complexes such as Ghirardelli Square, the Cannery, and Pier 39, as well as in Chinatown and on Fisherman's Wharf.

CHINESE RESTAURANTS: More than one-seventh of the population of San Francisco is Chinese, and so Chinese fare is long-established there and deserves a special note. Since the city is the gateway to the United States for most Chinese immigrants, there is a variety of cooking styles—from Canton, Shanghai, Hunan, Sichuan, and Peking—along with what are probably the best examples of dim sum to be found in the country.

Despite the variety that is available, the majority of the 100 restaurants in Chinatown remain Cantonese, and to eat their food here is to experience it unadulterated by Western adaptations. Most of the city's Chinese restaurants are in Chinatown, bounded loosely by Bush Street and Broadway, Kearny and Powell Streets; Grant Avenue and Stockton Street are its main arteries. An exception is the elegant and expensive Mandarin in Ghirardelli Square (noted earlier). The restaurants mentioned here are considered reasonably accessible.

Perhaps the best thing about eating Chinese food in San Francisco is that most of the restaurants can be included in the moderate and budget categories. Among those considered accessible and in the budget price range, is **Yuet Lee,** 1300 Stockton St. (tel. 982-6020), a storefront restaurant with a blackboard menu and an accent on seafood. Open from noon to 10 p.m. every day, but go early since it is very popular.

Another inexpensive Chinese restaurant is **Lichee Garden,** 1416 Powell St. (tel. 397-2290), which serves a Hong Kong-style Cantonese cooking (faster stir-frying). Open from 11:30 a.m. to 9:30 p.m. every day. It is advisable to make reservations on the weekend.

Dim sum, the seemingly endless varieties of small stuffed dumplings that are served for the Chinese tea, breakfast, or brunch, is a San Francisco custom among Chinese and non-Chinese alike. One of the best dim sum restaurants anywhere is fortunately also in the inexpensive category. It is the **Hong Kong Tea House,** 835 Pacific Ave. (tel. 391-6365), where only dim sum is served in a large, busy room, open every day from 9 a.m. to 3 p.m. Waitresses walk through the restaurant with their dim sum carts as you pick what takes your fancy. At the end of the meal, your bill is based on the number of empty plates at your table.

Slightly higher-priced but not much, the **Hunan,** 924 Sansome St. (tel. 956-7727), is a large barn of a place that is very popular and specializes in spicy Hunan-style dishes. Open Monday to Friday only, from 11:30 a.m. to 9:30 p.m.

Note: One of the handiest references to restaurants which have wheelchair accessibility is *California,* the weekly magazine you'll find on newsstands. Although these are subjective judgments of the restaurants themselves, they can be a good start. Follow up with a phone call to check on your specific needs. *California* Magazine has *three* different categories: The accessibility symbol followed by + indicates that the building and its facilities, including rest rooms and elevators, are suitable for patrons in wheelchairs, that doors are at least 32 inches wide, and that there are no steps. The wheelchair accessibility symbol alone indicates that the building is suitable for persons in wheelchairs, though not all the facilities. The wheelchair-access symbol with "call ahead" added, means that with advance notice, the management will make arrangements for persons in wheelchairs.

6. Sightseeing

Most standard guide books emphasize that much of San Francisco is to be explored *on foot.* For the nondisabled visitor the implication is for leisurely strolling and poking around at a slow pace, and there's no reason that the same style cannot be followed by visitors who don't necessarily do it "on foot." With that in mind, this brief guide will concentrate on those areas that are in the flatter sections of town, leaving the hill-climbing to be done by car or taxi if you'd like to get those unexcelled panoramic views from the higher elevations. Included are the special facilities available at each spot.

The **San Francisco Convention and Visitors Bureau,** at Market and Polk Streets in Fox Plaza (tel. 626-5500), has level entrance and elevator access. There is also a **Visitors Information Center** near Union Square at 476 Post St. (tel. 421-5074), which has level entry.

CHINATOWN: Once you are inside this seven-block-long and three-block-wide area, you are in the largest Chinese settlement outside Asia. Buildings have a pagoda shape, as do street lights and the telephone booths, but it's definitely not done just to attract tourists: the Chinese community has been here since the days of the Gold Rush of 1849, and it was prejudice that created the ghetto. Despite its reputation based on a past history of opium dens and Tong wars, the area that stretches roughly from Bush Street to Pacific Avenue is today one of the safest neighborhoods in America.

If you go there by car, you'll find a parking garage on Kearny beneath Portsmouth Plaza, which was the plaza of the original Spanish settlement. Grant Avenue is the main thoroughfare here, and if you go by taxi, you might want to get out near California Street since Grant Avenue goes slightly downhill from here in the direction of Jackson Avenue four blocks away. On **Grant Avenue** you'll get the full flavor of Chinatown, its shops full of all kind of things from the ordinary to the exotic, junk as well as genuine, and grocery stores purveying Oriental delicacies you may never have seen before. Most stores have level access. At this junction of Grant Avenue and California Street, you may want to drop in to the **Chinatown Wax Museum** (tel. 981-4298), where you will see depictions of Chinese history as well as of the early Chinese settlers in California and Old Chinatown as it was before the earthquake of 1906. Admission is $1.75 for adults, $1 for children 6 to 12. Open daily from 10 a.m. to 11 p.m.

The **China Trade Center,** 838 Grant Ave. near Washington, is the commercial essence of Chinatown in one building, with a complex of shops, and elevator access to different floors. The basement houses a discount center for Chinese food and kitchen supplies. At the top, on the sixth floor, is the Empress of China restaurant, a rather luxurious place whose decor is the re-creation of a temple and pleasure park.

Many of Chinatown's streets are narrow, so choose in-between times like midmorning or midafternoon to visit. At the Chinese New Year, celebrated with great gusto in late January or February, it is *very* crowded, to say the least.

JACKSON SQUARE: Close by Chinatown, two (steep-ish) blocks from Grant Avenue on Jackson Street at Montgomery Street, is Jackson Square, a three-block area of restored buildings, some of which are earthquake survivors. It was once known as the "Pit of Hell," one of the Barbary Coast's least salubrious spots. Now it is occupied by antique dealers, art galleries, gift and apparel shops, and primarily home furnishings showrooms, not open to the public, but where you'll see some exceptional window displays. It's worth a visit to see the extraordinary revival of the brick Federal-style buildings with their handwrought iron shutters and graceful façades. The oldest structure here is 472 Jackson Street, where William Tecumseh Sherman (later General) opened a bank in 1849 just in time for the Gold Rush. The original interior columns, still here, are made from ships' sailing masts. One of the accessible buildings is the Assay Office restaurant on Gold Street.

EMBARCADERO CENTER: Toward the waterfront end of Sacramento Street is the Embarcadero Center, eight acres of innovative architecture, plazas, malls, fountains, sculptures, restaurants, galleries, and shops. There's a BART stop here, and an underground garage with an elevator to the lobby level. Although the main means of access between floors in the four buildings is by escalator, you can take the office building elevators to reach the upper levels where you'll find accessible restaurants and rest rooms, as well as a multitude of shops of all kinds. You can travel between buildings (except from Embarcadero One to Embarcadero Four) on the podium and lobby levels. A map is available that carries the wheelchair-access symbol for elevators, rest-room locations, and routes between buildings.

Back down on the plaza, there are sidewalk cafes for refreshments and people-watching, including one at the Hyatt Regency Hotel (where the public rest rooms are wheelchair-accessible). All around is a constant street fair of craft offerings and other activities, along with millions of dollars worth of original paintings and sculpture.

UNION STREET AND COW HOLLOW: Another recently renovated area of San Francisco is the Cow Hollow stretch of Union Street (between Van Ness Avenue and Steiner Street), once the grazing ground of dairy cattle and then a drab commercial area, but now in full Victorian regalia of brick façades, gingerbread trim, gaslight, and flower-filled courtyards. Boutiques have antiques and handicrafts, but there's also almost everything you'd find in a shopping district, including restaurants (many accessible). Curbs are not ramped here, though.

FISHERMAN'S WHARF AND VICINITY: The place to eat seafood and watch the bay activity of all kinds is San Francisco's famous Fisherman's Wharf, surrounded by lots of other things to see and do, such as the Maritime Museum, Aquatic Park, Ghirardelli Square, the Cannery, and Pier 39.

Center of all the activity at Fisherman's Wharf is **Victoria Plaza,** a gaslight replica of a 19th-century park with its nonstop festival atmosphere.

Because of the lay of the land, it's a good idea to start at the **Maritime Museum** at the west end of Victorian Park at the foot of Polk Street (tel. 673-0700). It's a treasure house of sailing, whaling, and fishing exhibits from San Francisco's historic past, and although there is no elevator, there is plenty to see on the first floor. There's a level entrance through the Senior Citizens Center on the side of the museum. Admission is free.

From here you can get to **Ghirardelli Square,** 900 N. Point St. (tel. 775-5500), via the Beach Street arcade from where the elevator goes to the main plaza. If you go directly to Ghirardelli Square from elsewhere, (there is a garage which has rest rooms with stalls at least 25 inches wide), there is an accessible entrance at Larkin Street. Elevators go to all floors. This ten-level complex of shops, theaters, cafes, restaurants, and exhibitions is, once more, a loving conversion, this time from the old Ghirardelli chocolate factory and a wool mill. There's something here for everybody—street performers in the West Plaza, over a dozen restaurants, including the accessible Magic Pan, the Mandarin, and Paprika's Fono, and 80 stores surrounded by terraces for viewing the bay. Pick up a free guide at the information center to find your way around. Ghirardelli Square is open in the summer from 10 a.m. to 9 p.m. Monday through Saturday, 11 a.m. to 6 p.m. on Sunday. The rest of the year, hours are 10:30 a.m. to 6 p.m. Monday through Thursday, 10:30 a.m. to 9 p.m. Friday and Saturday, and 11 a.m. to 6 p.m. on Sunday.

There's a slicker version of the same idea at **The Cannery,** 2801 Leavenworth St. at the foot of Columbus St. (tel 771-3112), *downhill* on Hyde Street from Ghirardelli Square. The brick structure was once the Del Monte Cannery and a survivor of the 1906 earthquake. The conversion preserved the exterior and and created a three-story interior complex for shopping, eating, and entertainment, all accessible by a glass-enclosed elevator. There is a level entrance and a parking lot nearby if you are going straight there in your own car. Accessible restaurants here include El Sombrero, Hungry Tiger, and Shang Yuen. The Cannery hours are 10 a.m. to 6 p.m. on Monday through Saturday, 11 a.m. to 6 p.m. on Sunday, until 9 p.m. on holidays and during the summer.

At the Jefferson Street exit of the Cannery, you'll find yourself on **Fisherman's Wharf** proper, with its scores of seafood restaurants and stalls which, in the afternoon, serve the fresh catch from that morning's fishing fleet. It's paradise for lovers of shrimp and crab, which you can eat as you take in the other sights of vendors and stores selling just about everything.

At the bay end of Jefferson Street you'll come to **Pier 39,** a restaurant-shopping complex that resembles a turn-of-the-century San Francisco street scene. Built on an abandoned cargo pier and flanked by small boat marinas, it is yet another demonstration of San Francisco's flair for turning an ordinary work setting into a special place for everybody to enjoy. Here's the place for spectacularly sweeping views of the bay and the city! It has level access and wider rest room stalls equipped with grab bars. There's nonstop free entertainment at the three open-air stages (tips appreciated by the performers) and some 130 shops and lots of restaurants, many of which you will find easily accessible. Its restaurants are open from 11:30 a.m. to 11:30 p.m., cocktail lounges open until 2 a.m., shops from 10:30 a.m. to 8:30 p.m. Call 981-PIER for information on Pier 39 events and restaurants. The Pier has validated parking for 100 cars, and you'll find taxis out front.

GOLDEN GATE PARK: It's hard to imagine that the natural gardens, meadows, and groves of the Golden Gate Park were a stretch of barren sand dunes that the city bought for a park more than 100 years ago. You may want to make your tour of the park on the same day that you take the 49-mile Scenic Drive that San Francisco has mapped out (the route is part of the Visitors Map available from the San Francisco Convention and Visitors Bureau), or just spend half a day relaxing here, picnicking and leisurely touring the three-mile long and half-mile wide park, for which you will probably opt for four-wheel mobility. You can get a free map of the park at headquarters near the entrance at Fell and Stanyan Sts. (tel. 558-3706).

On Kennedy Drive near Arguello Boulevard you can visit the **Conservatory of Flowers** through the side entrance, which is level, and see a continuous flower show in bloom. It's open daily from 8 a.m. to 4:20 p.m. (4:50 p.m. during Daylight Saving Time). At the **Strybing Arboretum,** on the South Drive at 9th Avenue, there is level access and hard-surfaced paths through the 70 acres that display more than 6000 species of flowers and plants. The Hall of Flowers at the entrance to the arboretum has a level entrance. It is open from 9 a.m. to 4:30 p.m. and from 10 a.m. to 5 p.m. on weekends. At the **Japanese Tea Garden** on the South Drive there is roadside parking, but the paths here are narrow and there are steps, steep slopes, and arching bridges—to be expected in a replica of a Japanese garden. If you are wheeling, you may be able to see only part of it. Visitors in wheelchairs will need assistance at the thatched-roof Japanese Tea House, where you will be served tea and wafers by waitresses in kimonos. In March or early April you may catch the Japanese cherry blossoms, rivalled only by those in Washington, D.C. (and Japan, of course). Close to the Tea Garden on John F. Kennedy Drive near 16th Avenue, is **Stow Lake,** ideal for picnicking, which is surrounded by a hard surface walk. **Spreckles Lake,** on John F. Kennedy Drive near 36th Avenue, is also bordered by a hard-surfaced walk.

Among the other buildings in Golden Gate Park that you can visit on your tour, or on a special trip in order to savor them more fully, are the California Academy of Sciences, the de Young Memorial Museum (described under museums in this section), and the Music Concourse (described under theaters).

JAPAN CENTER: If you happen to be staying at the Miyako Hotel, you won't need to be told that you are in the Japan Center, opened as a showcase for Japan about 15 years ago. Around the hub, the Peace Pagoda, is a three-block area (bounded by Laguna, Fillmore, Geary, and Post Streets), of arcades, squares, shops and showrooms, teahouses, and restaurants, the majority of them wheelchair-accessible. You'll find it relatively easy to tour the Japan Center, much is flat and well ramped, with wheelchair-accessible rest rooms. There are Japanese festivals in April (Cherry Blossoms), July (Buddhist Bon Festival), and September (Aki Matsuri—autumn harvest). On most Saturdays during the summer there is traditional Japanese entertainment in the streets of the area.

CRUISE BOATS AND FERRIES: One way to see the hills of San Francisco without climbing them, as well as to sail under the Golden Gate Bridge and close to Alcatraz among other sights, is to take a bay cruise from Fisherman's

Wharf, either the **Red-and-White Fleet** (tel. 546-2810), Piers 41 and 43½, or the **Blue-and-Gold Fleet** (tel. 781-7877) from Pier 39. Both cruises take about 1¼ hours and cost $8 for adults and $4 for children 5 to 11 (under 5 free). They have frequent departures between 10 a.m. and late afternoon. You'll be able to enter the terminal and board the boats by ramps. Once on board, you can see the sights from the entry level deck, which has large panoramic windows (there is a staircase to the open deck). Refreshments available, but rest rooms not accessible.

The **Golden Gate ferries,** that were put out of business by the bridge in 1938, went back into service again in 1970 to take care of overflow commuting traffic between Marin County and San Francisco. The tourist can take advantage of them, too, to see the bay for less than it costs on the guided cruises. They leave from the Ferry Building at the foot of Market Street. You can board via ramps for destinations at Sausalito, Tiburon, and Larkspur, all picturesque communities in Marin County. Sausalito is built on steep slopes, but in Tiburon you can get around Main Street and browse in the shops or stop at a cafe on the waterfront for refreshments. This is a good idea for weekends or holidays when you won't get caught up with commuters. (The ferry to Larkspur runs on weekends only in the summer.) Weekend and holiday schedules are less frequent than on weekdays. Call 332-6600 for information. Fare on weekends is $2.50, on weekdays $2, half fare for children accompanied by an adult. Refreshments available, but rest rooms not accessible.

SCENIC DRIVE: The 49 Mile Scenic Drive has been mapped out to cover many of San Francisco's sights, and its route is shown on the city map available from the Visitors Bureau. (It is suggested that the congested downtown is to be avoided during the day on weekdays.) The drive will take you to downtown areas like the Civic Center, Japantown, Union Square, Chinatown, the Financial District, Telegraph Hill, and then skirt the waterfront toward the Golden Gate Bridge, through Lincoln Park and past the Palace of the Legion of Honor, near Seal Rocks and along the Pacific Ocean past the zoo and Harding Park, and back through Golden Gate Park, taking in Twin Peaks (the city lies spread out before you from here) and Mission Dolores on the way back to downtown.

Even if you don't use a car for the rest of your visit, you may want to consider renting one for the day for the Scenic Drive. It's a good idea to take food along with you.

BY BART: It's always a special treat to ride on public transportation if you are not accustomed to the opportunity, and especially when it has wall-to-wall carpeting (easy to wheel on), and is air conditioned.

Downtown, BART runs only along Market Street, stopping at the Civic Center, Powell Street, Montgomery Street, Embarcadero Center, and the Ferry Building, but you can take a 71-mile excursion ride along the system's three-county routes. It only costs $1 as long as you come back to the place you started at and don't exit anywhere. The rapid train that's capable of 80 mph, can take you from downtown to the countryside in just a few minutes.

BART runs Monday to Saturday from 6 a.m. to midnight, and on Sunday from 9 a.m. to midnight. The best time to tour is on the weekends and from 10 a.m. to 3 p.m. on weekdays.

ART MUSEUMS: San Francisco is the city of parttime artists who exhibit their work wherever the opportunity presents itself. You will be able to see most of it without being concerned about accessibility since the small galleries are usually in one street-level room, and every September, part of the Civic Center Plaza becomes a vast outdoor exhibition.

However, for the more formal art institutions, here are details of their access features:

The **San Francisco Museum of Modern Art** is in the Veterans Building near the Civic Center, Van Ness Ave. at McAllister St. (tel. 863-8800), and is a noted center of contemporary painting with emphasis on Abstract Expressionism. There is level access from Van Ness Avenue into the building lobby where the elevator goes to the fourth-floor exhibit area. Admission is from $1 to $3 depending on the exhibit, free on Thursday evening from 6 to 10 p.m. Museum hours are 10 a.m. to 6 p.m. on Tuesday, Wednesday, and Friday, and until 10 p.m. on Thursday; 10 a.m. to 5 p.m. on Saturday and Sunday. It is closed on Mondays and holidays.

The **M.H. de Young Memorial Museum,** in Golden Gate Park (tel. 221-4811), has an impressive collection of old masters and is the most diversified of the city's museums. The main entrance is ramped. There is adjacent parking. The museum is open from 10 a.m. to 5 p.m. Wednesday through Sunday (closed Monday and Tuesday). Admission is $1.50 for adults, 50¢ for children and senior citizens. Free on the first Wednesday of the month.

In the same building, and for the same admission fee, you can visit the **Asian Art Museum** (tel. 558-2993), which contains the Avery Brundage collection of Oriental art treasures, one of the largest of its kind in the world.

San Francisco's most beautiful museum is the **California Palace of the Legion of Honor** (tel. 558-2881) in Lincoln Park (which you'll pass if you take the Scenic Drive). It has three steps at the entrance, but if you can negotiate those, you'll see some treasures of 18th- and 19th-century French art. The museum itself is a replica of the Legion of Honor Palace in Paris. It is open from 10 a.m. to 5 p.m. Wednesday through Sunday. The admission, fee $1.50 for adults and 50¢ for children under 17 and senior citizens, entitles you also to admission to the de Young Museum and the Asian Art Museum.

7. Entertainment

In proportion to the city's size, San Francisco's theater, opera, symphony, and ballet scene is one of the liveliest in the U.S. outside New York City.

For programs and performance times, consult the weekly *Key,* found in hotel lobbies and newsstands, the daily papers, or the special entertainment section of the *San Francisco Examiner and Chronicle. California* Magazine (weekly) lists bay area theaters and movie houses with a wheelchair-access symbol. Call to confirm facilities before you go.

TICKETS: **San Francisco Ticket Box Office Service (STBS)** provides tickets at half price for day-of-performance sale to all kinds of performances in the major theaters and concerts hall. STBS also handles full-priced tickets for advance bookings, although not for everything. You will have to go in person, and all sales are in cash. It is located at Stockton Street between Geary and Post Streets on the east side of Union Square opposite Maiden Lane. Hours are Tuesday to Saturday noon to 7 p.m., Sunday, noon to 4 p.m. (subject to change).

THEATERS: The highly regarded American Conservatory Theater (ACT) company has a repertory season from late September through early June at the historic **Geary Theater,** 415 Geary St. (tel. 673-6440). There is a parking lot on the same block. The main entrance to the theater has two steps, but there is level access at the side entrance, and to the orchestra section. Tickets range from $10 to $20.

Broadway musicals are the major fare at the **Curran Theater,** 445 Geary St. (tel. 673-4400). You'll find a parking lot on the same block. The theater has two steps at the entrance and level access to the orchestra section. Tickets range from $12 to $24. Headsets for hearing-impaired patrons can be rented in the lobby, and so can headsets with induction loops for hearing-aid wearers.

There is good access at the **Golden Gate Theater,** 25 Taylor St. at Market St. and Golden Gate Ave. (tel. 775-8800), where Broadway musicals also reign. It has recently been reopened and restored to its 1920s marble-and-gilt splendor. Headsets for hearing-impaired or hearing-aid wearers are also available here for a nominal fee.

OPERA AND BALLET: Opera-lovers will find it frustrating to get tickets to the San Francisco Opera Company, whose season starts in September at the **War Memorial Opera House,** Van Ness Ave. at Civic Center (tel. 431-1210). However, if you want to try, know that the opera house only has one step, and the interior is level. Get your name on the mailing list, at least, by writing to Opera Box Office, Opera House, San Francisco, CA 94102.

If you're in San Francisco in the spring, however, you might want to give the Dollar Opera a try. At the end of the Western Opera Theater's road tour, it performs at the accessible **Herbert Theater,** McAllister St. and Van Ness Ave., where admission is only $2. Tickets go on sale about three weeks before each performance. Call 431-5400 for information.

In April, a small version of the company, the Spring Opera, has a season at the **Palace of Fine Art Theater,** Bay and Lyon Sts. (tel. 921-9968). (This building is also the home of the science activity museum, the Exploratorium.) There are wheelchair locations in the accessible theater.

The San Francisco Ballet, highly praised and the oldest permanent ballet company in the U.S., gives its season from January to May at the Opera House (see above for accessibility). Call 621-3838 for ticket information.

MUSIC: The San Francisco Symphony Orchestra plays from October to May in the new Louise M. Davies Symphony Hall at the **War Memorial Performing Arts Center,** CA 94102 (tel. 431-5400). The building is located on the corner of Van Ness Avenue and Grove Street, with the hall's entrance on Grove Street. The hall is very accessible with wide-door elevators and rest rooms with wide stalls and grab bars.

On Sunday afternoons in the summer, from early June to mid-August, you can enjoy free performances of the Symphony Orchestra given under the trees at the **Sigmund Stern Memorial Grove,** 19th Ave. at Sloat Blvd. (tel. 681-6844). There is a parking lot on the amphitheater level, reached via Sloat Boulevard and Vale Avenue, but get there early! The ascent from the street level to the amphitheater is rather steep, and the paths are not all smooth. It's a good idea to call ahead and explain your disability, so some special arrangements can be made for you.

Also in summer during July and August there are Municipal Pop Concerts, led by famous conductors, at the **Civic Auditorium,** Civic Center at Grove St. (tel. 558-5065), which has level access. It's also the auditorium for many other events, such as sports and circuses.

8. After Dark

There's a lot of nightlife in San Francisco, its liveliness not much hampered by 2 a.m. closings and stringent liquor regulations. You won't find many plush nightclubs or extravagant floor shows, but there's more bare skin on display on one block of North Beach than in lots of other cities rolled together (if that's your style). Then there are jazz joints, comedy houses, piano bars, and top-of-the-everything cocktail lounges. Here are some places that are reasonably accessible:

PANORAMIC COCKTAILS: There's a spectacular view of the city at sunset or later from many of the city's famous skyline bars.

If you go to the plush **Crown Room** (tel. 772-5000) of the Fairmont Hotel on Nob Hill at 950 Mason St. (valet parking at the Mason St. entrance), you'll ride up to the 29th floor by an exterior glass elevator, an experience in itself! Drinks average $4.25. Open until 1 a.m.

There are more breathtaking views from windows on all sides (and there's room for wheelchairs to get through to them) of that Nob Hill legend, **Top of the Mark,** at the Mark Hopkins Hotel (tel. 392-3434). Drinks here average $3.75 with a cover charge of $2 on week nights and $3 on weekends.

You can have a revolving view from the **Equinox** at the top of the Hyatt Embarcadero in Embarcadero Center (tel. 788-1234). There are accessible rest rooms here on the hotel lobby floor.

Henry's is at the top of the Hilton Tower, 333 O'Farrell St. at Mason (tel. 771-1400), which has level access from the street to the elevators. Here you can listen to dance music in romantic surroundings under a glass roof as you sip your drinks. There's a $3 cover charge.

You can get the highest view of all from the 52nd floor in the unlikely setting of the Bank of America headquarters in the financial district on the edge of Chinatown, at the **Carnelian Room,** 555 California St. (tel. 433-7500). It's between Montgomery and Kearny (level entrance to the building at Kearny). There's a prix-fixe dinner here for $19.50. Reservations essential.

Around Union Square, the **Holiday Inn** at 480 Sutter St. (tel. 398-8900), has a 30th-floor eyrie called the **S. Holmes Esquire,** where you can have drinks to musical accompaniment in a veritable Sherlock Holmes museum. Three steps at the entrance.

Music Etc.

Even if dancing is not included in your activities, perhaps you'd like to listen to the orchestra and enjoy a floor show that offers features by name stars. You can do that in the most elegant, and expensive, club in San Francisco, the **Venetian Room** (tel. 772-5163) in the Fairmont Hotel on Nob Hill. Cover charge varies from about $10 to $17 depending on the star of the show. Weeknights can be less expensive.

At the Fairmont, too, you can listen to dance music in a Polynesian setting at the **Tonga Room** where the former swimming pool is now a lagoon (the band plays on an island in the center!). Dinner menu emphasizes Polynesian and Chinese specialties and is served from 5 p.m., with music after 8 p.m. on weeknights and 9 p.m. on weekends. There's a $2 cover charge.

Jazz

San Francisco is a favorite place for jazz musicians and it thrives there. Accessible places include:

Earthquake McGoon's, on Pier 39 at Fisherman's Wharf (tel. 986-1433), is a large place, heavy on New Orleans-style jazz. It's open from 11:30 a.m., and the entertainment starts at 4 p.m. There's a cover charge of $4 after 8 p.m.

Big-name jazz entertainment is featured at **Keystone Korner,** 750 Vallejo St. between Powell and Stockton Sts. (tel. 781-0697), in an ornate setting with concert-style seating. There are two sets nightly, at 9 and 11 p.m., with a cover charge of $7.50 to $8.50 and a one-drink minimum. You can eat here, too, and the food is Middle Eastern-style. Tickets can be bought in advance.

There are often jazz greats as well as lesser lights at the **Great American Music Hall,** 859 O'Farrell St. between Polk and Larkin Sts. (tel. 885-0750). Cover is $5 to $12 depending on who is playing, and light fare and drinks are available. Open from 7:30 p.m. to 2 a.m. five to seven nights a week—so check before you go.

9. Shopping

There's probably *too* much shopping available in San Francisco for the good of your budget! It's a town primarily of small specialty shops with fashionable and unusual merchandise of all kinds, and it is also strong on bazaarlike establishments that sell anything under the sun and provide a lot of browsing. Citing accessibility of specific places is not feasible because of their numbers; you will be able to see as you travel through on your sightseeing which ones you will be able to get into and get around.

The major shopping areas coincide with many of the sightseeing areas and have already been covered in that section of this chapter, but here's a reminder of where you'll find them. Many are in the flatter areas of the city, and in the large complexes that have good accessibility.

There's downtown, centered on **Union Square** and bounded by Bush, Taylor, Market and Montgomery Streets, which has all the city's department stores and most of the specialty shops.

In **Chinatown,** along Grant Avenue (after it crosses Bush Street), store hours are flexible!

On **Union Street,** between Van Ness and Steiner Streets, you'll find a stretch of antique shops, handicrafts, and high fashion boutiques. Great for window-shopping as well as the real thing.

For the shopper who knows the famous Galleria in Milan, Italy, there's a reminder of it in the **New Galleria at Crocker Center** in the financial district, on Kearny St. between Post and Sutter Sts., a glass-enclosed tri-level complex that houses more than 60 specialty shops and restaurants. Accessible entrance is on Kearny Street, elevators give access to different levels, and there is a wheelchair-accessible rest room in the restaurant complex.

Last, but certainly not least, there are a lot of shopping possibilities at **Fisherman's Wharf,** an area that includes Ghirardelli Square, the Cannery, and Pier 39. You'll find accessibility notes and hours detailed in the sightseeing section of this chapter.

10. Excursions

If you want a change from city sightseeing, there are things you can see—and do—in the nearby areas across the bay.

One place you can visit *without* a car is **Berkeley.** Even if you only go there to try out BART at least once, you'll be able to get around Berkeley, site of the University of California campus, and famous as the spark of campus riots of the sixties. It is also one of the most barrier-free places anywhere, thanks to the pioneering efforts of the independent living movement of the seventies, which started here and produced the Center for Independent Living (CIL), the model for similar centers all over the country.

You can get to Sausalito and Tiburon by ferry (see sightseeing section of this chapter) and tour the waterfront sections of shops and restaurants of these charming bay-side "villages." If you want to see much of either town, however, you'll need a car to climb their picturesque hills. **Sausalito** is eight miles from San Francisco via the Golden Gate Bridge and Route 101. Its steep hills are not the kind of terrain you'd probably care to roam around on the sidewalks, but its marvelous views and slightly bohemian atmosphere make it a great place to visit by car. **Tiburon** is 18 miles from San Francisco by the same route. (Sabella's here is a seafood restaurant you may want to try. It's at 8 Main St. tel. 435-2636.)

Also in Marin County, 17 miles north of San Francisco, is a haven of towering grandeur at the **Muir Woods National Monument** in Mill Valley (tel. 415/388-2595), where you can see the world-famous California redwoods. You can reach Muir Woods on Route 101 via a well-marked turn-off past Sausalito. Admission is free. There is no other forest like it anywhere in the world. It's a National Park and there is easy access to the information station, all rest rooms, the snack bar and gift shop, and a one-mile paved trail. For sight-impaired visitors there's also a roped trail marked with large print text and braille signs. Muir Woods is open from 8 a.m. until sunset, but least crowded before 10 a.m. and late in the afternoon. You can drive to the top of **Mount Tamalpais** here and get sweeping views for 100 miles in all directions.

The peninsula north of San Francisco is noted for its long beaches backed by tall cliffs, and offshore bird and sea lion colonies, and if you're in the mood to drive further into Marin County on Route 1, there are spectacular ocean views and rolling headlands at another National Park, **Point Reyes National Seashore** (tel. 415/663-1701). Much of it can be seen from a car. There are parking areas at Point Reyes Station and at Drakes Beach Visitors Center, which has accessible rest rooms and a picnic area that is easy to get to.

Chapter 11

HAWAII

Aloha!

**1. Getting There
2. Getting Around
3. Orientation 4. Where
to Stay in Waikiki 5. Dining
in Waikiki/Honolulu 6. Sightseeing
in Honolulu and Around Oahu 7. Nightlife
8. Shopping 9. The Island of Hawaii 10. Maui**

TROPICAL PARADISE it is for sure, but for disabled visitors there's the added bonus of accessibility—at least in Honolulu and Waikiki—and the friendly and smiling assistance comes with the territory.

The undeniable lure of this archipelago in the Pacific Ocean doesn't need reinforcement here. Everybody has an image of Hawaii from decades of movies, television programs, travel posters, and their own fantasies. A visit will confirm it all, and then some. Don't expect solitude among the waving palms: Waikiki is the most popular vacation spot in the United States. But away from Waikiki and Honolulu you can see some of the sights that must have greeted Captain Cook in 1777 when he discovered and claimed the islands for England.

So, there should be something for everyone—the ramped curbs and flat sandstrip of Waikiki Beach, easy to get around and with plenty of amenable hotels and restaurants, plus the uniquely convenient Handi-cabs of the Pacific vans for wheelchairs, with a service that is available to take you or to pick you up to suit your schedule.

All this on the island of Oahu.

There are a few more challenges—and compensating rewards—on the neighbor islands, which have their own treasures to offer: the "Big Island" or Island of Hawaii, is covered in some detail here, and Maui is touched upon. Kauai, unfortunately, beautiful as it is, does not offer enough special facilities for visitors with mobility impairments to be part of this guide.

Most facilities in the Hawaiian islands do not have provisions for the visually handicapped visitor, such as braille menus and audible signals. A quarantine of 120 days is required for guide dogs as well as other dogs.

For general information, maps, and a hotel directory, write to the **Hawaii Visitors Bureau,** Suite 801, 2270 Kalakaua Ave., Honolulu, HI 96815 (tel.

808/923-1811), or request it from the bureau's offices in New York, Chicago, San Francisco, and Los Angeles.

Accessibility guides for Oahu, Hawaii, Maui, and Kauai are published by the **Commission on the Handicapped**, Old Federal Building, 335 Merchant St., Honolulu, HI 96813 (tel. 808/548-7606), for $1 each. A 1983 update for Oahu is available from the same address, although no restaurants are listed, and details of hotels and sightseeing are generally summarized without the fuller details included in the $1 booklet.

1. Getting There

Hawaii was once a faraway dream for most people—four days by ship from San Francisco, or a very expensive flight on the one or two airlines that went there—until the advent of statehood 25 years ago and, even more recently, jet air travel. Now, the 2500 miles of ocean between the mainland and Honolulu are covered in five hours' flying time from San Francisco or Los Angeles. The airlines that provide service to Honolulu are American, Continental, Northwest Orient, Pan American, United, and Western. Continental, United, Northwest Orient, and Western also go to Hilo on the island of Hawaii, and United now has direct flights to Maui from San Francisco and Los Angeles.

Interisland routes are served by Aloha Airlines, Hawaii Air, and Mid-Pacific, and the jet service between Honolulu, Hawaii, Maui, and Kauai provides short flight times from Honolulu to Hilo on Hawaii (40 minutes), Kona on Hawaii (35 minutes), Maui (30 minutes), and Kauai (25 minutes).

Air fares from the mainland are by no means inexpensive, but you or your travel agent can shop around for air/hotel packages that can save a great deal of money over arrangements for travel and hotel that are made separately. Also look into what island-hopping you can do at a small surcharge over the regular fare. Some packages also include a rental car.

HONOLULU INTERNATIONAL AIRPORT: This main airline terminal on the island of Oahu is where you'll arrive if you are heading for Waikiki. Access to the terminal from the plane is via the level jetway covered bridge, and all levels of the terminal are serviced by elevator. Although there are low phones in the main waiting lobby on the second level and in the center of the baggage claim area on the ground level, they have built-in seats, so use from a wheelchair may still present problems.

All but one of the 22 sets of rest rooms have 32-inch entry and 30-inch stall doors, with grab bars, and they are equally spaced throughout the terminal and next to each gate. There are curb cuts at 20-yard intervals at the loading zones on both arrival and departure levels and, should you have use for them, there are four "special" parking spaces on the fourth floor of the multideck parking lot, with elevator access from there to the interior of the main terminal.

You can take a taxi from Honolulu airport to Waikiki for about $12, or you can make arrangements in advance with Handi-Cabs to pick you up in a wheelchair-accessible van (cost is $10 for pick-up, plus $1.50 per mile). Their address is **Handi-Cabs of the Pacific**, P.O. Box 22428, Honolulu, HI 96822 (tel. 808/524-3866).

The Interisland section of the terminal, which you will use if you visit the other islands, is reached by a level pathway from the main terminal, and there are ramped curbs near the check-in counters as well as near the baggage claim areas 1 and 2. There is only one level in the Interisland terminal. Rest rooms in the Aloha Airlines check-in area, and in each waiting area for interisland

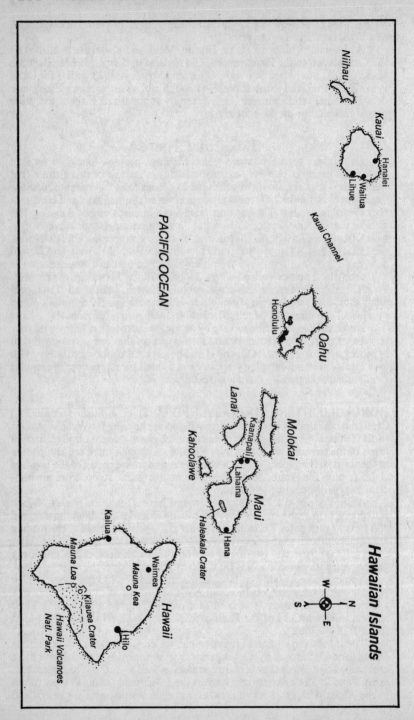

Hawaiian Islands

gates, have 32-inch entrances and a 30-inch stall door, with grab bars. (The one next to the restaurant is the only one that is *in*accessible.)

HAWAII-HILO AIRPORT: This is the main terminal on the island of Hawaii and serves both direct flights from the mainland and interisland flights. You deplane by level jetway to the second level of the terminal, and there is an elevator down to the baggage claim area available for passengers in wheelchairs. The three sets of rest rooms with 32-inch entry and 32-inch stalls and grab bars, are located at the Interisland check-in, Mainland check-in, and the boarding lounge.

HAWAII-KONA/KEAHOLE AIRPORT: This airport for Kailua, on the Kona coast of the island of Hawaii, is used by interstate services and has easy access all on one level. Airport and airline personnel will assist you in deplaning via steps. The rest room is accessible.

MAUI (KAHULUI) AIRPORT: There are no jetways here, but airlines will make arrangements for you to exit the plane (if you cannot walk) either by lift, or by being carried down the stairs. There are accessible rest rooms.

2. Getting Around

Once you're in a hotel in Waikiki, if that's your destination, you won't need much help running the length of Kalakaua Avenue since it is flat, with all its curbs ramped. This is Waikiki's main street, jampacked with stores, restaurants, and hotels, which runs parallel to the beach for about two miles and then goes, unobstructed, for a long stretch alongside the beach in the direction of Diamond Head.

When you want to go further to see the sights, here's a rundown on what's available in the way of mechanized transport:

TAXIS: Taxis are available all over the city, but they don't cruise and it's necessary to summon one by phone (hotels and restaurants can do it for you). If you're not moving far away from one spot and don't plan to do much touring, they would prove to be less expensive than renting a car.

SPECIAL TRANSPORTATION: Handi-Cabs of the Pacific provide wheelchair-accessible taxi service door-to-door 24 hours a day, 7 days a week. Rates are $4.75 per pick-up and $1.50 per mile. There is no charge for ambulatory companions. Advance notice is necessary if you need service outside dispatching hours, which are 8:30 a.m. to 5:30 p.m. Handi-Cabs also provides many sightseeing tours and packages tied in with harbor cruises (see sightseeing section of this chapter). For complete details of what they have to offer, write for the brochure to Handi-Cabs, P.O. Box 22428, Honolulu, HI 96822 (tel. 808/524-3866).

The city and county of Honolulu provide curb-to-curb service through Handi-Van, equipped with wheelchair lifts and ramps. Priority is given, of course, to essential trips, but it might be worth applying for a pass *well* in advance of your arrival. Write to the City Department of Transportation Services, Attn. Handi-Van Pass, 650 S. King St., Honolulu, HI 96813 (tel. 808/524-4626). Medical verification is required.

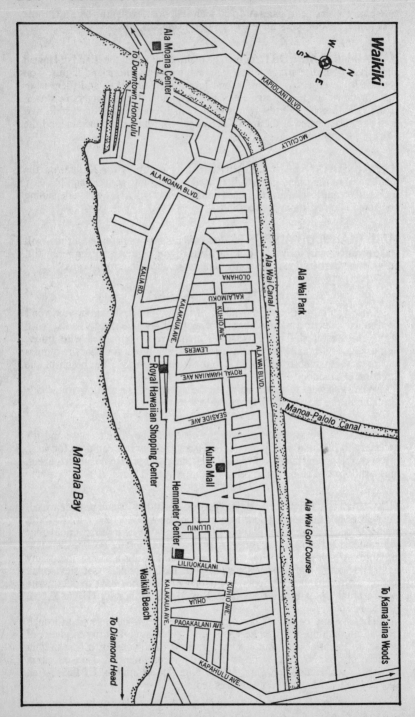

RENTAL CARS: You can order a rental car from **Avis** if you need hand controls (either right- or left-hand) with three weeks notice at least (tel. 800/ 331-2112). If you want to go to the trouble of bringing your own hand controls along, you can perhaps make arrangements in advance with your local office of Hertz.

One unique service you'll find in Honolulu is provided by **Lowell Grant** (tel. 808/533-2794), who rents hand controls and will meet you at the car rental office and install them. He also has a complete wheelchair repair shop and can also provide rentals on manual and motorized chairs, as well as on batteries. If you do *not* need hand controls, car rental is quite competitive in Hawaii, and you should check out the different companies in addition to the regular national companies on the spot, since prices change so frequently.

PUBLIC TRANSPORTATION: Buses run all over town, and service is frequent between Waikiki and downtown Honolulu, but they are not accessible to wheelchairs. Fare is 50¢. Customer service telephone is 808/531-1611.

3. Orientation

Hawaii is not just Honolulu and Waikiki, though most visitors do not get to see much more than that.

They are both on **Oahu,** by far the busiest of the Hawaiian Islands, but only one of the four largest of the eight islands that comprise the 50th state. It's also the easiest of the islands for a disabled visitor to negotiate, but it would be a shame not to think about visiting one of the other islands, since they do offer a degree of accessibility as well as a panorama of natural wonder unmatched anywhere else. Maui, the Valley Island, or Hawaii, the Big Island, with its Volcanoes National Park, are favorite vacation spots for the people who live in Honolulu.

Let's start with Honolulu/Waikiki.

As a beach, **Waikiki** is only one of dozens of equally breathtaking stretches of sand and ocean that surround most of these islands, which are peaks of a submarine mountain range thrown up by volcanic action thousands of years ago. It happens to be close to the capital, Honolulu, and of course convenient to the airport there, and so its development since statehood in 1959 has been phenomenal.

Once dominated only by the crater-topped Diamond Head at its far end, Waikiki has sprouted dozens of high-rise hotels that have given Diamond Head a run for its money, in a small area bordered on one side by the Pacific Ocean and on the other by the Koolau Mountains. It's about 2½ miles long, from the Ala Wai Yacht Harbor on the southwest, to Diamond Head on the southeast, and about three-quarters of a mile at its widest point from the Pacific Ocean to the inland Ala Wai Canal.

Note: When you're in Waikiki you won't hear much talk of north, south, east, or west. Rather, you'll hear reference to directions that relate to the mountains and the sea. For instance, anything toward the ocean is *makai,* toward the mountains is *mauka.* Toward Honolulu is *ewa* (eh-vah).

Waikiki itself has three major avenues running parallel to each other: nearest the beach is its main street, **Kalakaua Avenue,** lively and bustling with the big hotels, restaurants, and shops. A few blocks *mauka* is **Kuhio Avenue,** a bit quieter and less crowded. And a few more blocks *mauka* is the **Ala Wai Boulevard,** next to a quiet waterway created in 1920 when the swampland of Waikiki was drained.

So Waikiki's sights are compact, its terrain is flat, and its curbs are ramped. That's enough to make it paradise for anyone in a wheelchair.

As for the rest of the island of Oahu, it is circumnavigable by good roads that follow the coast line for the main part, and the valley between two lines of mountains, and there are sights to see along the way as you travel by car.

CLIMATE: Any time you go is the right time for weather. Hawaii's weather is nearly always wonderful, with gentle trade winds keeping the temperatures constant at an average of 75 degrees, a little higher than that during the summer. You may need a sweater for some of the mountain areas at night, and a light raincoat in February and March, although in some winters it hardly rains at all. The summer "rain" is usually a short, light shower, although most tourist centers are leeward of the rain-bringing northeasterly winds.

AREA CODE: The telephone area code for all of Hawaii is 808.

USEFUL REFERENCES: For information on a variety of special questions that you might have about Hawaii, try one of the following organizations: **Commission on the Handicapped,** 335 Merchant St., Honolulu, HI 96813 (tel. 808/528-7606); **Easter Seal Society,** 710 Green St., Honolulu, HI 96813 (tel. 808/536-1015); **Hawaii Center for Independent Living** (personal care attendants on a fee-for-service basis), 677 Ala Moana Blvd., Suite 402, Honolulu HI 96813 (tel. 808/537-1941); **Grant Wheelchair and Repair Service,** 636 Queen St., Honolulu, HI 96813 (tel. 808/533-2794); **Handi-Cabs of the Pacific,** P.O. Box 22428, Honolulu, HI 96813 (tel. 808/524-3866).

4. Where to Stay in Waikiki

If it's your first visit to the islands, you'll probably want to head for Waikiki Beach on the island of Oahu to be close to that fantastic combination of ocean and beach, and to have all the big-city amenities of Honolulu close by.

Because they offer some of the best bargains as a combination of air fare and hotel, plus some sightseeing, it's a good idea to consider one of the many packages offered through travel agents or the airlines. Even so, you'll want to know which of the hotels in the packages would be suitable for your particular needs, and details are listed below. As always, it is all but impossible to locate low-budget hotels that make sense for the traveler with mobility problems, but some of the hotels listed here are used by the tour packagers, and special rates will apply.

High season in Hawaii is usually from mid-December to April 1, when rates are about $5 to $7 a day higher than during the rest of the year. Rates also vary considerably depending on the view from your room. Advance reservations are always suggested, of course, when special accommodations are required. Some of the very popular hotels can even get booked up a year in advance for the Christmas-New Year period. Rates quoted here are subject to change.

Literally dozens of hotels front the beach on Kalakaua Avenue, Waikiki's main street, facing the Pacific Ocean, and dozens more are only a block away. There are walkways to the beach, and you'll find beachboys eager to help with carrying wheelchairs, or even you, over the sand.

Note: If you will be one of a group, say, of four people (same rate for any number), you may want to consider renting one of the many condominium apartments available on all the islands, on a daily, weekly, or monthly basis. Check the hotel guide for the ones that consider themselves suitable for people in wheelchairs—marked with (W)—in the guide available from the **Hawaii Visitors Bureau,** Suite 801, Waikiki Business Plaza, 2270 Kalakaua Ave., Honolulu, HI 96815. Because (W) designation does not always mean totally barrier-free, always check exact details before making reservations. Check also if daily maid service is included in the price quoted, or is an extra charge.

UPPER BRACKET: Most of the high-rise hotels on the beach are the upper-bracket resort-type establishments that offer multiple dining rooms, nightclubs, and beach and pool facilities, all in a setting of tropical flowers and foliage and soft trade winds. All of them are within easy distance of each other, and all are near Waikiki's other attractions.

One of the great showplace hotels in the country is the **Hyatt Regency Waikiki** at Hemmeter Center, 2424 Kalakaua Ave., Honolulu, HI 96815 (tel. 808/922-9292). Despite its size, it manages to create an oasis of calm and tranquillity amid the bustle of a heavily trafficked area, with its Great Hall replete with waterfalls, fountains, greenery, sculptures, paintings, and antiques that have made it a very popular place for shopping, dining, and promenading. Each room has a lanai (terrace), and all range in price from $75 to $105, depending on the view and floor. The beach is directly across the street, and there is an outdoor pool, with level access, on the third floor.

Some of the entrances have steps, but there is a level one on Kalakaua Avenue, and the interior has level access to all shops and restaurants. The ten special guest rooms here have bathroom entry at least 29 inches wide and grab bars. Although nearly everything is level, you may sometimes have to take two elevators at opposite sides of the hotel to get where you want to go (one serves the first through fourth floors, the other the second to the top floor). Check with the hotel for the most convenient room, to avoid too much long-distance traveling between floors. Public rest rooms on the second floor have 32-inch stall entry and grab bars.

The Waikiki hotel with more rooms designed with disabled guests in mind than any of the others, is the **Hawaiian Regent Hotel,** 2552 Kalakaua Ave., Honolulu, HI 96815 (tel. 808/922-6611, toll free 800/367-5370), a peaceful retreat around a cool, verdant courtyard in the midst of the activity outside. Waikiki beach is just across the street.

The special rooms are in the Kuhio Tower (two per floor) and they have wide doors, grab bars, easy touch lights, low locks, low refrigerators, and space under the counters to accommodate wheelchairs. There is a level entrance from Kalakaua Avenue and a ramped entrance at Ohua Avenue. The lobby is level except for two steps to the lobby bar, and there are elevators to all parts of both towers and to all restaurants except the Point After Disco. All other restaurants have level access. There is a low telephone in the main lobby, and all the shops have level entrances and wide double doors. Public rest rooms on the first three floors of the Kuhio Tower are totally accessible. The Hawaiian Regent has a physician's office staffed by a nurse, with a doctor on call.

Views from most rooms, and particularly from the third floor swimming pool and the sitting area, take in a panorama of the sea, the mountains, and Diamond Head. The rates range from mountain view for $62, to ocean front for $98, with variations in between, both single and double.

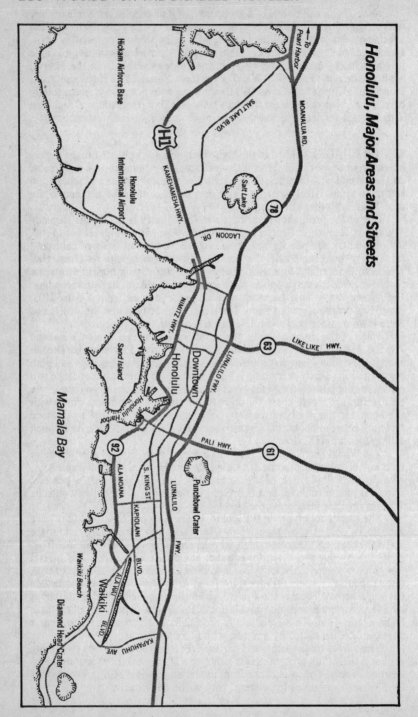

Honolulu, Major Areas and Streets

The high-rise **Sheraton-Waikiki**, 2255 Kalakaua Ave., Honolulu, HI 96815 (tel. 808/922-4422, toll free 800/325-3535), has one room with wide doors (no grab bars), but the larger rooms on each floor have 32-inch entry doors and 25½-inch bathroom doors (management is willing to remove the bathroom doors for easier access). There is a level entrance, and ramps lead to all parts of the hotel including the pool, shops, and restaurants. The Ocean Terrace, Safari, and Prow Lounges have barrier-free entrances off the lobby; the Hanohano Room, 30 stories up, is reached by an exterior glass elevator, and a regular elevator goes to the Kon Tiki Restaurant. All rooms have private lanais, and the unobstructed view from all rooms is spectacular. Rooms with a mountain view are $86 double, and those with a complete sweep of the ocean from Diamond Head to downtown Honolulu are $115—with variations in between, single or double.

MEDIUM-PRICE HOTELS: The Hilton-Hawaiian Village, 2005 Kalia Rd., Honolulu, HI 96815 (tel. 808/949-4321), is just that. Set on 20 acres, it has 2600 rooms, three swimming pools, a lagoon, a supper-club theater, acres of shops, and more than a dozen places to wine and dine, all next to one of the finest stretches of beach in Waikiki. It has 25 rooms with wide bathroom doors and grab bars, lowered telephones, and easy access to all the restaurants (except the Rainbow Tower Cafe) and shops, as well as the public rest rooms. Again, rates depend on the view from the room: they range from $57 and up with garden view; $64 for broader mountain views, and yacht harbor and ocean views begin at $70, double occupancy. An extra person in a room is $10, and single occupancy is $8 less. No charge for children staying in the same room. The hotel also offers a modified American plan which includes two meals ($30) or three meals ($37). Reservations can be made through any Hilton hotel or reservation office.

The **Waikiki Beachcomber**, 2300 Kalakaua Ave., Honolulu, HI 96815 (tel. 808/922-4646, toll free 800/227-4700), is in the heart of Waikiki, across the road from the beach. There are four rooms here that have 36-inch bathroom doors and grab bars at the bath. Rooms are spacious, and trapeze bars are available for both toilet and tub. There is elevator service to all areas, and the Veranda Coffee Shop and Don the Beachcomber dining room are easy to get into. Rates range from $57 to $85 single or double, $6 for an extra person in the same room, $5 less from April 1 to December 20.

The **Outrigger-Prince Kuhio**, 2500 Kuhio Ave., Honolulu, HI 96815 (tel. 808/922-0811, toll free 800/367-5170) has 11 rooms that have wider doors and grab bars in the bathrooms, and restaurants are accessible. There is a great sense of luxury and serenity here. Rates for double rooms start at $54 and go to $83 depending on the view.

There are two wheelchair-accessible rooms equipped with wider doors and bathroom grab bars at the **Holiday Inn Waikiki Beach**, 2570 Kalakaua Ave., Honolulu, HI 96815 (tel. 808/922-2511, toll free 800/238-8000). There are a ground level entrance off Lemon Road and elevator service to all the areas of the hotel. Rates here are $45 to $75 single, $50 to $80 double, depending on the view.

MODERATE-PRICE HOTELS: The combination of 20 wheelchair-accessible rooms and moderate prices is worth looking into. You'll find it two blocks from the beach at the **Waikiki Malia**, 2211 Kuhio Ave., Honolulu, HI 96815 (tel. 808/923-7621). These rooms are not only bigger than the regular rooms but they also have 31-inch bathroom doors, grab bars, low sinks and low refrigerators as well as color TV, air conditioning, and lanais. There is a low phone in the lobby. The elevator serves all the floors, and there is level access to the restaurants. Rates are $30 to $47 single and $37 to $52 double, with $5 additions from December 20 to April 1, and $7 extra for a third person (over 12) in the same room. For reservations write to Great American Management, Suite 190, 2255 Kalakaua Ave., Honolulu, HI 96815.

The **Waikiki Pacific Isle TraveLodge,** 1850 Ala Moana Blvd., Honolulu, HI 96815 (tel. 808/955-1567, toll free 800/255-3050), is across the street from Waikiki beach and has two rooms suitable for guests in wheelchairs, with 35-inch bathroom doors and grab bars. There is level entrance to the hotel and to the restaurants, and elevators serve all areas of the hotel. Rates start at $45 single and $56 double.

Two special rooms on each floor provide wheelchair accessibility, though rooms are small, at the **Waikiki Tower of the Reef,** not far from the beach at 200 Lewers St., Honolulu, HI 96815 (tel. 808/922-6424, toll free 800/367-5610). Bathroom doors in the guest rooms are 30 inches wide, and there are grab bars. There is a ramped entry to the lobby and level access to the restaurant. Rates refer to the location of the floor and range from standard at $28 to $32, to moderate $40, and deluxe $48, double occupancy.

5. Dining in Waikiki/Honolulu

Once in your hotel in Waikiki, you may prefer not to move too far from its amenities: most of the hotels listed in the previous section offer multiple choice in dining rooms, with a wide variety of menus from haute cuisine, Polynesian, Japanese, Chinese, and to American-style fare. You'll want to sample that special Hawaiian feast, a *luau,* at least once during your stay. (A luau is a traditional, barbecue-type feast consisting of roasted pig served with island fruits, poi—perhaps an acquired taste—and endless other dishes.

However, if you want to see what's going on in other hotels or in what are considered the more interesting restaurants, both for their food or for their views, or both, here are some that are accessible. Rest rooms are only mentioned where they are accessible. All the restaurants included have tables at least 28 inches from the floor with movable chairs, and with aisles at least 25 inches wide. Of course it is always a good idea to call the restaurant in advance if you use a wheelchair so that the most convenient location can be reserved for you.

The following list concentrates on the more expensive and moderately priced restaurants, for most of which you should make a reservation, or at least an advance call. The multiple fast-food outlets—you will find all the hometown familiars here—can easily be checked out as you pass by.

Although dress codes are not rigid, the better restaurants will look askance at shorts and bare feet!

THE BEST IN THE UPPER BRACKET: With a reputation as one of the most fabulous restaurants in town, and with many awards to back it up, the **Third Floor** in the Hawaiian Regent Hotel, 2552 Kalakaua Ave. (tel. 922-6611), offers the finest continental cuisine amid the most elegant decor, accoutrements, and strolling musicians. The entrances to the hotel and to the restaurant are barrier-free. Dinner is served daily from 6:30 to 11 p.m., and à la carte entrees range in price from $14 to $21. Reservations are necessary.

Bagwells 2424 is a sumptuously elegant restaurant in the Hyatt Regency Hotel, 2424 Kalakaua Ave. (tel. 922-9292), that serves French and American gourmet specialties amid a decor of original art and sculpture. Entrees here average $16 to $22, and dinner is served nightly from 6:30 to 10:30 p.m. Although sandals and T-shirts are not acceptable dress, men are welcome to wear aloha shirts if they would rather do without a jacket and tie.

In rather understated island elegance, the **Protea Dining Room** in the Outrigger-Prince Kuhio Hotel, 2500 Kuhio Ave. (tel. 922-0811), is gourmet all the way, with entree prices ranging from $11.50 to $18 at dinner, served from 6 to 10 p.m. daily. It might be the place to have a Sunday Champagne brunch for $13.50, served from 10 a.m. to 2 p.m. Reservations are necessary.

For the most lavish buffet in town, there is the Royal Hala Buffet served on the **Hala Terrace** on Sunday night at the Kahala Hilton Hotel, 5000 Kahala Ave. (tel. 734-2211). Both hotel and restaurant have level entry, and the public rest rooms in the hotel are wheelchair-accessible. This hotel is about 15 minutes drive outside Waikiki in a beautiful residential area.

One of Waikiki's famous oldtimers that attracts an enormous following for its beautiful garden setting and its good food, is **The Willows,** 901 Hausten St. (tel. 946-4808). Once a private estate, it is situated on a pond surrounded by trees and flowers in a natural, unspoiled atmosphere. The menu is full of island treats, and dinner entrees range from $12 to $23. However, prices are lower at lunch, which is served Monday through Saturday from 11:30 a.m. to 1:30 p.m. There is also a garden buffet brunch on Sunday from 10:30 a.m. to 2 p.m. Entrance is accessible, and the restaurant is very open and spacious, with large areas in the open air.

Opposite Fort de Russy, the **Canlis Charcoal Broiler Restaurant,** 2100 Kalakaua Ave. (tel. 923-2324), is intimate and romantic and specializes in steak and seafood served in handsome, modern decor. Entree prices range from $12 to $20. Open for dinner Monday to Saturday from 6 to 11 p.m. Reservations are necessary.

MEDIUM-PRICE RANGE ($7 to $15 A MEAL): To begin with suggestions for hotel restaurants, the **Colony Steak House** in the Hyatt Regency, 2424 Kalakaua Ave. (tel. 922-9292), re-creates the atmosphere of British colonial days in India with its rattan furniture and revolving ceiling fans. You can select your own piece of meat for your meal, reasonably priced by the ounce, and combine it with an extensive selection from the salad bar while the meat is being cooked. Entrances to the hotel and the restaurant are barrier-free. Another place to note at the Hyatt Regency is the **Terrace Grille,** which has a special breakfast buffet for $8.50, a most lavish spread, served in a beautiful setting in the open air overlooking Waikiki beach, Diamond Head, and the Pacific Ocean. The public rest room on the hotel's second floor is wheelchair-accessible with 32-inch stall doors and grab bars.

Also in the Hyatt Regency is one of the kickiest places in town, **Spats,** part restaurant, part disco. Italian specialties include pastas at $7.50 served nightly from 6:30 to 10 p.m.

In the Waikiki Tower of the Reef Hotel, 200 Lewers St. (tel. 923-8836), there's indoor/outdoor dining all day long at the **Waikiki Broiler,** starting with breakfast at 6 a.m. until dinner from 5:50 to 10 p.m., seven days a week. Entrance to the hotel is ramped and there is level entry to the restaurant. The public rest rooms in the lobby have 30-inch stall doors and grab bars.

The easiest entry to the **Trattoria** at 2168 Kalia Rd. (tel. 923-8415), on the grounds of the Edgewater Hotel, is through the companion Waikiki Towers of the Reef Hotel lobby. Here you can enjoy some of the finest Italian cuisine in the islands, with full dinners starting at $10.50; à la carte dishes are also available. Dinner is served seven days a week from 5:30 to 11:30 p.m.

Rudy's is a bright bistro with a level entrance at 2280 Kuhio Ave. at the corner of Nohonani St. (tel. 923-5949), that serves family-style Italian dinners priced from $7.75 to $12.95, from 5:30 to 10 p.m. daily.

There's a view of the ocean from the **Ocean Terrace** at poolside in the Sheraton Waikiki Hotel, 2255 Kalakaua Ave. (tel. 922-4422), where the dinner buffet is priced at $11.50 (lunch buffet is $8.75 and breakfast $7.50).

One of the prettiest medium-priced restaurants in town is **Trellises** in the new Prince Kuhio Hotel at 2500 Kuhio Ave. (tel. 922-0811), decorated with greenery overlooking a waterfall. There are special-themed buffets here four nights a week (in addition to regular meals) for $10.95. Dinner entrees range from $6.50 to $10.50.

The **Pottery Steakhouse**, 3574 Waialae Ave. (tel. 735-5594), is literally both. Dinners are served on distinctive ceramic ware that is also for sale. Open for dinner only, seven days a week. The entrance is level on Waialae Avenue.

There's a nautical decor and an appropriate view as well at one of the oldest seafood restaurants, **Fisherman's Wharf**, 1009 Ala Moana Blvd. at Fisherman's Wharf (tel. 538-3838), where there's a lot to choose from, priced between $5.95 and $11.95 (though steak and lobster are higher) in the Seafood Grotto part of the restaurant.

Hearty eaters can have their fill at the **Flamingo Chuckwagon,** 1015 Kapiolani Blvd. (tel. 538-1161), on the Honolulu side of the Ala Wai Canal—as much as you can eat from a bountiful chuckwagon for $8.50. The entrance is level.

If you find yourself at the Waikiki Shopping Plaza, 2279 Kalakaua Ave. at lunchtime or dinnertime, try **Lau Yee Chai** (tel. 923-1112), a branch of Honolulu's famous Chinese restaurant, here embellished with fine furniture and Chinese antiques to make it one of the most beautiful Chinese restaurants anywhere. Most dishes are between $3.50 and $6 at lunch served family-style. Dim sum is also available. There is a level entrance to the restaurant. The Waikiki Shopping Center has wheelchair-accessible rest rooms on each floor, with 30-inch stall doors and grab bars.

Japanese dishes are also represented on the fourth floor of the Waikiki Shopping Plaza at the corner of Seaside and Kalakaua Avenues. **Tanaka of Tokyo** (tel. 922-4702) serves Western-style portions, so the $8 to $18 price tag for full dinner is not unreasonable. If you've never been to Tokyo, this will give you a taste of it. The entrance is ramped.

When you are sightseeing in downtown Honolulu, there's a restaurant called **Oceania**, on a Hong Kong-built ship, moored (firmly!) at Pier 6 in the harbor (tel. 523-7011). Dim sum is served from 10:30 a.m. on, and there's also a buffet lunch for $4.25. Dinner is served from 5 to 10 p.m. and main course prices start at $5. There's plenty of parking at the gangplank, and there is a ramped entrance to the restaurant.

One of Waikiki's best French restaurants, **Chez Michel**, 444 Hobron Lane (tel. 955-7866), is in the Ala Moana area, in a gardenlike setting. There is ramp and elevator access. Lunch is served Monday through Friday from 11:30 a.m. to 2:15 p.m., when à la carte dishes range from $7 to $9. Entrees at dinner are from $11 to $18. Reservations suggested. There is valet parking.

6. Sightseeing in Honolulu and Around Oahu

When you are ready to tear yourself away from ocean-watching and sun-basking, there's much to be seen on the island of Oahu that will open your eyes to the real Hawaii, including 130 other delightful beaches and the exciting city of Honolulu.

Sightseeing tours are available if you can board the usual tour bus (**Gray Line,** tel. 808/922-8222). **E Noa Tours** (tel. 808/941-6608) uses an 11-passenger van (not wheelchair-accessible). Best bet for wheelchair users is **Handi-Cabs of the Pacific** (tel. 808/524-3866) at charter rates of $25 an hour with no mileage charge. They have a great number of sightseeing packages, and you should write for their brochure to P.O. Box 22428, Honolulu, HI 96822. Also check with them to see if you can join others in a whole island tour (their vans take four wheelchairs and four ambulatory passengers), and the total cost can then be shared.

And then, of course, there is a rented car if you want to explore at your own pace (see the Getting Around section of this chapter).

IN AND AROUND HONOLULU: Honolulu is, of course, the location of **Pearl Harbor** and the *Arizona* Memorial to that "day that will live in infamy" of 1941. There are a number of cruise boat companies that offer tours, and most are wheelchair-accessible with plenty of assistance always available. Handi-Cabs offers a package that includes the Pearl Harbor cruise and round trip transportation for $12.50 per person. Call 524-3866 for schedule details and reservations. There is also a free tour, on a first-come, first-boarded basis, run by the U.S. Navy, which leaves from Pearl City Pier via a launch that requires assistance for boarding. There is an accessible Visitors Center here with films and exhibits about the memorial. Call 471-3901 for details of sailing times and tell them the assistance you'll need.

Overlooking Honolulu in a spectacular setting is another solemn reminder of America's war dead from the Spanish-American War to the Vietnam War, the **National Memorial Cemetery of the Pacific** in Punchbowl Crater. The access road leads to the monument where there are ramps for wheelchairs on each side. Sunrise services are held here on Easter Sunday at the scenic lookout point that can be reached by visitors in wheelchairs.

If you are not going to see the real thing, you can see a semblance of a Hawaiian jungle at **Paradise Park** in the Manoa Valley at 3737 Manoa Rd. (tel. 988-2141). The 15-acre park, about five miles from Waikiki, is a somewhat tame but picturesque setting for hundreds of birds and tropical flowers. The paths are hard-surfaced, but wheelchair users may need assistance on some of the gradients. Trained birds go through their paces in the amphitheater, and there are reproductions of ethnic villages representative of Hawaii's many races. It is open daily, except Christmas Day, from 9:30 a.m. to 5:30 p.m. Admission for adults is $4.95, children (4 to 12) $3.

For horticulturists and just plain plant lovers, there's a treat in store at **Foster Botanic Gardens,** 180 N. Vineyard Blvd. (tel. 531-1939), another 15 acres of rare tropical plants and orchid displays. Easiest entrance is by the Nursery on N. Vineyard Blvd., and there is one main asphalt path around the major areas of the park. Admission is free and there are guided tours on Monday, Tuesday, and Wednesday. Open daily from 9 a.m. to 4 p.m.

The fascinating story of the early settlers from Polynesia, who made their way across the Pacific Ocean in outrigger canoes, comes alive at the **Bishop Museum,** 1355 Kahili St. (tel. 847-3511), where there is also a collection of primitive art of the Pacific islands. There is a level entrance in the rear, but if you use a wheelchair you will not be able to reach the second floor. However, there are many exhibits on the ground floor including music, dance, and crafts. Open daily from 9 a.m. to 5 p.m. Admission is $3 for those over 18, free for visitors in wheelchairs.

For a reverse view of Waikiki—from the ocean—you can take a **Windjammer Cruise** aboard a traditional sailing vessel for a sunset dinner cruise that lasts 2½ hours. The barkentine *Rela Mae* is recommended for wheelchairs since it is ramped and there is plenty of room on deck. It leaves Fisherman's Wharf at 5:15 and 7:45 p.m., and there is pick-up service available at most major Waikiki hotels on the beach. The mai tais are unlimited, and the buffet is lavish, all accompanied by a Hawaiian serenade; the cost is $32.50. Windjammer Cruises (tel. 521-0036, or toll-free 800/367-5000 for information) also has a four-hour luncheon cruise for $39 on Wednesday, Friday, and Sunday, and a Showboat cruise featuring entertainment and an open bar that sails on Friday at 9 p.m. and costs $14.

Another popular dinner cruise takes place on a catamaran, the kind of sailboat with a double hull, that leaves the Hilton Hawaiian Village dock every day at 5:30 p.m. for a two-hour **Sunset Dinner Sail** that includes dinner, entertainment, and an open bar. There are boarding facilities and deck space for those in wheelchairs. Cost is $30 for adults, $15 for children under 12. Phone 955-3348 for reservations.

A two-hour **Catamaran Dinner Cruise** from Fisherman's Wharf anchors off Waikiki Beach and Diamond Head, at 5:30 and 8:30 p.m. every day, with good flat deck space for wheelchairs. The Cruise includes an open bar, buffet dinner, and entertainment and costs $32 for adults, $20 for children under 15.

What would an image of Hawaii be without the hula? Although it's now mostly done for the benefit of the tourists, the hula has its roots in spiritual homage to the goddess Laka, sister of the volcano goddess Pele. You can see the **Kodak Hawaii Hula Show** presented free every Tuesday, Wednesday, Thursday, and Friday morning at 10 a.m. in Queen Kapiolani Park at the Diamond Head end of Kalakaua Avenue. Be there early and special arrangements can be made for wheelchair users to be taken to the front of the seating which is on a lawn next to the Waikiki Shell.

While you're in this neighborhood you may want to go an extra block to the **Honolulu Zoo,** where there is a smooth path throughout the 42 acres, and accessible snack bars and picnic tables. Rest rooms here have 32-inch stall doors and grab bars.

SPORTS: If you've energy left over and want to try your hand at an active sport, or want to keep your hand in at something you already enjoy, the Commission on the Handicapped provides the following references of recreational activities with programs for disabled participants: **Wheelchair Tennis,** Peter Burwash International (tel. 746-1236); **Scuba Diving,** Aloha Dive Shop (tel. 395-5922 or 8882); and **Flying Instruction,** Handi-Flyers (tel. 836-3134).

THE OTHER OAHU: Beyond the beautiful beach at Waikiki and the urban excitement of Honolulu, there's a whole 26-by-40-mile island out there—the **Windward Oahu** of suburbs, small towns, endless beaches, small bays, and pounding surf, pineapple plantations, picnic spots, natural parks, Polynesian model villages, and a visible underwater reef. You can enjoy it all.

Depending on the time you have to spare, you can circle the island slowly in one day, or make short direct trips of about an hour to the various attractions out there via the mountain tunnels. If you can get into a regular bus, there's one that leaves Ala Moana Center every 15 minutes during most of the day, and you can get around the island for a fare of 50¢. If you need a wheelchair-lift van, look into what Handi-Cabs has to offer—perhaps you can link up with one or two more people in wheelchairs and split the cost. Call them at 523-4083. For independent travel, this might be the day to get a rented car (see Getting Around section of this chapter), and a good map, and off you go! Take picnic fixings so that you can stop at one of the many accessible beach parks.

Heading out past Diamond Head on Rte. 72 you'll see **Hanauma Bay, a** brilliant green/blue, at the bottom of a volcanic crater to be viewed from an overlooking observation deck. If you can get on a bus, one will take you down to the water's edge and along a dramatic coastline to see ancient lava cliffs dropping down to the sea below, past a geyser in the lava called the Halona Blow Hole. At **Sandy Beach,** you'll find accessible rest rooms at both ends of the park, reached by a concrete path ramped from the parking lot, with 32-inch stalls and grab bars.

You'll be able to stop at **Sealife Park,** at the base of towering lava cliffs, for the dolphin show, and be able to get around a glass-enclosed Hawaiian reef full of rare Pacific marine life via a smooth circular ramp. Admission is $6.50, $4.75 for children 7 to 12. Open every day from 9:30 a.m. to 5 p.m. There's a luau here on Sunday evenings for $23.50. Call for information, 259-7933 at the park, or 923-1531 in Waikiki.

If you continue now on the coastal highway seeing its gorgeous views at every turn of the road, you'll be going in the right direction for the next big attraction at Laie: the Polynesian Cultural Center. But before you get that far, you may want to stop for refreshments at **Pat's at Punaluu,** a scenic beachside restaurant that has two steps at the entrance but lots of willing help if you are in a wheelchair. It is split-level inside, but the view is just as spectacular from the entry level part of the restaurant. Or you can picnic at the **Kaawa Beach Park,** which has a grassy park, level with the parking lot, and direct access to the sandy beach. Rest rooms have a ramped entrance, 32-inch stalls, and grab bars.

Next is Laie, a Mormon town (missionaries have been in Hawaii for over a century), and the **Polynesian Cultural Center** there is one of Oahu's leading attractions. It provides work for Pacific Islander students attending Brigham Young Hawaii University. Seven different authentic Polynesian villages have been re-created here, staffed by natives of each island who demonstrate their crafts and perform their songs and dances. There are events throughout the center, including a music show, the afternoon Pageant of the Long Canoes, and special buffets at lunch and dinner, as well as a nightly musical spectacular. The entrance is level off the parking lot, which has special spaces for disabled visitors, and the visitors' buildings are accessible, although some of the village buildings are not easily entered. Rest rooms are adapted for wheelchair users throughout the center. If you call and make reservations in advance, special arrangements can be made for a tour (tel. 293-8561 in Laie, 923-1861 in Waikiki). Admission packages, from $13 for adults, $6.50 for children, include a tour of the villages, canoe rides, and the shows. The evening spectacular is an additional $14 for adults, $7 for children. (The Polynesian Cultural Center is a place that can also be reached directly from Honolulu via the Pali or Wilson tunnels, if you are not making the round-the-island tour.)

If you are doing the coastal drive, you can now return to Honolulu, if you wish, in about an hour from Laie via those tunnels.

If you want to go the long way back, you'll go past the North Shore and surfer's territory. It's at **Sunset Beach** and **Waimea Bay** where the thundering breakers sometimes reach heights 30 feet to make those legendary "tubes." Peek in on the luxury **Kuilima Hyatt Resort Hotel**—it's fun to explore—just before you reach Sunset Beach. You can have a buffet lunch (about $9.50) on the Garden Terrace overlooking the pool and ocean, or dinner with entertainment in either of the two dining rooms. At sunset, the view is unforgettable from the cocktail lounge overlooking Turtle Cove. The Resort Hotel is ramped throughout.

Just across the road from Waimea Bay Beach Park is **Waimea Falls Park,** a narrow canyon extending into the Koolau Mountains, site of an ancient Hawaiian village, where you'll find two restaurants, an arboretum, a bird sanctuary, picnic spots, a hula show, and cliff-diving exhibitions. The pathway is paved throughout the park, and there are a few steep slopes where assistance may be needed. Wheelchairs can be assisted aboard buses for a guided tour (again, lots of willing help). Admission is $5.75; $3.75 for children over 7. The park is open from 10 a.m. to 5:30 p.m. Just before the road turns inland, you'll come to **Haleiwa Beach Park** on Waialua Bay (accessible rest rooms here).

There is no road around rugged Kaena Point, so the road goes inland back to Honolulu, through the largest pineapple plantation in the world on the Leilehua Plateau, where you'll find the **Dole Pineapple Stand** with the freshest pineapple you've ever tasted. (The rest room at Dole has a 32-inch stall door but no grab bars.) If you're still hungry on the way back, stop off at a favorite local restaurant on Highway 99 in Wahiawa, **Kemoo Farm,** which has a ramp to the door on Wilikina Drive and moderate prices.

Soon after, the Kamehameha Highway becomes a four-lane freeway (Rte. 90), goes into Pearl Harbor, then connects with Rte. 92 (Nimitz Highway) past Honolulu Harbor on into Waikiki.

7. Nightlife

Early dinners and an evening with TV are not the reason you're in Hawaii! Just join the throngs on the streets and in the clubs and bars of Waikiki, or see big-name entertainment at the big hotels, or enjoy a drink by moonlight with the still water lapping on the sand on a quiet terrace overlooking the ocean.

Most of the big-name entertainment takes place in the big hotels. Here are some suggestions of places with easy access (prices are subject to change):

An institution in Hawaii, the **Danny Kaleikini Show,** can be seen on the **Hala Terrace** of the Kahala Hilton, 5000 Kahala Ave. (tel. 734-2211), set against a romantic backdrop of sea and sky. The cover charge is $9, dinner about $25, for the 9 p.m. dinner show.

At the venerable **Royal Hawaiian Hotel,** 2259 Kalakaua Ave. (tel. 923-7311), there is a 9 p.m. dinner show for $35 (including tax and tip). You can see the show, usually the island's leading entertainers, for $16.50, which includes two drinks, at 9 and 11 p.m. Enter the hotel by the ramped side door. Wheelchair patrons can be assisted down the steps to the Show room.

Hawaii's best-known entertainer, **Don Ho,** performs at the **Hilton Dome Showroom** at the Hilton Hawaiian Village, 2005 Kalia Rd. (tel. 949-4321). The $32.50 price for the 8:30 p.m. show includes a steak dinner and one drink, tax, and tips. On Friday and Sunday only, there's a cocktail show at 10:30 p.m. for $16.50, which includes one drink, tax, and tip.

The **Polynesian Palace** at the Cinerama Reef Towers, 227 Lewers St. (tel. 923-9861), once Don Ho's place, is now the lavish home of another of Hawaii's best-loved entertainers, Al Harrington (of "Hawaii Five-O") and his revue. The price is $30 for the Sunday-through-Friday dinner show, including dinner, tax, and tip. It's $15 for the cocktail show package. There's a steepish ramp from the street to the lobby of the hotel and a gentle one from the parking lot to the entrance. The entrance to the Polynesian Palace is ramped.

Polynesian shows and buffets are offered at the **Bayan Court** of the Moana Hotel, 2365 Kalakaua Ave. (tel. 926-4474), twice nightly for $30.50 all inclusive. Rest rooms here are wheelchair-accessible. The best entrance is via the ramp at the Surfrider Hotel next door, connected to the Moana by level walkway. Similar offerings can be found at the **Hawaiian Hut** at the Ala Moana Hotel, 410 Atkinson Drive (tel. 941-5202), where the all-inclusive tab is $27; $16 for the cocktail show. The entrance to the hotel is ramped.

Among the many romantic spots is the **Hanohano Room** at the Sheraton-Waikiki, 2255 Kalakaua Ave. (tel. 922-4422), where there is a nonstop view from Diamond Head to Pearl Harbor and dance music with dinner from 8 p.m., or with a drink after 10:30 p.m.

The revolving restaurant, **La Ronde** (tel. 946-8080), atop the Ala Moana Building in the Moana Shopping Center, also has glorious views and soft background music for drinks and dinner. The 20th floor of the building has an accessible rest room.

8. Shopping

If you can't resist shopping, Honolulu is going to be a big temptation. Even though there's no favorable exchange rate or duty-free shopping (this is the U.S., remember) there are so many different and interesting things to buy, and they're all offered very conveniently in shops that line Kalakaua Avenue and in super-malls that have sprouted all over. So whether it's the bold Hawaiian prints of aloha shirts and muumuus, carved woods, ukeleles, shell jewelry, Macadamia nuts, or pineapples, make sure you have extra room in your luggage before you leave home!

Some shopping centers have better accessibility than others, so here's a rundown of the best:

Even if you don't like shopping centers, it's hard to resist the attractions of the **Ala Moana Shopping Center,** 50 acres of the best of island architecture connected by pools, gardens, fountains, and shady walks. It's on Ala Moana Boulevard, a ten-minute ride from Waikiki in the *ewa* direction of Honolulu. Parking is on all three levels—street, mall, and roof deck—with "special" spaces on the mall level. You'll find ramps on all three levels into the center. There is an elevator at the Diamond Head end near Liberty House, in the center at Penney's, and at the *ewa* end at Sears. Some stores have internal elevators. There is one totally accessible rest room near Liberty Bank on street level. Ala Moana Center is open from 9:30 a.m. to 9 p.m. Monday through Friday. It closes at 5:30 p.m. on Saturday. Sunday hours are 10 a.m. to 5 p.m.

The **Waikiki Shopping Plaza** at 2250 Kalakaua Ave., at the corner of Seaside, is an international center ranging from ethnic snackshops at the lowest level to luxurious international restaurants on the top floor. Free evening entertainment is often presented on the ground level. Level entrances from the sidewalk are at Kalakaua, Royal Hawaiian, and Seaside Avenues, and there are elevators to all floors. The freight elevator next to all regular elevators is larger and has lower controls. Each floor has a wheelchair-accessible rest room, with 30-inch stall doors and grab bars.

Near the Sheraton-Waikiki on Kalakaua Avenue is the brand new and grandiose **Royal Hawaiian Shopping Center,** three city blocks long and full of more than 100 shops and restaurants set in a tropical environment, along with free entertainment. It's accessible throughout, including the rest rooms. Open daily from 9 a.m. to 10 p.m.

Close to the Kewelo Boat Basin at Ala Moana Boulevard and Ward Avenue, the **Ward Warehouse** specializes in crafts of a high artistic level in a number of boutiques. There's a multideck garage with elevator access to the Warehouse, as well as ground level parking with ramps to stores at the end and middle of the building. Elevators have low controls near the Spaghetti Factory and Orson's restaurant, where you'll also find accessible rest rooms.

9. The Island of Hawaii

The island of Hawaii, a fascinating mixture of legend and reality, contains more variety per square mile than any other part of the islands: tropical black-sand beaches; snow-covered Mauna Kea mountain; an active volcano, Kilauea, on Mauna Loa; lush vegetation and a rain forest where orchids grow in abundance; cattle ranches; and coffee plantations. Hawaii is called The Big Island because it's more than 4000 square miles in size. To do it justice, four days would be a minimum here, dividing the time between sometimes cloud-shrouded Hilo on the eastern coast and sun-drenched Kailua on the western, Kona coast. There are a number of hotels on both coasts that have wheelchair-accessible rooms.

Unlike Oahu, most of the beach parks on Hawaii don't have facilities for visitors in wheelchairs, since the volcanic lava terrain is rugged and difficult to negotiate.

On the other hand, Volcanoes National Park is surely one of the reasons you've come to the island of Hawaii, and you'll be able to see it all from wheelchair-accessible overlooks or from the car.

The highway that takes the northern route from Hilo to Kailua-Kona is one of the most awesome road trips anywhere in the world.

Travelers to the Big Island can land on either the east or west coast. You can come direct from the mainland to the jetport at Hilo, or you can take an interisland flight (40 minutes from Honolulu to Hilo for instance), to either Hilo or Kona-Keahole airports (see Getting There section of this chapter). You will need a car on Hawaii if you are going to tour. **Avis** (tel. 800/331-2112) rents cars with hand controls in either Hilo or Kona, on at least three weeks notice. Taxis are available for shorter trips, and there are tour buses if you can board them.

HOTELS IN HILO: Resort hotels sprouted after the jetport opened, and a number of them have rooms with special facilities.

There are four special rooms at the **Sheraton-Waiakea Village Hotel,** 400 Hualani St., Hilo, HI 96720 (tel. 808/935-6705, toll-free 800/325-3535), where "villages" on a 15-acre garden are built on a self-contained island overlooking Waiakea Lagoon, which mirrors the Mauna Kea towering in the distance. Everything is on one level, and in the special rooms entrance doors are 35 inches wide. There is no door to the bathroom, which is equipped with grab bars and low switches, and there is space under the sink. Both single and double rooms are $60 to $80. A third person can stay in the same room for $10 additional.

The **Hilo Hawaiian Hotel,** 71 Banyan Dr., Hilo, HI 96720 (tel. 808/935-9361, toll free 800/367-5004), overlooks Hilo Bay and has seven special rooms, all very spacious, with 30-inch bathroom doors, grab bars, and low controls. The entrance to the hotel is barrier-free, and there are elevators to all floors. The entrance is level to the Queens Court restaurant. Rates here are $37 to $49 single, $40 to $52 double, depending on the floor. For reservations, write to

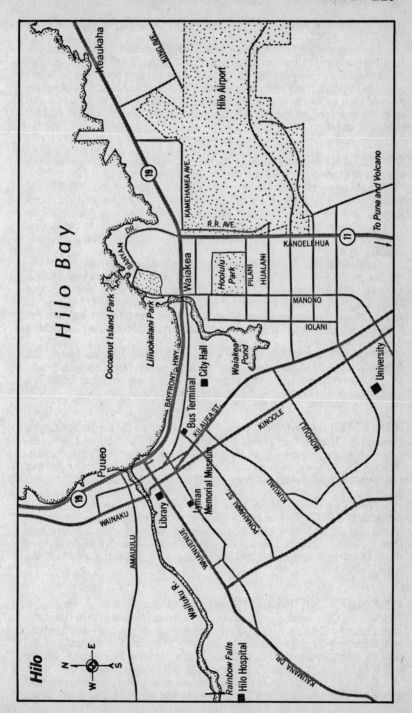

Hawaiian Pacific Resorts, 1150 S. King St., Honolulu, HI 96814, or call toll free 800/367-5004.

Also overlooking Hilo Bay is a TraveLodge with two special rooms, the **Hilo Pacific Isle**, 121 Banyan Dr., Hilo, HI 96720 (tel. 808/935-7171, toll free 800/255-3050), 1½ miles from the airport. Free parking here. The main entrance has a gentle ramp, and the restaurant has a level entrance. Special rooms have 34-inch bathroom doors, grab bars, low controls, and space under the sink. Rates depend on the location of the room and range from $42 to $57, single or double.

DINING IN HILO: If you want to try the restaurant at a hotel other than the one you are staying at, here are some suggestions:

The **Kupuna Room** at the Sheraton Waiakea Village Hotel, 400 Hualani St. (tel. 961-3041), is decorated in Hawaiian Monarchy style, and the menu features gourmet continental and Polynesian dishes. A meal here will run between $15 and $20. Dinner is served nightly from 6 to 9 p.m., to the accompaniment of classical guitar music. The entrances to both the hotel and restaurant are level.

Queens Court in the Hilo Hawaiian Hotel, 71 Banyan Dr. (tel. 935-9361), offers a great view of Hilo Bay and a well-priced meal in an elegant setting. Japanese, Korean, Italian, and Hawaiian lunch specials range from $2.95 to $6.25, and there are alternating Japanese ($9.75) and Hawaiian ($12.95) buffets at dinnertime. Sunday brunch is under $10. There are level entrances to the hotel and the restaurant. The public rest room in the hotel has a 26-inch stall door, but no grab bars.

Good budget-priced food can be had at the **Hilo Hukilau Hotel**, 126 Banyan Dr. (tel. 935-0821), with many luncheon entrees priced between $3 and $5. Dinner prices are around $5.95 to $8.95 for a complete meal. There is a level entrance to the Hukilau Restaurant from the street level.

HILO AFTER DARK: If you want to see a show, try the one at the **Crown Room** at the Naniloa Surf Hotel, 93 Banyan Dr. (tel. 935-0831), a Las Vegas-type club with top shows from the mainland, as well as Polynesian revues. Cover is $11 for the show, one drink, tax, and tip. Entrances to the hotel and restaurant are level. Public rest rooms are spacious with 27-inch stall doors, but no grab bars.

There's a generous Happy Hour in the **Voyager Restaurant** at the Hilo Pacific Isle Hotel, with free *pupus*—a variety of Hawaiian hors d'oeuvres—served with drinks from 4 to 6 p.m. Hawaiian music provides background here from 8 p.m. to midnight Tuesday through Saturday. There's a slight ramp at the front entrance to the hotel and level access to the Voyager Room from the hotel lobby.

VOLCANOES NATIONAL PARK: Hawaii's most famous resident is Madame Pele, the flaming goddess of the volcanoes, and she lives in Halemaumau Crater on Kilauea. You may even get to see her in action—she has been *very* active in 1983 as I write. If you see a very old woman in the area and she asks for a handout, be sure to respond. That's Madame Pele, as any islander will tell you, and if you don't respond, that will bring bad luck!

Call 967-7311 for news of the latest eruptions and viewing conditions, and check with Park Rangers for directions when you arrive. Active or no, you'll

want to see Madame Pele's home, now Hawaii's Volcanoes National Park and it's easy—Kilauea is known as the "drive-in" volcano.

Take Highway 11 out of Hilo all the way to Kilauea, where you should stop first at park headquarters. The rangers on duty will give you driving maps and information, and you will be able to see a movie here on volcanology. The **Kilauea Visitor Center** is fully accessible, and rest rooms have 32-inch stall doors. You can also get information here on accessible facilities elsewhere in the park.

Most overlooks and exhibitions on Crater Rim Road and Chain of Craters Road are accessible, and many features of the park can be seen from a car on the circular drive that surrounds the park and leads you alongside every major point of interest. The National Park Service advises that a self-guiding trail between the Kilauea Visitor Center and Volcano House (which also has accessible rest rooms with 32-inch staff doors and grab bars) is easily negotiated by visitors in wheelchairs. Other trails such as the Thurston Lava Tube and Bird Park have steps and steep grades.

Volcano House is an accessible hotel that stands a safe distance above the lip of Halemaumau, the firepit of the **Kilauea crater,** and provides a great opportunity, especially during active eruptions, to really see and experience the volcano amid eye-popping views, crisp air, and mountain foliage, so different from the tropical beaches below. You can have dinner here.

Road elevation in the park ranges from the luxuriant rainforest at sea level to 6000 feet at the craters, so bring a sweater for the higher altitudes.

If you want to go a different way back to Hilo, take the Chain of Craters Road, where you can see a series of active small firepits, to the Wahaula Visitors Center (accessible rest rooms) and go in the direction of the Puna area via Pahoa and Keaau through rain forests, papaya fields, orchid farms, and stretches of roadway along the seashore that will give you an unforgettable picture of the effects of volcanic eruptions.

HILO TO KONA: If you drive the 108-mile horseshoe of a highway, easily accomplished in less than three hours, from Hilo to Kona, you'll see such contrasts of landscape that it's hard to believe you're on the same island, as you pass sugar plantation fields, around the base of Mauna Kea on the Hilo coast, the grassy pastures of the Parker Ranch, and on into remote mountain regions and across barren lava landscapes to the luxuriant green of Kona. Since you will be staying in the car, a detailed itinerary from a regular guide book will serve you well for points of interest.

After Highway 19 from Hilo heads inland, you'll come to the **Parker Ranch,** where you can stop at the Parker Ranch Broiler if you're hungry. It specializes in steaks and prime ribs at dinner (entrees $11 to $15), or you might have a lavish buffet lunch for $5.95. It has a ramped entrance.

HOTELS IN KONA: There's a room with special features on each of the six floors of the **Hotel King Kamehameha,** Alii Drive, Kailua-Kona, HI 96740 (tel. 808/329-2911), a new establishment built on the site of an old landmark hotel and combining the best of Hawaii past and present. It has its own sandy beach, the only one right in the heart of town, where the Kona Beach Luau is held four nights a week. The special rooms have bathrooms with 35-inch-wide doors, grab bars, and low switches. There is a ground level entrance, and the interior is very spacious. Exterior grounds and shopping mall are accessible and so are the restaurants. Single and double rooms range from $49 for a standard

to $75 for a deluxe oceanfront view. Write for reservations to P.O. Box 8519, 2222 Kalakaua Ave., Honolulu, HI 96815.

In the Keauhou Bay area, six miles outside the town of Kailua-Kona, is the **Keauhou Beach Hotel**, 78–6740 Alii Dr., Kailua-Kona, HI 96740 (tel. 808/322-3441), in a setting of such great natural beauty that the area was a favorite retreat of Hawaiian royalty. There are two spacious, special rooms, with 33-inch doors and bathroom grab bars. Entrance is level, and the grounds and pool are accessible via ramps. There is a private swimming beach (rare for Kona), and if you are with a companion who likes to play tennis or golf, this resort hotel has all the amenities. You'll have a choice of three restaurants, all wheelchair accessible. Rates range from $49 to $75 single or double, depending on the view. From April 1 to December 20, all prices are $6 less. A third person in the same room is $6 additional. For reservations, write Island Holiday Resorts, Central Reservations, P.O. Box 8519, 2222 Kalakaua Ave., Honolulu, HI 96815.

Although it has no room specifically designed for disabled guests, you may want to consider the **Kona Hilton** (tel. 808/329-3111) if you can manage without grab bars, for instance, since the entry door to guest rooms is 31 inches wide, and there is a good deal of barrier-free access to all parts of the hotel—the beach building has a wheelchair ramp and so does the approach to the pool area, and the grounds and pathways around the hotel are also suitable for wheelchairs. Wherever you look, there are spectacular views of mountains and sea on this 12-acre oceanfront, half a mile from the center of Kailua-Kona village. Depending on the view, rooms are $57 to $90 double occupancy ($6 less for singles) and $10 additional for a third person in the same room; children stay free. There's a diverse program of dining and entertainment events here. You can make reservations at any Hilton Reservation Office, or write to the Kona Hilton Beach and Tennis Resort, P.O. Box 1179, Kailua-Kona, HI 96740.

DINING IN KONA: A long-time Kona favorite is **Huggo's** (tel. 329-1493) in a lovely waterfront location on Alii Drive, not far from the Kona Hilton. The entrance and interior are level. Huggo's is noted for fresh fish and seafood as well as meat and chicken entrees, priced from $7.50 to $12.50 (lobster slightly higher). Lunch is served weekdays from 11 a.m. to 2:30 p.m., and dinner every night from 5:30 to 10 p.m. There's live music nightly Thursday to Saturday after 8:30 p.m.

If you're not staying at the Kona Hilton, its wheelchair-accessible grounds and ground-floor lobby provide a pleasant stroll before dining at the elegant **Hele Mai** restaurant (tel. 329-3111). Dinner entrees, with salad bar, range from $19 to $25. The Hilton's **Kona Rib House** has a complete dinner for around $15, and the **Pasta Korner** complete dinners for around $8.95.

KONA AFTER DARK: Much of the action is centered around the luaus at the big hotels. There's a "Night in Hawaii," including an elaborate feast and show at the **Kona Surf Hotel**, on Alii Dr. (tel. 322-3411), which has a level entrance. It's held on Saturday through Thursday from 6 p.m. and costs $25 all-inclusive.

Another festive luau is held at the **Keauhou Beach Hotel** (tel. 322-3441), six miles outside town, on Sunday, Tuesday, Wednesday, and Friday at 6:30 p.m. for $24.50. There is a ground-level entrance to the hotel. And at the **Hotel**

King Kamehameha, on Alii Drive in town (tel. 329-2911), the luau tab is also $24.50 all-inclusive.

Note: Check any of the luaus before you go, since times and schedules may change.

AROUND KONA: Although one of the usual highlights of a visit to the Big Island is the **Pu'Uhonua O'Honaunau National Historic Park,** the restored temple complex formerly known as the City of Refuge, it does present difficulties for those with mobility problems since there is no paved path, only a sand or lava walkway. However, you can get to the Visitor Center here, easily approached from the parking lot, and a hand-railed ramp leads to the amphitheater with a terrific ocean panorama, and where orientation talks are given by park personnel. The fully accessible rest room is equipped with grab bars. This was originally a sanctuary over 400 years ago, in the days of warring chieftains, and was the place where refugees and defeated warriors could be safe from becoming victims of human sacrifices. Tabu-breakers could also be cleansed of their offenses here.

The drive to the park on the Kuakini Highway out of Kona will take you past coffee plantations (where they grow the rich Kona coffee) and small cattle ranches. Across the bay at Kealakekua, you'll see the white monument that marks the spot where Captain Cook was killed by natives in 1799 on his second visit to the islands.

10. Maui

Maui's glorious beaches, jungle valleys, and the sleeping volcano of Haleakala are only 88 miles from Honolulu, and only a 20-minute flight from there to Kahului airport (see Getting There section of this chapter).

Maui is a spectacular result of constant volcanic action: the western end began as a separate island with mountains that fold over on each other as they reach down to the marvelous beaches. On the eastern side, also once a separate island, is the awesome Haleakala Crater. Volcanic activity on both islands finally bridged the gap to create the island of Maui.

You really need a car here, so check with **Avis** (tel. 800/331-2112) if you need a car with hand controls, and give them at least three weeks notice. Check also on hotel packages that may include a car. There are tour vans, if you can get into one, but none with wheelchair lifts.

Accommodations for tourists on Maui are based around large resorts that encompass hotels and condominiums. Nearly all are in the luxury category. Hotels with rooms specifically designed for disabled guests can be counted on the fingers of one hand, but some hotels have large rooms and bathrooms (if you don't need grab bars), and the grounds, restaurants, and other public areas provide easy wheeling. Condos outnumber hotels and are a good idea for three or four people traveling together. However, beware when you check the official guide (which also shows the condos) for hotels marked with a (W), which indicates they consider their facilities suitable for guests who use wheelchairs. That (W) reflects a subjective judgement and often leaves something to be desired. Check details before you reserve.

A clearinghouse for information on services and resources such as transportation, equipment, medical support personnel, and sign language interpreters is at the Maui office of the **Commission on the Handicapped,** 54 High St., Wailuku HI 96793 (tel. 244-4441).

There is also a **Maui Center for Independent Living** (tel. 242-4966, TDD 242-4968) which also acts as an information and referral center.

HOTELS AT KAANAPALI BEACH:

HOTELS AT KAANAPALI BEACH: One of the great resort areas in the world, Kaanapali Beach has white sand, a clear-as-crystal ocean, and spectacular vistas oceanward and inland.

At the **Maui Surf Hotel**, Kaanapali, Maui, HI 96761 (tel. 808/661-4411, toll free 800/367-5630), it's hard to tell the difference between indoors and outdoors, because there's a summerhouse atmosphere throughout the hotel. There are two rooms with wide bathroom doors (30 inches) but no grab bars. The front entrance is ramped, and access to poolside and beach areas are level. There are also level entrances to the restaurants. The rates vary according to the height of the floor and the view, and range from $82 to $93 double. Make reservations through InterIsland Surf Resorts, P.O. Box 8539, Honolulu, HI 96815.

With rates a bit lower than most—and if you don't need a wide bathroom door—everything else is accessible at the **Kaanepali Beach Hotel**, Lahaina, Maui, HI 96761 (tel. 808/661-0011). It's in a lovely spot, right at the ocean, with acres of flowering grounds and plenty of restaurants. Entry to guest rooms is 40 inches, but bathroom doors are only 24 inches (management will remove the door to give an extra inch or so). Rates are $58 to $75, single or double. Restaurant prices are also moderate. Make reservations through Amfac Hotels, P.O. Box 8519, Honolulu, HI 96815.

HOTELS BETWEEN KAANAPALI AND NAPILI:

HOTELS BETWEEN KAANAPALI AND NAPILI: This is condo country on the miles of curving coastline in an idyllic setting.

A longtime favorite at Kaanapali is the **Royal Lahaina** resort, 2980 Kekaa Dr., Lahaina, Maui, HI 96761 (tel. 808/661-3611), on 52 acres of tropical gardens fronting the beach, nearly all of which is accessible on level surfaces. Entry doors to guest rooms are 35 inches wide, and to bathrooms 26 inches (no grab bars). There are small thresholds to the shops; all restaurants are accessible. Although the buffet area is down two steps, there's a lot of willing assistance. The rooms are spacious. Rates go from $66 to $86 double, and rates for suites that can accommodate up to six people are comparable in price. For reservations, write Amfac Hotels, P.O. Box 8519, Honolulu, HI 96815, or directly to the hotel.

Among the hotels on the gorgeous Napili Bay is the **Napili Kai Beach Club Hotel**, 5900 Honoapilani Rd., Lahaina, Maui, HI 96761 (tel. 808/669-6271, toll free 800/367-5030). Entry doors to the guest rooms are 31 inches wide, and to the bathrooms 28 inches wide (no grab bars). The interior, grounds, and restaurants are accessible. Rates are $85 to $125 double. All rooms here have kitchenettes.

The elegant and expensive **Kapalua Bay Hotel** near the northern tip of the island is a 600-acre resort complex surrounded by ocean and bay, landscaped with flowering gardens. Its three rooms designed for disabled guests have 35-inch entry and bathroom doors, with grab bars, bedside light control, and level access to the lanai. Room location determines the rates which, for double occupancy, go from $94 to $224. Make reservations through Kapalua Bay Hotel, Rte. 1, Box 333, Kapalua, Maui, HI 96761 (tel. 808/669-5656, toll free 800/225-1739).

You'll find more modest but accessible accommodations in two special rooms at the **TraveLodge**, 888 Wainee St., Lahaina, Maui, HI 96761 (tel.

808/661-3661), near the picturesque 18th-century town of Lahaina, once the capital of the islands and a historic whaling port. Entrance is ramped. Rooms 161 and 162 have 35-inch bathroom doors and grab bars, with pulley hooks in the ceiling above the toilet and the bed. Mirror and vanity table are lowered, with approach space underneath.

HOTELS IN KIHEI AND WAILEA: This dry, sunny area about 20 miles from Kahului (where the airport is located), developed relatively recently and has marvelous sand beaches and lashings of peace and quiet.

One of the few Maui hotels with special rooms is the **Wailea Beach Hotel,** 3550 Wailea Ave., Wailea, Maui, HI 96753 (tel. 808/879-4900, toll free 800/228-3000). Rooms 503 and 504 are very spacious and have low controls throughout. The bathroom door is 32 inches wide, and there are grab bars. The elevator to all floors has low controls, and the entrances to the restaurants are barrier-free. Rates at the Wailea Beach are $90 and $160 double occupancy.

The **Hotel Intercontinental Maui** is a luxury villa on the beach at Wailea that is at the same time comfortable and casual. The spacious terrain is level, and it has everything resorts are there for. There is one room with bathroom grab bars, and all entry doors to the guest rooms are 33 inches wide and to the bathrooms 27 inches wide. The rates are $70, $90, and $100, double occupancy, depending on the view from the room; higher rates from late December to mid-March. Make reservations through Hotel Intercontinental Maui, P.O. Box 779, Kihei, Maui, HI 96753 (tel. 808/879-1922, toll free 800/367-2960).

HALEAKALA CRATER: The dormant, colorful crater of the Haleakala volcano, a "not-to-be-missed" sight on Maui, is now a National Park accessible to visitors in wheelchairs. The home of the god Maui is a spacious one—7½ miles long and 2½ miles wide.

Choose a clear day for your visit to Haleakala—check weather conditions by calling 572-7749 before you go—and bring a sweater since it can get quite cool. When you arrive, check in at park headquarters and get maps and orientation on what to see and what will be accessible relative to your mobility. Rest rooms here have 28-inch-wide stalls.

The Haleakala and Puu Ulaula observatories are accessible via a small ramp. From the Haleakala Observatory you can see thousands of square miles of Pacific Ocean and the crater below, changing in a kaleidoscopic color show created by the sun and clouds. The Oheo section is a very scenic area of streams and waterfalls that can be reached by car.

Part III

Chapter 12

A PREVIEW OF CANADA

CANADA may be North America, but it's far from being a reflection of the United States, and that's what makes a trip there so revealing and so refreshing at the same time. Familiar on the surface to U.S. visitors are Canada's currency, its traffic, and fast-food and motel chains, but on closer view there are many aspects of the Canadian lifestyle that reflect a more orderly way of life.

In the big cities covered in this section—Montreal, Toronto, and Vancouver—there are few slums, no graffiti, and hardly any litter. Canadian drivers can safely leave their cars unlocked, except that it's against the law. And politeness is the norm of behavior.

The attitude to disability is quite advanced in Canada. Hotels, restaurants, theaters, and public buildings have been installing ramps and accessible bathrooms at a faster rate, it seems, than their U.S. counterparts, although some of the older facilities and buildings have, as everywhere else, presented obstacles to total accessibility.

CURRENCY: As far as money and credit cards are concerned, Canadians use dollars and cents, and coins are similar to American ones: dollar bills (which include a $2 denomination) are distinguished by different colors for different denominations. U.S. dollars are accepted in most establishments and you will get a "bonus" to account for the difference in exchange rates, which is usually posted. However, it is usually *less* than you will receive at the banks. (As we go to press, the Canadian dollar equals 81¢ in U.S. currency.) U.S. credit cards are widely accepted.

Currency Note: Unless otherwise stated, *prices are quoted in Canadian dollars* throughout this section.

CUSTOMS: Customs regulations and border formalities for U.S. citizens on vacation are usually minimal, but you should be prepared to show proof of citizenship (passport, voter registration, or birth certificate), and car registration if you are bringing an automobile. You are allowed up to U.S. $300 worth of Canadian goods duty-free per person when leaving Canada, unless you have been there for less than 48 hours, when the allowance is only U.S. $25.

CLIMATE: Most of the weather in Montréal and Toronto is similar to that of New England. Winters are very cold, and summer is warm, sometimes hot. The glorious autumn is probably the best time to visit those cities; days are on the warm side, and nights are cool, even chilly—a combination that produces spectacular foliage colors.

Vancouver's weather can best be described as balmy and pleasant, warmer in summer than in winter, of course, but never extreme. Be prepared for showers in this maritime environment.

Chapter 13

MONTRÉAL

Joie de Vivre!

**1. Getting
There 2. Getting
Around 3. Orientation
4. Where to Stay
5. Restaurants 6. Sights**

IN MODERNITY, SOPHISTICATION, AND VITALITY, Montréal has been the leader among Canadian cities for 150 years, although a number of others are rapidly catching up. It's Canada's largest city and the largest French-speaking city outside Paris. If all that sounds rather awesome, it is counterbalanced by a friendly and law-abiding citizenry that won't mind one bit if your knowledge of French is limited to *"oui"* and *"merci."* The bilingual language policy of the Province of Québec has brought with it a sense of linguistic security for the French-speaking population, but the city's English-speaking portion is still important, as you can see by the city's flag—on which English, Irish, Scottish, and French emblems each take equal territory.

The emphasis on friendliness and the de-emphasis of language mean that there won't be any problem asking your way around or getting a lot of help when you need it. Much of the city is flat, and there are curb cuts downtown; then there's the mountain of *Mont-Réal* ("Royal Mountain"), for which you'll need a car or taxi; and the Old City, which is a bit hilly and bumpy (cobblestones), but that won't deter an energetic wheeler with some valiant assistance. Montréal prides itself on the distinction of being both an above-ground and an underground city—the subterranean network of shops, restaurants, art galleries, and other attractions beneath the surface is unique in its concept and execution.

Montréal has one big disappointment for the traveler in a wheelchair: the Métro subway of which the city is so proud is *not* accessible. Its construction for the opening of Expo 67 just missed out on the awareness that came as a result of the advocacy movement of the 1970s. Transportation for any distance has to be by car or taxi.

There are Canadian Tourist Offices in most large cities in the U.S. (check the telephone directory). Or you can write directly to the **Greater Montréal**

Convention and Tourism Bureau, 155 rue Notre-Dame est, 2HY 1B5 (tel. 514/872-3561).

"Access Montréal" is a bilingual guide to many hotels, restaurants, places of interest, theaters, and shopping for travelers who use wheelchairs, and can be requested free of charge from the Paraplegic Association of Québec, 4545 Queen Mary Road, H3W 1W4 (tel. 514/344-3890).

1. Getting There

Montréal is a hub of transportation of any kind from any direction. Superhighways link it with the rest of Canada and with major cities in the eastern United States, as do express train and bus services. Its two international airports are serviced by most of the world's major airlines.

BY AIR: Most visitors to Montréal come by way of North America on Air Canada, CP Air, Delta, Eastern, USAir, and American Airlines. In addition, Pilgrim connects it with Connecticut, and Empire with upstate New York, among other locations. Most intra-Canadian and United States flights arrive at Dorval Airport.

Dorval Airport (tel. 516/636-5970), 13 miles southwest of the city, is level and accessible by elevators between floors, and there are wheelchair-accessible rest rooms in many locations. Restaurants and bars are accessible.

Mirabel Airport (information booth tel. 514/476-3010) is 35 miles northwest of the city and handles international traffic. Facilities here include accessible rest rooms, telephones, lockers, and restaurants, with elevator access between floors.

To go downtown, use taxis, or special transportation arranged in advance through **Medicar**, 2930 Guy St. (tel. 514/733-7969 or 342-9140), if you need a wheelchair-lift van.

BY TRAIN: Montréal is a major terminus on Canada's **VIA Rail** network (tel. 514/871-1331) and on the U.S. **Amtrak** service, which operates the *Montrealer* from Washington via New York (night train) and the *Adirondack* from New York (day train). The New York to Montréal run takes about 12 hours at night, nine hours by day. Amtrak goes into **Windsor Station**, 910 Peel St. at LaGauchetière St. (tel. 514/395-7109), which has a ramped exit at the rear of the building onto Peel Street. The interior of the station is all on one level, and there is Redcap assistance available by prior notice through Amtrak (ticket office tel. 514/395-6904). (See Chapter 2's section on train travel.) Lifts are required for getting on and off trains. Canadian VIA goes into **Central Station**, 935 LaGauchetière, and has a ramped entrance and electric doors. There is only escalator access to the lower level for boarding trains.

BY BUS: Montréal's main bus terminal is the **Terminus Voyageur**, 505 Blvd. de Maisonneuve Est (tel. 514/842-2281), served by Vermont Transit from Boston, Greyhound from New York, and the Voyageur Company from all parts of Québec Province. There is a ramp at the Berri St. exit and a wheelchair-accessible women's rest room on the ground floor in front of gates 2 and 10. The men's rest room on the ground floor near gates 2 and 4 has room to turn a wheelchair.

BY CAR: The Trans Canada Highway runs right through the city, connecting it with both ends of the country. There's expressway all the 400 miles from New York City, or the 320 miles from Boston. Highway distances and speed limits are given in kilometers per hour in Canada.

It is said that Montréalers drive with Gallic frenzy, so be ready for some defensive driving. In the Province of Québec, expressways are called autoroutes and although some highway signs in the Province are in French only, around Montréal they are in both English and French. Distances are shown in kilometers. Gasoline is sold by the imperial gallon or the liter, at prices comparable to those in the U.S. *Essence* means gasoline; *sans plomb* means lead-free; *huile* is oil; and *libre service* is self-service. You are required by law to wear your seatbelt while driving.

2. Getting Around

"Walking" is usually recommended by guide books as the nicest way to get around Montréal, but if you need wheels other than those on your chair, here are your options.

PUBLIC TRANSPORTATION: Neither buses nor Métro subway system are wheelchair-accessible. The city has a para-transit operation for disabled residents, but it would only be available for visitors on a long-term basis since there are application and registration procedures to be followed.

TAXIS: There is a $1.20 drop-meter charge plus 70¢ a kilometer for taxi fare, at the time of writing. You'll find taxis at stands outside the major hotels and at designated places throughout the city, as well as cruising the streets.

RENTAL CARS: The major U.S. companies do not have hand-control cars in Montréal. They are available from the Canadian company, **Tilden,** 1200 Stanley St., H3B 2S8 (tel. 514/878-2771) on 48 hours notice.

SPECIAL TRANSPORTATION: A private company that provides wheelchair-lift vans is **Medi-Car,** 2930 Guy St. (tel. 514/733-7969 or 342-9140).

GUIDED TOURS: The romantic way to tour Montréal is by calèche, the horse-drawn open carriages that wait at Dominion Square downtown and in Old Montréal. There's a very high step up to get into the carriage. And there are steps, too, into the regular sightseeing buses run by **Gray Line** (tel. 514/866-4641) and the **Murray Hill Co.** (tel. 514/937-5311).

Many taxi drivers will take you on a tour of the city for the same rate as the calèches ($20 to $30 an hour).

3. Orientation

The Mont Réal ("Royal Mountain") that Jacques Cartier, the French explorer, named when he sailed up the St. Lawrence River in 1535 still dominates the island he discovered. It's now Mount Royal Park and provides great views over the city.

Besides the view from Mount Royal, you can also get an orientation view of the city from the **45th floor of the Royal Bank Building,** the cross-shaped skyscraper in the Place Ville Marie. (You can have a buffet lunch here for $16

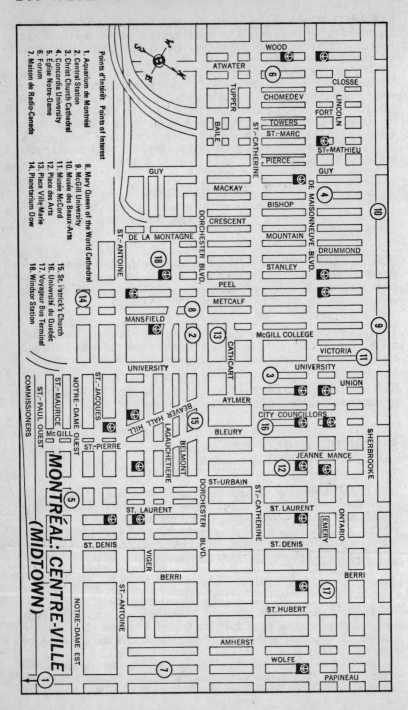

MONTRÉAL: CENTRE-VILLE (MIDTOWN)

Points d'Intérêt Points of Interest

1. Aquarium de Montréal
2. Central Station
3. Christ Church Cathedral
4. Concordia University
5. Église Notre-Dame
6. Forum
7. Maison de Radio-Canada

8. Mary Queen of the World Cathedral
9. McGill University
10. Musée des Beaux-Arts
11. Musée McCord
12. Place des Arts
13. Place Ville-Marie
14. Planetarium Dow

15. St. Patrick's Church
16. Université du Québec
17. Voyageur Bus Terminal
18. Windsor Station

from noon to 3 p.m. and a buffet dinner for $23 from 6 to 9 p.m. Call 861-3511 for reservations.) You'll clearly see from the views at the top that Montréal is a collection of islands surrounded by the St. Lawrence and its tributaries.

Downtown Montréal is just south of Mount Royal, an area that was, a century ago, divided into the English-speaking western half centered on Dominion Square, and the French-speaking eastern part around the Université de Québec and Rue St. Denis. Vestiges of the division still remain, even though the language barrier is long gone. For all its size, Montréal has a fairly logical street grid with wide boundaries such as St. Catherine Street, the major commercial thoroughfare.

The historic part of the city, **Old Montréal** *(Vieux Montréal)* is down by the seaport on the river. Though once neglected, it is now protected as an historic area.

INFORMATION AND REFERRAL: One organization that will be helpful in answering any special questions or helping you find the answers is the **Paraplegic Association of Québec,** 4545 Queen Mary Rd., H3W 1W4 (tel. 514/344-3890).

4. Where to Stay

Montréal has a lot of hotels that were built for the 1967 World's Fair and for the 1976 Olympics, and except for July and August, there is usually no problem with finding accommodations. The only problem is that there aren't too many with good access. The ones with features that make them suitable for disabled guests are, as usual, in the upper bracket. One consolation in Montréal is that the government has withdrawn its room tax. There *are* ways to stay at the upper bracket hotels at rates that are less than those that are cited: on Friday, Saturday, and Sunday nights nearly all the luxury hotels offer special weekend rates, sometimes as much as 50 percent lower than weekday rates. There are often other bonuses as well. It's always worthwhile to check the "specials," and always inquire about any other breaks the hotels might be offering at the time you plan to visit. The *prices here are quoted in Canadian dollars.*

UPPER BRACKET: The **Hyatt Regency Montréal,** 777 University St., Montréal, PQ H3C 3Z7 (tel. 514/879-1370; toll free in the U.S. 800/288-9000, in Canada 800/268-7530) has two rooms with special features located near the elevator. The doors to both guest room and bathroom are 30 inches wide. Entrance is via a ramp at the main door or by elevator from the garage. All the familiar Hyatt trademarks are found here: the glass-walled elevators, the greenery-draped atrium, a revolving rooftop restaurant, and no less than eight other restaurants or bars. Rates for double occupancy are $80 to $120.

Another very modern hotel is **Les Quatre Saisons** ("The Four Seasons"), 1050 Sherbrooke West, PQ H3A 2R6 (tel. 514/284-1110, toll free through Four Seasons reservations), which has two guest rooms with wider doors and grab bars. There is underground parking and a ramp from the entrance to the elevator level. Rooms are spacious, and TV is equipped with remote control, and the luxury is priced accordingly, at rates that range from $115 to $175 (but don't forget to ask about the special package rates).

There's solid comfort in the heart of Montréal at the **Queen Elizabeth Hotel,** 900 Dorchester Blvd. West, PQ H3B 4A5 (tel. 514 861-3511), which has wider doors and considers itself wheelchair-accessible. There is under-

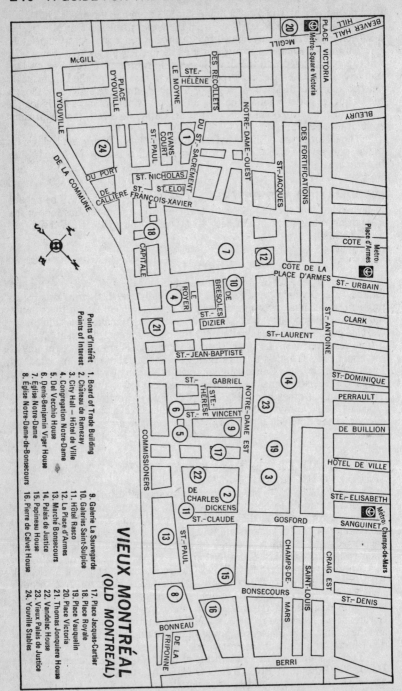

VIEUX MONTRÉAL
(OLD MONTREAL)

Points d'intérêt
Points of Interest

1. Board of Trade Building
2. Château de Ramezay
3. City Hall – Hôtel de Ville
4. Congregation Notre-Dame
5. Del Vecchio House
6. Denis-Benjamin Viger House
7. Église Notre-Dame
8. Église Notre-Dame-de-Bonsecours
9. Galerie La Sauvegarde
10. Galeries Saint-Sulpice
11. Hôtel Rasco
12. La Place d'Armes
13. Marché Bonsecours
14. Palais de Justice
15. Papineau House
16. Pierre de Calvet House
17. Place Jacques-Cartier
18. Place Royale
19. Place Vauquelin
20. Place Victoria
21. Thomas Jonquière House
22. Vandelac House
23. Vieux Palais de Justice
24. Youville Stables

ground parking and an elevator from there to the hotel lobby. The entrance on Dorchester Boulevard is level with the street. Public rest rooms on the mezzanine (reached by elevator) have a 30-inch stall door and grab bars. Restaurant entrances are level, and braille menus are available in each of them. It is in a prime location for downtown sightseeing. Rates range from $80 to $140 single, $104 to $140 double, but there are various discounts in the form of weekend and excursion packages.

Located right atop the city's Place Bonaventure shopping-and-exhibition complex in the center of town, you'll find five special rooms at the **Westin Bonaventure,** 1 Place Bonaventure, P.O. Box 779, H5A 1E4 (tel. 514/878-2232, toll free through Westin Hotels). These rooms are near an elevator and have 29-inch bathroom doors and grab bars. The entrance from the street is ramped, or if you come from the underground garage, there is an elevator to the lobby. The elevator has brailled buttons. The public rest room in the lobby near the restaurant is wheelchair-accessible. There are one or two steps to some of the restaurants, but assistance is available. Rates are $124 to $138 single, $140 to $154 double. There are good special packages.

Montréal's newest luxury hotel has ten rooms designed with wide doors and bathroom grab bars. It is **Le Centre Sheraton,** 1201 Dorchester Blvd., H3B 2L7 (tel. 514/878-2000, toll-free reservations through Sheraton). Some of those rooms have telephones in the bathroom, and amplifying controls are available for all telephones for hearing-impaired guests.

The entrance to underground parking is on Drummond Street, and there is an elevator from here to the lobby. Public rest rooms are wheelchair-accessible. The new Sheraton is in a very central location near Windsor and Central Stations and close to Dominion Square. Restaurant entrances are barrier-free (the Restaurant Le Point de Vue on the 32nd floor has a marvelous view of the St. Lawrence River and of the city). Rates here are $76 to $97 single and $89 to $110 double, with $18 extra for a third person in the same room. Again, look for the special weekend discounts.

The venerable **Ritz Carlton,** 1228 Sherbrooke West, H3G 1H6 (tel. 514/842-4212, toll free through Intercontinental 800/327-0200), has a classic elegance and 27-inch bathroom doors in all the guest rooms, with grab bars in the tub (not at the toilet). Guest-room entrance is 33 inches wide. The entrance to the hotel is level from the street, and there is elevator access to all floors. Rooms are priced at $84 to $97 single, $91 to $113 double.

One of Montréal's striking new architectural complexes is the Complèxe Desjardins, and the **Hotel Meridien** is an integral part of it at 4 Complèxe Desjardins, H5B 1E5 (tel. 514/285-1450, toll free through Air France). It has 11 rooms designed to be accessible to wheelchair guests, and the rest of the hotel is easy to negotiate since all the essential areas are ramped. There is valet parking ($6 a day) at Jeanne Mance Street, and an elevator from there to the lobby. The public rest rooms are wheelchair-accessible with 30-inch-wide stalls and grab bars. The swimming pool here, one of the most attractive in the city, is also accessible, although the changing rooms are not. Access to all the restaurants is barrier-free, and you can easily get to the Complèxe Desjardins from the hotel via a glass-enclosed elevator from the lobby to the various levels of the complex. In addition, the downtown shopping district and Old Montréal are not far away, and Chinatown is in the next block. Rooms are $95 to $115 single, $110 to $135 double.

Although in the luxury class, the prices are more moderate at **Le Park-Regent,** 3625 Avenue du Parc, H2X 3P8 (tel. 514/288-6666, toll free through Regent International Hotels), perhaps because it is not smack in the middle of things, about ten blocks from Dominion Square. In its favor are four rooms designed for disabled guests. Restaurants are accessible. Rates are $80 single, $95 double.

MODERATE: Hotels in this category are mostly chains that have rooms with wider doors and reasonable access from the street and in their interiors. They have the advantage of free parking.

The **Holiday Inn Place Dupuis**, 1415 Rue St. Hubert, H2L 3Y9 (tel. 514/842-4881, toll free through Holiday Inn reservations), is in the heart of traditionally French Montréal. There is indoor parking and rates are $75 single, $90 double.

Near the Place des Arts is the **Holiday Inn Downtown**, 420 Sherbrooke West, H3A 2L9 (tel. 514/842-6111, toll free through Holiday Inn reservations). Rates start at $72 single, $83 double.

Only about three blocks from downtown is the **Ramada Inn Downtown**, 1005 Guy St. (corner of Dorchester Blvd.), H3H 2K4 (tel. 514/866-4611, toll free through Ramada reservations). It has spacious rooms and wheelchair turn-space in the bathrooms. Although the front entrance has steps, the level entrance from the parking lot goes directly to the lobby. You may want to plan to eat elsewhere, since the restaurant off the lobby has six steps at the entrance. Rates start at $59 single, $67 double.

5. Restaurants

It is said that there are 5000 restaurants in Montréal and, with the French passion for good eating, you are going to be able to find pleasurable dining in the city. There's a great variety of cuisines, in addition to French, so you have a wide choice. If you use a wheelchair, you'll find very many of them quite accessible. Here's a guide to some, starting with those considered the city's best (and so, usually the most expensive), but the listing includes the moderately priced and some inexpensive as well.

Outdoor cafes usually provide a great way to have a meal in the summer, and there are a number of them on the Place Jacques Cartier in the Old City that you will enjoy. And it seems that in Montréal's Latin Quarter, on the rue St-Denis between Maisonneuve and Ontario, every restaurant puts out sidewalk tables in the summer. They are always crowded, so for lunch, go early or late. Crescent Street, too, has many outdoor cafes in the summer

The **Café de Paris** (tel. 842-4212), in the Hotel Ritz-Carlton at 1228 Sherbrooke St. West, is among Montréal's top restaurants. Entrance to the hotel is level and the restaurant has no steps from the lobby. Although dinner for two may cost you $75 here, you can have the same fine food at lunch for less. The Café de Paris is open daily for lunch from noon to 3 p.m. and from 6 to 11 p.m. for dinner.

There's classic French cuisine at **Le Saint-Amable,** 188 rue Saint-Amable (tel. 866-3471), in the heart of Old Montréal on the west side of Place Jacques Cartier. Although it's been described as small and cozy, I was told by the owner that people in wheelchairs would have no problem and that there are no steps at the entrance. Luncheon prices are surprisingly moderate; dinner is more expensive. Open for lunch Monday through Friday, and every day for dinner.

For an inexpensive Italian meal in the same area near the Place Jacques Cartier, try **L'Usine de Spaghetti Parisienne**, 273–277 St.-Paul Est (tel. 866-0963). There are two small steps at the entrance but assistance is available.

Prince Arthur Street between St. Louis Square and Boulevard St-Laurent is five blocks full of restaurants of all kinds and all prices, and now a pedestrian mall. One of the popular establishments there is the moderately priced **Restaurant Vespucci**, 124 Prince Arthur Est, at the corner of Bullion (tel. 843-4784). Although it has two small steps at the entrance, there is plenty of room inside its bright, modern interior.

For seafood at moderate prices, there's **Chez Delmo**, 211 rue Notre-Dame Ouest (tel. 849-4061), centrally located near the corner of St. Francis-Xavier. There is one step at the entrance. It's crowded at lunchtime, so either have a reservation or go early. Since it caters mainly to business clientele, it is closed Saturday at noon, all day Sunday, and Monday evenings.

Of course, there are inexpensive places to eat all over town, but even the lowly hamburger or a luncheon plate special, even a sandwich, gets the French touch. Beer is the prime reason for the existence of Montréal's brasseries, but the food that accompanies it usually provides good eating at a reasonable price. One with an un-French name is the **Old Munich**, 1170 rue St. Denis at the corner of Dorchester (tel. 288-8011), which is a traditional beer hall decorated Bavarian-style. There is one step at the entrance.

Delis are good places to have a filling, inexpensive meal or sandwich, and **Ben's Delicatessen and Restaurant** is conveniently located right next to the Sheraton Mount Royal Hotel at 990 Maisonneuve (tel. 844-1000). It's open every day, *almost* all the time.

6. Sights

Finding the sites of the sights is relatively simple in Montréal since, despite its size, it has a fairly logical grid system of streets with wide traversing boulevards. If you want to get your bearings from the top, you can get a good idea of the layout from the heights of Mount Royal or from the top of one of the skyscraper hotels.

OLD MONTRÉAL (Vieux Montréal): Do try and make a visit here, even though some of the streets are cobblestoned and it is hilly in part; perhaps drive through by car. Montréal's long and colorful history is preserved in the old city's ancient walls and streets and is alive today in its picturesque churches and houses. In the **Place d'Armes** you'll see a statue of Sieur de Maisonneuve, who established the settlement in 1642. It is on the spot where he defeated the Iroquois in a bloody fight to hold the ground. In the **Place Jacques Cartier,** one of the city's most enchanting squares, there are outdoor cafes, street musicians, and flower sellers, creating a lively activity.

Just across from City Hall in rue Notre-Dame is the **Chateau de Ramezay** (tel. 861-7182), built by Gov. Claude de Ramezay in 1705 and the home of French royal governors before being taken over by the English and used for the same purpose. It became a museum nearly 100 years ago and now has exhibits of old coins, furnishings, tools, and other objects from early Québec. It is accessible by using the main entrance for the main floor and the rear driveway for the lower level, via portable ramps. There is a wheelchair-accessible rest room in the basement (using the rear entrance to the building). There are special facilities here for hearing-impaired visitors. Open Tuesday through Sunday from 10 a.m. to 4 p.m.

From here along rue Notre-Dame you are at the top of the Place Jacques Cartier which slopes down to the **Vieux Port ("Old Port"),** a federal park with stage shows, an open-air theater, artists' booths, and an outdoor cafe. It is open from late June to early September from 11 a.m. to 11:30 p.m.

Down here toward the river at 401 Bonsecours St. is **Calvet House,** built in 1725 and recently restored as a museum to show a house of that period inhabited by a relatively wealthy family. It is not accessible for wheelchairs, but it does have special facilities for hearing- and sight-impaired visitors. Open from noon to 4:45 p.m. Tuesday through Sunday. Admission is free.

North on Bonsecours to rue Notre-Dame and six blocks left to the Place d'Armes you will come to the magnificent **Notre-Dame Church** built in 1829. It has a main entrance that is ramped but wheelchairs may need some assistance. The interior is noted for its architecture and decoration. Montréal's oldest stone walls, dating from the 1650s, are next door to Notre-Dame Church.

There are many other interesting places to be seen from the outside as you wander around, and they carry markers in explanation of their significance.

MODERN MONTRÉAL: Much of the look of modern Montréal downtown comes from the last 30 years or so, and its most ambitious building projects date even more recently from Expo 67 (the 1967 World's Fair) and the 1976 Olympics.

Downtown

Dominion Square, the center of so-called "West" Montréal when it was the center of the English section of the city, goes back to the Victorian era. If you can get into one of the great horse carriages, this is where they start the tour of the city. If you are touring on your own, you can go east along Dorchester Boulevard, the city's broadest downtown thoroughfare. Across from the Queen Elizabeth Hotel is the Place Ville-Marie (called just PVM by Montréalers). The cross-shaped skyscraper designed by I. M. Pei (and the square's name) recalls the cross planted by Cartier to claim the island of Montréal for France. There is a shopping promenade on the street level (a ramp at the entrance on University Street) and a number of accessible restaurants. There is also a Tourist Information Office at the eastern end of the complex.

Left on University Street and two blocks to rue Ste-Catherine, you'll come to **Christ Church Cathedral,** a Gothic building that is the seat of the Anglican bishop. The entrance is ramped.

Another left on Ste-Catherine will take you through the center of Montréal's shopping and entertainment district, where you'll find the large department stores. Near the corner of Crescent and Sherbrooke Streets is the **Musée des Beaux-Arts** (Museum of Fine Arts), 3410 Avenue du Musée (tel. 285-1600), Montréal's most extensive collection of art works, representative of Western art from ancient times to the present, as well as pre-Columbian statuary, Islamic art work, and African masks. Open from Tuesday through Sunday from 11 a.m. to 5 p.m. The entrance is ramped, and there are special facilities for visitors with sight or hearing impairments. There are many elegant antique shops, grouped near the museum and along Sherbrooke, which, if you go still further east, will bring you to the campus of **McGill University,** one of Canada's prestigious academic institutions. It has an attractive campus that stretches to the lower slopes of Mount Royal.

Place des Arts

This is part of the "new" Montréal that began to grow after World War II, and the Place des Arts, 175 Ste. Catherine West (tel. 842-2112), is a complex of handsome buildings for opera, concerts, and ballet, with two concert halls and one theater, constructed in the 1960s. Offerings are in French, and you can get a schedule of performances from the tourist office or from your hotel. There are wheelchair locations at the rear of the auditoriums and the best access is via the underground concourse (entrance on Maisonneuve Boulevard). The complex also has facilities for patrons with hearing or visual impairments.

MONTRÉAL UNDERGROUND CITY

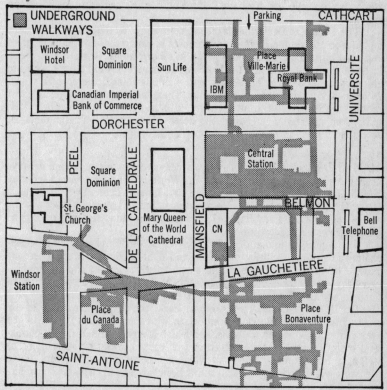

The Underground City

The major building complexes, such as Place des Arts, Place Ville-Marie, Place Bonaventure, and Complèxe Desjardins, have several underground levels connected to each other. Although the longer distances are designed to be covered by the Métro subway (*not* accessible to wheelchairs), there are many parts of it that can be explored without the Métro. Down there you'll find an underground city of hotels, restaurants, movie theaters, concert halls, shops, and even swimming pools. Each complex defines its own spatial levels, and though this may seem confusing at first, there are directional signs everywhere.

Where you begin your explorations underground doesn't really matter, but sooner or later you should see **Place Bonaventure** (Mansfield and LaGauchetière, where there is the Hotel Bonaventure, a swimming pool open to the sky, and Montréal's largest exhibition hall, and an international shopping area called Le Viaduc. There are also movies, restaurants, cafes, and nightclubs here. If you go there directly by car, there is parking underground and special spaces on odd-numbered levels and elevator access to other levels. If you are not going by car, take the Mansfield entrance below LaGauchetière, where there is an attendant. You should contact the information desk on the main level for elevator access to the Exhibition Hall and the Viaduc shopping level. There is a wheelchair-accessible rest room at the main level in Area A. In Cinema I (tel. 861-2725), there are locations for ten wheelchairs. From the Place Bonaventure, you can also take the elevator up to the Queen Elizabeth Hotel, or continue the stroll to Place Ville-Marie's underground shopping arcades.

The **Complèxe Desjardins** is the most striking of all the city's ultramodern building complexes, an exciting environment of waterfalls and fountains, trees and even birds. Lanes and shops go off in all directions. Beneath are several levels of parking garage, and the Hotel Meridien and four tall office towers are also part of the complex. There's always something going on here, and it's open 24 hours a day, with easy access all over. There is a wheelchair-accessible rest room at the St. Urbain entrance, which is also the preferred entrance for access to the complex, if you enter from the street. There are lots of restaurants, all accessible.

MAN AND HIS WORLD:
There are gardens and a couple of pavilions always open, but as we go to press, Man and His World is being reorganized and may be fully open for the 1984 season from mid-June to Labor Day. St. Helen's Island (Ile Ste. Hélène) and Ile Notre-Dame in the St. Lawrence River was the site of the World's Fair, Expo 67, and many pavilions still remain on the grounds, which are always open.

The **Aquarium** in the Alcan Pavilion (tel. 872-4656) is accessible to wheelchairs and also has facilities for hearing and sight-impaired visitors. There are exhibits here of marine fauna and flora and a performance by trained dolphins every day in May through September from 10 a.m. to 10 p.m., Tuesday through Sunday, and in the winter from 10 a.m. to 5 p.m.

On Ile Notre-Dame, too, is **Floral Park,** the spectacular legacy of the recent International Floral Exposition, to which many nations contributed their particular horticultural style, and which is now maintained on a permanent basis. There are hard-surfaced or well-packed gravel pathways here, as well as a mini-train that tours *and* which is accessible to wheelchairs. There are two pavilions on the grounds, with wheelchair access, that stage changing international exhibits each season.

The setting provides a panoramic view, as well, of the port of Montréal and the downtown area.

If Man and His World is fully open by the time you visit Montréal, check on admission prices, pavilion accessibility, and accessible rest rooms and any special parking facilities. Call 514/872-6220 for information. There will be an overall admission fee to the pavilions, so make sure they will be available to you before buying a ticket, which also admits you to La Ronde Amusement Park.

If you want to take a look at **La Ronde,** the amusement park with rides and restaurants on St. Helen's Island, there is a wheelchair entrance at the main turnstile. It is mostly accessible, with gravel and concrete paths.

MOUNT ROYAL PARK:
Montréal may be the only city to have a mountain right in the middle of the city and to have a public park all over that mountain.

Obviously, climbing is not an activity for anybody with a mobility impairment, but fortunately Mont Réal can be climbed by car via Remembrance Road on the west and Camillien Houde Parkway on the east, spiraling up to a parking lot and the Chalet Lookout, directly off Remembrance Road, which provides a spectacular view of the downtown area, the St. Lawrence River, and South Shore mountains.

An alternative to going directly to the top is to enter the Park from Peel or Drummond Streets and take the road to Beaver Lake (Lac aux Castors), a manmade pond and pavilion where you can park at the rest area (there's a "special" space at the front entrance) and enter the pavilion by ramp, with another ramp to the restaurant on the second level. There is a wheelchair-accessible rest room on the lower level (get the key from the attendant).

ST. LAWRENCE SEAWAY: The remarkable feat of the seaway that finally gave mid-America access to the ocean in 1959 and created a highway along which ocean-going vessels could go inland to the Great Lakes 2000 miles from the Atlantic, can be seen in operation at the St. Lambert Lock (tel. 672-4110). Drive across Victoria Bridge to the observation platform (wheelchair-accessible), where scale models and displays explain the operation of the huge dock. There are facilities here for visitors with hearing impairments. It is open from May through October from 8:30 a.m. to sunset.

THE BOTANICAL GARDENS (Jardin Botanique): On the eastern tip of Montréal Island, and one of the largest public gardens in the world, Montréal's Botanical Gardens at 4104 Sherbrooke East (tel. 252-1171) has 30 outdoor gardens and nine exhibition greenhouses, all of which have level or ramped access. Pathways are slate and concrete with wide aisles and double-width doors. There are major seasonal exhibitions in October, December, and March, and it is open from sunrise to sunset. Admission is free. The Botanical Gardens has special facilities for visitors with sight or hearing impairments. There are steps into the cafeteria.

ST. JOSEPH'S ORATORY: The great dome of St. Joseph's Oratory at 3800 Queen Mary St. (tel. 733-8211) has towered over the Westmount area of Montréal since its completion in 1960 and, although it is a Roman Catholic pilgrimage site, this impressive shrine can be appreciated by everybody for its imposing architecture and interior. Access is by ramp. It is open daily from 8 a.m. to 10 p.m., and the museum is open from 10 a.m. to 5 p.m. There is a free organ concert on Sunday at 3:30 p.m.

DOW PLANETARIUM: Right downtown only two blocks from Windsor Station, the Planetarium, on Chaboillez Square at 1000 St. Jacques St. West (tel. 872-4530), is wheelchair-accessible and provides special facilities for visitors with hearing or sight impairments. The 55-minute show here changes themes every eight to ten weeks, and English and French presentations alternate several times each day. It is closed on Monday. Admission for adults is $2.50; half price for children and seniors.

RADIO CANADA HOUSE: You can take a free guided tour (in both French and English) of the huge complex of multiple radio and television studios at Maison de Radio-Canada (Radio Canada House), at 1400 Dorchester East (tel.

285-2690), which is wheelchair-accessible and has special facilities for hearing- and sight-impaired visitors. Tours are held Monday through Friday from 9 to 11 a.m. and from 1 to 4 p.m.

RIVER CRUISES: Have a skyline view of the city from the water by taking one of the boats operated by **Montréal Harbor Cruises** (tel. 842-3871) that tour the harbor and the St. Lawrence. The M/V *Miss Olympia* has a boarding ramp and a crew very willing to assist. The M/V *Concordia* has more steps, but again there is a portable ramp and plenty of assistance. Deck space is good once you're on board. The trips last 1½ hours and depart at 2 and 4 p.m. from mid-May to mid-June and during the last three weeks of September. Fare is $6 for adults and $3 for children. Both boats leave from Victoria Pier at the foot of rue Berri in Old Montréal. There is free parking at the dock.

Chapter 14

TORONTO

"People City"

1. Getting There
2. Getting Around
3. Orientation 4. Hotels
5. Restaurants 6. Sights
7. Entertainment & Nightlife

WHEN I FIRST VISITED TORONTO in the late 1950s, it didn't seem too different from one of the rather dreary provincial cities in England where I grew up. When I returned a few years later, it was unrecognizable. A metamorphosis was taking place, giving it a look and an atmosphere of almost a fictional model city (where, among many other amenities, public telephones work, where parks have "Please walk on the grass" signs, and where you don't have to keep an eye on your wallet every minute of the day).

It had kept the best of the past, built for the future, and created a city that's a positive pleasure to live in and visit. Its cleanliness surpasses any Swiss town, but it hasn't traded excitement for hygiene.

Thanks to the influx of European immigrants after World War II who put a little élan into the more sedate ways of the original Anglo-Saxon inhabitants, Toronto is now an exciting cosmopolitan city.

Because so much of the construction has been done in recent years, the awareness of the needs of disabled people—the elimination of architectural barriers wherever possible and the provision of facilities for people with hearing and sight impairments—is relatively high.

The lakefront area has been restored and offers pleasant strolling as well as a trip in a glass-fronted elevator up the world's tallest free-standing structure, the CN Tower, and there's a whole entertainment complex at Harbourfront. Ontario Place is another waterfront spot for entertainment. There's impressive shopping and dining as well as theater and music. All of it is available to the disabled visitor.

One discouraging note: all this new construction came just a little too late for the public transportation system to be made accessible—especially the clean and efficient subway of which Toronto is so proud. Opened for the World's Fair in 1967, it has only steps and escalators for access. Buses are not wheelchair-accessible either.

In the lack of accessible public transportation, however, Toronto is not so different from a host of other big cities. In *other* things, there's a lot that will open your eyes and which you can particularly enjoy if you are from another big city, or from anywhere else for that matter.

For tourist information in advance of your visit, write to the **Convention and Tourist Bureau,** Eaton Centre, Suite 110, Box 510, 220 Yonge St., Toronto, ON M5B 2H1 (tel. 416/979-3143, or call the Ontario Tourist Office, if there is one in your city. When you arrive, you'll also find tourist information booths in a number of locations including City Hall, outside Eaton Center and at the corner of Bloor and Yonge Sts.

An accessibility guidebook, "Toronto with Ease," was published in 1980 and is available from the March of Dimes, 90 Thorncliff Park Dr., ON M4H 1M5.

"An Ontario Travel Guide for the Disabled" includes information on Toronto. It is available from the Ministry of Tourism and Recreation, Province of Ontario, Queen's Park, ON M7A 2E1.

INFORMATION AND REFERRAL: Among organizations which will either try to answer your questions or direct you to someone who can, are the **Easter Seal Society of Ontario,** 350 Rumsey Rd., M4G 3V9 (tel. 416/425-6220); the **Canadian Paraplegic Association,** 520 Sutherland Dr., M4G 1R8 (tel. 416/422-5640); and the **Community Information Centre,** 34 King St., East (tel. 416/863-0505).

1. Getting There

Like any other large city today, Toronto is the hub of many transportation networks.

BY AIR: The major North American airlines that serve Toronto include **Air Canada, USAir,** American Airlines, CP Air, and Eastern Airlines, and they all arrive at the **International Airport** about 17 miles from downtown, as do flights from overseas. Your airline will have made arrangements for you to deplane and will provide you with an escort to baggage, customs, or the exit (see the air travel section in Chapter 2). The efficient and multilingual **Transport Canada Information Centers** (tel. 416/676-3506) can provide answers to most questions. Elevators serve all floors (except the roof parking), and there are wheelchair-accessible elevators, signed with the international access symbol, throughout the terminals. Each bank of telephones includes one that is lower and has amplifying controls.

For transportation downtown, there is the usual choice between an airport bus service (not wheelchair-accessible) and a taxi or a wheelchair-lift van if you have made arrangements in advance. Among the private companies that provide this service is **PHIACS** (tel. 416/663-5544) and **Bay View Transportation** (tel. 416/229-4045). Some first-class hotels also run their own limousine services, so make inquiries when you make your reservations.

BY TRAIN: Union Station on Front Street is the terminus for Canadian National (VIA) passenger trains (tel. 416/366-8411 for information). Arrangements must be made in advance for boarding and detraining wheelchair passengers by special lift (there is a weight limit of 350 lbs. and VIA does not accept motorized wheelchairs). In most VIA trains, passengers must transfer to a seat,

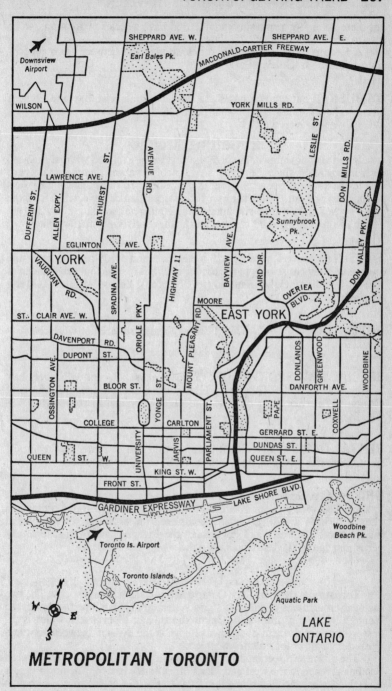

METROPOLITAN TORONTO

but there are a few new trains running that have wheelchair locations, so be sure to ask for the schedule on those.

A Redcap escort will arrange for elevator service between the main concourse and the track level.

BY BUS: All out-of-town buses use the bus terminal at Bay and Dundas Streets. There is one step at the entrance. No accessible rest rooms.

2. Getting Around

If you stay downtown, much of the city can be explored without the need for transportation, since the terrain is reasonably level and there are many curb cuts in the downtown area. A lot of it can be done on subterranean walkways (if you need protection from the rain, for instance), which are reached from the street by elevators in high-rise hotels and commercial buildings. You can get a map of the underground connections at the tourist information offices.

TAXIS: Taxi charges have a $1.20 meter-drop and a 60¢-per-kilometer rate after that. They cruise only in the central downtown areas, but cab companies that can be called include **Diamond** (tel. 366-6868), **Yellow** (tel. 363-4141) and **Metro** (tel. 363-5611).

PUBLIC TRANSPORTATION: Subway and buses are not wheelchair-accessible.

SPECIAL TRANSPORTATION: Companies that run vans with wheelchair lifts include **PHIACS** (Physically Handicapped Independent Advancement Community Services) (tel. 663-5544) and **Bay View Transportation** (tel. 229-4045).

RENTAL CARS: Cars with left-hand controls can be rented at the airport from Hertz (tel. 800/654-3001 from the US) on 48 hours notice.

DRIVING: Parking costs are, as in most other places, quite high. City-owned lots, marked with a green P, are a little cheaper. Toronto traffic ordinances allow a turn on a red light after a complete stop, except at certain marked intersections. The wearing of seat belts by the driver and any front-seat passenger is mandatory. Pedestrians have right of way at crosswalks.

3. Orientation

Toronto sits right on Lake Ontario and is Canada's largest city. The two major thoroughfares of Toronto's grid system are Yonge Street (pronounced Young), which runs from Lake Ontario north, and Bloor Street, which is the east-west artery through downtown. Yonge is the division between East and West designations for crosstown streets.

The downtown section is very large and usually refers to an area between Spadina Avenue in the west and Jarvis Street in the east; on the north it goes a few blocks beyond Bloor, and it extends to the lake on the south. Although many of the city's attractions are within this area, Toronto is a very spread-out

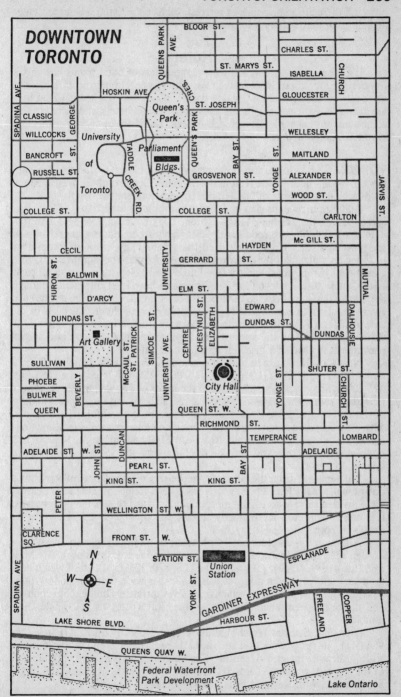

city, and there are some points of interest, such as the Ontario Science Center and the zoo, that require a longer trip.

4. Hotels

It's the same old story, sad to say: thousands of hotel rooms but only a few designed for guests in wheelchairs or with physical impairments. However, since all you usually need is just *one* room, let's look at the hotels where they are available. As usual, they are in the upper-bracket hotels, and there are also some standard chain motels included. Prices quoted are as of this writing and *are in Canadian dollars.*

TOP BRACKET: In the area of downtown that is closest to the lake, possibilities are the Harbour Castle Hilton, the Sheraton Centre and the Westin Hotel, all of which have "special" accommodations. Here are the details:

Adding a marvelous view of Toronto harbor to its other assets of luxurious surroundings, the **Harbour Castle Hilton,** 1 Harbour Sq., ON M5J 1A6 (tel. 416/869-1600), has two rooms with 33-inch bathroom doors and grab bars at the toilet and bath. If you don't need the extra facilities, the bathroom door is 26 inches wide in all the other regular guest rooms. The entrance off Queen Quay West is ramped; there is a level interior and elevator access to all parts of the hotel. Restaurants on the main floor also have level entrances, although there are a few steps between the different levels inside each of the restaurants. Every guest room has a view of Toronto Bay, a telephone extension in the bathroom, and TV control at bedside. Rates are from $99 single and from $119 double, depending on the floor (higher is more expensive). Look into special packages that provide a discount on the room rate.

Near City Hall in the center of downtown, the **Westin Hotel,** 145 Richmond St. West, ON M5H 3M6 (tel. 416/869-3456, toll free in the U.S. 800/228-3000), has given some attention to the needs of disabled guests. There are four guest rooms that have wide doors and grab bars, and ramp access to parts of the hotel (in addition to elevators, of course!). It's comfortably luxurious, with easy access to restaurants where braille menus are available. Public rest rooms are wheelchair-accessible. Rates are $110 and up single, $130 and up double. Weekend packages provide double rooms for $54 a night, single or double occupancy.

Further away from the lakefront, in the area of Bloor, but still very much downtown, are the Park Plaza, which has special rooms, and the Four Seasons Hotel, with adequate access but no specially designed rooms, included because it is one of Toronto's more quietly elegant and personal hotels. Here are the details of both:

Although it is an older hotel with an air of traditional graciousness, there *are* ten special rooms at the **Park Plaza,** 4 Avenue Rd. (at Bloor), ON M5R 2E8 (tel. 416/924-5471, toll free in the U.S. 800/323-7500), all of which have grab bars and bathroom doors at least 28 inches wide. There is underground parking adjacent to the hotel, which has a level entrance. Dining room, lounges, and coffee shop entrances are barrier-free. Rates start at $80 single, $105 double.

The **Four Seasons Hotel** is at 21 Avenue Rd., ON M5R 2G1 (tel. 416/964-0411), its entrance is level and the bathrooms in guest rooms are 26 inches wide. Otherwise no special features. The Four Seasons is home to Truffles, one of the top restaurants in Toronto (level entrance). Rates here are $120 single, $140 double, with weekend packages available.

MEDIUM-PRICE HOTELS: Sheraton Centre is a self-contained community of accommodations, dining, and shopping in the center of things in a convenient location at 123 Queen St. West, ON M5H 2M9 (tel. 416/361-1000, toll free from the U.S. 800/261-9330). It's atop one of Toronto's fascinating subterranean shopping malls with stores and movie theaters reached by elevator from the hotel. There's an underground garage (around $6 a day) at City Hall connected to this subterranean network, and the special parking spaces here are on the first level down. The door nearby is level with the lower concourse of the hotel, from where there is an elevator to the lobby. Rooms with wider doors and grab bars are available at the Sheraton Centre (regular rooms have 27-inch bathroom doors). Nearly all of the nine restaurants have barrier-free entrances. Rates are $55 to $70 single and $70 to $85 double; the special weekend packages are worth looking into.

Out at the airport, the **Airport Hilton,** 5875 Airport Rd., Mississauga, ON L4V 1N1 (tel. 416/677-9900), has two special rooms that have 32-inch doors. There are grab bars in the bath, but not at the toilet. There is level access at the main entrance and also to the restaurants (where braille menus are available). Rates run from $69 single, from $81 double, and children can stay free in the same room. Two nights accommodation in the packages brings prices down to $49 per person. Parking is free.

Fifteen minutes from downtown in an easterly direction via the Don Valley Parkway, but close to the Ontario Science Center, is the **Inn on the Park,** 1100 Eglinton Ave. East, Don Mills, ON M3C 1H8 (tel. 416/444-2561), surrounded by parkland on top of a vantage point overlooking the city and providing a lively resort atmosphere. There are some guest rooms here with wider doors and grab bars in the bathrooms. Ramps or level access connect all parts of the hotel, including the indoor and outdoor pools, and a wide variety of other facilities including the dining and entertainment rooms have barrier-free entrances and interiors. Rates start at $76 single, $91 double, and weekend packages are available. Parking is free. Reservations can be made toll free by calling 800/828-1188 in the U.S. (800/462-1150 in New York State).

Another resort hotel in the same area is the **Prince Hotel,** 900 York Mills Rd., Don Mills, ON M3B 3H2 (tel. 416/444-2511, toll free 800/323-7500 in the U.S.), where bathrooms in guest rooms have 27-inch-wide doors but otherwise no special features. However, rooms are oversize and the atmosphere of the 15 acres of grounds is peaceful and relaxed. Rates start at $80 single, $95 double.

MODERATELY PRICED HOTELS: Not *too* many, but here are some with special facilities:

In the downtown area closer to the lake, the **Delta Chelsea Inn,** 33 Gerrard St. West, ON M5G 1Z4 (tel. 416/595-1975), has a level entrance from the street, and three rooms designed for disabled guests. Among the luxury hotel facilities that are accessible are the indoor swimming pool, a whirlpool, and the sauna, as well as the dining room, the coffee shop, and the cocktail lounge. Rates start at $62 single, $72 double, and children under 18 in the same room stay free. There is paid parking in a surface lot across Gerrard Dr. or in an adjacent underground garage (from here there is one step up through doors that lead to the elevator for the hotel lobby).

Right behind City Hall, the **Holiday Inn Downtown,** 89 Chestnut St., ON M5G 1R1 (tel. 416/977-0707), has free parking and two special rooms with 30-inch bathroom doors and grab bars. The entrance is ramped over one step and the elevator serves all floors except the Top of the Inn nightclub. The revolving La Ronde restaurant, with a view and entertainment, is at the top of the building and is accessible by elevator. (An escalator goes from there to the Top of the Inn.) Parking is free. Rates start at $68 single, $85 double, depending on the floor height; children free in the same room.

Other **Holiday Inns** in the Toronto area with similar accommodations and prices are at the **Airport,** 970 Dixon Rd., Rexdale, ON M9W 1J9 (tel. 416/675-7611) and **Yorkdale,** 3450 Dufferin St., M6A 2V1 (tel. 416/789-5161), off Hwy. 401 on the way to the airport.

Because the moderately priced hotels with special accommodations for disabled guests are so few and far between, I'll mention a few without special equipment that have level access and bathroom doors that will accommodate a standard wheelchair. These include the **Windsor Arms,** just off Bloor at 22 St. Thomas St., ON M5S 2B9 (tel. 416/979-2341). Its larger dimensions derive from its era of construction, the 1920s, from which it also gets its ivy-covered walls and paneled interior. Room size varies, so request one with a larger bathroom, as long as it isn't on the first floor, since the elevator doesn't stop there. There is one step at the entrance, and parking is available in a multistory garage one block west at Colonnade off Bloor; valet parking can be arranged in advance. Rates are $55 to $95 single, $65 to $110 double.

Loew's Westbury Hotel, well located at 475 Yonge St., ON M4Y 1X7 (tel. 416/924-0611), has recently been refurbished, and rooms are large, with bathroom doors between 26 and 28 inches wide. Although there are steps at the main entrance (on Wood St.), there is a ramp at the Yonge St. entrance on the side of the building. Restaurants have level access (but there are three steps to the coffee shop). Rates are $54 to $70 single, $66 to $82 double, children under 14 in the same room stay free, and there are special weekend packages. There is underground or adjacent surface parking.

Further out, the **Muir Park Hotel,** at 2900 Yonge St., ON M4N 2J6, just south of Lawrence Avenue (tel. 416/488-1193), is also an older building with larger guest rooms and kitchenettes. Parking is free on an adjacent lot, and there is one step at the entrance. The interior has a ramp over the three steps to the elevator level. Rates are $46 to $56 single, $54 to $64 double. There are also one-bedroom suites (from $76) and two-bedroom suites (from $95).

If you can manage with a 25-inch bathroom door in spacious rooms, there's a better-than-moderate-price hotel at the airport (at the city end of the hotel strip there) called the **Cambridge Motor Hotel,** 600 Dixon Rd., Rexdale, ON M9W 1J1 (tel. 416/249-7671). If you want the 25-inch door, make sure you have rooms in the old wing, since bathroom doors in the new wing are much narrower. Parking is free in the adjacent lot, and there is a ramp over the one step at the entrance to the motel. Although the entrance to the coffee shop is level, there are two steps to the dining room and the cocktail lounge. Rates are from $55 single, $59 double, and weekend packages are available.

5. Restaurants

You would never know that eating out in Toronto can be quite expensive —there are so many restaurants, and most of them keep busy. Part of the amount on your bill, if it's over $6, is a 10 percent sales tax, and if you order imported wine, you will have contributed to the very large tax imposed on foreign wines by the Canadian government. There's also a 10 percent tax on all alcohol.

It is all but impossible to cover the city's restaurants for accessibility in a book of this size, so here are just a few from the very large selection you'll find there. It starts with the haute cuisine and goes on through the delis.

Although they are categorized by price here, you will see reference to the location as well—*downtown* refers approximately to the streets from the waterfront to about College Street; *midtown* is north of College as far as Yonge; and *uptown* beyond that.

All the restaurants previewed have level or ramped entrances unless otherwise noted, and as usual, do not look for wheelchair-accessible rest rooms.

Many of Toronto's fine restaurants are in hotel dining rooms. Here is a selection:

UPPER BRACKET: At the Inn of the Park Hotel, 1100 Eglinton Ave. (tel. 444-2561), and about a 15-minute drive from downtown, the **Cafe de l'Auberge** is famous for elegant French cuisine. The Westbury Hotel, 475 Yonge St. (tel. 924-0611), has **Creighton's** (level entrance on Yonge Street at the side of the hotel). In the Harbour Castle Hilton on the waterfront at 1 Harbour Square, the **Chateauneuf** restaurant is off the lobby. Other hotel dining rooms of some repute include the **Prince Arthur Room** at the Park Plaza, 4 Avenue R. (tel. 924-5471); the **Royal Hunt Room** at the Sutton Place Hotel, 955 Bay St. (tel. 924-9221) (one step at the entrance to the hotel); **Truffles** at the Four Seasons Hotel, 21 Avenue Rd. (tel. 964-0411); and the **Greenery** at Plaza II, 90 Bloor St. (tel. 961-8000).

Downtown, **Barberian's**, 7 Elm St. (tel. 597-0225), is a steakhouse in an original 19th-century building and a traditionally inviting interior. There is said to be room to turn a wheelchair in the men's rest room here. The steak and seafood entrees range from about $12.75 to $16.75. Make reservations—it's a popular place.

Three in midtown: for an Italian restaurant in the luxury class, there's always **La Scala,** 1121 Bay St. (tel. 964-7100), housed in an opulent town house with two steps at the entrance. For continental cuisine in elegant but relaxed surroundings, try **Fenton's,** 12 Gloucester St. (tel. 961-8485). Although it is on a number of different levels separated by steps and a staircase, you can dine in the Front Room on the ground floor in a setting of mahogany fixtures and a working fireplace. The entrance to Fenton's has two steps outside. Reservations are essential to make sure of getting a table in the Front Room. Prices are in the upper bracket.

In the Yorkville section, guess what they serve at **Noodles,** 60 Bloor St. West (tel. 921-3171), with very original decor (in tubular motifs) and original dishes that are quite-inspired Italian. Open at lunchtime, too, when prices are lower. There is a level entrance on Bay St., just north of Bloor.

MODERATE: Downtown, for good but not too expensive seafood, try the **Mermaid,** 724 Bay St. (tel. 597-0077), located just south of Hayter St. (stuffed shrimp, for instance, around $9.75 and a complete lunch for about $7.95). There's more seafood at another popular place, the **Old Fish Market,** 12 Market St. (tel. 363-0334), in a converted warehouse with plenty of room. The fresh fish dinners here are around $5 to $8.

In midtown, a long-established French bistro in the moderate price category, with one step at the entrance, **La Chaumière,** 77 Charles St. East at the corner of Church St. (tel. 922-0500), serves full dinners for $12 to $16.50. Open for dinner only, there are three sets of doors at the entrance, but staff can help with these.

Uptown, French elegance at moderate prices is available at **Antoine's,** 533 Eglinton Ave. West (tel. 483-8161). The entrance is at street level, and staff can help with the series of two doors. Open for dinner only. The reputation for live lobsters at reasonable prices is the attraction at the **Lobster Trap,** 1962 Avenue Rd. north of Lawrence (tel. 787-3211), where there are other fish dishes served as well. There is a ramped entrance. Open for dinner only from 4 p.m.

BUDGET: In the downtown area, even though there *are* two steps to the entrance, it's worth trying to get into **Sai Woo,** 130 Dundas St. West (tel. 977-4988), a very casual Chinese restaurant, for some of the best Cantonese food in Toronto at very low prices. The restaurant is on the second and third floors but there's an elevator. At **Le Papillon,** 106 Front St. east of Jarvis (tel. 363-0838), there are crepes of all kinds served in attractive, candlelit surroundings, most under $5. One step at the entrance. **Shopsy's Delicatessen,** 295 Spadina Ave. (tel. 977-5401), has two steps at the main entrance, but you don't have to go without their traditional thick deli sandwiches or soups, because there's a door with a level entrance they'll open for you, on the north side of the restaurant, to let you into the dining area. The deli itself is up two steps. Down toward the lakefront is the **Old Spaghetti Factory,** 54 The Esplanade (tel. 364-6517), where you can eat your pizza to the accompaniment of a vast theatre organ with built-in sound effects. There is one step at the door and wheelchair-accessible rest rooms on the main floor. **Mr. Green Jeans Emporium and Restaurant** is just that—small stores selling soap, plants, and novelties, and a restaurant featuring sandwiches, hamburgers, and salads. It is at 120 Adelaide St. (tel. 364-7484), and although the front entrance on Lombard Street has steps, there is another door, off Adelaide Street East (which the manager can unlock for you), that has just one step. There is another branch of Mr. Green Jeans in Eaton Centre.

Uptown, at budget prices you can pick from Cantonese, Mandarin or Szechuan at **China House,** 925 Eglinton Ave. West (tel. 781-9122), in attractive surroundings. There is free parking here and an entrance level with the street. Open noon to midnight. **Mount Pleasant Lunch,** 604 Mount Pleasant Rd. (tel. 481-9331), serves dinner, too, and at budget prices compared to many other restaurants, so it's always quite crowded. The menu is continental. Entrance is at street level. Perhaps the only Mexican food in Toronto is served at **Viva Zapata,** 2468 Yonge St. (tel. 489-8482), so that's one reason for its popularity. The other reason is its prices. There is one step at the entrance.

The specialties are Middle Eastern at **Jerusalem,** 955 Eglinton Ave. West, just west of Bathurst (tel. 783-6494). There is a level entrance from the street.

6. Sights

Toronto's development was planned to bring the city back to the people, and it's doing just that. Along with skyscraper office buildings, there's Ontario Place, a futuristic center for pleasure and leisure on the lakefront, the CN Tower (the world's tallest free-standing structure), the Ontario Science Center (spilling down a ravine), and even though the newest complexes like Eaton Centre are huge, the planning has all been done in terms of impact on people— and that includes disabled people. Although the public transportation system is not among the amenities we can use, most of the development in the last decade has kept us in mind.

There's Toronto Past as well as the stunning Toronto Present, and you'll see a lot of references in standard guide books to edifices preserved from the city's history (Old Fort York, Osgoode Hall, Campbell House, Black Creek Pioneer Village, and Casa Loma among them). If you don't find them included here, it's because they aren't easily visited or toured by anybody with mobility difficulties.

CN TOWER: Billed as the tallest (1815 feet) free-standing structure in the world—and moreover, totally accessible—the CN Tower is at 301 Front St. West (tel. 416/360-8500). Top-of-the-tower indoor and outdoor observation decks are reached by glass-walled elevators that run up the outside walls to the seven-level pod, if you want a spot where you can see the whole city, and about a hundred miles beyond on a clear day. There's the world's largest revolving restaurant on one of the levels up there (all can be reached by elevator) where you can have lunch, dinner, or Sunday brunch (tel. 362-5411 for reservations). If you are driving there, follow the accessibility symbol as you come off Lakeshore Boulevard directing you to the entrance off John Street, where there are special spaces available and parking is free. Wheelchair-accessible rest rooms are located up a ramp from the lobby level. The CN Tower is open daily from 9 a.m. to midnight. Admission is $3.50 for adults, $2.75 for children 13 to 17 and seniors, $1.75 for children under three.

ONTARIO PLACE: This centennial project of the Province of Ontario is a mostly outdoor recreational area on the Lake Ontario waterfront, west of downtown, with activities galore, set on 96 acres at 955 Lakeshore Blvd. (tel. 965-7711), and built on or over the lake on three man-made islands. There is parking in adjacent lots, and passengers can be dropped off within 20 feet of the entrance, which has a ramp. The entire area has hard-surfaced paths throughout, and though it is not all flat, it can be negotiated in a wheelchair with some assistance. There's a rather space-age look to Ontario Place which was constructed in 1971, much of which comes from the pods suspended on columns above the lake, and a large geodesic dome that houses the **Cinesphere,** a six-story movie theater showing special films (wheelchair locations here).

The **Forum,** an outdoor amphitheater, has some seating under a canopy; the rest is on grassy slopes where the summer entertainment runs the gamut from classical music to rock. Restaurants and snack bars abound throughout the park, and it has a wheelchair-accessible rest room on East Island. Ontario Place is open from mid-May to mid-September, from 10 a.m. to 1 a.m. Monday to Saturday, and until 10 p.m. on Sunday. Admission is $3.50 for adults and $2 for anybody under 18.

EATON CENTRE: At some point, everybody in Toronto goes to Eaton Centre, one of the most popular single tourist attractions in the city. A mallmaker's dream come true, opened in 1978, it is a modern downtown galleria of 302 stores, restaurants, and boutiques built under one roof and spread over a three-block area in the heart of Toronto—and with no architectural barriers to speak of. It runs from Dundas and Yonge Streets south to Queen Street.

There is a parking arcade at 1 Dundas St. West, adjacent to Eaton Centre, with special parking spaces at 6P. From here you can get into Eaton's department store via elevators on levels 2 or 5. From the street, the best entrance is just south of the Albert Street entrance, where you'll see the access symbol on a large square button that activates the double doors. Although escalators and stairs are the main links for the three shopping levels, there are also elevators to all floors located in the center of the shopping galleries.

The Centre's focus on the north side is the main downtown Eaton's store, and on the south side, connected by a second-story enclosed causeway, is

Simpson's department store. Other establishments are conveniently arranged on the three levels by *price*—budget at the lower level, medium on the second level, and higher-priced appropriately on the highest level. There are also 40 fast-food outlets and 20 sit-down restaurants in the Centre.

Among the variety of shops, boutiques, restaurants, and snack bars, there is also **Cineplex** on the ground floor. It has 21 small theaters with wheelchair locations (take the south entrance from Trinity Square, ring the bell for the attendant to open the doors if you are going directly from the street).

There are wheelchair-accessible rest rooms in Eaton's on floors marked 1 Below, 2 Below, 3, and 6.

Eaton Centre never closes, but most stores shut at 9 p.m., and restaurants and bars close by 1 a.m.

A brochure including a map and shop listings is available from Eaton Centre, Box 511, 220 Yonge St., ON M5B 2H1 (tel. 416/979-3300).

HARBOURFRONT: This waterfront development, a recent project of the federal government, has enabled Toronto to rediscover its waterfront, as many other cities have in recent years. The lakeshore park has been created around the old piers where once only crumbling warehouses and rundown depots stood. These days there's always something happening at Harbourfront. From the foot of York Street, stretching along the harbor west to Bathurst Street, it's an indoor/outdoor recreational complex. Admission is free. The focal point is **York Quay,** the building at 235 Queen's Quay West (tel. 364-5665), where there are specially designated parking spaces in the northeast lot at the corner of York and Queen's Quay West. Best drop-off for passengers is at the loading dock on the northeast side of the building. There is a ramped entrance.

ONTARIO SCIENCE CENTER: Part museum, part fun-fair, the Ontario Science Center is located eastward in the Don Mills area, a few miles from downtown but worth a trip to see the futuristic building in its ravine setting, and to experience the more than 500 hands-on things to do inside. It doesn't matter how old or young you are! In the small theaters there are film shows and demonstrations, and you'll also find a restaurant, a cafeteria, and a bookstore. The address is 770 Don Mills Rd. (tel. 429-4423), and to get there by car, take the Don Valley Parkway and follow the signs from Don Mills Road north. There is a parking lot ($1 fee) adjacent to the Science Center; the best entrance for passenger drop-off is on the lower level front entrance, where a ramp leads to the main level. Elevators service all floors, and all the facilities have level access. Five wheelchair-accessible rest rooms are located on the main level near the entrance, in the lower auditorium area, in the Hall of Space, in the Hall of Transportation and in the Hall of Communication.

The Science Center is open daily from 10 a.m. to 6 p.m. and longer in the summer. It's always crowded, and so earlier is better. Admission is $2 for adults, $1 for students, 50¢ for children under 12, and free for senior citizens.

ART GALLERY: If you are a fan of the sculptor Henry Moore, this is the place to see hundreds of his pieces in the Henry Moore Sculpture Centre at the Art Gallery, 317 Dundas St. West (tel. 361-0414). But as one of Canada's most important fine art museums, the gallery also has collections of Old Masters and of Canadian painters, all exhibited in a beautiful gallery belied by the exterior of the building.

Although there are steps at the main entrance, you'll find an entrance level with the street just below the main entrance. An elevator goes to all floors, and there are wheelchair-accessible rest rooms on the ground floor. There's a restaurant and a cafeteria as well as an auditorium for films, concerts, and lectures that has a wheelchair location. It is open 11 a.m. to 5:30 p.m. on Tuesday, until 9 p.m. on Wednesday and Thursday, and until 5:30 p.m. on Friday, Saturday, and Sunday. Admission is $2 for adults, 75¢ for students, free for children under 12 and seniors. You can find metered parking on the street, underground parking at the "Village by the Grange" shopping complex on McCaul Street.

ROYAL ONTARIO MUSEUM: The recent renovation of the Royal Ontario Museum, Avenue Rd. at Bloor (tel. 978-3692), has not only enabled it to expand its space, but also made the museum totally accessible to wheelchair visitors. The adapted rest room is on the first floor. The ROM, as it is known in Toronto, is noted for its exhibits of Life Sciences and the Ancient World, dinosaurs and Egyptian mummies, as well as extensive Chinese, Middle Eastern, and Classical collections. It's open Monday to Saturday from 10 a.m. to 8 p.m., and on Sunday from 10 a.m. to 6 p.m. Admission is $5.50 for adults, $4 for seniors and students, and $3 for children under 12.

CITY HALL: When did you last see a city hall included in a sightseeing guide? Well, in Toronto it's worth a trip. The exciting building, unique in its daring design, is at 100 Queen St. West, surrounded by Nathan Phillips Square with its flower gardens, fountains, and reflecting pool, and is the scene of much activity at all seasons. The interior is worth seeing, too, and free tours are conducted daily from 10:15 a.m. to 5:15 p.m. (tel. 367-7341 for information).

There's a good view over the city from the observation deck. You can get inside either from the underground parking lot off Queen and Bay Streets (with designated parking spaces for disabled visitors in the first level) via elevator to Nathan Phillips Square, or from the Sheraton Centre through the underground parking lot. Entrance from the square is level. Elevators serve all floors, and there are wheelchair-accessible rest rooms on the ground floor—ask the security guard at the east elevators for the key. The rest room in the cafeteria has a 28-inch stall door and grab bars. Hearing aids are available in the Council Chamber.

THE METROPOLITAN ZOO: Toronto's large zoo has 700 acres of African savannah, Malaysian rain forest, and other exotic climes in indoor habitats and huge free-form pavilions. Not only are the animals accommodated, but so are *all* visitors: Walkways are paved (though some can be a bit hilly), and all the pavilions are ramped. Wheelchairs can go aboard the **Monorail,** from which you can see the animals in their outdoor settings.

There is a special elevator for wheelchairs in the **African Pavilion.** Wheelchair-accessible rest rooms are located throughout the zoo and are well signed with the accessibility symbol.

The zoo (tel. 284-0123) is located in Scarborough, and to get there by car from downtown take the Don Valley Parkway to Hwy. 401 and exit on Meadowdale Road. There is a parking lot on the site ($1 in the summer, free in winter); best drop-off area is at the front entrance. Open daily in winter from 10 a.m. to 4:30 p.m., in summer from 9:30 a.m. until 7 p.m. Admission is $3.50 for adults, $1.50 for seniors and students, $1 for children under 12, and free for children under 5.

EXHIBITION STADIUM: For sports fans, Exhibition Stadium is the home of the Blue Jays baseball team, the Toronto Argonauts football team, and the Toronto Blizzard soccer team. Gate 9 to the south stands is used for games, and there is an elevator from here to wheelchair locations. There are wheelchair-accessible rest rooms throughout the building. (Gate A to the south stand is used for concerts and shows.)

HOCKEY HALL OF FAME: For true ice hockey fans who want to see *the* Stanley Cup (the original) dating from 1893 and other memorabilia of the hockey greats, this is part of Exhibition Place (over the bridge that crosses Lakeshore Boulevard from Ontario Place), grounds of the Canadian National Exhibition that takes place every year for three weeks before Labor Day. Open Tuesday through Sunday from 10 a.m. to 4:30 p.m. in the summer, open until 8 p.m. Tuesday through Sunday, and on Monday from 10 a.m. to 5 p.m. The entrance is ramped at the south end of the building.

7. Entertainment & Nightlife

Today in Toronto you can always see big shows and top performers—Broadway tryouts, hit shows on tour, rock groups, symphony orchestras, ballet companies, and folk singers. And they are there because Toronto has its own local boom in theater, dance, and music. As well as a resident symphony orchestra, a ballet company, and an opera company, there are dozens of small groups performing . . . you name it.

And many of the buildings in which they perform are accessible to people in wheelchairs. The brand new Roy Thomson Hall is equipped for hearing-impaired patrons as well as having wheelchair locations at all levels (and all prices). Check the local newspapers and the many going-out guides to find out what's playing where.

OPERA, BALLET, AND SYMPHONY: The **O'Keefe Centre**, 1 Front St. East (tel. 366-8131, box office tel. 365-9744) is a vast, modern concert hall where you can catch performances by the Canadian Opera Company, the National Ballet of Canada, and some of the world's leading companies on tour. Ticket prices vary according to the performance. Entrance is via a steep-ish ramp at Front Street, or is more level from the parking lot at the Terrace entrance (advance arrangements should be made to enter here). Wheelchair locations are available and, of course, must be requested when buying tickets. Wheelchair-accessible rest rooms are located on the main level.

The Toronto Symphony and the Toronto Mendelssohn Choir have a brand-new home in **Roy Thomson Hall**, King St. West, between Wellington and Simcoe Streets. Opened in September 1982, it is considered a "shining example of accessibility" by a representative of the Canadian Paraplegic Association. Among the amenities are curb cuts, extra space for transferring from cars, threshholds as level as possible, carpets as tightly woven as possible, wheelchair-accessible rest rooms (even larger unisex washrooms for those who need assistance from a companion), lowered drinking fountains and telephones, and amplified telephones.

The best entrance for wheelchair patrons is on the north side of the building at King and Simcoe Streets. Ramps connect the multilevel interior to the elevators. Underground parking can be reached from Wellington Street, and there are special spaces on the upper level near large elevators with indicators that are lowered and also in braille.

In the auditorium there are 28 seats in different price ranges that can be removed so that a wheelchair can take their place. There's also a choice of special seats in the orchestra, mezzanine, and balcony, so you can choose what suits your needs—a swing-arm to make transferring easier, for example. Make sure you specify your special requirements when buying tickets.

For hearing-impaired patrons there's an audio-inductive loop system (special receivers are available at the box office).

THEATER: Toronto has a very active theater in both large and smaller houses. Among the large ones, the **O'Keefe Centre** presents many musicals and other theatrical events in addition to the ballet and opera (see previous section for accessibility details).

Shows from Broadway can be seen at the **Royal Alexandra Theatre,** 260 King St. West (tel. 593-4211), where there is a ramped entrance and in which wheelchairs can be accommodated in four boxes on the main floor. Zip code if you write for tickets in advance—a good idea—is M5V 1H9.

The third large theater in Toronto is the **St. Lawrence Center for the Arts,** 27 Front St. East (tel. 366-7723), where wheelchair locations are available. There are wheelchair-accessible rest rooms at street level in the Town Hall auditorium of the St. Lawrence Center.

One of the city's oldest theatrical institutions is the **Toronto Workshop Productions,** 12 Alexander St. (tel. 925-8640), which presents a season of plays between October and June. Tickets are inexpensive. The best entrance is from the east parking lot to the stage door on the north side of the building, where there is level access to the seating and to the wheelchair locations.

Inexpensive and innovative drama and musicals can be seen at the **Bayview Playhouse,** 1605 Bayview Ave. (tel. 481-6191). The entrance has one step, and there are wheelchair locations in the back of the theater.

FILM: Because it's no ordinary movie theater, you should know about **Cineplex in Eaton Centre** (tel. 593-4535), where there are 21 different theaters, all of which have wheelchair locations. The same movie may be showing at more than one theater at a time, but at different hours, so waiting lines are pretty well eliminated. Best entrance from the street is from Trinity Square; use the south entrance with the special bell beside double doors (there are steps at the north entrance).

JAZZ: Believe it or not, Toronto is a jazz city. And it starts on Saturday afternoons in many hotel lounges and goes on from there. Two places that are reasonably accessible are Bourbon Street and George's Spaghetti House.

As probably the most famous jazz place in Toronto, **Bourbon Street,** 180 Queen St. West (tel. 598-3020), is busy, and there is jazz here every night except Monday from 9 p.m. to 1 a.m. There are a couple of steps to negotiate at the entrance. Minimum is $4 for drinks or a meal in the Italian restaurant adjacent, and no cover (except on Saturday from 3 to 5 p.m. when it is $2).

George's Spaghetti House, at Dundas and Sherbourne (tel. 923-9887), is also a jazz/Italian restaurant combination. There is one step at the entrance.

In the hotels that are accessible, you'll find jazz in the **Chelsea Bun** at the Chelsea Inn, 33 Gerrard St. West on Saturday afternoons, and at **Beaton's** in the Westbury, 475 Yonge St. (tel. 924-0611), where there is a jazz/buffet brunch on Sunday.

Chapter 15

VANCOUVER

Scenery Plus

1. Getting There 2. Getting Around 3. Orientation 4. Where to Stay 5. Restaurants 6. Sights 7. Entertainment 8. Shopping

VANCOUVER IS CRADLED between mountains on one side and ocean on the other, and the vistas that greet you at every turn make it one of the world's great harbor cities. It sits in the southwest corner of British Columbia, just 25 miles from the U.S. border. Canada's third largest city—after Montréal and Toronto—has a relatively balmy climate, some of the country's best restaurants, parks, and greenery, unforgettable views, and a downtown that is reasonably flat.

Public buses are *not* among its accessible amenities, but there is a paratransit system of wheelchair-van transportation, even for visitors if vehicles are available. You can also ride the ferries comfortably in a wheelchair to get your fill of more beautiful views from the harbor.

General tourist information is available from **Tourism British Columbia**, Parliament Buildings, 1117 Wharf St., Victoria, BC V8W 2Z2.

"Access Vancouver" is a pocket-size guide to the architectural access features of hotels, restaurants, museums, parks, pubs, nightclubs, and theaters. It is available for Canadian $1.50 from the Canadian Paraplegic Association, B.C. Division, 780 S.W. Marine Drive, Vancouver, BC V6P 5X7 (tel. 604/324-3611).

The British Columbia Tourism Office offers "B.C.: Travel Guide for the Disabled," with wheelchair access indicated for accommodations and leading attractions. The address is Information Services, Tourism British Columbia, 1117 Wharf St., Victoria, BC V8W 2Z2, or check your local Canadian Tourist Office for availability.

Organizations that can provide information and referral include the **Canadian Paraplegic Association** (see address above); the **Canadian Institute for the Blind,** 350 E. 36th Ave., Vancouver, BC V5W 1C6 (tel. 604/321-2311), and **Western Institute for the Deaf,** 2125 W. 7th Ave., Vancouver, BC V6K 1X9 (tel. 604/736-7391).

1. Getting There

BY AIR: Vancouver International Airport (tel. 604/273-2311) is on Sea Island, a short drive from downtown. It is wheelchair-accessible, including the rest rooms. The usual procedures of boarding and deplaning apply here (see the section on air travel in Chapter 2).

BY TRAIN: If you use a wheelchair, it's unlikely that you'll arrive in Vancouver by train since Canada's VIA rail system is not yet readily accessible. Amtrak service from the U.S. runs only a connecting bus service from Everett, Washington.

However, if you have been able to board either VIA trains or the Amtrak bus, you will arrive at the rail terminal at 1150 Station St. (tel. 604/682-5552), which has a reasonably level interior. Rest rooms are not accessible to wheelchairs.

2. Getting Around

Although many of the residential areas are hilly, downtown is flatter and good for wheeling since it is well provided with curb cuts.

PUBLIC TRANSPORTATION: Public buses are not wheelchair-accessible, but there is a paratransit system for disabled passengers in Vancouver, run by **Pacific Transit** (tel. 873-5247), and they are willing to provide a ride for visitors in wheelchairs if there is a vehicle available.

TAXIS: Taxis are plentiful, but they do not cruise. There are taxi stands at the major hotels, or you can call one of the radio cab companies, which include **Advance** (tel. 876-5555), **Diamond** (tel. 683-2111), and **Yellow** (tel. 681-3311).

RENTAL CAR: There are no rental cars with hand controls available in Vancouver. If you rent a regular car, you'll find driving is fairly disciplined here. Right turns are allowed on red lights.

3. Orientation

Vancouver lies on a narrow peninsula, between Burrard Inlet to the north and the Fraser River to the south, with bridges spanning the waterways, all dominated by the peaks of the Coast Mountains. You are practically in the center of town at the **Visitors Information Bureau,** 800 Robson St. BC V7X 1K8 (tel. 668-2300), which is accessible, and you are also on the main restaurant and shopping street. Robson Street runs westward all the way to Stanley Park and the Pacific Ocean.

Parallel to Robson Street is Georgia Street where there are many of the leading hotels and stores. Toward Burrard Inlet in a northeasterly direction, Gastown and Chinatown are close to the harbor, and nearby is the terminal for the Seabus ferries and Harbor Center.

Southward across the Strait of Georgia is Victoria, the capital of British Columbia, at the southern tip of elongated Vancouver Island.

AREA CODE: Vancouver's telephone area code is 604.

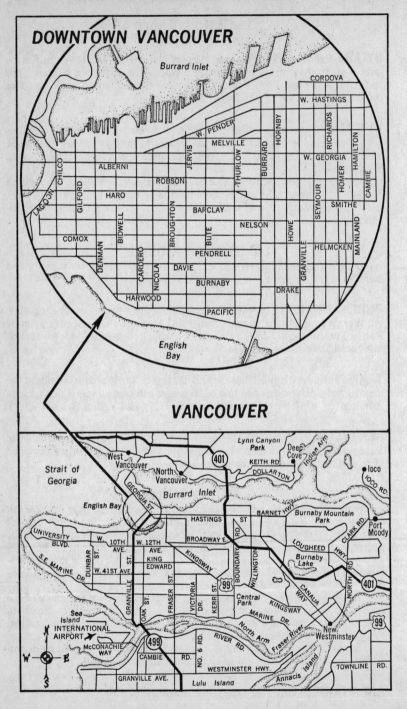

DOWNTOWN VANCOUVER

Burrard Inlet

CORDOVA
W. HASTINGS
W. PENDER
MELVILLE
ALBERNI
ROBSON
HARO
BARCLAY
NELSON
COMOX
PENDRELL
DAVIE
BURNABY
HARWOOD
PACIFIC

CHILCO
GILFORD
LAGOON
DENMAN
BIDWELL
CARDERO
NICOLA
BROUGHTON
BUTE
JERVIS
THURLOW
BURRARD
HORNBY
RICHARDS
HAMILTON
CAMBIE
HOMER
SEYMOUR
HOWE
GRANVILLE
HELMCKEN
MAINLAND
DRAKE
W. GEORGIA
SMITHE

English Bay

VANCOUVER

Strait of Georgia

Lynn Canyon Park
West Vancouver
North Vancouver
Burrard Inlet
English Bay

Deep Cove
Indian Arm
KEITH RD.
DOLLARTON
BARNET HWY.
HASTINGS
BROADWAY E.
loco
IOCO RD.
Port Moody
Burnaby Mountain Park
CLARK RD.

GEORGIA ST.
UNIVERSITY BLVD.
S.E. MARINE DR.
DUNBAR ST.
W. 10TH AVE.
W. 12TH AVE.
KING EDWARD
W. 41ST AVE.
GRANVILLE ST.
OAK ST.
FRASER ST.
VICTORIA DR.
KERR ST.
KINGSWAY
BOUNDARY RD.
WILLINGTON
LOUGHEED HWY.
Burnaby Lake
CANADA WAY
NORTH RD.

401
99
499

Central Park
KINGSWAY
MARINE DR.
New Westminster
Sea Island
INTERNATIONAL AIRPORT
McCONACHIE WAY
CAMBIE
NO. 6 RD.
RIVER RD.
North Arm Fraser River
Annacis Island
TOWNLINE RD.
GRANVILLE AVE.
WESTMINSTER HWY.
Lulu Island

4. Where to Stay

I'm sure you won't be surprised to learn that the hotels with guest rooms designed for disabled visitors are mainly in the upper price bracket, but there *are* some in lower price categories which offer accessible possibilities.

UPPER BRACKET: Among the luxury hotels that have specially designed rooms for disabled guests is the **Four Seasons**, 791 W. Georgia St., BC V6C 2T4 (tel. 604/689-9333, toll free in the U.S. 800/828-8188), designed in the usual luxuriously understated character of the chain. It is located in midtown and is part of the Pacific Center complex. There is underground parking and a level entrance. Elevators service all parts of the hotel and are equipped with braille floor indicators. Although there are three steps up to Le Pavillon restaurant, the staff is very willing to assist; there is an accessible entrance to the Grill. Rates are from $80 to $95 single, $96 to $111 double.

Surprisingly for an older hotel, there are specially designed rooms for disabled guests, too, at the stately landmark **Hotel Vancouver**, 900 W. Georgia St., BC V6C 1P9 (tel. 604/684-3131, toll free outside B.C. 800/268-9275). There is one step at the entrance, but the doorman is very willing to assist. There is a feeling of spaciousness here, and the regular guest rooms all have wide doorways and plenty of room to move about. Public rest rooms are wheelchair-accessible. The hotel houses the Panorama Roof, one of Vancouver's noted nightspots, and it is accessible. Rates go from $65 single, and $85 double.

Although they have no so-called "special" rooms, the Hyatt Regency and the Westin Bayshore Inn have the generously sized rooms and doorways and level access to most of the facilities that are typical of those chains. The **Hyatt Regency** is at 655 Burrard St., BC V6C 2R7 (tel. 604/687-6543, toll free in Canada 800/268-7530). There is parking in an underground lot. The entrance to the hotel lobby is level from the garage; the main entrance has one step (doorman will help). Regular guest rooms have wide doors and access to bathroom facilities is easy, but there are no grab bars. Singles at the Hyatt are $69 to $105, doubles from $84 to $120.

The **Westin Bayshore Inn**, 1601 W. Georgia St., BC V6G 2V4 (tel. 604/682-3377), has a steep-ish ramp at the entrance, but there's always plenty of help available. Guest rooms, with picture windows to take in the great views, have wide doors and plenty of turning space at the sides of the bed. If necessary, the management is willing to remove the door to the bathroom. The Bayshore Inn is right next to Stanley Park and it's also close to the main shopping streets. Trader Vic's restaurant is accessible. Rates start at $72 single, $84 double.

MODERATE: Although the rates are not too far below the luxury hostelries, the **Chateau Granville**, 1100 Granville St., BC V6Z 2B6, (tel. 604/669-7070, toll free in Canada 800/268-8990), is included in the moderate category, because each unit is a whole suite consisting of a living room, bedroom, and bathroom. There are two rooms designed for disabled guests; all the others have wide doorways and good turning space for wheelchairs. There is underground parking, and the hotel has level entrances from both the parking lot and from the street. Restaurants have level entrances. Rates, based on floor level, run from $55 to $65 for singles, $62 to $72 for doubles, and children under 18 stay free in the same room.

Wide doors and good turning space are also available at the **Sheraton-Landmark**, 1400 Robson St., BC V6E 1C5 (tel. 604/687-0511). The entrance is level from the street, and elevators service all 42 floors. All the restaurants, including the revolving rooftop Cloud 9 and the Robsonkeller Pub, are accessible. Rates are $45 to $68 single, $55 to $78 double.

Another moderately priced hotel with wider doors is the comfortable and cared-for **Grosvenor,** 840 Howe St., BC V6Z 1N6 (tel. 604/681-0141). Entrance is level to the hotel lobby and to the restaurants. Rates depend on whether you want extra-long or standard beds and range from $33 to $37 single, $41 to $43 double.

Among the chains downtown in Vancouver that offer special accommodations for disabled guests are the **Vancouver Center TraveLodge,** 1304 Howe St., BC V6Z 1R6 (tel. 604/682-2767), where rates are $45 single, $50 double, and the **Century Plaza Downtown TraveLodge** at 1015 Burrard St., BC V6Z 1Y5 (tel. 604/687-0575, toll free in Canada 800/268-3330, in U.S. 800/255-3050), where rates are $54 to $65 single, $62 to $75 double.

5. Restaurants

Vancouver has thousands of restaurants and almost every type of cuisine. Above all, it has salmon and Alaskan King crab, and you could conceivably eat your way through the day solely on seafood. Only a few restaurants in top and medium-price categories can be included here, but they are ones with reasonable accessibility. As usual, you won't find accessible rest rooms, however. Entrances are level except where noted.

TOP CHOICES: At the top of the Sheraton-Landmark Inn, 1400 Robson St., you can get the view from 42 stories high at the revolving **Cloud 9** (tel. 687-0511). It is open six days a week till 1 a.m., Sunday till 10 p.m.

Looking like a hunting lodge, the **Hungry Pilgrim,** 835 Hornby St., (tel. 688-2255), serves game as its specialty, including Black Forest boar or buffalo steak from Alberta, in addition to other game, all presented as veritable feasts. Open daily.

In the same class, and with the same degree of accessibility, are the **Three Greenhorns,** 1030 Denman St. (tel. 688-8655), where seafood is the specialty, and **Hy's Mansion,** 1523 Davie St. (tel. 683-2251), specializing in roast beef and steaks.

MODERATELY PRICED: Two with German and Austrian accents on Robson Street, a versatile restaurant row, are the **Schnitzel House,** 1060 Robson St. (tel. 682-1210), where you can have a variety of dishes in addition to the specialty for which it is named, and the **Robsonkeller,** 1400 Robson St. (tel. 687-9312), famous both for its food and its jazz. It is open until midnight, closed on Sunday.

In Gastown, the restaurants are almost as prolific, and are open every day. Among them are **Brother Jon's,** 1 Water St. (tel. 685-3285). Although there is one step at the entrance, it's worth negotiating to see the monastery setting, to hear the unmonastic musical accompaniment, and to sample the long menu that emphasizes ribs and steaks. The **Town Pump,** 66 Water St. (tel. 683-6695), has a relaxed pub setting; **La Brasserie de l'Horloge,** 300 Water St. (tel. 685-4835), is very Parisian-looking with menu to match (closed on Sunday), and the **Old Spaghetti Factory,** 53 Water St. (tel. 684-1288), speaks for itself.

In Chinatown, a block away from Gastown, the food is primarily Cantonese in dozens of eating places. A Vancouver innovation, the Chinese smorgasbord, is the specialty of the **Marco Polo** at the corner of Pender and

Columbia Sts. (tel. 682-2875), where it is served in ornate surroundings; and at the **Noodle Makers,** 122 Powell St. (tel. 683-9196), which looks rather like a museum and has a fish pond and soothing Oriental music to eat by.

Gizella's, 775 Burrard St. (tel. 682-4588), has an accessible ground-floor dining room (although there is also one upstairs that isn't). There is one step at the entrance. The menu is an interesting mix of Swiss, German, French, and English dishes. Open all week, but only until 6 p.m. on Sundays.

6. The Sights

Much of your sightseeing in Vancouver downtown can be done by wandering around—there are a lot of pedestrian malls as well as curb cuts. A car or taxi is useful for some of the longer trips.

The regular sightseeing buses are not accessible to passengers who use wheelchairs unless you can be carried aboard. However, if you have a car, there is an auto-tape tour that takes about two hours, available for $10 a day from the Gray Line Desk at the Sheraton-Landmark Hotel, 1400 Robson Street.

All admission prices quoted here are in Canadian dollars.

HARBOUR CENTRE: One of the best views of the city is from the top of one of Vancouver's landmarks, the Harbour Centre at 55 West Hastings St. on the waterfront, where there is an Observation Deck and a revolving restaurant on the 40th floor. Admission to the deck is $1.50 for adults, 75¢ for children, which is deductible from your bill in the restaurant if you eat there. There's also a panoramic audio-visual show here describing the city's past and present, with an admission of $1.50 (children $1). Open all week until 10 p.m.

Nearer the ground at the Centre is the Harbour Mall, which has some 50 shops and restaurants.

GASTOWN: Near the Harbour Centre and within "walking" distance of downtown, is Gastown, a formerly rundown area where Vancouver was originally settled and now one of its major attractions. It's a lively section with restaurants radiating out from Maple Tree Square at its center.

CHINATOWN: Right next to Gastown is Chinatown, one of the largest and most prosperous Chinese communities in North America, a three-block area off West Pender Street, where shopping and eating are the main activities. Sunday brunch at the huge dim sum halls can be fun.

STANLEY PARK: Vancouver has 144 parks, and the most spectacular is Stanley Park, a place where you could spend a whole vacation. Only about a $3 taxi ride from downtown, or a ten-minute "walk," the more-than-1000 acres of gardens, picnic sites, woodland, and beaches start at the foot of West Georgia Street. If you go by car, an eight-mile-long perimeter road offers glorious views of the bay and the mountains beyond. There are forests of Douglas fir here, as well as a zoo, a live theater auditorium, and an aquarium, largest of its kind in Canada.

The aquarium is accessible through the gift shop, and there is a ramp (quite steep) to the underwater viewing area. Rest rooms are accessible. There's a special pool for Beluga whales, and the Marine Mammal Complex stages performances by sportive dolphins. Admission is $3.75 for adults, $1.50 for children.

MUSEUMS: The **University Museum of Anthropology,** 6393 N.W. Marine Drive (tel. 228-3825), has a magnificent collection of art by the Indians of the northwest. Instead of traditional labels for its exhibits, the museum displays are explained by sight-and-sound programs. Its totem poles are impressive. The entrance is level, all the facilities are accessible, and rest rooms have wide doorways. Closed on Monday. Admission is $1.50 for adults, 75¢ for children and seniors.

The **Centennial Museum** and **Planetarium** are at 1110 Chestnut St., and completely accessible. The museum features the story of Vancouver's history and a great many changing exhibitions; admission is $1.50, 75¢ for children.

The planetarium has shows and technological gadgetry on the subject of extraterrestrial sciences. There are wheelchair locations in the auditorium, and wheelchair-accessible rest rooms on the lower level. Admission to the planetarium is $1.50 in the daytime, $2.50 in the evenings. Closed Monday.

EXCURSIONS: One great way to see the **port of Vancouver,** one of the busiest harbors in the world, and its mountain backdrops, is to take one of the B.C. Ferry Corporation's boats that can be boarded by people in wheelchairs. Call 669-1211 for information.

If you have a car, another place to get more great views is by taking the **Marine Drive,** which runs past beaches and the University of British Columbia, lying on the western tip of Vancouver Peninsula.

Also by the car, see the lights come on in Vancouver and as far away as the state of Washington from the top of **Grouse Mountain** on the north shore, by heading north in late afternoon from Stanley Park across Lions Gate Bridge and up Capilano Road. There you can take the cable car to the top—it's accessible to wheelchairs—where there is a restaurant as well as a fantastic view. Call 984-0661 for information.

You can make a day trip by car to **Victoria,** the capital of British Columbia, by taking the ferry to Vancouver Island. It costs $11 per vehicle. Call 386-3431 for ferry information. It's about a 40-minute drive from the ferry terminal to Victoria, which looks exactly like an English seaside resort, with tea shops, antique stores, and even red doubledecker buses. There's practically no industry here, nor high-rise buildings, so you can wander or drive around among the lawns on the oceanfront, the little squares and alleys of Old Town, and find everything spotless. You'll find the **Visitor Information Centre** at 1117 Wharf St. (tel. 387-6417), on the waterfront.

7. Entertainment

For theater or other entertainment with your dining, there are several neighborhoods that are having their particular moment in the limelight.

GRANVILLE ISLAND: One of the most popular nightspot areas is Granville Island, formerly landfill on the waterfront, where once-decaying warehouses and workshops have been transformed into an area of specialty shops, theaters, art galleries, and restaurants. Lots of activity here all the time, and level for wheeling. Get there by car or taxi across the Granville Street Bridge.

GASTOWN: Another entertainment area is Gastown (see more about it in the Sights section). The **Queen Elizabeth Theatre and Playhouse** at 600 Hamilton St. (tel. 683-2311), is a stage complex for opera and the Playhouse Theatre

Company, as well as an auditorium for a long list of local and imported musical, dramatic, and dance performances. Tickets run from $5 to $15. Three wheelchair locations are available in the orchestra section of both the theater and the playhouse.

There is level access, but no specific wheelchair locations, at the **Metro Theatre**, 1370 S.W. Marine Dr. (tel. 266-7191), which presents amateur companies performing in English and French.

Check the daily papers, or the free directory called "Vancouver Guideline," for what's on where.

SPECIAL EVENTS: Folkfest, which takes place on July 1 in Gastown and at the Orpheum Theatre, is a celebration of native costumes and ethnic foods, with dance and choral performances. All events are free.

From late August to Labour Day, it's the **Pacific National Exhibition** at the Exhibition Grounds (accessible), with free indoor and outdoor entertainment.

On weekends in late September and early October comes **Oktoberfest,** also at the Exhibition Grounds, a lively Bavarian celebration of bands and folk dancers, eating and drinking.

8. Shopping

Canada's specialty—the subterranean shopping mall—is very much part of Vancouver's shopping picture, linking large areas of the downtown area.

Biggest is the **Pacific Centre Mall,** 791 W. Georgia St. (tel. 688-7326), which connects with department stores and the Four Seasons Hotel above ground. It also gives direct access to the Vancouver Centre Mall. The entrance is accessible and all floors are connected by elevators. Both malls lie beneath the Granville Mall, which is at street level.

The **Royal Centre Mall** is beneath the Hyatt Regency Hotel (655 Burrard St.), and the **Harbor Centre Mall** lies below Harbour Centre (55 West Hastings St.) on the waterfront, and also makes underground connection to Gastown.

All the malls can be reached by elevator from the buildings above them, and provide a splendid way to enjoy a rainy day.

Part IV

EUROPE

LONDON

Let's All Go Down the Strand!

IF LONDONERS had really thought about it, they might have planned the city's 1941st birthday in 1984. That's by way of saying that it's a very old city that has been thriving (on and off) and growing ever since the Romans founded it. You probably don't need a history lesson, but London's age *is* relevant, in many ways, to a visitor who has a mobility disability. Of course, there isn't much left of that original settlement, but from the time of the Tower of London, (parts of which are nearly a thousand years old) on through the centuries to the Victorian age of ambitious and grandiose buildings, there really wasn't much thought given to wheelchair access! Much of central London architecture dates from the 19th century, and sometimes it seems so do many of its hotels. The London Tourist Board guide book points out that London, which can only just cope with the car, is not an easy city for the wheelchair visitor, and adds that Londoners who use wheelchairs say you have to be determined and resourceful.

Ah, but what compensations!

Congested, desperately short of parking spaces, and offering no public transportation to people who use wheelchairs, London makes up for all that in its landmarks, institutions, neighborhoods, pubs, museums, galleries, theaters, parks, and its people. London is not all history and culture and quiet gardens. Rock groups, discos, nude shows, experimental theater, and way-out dressing for the young generation all exceed other cities in the world. And it's still the only capital city that permits gambling clubs.

London *is* a place for careful planning, advance checking, and an approach that is about as adaptable as you can make it. But the effort will pay off. The city really *is* trying to put out the welcome mat, the ramps, and the helping hands. Theaters are getting induction loops for patrons with hearing aids, museums are making provisions for visually disabled visitors, and new developments, such as the Barbican Centre of the Arts, have been built with disabled people in mind at every stage.

1. A Tourist Survey

CLIMATE AND CLOTHING: Don't expect the fogs that were always an essential part of old thrillers—pollution control has taken care of that—but the control of rain showers is unfortunately not yet achieved. One nice thing about a typical English day is how many times the weather can change—if it's raining, there's always a chance of sunshine later. Temperatures rarely go to heat-wave levels (though the English believe that is around 75 degrees) and rarely go below freezing in the winter. Don't expect too much indoor heat or air conditioning: the English really don't think either is too healthy. Whatever else you pack, the essentials are a raincoat and a sweater; plan your wardrobe in layers so that you can don or doff as the weather demands, even in the course of one day.

There's more formality at the theater and concerts and the better restaurants than you might be used to, since the English like to dress up for occasions, though the younger generation is usually as casual as any all over the world.

CURRENCY: Britain has gone metric, primarily in its currency (you are spared the incomprehensibility of the pounds, shillings, and pence that earlier tourists faced). The current system is based on the pound (£), which is worth, as of this writing, around $1.50 in U.S. currency. The pound consists of 100 new pence, called "p." As I write this, the dollar is strong, so conversion rates are favorable and make English prices seem even more of a bargain. The denominations of pound notes (never called "bills") are distinguished by different colors, and coins are in denominations of ½p (just under 1¢), 1p (just under 2¢), 2p (3¢), 5p (7¢), 10p (15¢), 20p (30¢), and 50p (75¢).

MEDICAL TREATMENT: Make sure you have adequate medical insurance coverage. At one time, Britain's socialized medical system allowed free treatment to everybody, visitors included. That is now history. Overseas visitors must pay a regular fee for doctor or hospital treatment, although treatment at accident or emergency departments of hospitals continues to be free of charge, if the circumstances qualify.

If you need an ambulance in an emergency, dial 999. Nursing services are listed in the telephone directory Yellow Pages.

GUIDE DOGS: Britain has extremely strict anti-rabies laws that require animals, including guide dogs, to spend six months in quarantine.

LANGUAGE: It's obviously no problem, but just a note on a few words and phrases that can cause misunderstandings: "subway" means underground passage, *not* the underground train system; "ring" means making a phone call; "biscuits" are cookies; you "queue up" when you form a line; "walking stick" is better than "cane" (used only to punish schoolboys); a "lavatory," "loo," "convenience" or "WC" is a bathroom or public rest room; and of course "petrol" for gas, "boot" for the "trunk," "bumpers" for "fenders," and "lift" for elevator. Otherwise you shouldn't get into any trouble.

ELECTRICITY: Electrical current in Britain is 220 volts (American standard is 110 volts), so you will need a transformer for electrical equipment you take.

TELEPHONE: The country code for the United Kingdom is 44; the area code for London is 1.

BUS TRAVEL: Long-distance buses are called "coaches" and are a comfortable, fast way to travel around England. They are not equipped with either wheelchair lifts or rest room facilities, but folding wheelchairs can be carried as baggage at no charge, and drivers and terminal staff are willing to assist boarding. If you are nonambulatory, a companion is advised. The British Tourist Authority has a booklet with details and routes.

TRAIN TRAVEL: It's possible to use the British trains for travel from one city to another, especially by making advance arrangements. Generally speaking, you'll find the British Rail staff anxious to be helpful. Platforms at main-line stations are usually level with the train entrance, but baggage handling ramps and routes sometimes have to be used to board you if you are in a wheelchair. Many main line stations also have narrow chairs, similar to the ones used by airlines, to board nonambulatory passengers.

The Inter-City trains have coaches with wide doors and an open-plan layout; on new Mark III first-class coaches, a seat and table can be removed to accommodate a passenger in a standard wheelchair. Inter-City trains operate between London and Scotland, in Northern England, northwest England, South Wales, and the West Country. A list of stations served by these trains is included in "British Railways: a Guide for Disabled People," available from the Royal Association for Disability and Rehabilitation, 25 Mortimer St., London W1N 8AB.

On other trains, travel for a passenger in a wheelchair involves transfer to a regular seat or a ride in the baggage car (called the guard's van). A permit is necessary for this, but it can be obtained by advance planning.

Rest rooms on trains are not wheelchair-accessible, although main-line stations have such facilities.

Advance notice should be given to the area manager of the departure station, giving specific details of your journey and your disability. Discuss what facilities are available for your needs at both departure and destination station, and where you can be met by British Rail staff if advance notice is given.

Fares for train travel (even if you travel in the first-class section) is half the second-class fare. The same concession applies to the companion traveling with a disabled passenger.

USEFUL ADDRESSES AND PUBLICATIONS: The **British Tourist Authority** has many brochures and booklets that carry the wheelchair-accessible symbol in hotel listings. In the U.S.A. offices are located at 40 W. 57th St., New York, NY 10019 (tel. 212/581-4700); John Hancock Center, Suite 3320, 875 N. Michigan Ave., Chicago, IL 60611 (tel. 312/787-0490); 612 S. Flower St.,

Los Angeles, CA 90017 (tel. 213/623-8196); Plaza of the Americas, 750 North Tower, Dallas, TX 75201 (tel. 214/748-2279).

AA Guide for the Disabled Traveler, published by the Automobile Association, Fanum House, Basingstoke, Hampshire, England RG21 2EA ($6 surface mail, $10 air mail), gives access details of hotels and restaurants throughout Britain. *Britain for the Disabled* (free pamphlet) and *London for the Disabled* (book, about $3), both available through the British Tourist Authority (address above). *British Rail and Disabled Travelers,* available from British Tourist offices, or from the British Railways Board, Central Publicity Unit, 22 Marylebone Rd., London NW1 (free). *Who Looks After You at Heathrow Airport* and *Who Looks After You at Gatwick Airport,* both available from Airport Services, British Airport Authority, 2 Buckingham Gate, London SW1E 6JL. *Holidays for the Handicapped* is a brochure outlining organizations offering both group and individual vacation facilities throughout Britain. Available at no charge from the Greater London Association for the Disabled, 1 Thorpe Close, London W10 5X11.

Holidays for the Physically Handicapped is a comprehensive 588-page book listing accessibility features of accommodations of all kinds throughout the British Isles. It costs £1 in England, but write first asking how much to add for postage since it is very heavy. Available from RADAR, 25 Mortimer St., London W1N 8AB (tel. 01/637-5400). **The Royal Association for Disability and Rehabilitation (RADAR)** also has many access guides to individual British cities and towns. Write to them for a listing of their publications.

2. Getting There

Since you'll undoubtedly be arriving by plane, all you'll need to know about getting there are the facilities at the airports and how to get out of them. The two major airports that serve overseas flights are Heathrow in Hounslow, Middlesex, and Gatwick in Horley, Surrey.

Each airline makes its own arrangements for your embarkation and deplaning, and all the major carriers have staff who are knowledgeable about procedures. It is a good idea to discuss with the airline what methods of transport to and from the aircraft will be used and compare arrangements before choosing an airline. You will, of course, have discussed your needs with the flight attendant before the plane lands, and those needs can be communicated to the agent who meets the plane at the arrival gate.

Both airports have 24-hour medical service staffed by qualified nurses, and there are doctors on call in case of an emergency. Services can be contacted through the Airport Information desk or any uniformed employee of British Airports or the airlines.

HEATHROW AIRPORT: Heathrow is so vast and so busy that various methods of people-movers are used, including mobile lounges and minibuses, to get passengers from the planes into the terminal. Jetways are not always available at Heathrow. Whatever the method, airline personnel will make sure you have an escort, and will carry you whenever necessary.

Intercontinental traffic comes into Terminal 3 (except British Airways flights to and from Chicago and Miami, which depart and arrive at Terminal 1). Once inside the terminal you'll get an escort, if you are in a wheelchair, as far as the baggage claim. The airport personnel there will give priority to disabled passengers. These terminal buildings are well equipped with ramps, elevators, and lowered and amplified telephones, and there are plenty of wheelchair-accessible rest rooms, all marked with the international accessibility symbol. But make note that there are none beyond passport control when you are departing. Complete details of the location of all the facilities is clearly diagrammed (to the extent that even right-hand and left-hand transfers in the rest rooms are included) in *Who Looks After You at Heathrow Airport,* available from the Publications Dept., British Airports Authority, 2 Buckingham Gate, London, SW1E 6JL.

Customs facilities are speeded up at British airports by having a section for those with nothing to declare, but passport checking still means that you will have to "queue up" (unless your escort has influence and whisks you through a special gate, as has happened to me on occasions).

Airport Information desks often have staff on duty who are proficient in sign language.

If you are being escorted, you will be finally taken to the place where you are being met, or to the transportation previously arranged, or to the taxis. The usual doubledecker public-transportation buses between Heathrow and central London (Victoria or Paddington Stations) present insuperable problems to somebody in a wheelchair unless your companion is prepared to carry you aboard.

Taxi fare from Heathrow Airport to London in the neighborhood of Hyde Park Corner will be about £10 ($15), depending on traffic conditions, but the correct fare will show on the meter, of course. A larger-than-usual tip is in order if the driver has been especially helpful.

The new Underground connection from the airport to downtown London is not recommended for travelers in wheelchairs: getting on is easy, getting off is a problem since none of the stations in central London is equipped to handle wheelchair passengers.

GATWICK AIRPORT: General guidelines for air travel also apply to Gatwick Airport, which is noted for being one of Europe's most amenable airports for disabled travelers. Ramps, elevators, rest rooms, and public telephones are all designed for easy access by passengers in wheelchairs and are identified by the international symbol of access. Facilities for deaf and hard-of-hearing passengers, identified by the "ear" symbol, include induction loop attachments for public address system announcements and telephones, and staff at the airport information desk who are proficient in signing. Facilities for blind and partially sighted passengers are indicated by a system of directional and location signing comprising a symbol or word display in black on a contrasting yellow background. Essential flight information is broadcast over the public address system in addition to the television displays, and changes in floor level are marked by contrasting floor treatment. There are braille menus in the restaurant and coffee shop on the third floor. The exact location of all these facilities is detailed in *Who Looks After You at Gatwick Airport,* available from the Publications Dept., British Airports Authority, 2 Buckingham Gate, London, SW1E 6JL.

It *is* possible to travel by train from Gatwick Airport to London's centrally located Victoria Station. It takes about 40 minutes, and trains run every 15 minutes. However, since arrangements should be made in advance with the station manager, you or your travel agent should check with your airline to see if these arrangements can be included in your travel plans. You could certainly make the advance arrangements for the return journey to Gatwick from Victoria Station in London by notifying the station manager at Victoria of your intended departure time (tel. 01/928-5151). You will then be met at Gatwick by the airport's rail/air hostess. This journey has to be made in the guard's van (see the train travel information earlier in this chapter), since the trains on this line don't have special wheelchair access.

3. Getting Around London

Good news: most of the London you will want to see is on flat terrain. Bad news: there aren't *too* many ramped curbs (spelled "kerb" in England), and the public transportation system is not available to people in wheelchairs. Even if you can use an escalator, there are Underground (subway) stations that have long flights of stairs as well.

TAXIS: The famous London taxis look spacious and the doors wide, but there is a step up and the seat is toward the rear, so transfer from a wheelchair is not simple. There are jump seats that could be used for intermediate transfer, but they are still quite high up from the ground. Drivers are very helpful. (The official guidebook claims that London taxi drivers "are accustomed to coping with problems of disabled passengers and will lift the disabled person into the taxi," but that probably depends a lot on the burden involved!) Taxi doors are about 24 inches wide, and there is plenty of headroom, so smaller wheelchairs could be accommodated. London taxis have no trunks, but luggage (or wheelchairs) are stowed beside the driver (there is no front passenger seat). If you are at all ambulatory, they are the most comfortable and spacious taxis you will ever ride. They cruise, or can be called at 286-4848, 286-6010, or 272-3030.

For transfers from wheelchairs, it might be better to use the minicabs which are *not* allowed to cruise and must be called by phone. Telephone numbers will be found in the Yellow Pages of the telephone directory. It's important to agree on the fare beforehand, since there is no meter or fare rate in the cab.

You can hire a taxi with a qualified driver-guide for your sightseeing from **Prestige Tours Ltd.** (London Taxi Guides) (tel. 01/584-3118).

Note: Wheelchair-accessible taxis are scheduled, it's said by the British Department of Transport, to be introduced at the end of 1984!

RENTAL CARS, DRIVING, AND PARKING: For the very brave who can adjust to driving on the left-hand side of the road, at the same time tackling the congested traffic and the confusing street layout, to say nothing of all the one-way streets, there are automatic gear-shift cars with hand controls available from **Kennings Ltd.,** 477 Green Lane, Palmers Green, London N.13 (tel. 01/803-1488), who will deliver them to airports or hotels. And **Hertz** (tel. 01/679-1799) will fit hand controls for right-handed use on their Vauxhall Astra rental cars at no extra charge. Reservations should be made at least seven days in advance.

Street parking is restricted all over central London and allowed only at meters during weekdays (Saturday varies according to the district). In outer areas, the broken single or double yellow lines alongside the curb indicate restrictions that are detailed on nearby posts.

GUIDED TOURS: For travel planning and tours of London and England by a guide who has first-hand experience of what is needed for disabled travelers, write to **William Forrester,** 1 Belvedere Close, Guildford, Surrey GU2 6NP (tel. 0483 575401). An Oxford-educated historian, he is the first person in a wheelchair to become a London Tourist Board Registered Guide. His services

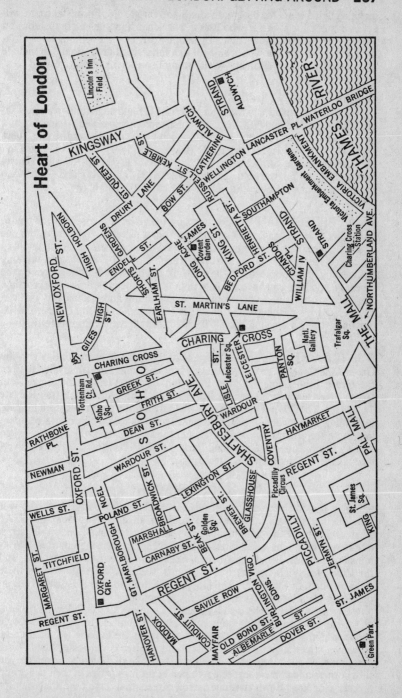

Heart of London

include guided tours for both individuals and for groups. For instance, he will act as a guide for a visitor who uses a wheelchair (and has a companion) on a day's tour of the London sights by taxi, by car, or even without transportation. He can also use a wheelchair-lift van for a small group that can include two passengers in wheelchairs. Write to him for details of services and fees.

Guided Tours by Hired Car

Car-hire companies with larger makes of car and sometimes station wagons (called "estate cars" in England) offer tours for disabled passengers and have drivers who will assist. Among these companies are: **Cavendish Car Tours Ltd.,** 441 Edgware Rd., London W2 (tel. 01/723-6641); **Take-A-Guide Ltd.,** 285 Lower Sloane St., London SW 1 (tel. 01/730-9144); **Relionus Travel Service Ltd.,** 87 Edgware Rd., London W2 (tel. 01/723-2243); and **Globe Cars** (station wagons), 30 Foley St., London W1 (tel. 01/636-6161).

AS A "PEDESTRIAN": When crossing the street it is essential for you to remember that the traffic will be coming from a direction opposite to the one you're used to: it will be coming from the right (except sometimes in one-way streets). Pedestrian crossings are clearly marked. The "Zebra" street crossing has flashing orange beacons on the sidewalk and black-and-white stripes on the roadway, and here you have absolute right of way once you are on the crossing. At "Pelican" crossings, you'll find two lines of studs and traffic lights that can be operated by pushing a button to halt the traffic. At some experimental crossings, there are sound signals to direct people with sight difficulties.

BUS (COACH): You can get to some of the outlying areas for day trips by **Green Line Coaches** (country buses). Maps and timetables are available from the Green Line Enquiry Office, Eccleston Bridge, Victoria, or direct from Green Line Coaches, Lesbourne Rd., Reigate, Surrey RH2 7LE (tel. Reigate 74/42411). Though not accessible to wheelchairs, the coach has storage space for folding wheelchairs, if the passenger can be carried on board by a companion (there are generally two steps to enter the bus). Some of the places you can visit by Green Line are Richmond Park, Windsor, Kew, and the pretty riverside village of Strand-on-the-Green.

4. Orientation

The London you've come to visit is a relatively small area of the vast London that sprawls for miles and miles in all directions from the River Thames. Even the five-mile-square area that is the tourist's London is a series of different boroughs and districts—Mayfair, South Kensington, Soho, Westminster, Holborn, Belgravia, Chelsea, Brompton, Bloomsbury, Barbican, and the City. Nearly all the hotels, restaurants, theaters, and sights are in these districts north of the river. The National Theater and Royal Festival Hall on the South Bank are practically the only exceptions.

Getting the lay of the land is not easy: London's streets follow no pattern, and there is no grid street system of letters and numbers to guide you. Logic and common sense are no good either when you are looking for an address. However, street signs are very legible, and courteous help is available from everybody. A good map goes a long way to make it all come clearer, as you turn corners and come unexpectedly upon beautiful squares in their peace and greenery, or head down twisting narrow streets that have been that way for

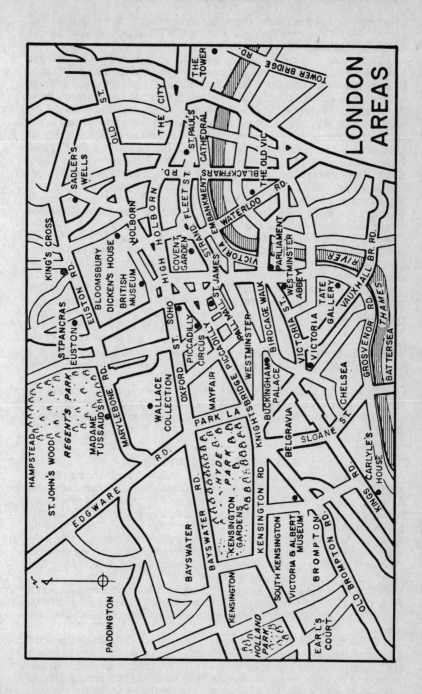

LONDON AREAS

centuries. The **London Tourist Board** has some excellent maps: their mailing address is 26 Grosvenor Gardens, London SW1W ODU, or your nearest British Tourist Authority.

To get your bearings by looking at a map, imagine you are in Trafalgar Square with its fountains splashing around you and Nelson atop his column. In the northwesterly direction beyond the National Gallery is Piccadilly Circus and the maze of Soho, on to Oxford Street and further on toward Regents Park. In the opposite direction, Whitehall (Downing Street, with the Prime Minister's residence at no. 10, is a small turn-off about halfway down) leads to the Houses of Parliament and Westminster Abbey. Off the westerly side of Trafalgar Square is The Mall, flanked by St. James's Park, leading to Buckingham Palace and on toward Knightsbridge and south to Chelsea and the King's Road. The northwest corner of Trafalgar Square leads to the Haymarket, Regent Street, and Piccadilly (the long street that eventually meets up with Hyde Park and merges into Knightsbridge). North from Trafalgar Square is Charing Cross Road, Leicester Square, Shaftesbury Avenue, and the West End theater district, on to Bloomsbury and the British Museum. Eastward from Trafalgar Square is The Strand (with Covent Garden lying a little north of it), and on to Fleet Street, the address of most national newspapers and synonymous with English journalism, which leads to St. Paul's Cathedral and eventually The City.

A word of explanation: "The City," as it's called by Londoners, is the City of London and is only that part of London that was originally the walled settlement. Today it is the financial center as well as the location of St. Paul's Cathedral, the Tower of London, and Barbican Center on the tourist trail. The City has its own police force and its own Lord Mayor, and whereas its winding, narrow streets are full of bankers and stockbrokers Monday to Friday, it is almost deserted on weekends since there are no residential areas (except, now, in the Barbican).

Note: Those circuses—Piccadilly, Oxford, Cambridge, etc.—are not the three-ring kind, of course you know. At one time they really did serve as traffic circulators, but much of that has been lost in the "one-way" and "do-not-enter" age of London's modern traffic movement.

5. Hotels in London

When you hear that most of London's hotels were built around the turn of the century, you'll know right away that accessibility is not their redeeming feature. Certainly, there have been American-style high-rise hotels constructed in recent years, and we can list a few that even have special features for disabled guests, but nearly all of those are in the upper price bracket. Many more list themselves in hotel directories as having wheelchair accessibility, but the judgment is strictly subjective and often does not take into account the access to the bathroom. So you can see it won't be simple. (See the details of the Tara Hotel before you get discouraged.)

In most of the hotels, the quoted price includes breakfast and a Value Added Tax (VAT). Many also add a service charge of 10% to 15%. So always check if prices quoted by the hotels include breakfast, the VAT, and the service charge.

Be warned about some hotel practices in England. Only the deluxe hotels provide washcloths and soap (so these are things you may want to include in your luggage), and orange juice is usually not included in the breakfast provided. You do know, of course, that elevators are called lifts, and that heating or air conditioning may not be what you are used to at home.

The hotels previewed here are in the central areas of London and are listed according to their feasibility for disabled travelers. Prices quoted in dollars are at the rate of $1.50 per pound sterling, which is the rate at the time of writing, but may have changed by the time you read this.

SPECIAL FACILITIES PLUS: All the access you need, with gadgets and assistive devices on tap, and moderate prices (even possibly a discount) in a first-class, centrally located hotel? A hotel in wishful-thinking-land? Well, it may be more real than you think.

There are ten rooms on the mezzanine floor at the **Tara Hotel**, Scarsdale Place, Kensington, W8 5SR (tel. 01/937-1115), which were recently adapted and ready for occupancy in late 1983, that have extensive facilities for disabled guests. These include level access, large elevators with low buttons, no steps to the restaurant and coffee shop, ramps to the bar, and rooms with automatic door opening devices, enlarged bathrooms, grab bars, access to washbasins, television controls from bedside, and room for wheelchair maneuvering in both bedroom and bathroom. Moreover, two of those rooms have been designed for severely disabled guests and are fitted with a ceiling track and sliding door to the bathroom that allow a self-operated hoist to travel from bed to bathroom, and with a toilet that has an automatic douche-and-dry mechanism. There is one 3-foot, 6-inch bed in these rooms; other rooms have two single beds. There are also adjoining rooms with communicating doors for the use of able-bodied companions, if required. A bedside console in all the rooms includes alarm and assistance call-systems, together with a remote control for door entry.

To assist guests with hearing impairments, each of the bedrooms has a telephone fitted with a flashing light, amplifier, and hearing aid couple.

The Tara's location is in back of Kensington High Street, close to Kensington Gardens and the the other attractions in the Boroughs of Kensington and Chelsea, such as Harrod's department store, the Victoria and Albert Museum, and the other museums clustered in that area. Kensington High Street is also the address of the **Disabled Living Foundation** (at no. 346, not far from the Tara Hotel), which is an information center for all facilities, services and equipment.

Kensington is about a 15-minute drive from London's many other attractions in the West End. The Tara's regular rates, as I write, and subject to change, are £36 ($54) single, £44 ($66) double, including VAT but not breakfast.

There's a unique arrangement here, though, that means you could be eligible for discounted room rates. The idea behind the adapted rooms came from a nonprofit organization called the London Hotel for Disabled People, which originally set out to be just that, but also undertook this interim project to encourage the integration of disabled guests into a regular hotel. The organization is operating a **Visitors Club** with annual dues of £1 ($1.50), that entitles disabled members to discount rates (subject to change) of £20.40 ($30.60) single, £33 ($49.50) double, including continental breakfast. For membership application write to the Secretary, The Visitors Club, Juxon House, 94 St. Paul's Churchyard, London EC4M 8EH.

Reservations for rooms at regular rates can be made through Aer Lingus Reservation Service, toll free from the U.S.A. (except Alaska, Hawaii, and New York City), at 800/223-6537, and in New York City 212/557-1110.

HOTELS WITH SOME SPECIAL FACILITIES: There aren't many, but here they are—in different price categories, most expensive first.

The **Holiday Inn Marble Arch,** 134 George St., W1H 6DN (tel. 01/723-1277), is a few blocks away from the northeastern corner of Hyde Park, and close to Oxford Street and Mayfair. It has one room with special features for disabled guests, and the restaurants are accessible. There is one step at the entrance. Rates here are $132 single, $151 double.

The **Hilton International London,** 22 Park Lane, W1A 2HH (tel. 01/493-8000), was controversial as London's first "skyscraper" 20 years ago, but is now an accepted part of the landscape opposite Hyde Park, in a location on the edge of Mayfair, close to Piccadilly and within "walking" distance of Buckingham Palace. The entrance is level, and the entrance from the rear car park is ramped. One snag—there are three steps to the elevators, but there is always plenty of help around. The hotel has two rooms with grab bars in the bathroom. All guest rooms have 31-inch-wide entry and 25½-inch bathroom doors and are air conditioned. TV is controlled from the bed, and there are ceiling hooks for lifting apparatus in the bathroom. All the many restaurants and the new casino are accessible, and so are the public rest rooms. Rates start at £85 ($127.50) double.

If you have a car or are willing to take taxis, you may want to consider the **Hilton International Kensington,** 179 Holland Park Ave., W11 4UL (tel. 01/603-3355), because it has two special guest rooms with 29-inch bathroom doors and grab bars in the bathroom. It is a bit further from the center of things, but is in the medium-price bracket, with double rooms from £44 to £62 ($66 to $93).

The **New Berners Hotel,** Berners St., W1A 3BE (tel. 01/636-1629) (off Oxford Street, a major shopping area), has a large number of rooms with bathrooms especially equipped for disabled guests. There is a level entrance to the hotel and large elevators. The public rest room is also wheelchair-accessible. Rates here are £45 ($67.50) single and £58 ($87) double.

Bayswater Road runs along the northern edge of Hyde Park, and that is the location of the **Coburg Hotel,** 129 Bayswater Rd., W2 4RJ (tel. 01/229-3654), where there are some large guest rooms with grab bars in the bathrooms (acceptable access in others). The entrance is level and an elevator goes to the restaurant. Rates are £18.50 ($27.75) single and double.

HOTELS WITH REASONABLE ACCESSIBILITY (no special features): Although there are no assistive devices in these following hotels, at least they have some guest rooms where the bathroom door is wide enough for the standard wheelchair to get through, and enough room in the bathroom to turn around. When you make reservations be sure to specify the width of bathroom door that you need, since they are not all the same size even in the same hotel. Most of the entrances of the hotels mentioned here are level or with one or two steps only.

Deluxe

The **Dorchester,** Park Lane, W1A 2HJ (tel. 01/629-8888), facing Hyde Park on the edge of Mayfair, is a legendary hostelry from the elegantly modern thirties era, with wide doorways and large bathrooms, some of which are equipped with grab bars. There *are* four steps at the entrance, but help in abundance is available. The restaurant, bar, and lounge areas on the lobby level have no steps. Singles start at £75 ($112.50), and doubles at £95 ($142.40) including tax and services.

At Hyde Park Corner, overlooking Green Park, the Hotel Inter-Continental, One Hamilton Place, W1V 0QY (tel. 01/409-3131, toll free in the U.S. 800/327-0200), has six rooms with 31-inch bathroom doors. The two entrances from the street are level, but only one of them gives direct access to the lobby (the other has five steps inside). TV can be controlled from bedside. Rates start at $150 single, $169 double.

The **Mayfair Hotel,** Berkeley St., W1A 2AN (tel. 01/629-7777), is centrally located in the fashionable area of the same name just north of Piccadilly and near Berkeley Square. What this comfortable hotel has to offer are large bedrooms, *some* of which allow access to the bathrooms. There is one step to the lobby and level access to the bar and restaurants. The rates here are from $145 double.

Upper Bracket

In Kensington, the **De Vere Hotel,** Hyde Park Gate, W8 5AS (tel. 01/405-2006), has about four large guest rooms with bathrooms that allow wheelchair access. Its spaciousness is typical of the Edwardian era when it was built in a location that overlooks Kensington Gardens near the South Kensington museums, including the Victoria and Albert. The hotel has kept up with the times, though, and service and other amenities are modern. There is one step at the entrance. Rates are £50 ($75) single, £70 ($105) double.

On the other side of town, near Trafalgar Square and close to the theaters, is the **Charing Cross Hotel,** Strand, WC1N 1NT (tel. 01/839-7282), with large bedrooms and wheelchair access to the bathroom in some of them. The entrance to the hotel is through the forecourt of Charing Cross railway station (but the station noise does not intrude on the interior of the hotel at all), and there is a ramped entrance through single doors next to the revolving one. Rates, including continental breakfast, are £60 ($90) single, £71 ($106.50) double.

One of the advantages of the majestic railway hotels that were built in the heyday of the steam engine is their dimensions. Attached to London's great Paddington Station is the **Great Western Hotel,** Praed St., W2 1HE (tel. 01/723-8064), in the Bayswater area north of Hyde Park. It has huge bedrooms and lofty ceilings in the Victorian manner, but is now well modernized. There is a portable ramp for the four shallow steps at the entrance (and also a ramped entrance from the station side). Elevators are large. There are as many as 12 bedrooms with bathrooms large enough to allow wheelchair access. Doubles here are £69 ($103.50).

Moderate

Not far from the British Museum, in Bloomsbury, is a lower-priced establishment, the **Grand Hotel,** 126 Southampton Row, WC1B 5AD (tel. 01/405-2006). This has a level entrance and easy access to the restaurants and lounge, as well as a few larger bedrooms with bathrooms big enough for wheelchairs to maneuver. Doubles here go from £25 ($37.50) including breakfast.

Note: There are, of course, dozens of other hotels in inner London that would be suitable for those with ambulatory-mobility impairments who do not need width and space for access to bathrooms. Some of these are listed in the London Tourist Board's *London for the Disabled* directory, including such hotels as the **Bloomsbury Crest Hotel**, Coram St., WC1N 1NT, (£36.50 or $55.25 double); the **Clifton Ford Hotel**, Welbeck St., W1M 8DN (£51 or $76.50 double); the **Cumberland Hotel**, Marble Arch, W1A 4RF (£65 or $97.50 double); the **Kenilworth Hotel**, Great Russell St., WC1B 3LB (£47 or $70.50 double); the **London Metropole Hotel**, Edgware Rd., W2 1JU (£51 or $76.50 double); the **Piccadilly Hotel**, Piccadilly, W1A 2AU (£65 or $97.50 double); the **Royal Lancaster Hotel**, Lancaster Terrace, W2 2TY (from £67.50 or $101.25 double); the **St. George's Hotel**, Langham Pl., W1N 8QS (£67 or $100.50 double); **St. James's Hotel**, Buckingham Gate, SW1E 6AF (from £ 39 or $58.50 double), and the **Westbury Hotel**, New Bond St., W1Y 0PU (£80 or $120 double).

A hint to London locations is in the first letters and number of the zip codes: these correspond to the old postal districts that are usually indicated alongside the names of the areas on most maps.

6. Restaurants

Of course, everybody knows that English cooking has a bad reputation and is usually not one of the main reasons for a visit to London, even though London has always had its share of fine restaurants in the deluxe class. But now quite a few improvements have been brought about because of tourists, imported chefs, and competition from "foreign" establishments, and so your English meals will do much more than just sustain you, especially if you eat in the West End. (The outskirts may be another matter!)

On the question of English eating habits, here are a few pointers.

Breakfast is one of England's specialties, so you can feast well if you are a breakfast eater. Even if you're not, perhaps this is the time to become one, since an English breakfast can keep you going right through a hectic day.

Tea, the late afternoon meal of thin sandwiches, scones, cake, preserves, and pots of hot brew, is no longer a universal habit except perhaps in private homes on Saturday and Sunday, but you'll still be able to sample it in most hotel lounges.

Fast-food establishments are clones on the American style, complete with hot dogs and hamburgers, and have superseded the once ubiquitous fish-and-chips shop. Among the English chains that may not be familiar to you, and which can be recommended for casual meals or snacks, are the Lyons Corner Houses, Quality Inns, Kardomah cafes, and Richoux restaurants.

And then there's the **pub**, that British institution that is so much more a center of social life than an American bar, and an eminently respectable place even for unescorted women. Although pub food is not what it once was, it's still a great way to lunch on sandwiches, sausage or meat pie, downed with one of the dozens of lagers, beers, or ales, amid some camaraderie with the local patrons.

Pubs *can* sometimes present problems if you are in a wheelchair, since they are often in old buildings, and doorways can be narrow. Crowds present another barrier, but a little patience and some help will get you your drink and your lunch, and it will be worth it. And would you believe . . . there's a Pub Information Centre. Call 01/222-3232.

Among the more famous pubs that have a degree of accessibility are two in Hampstead: the **Bull and Bush**, North End Rd. (tel. 455-3685), with parking space available, and the **Spaniards Inn** on Spaniards Lane (tel. 455-3276), a 16th-century inn; then there's **Feathers**, at 20 Broadway in Westminster (tel. 222-3744); the **Sherlock Holmes** in Northumberland St., WC2 (tel. 930-2644), decorated in Holmesian style; two on Fleet St., EC4, newspaper row: **Ye Olde**

Cheshire Cheese (tel. 353-6170), associated with Dr. Johnson, and **Ye Olde Cock Tavern** (tel. 353-8570), a favorite of Charles Dickens, both very crowded at lunchtime, though. Although the restaurant is inaccessible to wheelchairs, you can reach the bar at the **Prospect of Whitby,** 57 Wapping Wall, E1 (tel. 481-1095), an East End riverside pub steeped in history, which has live jazz at night. Closed Sunday and Monday.

London pubs are allowed to be open only from 11:30 a.m. to 3 p.m. and then from 5:30 to 11 p.m. (7 to 10:30 p.m. on Sundays).

Wine bars are a relatively recent innovation, often rivalling the pubs. You'll find them scattered all over the West End and in central London.

As far as prices are concerned, all restaurants and cafes are required to display them in a place where they can be seen from the outside. Charges for service, minimum charges, and cover charges must also be clearly shown, and prices quoted have to be inclusive of VAT (Value Added Tax).

In central London and especially Soho, London offers a surprising variety of international restaurants in all price ranges.

This section is not going to attempt to analyze the accessibility of London's thousands of eating places. It will point you in a few directions with a sampling of the restaurants, but the best advice is for you to observe the restaurants you pass, for a meal at the time you may be sightseeing, or to return to later.

Here are some that have been surveyed for wheelchair accessibility by the London Tourist Board:

The Ivy, 1 West St., WC2 (tel. 836-4751), is one of London's longest-established French restaurants, famous in years past as the haunt of the great stars of the theater, and now apparently regaining its tradition of star-spotting. The location is just north of Leicester Square. Prices are moderately expensive (£12 and up) for a table d'hote dinner, and it's open Monday to Saturday from 6:15 to 11:15 p.m. for dinner; lunch is served Monday to Friday from noon to 2:45 p.m.

Flanagan's, 11 Kensington High St., W8 (tel. 937-2519), is an Edwardian fish parlor with all the imagined gaiety and madness of that turn-of-the-century era, including honky-tonk piano, gaslight, and sawdust on the floor. It's in the moderate price category, meaning between £5 and £10 ($7.50 to $15), and is open from noon to 2:30 p.m. for lunch, 6 to 11 p.m. for dinner daily. There's one step at the entrance; access to all parts of the restaurant is not possible for wheelchairs. Another **Flanagan's** offers the same fare and facilities at 100 Baker St., W1 (tel. 935-0287), north of Oxford Street at the Hyde Park end.

There's Edwardian atmosphere, too, at the **Contented Sole,** 19 Exhibition Rd., SW7 (tel. 584-8359), in the neighborhood of the Victoria and Albert Museum. Prices are moderately expensive.

Tiddy Dols Eating House, 2 Hertford St., W1 (tel. 499-2357), in the heart of Shepherd's Market in Mayfair, re-creates another era, this time the 18th century, but it's entitled to it, since the building dates from 1785 and is full of twisting staircases (don't worry!) and alcoves tucked away beneath low-beamed ceilings. They have plenty of room for diners in wheelchairs. Food is traditionally English, authentic and good, with recipes from old English cookbooks, served with music from madrigal to modern from 7 to 11 p.m. It becomes a disco after 11 p.m. until 2 a.m., when a budget menu offers all you can eat for £2 ($3). There are also light suppers before and after the theater. If you have a full dinner here the bill will be about £13.50 to £17.50 ($20.25 to $26.25) including wine, cover, service, and VAT. Open from 6 p.m. to 2 a.m. daily.

An upper-bracket restaurant with good accessibility in the Covent Garden area is **L'Opera,** 32 Queen St., WC2 (tel. 405-9020), a plush, elegant place; and the Thomas de Quincey, 36 Tavistock St., WC2 (tel. 240-3972), in a 16th-century building once the home of the essayist after whom it is named.

If you're hungry for American-style hamburgers, you can get them at the other end of the price scale in Covent Garden at the **Rock Garden**, 6 The Piazza, Covent Garden, WC2 (tel. 240-3961), where there's live music every night.

For authentic Pekinese dishes, there's wheelchair accessibility at **Soho Rendezvous**, 21 Romilly St., W1 (tel. 437-1486). Prices range between £5 and £10 ($7.50 and $15).

And if you're in the mood for pasta while you're in Knightsbridge, there's the accessible **Spaghetti House**, 77 Knightsbridge, SW1 (tel. 235-6987), at moderate prices.

Steak, English-style, is the specialty at **Berni Steak Bar**, 185 Oxford St., W1 (tel. 437-5032), near Oxford Circus. Prices are moderately expensive.

7. London's Sights

Maybe it was a compromise that was meant to be. Since so many of London's museums and historic buildings present barriers to people with mobility problems, the city seems to compensate with lots and lots of outdoor attractions like the Changing of the Guard at Buckingham Palace, the "new" Covent Garden, the open-air concerts in London's magnificent parks in the summer, its winding River Thames spanned by so many bridges, and the silhouettes of all the picture-postcard edifices like Big Ben and the Tower of London. There's much, though, that *is* accessible, and you can see the national museums and galleries without having to part with a penny!

To get your bearings, of course, there is nothing like a sightseeing tour by coach (as the English call their long-distance buses and touring buses), and it is the cheapest way to do it if you can manage a few steps. But at present there are no sightseeing operators who have wheelchair-accessible coaches. The two-hour **London Transport Sightseeing Tour** on a regular London bus (no guide but a descriptive route map provided) is also a great value, if you can make it up to the entrance platform of the bus and then the one step inside. You'll have plenty of time to board. This tour starts from Piccadilly Circus, Victoria Station, or Marble Arch.

There are **tourist information centers** at Victoria Station, on the ground floor of Selfridges department store in Oxford Street, and on the third floor of Harrods in the Brompton Road. There is also telephone information service Monday to Friday from 9 a.m. to 5:30 p.m. (730-0791).

Registered guides are available, and for their services you should contact the **London Tourist Board** (tel. 01/730-3450). One of their special guides is William Forrester, a wheelchair user himself, whose services are described in the Getting Around section of this chapter, together with other guided tours and guide-drivers who are available.

Let's look first at some of London's best-known institutions that are feasible for the visitor in a wheelchair.

BUCKINGHAM PALACE: We don't have to worry about accessibility here because there are no tours! But you'll want to see Her Majesty's official residence in its great setting at the end of The Mall, the long stretch of roadway that runs between Trafalgar Square and the Palace, with St. James's Park on one side and a row of Regency buildings on the other that are residences of other members of the Royal Family or house exclusive clubs and embassies.

If Queen Elizabeth is at home, you'll see the Royal Standard flying at the masthead.

Changing of the Guard

You can see the Changing of the Guard every morning at Buckingham Palace, but the ceremony always draws huge crowds so perhaps "see" is not a good word. However, if you plan in advance, you can apply to watch the Changing of the Guard from the forecourt of the palace: disabled visitors can get permission from the Master of the Household, Buckingham Palace, London SW1. The ceremony lasts about half an hour and takes place on weekdays at 11:30 a.m., at 10 a.m. on Sunday. You can also see another Changing of the Guard on the far side of St. James's Park at the Horse Guards Parade in Whitehall.

Royal Mews

While you're at Buckingham Palace, you can visit the Royal Mews in Buckingham Palace Road (tel. 930-4832, ext. 643), which is accessible to wheelchairs and where you can see the magnificent Royal carriages, their horses and equipage. It is open Wednesday and Thursday afternoon from 2 to 4 p.m. Admission is 25p (38¢), children 10p (15¢).

TOWER OF LONDON: On the very edge of tourist London, in the City of London, (as compared to the City of Westminster where so many of the other attractions are located), standing on Tower Hill at the bank of the River Thames, is the formidable Tower of London, a name that for centuries struck terror in the ruler's enemies and, in the case of Henry VIII, his discarded wives. It is the oldest structure in London, some of it built nearly a thousand years ago, but you can have a look at most of it. The exception, for visitors in a wheelchair, is the Jewel House, guardian of England's Crown Jewels.

It is not, however, the easiest place in the world to navigate if you are in a wheelchair, but a little determination and some good assistance will go a long way. There are some cobblestones, but there is enough modernization of pathways to make the tower a feasible target for your sightseeing. The tower is open Monday to Saturday, March 1 to October 31, from 9:30 a.m. to 5 p.m., November 1 to February 28, 9:30 a.m. to 4 p.m.; on Sunday from March 1 to October 31, from 2 to 5 p.m. In July and August, admission is £3 ($4.50) for adults, £1.50 ($2.25) for children. In January, February, November, and December it is £2 ($3) for adults for £1 ($1.50) for children; in other months, £2.50 ($3.75) for adults and £1.50 ($2.25) for children. Closed on holidays. Telephone 480-6593 for information.

HOUSES OF PARLIAMENT: On the River Thames, too, but back in the City of Westminster, are the Houses of Parliament (Commons and Lords). The buildings were originally mid-Victorian, but the House of Commons has been rebuilt since it was destroyed by bombs in 1941, though the reconstruction remained faithful to the original.

The **Palace of Westminster** is open to the public on Saturday and holidays (except Christmas, New Year's, and Bank Holidays), and on Monday, Tuesday and Thursday in September from 10 a.m. to 5 p.m., provided neither House is sitting on those days. The House of Commons sits normally from mid-October to the end of July (except the week following Christmas and Easter).

Tours are available, with a limit of four wheelchairs in each group. Call 219-3090 for information. Visitors are allowed to listen to debates from the Strangers' Gallery, but it is difficult for wheelchair users to reach the gallery and even so, prior permission has to be arranged with a member of Parliament.

Westminster Hall, also part of the Palace of Westminster in Parliament Square, is the oldest public hall in London, dating from 1097. Its vast interior was the scene of many trials such as those of Sir Thomas More, Guy Fawkes, and Charles I. Enter via the Carriage Gates in the Palace of Westminster. It is open, providing neither House is sitting, even when Parliament is in session, from 10 a.m. to 1:30 p.m. Monday to Thursday, and from 10 a.m. to 5 p.m. on Saturday. Call 219-3090 for information.

WESTMINSTER ABBEY: On the other side of Parliament Square from the Houses of Parliament is the Gothic Westminster Abbey, parts of it here for 900 years, where kings and queens have been crowned since 1066, and now a shrine to many kings and even more to England's celebrated men and women through the centuries. The entrances are level, but there are a few steps inside to the various chapels, such as the Henry VII Chapel (four steps), that can be negotiated with assistance. The abbey is open to visitors daily from 8 a.m. to 6 p.m.; on Sunday the Royal Chapels are closed to visitors, but the Nave, Cloisters, and Exhibition of Treasure are open between services. Call 222-5152 for full information.

ST. PAUL'S CATHEDRAL: St. Paul's sits atop a large flight of steps at the main entrance, but there is a wheelchair entrance on the south side (on the right as you face the cathedral) through the gardens. It has a self-operated lift which takes you to the Nave level, but a mobile companion should request that the door be opened. You can, of course, admire Sir Christopher Wren's domed masterpiece from the outside, built in 1666 at the top of Ludgate Hill (up from Fleet Street). It is now surrounded by rather dreary modern office buildings constructed after World War II bombings razed all the older buildings around St. Paul's. The interior may seem rather bare, but it does contain many monuments to Britain's history. The Dome is off-limits to mobility-impaired visitors, as is the Crypt, but it can be admired from below as an illustration of Wren's genius. St. Paul's is open from 8 a.m. to 6 p.m. from mid-April to mid-September. The rest of the year hours are 8 a.m. to 5 p.m.

MADAME TUSSAUD'S: The famous wax museum can certainly be included in a listing of London's institutions. You'll find it on Marylebone Rd. (pronounced Marr-uh-ben), in a northerly direction toward Regents Park (tel. 935-6861). It is much more than a wax museum, indeed it is a whole entertainment. The collection of moving (literally) and terrifying famous and infamous figures worldwide, with a brand new Chamber of Horrors, collages of stage settings, panoramas, and other exhibitions, is augmented by snack bars and gift shops. It is wheelchair-accessible, but because of traffic circulation inside, the number of wheelchairs is limited to ten at any one time. An advance phone call is suggested. In the busiest months of July and August, admittance of people in wheelchairs is restricted before 4 p.m., and it would probably be impossible anyway to see most of the exhibits during the very crowded hours. There is a wheelchair-accessible rest room on the ground floor. It is open daily from 10 a.m. to 5:30 p.m. including weekends (until 6 p.m. April to September). Closed on Christmas Day. Admission to Madame Tussaud's is £2.75 ($4.10) for adults, £1.50 ($2.25) for children under 16.

THE STOCK EXCHANGE: One of the world's most famous financial centers —and a modern building for a change—is in Old Broad St., EC2 (tel. 588-2355) in "The City" as the financial district of the City of London is usually called. The Visitor's Gallery overlooks the trading floor and is open Monday to Friday from 9:45 a.m. to 3:15 p.m. Action is explained by guides, and there is also a cinema where documentary films are shown. Closed on holidays. It is recommended that visitors in wheelchairs have a companion for assistance here, and there is a limit to the number of wheelchair visitors allowed in at any one time, so it is a good idea to call in advance. Admission is free.

THE BRITISH MUSEUM: People have been rumored to have spent a lifetime in this immense museum whose collections of history, archeology, and art have been accumulating for more than 200 years. But don't let that put you off: you can just dip anywhere and find exciting treasures. Some of the most well-known are the **Rosetta Stone**, the key to deciphering Egyptian hieroglyphics, and the **Elgin Marbles** from the Parthenon, among the treasure trove of centuries. It is located in Bloomsbury on Great Russell St. (tel. 636-1555). The staff is helpful, and elevators between floors are large. One rest room and the restaurant are wheelchair-accessible. There are facilities for visitors with visual impairments. Wheelchairs are available on loan. The museum is open Monday to Saturday from 10 a.m. to 5 p.m., on Sunday from 2:30 to 6 p.m. Closed Good Friday; December 24, 25, and 26; New Year's Day; and May 1. Admission is free.

In the exhibition galleries of the **British Library** in the east wing of the British Museum are displayed a notable collection of autographs of England's legendary men of letters and science, first folios of Shakespeare's plays, and the Gutenberg Bible, among an extraordinary collection of other priceless manuscripts.

NATIONAL GALLERY: Overlooking the north side of Trafalgar Square and the monument to Admiral Nelson, is the National Gallery (tel. 839-3321), housing one of the world's great collections of art of every period except modern. There is a particularly impressive number of British masters such as Turner, Constable, Gainsborough, and Reynolds, as well as a feast of others such as Rembrandt, Rubens, Leonardo da Vinci, Titian, Michaelangelo, El Greco, and the French Impressionists.

The wheelchair entrance is in the rear of the gallery on Orange Street, where there is a lift that gives access to the main floor. Elevators provide access between floors. There is an adapted rest room, and the restaurant is accessible. Wheelchairs are available for the use in the gallery. The National Gallery is open Monday to Saturday from 10 a.m. to 6 p.m. Call 839-3526 for recorded information on exhibits.

COURTAULD INSTITUTE: A little north of the British Museum is a gem of an art gallery of the University of London for connoisseurs of Impressionist and Post-Impressionist painting, as well as old master paintings and drawings. The address is Woburn Square, at the corner of Torrington Place (tel. 580-1015). There *are* four steps to negotiate at the entrance here, and it is suggested that wheelchair visitors have a companion who can assist. The Courtauld is open weekdays from 10 a.m. to 5 p.m., and on Sunday from 2 to 5 p.m. Closed on holidays. Admission is £1 ($1.50) for adults and 50p (75¢) for students and children.

TATE GALLERY: Upriver from Westminster Abbey, but still in the City of Westminster, is one of Britain's most prestigious art museums, the Tate Gallery (tel. 821-1313), on Millbank near Vauxhall Bridge. It houses national collections of paintings and sculpture from the 16th century to the present. Best access is by ramp at the Atterbury Street entrance, where an elevator goes to the main floor. There is also a wheelchair-accessible rest room. Admission is free, but there is sometimes a charge to the special exhibits. Free lectures are offered every day, and free guided tours are provided Monday to Friday. Call 821-7128 for recorded information. The Tate Gallery Restaurant (accessible) is noted for its cuisine, and tables must be reserved in advance. There is also an accessible coffee shop. Wheelchairs are available on loan for touring the gallery. The Tate is open Monday to Saturday from 10 a.m. to 6 p.m., on Sunday from 2 to 6 p.m. Closed on Christmas and New Year holidays.

VICTORIA AND ALBERT MUSEUM: Yet another of the world's great museums, the Victoria and Albert, is in South Kensington at the corner of Cromwell and Exhibition Rds. (tel. 589-6371). Although the entire building is not accessible to wheelchairs, you can see most of the collections of fine and applied arts of all countries, periods, and styles, including Oriental art. Despite the fact that it is named for two of the most proper people of the 19th century, it is a lively and imaginative place.

Best access for wheelchairs is through the ramped entrance on Exhibition Road. Inside floors are level or ramped. One rest room has been adapted for use by visitors in wheelchairs, and the restaurant is accessible. Open Monday to Thursday, and on Saturday from 10 a.m. to 5:50 p.m., on Sunday from 2:30 to 5:50 p.m. Closed Friday and holidays.

SCIENCE MUSEUM: Across Exhibition Road from the side of the Victoria and Albert is the intriguing Science Museum (tel. 589-3456), which traces the history and development of both science and industry. There are veteran cars, trains (Stephenson's original *Rocket* among them), and airplanes, as well as a gallery devoted to the history of domestic appliances, and a children's gallery.

The main entrance is ramped and elevators give access to all floors except the basement. Facilities are provided for visitors with visual impairments. The museum is open on weekdays from 10 a.m. to 6 p.m. and on Sunday from 2:30 to 6 p.m. Closed on holidays.

WALLACE COLLECTIONS: A couple of blocks north of Oxford Street, close to Baker Street, is the Wallace Collection on Manchester Square (tel. 935-0687). It has important collections of works of art of all periods and is especially noted for its French 18th-century paintings, sculpture, furniture, porcelain, and goldsmiths' work, as well as an extraordinary collection of European and Oriental arms and armor. It is housed in the grand setting of the town house of the late Lady Wallace and has two steps at the entrance. Elevators are large enough to accommodate wheelchairs, and it is suggested that wheelchair visitors are accompanied. Because of the layout, the Wallace must restrict visitors in wheelchairs to one at a time. It is open weekdays from 10 a.m. to 5 p.m. and on Sunday from 2 to 5 p.m.

ROYAL ACADEMY OF ARTS: The prestigious showcase of the art establishment, the Royal Academy of Arts in Burlington House, Piccadilly (tel. 734-9052), was founded by Sir Joshua Reynolds in 1768 and holds its Annual Summer Exhibition of the work of living artists from May to August each year. There are major exhibits mounted throughout the year as well, details of which are published in the London newspapers and Visitors Guides. There is a ramped entry and the academy has large elevators, but suggests that wheelchair visitors be accompanied. Staff is helpful. The cafe is accessible. Open daily, including Sunday, from 10 a.m. to 6 p.m. Admission varies up to £2 ($3).

MUSEUM OF LONDON: Near St. Paul's Cathedral, at the corner of London Wall and Aldersgate Street, is the new Museum of London (tel. 600-3699). Its collections, originally in Guildhall and London museums, illustrate the history and topography of London from prehistoric times to the present day. The combination enables visitors to trace the history of London through relics, costumes, household goods, and models, all arranged chronologically. There's the Lord Mayor's State Coach dating to the 18th century and an audio-visual exhibit of the Great Fire of 1666, which wiped out most of the City of London at that time. The museum is open Tuesday through Saturday from 10 a.m. to 6 p.m. and on Sunday from 2 to 6 p.m. Admission is free.

There are steps at the main entrance, but wheelchair users are given access by a lift at the back entrance. It is a good idea to call in advance for instructions on where to park and how to reach the accessible entrance. Inside, everything can be reached by ramp or elevator. There is also an adapted rest room. The staff here is very helpful, and wheelchairs are available for visitors with mobility difficulties. There are also special facilities for visitors with visual impairments, and induction loop systems in the theater/auditorium.

IMPERIAL WAR MUSEUM: For military buffs, there are records of the two World Wars at the Imperial War Museum (tel. 735-8922), on the Lambeth Road, which is south of the Thames across Lambeth or Westminster Bridges. The building itself is the original "Bedlam," which may be quite appropriate for the relics it houses of those deadly battles—airplanes, submarines, bombs, weapons, and an extensive art collection of works related to the subject.

A side door can be opened to avoid the steps at the main entrance. All floors inside can be reached by elevator, and there is a specially adapted rest room. The restaurant is wheelchair-accessible. The museum suggests that visitors in wheelchairs be accompanied. Open Monday to Saturday from 10 a.m. to 5:50 p.m. and on Sunday from 2 to 5:50 p.m. Film shows on weekends at 3 p.m. Closed on holidays. Admission is free.

OTHER MUSEUMS: Among the more than 50 museums and exhibitions in London that are wheelchair-accessible and have special interests at their focus, are the **Geological Museum,** Exhibition Rd., SW7 (tel. 589-3444); the **IBA Broadcasting Gallery,** 70 Brompton Rd., SW3 (tel. 584-7011); the **National Army Museum** on the Royal Hospital Road, Chelsea, SW3 (tel. 730-0717); the **Natural History Museum,** Cromwell Rd., South Kensington, SW7 (tel. 589-6323); **Guildhall,** King St., Cheapside, EC2 (tel. 606-3030); the **National Postal**

Museum, King Edward St., EC1 (tel. 432-3851); the **Commonwealth Institute**, Kensington High St., W8 (tel. 602-3252); the **Jewish Museum**, Woburn House, Upper Woburn Pl., WC1 (tel. 387-3081); and the **London Transport Museum**, Convent Garden, WC2 (tel. 379-6344). (The first digits of the postal code after each address will give you a clue to the location, since these are usually marked on tourist maps.)

THE LONDON PARKS: Londoners owe some of their best parkland to their monarchs' love of the hunt: Royal decrees set aside hunting preserves that ultimately became public parks—among them Hyde Park, St. James's Park, Green Park, and Regents Park, all in the heart of modern London. They are green islands in an ocean of stone and brick and give the central part of the city the spaciousness of the country. They are places to picnic, listen to the band, watch open-air plays, and a dozen other pleasurable pastimes. Several parks have their own restaurants.

The sports facilities in the parks can be used by disabled people who can sail and row, by arrangement with the instructor. There is also swimming, horseback riding, and tennis available. Call the Royal Parks Department at the Department of Environment (tel. 212-3833) for information on these activities, and also on parking. There are no special parking arrangements at St. James's or Green Parks, but most of the other parks have spaces reserved for disabled drivers.

The parks are nearly all quite flat and interlaced with smooth pathways—the only trouble is that they can go on for miles and miles!

Hyde Park, London's largest, is also the world's largest, covering nearly 650 acres of central London and including a 40-acre lake called the Serpentine. The paths around the Serpentine are smooth and obstacle-free. It is the northeastern corner of Hyde Park at Marble Arch, where there was once the notorious Tyburn gallows big enough for 24 nooses at once, that becomes **Speakers Corner** on Sunday and attracts any orator who wants to declaim his opinion and expects to be heckled by enthusiastic onlookers, usually with opposing viewpoints. Hyde Park also is the site of **Rotten Row**, the 1½-mile sand track reserved for horseback riding, which attracts a Sunday crowd of onlookers.

Across Picadilly to the south are **Green Park** and **St. James's Park**, through which you can stroll past a romantic lake all the way from Buckingham Palace to the Houses of Parliament.

Regents Park is father north in the St. Marylebone district; it was designed in the 18th century by John Nash for the Prince Regent and is, therefore, the most classical and formal of London's parks. It has public rest rooms near Queen Mary's Rose Garden that are wheelchair-accessible. It contains the Open Air Theater and the London Zoo (tel. 722-3333), one of the most comprehensive collections of animals in the world. The zoo is accessible to wheelchair visitors and open every day except Christmas, with an admission of around £3 ($4.50) for adults and £1.50 ($2.25) for children.

ALONG THE THAMES: There are river excursions to many of the sites along the Thames, but for wheelchair visitors some are more easily reached by car.

The River Thames is as much a part of the London scene as the historic buildings, many of which can be seen during a river trip. Although assistance will be needed to board the river sightseeing boats, most operators are very willing to do all they can, especially if they have advance notice. To let them know you are coming and to discuss your particular needs, telephone any of the following numbers: 930-5947, 930-4097, 930-2062, or 709-9855.

The all-year-round river services from Westminster to the Tower of London and on to Greenwich are a marvelous way for disabled visitors to relax and enjoy some of the best views of London. There are also services upstream to Kew Gardens, Hampton Court, and Richmond that operate from April through October. For information on departures, phone the London Tourist Board's special **river information service** at 730-4812.

Westminster Pier is accessible with assistance (there is a wheelchair-accessible rest room here), and the piers at Kew, Greenwich, and Tower have a steep slope. Unfortunately, the piers at Charing Cross and Hampton Court are not feasible for wheelchairs.

Note: At Hampton Court, the palace is not wheelchair-accessible, but the gardens can be toured free of charge.

On Greenwich Pier, in permanent dry dock, you'll see the *Cutty Sark,* the last and most famous of the tea clipper ships. You can tour the area around the clipper and board it to see part of the exhibits. There is no admission charge for disabled visitors. Nearby is the *Gipsy Moth IV.* in which Sir Francis Chichester raced single-handed around the world in 1966.

Greenwich is also home to the **National Maritime Museum** (tel. 858-4422) with exhibits of all kinds illustrating Britain's great maritime and naval heritage. If you are in a wheelchair, a companion is useful here. Facilities are provided for visitors with visual impairments. Closed on holidays.

While I'm talking about Greenwich, let me mention the **Royal Observatory,** source of Greenwich Mean Time, which stands in Greenwich Park. The observatory has a lot of steps and stands on the crest of the ridge that leads in a long slope of Greenwich Park down to the river.

ROYAL BOTANIC GARDENS: Located at Kew Road, Richmond (tel. 940-1171), the *gardens* are a great spot for a day excursion by river boat or by car. They are considered the world's greatest botanic gardens, legendary for their plant collections for more than 200 years. Huge greenhouses grow blooms and trees from every part of the world and, of course, the attractions vary with the seasons. The gardens make for easy strolling, except for their size. You can rent a wheelchair here, and there are facilities for visually impaired visitors. The restaurant is accessible. Kew Gardens are open daily from 10 a.m. to 7 p.m. in the summer and until 8 p.m. from the end of July to the end of August. In winter, hours are 10 a.m. to 4 p.m. Admission to the Botanic Gardens is 10p (15¢).

Kew Palace, a 17th-century house with a collection of paintings, which stands in the grounds, has three steps at the front entrance and not all of the house can be seen by visitors in wheelchairs. Admission is 40p (60¢).

Note on rest rooms: What the English call public conveniences, and you probably know as public rest rooms, have always been relatively prolific in England, but very few are suitable for wheelchair users. However, there are a few near the tourist attractions, including Tower Hill and opposite Madame Tussaud's in the Marylebone Road; in the parks: Regents Park (Broad Walk, Chester Road, the Rose Garden, and near New Lodge), Hyde Park (near the police station and by the reservoir), St. James's Park (near the Marlborough Gate), and in Kensington Gardens (near the Flower Walk); at railway stations: Charing Cross, Victoria, Waterloo, and Paddington; in department stores: the Army and Navy store on Victoria Street, and John Lewis on Oxford Street.

8. Theaters

With London's reputation as the theatrical capital of the world, a visit to the theater is usually high on the list of priorities for any visitor. Although many of London's theaters are in old buildings, and that's usually bad news, a surprising number make provisions for patrons in wheelchairs. Be flexible about what you plan to see, and be prepared to enjoy what is playing in the most accessible ones. There is good accessibility at the National Theatre and the Festival Concert Hall on the South Bank, built since World War II, and Barbican Centre is another complex that has just been completed.

It is the policy of most theaters, because of fire regulations, that disabled people unable to walk must have a companion who can provide assistance.

You'll find ticket prices cheap by U.S. standards and more readily available at short notice. Performances are listed in newspapers and in most entertainment guides available in hotel lobbies, or in copies of *What's On In London,* available on newsstands. Tickets can be bought from the box office of the theater or from ticket agencies. There is also the Ticket Booth in Leicester Square that sells tickets on the day of a performance for half price plus a 50p (75¢) service charge, open from noon to 2 p.m. for matinee performances and from 2:30 to 6:30 p.m. for evening performances. Check on performance times, since they differ from custormary American curtain times. In New York, the British Tour and Theater Center offers the opportunity to buy tickets for London attractions (Stratford-on-Avon, too) at a price $5 above the price paid in London. Information from the **British Tour and Theater Center, Inc.,** The Berkeley Building, 19 W. 44th St., Suite 718, New York, NY 10036 (tel. 212/719-1223).

Some of the more notable theaters that you will find in the following list of possibilities are the **Theatre Royal,** Drury Lane, one of London's oldest and best-known theaters, associated with Nell Gwynne, notorious mistress of King Charles II; the **Mermaid,** on the banks of the river quite outside the theater district but a complex of two riverside restaurants, a coffee bar, as well as the theater; the **Royal Court** in Chelsea, where the new wave of British theater got its start with John Osborne's *Look Back in Anger;* the **Palladium,** renowned variety house; and the **National Theater,** home of Britain's great national theater company, where there are three theaters under the same roof that offer a wide variety of plays, and a complex of bars, restaurants, buffets, river walks, and terraces along the Thames. Newest addition to London's theater scene is the **Barbican Theatre** in the Barbican Center in the City of London, home of the Royal Shakespeare Company when it isn't in Stratford-upon-Avon, and where it performs a wide spectrum of great drama.

Here is a guide to the situation at the leading theaters: the ones listed have wheelchair locations as noted, and are level access unless noted.

Adelphi, The Strand, WC2 (tel. 836-7611): there are six wheelchair locations in boxes. Transfer to seats possible in the orchestra. Staff will assist.

Albery, St. Martin's Lane, WC2 (tel. 836-3878): four wheelchair locations in boxes; transfer to seats possible in orchestra. Staff will assist. Three steps to negotiate.

Aldwych, The Aldwych, WC2 (tel. 836-6404): no wheelchair locations available but suitable for transfer to seat. Two steps; staff will assist.

Ambassadors, West St., Cambridge Circus, WC2 (tel 836-1171): no wheelcair locations, but suitable for transfer to orchestra seat. Six steps; staff will assist.

Coliseum, St. Martin's Lane, WC2 (tel. 836-3161): nine wheelchair locations; two steps.

Comedy, Panton St., SW1 (tel. 930-2578): no wheelchair locations, but suitable for transfer to seat.

Criterion, Piccadilly Circus, W1 (tel. 930-3216): no wheelchair locations but suitable for transfer to seat.

Drury Lane Theatre Royal, Catherine St., WC2 (tel. 836-8108): ten wheelchair locations.

Duke of York, St. Martin's Lane, WC2 (tel. 836-5122): suitable for transfer to seat. Induction loops available.

Fortune, Russell St., WC2 (tel. 836-2238): no wheelchair locations but suitable for those who can transfer to seat.

Garrick, Charing Cross Rd., WC2 (tel. 836-4601): two wheelchair locations.

Globe, Shaftesbury Ave., W1 (tel. 437-1592): no wheelchair locations but suitable for transfer to seat.

Haymarket Theatre Royal, Haymarket, SW1 (tel. 930-9832): suitable for transfer to seat.

Her Majesty's Theatre, Haymarket, SW1 (tel. 930-6606): one wheelchair location; also suitable for transfer to seat.

Lyric, Shaftesbury Ave., W1 (tel. 437-3686): six wheelchair locations in boxes only.

Mermaid Theatre, Puddle Dock, EC4 (tel. 236-5568): a large number of wheelchair locations available.

National Theatre, South Bank, SE1 (tel. 928-2252, 633-0880 for information); four wheelchair locations in the Lyttelton Theatre; two in the Cottesloe Theatre; six in the Olivier Theatre. All theaters have induction loop facilities for patrons with hearing impairments, as well as wheelchair-accessible rest rooms.

Palace, Cambridge Circus, W1 (tel. 437-6834): two wheelchair locations.

Palladium, Oxford Circus, W1 (tel. 437-7373): three wheelchair locations.

Phoenix, Charing Cross Rd., WC2 (tel. 836-8611): two wheelchair locations.

Piccadilly, Denham St., W1 (tel. 437-4506): six wheelchair locations.

Prince Edward Theatre, Old Compton St., W1 (tel. 437-6877): two wheelchair locations.

Queens, Shaftesbury Ave., WC1 (tel. 734-1166): transfer to seat required.

Royal Court, Sloane Sq., SW1 (tel. 730-1745): no wheelchair locations but suitable for transfer; three steps.

Royal Opera House, Covent Garden, WC2 (box office tel. 240-1066, manager tel. 240-1200): not the easiest access, but you may want to visit since it's one of Europe's great opera houses as well as the home of the Royal Ballet. The staff here is very willing and accustomed to handling wheelchairs up the staircase to either the Grand Tier, where there is a wheelchair-accessible box, or to the stalls (orchestra section), where transfer to a regular aisle seat is needed. The opera house seats have to be booked well in advance, and it is just as well to do this in writing since you can then also be on record for assistance. This information is passed to the manager's office.

Shaftesbury Theatre, Shaftesbury Ave., WC2 (tel. 836-4255): two wheelchair locations in boxes.

St. Martin's, West St., Cambridge Circus, WC2 (tel. 836-1443): one wheelchair location.

Savoy, The Strand, WC2 (tel. 836-8888): two wheelchair locations; two steps.

Strand, Aldwych, WC 2 (tel. 836-2660): one wheelchair location, but there are a number of steps here.

Vaudeville, The Strand, WC2 (tel. 836-9988): one step; suitable for transfer.

Victoria Palace, Victoria St., SW1 (tel. 834-1317): one wheelchair location.

Westminster, Palace St., SW1 (tel. 834-0283): six wheelchair locations; three steps.

Wyndhams, Charing Cross Rd., WC2 (tel. 836-3028): two wheelchair locations; three steps.

BARBICAN CENTRE: Barbican Centre, located in the City, is getting a separate mention here because it offers an array of cultural facilities all under one roof, with a permanent home for the Royal Shakespeare Company in the Barbican Theatre, concert seasons of the London Symphony Orchestra and the English Chamber Orchestra in **Barbican Hall,** and programs of art exhibitions, films, and free events in the foyers.

The main entrance is at the junction of Silk Street and Whitecross Streets with an unloading zone for taxis and cars for the Level 5 Foyer.

Historically, it is the completion of an ambitious project that has been taking place over a number of years, and it stands in the Barbican area of the City of London that was virtually wiped out by bombing 40 years ago. A detailed survey of all its facilities is available from Barbican Centre for Arts and Conferences, Barbican, London EC2Y 8DS. Box office telephone number is 628-8795, and house management telephone number to call, prior to your visit, to make special arrangements is 628-3351, ext. 412. For performance information, call 928-9760 for concerts and 628-2295 for theaters.

There is special parking, wheelchair-accessible rest rooms, and ramps for easy access, as well as 16 wheelchair locations in **Barbican Hall** and four in the **Barbican Theatre.** (In the theater, the locations have an electric lift which allows adjustment to sight lines!) Both theater and concert hall are equipped with induction loop systems for those who wear hearing aids. The cinema also has box locations equipped for two wheelchair patrons and their escorts, as well as induction loop systems for people with hearing impairments.

You can take a guided tour, and although part of the tour usually includes stairs, it is possible to take the elevators instead for most of the tour. All levels are connected by elevators, and the entrance to the **Art Gallery** on Levels 8 and 9 is near the elevator on Level 8. There's access to raised areas in the Sculpture Court via a ramp at the north side of the Sculpture Court, which is on Level 8. Wheelchair-accessible rest rooms are on Level 1 (Cinema 1), Level 4 (Barbican Theatre), Level 7 (Administration Offices), and Level 9 (Frobisher Crescent).

Restaurants are the Waterside Cafe on Level 5, and the Cut Above on Level 7, with good access and plenty of wheelchair circulation space.

CONCERT HALLS: Best known of London's concert halls, perhaps because it is the oldest, is the **Royal Albert Hall,** Kensington Gore, SW7 (tel. 589-8212), opposite Kensington Gardens in Hyde Park. Although this grand example of Victorian architecture isn't ideally accessible (some steps), there are wheelchair locations and facilities for patrons with sight impairments. Call 589-0417 for details relating to your particular needs.

Newest, and therefore more accommodating, is the complex on the South Bank side of Waterloo Bridge, where there are three of the most comfortable and acoustically perfect concert halls anywhere. They are part of the same complex as the National Theatre, and are the **Royal Festival Hall, Queen Elizabeth Hall,** and the **Purcell Room.** They all have wheelchair locations and accessible restaurants, as well as induction loop systems for hearing-impaired patrons. Call 928-3002 for information.

9. Shopping in London

A guide to London shopping deserves a book all to itself, so this will have to be a fast overview of major department stores, main shopping areas, and the open-air markets that are among London's unique attractions.

For the disabled visitor particularly, shopping can turn into an obstacle course however, because in London's old-fashioned shopping streets, parking is limited and private cars are banned altogether from parts of Oxford Street. King's Road in Chelsea is known world-wide, but many of its boutiques have narrow entrances and inaccessible upper or lower floors. The same comment applies to the recent development of Covent Garden, where shop entrances and interiors are a problem for wheelchair-users, but this is a fun place just to browse around. It is a good idea to avoid the Saturday crowds anywhere.

In many shops and stores you can avoid the hefty tax (VAT) on luxury items by presenting your passport, but only if you have your purchase sent to your home address or have it delivered to the plane on which you are returning home.

REGENT STREET: The gracefully curved thoroughfare that runs between Oxford Circus and Piccadilly Circus was designed by John Nash in the early 19th century as a processional way for the Prince Regent. Now it's the location of many fashionable stores, which include **Dickins & Jones** (tel. 734-7070), and **Liberty's** (tel. 734-1234). Both have level entrances, elevators between floors, and accessible restaurants.

OXFORD STREET: Considered London's main shopping street, it is a long stretch from St. Giles Circus to **Marble Arch,** with an endless procession of retail establishments including six of London's major department stores. Those with easy entrance and elevators between floors at the Marble Arch end include **Marks & Spencer** (tel. 486-6151), and **Selfridges** (tel. 629-1234) (where there is a perhaps-accessible rest room in the basement) and an accessible restaurant; in an easterly direction along Oxford Street from Selfridges is **John Lewis** (tel. 629-7711) with an accessible restaurant *and* a wheelchair-accessible rest room; and **D.H. Evans,** also with an accessible restaurant.

PICCADILLY: Leaving the circus behind, Piccadilly is an upper-crust stretch of shopping all the way to Green Park and includes the venerable **Fortnum & Mason's** which supplies groceries to the Royal Household. It has a level entrance and an elevator between floors, and an accessible restaurant.

On the north side of Picadilly is the **Burlington Arcade,** the glass-roofed Regency-style covered walkway of fine shops. It connects with Regent Street at its other end. There are a couple of steps into the arcade, and many of the shops are small, but if you want to see the elite of specialty merchandise, it's great for browsing.

BOND STREET: The haunt of Beau Brummel and his Regency dandies runs in a northerly direction off Piccadilly in the direction of the heart of Mayfair.

and is synonymous with the carriage trade for antiques, jewelry, shoes, and fine art. Again, more for browsing.

KNIGHTSBRIDGE: This elegant stretch south of Hyde Park is the site of **Harrods** on Brompton Rd. (tel. 730-1234), the largest store in Europe, a British institution and the one with a reputation for selling everything you could possibly ask for. Harrods has an information sheet for disabled shoppers. Entrance is level, there are elevators between floors, and the restaurant is accessible.

CHARING CROSS ROAD: The place for scholars and musicians with its shops for musical instruments, music, and bookshops, especially **Foyle's** at no. 119 (tel. 437-5660), which claims to have more than 4 million books in stock. Although the entrance is level, the building inside is not wheelchair-accessible in all parts.

COVENT GARDEN MARKET: Off the Strand, this area used to be the most famous market in all England for fruit, vegetables, and flowers. After four centuries, the Market has moved away and taking its place in the legendary buildings (for one thing, the setting for *Pygmalion/My Fair Lady*) is a new complex of restaurants, bars and shops designed to provide an authentic 19th century atmosphere. There is access to the arcades and the outdoor cafes, but stores are rather too compact for wheelchair users.

KING'S ROAD: Now itself legendary for setting off the trendy boutique era, is the area of Chelsea at the other end of Sloane Street from Knightsbridge. King's Road starts at Sloane Square (where **Peter Jones,** tel. 730-3434, is an upper-bracket department store with wheelchair access, including to the restaurant), and meanders on along what used to be the main street of the village of Chelsea. Lots of small boutiques here for window-shopping but not much wheelchair-accessibility inside them.

STREET MARKETS: Even if it seems that negotiating the space between stalls and shoppers may be too much of a challenge, it would be a pity to miss a visit to at least one of London's colorful street markets for all the free and lively entertainment they provide. An able-bodied companion will help if you are in a wheelchair. Arrive a little ahead of the lunchtime crowds and remember that most of them close down after 3 p.m. in the afternoon. Weekend markets such as Portobello Road and Petticoat Lane usually attract large crowds, but you may find parking nearby if you arrive early enough. Although the streets are narrow, they are closed to traffic, and stalls back onto the sidewalks, so the best route is probably the middle of the street. Here's a rundown on the major ones.

Petticoat Lane, Middlesex St., E1, makes for a lively Sunday morning in the heart of Cockney-land, with everything possible for sale, from old clothing to potentially valuable antiques. There is refreshment here, too. The market operates from 9 a.m. to 2 p.m., but early arrival is advised. Parking is possible on the side streets, and there is a public car park as well.

Portobello Road, off Westbourne Park, W11, a bit further out, is a Saturday activity for antiques (daily for vegetables, fruit, and flowers). It's a lure for collectors of just about anything. Operates 9 a.m. to 5 p.m., but nothing on Sunday. There is parking in the side streets.

Berwick Street Market, Berwick St., W1, is in the heart of Soho's narrow streets, bustling six days a week with fresh fruit and vegetables, as well as "collector's" items in records, books, and old magazines. Parking is impossible, but you'd want to walk through Soho anyway. (Don't be put off by the strip clubs and porno stores all around: there are famous international restaurants and a host of colorful characters here as well.)

.The **New Caledonian Market** in Bermondsey, Tower Bridge Rd., SE1, is the dealers' antique market. If you get there early, you may snag a few for yourself. Friday only, 7 a.m. to 2 p.m. Parking nearby.

10. Postscript: And After London . . .

Small as they may be, the British Isles are packed with a range of travel experience of such contrasts that you might even be in a different country with each one. By North American standards it seems there is no distance between any of them.

The are good rail and coach (bus) connections in a convenient network of transportation, if you are not going by car. (See the beginning of this chapter for sources of information.) Indications of wheelchair-accessibility are to be found in a number of publications, including many put out by the British Tourist Authority, and in the *AA Guide for Disabled Travelers* (see the front of this chapter for addresses). These ratings are subjective ones by the institutions listed, so a careful check in advance is always called for. The guides offered by RADAR (see beginning of chapter) have often been checked out by local organizations and so offer what might be more reliable information.

It may be encouraging to know that there are hotels in which wheelchair guests can be accommodated in popular cities like Oxford, Stratford-upon-Avon (where there is a Hilton International with two specially equipped rooms), and Bath, for instance. Details are to be found in booklets available from RADAR at minimal charges.

The interiors of many of the famous buildings in **Stratford**—Shakespeare's Birthplace and Anne Hathaway's Cottage—are not accessible for visitors in wheelchairs, but the Royal Shakespeare Theatre is reasonably accessible, and there are wheelchair locations. In any case, the town itself is a place to be savored just by strolling its streets. You can get an access guide from RADAR.

In **Oxford,** although the choice of accessible hotels is not large, there are some possibilities, and the city is eminently suited for wandering around the many quadrangles of the famous colleges that make up the ancient university. RADAR has an access guide to Oxford.

Farther west, as you may be touring through Stonehenge, Salisbury, and the Cotswolds, you may end up at **Bath** where there are also some hotels that are reasonably suitable for guests in wheelchairs. Even though most of them have no special facilities, they are generally very spacious. The most important sightseeing attractions in Bath, such as the Assembly Rooms, the Abbey, the Pump Room, and the Roman Baths are available to visitors in wheelchairs who have companions to assist. (Access Guide available from RADAR.)

If you are touring by car, the excellent brochures published by the British Tourist Authority cover every part of the country and include accommodation information with the wheelchair accessibility symbol where appropriate, a start for more detailed checking of the facilities available.

For other parts of the British Isles, there is information on Wales and Scotland available, too, on accommodations and facilities for disabled visitors.

A Guide for the Disabled Visitor is available from the Wales Council for the Disabled, Llys Ifor, Crescent Rd., Caerphilly, Mid-Glamorgan CF8 1XL, Wales (tel. 0222/869224) for $2 ($3 airmail).

The Scottish Tourist Board publishes *Accommodation with Facilities for Disabled Visitors,* as well as *Holidays with Care in Scotland,* with information and advice for people with special needs. The address is 23 Ravelston Terrace, Edinburgh EH4 3UE, Scotland. *Edinburgh and Lothian for the Disabled* is available from the Edinburgh Committee for the Co-ordination of Services for the Disabled, Simon Square Centre, Howden St., Edinburgh EH8 9HW, Scotland.

For other listings of access guides consult the *International Directory of Access Guides,* published by Rehabilitation International USA Inc. 1123 Broadway, New York, NY 10010 (tel. 620-4040).

There are two hotels, one in Llandudno, Wales, and one in Somerset, England, that have been built especially for travelers with disabilities. For more information, write to John Grooms Association for the Disabled, 10 Gloucester Drive, London N4 2LP, England.

Group tours for both visitors in wheelchairs and those with visual impairments are organized by **Anglo World Travel,** 130-136 Poole Rd., Bournemouth, BH4 9EF, England.

Chapter 17

PARIS

City of Light

**1. Getting There
2. Getting Around
3. Orientation 4. Where to
Stay? 5. Sightseeing in Paris
6. Entertainment 7. Shopping**

PARIS IS gay, chic, romantic . . . Paris is mostly flat. . . . Paris can be a problem for people in wheelchairs. Put it all together and you have the chance for an indescribable experience of one of the world's great cities, on good wheeling terrain, but with a terrible lack of accessibility in hotels, on public transportation, and in public buildings. But what's worth while in life that comes easy?

Here's a city that is the River Seine, the broad tree-lined boulevards, the elegant architecture, the sidewalk cafes, great food in the most modest bistros, the Left Bank, the Champs-Élysées. . . .

Ideally, find yourself somebody who lives there (in a wheelchair-accessible apartment), with a car, and we'll show you the places you can go. Realistically, this chapter will offer details of hotels that may suit—you'll really have to decide from the dimensions and access details if one is suitable for *you.*

Restaurants are not included in this chapter, since you will come across easy-access bistros, brasseries, and cafes as you stroll the different districts around your hotel or wherever you have gone for a day's sightseeing. Best of all, if you're in Paris in the summer, of course, are the most accessible eating and drinking spots of all—the sidewalk cafes. And Paris is certainly the place for those marvelous institutions: somewhere you can sit for hours for the price of a cup of coffee and have the passing show as free entertainment.

1. Getting There

From anywhere outside France it's likely you'll be arriving by air at one of the three major airports—Roissy-Charles de Gaulle, Orly Sud (South) or Orly Ouest (West). When you arrive on any airline at any of them, you will be met, escorted, and generally looked after by the **Bel Air Company,** which services all the airlines and whose representatives are recognizable by the badges on their jackets that carry the international symbol of access.

Your airline will contact Bel Air when they know your flight is arriving (you will, of course, have told the airline in advance of your needs and repeated them to the flight attendant on your plane). You are then met with an airport wheelchair and escorted through customs and immigration to the baggage claim area, where you claim your own wheelchair along with your luggage. Then you are escorted to whatever transportation you are taking into Paris. The agent is authorized to help you with flight connections if necessary and with customs clearance, as well as take care of your baggage, and even do some shopping if you wish.

When you *leave* from any of the Paris airports, you will find a special unloading zone marked with the access sympol. There is a special telephone that you can use to call for an escort. If you prefer to check-in yourself first, the airline will call for the escort who will provide all the services described for arrival in reverse—take you through customs and passport control and put you on the plane. If you arrive a little early and want to do some shopping or have a meal, a drink, or a snack, an escort will come and pick you up wherever you may be at an assigned time.

At each airport there are lowered telephones and wheelchair-accessible rest rooms, and all shops and most restaurants have level access. (If the shop has a turnstile blocking your entrance, it can be removed.) The special rest rooms are kept locked but the attendant at the adjacent rest room has the key.

You can get a booklet with complete diagrams of the airports and their facilities from **Paris Airport Authority**, 1 World Trade Center, Suite 2551, New York, NY 10048 (tel. 212/432-1093).

Here are some details of the facilities at each airport.

ROISSY-CHARLES DE GAULLE: Most gates at this airport are serviced by level jetways directly from the plane into the terminal, but if it is necessary to use ground transportation, the agent will make all the arrangements. There are moving sidewalks, but they are not all flat. For those with an incline, the agent may request that you use a motorized wheelchair. However, if you prefer, you can request to use the elevator instead.

There is a low phone at the post office on the shopping floor; rest rooms are on the transfer floor near satellites 3, 4, and 7, and in the medical center on the shopping floor.

When you're leaving Paris, the special unloading zone, where you can call for an escort, is at door 8 on Departures level. The duty-free shops are on the transfer level. All the restaurants are accessible except the snack bar.

For reference, the **Bel Air escort desk** is located near door 12 on the departures level (tel. 862-28-24).

ORLY SUD: Jetways are not always available at Orly Sud for direct access to the terminal from the plane, but the agent meeting you will make whatever arrangements are necessary for you to reach the terminal, where there are elevators between floors. The wheelchair-accessible rest rooms at Orly Sud are on the upper level (where you arrive and depart), in the halls leading to and from gates 1 and 2, and from gates 30 to 43. There is a low phone on the upper level beyond customs.

For departure from Orly Sud, you'll find the special unloading zone with the phone to call the escort, located at door N in the check-in hall. All the shops and restaurants have level access, with the exception of the ground-floor bar, which has one step up.

For reference, the **escort desk** (for Orly Sud and Orly Ouest) is located near door K (tel. 687-12-34, ext. 3071).

ORLY OUEST: Again, fewer jetways here, but the escort will take care of your transportation into the terminal. The wheelchair-accessible rest rooms are near the flight departure boards at the entrance to lounges 2 and 3 on the upper level. There are also low phones going toward lounge 2 on the upper level and two on the ground floor arrivals level (near the escalators to parking). All shops and restaurants have level access except the upper level bar. The same escort desk services both Orly Sud and Orly Ouest.

The Bel Air escorts are a service provided free of charge by the airports, and most of the escorts are multilingual.

2. Getting Around

You don't find too many curb cuts in Paris, but boulevards like the Champs Elysées have long stretches of wide sidewalks between intersecting streets. Side streets, of course, are another matter, and some have rough surfaces, but the terrain of the central district is comfortably flat. At least unless you undertake the climb to Montmartre, and you can always go there by car or taxi (or even the funicular!).

PUBLIC TRANSPORTATION: The Métro (subway) is a great transportation network for those who can use it, but long flights of stairs and escalators put it beyond the challenge of most visitors in a wheelchair. Public buses aren't exactly accommodating either.

TAXIS: Taxicabs in Paris are, as in most cities except London, regular automobiles. If you find the rear door as narrow as in most other taxis for transfer from a wheelchair, you can ask to sit in the front, but it will depend on the driver. (You may have competition from a small dog, which many Paris cab drivers take along with them for company!) All legitimate taxicabs have meters and, at the time of writing, the flag drops at 8F ($1), and then it's 1.80F (15¢) per kilometer. There are surcharges to which the driver is entitled, such as large baggage or a wheelchair, or a nighttime trip. You don't have to pay for the taxi's empty return ride between the airport and the city (as you do in some European cities). Tips should be between 12 percent and 15 percent, a little extra if the driver has been particularly helpful. "Libre" is the word that indicates a taxi is available.

3. Orientation

Paris is not a big city by world standards and its central part, the areas with the tourist attractions, are reasonably compact. The **River Seine** divides the city into the **Right Bank** (north) and the **Left Bank** (south), and 32 bridges span the river to link the two halves of the city. Different districts, called *arrondissements,* are referred to by their number rather than by name as a rule, and by written numerals followed by "e" or "er." Although, like nearly everywhere else, Paris now has its zip codes, the last two digits refer back to the arrondissement number. You'll find that most city maps thoughtfully delineate the arrondissements by different colors.

Fanciest arrondissements (on the Right Bank) are the **First, Second,** and **Eighth,** locations of the expensive restaurants, elegant hotels, and the fashion

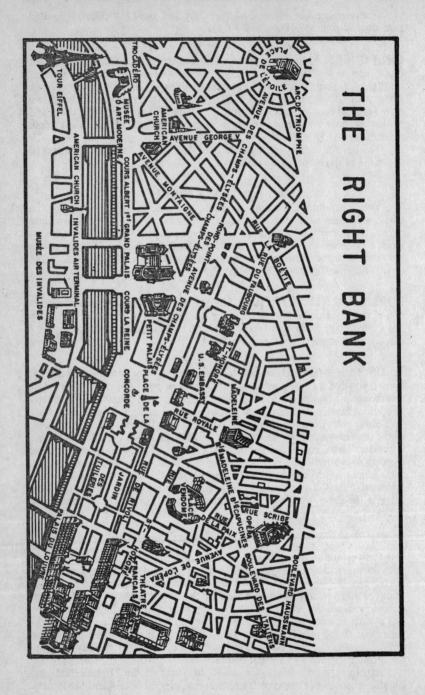

and perfume houses. All of which has its contrast south of the river, in the **Fifth** and **Sixth** on the Left Bank, the Latin Quarter and the student territory of the Sorbonne University, and the colorful world of aspiring artists and writers. The **Seventh,** still south of the Seine, runs westward as far as the Eiffel Tower and is a residential district, interspersed with ministries and embassies, with Les Invalides, site of Napoleon's Tomb, in the center. Further west across the river is the **Sixteenth,** with the Palais de Chaillot on the north bank of the Seine, and reaching across smart residential areas as far as the Bois de Boulogne. One of the others you might be visiting is the rather off-center **Eighteenth** where Montmartre climbs northward from Boulevard Clichy to the white dome of Sacré Coeur.

CURRENCY: The French franc (F) is a metric unit of 100 centimes (c), which are coins in units of 1, 5, 10, 20, and 50 centimes. Francs, as bills, are in denominations of 5, 10, 50, 100, and 500. Banks or *bureaux de change* are usually the best places to exchange currency, since there is often a discount taken by shops, hotels, and restaurants. You'll find large banks with exchange departments open on Saturday morning, in addition to their regular weekday hours of 9 a.m. to noon and 2 to 4 p.m.

CLIMATE: High temperatures range from a winter average of 45 degrees to a summer average of 75 degrees, with spring and fall around 65 degrees, although there can be very hot summers and very cold winters. Spring is a lovely extended season lasting sometimes from early April to the end of May and is one of the most pleasant seasons to visit Paris. Fall has similar appeal in temperature and scenery.

VOCABULARY: Most of what you need can be found in a phrase book (if you do not already know some French), but specialty phrases are often not included, such as the word for wheelchair, which is either *le fauteuil roulant* (pronounced something like luh faw-teh-yuh roo-long), or *la chaise roulante* (lah shez roo-lont); cane is *la canne* (lah can); crutch is *la bequille* (lah bay-kee). You'll recognize *la rampe* of course, and *l'ascenseur* (la-son-ser) also speaks for itself as the elevator. You don't want to see *des marches* (day marsh) or "steps"; and equally unpopular will be *l'escalier* (less-kal-yay) or "staircase."

EMERGENCIES: Call the police by dialing 17.

ELECTRICAL CURRENT: Paris electricity is the same as the rest of Europe —220V—but you'll need a converter for any appliances brought from the U.S.

WHEELCHAIR SERVICE: The Everest & Jenning agency in the Paris area is Jonk, 14 rue Henri-Martin, 93310 Le Pré Saint Gervais (tel. 865-1365).

TELEPHONE CODES: The country code for France is 33; the area code for Paris is 1.

4. Where to Stay?

The headline of this section carries that question mark for a very good reason. Very few hotels can be called accessible according to international standards; charm, quaintness, Parisian character, and even elegance are not always compatible with level entrances or elevators that are big enough for a wheelchair. The small elevator (where there is one) is typical of many European hotels, and its dimensions can be dealt with, in many cases, by taking the footrests off the wheelchair, and by having a companion maneuver the chair, since the elevators are usually wider than they are deep and require a sharp left turn to enter. Other vagaries of many hotels include different levels on the same floor. Another possible problem situation for somebody in a wheelchair in many European hotels is the separate toilet, usually with a narrow door. Since most hotels often have both arrangements, it is preferable to request a room where bath and toilet are combined.

Best accessibility, of course, is in the newer, higher-priced hotels, but I have tried here to give a wider range of possibilities that include hotels with generally larger rooms and entrances with level access or just one step. Where possible, I have also given the dimensions of the elevator as well as the door widths of the guest rooms and bathrooms. Unless it is mentioned, it can be assumed that the main entrance door is wide enough for a standard wheelchair.

Breakfast is often included in the price of the room and usually consists of rolls or croissants, butter and jam, and coffee or other beverage. Juice is usually an extra charge. It is normally brought to your room and arrives, as a rule, at the time you have ordered it.

Hotels included here are grouped geographically and by price, and you will find the arrondissement number in the last one or two digits of the zip code, a clue as to their location. Prices quoted (subject to change) are based on a conversion rate of 8 francs to $1.

RIGHT BANK: *The* famous Paris hotels on the Right Bank often carry the wheelchair-accessibility symbol in hotel listings, but since that is the hotel's own judgment, details should always be checked carefully. However, they *are* the ones that are likely to have the larger elevators and the larger rooms with wider doors. Here are details of some in the deluxe class, followed by the first-class, moderate priced, and then a couple of inexpensive hotels (though not entirely barrier-free).

Deluxe

Hotel Meurice, 228 rue de Rivoli, 75001 (tel. 260-38-60, toll free in the U.S. 800/327-0200), has been home to royalty and celebrities for a long time. Looking much like an 18th-century palace, it does have large guest rooms and doors to both room and bathroom that vary from 27 inches to 33 inches. There is one step at the entrance but plentiful assistance. The elevator provides access to the restaurant. Rates are $111 to $149 single, $149 to $181 double.

Prince de Galles, 33 avenue George V, 75008 (tel. 723-55-11) toll free in the U.S. 800/327-0200), is right off the Champs Elysées and is built around an open courtyard with a fountain in the center. Rooms are spacious and furnished in traditionally elegant style. There is one step at the entrance and level access to the restaurant and to the elevator, which has a 29-inch-wide door and measures 47 inches deep by 41 inches wide. Rooms have 33-inch entry doors and 30-inch doors to the bathroom. A separate toilet has a 26-inch door. Rates start at $121 single, $149 double.

Hotel Scribe, 1 rue Scribe, 75009 (tel. 742-03-40) is also centrally located, this time near the Opéra. It has a level entrance and level access to the restaurant, and an elevator that has a 28-inch door and 35-inch depth by 58-inch width. Rooms are either level with the elevator or up one step. Guest-room doors are in the 30-inch range and bathroom doors 29 inches wide. However, this is one of the hotels in which most rooms have a separate toilet with doors only 23 to 25 inches wide. Check carefully when making reservations. Rates start at 785F ($98.10) single, 1040F ($130) double, inclusive of breakfast.

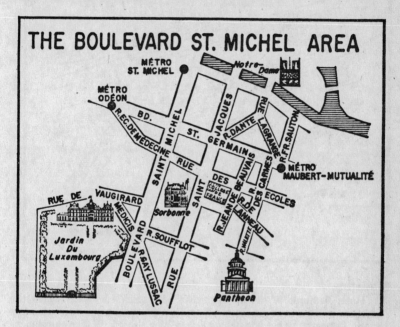

THE BOULEVARD ST. MICHEL AREA

First Class

Le Grand Hotel, 2 rue Scribe, 75009 (tel. 260-33-50, toll free in the U.S. 800/327-0200), opposite the Opera House, has always been one of the city's elegant old hotels, and now it has been appropriately refurbished by Inter-Continental. It has a ramped entrance and 34-inch doors all over, including bathrooms! Single rates go from $78 to $100, and doubles from $109 to $131, including tax and continental breakfast.

Ambassador-Concord, 16 boulevard Haussmann, 75009 (tel. 246-92-63), is behind the Opéra and near Galeries Lafayette. It has a level entrance, and level access to the restaurant and to the elevator (28-inch door, 50-inch depth and 40-inch width). Rooms are on a level with the elevator, and doors range from 29 to 32 inches wide. The bathroom door is 26 inches. Rates start at 525F ($65.50) for both single or double, and at 630F ($78.75) for a twin-bedded room.

Le Pavillon L'Horset, 36 rud de l'Echiquier, 75010 (tel. 246-92-75) is on the border of the 9th and 10th arrondissements and so is near the center of things. There is one step at the entrance, but there is level access to the restaurant and to the ample-sized elevator, which has a 40-inch door and measures 51 inches deep by 40 inches wide. Rooms are on the same level as the elevator on each floor and have 29-inch entrance doors, with 28- to 30-inch doors to the bathroom. Rates here start at 350F ($43.75) single and 410F ($51.25) double.

Moderate

Hotel Bedford, 17 rue de l'Arcade, 75008 (tel. 265-40-32) is near the Madeleine in the area of the Opéra off boulevard Haussmann, and so centrally located. The entrance has one step and everything else is level. Elevator dimensions are 51 inches deep by 39 inches wide. Guest-room doors are 28 inches wide, and the doors to the bathroom are 26 inches. Rates start at 240F ($30) single and 324F ($40.50) double, breakfast included.

The **Astra Mapotel,** 29 rue Caumartin, 75009 (tel. 266-15-15) is another centrally located hotel in the same area of the Madeleine and the Opéra. There are two steps at the entrance, separated by a landing, and three steps to the restaurant, but some of the rooms here are spacious. A few have a 31-inch door and a 29-inch door to the bathroom. The elevator door is 27½ inches wide, and the interior measures 52 inches deep and 31 inches wide. The single rates start at 350F ($43.75) and the doubles from 360F ($45).

There are two medium-priced hotels in the 8th arrondissement. The **Hotel de l'Arcade,** 7 rue de l'Arcade, 75008 (tel. 265-43-85) is also in that central area around the Opéra and the Madeleine. It has one step at the entrance and level access to the elevator, which has a 26-inch door and is 42 inches deep and 57 inches wide. Guest-room doors are 26 inches wide and *some* bathroom doors are 25 inches wide (others are narrower). Rates are $28 single and $34 double, breakfast included.

The **Hotel Rochambeau,** 4 rue la Boétie, 75008 (tel. 265-27-54) has a level entrance and level access to the elevator (27-inch door, 52-inch depth and 29-inch width). Both guest-room and bathroom doors are 26½ inches wide.

Rates are 227F ($28.50) to 265F ($33) single; 290F ($37.50) double, breakfast included.

Hotel Helios, 75 rue de la Victoire, 75009 (tel. 874-28-64) is close to boulevard Haussmann at the Galeries Lafayette, and there is one step at the entrance. The elevator is small, but this hotel has one room on the ground floor with a 28-inch entry door and 27-inch bathroom door. Rates are 169F ($21.50) to 195F ($24.50) single and 202F ($25.25) to 232F ($29) double.

Three medium-priced hotels in the Mapotel chain (Best Western) are listed as having accessible rooms by the Comité National Français de Liaison Pour la Réadaption des Handicapés (CNFLRH), an organization concerned with the rehabilitation of disabled people. They are **Mapotel Colisée,** 6 rue Colisée, 75008 (tel. 359-95-25); the **Bergère,** 32 rue Bergère, 75009 (tel. 770-34-34), and the **Mapotel Victor Hugo,** 19 rue Copernic, at the Arc de Triomphe end, 75016 (tel. 553-76-01). Rates are in the range of $35 single and $40 to $50 double.

Inexpensive

In a great location just off the rue de Rivoli and handy to the Louvre, Notre Dame, the Ile de la Cité, and the Left Bank (via the Pont Neuf), is the **Hotel des Ducs de Bourgogne,** 19 rue du Pont Neuf, 75001 (tel. 233-95-64). It is mentioned here even though it has a few barriers to overcome and is closed for the month of August, but considering the desirable location and the price, it's worth knowing about, and what those barriers are. The entrance has one step, and there is level access to rather small elevator (door is 26 inches, depth is 34 inches, and width 32 inches). Guest rooms have 29-inch doors, but the bathroom has one step, and the door is only 24 inches wide. Some bathrooms have separate toilets, but others are combined. Rates start around 175F ($23) single, 200F ($25) double, breakfast included.

Also in the 1st arrondissement, the **Hotel Montpensier,** 12 rue de Richelieu, 75001 (tel. 296-28-50), is another hotel with a very small elevator but there are rooms on the ground floor, up two steps. The entrance to the hotel itself has one step. Guest rooms have 26-inch doors, but bathroom doors don't go much wider than 23 inches. Rates are in the range of 202F ($26) single and 240F ($30) double.

LEFT BANK: There is one deluxe hotel on the south side of the river that has two rooms designed for accessibility and that is the **Hilton International,** close to the Eiffel Tower at 18 avenue de Suffren, 75015 (tel. 273-92-00), where its modern 11-floor silhouette caused consternation at first but is now an accepted part of the Parisian scene. Every room has color TV. The two special rooms have wider doors, bathroom grab bars, and ceiling hooks for hoist installation in the bathroom. All the public rooms are accessible, including the rooftop restaurant and cocktail lounge, Le Toit de Paris, and the coffeeshop. Rates range from $60 to $80 single, $70 to $95 double.

First Class

The **Victoria Palace Hotel,** rue Blaise Desgoffes, 75009 (tel. 544-38-16), is in Montparnasse, an elegantly comfortable hotel behind an ornate facade. It has one step at the entrance, level access to the restaurant (that opens on to the courtyard and its greenery), and to the elevator, which has a 27-inch door and 42-by-40-inch dimensions. Guest rooms have 28-inch entry doors and 26-inch doors to the bathrooms, many of which are decorated in Italian marble and equipped with hand showers. Rates are around 480F ($60) single, 680F ($85) double).

Le Grand Littré, 9 rue Littré, 75006 (tel. 544-38-68), on a quiet street in the heart of Montparnasse, is an old hotel that has undergone a complete remodeling, and is furnished in reproductions of traditional French pieces. The entrance from the street is level, but there are three steps inside to the lobby and elevator (which has a 27-inch door and is 50 inches deep by 28 inches wide. Guest rooms have 32-inch doors and bathroom doors vary from 28 to 30 inches wide. Rates average around 360F ($45) for single and double rooms, breakfast included.

Among the many hotels in the 7th arrondissement, south of the river between the Eiffel Tower and St. Germain des Prés, are three that have reasonable accessibility. The **Saxe Residence,** 9 villa de Saxe, 75007 (tel. 783-98-28), is in the area behind the Hotel des Invalides at the other end of the Champ de Mars from the Eiffel Tower. The entrance has one step, and there is level access to the elevator, which has a 26-inch door and is 40 inches deep by 35 inches wide. However, there *are* rooms on the ground floor, in addition to ones on a level with the elevator on upper floors, that have 28-inch entry doors and 25-inch doors to the bathroom. Rates are 306F ($38.25) single and 362F ($45.25) double, breakfast included.

La Bourdonnais, 111 avenue de la Bourdonnais, 75007 (tel. 705-45-42), has level access throughout. The elevator has a door that is 27 inches wide and is 40 inches deep by 32 inches wide. Guest rooms have 27-inch doors with 25-inch doors to the bathroom. Rates are around 320F ($40) single; 350F ($43.75) double, breakfast included.

Also in the area behind Les Invalides is the **Hotel de Duquesne,** 23 avenue Duquesne, 75007 (tel. 705-41-86), with one step at the entrance but with level access elsewhere. The elevator has a 27-inch door and is 46 inches deep by 33 inches wide. Guest rooms have 28-inch doors, and bathroom doors vary from 24 to 27 inches. Rates are 240F ($30) single, 320F ($40) double.

KEY TO THE NUMBERED REFERENCES ON OUR PARIS MAP: 1—Arc de Triomphe; 2—Basilique du Sacré-Couer; 3—Bibliothèque Nationale; 4—La Bourse; 5—Catacombes; 6—Cathédrale de Notre-Dame de Paris; 7—Sainte-Chappelle; 8—Georges Pompidou National Center (Beaubourg); 9—École Militaire; 10—Église de la Madeleine; 11—Église Saint-Pierre de Montmartre; 12—Les Égouts (Sewers); 13—Grand and Petit Palais; 14—Hotel des Invalides; 15—Institute de France; 16—Jardin des Tuileries; 17—Jardin du Trocadero; 18—Marché aux Fleurs; 19—Musée Carnavalet; 20—Musée de Cluny; 21—Musée de l'Armée; 22—Musée de l'Histoire de France; 23—Musée de l'Orangerie; 24—Musée des Arts Décoratifs; 25—Musée de Jeu de Paume; 26—Musée Grevin; 27—Musée National d'Art Moderne; 28—Musée Rodin; 29—Musée Victor Hugo; 30—Palais Bourbon; 31—Palais de Chaillot; 32—Palais de Justice; 33—Palais de l'Élysée; 34—Palais du Louvre; 35—Palais and Jardins du Luxembourg; 36—Palais-Royal; 37—Panthéon; 38—Paris Opéra; 39—Place de la Bastille; 40—Place de la Concorde; 41—Place du Tertre; 42—Place Vendôme; 43—St-Etienne-du-Mont; 44—St-Germain-des-Pres; 45—St-Julien-le-Pauvre; 46—St-Séverin; 47—St-Sulpice; 48—Sorbonne; 49—Tour Eiffel; 50—Val-de-Grâce.

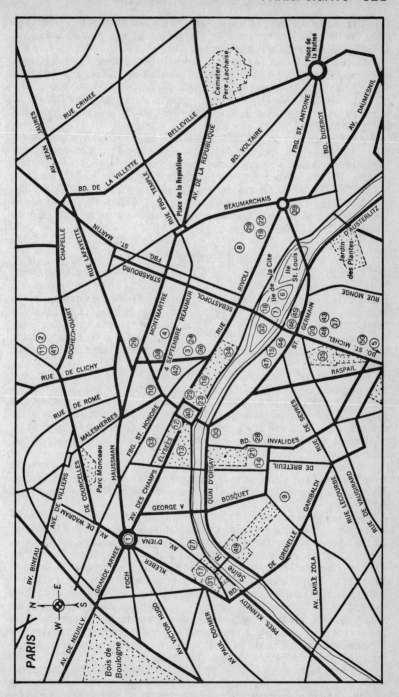

AT THE AIRPORTS: The hotels built at Orly and Charles de Gaulle Airports for the overnight convenience of travelers are new and do have good accessibility. Here are details of some:

Sofitel Paris Roissy, Aeroport Charles de Gaulle-Zone Central, Roissy-en-France, 95500 (tel. 1/862-23-23), has wheelchair-accessible rooms and rates that start at 320F ($40) single, 340F ($42.50) double.

Also at Charles de Gaulle Airport, there is the **Holiday Inn Roissy,** 54 rue de Paris, Roissy-en-France, 95500 (tel. 1/988-00-22), with rates around $63 single, $69 double.

At Orly Sud Airport, the **Hilton International,** Orly Sud Aérogare, 94310 (tel. 1/687-33-88), has one room with a 33-inch entry door, a 26-inch door to the bathroom, which is equipped with grab bars, and ceiling hooks for hoisting devices. TV can be controlled from bedside. Single rates range from 250F ($31.25) to 378F ($47.25), and doubles from 314F ($39.25) to 475F ($59.35).

Motel PLM Orly, Orly Ouest, 94310 (tel. 1/687-23-37), has six rooms that are designed to be wheelchair-accessible. Rates start at 212F ($26.50) single and 238F ($29.75) double.

5. Sightseeing in Paris

Paris itself—its streets, boulevards, and squares—*is* the main attraction, and the accessibility of most of its buildings is not. So, that works out well, and most of your sightseeing may be mostly outdoors. With the exception of the brand-new Pompidou Center, there really isn't one building of note that has anything like convenient accessibility for anybody who uses a wheelchair. Even if you have assistance for the steps that seem to sprout at every entrance, there is often another obstacle inside many buildings where the elevators are tiny or nonexistent.

Not to worry. The main daytime attractions of Paris can keep you busy for a long time as you explore the grand squares and boulevards, wander down the narrow winding streets, enjoy the space and greenery in the gardens and parks, and get your refreshment and entertainment at the same time in the sidewalk cafes. And you don't really need access information to get your fill of all those attractions. Just a good map so that you can concentrate on one district at a time without getting lost.

So what *are* those sights? The names should be familiar even if you've never been to Paris before. Arc de Triomphe, Eiffel Tower, Champs-Elysées, Place de la Concorde, Trocadéro, Place Vendôme, Latin Quarter, Montmartre, for a start.

Most of them provide fairly level going except Montmartre, which probably deserves a special word, since the elevation may seem rather forbidding for the disabled visitor. It's the site of the church, Sacré Coeur (difficult access), and its street surfaces are rather uneven, but it's hard to go to Paris and not visit the **Place du Tertre,** looking like a village square, the scene of the early struggles of famous artists like Picasso. You can always take a taxi up and roll back down! Or even try the **funicular** (cable railway) that takes care of the steepest climb. It starts about a block away from the Place d'Anvers at the Square Willette, and there's only one step at the entrance to the cable car, which has a wide door and 32-inch space each side of the central pole inside, with handrails all round. The exit at the top is level. It runs between 6 a.m. and 11 p.m. and charges 3F (38¢). Quite a view from the top!

Still outdoors, don't forget that the sidewalk cafes should not be considered just a place for refreshment, but as a a ringside location for sightseeing as well. The kaleidoscopic activity of Paris streets and boulevards becomes the free-of-charge sideshow where you can get lots of different shows, from the Champs-Elysées on the Right Bank to the Boulevard St. Michel on the Left Bank. Cafes are taken for granted as places to relax, read the paper, or even write home. A single block in the central part of the city may have three or four, so you won't have to look too far for one. You can stay as long as you want on just one cup of coffee, and you don't have to pay until you are ready to leave. Don't tip if the bill is *"service compris."*

Sightseeing tours do not have wheelchair-accessible vehicles, but if you *are* able to board, you can get details of the commercial tours from your hotel or from the tourist offices. The main **tourist office** is at 127 avenue des Champs-Elysées, 75008 (tel. 720-04-96), where the entrance has one small step. There are others in the main halls of the railroad stations at the Gare du Nord, the Gare de l'Est, or the Gare de Lyon.

A great sightseeing tour that can be taken even by visitors in wheelchairs is provided by the **Bateaux Mouches,** Pont de l'Alma, 75008 (tel. 225-96-10), which offer a wonderful way to see Paris from the river. The boats are spacious, and the staff is helpful and will deal with any difficulties there may be in boarding; the boats differ slightly from each other, and some are more convenient than others. Lunch and dinner are served on the boats that leave at 1:30 and 8:30 p.m. At the debarkation point there are four steps, but again, the staff can provide the necessary muscle or helping hand, depending on your needs.

Before it seems that you are *never* going to be able to go indoors while you are in Paris, here are details of most of the top sights, and you'll see there are possibilities all over, with varying degrees of accessibility. When preparing your day, remember that nearly all the museums and monuments are closed on Tuesday. The following places are listed in a rough order of "top sights" and not by area, but you will be able to locate them on that good tourist map you will have acquired.

EIFFEL TOWER: Although the second and third platforms of that symbol of Paris, the Eiffel Tower, have parapets that block the view from a wheelchair, there *is* good access and a good view from the first platform. The best elevator is at the North Tower since it has level entry and is a large one, relatively. If you are ambulatory, you will be able to reach the second level by the same elevator, but you have to change elevators to go to the third level. The first and second levels are open from 10 a.m. to 11 p.m., and the third from 10 a.m. to 6 p.m. The Eiffel Tower is notorious for its hours-long line, so plan your visit early in the morning, even though the staff is helpful to visitors in wheelchairs or others who are unable to stand for long periods. Admission charges vary by level: 8F ($1) to the first level, 18F ($2.25) to the second level, and 26F ($3.25) to the third level. Don't forget to take the North elevator back down. There's refreshment available at each level. (If you need a rest room in this neighborhood, note the details that follow for those underneath the steps at the Palais de Chaillot, which is just across the Pont d'Iéna over the Seine.)

PALAIS DE CHAILLOT: Don't miss the magnificent view from the Place du Trocadéro, between the two wings of the Palais de Chaillot, out over the Jardins du Trocadéro with its fountains, and across the river to the Eiffel Tower and the Champ de Mars beyond. There are steps—one and then three—but the view is worth the haul.

On the ground floor of the Palais de Chaillot is the **Musée de la Marine** (tel. 727-96-31), which has five steps at the entrance. On the first and second floors is the rather more inaccessible **Musée de l'Homme,** where visitors in wheelchairs must be accompained—the elevator door is only 25 inches wide, and there are a number of steps after you get off the elevator!

However, the public rest rooms at the Palais de Chaillot deserve a mention: there are stalls with 27-inch doors underneath the main flight of steps to the building, and they are signposted from within the gardens. There is one step to reach them.

NOTRE DAME: You can probably get almost as much pleasure looking at the outside of this magnificent Gothic cathedral that has seen so much of French history as you can from going inside. There is one step at the main entrance (which isn't always open, however, and the alternative is the Cloister Portal in the rue de Cloître which has three steps). The Nave is level, but there are three steps to the Ambulatory and the Treasury. (Other visitors may climb the 387 steps to the top of the twin towers, but that probably won't be on your itinerary.)

THE LOUVRE: Be prepared to have access problems at the Musée du Louvre (tel. 260-39-26), the most famous museum in Paris and the largest palace (its original function) in the world. Many of the galleries are reached only by staircase, but since it might be impossible to see it all even in one lifetime, there *are* parts that can be reached, once you have overcome the series of steps at the Porte Denon entrance (three, then five, then six to get to the main entrance lobby). There are even more steps at the other entrance, the Porte Barbet de Jouy. First compensation for making it this far is the view of the *Winged Victory* to the left of the main entrance.

You can reach the painting galleries on the first floor (the entrance lobby is the ground floor) by taking the elevator to the right of the main entrance. Here, the right wing galleries (home of the *Mona Lisa*) are level, with the exception of the step to the Flemish gallery. There is another elevator on the ground floor that will take you down to the *Venus de Milo,* but you may have to look for it carefully at the end of the Sept Cheminées Gallery.

Rest rooms are not specifically adapted, but there are some on the first and second floors near the elevators that have stall doors 25 inches wide. On the first floor between the buffet and the Grand Galleries there is a women's rest room with a 26-inch stall door.

The Louvre is open daily except Tuesday from 9:45 a.m. to 6:30 p.m. Admission is 9F ($1.12) and is free on Sunday and Wednesday (also more crowded therefore).

GALERIE DU JEU DE PAUME: At the other end of the Tuileries Garden from the Louvre are the works of artists who were at the other end of the art establishment at one time. The Impressionists' showcase is the Galerie du Jeu de Paume (tel. 260-12-07), on the corner of the rue de Rivoli and the Place de la Concorde. It is a relatively easy museum to visit and a treasure house for all the admirers of Manet, Monet, Renoir, Rousseau, Degas, Pissarro, Van Gogh, Gauguin, et al. There are two steps, or a rather rough-faced ramp, at the entrance, and an adequately sized elevator connects the two floors of the museum. It is open daily, except Tuesday, from 9:45 a.m. to 5:15 p.m. Admission is 7F (90¢), half-price on Sunday.

CENTRE GEORGES POMPIDOU: Now we're finally into the present at the avant-garde and completely accessible building, often referred to as the **Beaubourg** because it's on the Plateau Beaubourg, east of the boulevard de Sebastopol in the 4th arrondissement, near all the new construction that has also transformed the ancient Les Halles market area. It now rivals the Eiffel Tower as the most popular tourist attraction in Paris, and was a project destined to be a temple devoted to every form of 20th-century art.

The Musée National d'Art Moderne has been moved here and is now the center's most significant section. Each season there are special exhibitions as well. Other parts of the Beaubourg house the first public library in Paris, a center for industrial design, and a cinema that offers an historic perspective of filmmaking. The top floor restaurant and cafeteria have views that cover most of Paris. All floors are accessible by special elevator, and there are wheelchair-accessible rest rooms in the Pavillon des Arts.

The Centre Pompidou is open daily, except Tuesday, from noon to 10 p.m. and from 10 a.m. to 10 p.m. on weekends. Admission is 16F ($2) for an all-day pass to everything. Admission to the museum only is 8F ($1) and is free on Sunday. No admission fee for under-18 or over-65 visitors.

GRAND PALAIS: Although there is no permanent art collection at the Grand Palais, rue de Selves, 8e (tel. 231-81-24), which is between the Seine and the Champs-Elysées, it is one of Paris's leading cultural centers and has outstanding exhibits from time to time. You'll see them advertised on colorful posters around the city, or noted in the English-language *Paris Weekly Information,* which you can get from the Tourist Office at 127 Champs-Elysées.

Although there are 26 steps at the main entrance, there's a 1:10 ramp from door B at 3 rue de Selves, leading to the basement where you can take an attended elevator up to the exhibit hall. The galleries are all level. The Grand Palais is open daily from 10 a.m. to 7:45 p.m., on Wednesday until 9:45 p.m. Closed Tuesday.

PETIT PALAIS: There are also frequent exhibits at the Petit Palais across the street from the Grand Palais, on the Avenue Dutruit, 8e (tel. 265-99-21). It presents some access problems with the six steps at the rear of the building (there are 21 steps at the main entrance), but once you are inside, there is a large elevator to the floor where the exhibits are held. The rest room near room 13 on the ground floor has a 28-inch stall door (the attendant has the key).

SIGHTS WITH SOME PROBLEMS: Rather than leave them out or go through a more lengthy litany of some of the famous sights in Paris and all their steps and obstacles, I thought it best to mention some you might wonder about if they are not included at all. From the point of view of somebody who uses a wheelchair all the time, it seems that most of the venerable buildings included in most sightseeing guides were not to be considered, or were marginal. (No accessible rest rooms, of course.) It's up to you—here are the facts:

The **Hôtel des Invalides**; Napoleon's tomb has 13 steps and a 35-inch parapet around it; the Musée de l'Armée has 4 steps at the entrance, which is from the courtyard, but some halls on the ground floor that are barrier-free.

The **Conciergerie,** the medieval royal palace that became a prison during the Revolution, has steps at the entrance and only a spiral staircase to the palace kitchen, but once inside there is a one-step access to most of the rooms.

La Sainte Chapelle is one of the oldest and most beautiful churches anywhere, noted for its great stained-glass windows in the upper chapel. It has six steps at the entrance and only the lower chapel is accessible to wheelchairs.

The **Panthéon,** the former church that since the Revolution has housed the tombs of some of France's famous men, including Rousseau, Voltaire, Victor Hugo, and Emile Zola, towers over the Left Bank and is one of the landmarks of Paris. It has 11 steps at the entrance and 4 more inside.

La Madeleine, the patron church of Paris, is a beautiful building that stands between the Opéra and the Place de la Concorde, but you'll have to admire it from the outside (which it well deserves) unless you want to tackle the 28 steps at the entrance.

The **Musée de Cluny,** on the Left Bank, has beautiful medieval art and can be entered with only one step, but there is no elevator so that only the ground floor is accessible to wheelchairs and even that is not always level.

The **Rodin Museum** is in the 18th-century mansion where Auguste Rodin, the sculptor, once lived and worked. Many of his pieces can be seen in the courtyard, including *The Thinker* and *The Burghers of Calais*. The house has four steps at the entrance, and inside there are nine rooms on the same level, but only a spiral staircase to the upper floor.

Sacré Coeur, atop the hill that is Montmartre, is one of the best-known sights in Paris, and the terrace in front of it provides fine panoramic views of the city. There are lots of steps at the entrance and also down to the crypt and up to the dome. The nave is level.

CHATEAU DE VERSAILLES: Not a *Paris* sight, and not an easy one to visit, but so famous that you may want to know some details of the obstacles since it is only 15 miles from Paris.

The best way to visit Louis XIV's magnificent palace in its splendid and ornate setting is by car, because a disabled visitor can be driven into the vast cobbled courtyard (about 300 yards from gate to building entrance), although the car must then be parked in the Place d'Armes. If you go by train from the Gare des Invalides in Paris, the station at Versailles is about 600 or so yards from the courtyard gate (the train will have wide doors and a place to stay in a wheelchair, but two steps to board.)

Perhaps I should mention, before you get too eager, that the State Rooms and the Royal Apartments are reached only by a staircase with 40 steps. Once up there, the floors are level! The entrance to the ground floor has two sets of three steps at the main entrance, and three steps at the Queen's Staircase entrance.

It may be better to save your energy for the vast gardens, the ultimate of French landscaping, with fountains, lakes, and hundreds of statues. Most of the park is accessible via ramps and slopes, and the surface is hard gravel for the most part. There are plenty of seats available for resting if you are not already in your own. One of the buildings in the park that is reasonably accessible is the **Grand Trianon,** a *long* way from the main palace. It has level entrance and is open from 2 to 4:40 p.m. each day except Tuesday, with an admission charge of 9F ($1.12). The park and gardens at Versailles are open daily from early morning until dark, when there is often a spectacular *son et lumière,* sound and light, show at the Neptune Lake.

6. Entertainment

THEATERS: It's difficult to be too encouraging about Paris theaters since nearly all of them have steps either outside or inside, and where there *are* elevators at all, they are usually small ones.

The **Opéra** is pretty much out of bounds with its sweeping staircases both inside and out, but there is light opera at the **Opéra-Comique,** 5 rue Favart, 75002 (tel. 742-72-00), which has a level entrance on the rue Marivaux, a small elevator, and accessible balcony boxes.

If you have a minimum knowledge of French, you might enjoy a performance of Molière, for instance, at the **Comédie Française,** Place du Théâtre Français, 75001 (tel. 742-27-31), but there are steps to the foyer and a small elevator to the auditorium. There are wheelchair locations in the orchestra, but a couple of steps to get there.

You won't need to know the language for the concerts and ballet performances held at the **Théâtre des Champs-Elysées,** 15 avenue Montaigne, 75008 (tel. 359-37-03), but there are two sets of three steps at the entrance and transfer to a seat is required.

Among theaters with level entrances and wheelchair locations are: **Madeleine,** 19 rue de Surène, 75008 (tel. 265-06-28); the **Marigny,** Carré Marigny, 75008 (tel. 256-04-41); and the **Salle Genier,** Place du Trocadéro, Jardins du Trocadéro, 75016 (tel. 533-74-27).

Theaters with level entrances, but requiring transfer to theater seats, include the **Antoine,** 14 boulevard de Strasbourg, 75010 (tel. 208-77-71); the music hall **Gaité Montparnasse,** 26 rue de la Gaité, 75014 (tel. 633-16-18), and via the rear entrance at the Théâtre de la Ville, 2 place du Chatelet, 75004 (tel. 887-35-39).

Wheelchair locations, but with steps at the entrance, are available at the **Athénée** (five steps), 4 avenue de l'Opéra, 75001 (tel 073-16-45); the **Comédie des Champs-Élysées** (two steps), 15 avenue Montaigne, 75008 (tel 359-37-03), where the wheelchair location is in a ground-floor box in the orchestra; **La Bruyère** (one step), 5 rue la Bruyère, 75009 (tel. 874-76-99); **Michel** (two steps), 38 rue des Mathurins, 75008 (tel. 265-35-02); **Mogador** (two steps), 25 rue Mogador, 75009 (tel. 285-25-80); **Montparnasse** (two steps), 31 rue de la Gaité, 75014 (tel. 326-66-00); **Oeuvre** (four steps), 55 rue de Clichy, 75009 (tel. 874-42-52), and the **Théâtre de Paris** (four steps), 15 rue Blanche, 75009 (tel. 874-20-44).

CONCERT HALLS: There are two concert halls that have better accessibility than most of the theaters, and which give priority to patrons in wheelchairs.

Salle Gaveau, 45 rue la Boétie, 75008 (tel. 225-29-14), has one step at the main entrance and the elevator door here is narrow, but the entrance on the avenue Delcassé has a larger, attended service elevator. There are wheelchair locations on the second floor.

At the **Salle Pleyel,** 252 rue du Faubourg St. Honoré, 75008 (tel. 227-06-30), there is one step at the entrance and one step into the elevator. This hall has a number of wheelchair locations.

CABARETS: Among the cabarets and night clubs with level entrances and wheelchair locations are the famed **Folies Bergére,** 32 rue Richer, 75009 (tel. 770-98-49), and the **Olympia,** 28 boulevard des Capucines, 75009 (tel. 742-25-49).

Note: It is customary to tip the attendant who shows you to your seat a minimum of one franc, but more, of course, if you have received special assistance.

You can get entertainment information in English by calling 720-88-98, or from the English language *Paris Weekly Information,* available at newsstands, or from tourist offices. You'll also see billboard announcements of shows and concerts on the round kiosks all over Paris streets.

7. Shopping

It's *your* decision whether you want to pay the rather high prices you'll find in Paris, but there's a lot of window-shopping that can be done.

The **rue du Faubourg Saint-Honoré** is the home of the *haute couture,* and around the **Place Vendôme** you can feast your eyes on the jewelry, with more temptation in the boutiques on the **avenue Montaigne,** the **avenue Victor Hugo,** the **rue de Passy,** and the **rue de Sèvres,** among others.

Perfumes and gloves are usually good buys in Paris, but remember that the tax-free shops at the airports stock many of the perfumes and other items you'll see in the stores and give a considerable discount. However, if you spend more than 400F ($50) in any one store, you are entitled to a foreigner's discount, which means that you don't have to pay the 15 percent sales tax (but there's a lot of paperwork involved).

If you'd like to browse in a couple of the large department stores, here is some access information. Most Paris stores are open Monday to Saturday from 9:30 a.m. to 6:30 p.m.

Galeries Lafayette is next door to the Opéra, at 40 boulevard Haussmann, 75009 (tel. 282-34-56), and entrance doors are level except for the ones marked Antin, Victoire, and Trinité. The elevator is sizable and goes to all floors.

Printemps is not far away, near the Madeleine, at 69 boulevard Haussmann, 75009 (tel. 285-22-22). It is actually three stores connected by bridges on the third floor. There are level entrances to the new store at the corner of boulevard Haussmann and rue Charras, and at the men's fashion store (Brummel) on the rue de Provence. At the old store, there are level entrances on the corner of rue Caumartin and boulevard Haussmann, and a ramped entrance on the rue du Havre. The restaurant on the sixth floor in the new store is accessible. Rest rooms in the new stores have a stall with a 26-inch-wide door on the third floor and a 28-inch stall door on the sixth floor.

Something new for Paris is the multilevel underground shopping mall. At the easterly end of the 1st arrondissement, behind the fashionable rue de Rivoli and bordering on the boulevard de Sebastopol, the produce market of Paris, Les Halles, stood for centuries. A few years ago, like many other urban markets, it was moved to the outskirts of the city, and in its place is now the **Forum des Halles,** a four-level pedestrian mall of boutiques and cafes. Some of the streets on the surface level still have their original cobblestones, but there are three more levels, including a garage underground, which are all connected by elevator.

Chapter 18

VIENNA

The Waltz and the Woods

1. Getting There
2. Getting Around
3. Orientation 4. Some
Suggestions on Hotels
5. Eating in Vienna 6. Seeing
the Vienna Sights 7. Opera and Concerts

VIENNA CONJURES UP many romantic images—the Danube, the Vienna Woods, the waltz, the heyday of the Austro-Hungarian Empire. . . .

Today Vienna retains the special charm that attracted artists, musicians, and the *beau monde* in the past, and has settled into a gracious, friendly city, with 18th-century baroque palaces and 19th-century imperial grandeur reflecting the glorious time when it was the hub of Europe. It has great architecture, treasurehouses in its museums, and splendid music for the intellectual senses; restaurants, pastry shops, and coffee houses galore for pleasurable senses of another kind.

And the center of the city is flat and easy to get around. *Wien* (Vienna) is a convenient city. Nearly all its main attractions are within "walking" distance in the city center (*inner Stadt*), which has large areas of pedestrian malls and narrow streets that are less-trafficked for the most part, and all on flat terrain.

Hotels, as always, have to be carefully screened before you make reservations. Their accessibility is related to the energy and tolerance of the visitor in a wheelchair, as in most European cities where interiors with odd floor levels, tiny elevators, and separate toilets with very narrow doors are often the norm in the older hotels, even the grand ones. But there *are* possibilities!

The "sights" were obviously not designed with wheelchairs in mind either, and there are a number of places that have formidable steps. However, many places do offer alternative ways around the obstacles and staff that are eager to help you see their treasures.

Door widths and other access information for some hotels, restaurants, theaters, and museums, among other institutions in Vienna, are given in a booklet, "Vienna: City Guide for Disabled Persons," available from the Verband der Querschnittgelahmten Oesterreichs, Liechtensteinstrasse 61, 1090 Vienna, Austria.

1. Getting There

Coming from overseas, you will land at **Schwechat Airport,** some ten miles from downtown. It is a reasonably easy airport to cope with. As always, airlines make the arrangements for disabled passengers to be deplaned and escorted through formalities. It does have adapted rest rooms, but they are not too obvious, and airport staff should be able to direct you.

Transportation to the center of the city has to be by taxi if you can't use the regular transfer bus connections. Taxi fare will cost about AS 300 (approximately $16).

2. Getting Around

Most of what you will want to do in Vienna is within a compact area. There aren't any curb cuts on the streets where there is traffic, but there are plenty of pedestrian-only thoroughfares that are quite level. Sidewalks, of course, are narrow in the old city, but you won't usually find them crowded.

As a paraplegic with an able companion, I found Vienna a delight, and easy to get around. You won't really need the subway to get anywhere, but if you don't mind riding escalators in a wheelchair, you can even use the relatively new **U-Bahn,** although some stations only have "up" escalators. Don't make my mistake (unless you've lots of help), and board at the brand-new station at Stephansplatz to go to Schönbrunn Palace, only to find an old-fashioned station with a long flight of stairs at the other end. Whatever the surprises, it was another cherished experience of riding with the rest of the world on a public transit system, and this one is a beauty. The subway can also be a way to get to the top of the hill on which the Upper Belvedere Palace stands, and even though it is a medium distance from the station to the palace, it is all on level terrain.

Vienna's surface public transportation is in the form of **trolleys** that have very high steps to enter, and certainly no place inside for a wheelchair.

There are no **rental cars** with hand controls available in Vienna, but there are plenty of companies such as **Avis** (14 Kärntnerring) if you do not need hand controls, or are with a companion who drives. The only time you will need a car, though, is if you decide to spend a day in the Vienna Woods with its hilltop castles, or want to visit the *Heurigens,* the taverns where the products of the local vineyards can be sampled in rustic surroundings. It makes a wonderful outing.

Vienna recently replaced its **taxi** fleets with brand-new Mercedes cars (even some station wagons), and you will find them at taxi stands. Taxis can also be called by dialing 3130, 4369, or 6282. Fares are metered within the city, but for trips outside, rates should be agreed with the driver beforehand. One driver told me, as he took me ahead of the other two people in line at the taxi stand, that it was the policy of Viennese taxis to give priority to disabled passengers. As a New Yorker, I'm still reeling from that one.

3. Orientation

The heart of Vienna is the old city that was founded on a Roman settlement (Vinaboda) on the south bank of the **Danube** (which is called the Donau by Austrians). It was surrounded for centuries by a city wall that protected it

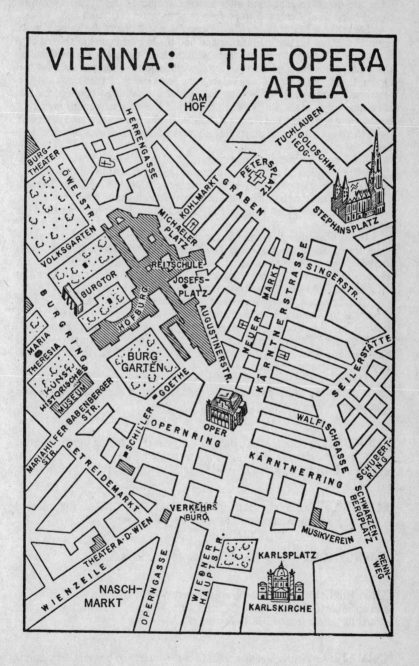

from one would-be conqueror after another, including the Turks, who were turned back from Central Europe forever at its gates 300 years ago.

Less than a century ago, when Vienna was still one of the world's most important cities, Emperor Franz Joseph had the last remnants of the old city walls pulled down and replaced them with the impressive **Ringstrasse**, one of the grand boulevards of Europe, lined with majestic buildings such as the Opera, the Hofburg (the Royal Palace), the Art Gallery, Parliament, and the University, among others. Within the relatively small area bounded by the horseshoe curve of the Ringstrasse are most of Vienna's attractions including its shopping and cafes. The Ring is completed by the Danube Canal, a diversion from the main river, that starts just above Vienna and rejoins the river just below the city.

Focal point of Vienna is, undeniably, **St. Stephan's Cathedral,** whose tall, distinctive steeple and roof can be seen for long distances in all directions.

The oldest part of the city extends between St. Stephan's and the **Danube Canal** where the narrow streets of the former Jewish ghetto lead from Hoher Markt to Vienna's oldest church, **St. Ruprecht's,** which dates from the 11th century.

In the other direction from St. Stephan's are Vienna's most elegant shopping streets, **Kärntnerstrasse** and **Der Graben,** running south and east. Both are pedestrian malls with many outdoor cafes. If you follow Kärnterstrasse, it eventually leads to the State Opera and the Ringstrasse. If you follow the Graben and Kohlmarkt, you'll come to the Hofburg, one-time Imperial Palace.

The **Prater,** a former Imperial hunting reserve, lies between the Danube Canal and the Danube River, and is now a 4000-acre recreation area of gardens and parks and has one of the oldest amusement parks in Europe.

Belvedere Palace stands on a hill just south of the Ringstrasse, and **Schönbrunn Palace,** once deep in the country, is now enclosed by the extended city in a southwest direction.

On the northeastern bank of the Danube, the modern office blocks that tower above the older buildings are headquarters of some United Nations agencies.

CURRENCY: The unit of currency in Austria is the schilling (often indicated as "S" but here referred to as "AS" for Austrian schilling), which contains 100 groschen. I have used a rate of AS 18.8 to $1 to convert prices in this guide.

ELECTRICITY: Electrical current in Vienna is 220 volts AC, so you will need a converter for appliances brought from the United States.

EMERGENCIES: Phone 133 for police; 144 for ambulance.

SHOPPING: Shops are usually open Monday to Friday from 9 a.m. to 6 p.m. and on Saturday from 8 a.m. to 12 noon. Food shops open earlier but are often closed for lunch from 12:30 to 3 p.m.

CLIMATE: In Vienna, weather tends to cold winters and hot summers. Spring and fall with their mild, sunny days are ideal times to visit.

LANGUAGE: German, with a distinct Austrian accent and sometimes a slightly different vocabulary, is the principal language, but English is widely understood and spoken. The word for wheelchair is *Rollstuhl* (pronounced rol-stool).

TELEPHONE: The country code for Austria is 43, the area code for Vienna is 222.

4. Some Suggestions on Hotels

Vienna has its share of Europe's grand hotels, charming pensions, and modern chains, but the only hotel in the center of the city that has special facilities for wheelchair visitors is the Hilton International. Dozens of others mark themselves with the international symbol of access in the official hotel directory, but it is based on their own criteria, which are probably confined to wide doorways, not too many steps, and staff that is willing to lend a hand. The elevators built in the older hotels were never meant to carry more than a couple of vertical guests, and the size was often dictated by the size of the stairwell into which the elevators were installed. Hoteliers don't always realize that the width of the door to the separate toilet is also crucial to a guest who uses a wheelchair all the time, despite the fact that the door to the bathroom may be huge.

With all those caveats expressed, I have to add that it *is* possible to find somewhere to stay, as long as there is plenty of checking done before you make a reservation. Most European hoteliers are true professionals, carefully trained in the care of guests, and are usually prepared to find you accommodation in their establishment as long as you are very specific about your needs. The hotels included here are only those around the **Inner City (First District):** Vienna is such an easy place to visit if you are based in the center, since most of the museums, restaurants, and other sights are then within "walking" distance. They are arranged here in order of price, converted from schillings into dollars at the rate of AS 18.8 to $1, the exchange rate.

Note: European hotels often quote rates for double rooms as "per person." Rates quoted here for double rooms are double the "per person" rate.

The addresses are given here Austrian-style, with the street first, then the house number, then the zip code, which should be written before the city name, as is usual in most European countries.

DELUXE: The **Hilton International Wien,** Am Stadtpark, 1030 Vienna (tel. 222/75-26-52) overlooks the Stadtpark (City Park), and has level access throughout and elevators to all floors. There are two rooms with 34-inch entry and bathroom doors, and grab bars at the toilet and bath. The public rest room in the Cafe am Park is also wheelchair-accessible. Rates are AS 1090 to AS 1650 ($58 to $67.75) single; AS 1470 to AS 2200 ($78 to $117) double.

The **Hotel Intercontinental,** Johannesgasse 28, 1030 (tel. 222/56-36-11), also at the Stadtpark, has an entrance on Lothringerstrasse that has no steps. Because it is also a relatively new hotel, there is an adequate elevator and access to guest rooms. Rates are AS 1250 to AS 1750 ($66.50 to $93.10) single; AS 1590 to AS 2090 ($84.60 to $111.20) double.

One of Europe's grand luxury hotels has always been Vienna's **Hotel Imperial,** Kärntner Ring 16, 1010 (tel. 222/65-17-65), located on the Ringstrasse. There is one step at the entrance and another to the restaurant. The elevator is adequate with a 32-inch door. Bathroom entry is 27 inches and toilets are in the bathroom. Rates are AS 1100 to AS 1700 ($58.50 to $90.45) single; AS 1700 to AS 2600 ($90.50 to $138.30) double, including breakfast.

Another world-renowned and elegant grand hotel in Vienna is the **Hotel Sacher,** Philharmonikerstr. 4, 1010 (tel. 222/52-55-75), located behind the State Opera House. The entrance is level and the elevator has a 27-inch door. Many of the guest-room baths have doors that are only 24 inches wide, so you should indicate your specific requirements if you make reservations here. Single rates range from AS 980 to AS 1400 ($52.15 to $74.50) and double from AS 1750 to AS 2050 ($93.10 to $109.10) including breakfast.

Just off the Ring in a wing of the baroque Schwarzenberg Palace, the **Hotel im Palais Schwarzenberg,** Schwarzenberger Platz 9, 1030 (tel. 222/72-15-25), has very convenient dimensions for access. The entrance has no steps, but the restaurant has three. Elevator door is 35 inches, and bathroom doors in guest rooms are also 35 inches wide. Single rates range from AS 1290 to AS 1600 ($68.60 to $85.10), and doubles from AS 1750 to AS 3150 ($93.10 to $167.55) including breakfast.

Right on the Ring opposite the Opera is the **Hotel Bristol,** Kärntner Ring 1, 1010 (tel. 222/52-95-52), which has no steps at the entrance. The elevator door is 31 inches wide, and its inside dimensions are 55 by 55 inches. Width of bathroom doors varies from 23 to 26 inches so specify when you reserve if you want a room with the wider door. Single rates here range from AS 1100 to AS 1700 ($58.50 to $90.45), and doubles from AS 1700 to AS 2400 ($90.45 to $127.65) including breakfast.

FIRST CLASS: With hotels outside the "grand" category, you can expect dimensions to diminish too, but that is not to say that all is impossible.

Very centrally located, the Hotel Astoria, Kärnterstrasse 32, 1015 (tel. 222/52-65-85), has one step at the entrance and a 31-inch door to the rather small elevator. Bathroom doors are 27 inches wide and toilet doors are 25 inches wide. Single rates are AS 980 ($52.15) and doubles range from AS 1360 to AS 1540 ($72.35 to $82) including breakfast.

In the same central area, just off the Kärnterstrasse, is the **Hotel Kaiserin Elisabeth,** Weihburg Gasse 3, 1010 (tel. 222/83-86-10), which I found reasonably accessible in a standard wheelchair. There is one step at the entrance, and the elevator door is wide enough, but my chair had to be maneuvered for a turn inside it. The interior of the hotel is level to the elevator and to the restaurant. Doors to guest room and bathroom were wide enough. Single rates go from AS 595 to AS 710 ($31.65 to $37.75), and doubles from AS 840 to AS 1540 ($44.70 to $81.90) including breakfast.

The **Hotel de France,** Schottenring 3, 1010 (tel. 222/34-35-40), is located on the westerly part of the Ring. The entrance has no steps; there are three steps to the restaurant. Elevator door is 28 inches wide and interior dimensions are 51 by 45 inches. Bathroom and toilet doors here are only 23 inches wide but open outward. Single rates range from AS 805 to AS 1005 ($42.80 to $53.45), and double rates go from AS 1230 to AS 1870 ($65.40 to $99.50).

MODERATE: Many of the hotels in this category have fewer rooms *with* baths than without, so be very specific in making reservations.

In the older part of town, between St. Stephan's Cathedral and the Danube Canal, is the **Hotel Kärntnerhof,** Grashofgasse 4, 1010 (tel. 222/52-19-23). The entrance has one step. Elevator door is 35 inches wide (interior is 43 by 59 inches), and bathroom doors are 29 inches, with variations in the toilet doors from 27 inches and wider. Single rates are AS 620 ($33) and doubles are AS 960 ($51) including breakfast.

Also in the older part of the city is the **Hotel Post,** Fleischmarkt 24, 1010 (tel. 222/52-66-87), which has no steps at the entrance and one step to the restaurant. The elevator door is 35 inches wide, and the inside of the elevator is 55 by 47 inches. Bathroom and toilet doors are 27 inches. Rates are AS 560 ($30) single, AS 740 to AS 880 ($39.40 to $47) double including breakfast.

The **Hotel Mozart,** Julius Tandler Platz 4, 1090 (tel. 222/34-15-37), has one step at the entrance, and the elevator door is 28 inches wide (41 by 43 inches inside). Bathroom and toilet doors are 29 inches, with the toilet door opening outward. Rates range from AS 270 to AS 500 ($14.35 to $26.00) single, and AS 520 to AS 820 ($27.65 to $43.65) double, including breakfast.

Although there are three steps at the entrance, the staff entrance is level at the **Hotel Wandl,** Petersplatz 9, 1010 (tel. 222/63-63-17). It has an adequate elevator, and bathroom and toilet doors are at least 27 inches. Rates go from AS 430 to AS 560 ($22.85 to $29.80) single, AS 730 to AS 850 ($38.85 to $45.20) double.

5. Eating in Vienna

In Austria, you are in a country where everybody loves to eat even between meals, and for very good reason: there are endless temptations. Although it is not a large country, its cuisine has tremendous variety because it is derived from the different nationalities of the old Austrian Empire—what is now Czechoslovakia, Hungary, Yugoslavia, Italy, parts of Germany, and Poland. The price range is wide, too, from the elegant and expensive to the modest *Beisels,* which are plain, pub-like places serving good home-style food. The thoroughly Austrian *Konditoreien* (pastry shops) and their sidewalk cafes are an integral element of the Viennese scene. Although there are good ones all over town, the most famous cafe in Vienna is **Demel's** at Kohlmarkt 14, near the Hofburg gates.

A word about Viennese coffee, which is an institution in Vienna, the city that introduced coffee to Europe through old Turkish connections. Among its more than 20 varieties are the *kleiner schwarzer* (small cup without milk); a *kleiner brauner* (small cup with just enough milk to make it brown); *melange* (large cup with milk); the *melange mit schlag* (whipped cream on top); Eiskaffee (iced coffee with vanilla ice cream and milk), and many, many more.

No need to elaborate on the pastries—just point!

Among the more expensive restaurants in central Vienna that have reasonable accessibility are the **Kervansaray,** Mahlerstr. 9 (tel. 52-88-43), with Turkish specialities, which has one step at the entrance and one step inside, and **Zu den 3 Husaren** (The Three Hussars), Weihburggasse 4 (tel. 52-11-92), with a level entrance.

In the top bracket are the **Coq d'Or,** Fuhrichgasse 1 (tel. 52-12-75), with one step at the entrance; the **Falstaff,** Wahringerstr. 67 (tel. 42-27-41), also with one step at the entrance, and the **Restaurant Schöner,** Siebenstern Gasse 19 (tel. 93-72-06).

Two of the grand hotels that recall the plush era of the Hapsburgs provide top restaurants but also pleasant lounges and cafes where the tab will not be *so* high. At the **Sacher,** Philharmonikerstr. 4 (tel. 52-55-75), home of that delicious chocolate cake, the Sachertorte, there is a level entrance. The **Imperial,** on the Ring at Kärntner Ring 16 (tel. 65-17-65), has music in the cafe in the afternoon and in the restaurant in the evening. There is one step at the entrance to the hotel and another step to the restaurant.

The moderate price category includes the **Alter Rathauskeller,** Wipplingerstrasse (tel. 63-14-41), which has a level entrance; the **Kursalon Stadtpark,** Johannesgasse 33 (tel. 73-21-81), with one step at the entrance; **Zum Schottentor,** Schottengasse 7 (tel. 63-93-81); **Marhold,** Fleischmarkt 9 (tel. 63-28-73), with two steps at the entrance; **Mullerbeisl,** Sellerstätte 15 (tel. 52-42-65), with a level entrance; **Wienerwald,** Hellariastrasse 12 (tel. 93-72-79), and also the Wienerwald at Triesterstrasse 56 (tel. 62-01-82), both of which have one step at the entrance and two steps inside; and **Zum Laterndl,** Landesgerichtstrasse 12, (tel. 43-43-58), which has one step at the entrance.

Medium-priced meals can be had at the **Drei Hüte** (Three Hats), Elisabeth Platz 7 (tel. 65-41-49), which has one step at the entrance; the **Gösser Bierhaus,** Stubenbastei 2 (tel. 52-48-39), with two steps at the entrance; **Schweizerhaus,** Prater 116 (tel. 24-23-17), which has no steps; and the **Batzenhäusl,** Dr. Karl Jueger Ring 12 (tel 63-53-44), with one step.

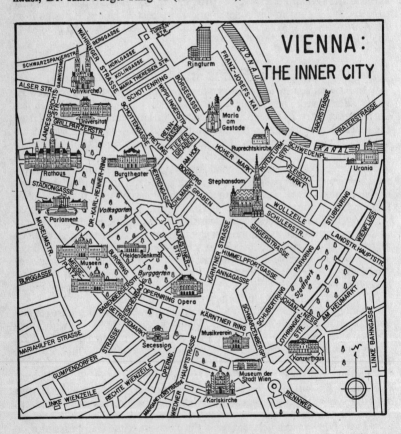

VIENNA:
THE INNER CITY

6. Seeing the Vienna Sights

Vienna is a place to wander. Poke down the narrow street where Mozart died, or where Beethoven or Liszt lived for a time. Come across a palace or two in the center of town from the days of the nobility's love affair with the baroque. Stroll around Stephan's Platz and the shopping areas of Kärntnerstrasse and the Graben, all closed off to traffic now for the convenience of the pedestrian. And then stop at one of the busy sidewalk cafes for one of the dozens of kinds of coffee, for a sinful pastry or two, and become the observer. Refreshed, stroll through the gates of the Imperial Palace, the Hofburg, where Emperor Franz Joseph rode in his carriage not *so* long ago; look in on all the buildings he erected as the trappings of empire, and experience the art and other treasures they house. Promenade along Ringstrasse past the Opera house and on into Stadt Park where Johann Strauss's waltzes may be playing at the bandstand.

For this you won't need much more than a good map and some standard tourist information that is available from any **Austrian National Tourist Office** before you leave home. There is one in New York at 545 Fifth Ave., New York, NY 10017 (tel. 212/697-0651). In Vienna the address is **Vienna Tourist Board**, Kinderspitalgasse 5, A-1095 Vienna.

All the chief buildings in Vienna sport small numbered flags in the summer, and for AS 25 ($1.32) you can get a booklet from the tourist board that identifies the buildings and gives background on each.

If you can board a regular sightseeing bus, you can take the guided tour for a good orientation of the city. There are other tours to the Vienna Woods and to Mayerling where Crown Prince Rudolph and Maria Vetsera died (but the hunting lodge is no longer there).

MUSEUMS: There are more than 40 important museums in Vienna. Among them are the homes of Mozart, Beethoven, Haydn, and Schubert, but since these are houses with staircases, you may just have to absorb the musical genius from the outside. Larger, and more amenable, are the grand buildings that Emperor Franz Joseph had erected on the Ringstrasse that house incomparable art treasures.

In the museums and other buildings described, there are no wheelchair-accessible rest rooms unless noted.

The **Kunsthistorische Museum (Museum of Fine Arts)**, Maria-Theresien-Platz (tel. 93-45-41), across from the Hofburg, is one of the most important art galleries in Europe. It contains the world's largest Breughel collection and many works by Rembrandt, Rubens, Velasquez, and Dürer among the world's great painters. It is quite overwhelming in its offerings. Although the main entrance has steps, there is a ground-level door on the Burgring side that can be opened by a staff member who will guide you to the elevator that gives access to all the floors. You will have to notify a guard when you want to return by this route. If you don't have your own wheelchair and need one to tour the vast exhibits, they are available from the museum. It is open from 10 a.m. to 3 p.m. Tuesday to Friday, 9 a.m. to 1 p.m. Saturday and Sunday. Admission is AS 30 ($1.60).

There's another part of the Fine Arts Museum in the **Neue Burg** at Heldenplatz, the building behind the Prince Eugene monument (tel. 93-45-41), where there is the world's second largest collection of weapons and armor, and a unique collection of musical instruments, including pianos that belonged to Beethoven, Schubert, and Mahler. The best entrance here is by a service ramp (often the best way!), which is on the side of the building. You can reach the various levels inside by a special elevator (27-inch door). Open Tuesday to Friday 10 a.m. to 3 p.m., Saturday and Sunday 9 a.m. to 1 p.m., with an entrance fee of AS 20 ($1.06).

The **Albertina**, Augustinerstrasse 1 (tel. 52-42-32), between the Hofburg and the State Opera, is a treasurehouse of graphics, especially drawings by

Dürer. It has one step at the entrance, and there is an elevator you can use, with special staff escort, to reach the third floor where the graphics collection is exhibited. The Albertina is open Monday, Tuesday, and Thursday from 10 a.m. to 4 p.m., on Wednesday from 10 a.m. to 6 p.m., Friday from 10 a.m. to 2 p.m., and Saturday and Sunday from 10 a.m. to 1 p.m. It is closed on Sunday in July and August. There is a minimal admission charge.

The **Historische Museum der Stadt Wien (Museum of the History of Vienna)** (tel. 42-8-04), is in the Karlsplatz. It does have four steps at the entrance, but there is an elevator inside with a 26-inch door that can be used to reach the second and third floors. Admission is free, and the museum is open from Tuesday to Friday from 10 a.m. to 4 p.m., on Saturday from 2 to 6 p.m., on Sunday from 9 a.m. to 5 p.m., and Thursday until 7 p.m.

SPANISH RIDING SCHOOL: The white Lippizaner stallions and their riders of the Spanish Riding School are world-famous for their show of horsemanship that hasn't changed in four centuries, and their performances in the Hofburg of the special prances and pirouettes are often booked up as much as a year ahead. However, if you plan far enough in advance, they can make special accommodation for visitors in wheelchairs in the ground-floor box seats. There are a couple of steps to the entrance at Michaelerplatz. Performances are not given in the summer as a rule, and dates differ from year to year. Information on the schedule can be provided by the Austrian Tourist Office.

Throughout the year you can take tours of the stables from 2 to 4 p.m. Monday through Saturday, and from 10 a.m. to noon on Sunday. Admission is AS 10 (53¢).

ST. STEPHAN'S CATHEDRAL: As the focal point of Vienna, with its Gothic spire and its location literally in heart of town, it's hard to miss 700-year-old St. Stephan's, Vienna's most revered landmark. The roof is new, since the original went up in flames at the end of World War II, but the 14th-century Gothic exterior, overlaid inside with some Romanesque and even a little baroque, make it an interesting church to visit. There's a level entrance at Riesentor. Other entrances have no more than one or two steps down. Although there is an elevator to the Bell Tower, it's tiny.

THE HOFBURG: The official residence of the Hapsburgs, the Hofburg, is an enormous complex of buildings erected at intervals over seven centuries.

To get to the Imperial State Rooms your best way is through the side entrance, where there is one step and two doors to reach the elevator, which has a 25½-inch door. You can take a tour of the apartments of Emperor Franz Joseph, Empress Elisabeth, and Czar Alexander I of Russia, who stayed there in 1814 when the Vienna Congress that ended the Napoleonic Wars was in session.

The Swiss Court (Schweizer Hof) is the oldest part of the palace and houses the Imperial Treasures; the oldest building is the Chapel (Burgkapelle) where the Vienna Boys Choir sings. But there are lots of steps in the interiors of both.

The famous Imperial Crypt (Kapuzinergruft), where 54 urns contain the hearts of the Hapsburgs, is down many steps from the street level.

BELVEDERE: On a hill overlooking Vienna is the summer palace built for Prince Eugene of Savoy, who successfully defended Vienna against Turkish invasions. The Upper Belvedere is now the home of the Austrian Gallery of 19th and 20th Century Art, including such notables as Gustav Klimt and Oskar Kokoschka. There are wonderful views from the top floors.

The entrance, near the top of Prinz Eugen Strasse, is level across a gravel walk to the main door, where there is one step into the building. Inside, there is a special elevator you can use with staff escort. If you have gone there by taxi or even subway, you can get back to town under your own steam, downhill all the way, by using the paved side paths of the gardens with their cascading fountains and terraces. The gallery is open Tuesday through Thursday and on Saturday from 10 a.m. to 4 p.m., on Friday from 10 a.m. to 1 p.m., and on Sunday from 9 a.m. to noon. There is an admission charge of AS 10 (53¢).

In summer, from mid-May to the end of September, weather permitting, a *son et lumière* show tells the history of the palace. Seating is reached without steps on the paved side walkways of the garden and then on the gravel paths. Entrance is at the main gate on Prinz Eugen Strasse.

SCHÖNBRUNN: The beautiful imperial summer palace of Schönbrunn, Schönbrunner Schloss Strasse (tel. 82-32-44), is so much a part of a visit to Vienna and should not be missed. It is on the edge of the city, a distance that is normally a short streetcar ride, but if that form of transportation is denied you, the taxi fare will be approximately AS 100 ($5.35). Access is quite easy into the palace (one step), and the guided tour (offered in a variety of languages), is without obstacles throughout the fantastic white and gilt rococco State Apartments that look much as they did when the Empress Maria Theresa redesigned the palace in the mid-18th century. A good example of why it always pays to check things out is that the very detailed guide to Vienna for disabled visitors does *not* mention the elevator I used with a staff escort when I visited Schönbrunn! Tours are offered from 9 a.m. to noon from 1 to 4 p.m. daily. Admission is AS 20 ($1.06).

Most visitors emerge from the palace and explore the beautiful grounds, then climb the hill to the Gloriette that commands views for miles all round. I can vouch for the view, since I got there with the help of *two* able-bodied companions, but the path *is* steep. No problem coming down, though!

7. Opera and Concerts

Music is a universal language, and there's plenty of it in Vienna. If you are an opera lover, you could try to get tickets to the famous State Opera (Staatsoper), or to the Volksoper, if operetta is more your style. The **Vienna Tourist Board,** Kinderspitalgasse 5, A-1095 Vienna, can supply tentative advance programs and order forms for both.

At the **Opera House** on the Opernring (tel. 52-76-36), there are eight steps inside to get to the elevator (its door is 30 inches wide), but there *are* two wheelchair locations available.

There are also wheelchair locations at the **Volksoper,** Wahringerstrasse 78 (tel. 34-36-27). The best entrance is the emergency door on Wahringerstrasse, where there are just two steps leading to the loge section. (Many more steps elsewhere.) Give the theater advance notice so that the door can be opened from the inside.

Another auditorium with wheelchair locations is Vienna's **English Theater,** Josefgasse 12 (tel. 42-12-60), where staff assistance is offered if you need it. The entrance is level.

The Vienna Philharmonic Orchestra plays at the **Konzerthaus,** Lothringerstrasse 20 (tel. 72-12-11), but this does not have easy access. There are three steps at the entrance and 12 more to the special elevator, which must be operated by a staff member.

Another concert hall, the **Musikverein,** Dumbastrasse 3 (tel. 65-86-81), has steps, but the entrance on Bösendorferstrasse has the fewest, with two steps to the special elevator (27-inch door).

AMSTERDAM

The Dutch Treat

1. Getting
There 2. Getting
Around 3. Orientation
4. Where to Stay 5. Eating
& Drinking 6. What to See
7. After Dark 8. Shopping 9. Excursions

THE NETHERLANDS is very proud of its Golden Age—the navigators, merchants, and painters of the 17th century. That may sound like ancient history to you, but in Amsterdam's old center, especially, things haven't changed much, at least in appearance. You're right in the heart of the Old World there amid tree-lined canals, medieval churches, and centuries-old town houses: somehow or other Amsterdam has managed to move into the 20th century without unduly disturbing its heritage.

For all visitors, the Netherlands offers much more than clogs and windmills and tulips, although all of these are present in abundance with all their appealing charm. This very compact country is only about half the size of Maine, and its big three cities—Amsterdam, Rotterdam, and The Hague—are only a few miles apart. You can even visit them all in a day.

For the disabled visitor, the country has two particular things in its favor: one is the flat terrain, most of it reclaimed from the sea over centuries by the remarkably patient and enduring Dutch people, and the other is the Dutch people themselves, who are friendly and helpful and display an attitude to disability that is as enlightened as I've encountered. The Dutch make a very conscious effort to make things easier.

Another advantage: this is still the land of bicycles, encouraged by the easy flat terrain, special paths, and their own traffic signals. All that has to have *some* implication for a visitor in a wheelchair, even if you are only thinking about what you'd do if you'd get a flat!

You won't need motorized transportation much while you're touring Amsterdam—there are no great distances between any of its sights, and much of its appeal, of course, is in just wandering. But if you do, there are wheelchair-accessible taxis! You can also take a boat ride on the canals to see the city without effort, and when you want to take a day trip to another city or town, consider the train, a rented car, or even a taxi, since distances are not that great and you get to see the countryside as well on the way.

There are hotels with "special" rooms, though you may have to forgo the historic, the quaint, and the budget-priced to stay in one of them.

Eating needn't present too many accessibility problems because of the abundance of sidewalk cafes, though it may present other types of problems in the overabundance of delicious food.

Write for all the tourist information you can get before you go. There are **Netherlands Tourist Offices** in the U.S.A. at 576 Fifth Ave., New York, NY 10036 (tel. 212/245-5320); at 881 Market St., San Francisco, CA 94105 (tel. 415/781-3387); and at 36 S. Wabash Ave., Chicago, IL 60603 (tel. 312/236-3636). In Canada, the tourist office is at 327 Bay St., Toronto, ON M5H 2R2 (tel. 416/363-1577). Ask also for a booklet (in English) called "Holidays in Holland for the Handicapped," which lists hotels, motels, guesthouses, camp sites, and youth hostels as well as details of highway facilities and other useful information.

Every major town in Holland has a tourist office, called **VVV**, which can provide you with more detailed and specific information when you arrive.

KLM's booklet "Budget Travel Tips" is a storehouse of useful tips about Holland and is available from any KLM office.

1. Getting There

If you're traveling from the U.S. or Canada, you'll arrive at **Schiphol,** Holland's only international airport (tel. 020/49-91-23), well equipped with facilities for getting you around, and with wheelchair-accessible rest rooms. Your airline will have made arrangements for you to be deplaned and escorted through the airport formalities (see the general section on air travel). Although Schiphol is a sprawling terminal, there are moving sidewalks from the gates to the main terminal building. If you can get into an electrocar (like a golf cart), KLM will provide a driver for the long-ish journey through the airport.

Dutch customs operates on the honor system, and you are allowed to decide whether you have anything to declare; if not, there is no need to go through inspection.

The airport is not far from downtown Amsterdam. There are bus services to the central railway station, but vehicles are not suitable for passengers unable to board a regular bus.

Taxis operating from the airport are all metered, and you can expect the ride to be about Dfl. 30 ($10.25) to Dfl. 40 ($13.75), depending on the part of town where you're staying. One thing you'll want to remember in Holland—the tip is already included in the price shown on the meter. If you need it, you may be able to get assistance in calling for a wheelchair-accessible taxi through the **Central Taxi Exchange** (tel. 77-77-77).

2. Getting Around

Most of what you'll want to see in Amsterdam can be reached "on foot," which is just as well since the regular means of public transportation—the tram—is off-limits, at least to somebody in a wheelchair.

The terrain is quite flat, and the biggest rises you'll find are the sloping approaches to the bridges over the canals, some a little steeper than others.

TAXIS: For the wheelchair-accessible taxis (or any others), call the **Central Taxi Exchange** at 77-77-77. No taxis cruise, but they can be picked up at taxi stands around the city, at the large hotels, or in the major squares. The amount shown on the meter includes the tip, and fares start at Dfl.2 (69¢) with Dfl. 1.75 (60¢) per kilometer after that, slightly higher after midnight. You can also find taxi drivers who will give you a city tour (or take you on an excursion). Ask the estimated cost first.

THE METRO: Although it was built to serve the suburbs primarily, the new Metro system is accessible to wheelchairs, and there are a couple of stops downtown that you might find useful. The tourist maps will indicate the Metro route.

SPECIAL VANS: If you need a wheelchair-lift van to pick you up from the airport, or in order to take an excursion outside the city, there are two companies that have vehicles able to handle one wheelchair: **Bloemkolk,** Groestraat 76 (tel. 020/36-08-36), and **Ver. Ziekenvervoer,** Valentijnkade 57 (tel. 020/35-42-13). There are others that handle more than one wheelchair, but it is assumed that their rates would therefore be higher. Charges fluctuate too much to be quoted here.

TRAINS: Many other interesting cities and towns, like The Hague, Haarlem, Rotterdam, Leiden, and Delft, are all within day-trip distance from Amsterdam, some less than an hour away on the train. (See the Excursion section of this chapter for accessibility information.)

CARS: The only time it makes sense to rent a car in Amsterdam is to take an excursion. Otherwise you'll be handicapped by impossible parking and confusing, narrow one-way streets and bridges. The **VVV tourist offices,** 9–15 Rokin (tel. 22-10-16), near the Central Station, can give you details of rental companies and also indicate the possibilities of hand controls. (Neither Avis nor Hertz have hand controls available in Amsterdam.) If you are driving around the Netherlands, you can be sure of good roads that are well maintained and signposted. Distances are short.

BUS TOURS: Both sightseeing tours and intercity buses use vehicles that are not wheelchair-accessible.

3. Orientation

Amsterdam has its share of the modern world's architecture in high-rises and elevated highways, as well as along the bustling waterfront. But as a visitor, you've come to see that 17th-century city that still centers on **Dam Square,** around which hangs the five-strand necklace of concentric canals originally dug around the medieval city walls. At first, there may not seem anything to distinguish one canal from another, or one street from the next; be sure to follow the map carefully so you don't cover more territory than you intend.

AREAS: The three major squares on which you may want to orient yourself while you tour, are Dam, Leidseplein and Muntplein. **Dam Square** is the site of the original dam across the Amstel River (the city was originally called Amstelledamme), and is in the heart of the city, surrounded by the Royal

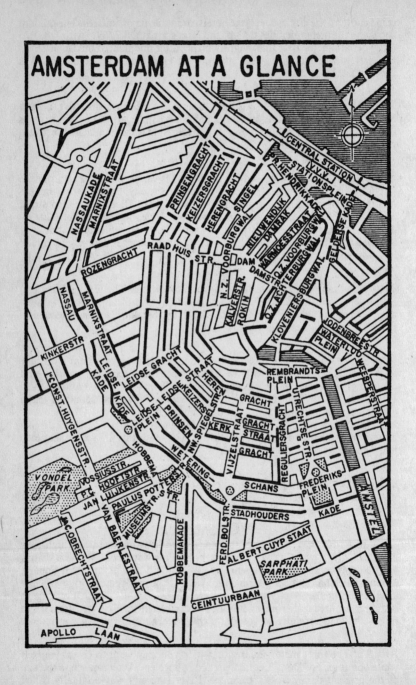

Palace, the Nieuwe Kerk (New Church), some department stores, and hotels. This is also the location of the Central Railroad Station.

Moving outward from the Dam, you'll come to busy **Muntplein** with its Mint Tower, one of the original fortresses of the city. It's now the hub of the public transportation system.

Leidseplein, still a little farther out from Dam, is also bustling, with restaurants, nightclubs, movie theaters, and the Stadsschouwburg theater (opera and ballet).

On the same canal as the Leidseplein, but on the other side, is the **Museumplein** and its surrounding streets, where you'll find the three major art museums—the **Rijksmuseum,** the **Vincent Van Gogh,** and the **Stedelijk,** as well as the **Concertgebouw concert hall,** and some of Amsterdam's most elegant shopping streets.

A little south of central Amsterdam is the wide boulevard of **Appollolaan,** an area of prestigious residences and top hotels.

To the east, on the far bank of the Amstel River, is another residential area and also the site of sightseeing attractions such as the Maritime and Tropical Museums.

ADDRESSES: Finding a street address in Amsterdam means focusing on the center, where the low numbers start on streets that lead away from it. To find addresses on the canal streets that form a semicircle around it, begin on your left hand as you face the center. Wherever possible, the approximate location of anything mentioned here will be given.

LANGUAGE: English is the Netherlands' second language, and nearly everybody is fluent in it, so there's no need to try and get your throat around some of those guttural consonants unless you want to. Apart from the pronunciation, some of the words may seem familiar, such as *straat* for street. Other identifying suffixes for locations in the city include *-gracht* for canal, *-plein* for square, and *-laan* for boulevard.

CURRENCY: The decimal currency system in the Netherlands is based on guilders and cents, but the abbreviation you'll see for Dutch guilders is Dfl., which comes from the old florin. Bills are in denominations of Dfl. 5 (green), Dfl. 10 (blue), Dfl. 25 (red), and Dfl. 100 (brown). The bills all have a braille indication of their value in one corner. It is always advisable to change money or travelers' checks in a bank—hours are 9 a.m. to 4 p.m. Monday to Friday, and until 7 p.m. on Thursday. A currency exchange at the Central Station is open over the weekend from 7 a.m. (8 a.m. on Sundays) until 11 p.m.

ELECTRICAL CURRENT: As in most European countries, the voltage in the Netherlands is 220, so you will need to take a voltage converter for any small appliance or respirator you take with you from the United States or Canada.

CLIMATE: The Netherlands has typical northerly maritime weather—mild winters and never-very-hot summers. Rain is frequent in the winter, and summer has its heavy showers, but they don't last too long. Because half of the country is below sea level, it's common to have early-morning fog, when it will be quite chilly, but the fog usually clears off before noon and skies can turn clear and sunny. So dress accordingly, with a layering system that includes a removable sweater, even in the summer.

MEDICAL SERVICE: Your hotel will always be able to refer you to medical assistance when you need it; or you can call the **Central Medical Service** *(Centrale Doctersdienst)* at 64-21-11, if there is an emergency at night or on the weekend.

TELEPHONE CODES: The country code for the Netherlands is 31, and the area code for Amsterdam is 20.

4. Where to Stay

Amsterdam used to have a reputation as one of the more moderately priced cities of Europe, but that is no longer true, it seems. The one thing, however, you can always be sure of is that you will get value for money, both in style and service, in Amsterdam hotels.

As in most European hotels, private baths are not always taken for granted, but this guide assumes that a room with a bath will be your choice. Given that, and given the usual problems of lack of access in the lower-priced hotels, this section cannot include much information for budget accommodations, unfortunately. However, you can be sure of having all the amenities that modern hostelry has to offer in the ones that are listed—except that few have any "special" rooms. Door dimensions are given so that you can decide for yourself if a hotel will be suitable for your individual needs. (For some reason, Amsterdam hotels seem to have slightly larger elevators than those in many other European cities, thank goodness.)

Hotels here are all convenient to the center of the city so that you'll be able to tour without the need for transportation most of the time.

Room rates are quoted in guilders (Dfl.) with dollar equivalents based on a rate of Dfl. 2.92 to $1—although this is subject to fluctuation—and it can also be assumed that some of the rates will rise as well. It has been noted where breakfast is included in the room rate: "breakfast" in the Netherlands is a hearty meal that can include a variety of breads, cheeses, cold meats, jam, and a beverage. Fruit juice is not usually included and may be a rather expensive extra. Most of the rates include the 15 percent service charge, which eliminates the need to tip unless you want to acknowledge any extra special assistance or service. The hotels are listed here according to the official Netherlands Tourist Office rating, in which five stars is the luxury category. Addresses given here include the Amsterdam postal code after the street address.

FIVE-STAR HOTELS: The **Amsterdam Hilton,** 138 Apollolaan, 1077 BG (tel. 020/78-07-80), is one of the few hotels in the city that can provide rooms specifically designed with wider doors and other amenities for wheelchair visitors. It is located on one of Amsterdam's only boulevards, in the "Gold Coast" neighborhood to the south of the city center. The entrance is ramped and the interior is level. Two special rooms have 32-inch entry doors and 27-inch doors to the bathrooms, which have grab bars and ceiling hooks. Restaurants are on the same level as the lobby. Rates range from Dfl. 155 to Dfl. 265 ($53 to $90.75) for single rooms, and Dfl. 195 to Dfl. 335 ($66.80 to $114.75) for doubles. Reservations can be made through any Hilton hotel.

There are also some wheelchair-accessible facilities at the **Amsterdam Sonesta,** 1 Kattengat, 1012 SZ (tel. 020/21-22-23, in Canada 416/281-3734, toll free in the U.S. 800/343-7170). It is near Dam Square in the heart of the city and on the banks of the oldest canal. Although there are steps at the main entrance, the service elevator alongside can be used to reach the lobby. The interior elevator for access to other floors and to the restaurant is of adequate size for a large wheelchair. All the rooms have 33-inch entry doors, but two rooms have wide doors to the bathrooms, where there are grab bars. Rates for single rooms go from Dfl. 190 to Dfl. 260 ($65.06 to $89.05), and doubles from Dfl. 230 to Dfl. 305 ($78.75 to $104.45). The new, all-American six-story Sonesta is built around an open central courtyard and styled to blend with its gabled neighbors. Accessible facilities include shops, a restaurant, a sidewalk cafe, and a restored 17th century church that's used for concerts.

Wide doors are to be found at the **Amsterdam Marriott,** 21 Stadhouder-skade, 1054 ES (tel. 020/83-51-51, toll free in the U.S., except Alaska and Hawaii, 800/228-9290), which is located right on the Leidseplein with its restaurants, cafes, and the Stadsschouwburg theater, where the National Opera and National Ballet companies perform. Double-glazed windows protect rooms from the noise of the busy neighborhood. The main entrance has two steps, but the side entrance is level to the lobby. The elevator is sizable and gives access to all rooms and some of the restaurants. Two rooms have 29-inch bathroom doors (other rooms are 21 inches), but there are no grab bars. Single rates are Dfl. 185 to Dfl. 275 ($63.25 to $94.20).

You can find one room with wider doors at the **Apollo Hotel,** 2 Apollo-laan, 1077 BA (tel. 020/73-59-22), which, like the Hilton, is on the boulevard south from city center. The best entrance is on Stadionkade and leads to the ground floor (there are steps at the main entrance). A good-sized elevator gives access to upper floors. Entry doors to all rooms are 30 inches wide, and one room has a 30-inch door to the bathroom, where there is a grab bar at the bath. The restaurant entry is level. Rates are Dfl. 200 to Dfl. 240 ($68.50 to $82.20).

FOUR-STAR HOTELS: Facing the Royal Palace in the city center is the **Grand Hotel Krasnapolsky,** 9 Dam Square, 1012 JS (tel. 020/26-31-63), a landmark hotel with one adapted room that has a 27½-inch bathroom entry with a sliding door. There is a level entrance, marked with the wheelchair-access symbol, at the side of the hotel. (The main entrance has four steps.) Since this is a hotel that was opened 100 years ago and has subsequently spread over a number of neighboring buildings, some of the floor levels vary, but the elevator, special guest room, and restaurant are all on the same level. Rates are Dfl. 179 to Dfl. 240 ($58.25 to $82.80) single, and Dfl. 220 to Dfl. 279 ($75.35 to $92.47) double, including breakfast.

By a canal near the Leidseplein and the Museum Quarter, the **Parkhotel,** 25 Stadhouderskade (tel. 020/73-09-61), has some rooms on each floor with a 29-inch entry and bathroom doors. There are four steps at the main entrance, but entry via the garage is level. Guest rooms and the restaurant can be reached by the elevator, which is of adequate size. Single rates go from Dfl. 129 to Dfl. 133 ($44.20 to $45.55), and doubles from Dfl. 184 to Dfl. 190 ($63 to $65.10) including breakfast.

THREE-STAR HOTELS: If you don't need wide access to the bathroom, there is otherwise spaciousness and accessibility at the **Carlton,** 2–18 Vijzel-straat, 1017 HK (tel. 020/22-22-66), located near the Muntplein in the town center. It is an older hotel with a variety of room sizes, but most of the bathroom doors are only about 21 inches wide. Elevator size is good. There is no restaurant, but breakfast is included in the rates, which are Dfl. 167.50 ($57.35) single, and go from Dfl. 193 to Dfl. 228 ($69.10 to $78.10) double.

There are bathroom doors that are 23½ inches wide (perhaps negotiable if you have a narrowing device for a wheelchair) at the **Caransa,** 19 Rembrandtsplein (tel. 020/22-94-55), also close to the city center. The entrance is level and has an automatic sliding door. The elevator size is good. Doors to guest rooms are 29 inches wide. Single rate is Dfl. 155 ($53.10) and double is Dfl. 200 ($68.50) including breakfast.

Ground-floor rooms are suitable for wheelchair guests (they have 27-inch-wide bathroom doors) at the **Delphi,** 101–105 Apollolaan, 1077 BG (tel. 020/79-51-52). There is a ramp over the two steps at the entrance. The hotel is located west of Beethovenstraat on the Apollolaan in a quiet, residential neighborhood south of the city center and not far from the Hilton. Breakfast is included in the room rates, which are Dfl. 103 ($35.25) single, Dfl. 142 ($48.65) double.

TWO-STAR HOTELS: A smaller hotel that also has rooms on the ground floor, the **Napoleon,** 72–74 Valkenburgerstraat (tel. 020/24-96-87), has 31-inch entry doors to its guest rooms, and bathroom doors that are 26 inches wide. There is a ramp over the one step at the entrance, and a good-sized elevator. It is located very close to the city center, a few canals eastward, and open only from March to November. Rates, which include breakfast, are Dfl. 50 to Dfl.75 ($17.15 to $25.70) single, and Dfl. 75 to Dfl. 110 ($25.70 to $36.70) double.

AT THE AIRPORT: There is one special room with a 26-inch bathroom door and grab bars, at the **Sheraton Schiphol Inn,** 495 Kruisweg, Hoofdorp 2132 NA (tel. 02503-15851, toll free in the U.S. 800/325-3535). It has a level entrance to the hotel and to the restaurant. Rates are Dfl. 191 ($65.40) single, Dfl. 232 ($79.45) double, including breakfast.

5. Eating and Drinking

These are brief guidelines, gastronomic rather than architectural, since accessibility will be more or less obvious as you pass the many eating and drinking establishments while wandering around the city.

Amsterdam offers a very wide variety of international food, which may seem surprising in a small country until you remember how extensive Dutch influence has been in its history throughout all parts of the world. You can choose from dishes of scores of nations, with multi-dish Indonesian *rijstafel* (rice table) high on the list of culinary specialties. If you choose, literally, to go Dutch, look for "Neerlands Dis" signs outside restaurants: it indicates that traditional dishes of Holland are served at reasonable prices. The Dutch are hearty eaters, so be prepared for generous portions that will probably serve to keep you going on one meal a day. A good idea is to have one of these large meals, whether it be lunch (if you haven't already had a large Dutch breakfast!), or dinner, and then snack as you tour. This can be done on *broodjes,* the bread-roll sandwiches with delicious fillings that you can order by pointing, available at the *broodjeswinkels;* open-faced sandwiches *(uitsmijter);* or the thin, crepe-style Dutch pancakes *(pannekoeken).*

The **Tourist Menu** is an official Tourist Office program that offers you a three-course meal for a fixed price of Dfl. 16.25 ($5.50), including tax and service, though it may be slightly higher by the time you visit. Although the price is the same everywhere, the offerings on the menu will vary widely according to the specialties of the restaurant, which are identified by a blue-and-white symbol showing a fork wearing a hat and a camera. Only those restaurants that reach certain quality standards are allowed to offer the Tourist Menu, and they are regularly checked out by hotel and restaurant authorities. You'll find the Tourist Menu at some of the first-class hotels such as the Sonesta.

If the Dutch like to eat, drinking is not far behind in popularity. And one of the favorite places to do it is in the *bruine kroeg* (brown cafe), which are popular meeting places for Amsterdammers before and after dinner. They are unique to the Netherlands, and are not really to be compared with either an English pub or an American tavern. You should sample the atmosphere there, even if not every one of the dozens of different types of beer served, including the Netherlands' own. There are so many "brown cafes" that you will surely come across at least one or two in your wanderings along the canals and old streets of the city center.

6. What to See

One of the best things to see in Amsterdam is the city itself. Its historic buildings and arching bridges are an outdoor exhibit of museum quality that has no equal, and will thankfully remain unchanged because city landmarks are protected by strict government regulations against alteration.

Amsterdam is a place to go for a leisurely visit to its main attraction, the city, with a couple of side trips to one or two of its outstanding museums, particularly those accessible to wheelchair visitors, of course. In case you wonder about the **Anne Frank house,** it is, as you might guess, *not* accessible, since it was one of Amsterdam's small buildings with not much space inside and only staircase access to the top floors. You'll see it at 263 Prinsengracht (marked on most tourist maps). There are similar restrictions to another famous house from an earlier era, the one where Rembrandt lived and worked. But you will pass it as you tour the city center, at 4–6 Jodenbreestraat, near Waterlooplein.

Fortunately, Amsterdam's great heritage of paintings, and its contemporary art, are accessible in its famous museums.

CANAL BOAT RIDE: To sample the atmosphere of the city, you can hardly do it better than by a trip in a glass-topped launch around the canals and the harbor, by day or night. One operator who is willing to help disabled passengers aboard is **Rederij Lovers,** (tel. 25-93-23). Boats leave at about 15-minute intervals in the summer from various locations, and most have their main dock at Prins Hendrikkade near Central Station. Commentary is multilingual. Fare is about Dfl. 7 ($2.40).

VINCENT VAN GOGH MUSEUM: The accessibility of the Vincent Van Gogh Museum has been officially recognized by the Netherlands Society for Rehabilitation with criteria based on independent use by people in wheelchairs. This also means wheelchair-accessible rest rooms. The best entrance is on Van de Velderstraat. You can see more than 200 of the artist's paintings here—in fact nearly everything he ever produced. The Vincent Van Gogh Museum is at 7 Paulus Potterstraat at the Museumplein (tel. 76-48-81), and is open Tuesday through Saturday from 10 a.m. to 5 p.m., and on Sunday and holidays from

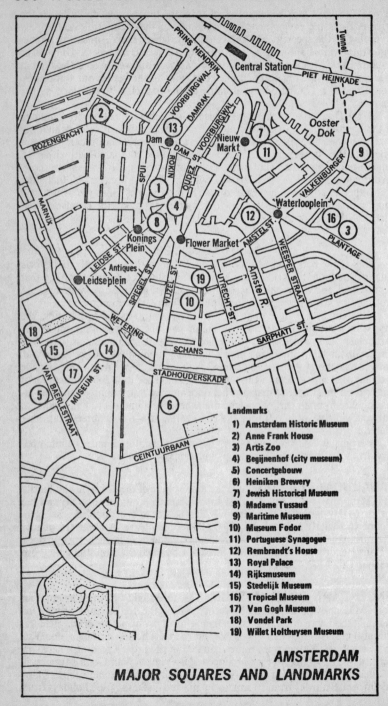

**AMSTERDAM
MAJOR SQUARES AND LANDMARKS**

Landmarks

1) Amsterdam Historic Museum
2) Anne Frank House
3) Artis Zoo
4) Begijnenhof (city museum)
5) Concertgebouw
6) Heiniken Brewery
7) Jewish Historical Museum
8) Madame Tussaud
9) Maritime Museum
10) Museum Fodor
11) Portuguese Synagogue
12) Rembrandt's House
13) Royal Palace
14) Rijksmuseum
15) Stedelijk Museum
16) Tropical Museum
17) Van Gogh Museum
18) Vondel Park
19) Willet Holthuysen Museum

1 to 5 p.m. Admission is Dfl. 3.50 ($1.20) for adults and Dfl.1 (35¢) for children under 18.

STEDELIJK MUSEUM: The contemporary art museum, Stedelijk, also in the Museumplein area, has also received the official wheelchair accessibility symbol. The address is 13 Paul Potterstraat (tel. 73-21-66), but the recommended entrance is on Van Baerlestraat. The Stedelijk Museum is open Tuesday to Saturday from 10 a.m. to 5 p.m. and on Sunday and holidays from 1 to 5 p.m. Admission is Dfl. 3.50 ($1.20) for adults and Dfl. 1.75 (60¢) for children under 17.

RIJKSMUSEUM: Although you won't be able to get into Rembrandt's house if you use a wheelchair, you can certainly see many of his famous paintings in the Netherlands National Gallery, the Rijksmuseum, including his spellbinding *Night Watch*. It is at 42 Stadhouderskade at the Museumplein (tel. 73-21-21). The museum also contains the world's largest collection of paintings by other Dutch masters like Frans Hals and Vermeer, as well as other treasures that rank it along with the other major museums of Western European painting.
 The wheelchair-accessible entrance is via the service elevator on the side. There *are* rest rooms adapted for wheelchair access. The Rijksmusuem is open Monday through Saturday from 10 a.m. to 5 p.m., on Sunday and holidays from 1 to 5 p.m., closed on January 1. Admission is Dfl. 3.50 ($1.20) for adults and Dfl. 1 (35¢) for children under 18; under 11 free.

AMSTERDAM HISTORICAL MUSEUM: One institution that will give you a marvelous insight into the city that you are visiting is the Amersterdam Historical Museum, 92 Kalverstraat (tel. 25-58-22). The entrance is wheelchair-accessible, and there is an elevator inside the museum, although there are *some* areas that you will not be able to reach by elevator. Although exhibits are described in Dutch, there are English-language introductions in each gallery. Open Tuesday through Saturday from 10 a.m. to 5 p.m., Sunday and public holidays from 1 to 5 p.m. Admission is Dfl. 3 ($1) for adults and Dfl. 1.50 (50¢) for children between 11 and 16, under 11 free.

DIAMOND CUTTING: The skill of Amsterdam's diamond cutters made it the diamond center of the world, and you can take a tour of one of the cutting and polishing factories. Check at the VVV tourist office for ones that may be suited to your particular mobility needs, or check when you see signs for diamond-cutting demonstrations outside the factories, which are all over the central area of the city.
 In case you're wondering about other sights listed in the tourist brochures, there aren't too many others with wheelchair access, and that includes Madame Tussaud and the Heineken Brewery.

7. After Dark

 The title of this section can encompass much in Amsterdam—jazz, the brown cafes, the ballet, the opera, the Concertgebouw Orchestra, or even the more infamous aspects of Amsterdam nightlife.
 One of the cheapest activities is a stroll along the canals, fairy-lighted and floodlit for a spectacular show, free of charge. But don't forget that Amster-

dam, for all its quaintness, is still a modern city, so check with somebody who knows the more congenial places to go.

You can have your before- or after-dinner refreshment in one of the "brown cafes"; or go to the top for cocktails-with-a-view from the **Ciel Bleu Bar** on the 23rd floor of the Hotel Okura Amsterdam (level entrance) at 175 Ferdinand Bolstraat, which is in the southern section of town. It's particularly attractive at sunset since the view is over the city toward the harbor.

CONCERTGEBOUW: If music is one of your interests, you surely know the reputation of the Amsterdam Concertgebouw Orchestra, whose home is one of the most acoustically perfect concert halls in the world at the Concertgebouw, 98 Van Baerlestraat, facing the Museumplein (tel. 71-83-45). The entrance, which is accessible to wheelchairs, is on Jan Willem Brouwersplein, and there is an elevator from here to the concert hall. There are no wheelchair locations, however, and transfer to a seat is required.

STADTSSCHOUWBURG: Holland's two major dance companies, the National Ballet and the Netherlands Dance Theater make their homes at the Stadtsschouwburg theatre, 26 Leidseplein (tel. 24-23-11). They are not always in residence, but if you are lucky enough to be there when they are giving performances, there is an accessible entrance (used by the artists) in Marnixstraat, where there is an elevator to the auditorium. There are two wheelchair locations. Tickets are relatively inexpensive—Dfl. 20 ($6.85) is the top price.

8. Shopping

You probably can't walk around Amsterdam without wanting, at least, to *look* at what is being offered for sale: the Dutch are traditional traders and their heritage shows in their commercial enterprises today. There's good window-shopping all the way from Central Station to the Concertgebouw, sometimes along pedestrian malls, then canalside, or busier major thoroughfares. The **pedestrians-only shopping centers** are at Nieuwendijk, Kalverstraat, Heiligeweg, and Leidsestraat.

The most famous shopping area in Amsterdam is **Kalverstraat** between Dam Square and the Muntplein, one of the most popular streets for strolling because it has everything.

Rokin runs parallel to the Kalverstraat (it's a busy tram route) and has **art galleries** and **antique shops** as well as **fashion boutiques.**

Near the museum area are the elegant and expensive shops on **P.C. Hoofstraat.**

At the Dam Square is Amsterdam's big department store, **De Bijenjorf,** which has accessible entrances on the square and at Beurssquare. There are elevators between floors *and* a wheelchair-accessible rest room.

Street markets are a permanent part of the Amsterdam shopping scene. You'll find the large **Waterlooplein flea market** at Valkenburgerstraat, and there's a floating **flower market** on the Singel canal where it meets Muntplein. You'll also come across specialized markets for books, textiles, and stamps as you stroll around the city.

9. Excursions

Windmills, tulips, clogs, and starched white headdresses, more canals, cheese markets, and all the things you may associate with the Netherlands are all around you if you take an excursion from Amsterdam, even for half a day. You can visit Rotterdam, The Hague, Haarlem, Leiden, Delft, and Utrecht, perhaps not all at once, but certainly one or two, on a day's trip from Amsterdam. Some of them are much less than an hour away on the train; Rotterdam, the furthest, is only just over an hour away. And you won't find anything but flat terrain.

Train travel presents a possibility for getting around. The Netherlands has one of the most efficient railroad systems anywhere, with trains leaving frequently from Amsterdam to all other towns. A portable ramp is available at the major stations, and many of the others, to facilitate entrance to the cars marked by the international symbol of access.

If you need special assistance, give at least 24 hours notice. You can call 030/33-12-58, or if you want to write in advance, the address is N.V. Nederlandse Spoorwegen, Dienst van Exploitatie, Afd., 6 Postbus 2023, 3500 HA Utrecht. Give advance notice the previous Friday if you want to travel on Saturday, Sunday, or Monday.

Car, of course, is another means of touring for these short distances. Highways are well signposted. There are quite a few gas stations with "adapted" rest rooms; they are listed in "Holidays in Holland for the Handicapped," available from the Netherlands Tourist Offices.

You'll find a local VVV tourist information office (with English-speaking staff) nearly everywhere you go, either at the railroad station or in the town square, where you will be able to find out what are the easiest and most convenient ways for you to take a brief tour of the city or town, and see the sights.

In addition to the brief outline here of some of the cities you can visit, there are the flower centers such as the **Keukenhof Gardens** at Lisse, or the **Aalsmeer Flower Auction;** the cheese towns of **Alkmaar** and **Gouda,** where the markets are very lively places; the famous windmills of **Kinderdijk;** and the picture-postcard villages of **Volendam** and **Marken.**

You *know* they will all be on very flat terrain. Any tourist brochure will give you other details.

THE HAGUE (DEN HAAG): There's a spacious grandeur in The Hague that recalls the past in this seat of government and official residence of the Dutch monarchs. The VVV tourist office there can give you an **Antique Walking Tour** guide through the heart of The Hague, and you'll pass some good places for lunch or snacking as well. While you are at the tourist office, check out the availability of tours of the Parliament (Binnenhof) and the Peace Palace.

If you go to The Hague by car, you'll be able to take the short side trip to **Madurodam,** 175 Haringkade, in the Scheveningen Woods, where you can see the Netherlands in a nutshell as you wander through this unique miniature village that represents a Dutch town on a 1:25 scale, with its historic buildings, railways and motorways in action, its ports and canals. Madurodam has been given the international symbol of wheelchair access by the Netherlands Society for Rehabilitation. It is open Monday to Saturday, from 9:30 a.m. to 10:30 p.m. from April 1 through June 30, and open until 11 p.m. in July and August. Hours in September and October are 9:30 a.m. to 9:30 p.m.

ROTTERDAM: In contrast to The Hague's wealth of parks and elegant homes, Rotterdam is a modern city that was built on the ruins of a city nearly completely razed in World War II. Its Europoort is the busiest harbor in the world, and you should take the **Spido Harbor Trip** to see at least some of it. Wheelchairs can get aboard the boats.

One of the areas that survived the World War II bombing was the historic area of **Delftshaven** (Delft harbor), the initial port of departure for the Pilgrim Fathers as they set out for the New World.

You can get a bird's-eye view of Rotterdam harbor from the top of **Euromast**, 20 Parkhaven, where you'll be able to reach the top of the 600-foot structure in an observation elevator. The revolving top has a restaurant and a coffeeshop.

You can also wander around the **Lijnbaan shopping mall** where there are plenty of restaurants in all price brackets.

UTRECHT: In the heart of the old town of Utrecht there are more medieval churches than anywhere else in Europe. One of them, **Het Catharijneconvent (St. Catherine's Convent),** is a state museum that is also officially wheelchair-accessible by standards of the Netherlands Society for Rehabilitation (even though it is a 16th-century building!). It is at 63 Nieuwegracht and houses a museum of the history of Christianity in the Netherlands.

Along the wharf at the Oude Gracht Canal that runs through the center of town, there are lots of outdoor cafes in the summer since Utrecht is no longer the active port it once was.

DELFT: Along with its share of tree-lined canals, flower boxes, and a wealth of old buildings and intriguing facades, some from the 14th century, Delft is, of course, also home of the famous blue-and-white ceramic that bears its name. There are a couple of steps at the entrance and one or two more inside between levels, but you can tour **De Porceleyne Fles,** 133 Delftweg, and see demonstrations of the art of painting Delftware. Delft was also the home of the famous 17th-century painter Johannes Vermeer.

It's a pretty town that you can wander around with ease and pleasure, with plenty of places to eat in the area of Market Square.

LEIDEN: This historic university town has a picturesque old town center. You can follow one of the special city walking tours that were marked on the sidewalks by the University of Leiden to commemorate its 400th anniversary in 1975. The tours vary in length, so you may want to get details from the VVV tourist office.

The **Pilgrim Fathers Documents Center,** 2a Boisotkade, carries the official international symbol of wheelchair accessibility. It has a recorded commentary on the Pilgrims who spent 11 years in Leiden before they set sail on the *Mayflower,* and an exhibit of documents relating to their residence here. It is open Monday to Friday from 9 a.m. to noon and 2 to 4:30 p.m.

Leiden may be the only town where there are two buildings that are officially wheelchair-accessible (according to the Netherlands Society for Rehabilitation standards), and both are in the same neighborhood. The other is the **National Museum of Antiquities,** 28 Rapenburg, which houses the *Temple of Taffeh,* the Egyptian government's gift to the people of Holland for helping to save monuments when the Aswan Dam was built. The musuem is open Monday to Saturday from 10 a.m. to 5 p.m., and on Sundays and holidays from 1 to 5 p.m.

Part V

POSTSCRIPT

Chapter 20

A TRAVEL INFORMATION GUIDE

. . . Where Else?

1. Travel Reference Sources
2. Travel Agents & Group Tours

THE MOST EXPERIENCED traveler can only be in one place at a time—with a need to know everything possible about that one place—so this guide has focused on providing a lot of detail about a large number of places. It doesn't exhaust all the possibilities by any means. There is the rest of the world, after all.

1. Travel Reference Sources

As I said in the introduction, researching from scratch can produce some puzzling contradictions and can require a great deal of time and patience. However, a guide for disabled travelers isn't really complete without mention of organizations that have services to provide travel information, or at least to lead you to sources of information about other places than the ones included in this book.

Travel is one of the interests of **Rehabilitation International USA (RI-USA)**, 1123 Broadway, New York, NY 10010 (tel. 212/620-4040), the U.S. affiliate of a world-wide organization. The latest edition of its *International Directory of Access Guides* contains more than 450 entries covering cities, towns, parks, and transportation systems in the U.S.A. and other countries around the world. Individual copies are available at no charge.

There is a unique **Travel Information Center at Moss Rehabilitation Hospital**, 12th St. and Tabor Rd., Philadelphia, PA 19141 (tel. 251/329-5715, TDD 215/329-4342). Moss will provide information free of charge to disabled people about hotels, motels, tourist attractions, cruises, or anything else you may need to know, if it is available in their files, or they will tell you where it may be obtained. They do not make any travel arrangements.

Mobility International USA (MIUSA), P.O.Box 3551, Eugene, OR 97403 (tel. 503/343-1284), is a nonprofit organization affiliated with the parent organization in London, whose purpose is to promote international educational exchange and recreation travel experiences for people with disabilities. One of its activities is a travel information and referral service. MIUSA membership dues range upward from $10 depending on income.

An organization that can direct you to a travel agent who may be familiar with the needs of disabled travelers is the **Society for the Advancement of Travel for the Handicapped (SATH)**, Suite 1110, 26 Court St., Brooklyn, NY 11242 (tel. 212/858-5483). It is a nonprofit membership organization of professionals in the rehabilitation field, travel agents, and consumers. Full membership provides travel information as well as a newsletter. Enclose a self-addressed, stamped envelope if you write.

2. Travel Agents and Group Tours

Just as some travelers prefer to head out on their own—the ones to whom this guide is primarily directed—others enjoy the convenience and camaraderie of the group tour. For those who have never traveled as a disabled person, the group tour may be a good way to begin, as you'll have somebody else smooth the way: the organized tour sometimes has the merit of taking the travail out of travel.

Even so, there are things to check out. Although the tour may be specifically designed for disabled travelers, nobody knows better than you what your specific needs are. Most of the reputable group tour operators know that too, and it's essential that they have every detail of your function and what you will require to make your trip enjoyable. For more assurance, you may even consider checking for yourself the facilities at the hotels on the itinerary, as well as making sure that the ground transportation planned is suitable for you. If you want a leisurely trip, check on the amount of sightseeing and one-night stopovers. This, however, is usually more of a problem with regular tours rather than ones organized for groups of disabled travelers, which tend to go at a leisurely pace. Then again, if you want a little more action, check it out for that too!

The travel agencies who sepcialize in making arrangements for disabled clients vary in the services they offer. Some do only group tours, some do no group tours, some make both group and individual arrangements. Some require a companion to travel with you, if you do not meet certain levels of independence, although they will always take the responsibility for getting you in and out of trasportation, and up and down any steps involved in sightseeing.

One caveat about the group tour. Even similar disabilities do not necessarily create compatible companions, and the problems of disparate personalities are as possible in a group of disabled travelers as in any other. Your choice . . .

Here are some leading operators of group tours for travelers who have physical disabilities:

Evergreen Travel Service, Inc.'s Wings on Wheels division, 19505L 44th Ave. West, Lynnwood, WA 98036 (tel. 206/776-1184, toll free inside Washington State 800/562-9268), was a pioneer and has 25 years experience in organizing groups of disabled travelers. It's run by Betty Hoffman and her son, Jack, and their trips range all over, from China to Alaska to Afghanistan, around-the-world and literally everywhere except Russia. Some of their tours are built around specific disabilities, such as their "white cane" tours for blind travelers.

Flying Wheels Travel, 143 West Bridge St., Box 382, Owatonna, MN 55060 (tel. 507/451-5005, toll free 800/533-0363, in Minnesota 800/722-9351) is run by Judd and Barbara Jacobsen (he is quadriplegic) and will handle independent travel plans as well as the group tours they arrange in the U.S.A., Europe, and on cruises. Tours are usually limited to 25 people, including companions. Flying Wheels can make arrangements for personal assistance if you're not independent, added to the cost of course.

The Guided Tour, 555 Ashborn Rd., Elkins Park, PA 19117 (tel. 215/782-1370), is a nonprofit membership organization headed by Irv Segal, who arranges escorted tours all over the world.

Handy-Cap Horizons, 3250 E. Loretta Dr., Indianapolis, IN 46222 (tel. 317/784-5777), is a nonprofit group run by volunteers who organize tours for its members ($10 dues). The pace is leisurely, though the itineraries are global. Costs tend to be lower than the commercial ventures. When you write to Mrs. Dorothy Axsom for details, enclose a stamped, addressed envelope.

In Canada, **Handi-Travel,** First National Travel, 151 Bloor St. West, Suite 680, Toronto, ON M5S 1S4 (tel. 416/920-7560), were pioneers in organizing tours for disabled travelers. They offer tours to Hawaii, Florida, and Europe, among other places, as well as to the Winter Games for the Disabled.

Happy Holiday Travel, 2550 N.E. 15th Ave., Wilton Manors, Fort Lauderdale, FL 33305 (tel. 305/561-5602), is a full service travel agency that specializes in making arrangements for individuals, but has some group tours too. It is run by Ancill Miers, who is himself disabled.

If you already have a group (minimum ten people) that wants to tour Washington, D.C., Orlando, New York, Williamsburg, New England, and a few other places on Amtrak routes, **Helping Hand Tours,** Suite 418, 1155 15th St. NW, Washington, DC 20005 (tel. 202/ 659-0245) will make the arrangements.

Incentive Tours America, 12077 Wilshire Blvd., Suite 556, West Los Angeles, CA 90025 (tel. 213/826-2661), organizes group tours throughout the western United States and in Europe, using special buses for groups of 25 to 35 passengers, including wheelchair-users.

Mobility Tours, 26 Court St., Brooklyn, NY 11242 (tel. 212/858-6021, TDD 212/625-4744), makes travel arrangements for existing groups.

Rambling Tours, P.O. Box 1304, Hallandale, FL 33009 (tel. 305/456-2161), is a family-run agency experienced in tours to Europe, Israel, and the Orient. A companion is not required if you are reasonably independent.

A full-service travel agency that's also a membership organization, is **THETA Association Inc.,** 1058 Shell Bldg. #1, P.O.Box 4850, Foster City, CA 94404 (tel. for voice and TDD 415/573-9701, toll-free 800/25-THETA, in California 800/336-1273). The Handicapped & Elderly Travelers Association Inc. (THETA) provides all travel information at no cost to members, arranges for medically trained aides and escorts when required, airport assistance, medical travel protection at special rates, and 24-hour protection insurance as options.

Whole Person Tours, Inc., 137 W. 32nd St., Bayonne, NJ 07002 (tel. 201/858-3400), runs group tours in the United States and to Europe. This organization also publishes "The Itinerary" six times a year, dealing with topics of interest to disabled travelers, each issue focusing on a specific theme. Annual subscription is $6 in the U.S, $7 in Canada, $10 overseas.

NOW, SAVE MONEY ON ALL YOUR TRAVELS!
Join Arthur Frommer's $25-A-Day Travel Club

Saving money while traveling is never a simple matter, which is why, over 22 years ago, the **$25-A-Day Travel Club** was formed. Actually, the idea came from readers of the Arthur Frommer Publications who felt that such an organization could bring financial benefits, continuing travel information, and a sense of community to economy-minded travelers all over the world.

In keeping with the money-saving concept, the annual membership fee is low—$15 (U.S. residents) or $18 (Canadian, Mexican, and foreign residents)—and is immediately exceeded by the value of your benefits which include:

(1) The latest edition of any TWO of the books listed on the following page.

(2) An annual subscription to an 8-page quarterly newspaper *The Wonderful World of Budget Travel* which keeps you up-to-date on fastbreaking developments in low-cost travel in all parts of the world—bringing you the kind of information you'd have to pay over $25 a year to obtain elsewhere. This consumer-conscious publication also includes the following columns:

Travelers' Directory—members all over the world who are willing to provide hospitality to other members as they pass through their home cities.

Share-a-Trip—requests from members for travel companions who can share costs and help avoid the burdensome single supplement.

Readers Ask ... Readers Reply—travel questions from members to which other members reply with authentic firsthand information.

(3) A copy of *Arthur Frommer's Guide to New York.*

(4) Your personal membership card which entitles you to purchase through the Club all Arthur Frommer Publications for a third to a half off their regular retail prices during the term of your membership.

So why not join this hardy band of international budgeteers NOW and participate in its exchange of information and hospitality? Simply send $15 (U.S. residents) or $18 U.S. (Canadian, Mexican, and other foreign residents) along with your name and address to: $25-A-Day Travel Club, Inc., 1230 Avenue of the Americas, New York, NY 10020. Remember to specify which *two* of the books in section (1) above you wish to receive in your initial package of members' benefits. Or tear out this page, check off any two books on the opposite side and send it to us with your membership fee.

FROMMER/PASMANTIER PUBLISHERS Date_____
1230 AVE. OF THE AMERICAS, NEW YORK, NY 10020

Friends, please send me the books checked below:

$-A-DAY GUIDES
(In-depth guides to low-cost tourist accommodations and facilities.)

☐ Europe on $25 a Day $10.95
☐ Australia on $25 a Day $9.95
☐ England and Scotland on $25 a Day $9.95
☐ Greece on $25 a Day $9.95
☐ Hawaii on $35 a Day $9.95
☐ India on $15 & $25 a Day $9.95
☐ Ireland on $25 a Day $9.95
☐ Israel on $30 & $35 a Day $9.95
☐ Mexico on $20 a Day $9.95
☐ New Zealand on $20 & $25 a Day $9.95
☐ New York on $35 a Day $8.95
☐ Scandinavia on $25 a Day $9.95
☐ South America on $25 a Day $8.95
☐ Spain and Morocco (plus the Canary Is.) on $25 a Day $9.95
☐ Washington, D.C. on $35 a Day $8.95

DOLLARWISE GUIDES
(Guides to accommodations and facilities from budget to deluxe, with emphasis on the medium-priced.)

☐ Austria & Hungary $10.95
☐ Egypt $9.95
☐ England & Scotland $10.95
☐ France $10.95
☐ Germany $9.95
☐ Italy $10.95
☐ Portugal (incl. Madeira & the Azores) . $9.95
☐ Switzerland & Liechtenstein $9.95
☐ Canada $10.95
☐ Caribbean (incl. Bermuda & the Bahamas) $10.95

☐ Cruises (incl. Alaska, Carib, Mex, Hawaii, Panama, Canada, & US) $10.95
☐ California & Las Vegas $9.95
☐ Florida $9.95
☐ New England $9.95
☐ Northwest $10.95
☐ Southeast & New Orleans $9.95
☐ Southwest $10.95

THE ARTHUR FROMMER GUIDES
(Pocket-size guides to tourist accommodations and facilities in all price ranges.)

☐ Amsterdam/Holland $4.95
☐ Athens $4.95
☐ Atlantic City/Cape May $4.95
☐ Boston $4.95
☐ Dublin/Ireland $4.95
☐ Hawaii $4.95
☐ Las Vegas $4.95
☐ Lisbon/Madrid/Costa del Sol $4.95
☐ London $4.95
☐ Los Angeles $4.95

☐ Mexico City/Acapulco $4.95
☐ Montreal/Quebec City $4.95
☐ New Orleans $4.95
☐ New York $4.95
☐ Orlando/Disney World/EPCOT $4.95
☐ Paris $4.95
☐ Philadelphia $4.95
☐ Rome $4.95
☐ San Francisco $4.95
☐ Washington, D.C. $4.95

SPECIAL EDITIONS

☐ How to Beat the High Cost of Travel ... $4.95
☐ New York Urban Athlete (NYC sports guide for jocks & novices) $9.95
☐ Where to Stay USA (Accommodations from $3 to $25 a night) $8.95
☐ Fast 'n' Easy Phrase Book (Fr/Sp/Ger/Ital. in one vol.) $6.95

☐ Marilyn Wood's Wonderful Weekends .. $9.95 (NY, Conn, Mass, RI, Vt, NJ, Pa)
☐ Museums in New York $8.95
☐ Guide for the Disabled Traveler $10.95
☐ Bed & Breakfast-No. America $7.95

In U.S. include $1 post. & hdlg. for 1st book; 25¢ ea. add'l. book. Outside U.S. $2 and 50¢ respectively.

Enclosed is my check or money order for $_____

NAME_____

ADDRESS_____

CITY_____ STATE_____ ZIP_____